Leningrad 1941–1942

Leningrad
1941–1942

Morality in a City under Siege

Sergey Yarov

Translated by
Arch Tait

polity

First published in Russian as *Блокадная этика. Представление о морали в Ленинграде в 1941–1942гг.* © Sergey Yarov, 2012

This English edition © Polity Press, 2017

This publication was effected under the auspices of the Mikhail Prokhorov Foundation TRANSCRIPT Programme to support translations of Russian literature.

Polity Press
65 Bridge Street
Cambridge CB2 1UR, UK

Polity Press
350 Main Street
Malden, MA 02148, USA

ISBN-13: 978-1-5095-0798-6

A catalogue record for this book is available from the British Library.

Library of Congress Cataloging-in-Publication Data

Names: Yarov, Sergei Viktorovich, author.
Title: Leningrad, 1941-42 : morality in a city under siege / Sergey Yarov.
Other titles: Blokadnaia etika. English
Description: English edition. | Cambridge, UK ; Malden, MA : Polity, 2017. | Includes bibliographical references and index.
Identifiers: LCCN 2016043509 (print) | LCCN 2016046586 (ebook) | ISBN 9781509507986 (hardback) | ISBN 9781509508006 (paperback) | ISBN 9781509508013 (Mobi) | ISBN 9781509508020 (Epub)
Subjects: LCSH: Saint Petersburg (Russia)--History--Siege, 1941-1944. | Saint Petersburg (Russia)--History--Siege, 1941-1944--Personal narratives. | Blockade--Social aspects--Russia (Federation)--Saint Petersburg--History--20th century. | World War, 1939-1945--Moral and ethical aspects--Russia (Federation)--Saint Petersburg. | World War, 1939-1945--Social aspects--Russia (Federation)--Saint Petersburg. | Saint Petersburg (Russia)--Social conditions--20th century. | Saint Petersburg (Russia)--Moral conditions--History--20th century.
Classification: LCC D764.3.L4 I27513 2017 (print) | LCC D764.3.L4 (ebook) | DDC 940.54/21721--dc23
LC record available at https://lccn.loc.gov/2016043509

Typeset in 10 on 11 pt Times New Roman MT by
Servis Filmsetting Ltd, Stockport, Cheshire
Printed and bound in Great Britain by CPI Group (UK) Ltd, Croydon

For further information on Polity, visit our website: politybooks.com

Contents

Foreword

No city in the history of warfare has known a catastrophe like that suffered by Leningrad in World War II. While the exact number who died during the siege by the German and Finnish armies from 8 September 1941 to 27 January 1944 will never be known, available data point to 900,000 civilian deaths, over half a million of whom died in the winter of 1941–2 alone.[1] Many other cities were devastated in World War II, but none saw death on such a scale as Leningrad. And, unlike others, it was not bombing, fighting or shelling that caused the massive number of deaths. The overwhelming majority of those who perished in Leningrad died of hunger.

That Leningrad would be besieged was unforeseen by either side in the titanic struggle that began when Hitler launched Operation Barbarossa, the surprise invasion of the USSR by 3½ million German troops and their allies, on 22 June 1941. After the crushing defeat of France the previous summer, both he and the Wehrmacht high command were confident that *Blitzkrieg* would see the fall of Leningrad within a few weeks. For Stalin, the idea that enemy forces could penetrate Soviet defences and advance deep into Soviet territory had been unthinkable. Red Army commanders faced the charge of treason if they planned for defence in depth. No preparations had been made to defend Leningrad, let alone endure a long siege.

By the end of July, the fierce resistance of the Red Army, even as it retreated with staggering losses, caused Hitler to begin rethinking his strategy. The immediate task for Army Group North was now to encircle Leningrad; and, for the first time, the word 'starve' appeared in his war notes. On the Soviet side, the speed of the German advance forced Stalin and the Soviet leadership to realize that Leningrad was highly vulnerable. Thousands of volunteers were mobilized in people's militias and, with little or no training, thrown into battle alongside the Red Army to halt the Germans at the Luga River line, suffering huge casualties in the process. Meanwhile, thousands more, mainly women, were drafted to work day and night to construct extensive fortifications outside and inside the city.

It was only on 21 August, however, that Leningraders were told that their city was in danger of attack. Eight days later, the last rail line out of the city was cut, and on 8 September German forces captured

Schlisselburg, cutting its last land link with the rest of the USSR. Hitler's strategy was now decided. Rather than attempting to take Leningrad by storm and risking heavy losses of forces needed for the imminent battle for Moscow, hunger would bring the Nazis victory. The population of 2½ million would be starved to death and the city razed to the ground. The siege had begun; it would last for 872 days.

With the destruction by bombing of the large Badaev food stores on the first day of the blockade, and supplies by air or water drastically limited, Leningrad's leaders knew that disaster threatened. In the weeks that followed they cut the bread ration five times. By 20 November, it had been reduced for most Leningraders to 150 grams, a fraction of the amount needed to sustain life. Of this, half was composed of additives with no nutritional value – sawdust, cellulose, malt and other surrogates – and almost no other rations were provided. Leningraders were left to their own devices to supplement their meagre bread ration with anything remotely edible – wood glue, tank grease, oilcake, leather belts and many other surrogates – or to barter their possessions for food.

The result was mass starvation. The first such deaths occurred in late October and they grew inexorably. By November, the first arrests were being made for cannibalism. By December, death from 'dystrophy', atrophy of the vital organs, was common. Victims collapsed and died at home or work, resting or walking. With the cessation of electricity and water supply, heating and sewerage, with starving people forced to stand for hours, often at night, in bread queues, even then not always receiving their ration, and in one of the bitterest winters on record, the death rate rose in January and February to thirty times its peacetime level. Leningrad was in the grip of a famine unprecedented in its scale and intensity. The Leningrad famine in the 'Hungry Winter' of 1941–2 would belong in the same category as major famines of modern history: Ireland in 1846, India in 1876–9, Bengal in 1942, China in 1959–61.

As a description, 'Hungry Winter' is an understatement. It was, as Sergey Yarov says, the Time of Death. With the Leningrad Funeral Trust unable to cope with the huge number of dead, corpses lay everywhere – in homes, courtyards, on the streets, in improvised morgues and hospitals. When eventually collected, they were transported in lorries full to the brim, and left in piles of hundreds, sometimes thousands, at cemeteries, awaiting burial in mass graves or cremation. Not until March would the death rate begin to diminish. With increased food supplies reaching Leningrad and the evacuation of half a million people via the Road of Life across Lake Ladoga, and fewer people alive to be fed, by spring rations had reached a level capable of sustaining life. The effects of extreme malnutrition during the winter, however, would last for months. People were still dying from dystrophy, if in fewer numbers, for the rest of 1942. Hundreds of books have been published about the siege of Leningrad. Already during the blockade itself, the authorities decided that its immense human cost should be recorded in order to write its history

They called on Leningraders to provide personal records of it, including diaries they were writing – or had been until they died; and many were collected. This project was brought to a sudden halt, however, in 1949–50 in the Leningrad Affair, when Stalin ruthlessly purged many who had been leading figures during the siege on the grounds of their supposed ambition to challenge Moscow's preeminence. For the rest of the Stalin period, Leningrad's role in the Soviet war effort would receive minimal attention from historians. The diaries, along with other materials, were consigned to remote corners of the archives. [2]

From the Khrushchev period, it became possible again to write about the siege, though almost exclusively in ways that emphasized the role of patriotism and heroism in victory over Nazi Germany.[3] But it would take Perestroika from 1985, and above all the collapse of the Soviet Union in 1991, to open Soviet archives and make research into previously ignored or taboo areas of the siege's history possible for both Russian and Western historians.[4]

Unique among these was Sergey Yarov. In the ten years that this brilliant and original St Petersburg historian devoted to study of the history of the siege, until his untimely death in September 2015,[5] he read hundreds of diaries, letters, memoirs, reminiscences and reports, and interviewed many survivors of the siege. His aim was to show the full tragedy of the siege, the impact that the terrible conditions in which the great majority of the population lived and died during the siege had on their attitudes, behaviour and psychology. More than anyone who has written about the siege, he showed the terrible choices that desperate and famished people could be forced to make – to feed one child at the cost of another's life, to keep the body of a dead relative in the apartment to use his or her ration cards to keep others alive, to use the flesh of a corpse to feed dependants or oneself. Was it possible to remain human in inhuman conditions? Yarov argued that, from late October 1941 to spring 1942, Leningrad saw a 'degradation' of collective morality, and that the foundations on which the ethics of daily life rested broke down. While many people strove to retain a sense of what being human meant in their relations with others – family members in particular – for others the imperatives of survival dictated very different norms. That the great majority of those arrested for cannibalism were women refugees without the right to bread rations speaks volumes about the unimaginably appalling conditions of the blockade.[6]

Sergey Yarov's book poses questions not only about the history of the Leningrad siege. How, in such appalling circumstances, would people today – we ourselves included – behave? What would the impact of mass starvation and death be on a modern city in a developed society, with a great cultural history and a highly educated population – all of which describes Leningrad in 1941. War, with all its catastrophic and unforeseen results, is a ubiquitous and unpredictable phenomenon in the contemporary world, just as hunger, malnutrition and starvation remain the fate of millions of its inhabitants. For this reason above all, the knowledge and understanding of what the people of Leningrad suffered in the winter of 1941–2 provided in this outstanding book have a relevance and importance that go far beyond its historical interest.

John Barber

Notes

1 When military deaths in nearly three years of fighting in or near Leningrad – the longest battle in World War II – are added, the total Soviet death toll there may well have been as high as 2 million.
2 Where they would remain until after the collapse of the Soviet Union. In 1994, when I was in Leningrad working in TsGAIPD, the former Communist Party archive, I asked an exceptionally helpful archivist, Taisa Pavlovna Bondarevskaya, for files that would show people's reactions to the German invasion and its aftermath. To my pleasant surprise, she showed me the catalogue of *blokadniki*'s diaries, many of which I was able to read in the following weeks. For a detailed description of the blockade diaries, see Alexis Peri, *The War Within: Diaries from the Siege of Leningrad*, Cambridge, Mass., 2017.
3 A rare exception which included previously taboo subjects such as crime, defeatism and cannibalism, based on interviews with survivors of the siege, was Ales' Adamovich and Daniil Granin, *A Book of the Blockade*. Translated by Hilda Perham, Moscow, 1983.
4 Among them, Cynthia Simmons and Nina Perlina, *Writing the Siege of Leningrad: Women's Diaries, Memoirs, and Documentary Prose*, Pittsburgh, 2002; John Barber and Andrei Dzeniskevich, eds., *Life and Death in Besieged Leningrad*, Basingstoke, 2005; Michael Jones, *Leningrad: State of Siege*, London, 2008; Anna Reid, *Leningrad: Tragedy of a City Under Siege, 1941–44*, London, 2011; Richard Bidlack and Nikita Lomagin, *The Leningrad Blockade, 1941–1944: A New Documentary History From the Soviet Archives*, London, 2012; Peri, *The War Within*.
5 A professor at the European University of St Petersburg and the Herzen Pedagogical University, he was described by in a eulogy by Sergy Erlikh as 'blessed' both in his relations with students and colleagues, and for his total dedication to teaching and research: 'Zhurnal'nyi zal', *Zvesda*, No. 4, 2011.
6 Two years before he died, Sergey Yarov published a book on daily life in blockaded Leningrad, *Povsednevnaia zhizn' blokadnogo leningrada* (Moscow, 2013). In it, he described in detail the horrific reality that underlay the changes in morality described in the present book. Those who know Russian may wish to read about the unutterably wretched conditions in which *blokadniki* lived and died – or they may not wish to.

Preface

Lord! we know what we are but know not what we may be.
                                        Shakespeare, *Hamlet*

Anybody embarking on a description of morality during the siege of
Leningrad must expect to be distressed by an abyss of incredible suffering,
incalculable loss and inconsolable grief. It is impossible to provide a cool,
dispassionate account of the nightmare that was Leningrad in 1941–2.
Human beings empathize, and we must expect to be seared even today by
the horror of a past lit by the glare of countless fires, set among the city's
bomb-ravaged streets, and filled with images of the shocking deaths of so
many Leningraders in full view of their families and friends.

To subject this era to the measured, deliberate approach and scholarly
language of research methodology may seem improper, but it is the only
way. If we are to understand how people endured, we have to accept them
as they really were, without sparing our own feelings, without distortion
or omission. Only if we see those caught in the siege in all their self-
contradicting diversity, where the light is mixed with darkness, will we do
justice to the ordeal they were subjected to and understand the price they
had to pay to retain their human dignity.

The tragedy of Leningrad is reflected in thousands of documents. No
other event in Russia's Great Patriotic War of 1941–5 has been described
in such detail, literally day by day. These memoirs, diaries and letters
are immensely valuable for the light they cast on the siege, but until very
recently have been handled with an excess of caution. Life during the siege,
as it appears from these sources, was exceptionally brutal and harsh. In the
scholarly and popular literature, there has been an attempt to gloss over
descriptions of human weakness and helplessness. Certain episodes have
been highlighted while others were left in the shadows. This was not an
easy task. Documents could be edited and toned down, but it is difficult
to disrupt linked diary entries, or to patch together passages from letters
deliberately taken out of context. In publications of the 1970s and 1980s,
we find the authors themselves trying to rewrite their wartime diaries.

They watered down the diaries and letters to try to make them conform to the official Soviet trope of ordeals engendering heroism, which was rewarded by victory. The myth became part of the history. Until the mid-1980s, major obstacles were placed in the way of any attempt to publish the most revealing notes and diaries. If they were published at all, it was only with severe curtailment. *Blokadnaia kniga* [*The Book of the Siege*], by Ales Adamovich and Daniil Granin, could at first be published only in Moscow, by Raduga in 1983. The Leningrad censors reproached Lydia Ginzburg for dwelling unduly on the issue of food. Selection of documents for publication was biased heavily in favour of those which were predominantly optimistic and which played down distressing details of personal degeneration. Such unbiased eyewitnesses of the tragedy as Academician Dmitry Likhachev and historian Vladislav Glinka are withering in their assessment of the 'siege literature' which appeared between the 1940s and 1970s.[1]

Self-censorship by other authors writing about the siege of Leningrad also hindered the presentation of a full and accurate picture. This is a sensitive topic, but we cannot just ignore it. The authors of actual documents are least guilty of this. Nearly all their reminiscences, diaries and letters are now available to researchers, and we have every reason to suppose they have tried to tell the story of what they endured honestly, if sometimes selectively. 'You've come to the wrong place if you want to hear a lot of positive stuff', one siege survivor stated forthrightly at the beginning of her interview.[2]

Not all descriptions of the siege reflect the dark aspects of everyday life. We can identify self-censorship wherever we find an overabundance of emotive exclamations, which are rare in most of the documents. We see it where those writing have made later deletions to their original text. We see it in rewriting intended to tone down criticism. One diarist changed her sentence, 'How rapidly we deteriorated' to 'How rapidly our canteens deteriorated.'[3]

Some documents have introductory notes. 'I feel I should mention that in some cases I have recorded not only facts but also "rumours", which were vital and eagerly sought out by Leningraders at a time when there were no newspapers, no radio, no telephone or postal service.' This covering letter of 9 June 1943 to the Goslitizdat publishing house, which accompanied Maria Konoplyova's diary, reads less like an explanation than an excuse for telling the truth. In other, later, cases, there is an apology for toning down some of the descriptions.[4]

A significant influence was the canonical view of the siege, which was firmly established by the mid-1960s and which many survivors saw as unambiguous confirmation of their heroism. Eyewitnesses tailored their testimony to the conventional rhetoric.

We barely encounter entries soberly recording minor details. What finds its way into the documents tends to be what seemed unusual or dramatic at the time, which is perfectly understandable but limits our picture of the variety of daily life.

Reticence about passing on every detail is also due to moral taboos. Not everyone is willing to describe the more extreme forms of degradation, especially if those invoved are their family and friends. To do so would have seemed insensitive towards people who were victims of war, an offence against family history, or just needless unkindness. Our human sympathy debars us from dwelling on lamentable scenes of the foundering of personal integrity.

It is not only self-censorship by the eyewitnesses which complicates use of their testimony. That Leningraders are emotionally involved when talking about the war is only to be expected when we consider what they went through, but it can blind them to some nuances of events, which they replace with sweeping generalization. They want to express unstinting admiration for those who helped them when times were bad, but this can make them uncritical. Many who endured the siege observed only a small portion of what was taking place. Thousands became bedridden, and tend to generalize the actions of the few people they came into contact with as if they were representative of all their fellow Leningraders.

Thousands of citizens of Leningrad wanted to communicate what they had seen in the most vivid form possible, as works of literature, and this can lead to a chaotic and less than reliable narrative. As we ponder the testimony of those in the siege, we need to remember that the attention they pay to a particular event may be disproportionate, and that their opinions may not be representative. We need also to weigh their personal cultural level, their interests, and their capacity for realistic self-analysis. They have their likes and dislikes, and a natural wish to present their own actions in a good light. Only then will we be able to understand their behaviour objectively.

This is a book about the price that had to be paid in order to remain human in a time of inhumanity. Those who did not flee Leningrad hoped misfortune would pass them by. None could have imagined what they would have to endure. By the time they did understand the extent of the calamity they were facing, it was too late. They were to plumb the very depths of human suffering, callousness and cruelty. They were confronted by children maimed by bombing, a dying mother begging for bread in the moments before death but denied it, and an endless stream of other people, like themselves trapped in the siege and begging for help.

I dedicate this book to the blessed memory of those to whom death came only after unimaginable sufferings.

Part I

Concepts of Morality in 1941–1942

1

The tragedy of Leningrad

The Time of Death

1

'The Time of Death': that, according to Vitaliy Bianki, is the name given by many Leningraders to the most terrible months of starvation at the end of 1941 and beginning of 1942.[1] Starvation, the cold, the absence of civilized amenities, disease, apathy in all its manifestations, and a weakening of family ties all affected how people behaved.

In the first months of the war, despite the introduction of ration cards, until September 1941, there was no talk of starvation.[2] As time passed, however, it became increasingly apparent that the variety of food on offer was decreasing.[3] On 12 September 1941, there was a reduction of rations, with manual workers now entitled to 500 grams of bread a day, non-manual workers to 300 grams, and children to 200 grams.[4] The ensuing panic was predictable. It was the result of, among other things, disturbing reports from the front and 'alarmist' rumours about Leningrad's food stocks. In October, talk of starvation became more common. It was now no longer possible to buy meat without coupons, and the sugar and grain rations fell below the minimum for normal physiological needs.[5] This was the point at which crowds of Leningraders began combing through the ashes of the Badaev warehouses, bombed in September, in search of 'sweet' earth which they could wash, strain off the mud, and use as sugar. People no longer turned up their noses at unconventional, 'gross' food. When a notice appeared in a restaurant window in October 1941 offering 'horsemeat chops' for sale, 'people just walked on by, shaking their heads. Few went in.'[6] The next day, however, the announcement had been torn down and there was a crowd outside the door.[7]

'I usually ate hardly any meat and took my meals in a vegetarian restaurant, but now I devour it greedily and would be glad to do so every day', Maria Konoplyova wrote in her diary on 5 October 1941.[8] The person sitting next to her in the Hermitage canteen on 9 October 1941 asked her directly whether she was hungry, and himself admitted, 'I always feel hungry now.' 'We hear the same thing from all the young people', she notes. What Ksaveriy Seltser described as 'a constant gnawing in the pit of your stomach', is something many people mention in October 1941, and it became more oppressive with every day that passed.[9] There was nothing that could be done about it. Everybody's stocks were running out and rations were constantly being reduced. No one could think of an answer. Scouring the shops for whatever food remained was how most people tried to find more to eat, but with little success. Nothing else came to mind and, in many cases, people did not know how to improvise. They just hoped the situation would improve soon, or at least not become more serious.

Hopes of being able to rely on the black market were rapidly dispelled. In late 1941 and early 1942, directors of laboratories and institutions, and skilled workers, were being paid a monthly salary of 800–1,200 rubles; a university professor got 600 rubles; middle-ranking researchers and accountants were receiving 500–700 rubles; and cleaners were paid 130–80 rubles. The official price of bread was 1 ruble 70 kopeks per kilogram, and from 1 January 1942 this was increased to 1 ruble 90 kopeks. The black-market price of 1 kg of bread in December 1941 was 400 rubles; of meat, 400 rubles; of butter, 500 rubles.[10]

Already, however, some vendors were refusing to exchange food for money. From January or February 1942, bread was increasingly bartered for valuables like gold or jewellery, and more often only for other foodstuffs.

The first signs of real, frightening famine became evident in November 1941, the beginning of the Time of Death, with an endless succession of funeral processions, people trying to share out tiny pieces of bread, and a feverish search for food substitutes of any description. 'Somehow the hunger accumulates and grows, and what recently would have been a satisfying meal is now hopelessly inadequate. I am experiencing an acute sense of deprivation, a nagging emptiness in my stomach. Within an hour of a fairly decent meal, I am gathering up the tiniest scrap of anything edible and scouring the pans and plates', Irina Zelenskaya wrote in her diary on 9 January 1942.[11]

Having examined the bodies of people who had starved to death, the pathologist Professor Vladimir Garshin noted that their livers had lost two thirds of their mass, their hearts over a third, while their spleens were several times smaller than normal: 'The starvation had consumed them . . . the body had not only drawn on all its reserves, but had destroyed the very structure of its cells.'[12] Each month during this period had its particular feature, not unique to it but typical of it: sledges bearing mummy-like 'swaddlings' in December, numerous unburied corpses in the streets in January, and bodies piled up in stacks in February.

2

There were some obvious consequences of starvation, of which the most evident was apathy.[13] This presented as impaired movement, lethargy and the 'torpor' frequently referred to in diaries and notes about the siege.[14] It was physical frailty or, more forcefully, 'decrepitude'.[15] Memoirs repeatedly refer to the wizened features of famine victims, irrespective of their age. Many were unable even to move around their rooms, and would sit or lie on their beds for long periods. A. P. Bondarenko recalled her brother standing motionless for hours at the table, and her sister who just lay in bed, showing no interest in the doll beside her.[16] Z. V. Vinogradova, searching for children in 'escheated' apartments where everybody had died, wrote of her shock at how indifferent survivors were: 'A person would be lying in bed beside a dead family member, in a state of complete torpor.'[17]

Children, just like the adults, very soon became inured to death. It was in evidence everywhere, even at a New Year celebration. Those who came to the party at the Musical Comedy Theatre in January 1942 saw an usher in livery, who had died of starvation, being carried out. 'Nowhere do you see children playing. There are never any just running about', I. I. Zhilinsky wrote in his diary.[18] 'Children talked about the same things as adults: bread, and the fact that "they're going to give us some today".'[19] The Time of Death left its mark even on their games. N. A. Bulatova, who then was seven years old, recalls that when they received a piece of bread 5 cm x 5 cm, she and her sister would have a competition to see 'who could eat it for longer, a crumb at a time, and at the same time we counted how many dead people there were on our and the other side of the street'.[20]

People's actions appeared mechanical, without the least trace of emotion. 'Everybody looked very serious, nobody smiled', O. Soloviova recalled of those she met in the all but deserted streets.[21]

In late 1941 and early 1942, it became particularly noticeable that those in the siege were becoming slow and cloddish; as if no longer seeing each other, they would fail to move aside and collide.[22] Some already seemed doomed: 'They had a detached look, as if already taking leave.'[23] They said nothing and lacked all emotion: surprise, joy, even acute grief. As Yevgeny Schwartz put it, life was 'losing its warmth'.[24] People too were losing their sense of self-preservation and danger, and their interest in other people. Their sole interest now was food, and when they ceased to be interested in that, death was imminent. In his memoirs, artist Ilya Glazunov recalls stages on the road to extinction: 'There was an extraordinary facility about moving from one state to another. Images from books you had read or of people or events you had seen came to life and took shape in your mind. You no longer wanted to eat. Your mind gradually became as confused as that of a drug addict. You might suddenly black out.'[25]

Apathy weakened the ties between people and often led to social exclusion, which had consequences. It is as a member of the community that a person is reminded every day of moral principles, about being a decent, honest, fair, responsive, generous person. He may not always live up to these criteria, and will dissimulate, but even then he is bearing in mind how he is expected to behave. He knows that others are watching, assessing and correcting him, approving or disapproving. Ethical standards need these interactions, disputes and emotional setbacks if they are to survive. These 'transactions' are no mere formality, and without them the understanding of morality becomes blurred. Standards are only felt when people are monitoring themselves, scrutinizing the motivation behind their actions, and receiving critical feedback from others. They wilt where there is no interest in books and art, and a lack of concern about the moral evaluation of actions.

A person who became indifferent to everything, who became reclusive and turned in on himself, lost the ability to feel emotions, to experience joy, surprise, fear, grief and hope. This blunting of emotion was actually seen by some as salutary: Leningrad had become a grim, cold, dark city, and the only way not to break down completely was to become aloof and immune to suffering. This is the gist of an entry on 19 November 1941 in Lyudmila Eliasheva's diary.[26] The only salvation, Maria Mashkova noted in her diary a few months later, was to become brutally indifferent to human suffering.[27]

The atrophy of emotion was evident in many episodes during the siege, but perhaps the most startling was indifference to the bombing and to death in general. The first shelling of Leningrad in early September 1941 caused great concern. Citizens needed no persuading to take cover in the bomb shelters, and were anxious to find out how many casualties there were and which buildings had been destroyed.[28] Soon, however, they became used to it and, only a month later, in October 1941, we read in the diary of Vladimir Kulyabko, an engineer: 'I have little interest now in where has been bombed or how many victims there were. People get used to everything, even horror.'[29] Hunger rather than the shelling was soon the main topic of conversation. In the Time of Death, no one found this lack of interest in the bombardment surprising.[30] Some had the resilience to joke about it.[31] The police had sometimes to fine people reluctant to take shelter, and literally force them to get off the streets. What the writer Vitaliy Bianki noted about a friend who lived in Leningrad was not untypical: 'At first she would get everybody in her apartment out of bed if there was bombing even in the far distance, but later it ceased to disturb her. Now she gets fined for not taking cover during air raids, and doesn't wake her children in the night if there is bombing.'[32]

3

Instances, during bombardment, of some hiding from the bombs while others hid from the police, had a certain logic to them. The siege encouraged development of a phlegmatic pragmatism, with people preferring to conserve what little strength they had left by staying at home and hoping for the best. In their debilitated state, some doubted they would make it to the shelter down ice-covered staircases fouled with excrement before the all-clear sounded. Others did not want to risk losing their place in a queue, even though the shops were obliged to close.[33] It was a real enough predicament: queues re-formed rapidly, and people would have no inclination to recognize a pre-existing priority.

This pragmatism surprised later visitors to the city. Vitaliy Bianki, sitting with a local policeman during shelling, noticed he seemed less concerned about their building being hit than about whether the lights would go out.[34] Bianki emphasizes that there was no suggestion of bravado about this.[35]

For Leningraders, these survival mechanisms became commonplace, as the behaviour of some when the Sytny Market was shelled in December 1941 served to confirm.[36]

Indifference to the shelling, resulting from severe malnutrition and exhaustion, did, inevitably, affect Leningraders' moral standards. In the first place, there was a loss of the sense of responsibility for looking after the vulnerable: children, the elderly and invalids. Accepting the futility of attempting to get them to shelter in time was at least more moral than hoping the bombs would fall somewhere else. Excusing themselves for this not inconsiderable lapse opened the way to justifying other departures from traditional morality.

In the second place, indifference to the shelling weakened, and often led to the loss of, fear and awareness of danger. No longer fearing for themselves, they saw no need to protect others, and had no sense that this was immoral.

People got used to bombardment and, with bodies lying everywhere, also to death. There were bodies next to hospitals and in the streets, in apartments and stairwells, in basements and courtyards. A.Ya. Tikhonov, chairman of the Vyborg District Executive Committee, reported that 'the highest number of bodies collected in our district in a single day was 4,500, but that counts only corpses collected from the streets.'[37] Neighbours would pile dead bodies up or take them to rubbish tips.[38] They were not always removed promptly.[39] In trucks, they were stacked like logs, and Leningraders shuddered at the sight of the hair of the dead fluttering in the wind. Lyudmila Ronchevskaya was shocked to see stiff corpses propped up against the wall of the mortuary by the Rossi Pavilion.[40] Bodies lay uncollected in apartments, hostels and evacuation centres, while people ate and slept next to them.[41] Pedestrians stepped over corpses, not having the strength to push them to the side of the road.[42] People registered neither fear nor disgust. V. Nikolskaya recalled people collecting snow for drinking water in a square which had bodies lying in it.[43]

A boy was coming towards us pulling a sledge with swaddlings. Some people, talking away, came past me and made way for him, paying not the slightest attention to what was on his sledge, not even exchanging a glance with each other. That same evening, I heard the expression 'this time of death' again on a street in the city centre, and again the people talking paid no attention at all to the load moving towards them: a young, exhausted woman was pulling a sledge with one large and two small swaddlings. At the turning by the little park opposite the Russian Museum, the long swaddling slipped off the sledge and

half-way into the snow. The weary woman stopped, crossly pushed it
back into place with her foot and again strained at the rope.[44]

This indifference to death is described by Bianki and other witnesses of the
terrible first winter of the siege.[45]

Dmitry Lazarev writes of the kind of funeral he was able to give his
friend, helping a member of the man's family. They had no coffin, and had
to take the body not to the cemetery but to a mortuary. They intended
even so to observe civilized customs, but found it impossible. There was
a searing −35° frost and their hands were numb. They took turns pulling
the sledge so that the other person could turn away for a time from the
icy wind. They had not very far to go but the journey seemed endless. The
mortuary was a shed and, when they opened the door they saw a mountain
of corpses piled up like logs. The doorkeeper, 'herself barely alive because
of the cold', did all she could to hurry them along, 'spurring us on': she just
wanted to get back home out of the intolerable cold.

There were no rites or rituals of leave-taking, no tears. Every aspect of
the 'funeral' was an offence against custom:

> The doorkeeper stood aside, plainly disinclined to give us any help.
> We untied the body from the board, tried and failed to lift it; there
> was no strength in our wasted muscles. We had no choice but to try
> to drag the body to the pile. The easiest way, we found, was to take
> it by the legs and climb backwards over other people' bellies, backs
> and heads, which were as hard and slippery as ice. The doorkeeper
> shoved his head further in using the door, to be sure she would be
> able to shut it.'[46]

The end result of their journey? 'I remember we felt a dull indifference to
the death of someone we had loved, and were only too glad to be shot of a
burden we had barely managed to cope with.'[47]

A lack of concern for the dead could lead to callousness towards the
living.[48] It drove out humane feelings of sympathy and compassion, and
the willingness to shield others from hardship. A woman died during construction of the city's defences: 'We pushed her to one side, abandoned her
log, and dragged our own one further.'[49] M. S. Konoplyova writes also
of the 'sad irony' with which they came to view the dead, and gives examples.[50] People saw not the mystery of death, but its seamy side: desecrated
bodies stripped of all decency which had to be stepped over, corpses
gnawed at by rats, in rags or naked, often with their ransacked pockets
turned inside out.

4

The realities of the siege radically altered the old way of life. In the past,
even in communal kitchens, which were seen as hotbeds of conflict, rules
of how people should behave towards each other came eventually to be

accepted. They shared food and turned to each other when they needed help. During the siege those communal rules broke down. Everything changed suddenly. The human contact, which required on a daily basis that moral values should be maintained, broke down. New rules were needed, but circumstances during the siege changed so rapidly and so horribly that there was no time for them to evolve.

Fits of irascibility, quarrels and fights tended to occur where bread was being shared out, or a bowl of soup or cup of hot water provided, and that was most often in canteens. Huge queues were to be observed in canteens and cafes already in September 1941. Until late October, soup and porridge were often still being served without the need for ration coupons. 'There was bedlam: everyone was shouting and swearing', Konoplyova notes in her diary on 12 September 1941,[51] and on 19 October she notes that in a canteen serving coupon-free sorrel soup, 'there is a noisy, excited crowd entirely capable of beating up anyone trying to get to the payment desk out of turn'.[52]

This disorder affected even educated, intelligent people. If you showed a moment's hesitation or the least fussiness you could be crushed, pushed aside, expelled from the queue. 'It seemed natural to fight for that meal, which could save you from starvation, at all costs', Lydia Ginzburg said later.[53] Quarrels could break out even in the restaurants of the Writers Union and the Public Library.

Outbursts occurred for a variety of reasons: the cashier might tear off too many coupons; if someone was late they might discover their ration had been eaten by someone else. There were arguments over priorities, who got served first, or because the service was too slow. Insufficient porridge might have been cooked, meaning that there was not enough to go round. Finally, and most commonly, someone might not want to wait their turn for their lunch or dinner. The same scene is described in different notes: hungry people ran out of patience, could wait no longer and, not caring what others might think, demanded loudly and insistently that they should be served first. Ill-tempered waitresses, visibly better fed, were openly contemptuous of would-be diners who alternately insulted them and begged them for food.[54] The memoirs of Georgiy Kulagin contain a hard-hitting description of such squabbling in a canteen for 'directors', where the food was better, good manners should have been more in evidence, and the diners were educated and clever people:

It was December, but people were not starving yet and behaved respectably. They still had food stores at home to draw on. Some had contacts in the food distribution network who could indent for starch and industrial gelatine from the central stores, but when that came to an end the restaurant was no better than any other. The ranks of diners thinned and polite conversation became a thing of the past. Directors began waiting impatiently for it to be lunchtime, and by one minute to the hour all the seats were taken.

The clientele look silently and with anticipation at the soup pot. Each unfolds a piece of paper with a small piece of bread kept since breakfast, some produce test tubes with pepper or have a supply of salt, but within a minute or two their patience is at an end:

'Anastasia Ivanovna, may I have a bowlful now, please!'

'Anastasia Ivanovna, I am waiting!'

'Tasenka, 200 grams of bread, please!'

'Anastasia Ivanovna, do please serve me!'

Everybody suddenly became very animated, jumping up from their places, reaching out for soup at the risk of spilling it over their neighbour.

When the soup had finally been served to everyone, the silence was disturbed only by the sound of slurping and munching. Then there was again a commotion and shouting as people ordered their next course.

'Tasya, Tasenka bring me a double portion of boiled grain', booms the mighty voice of Vishnyakov.

'Anastasia Ivanovna, am I ever going to be served?' someone's pleading, reedy voice breaks through the general hubbub.

Tasya blinks, annoyed and confused. Someone accuses her of being slow, someone else deliberates on the rudeness of waitresses, someone else again looks doubtfully at their plate of porridge and, seeking support from their neighbour, queries, 'Is this really a double helping?'

Then everybody calms down again. When the meal is over, they queue to pay. The waitresses openly question the honesty of the diners and have no hesitation in querulously disputing who has eaten how much of what.[55]

Irascibility was not confined to canteens. 'Everybody was extraordinarily irritable', Dmitry Likhachev recalled.[56] Conflict and quarrelling between people is common in every period, not only in wartime. What was different here was the causes and how heated the arguments became. There was irritation at people slow to adapt to the hardships of the siege, at citizens unable to cope, but also at those who seemed in suspiciously good health. Shop assistants were hostile towards customers prepared to queue for hours at empty counters.[57] Passengers were irritated by others trying to squeeze into already overcrowded trams. People in queues rounded on would-be queue-jumpers with all sorts of claims to priority. Pedestrians complained about someone shambling along slowly and getting in their way. They objected to the crying of a hungry child, and gave a hard time to the cleaner who heated up the tea half an hour before the lunch break so that nobody got to drink it hot.

'It was the hunger made everyone ratty', Alexandra Zmitrichenko noted, and was indubitably right.[58] During the siege, however, as at any other time, many aspects of everyday life reflected how people had been brought up and educated, their culture, and realities they were powerless to alter. Often enough, Leningraders could not explain their irritability themselves. They felt their own emotional reactions had been excessive when they saw what had caused them.

5

The major cause of physical and moral deterioration was hunger. Its most visible sign was a person's external appearance. On 17 January 1942, Lev Khodorkov noted, 'People take a second look at anyone in the street who has a normal, pink complexion.'[59] It was often remarked on that victims of the siege had swollen faces, which was usually ascribed to excessive consumption of salt water to alleviate hunger pangs. A contributing factor may also have been the 'coupon-free' soups served in institutional and factory canteens.[60] People were sometimes allowed several helpings of this turbid liquid, of almost no nutritional value, without pasta, grains or meat. Some of it would be taken home, and the consequences soon made themselves felt. The legs would swell, and then the 'dropsy' would spread to the rest of the body, affecting even the eyes. Walking became difficult, there was great pain in the legs, and shoes no longer fitted swollen feet.

Eyewitnesses' observations concur, and enable us to produce a portrait of the average siege victim without privileged access to food. They were pale, emaciated, puffy, swollen ('bloated and sagging', in the words of Irina Zelenskaya),[61] with a jaundiced or ashen complexion. They had wrinkles, bruises, milky, watery bags under the eyes, and walked in an 'odd', 'ungainly' manner,[62] 'unable to control their legs properly, and as if they had the heavy weights of religious penitents attached to their feet'.[63]

This was not really walking: with great effort they were placing one foot in front of the other an inch at a time. M. I. Chaiko wrote of the 'highly practical gait of one woman': 'No elegance, legs apart, a walking stick, and forward.'[64] Their movements were slow and they crept forward carefully. Quite often even children were leaning on sticks and crutches.[65]

Many spoke very slowly. I. Byliev reproduces their speech in his account of the artist, Ya. Nikolaev. He had spilled his soup and offered an exchange: 'He went on, making the same extraordinary effort, "I'll give you my coupon for grains and you . . . what do I mean? . . . you know . . . and you'll get, and we can . . . what do I mean? . . . you know . . ."'[66]

The symptoms of scurvy were particularly distressing, and much in evidence in spring 1942. The skin on people's legs turned purple and was covered in inflamed pustules. These would harden and walking became very painful. Some people were still lame many months later. There were stomach pains, the body was covered in boils, the face in congealed sores. The tongue would swell, sour food tasted bitter and sweet food tasted sour.[67] Another of the symptoms of scurvy was loss of teeth as the result of gum disease. Mina Bochaver accompanies her dry but medically precise listing of symptoms with a metaphor: 'We could easily extract them ourselves, like pulling cigarettes out of a pack.'[68]

Local people soon grew used to 'siege' faces, but those from further away found them horrifying. Boris Babochkin, who came to Leningrad in spring 1942, later recalled, 'An actress arrived. She had been a great beauty but now her teeth had fallen out and she was a wreck. She kept herself alive by picking up rats run over near the stores by trucks during the night.'[69] The appearance of some people, however, appalled even those who had become inured to most things during the siege. 'I just don't know how to describe it. If I had not met him in the street I would never have recognized him'; 'It gave me a fright: he looked so horrible, his face all swollen'; 'I was shocked by the sight of him, he was terribly swollen'; 'How he has changed. I can't put it into words. It is unimaginable.'[70] It was difficult to be with such people. They themselves were ashamed of their appearance (especially the women), and would try to keep their face turned away.[71] And what else could they do when it was obvious that the people talking to them could barely control their fear and did not want to look them in the face? How could the 'dystrophics', disfigured by starvation and with their slow speech and gestures, conduct a normal conversation when everybody who saw them was stunned and overcome by pity? There was nothing they could do to improve the situation. Indeed, every further day of famine made them less recognizable and more frightening. This may have been why people stopped bothering to keep their clothes clean and tidy, to wash themselves and take care over personal hygiene. Other causes, perhaps more impor-tant, were the general frailty of the people suffering from starvation, the lack of light, heat and running water in their rooms, and the closure of the bathhouses and other communal services.[72] The ubiquity of grimy, smoky faces is regularly commented on in testimony about the winter of 1941–2. T. Nezhintseva wrote of how ashamed she was to be going unwashed to the maternity hospital but, 'I found everyone had the same problem.'[73]

There was no firewood because people had not the strength to fetch it, so there was no heat. There was no water, and emaciated citizens who had difficulty getting to standpipes or holes in the ice had to save every drop, using it only for drinking and cooking.[74] There were few bathhouses and no fuel to heat them. Entry was only by official permit or ration coupons, for which not everyone was eligible. It could come to the point, as Irina Zelenskaya notes, where 'even the bathhouse becomes an inaccessible luxury, because it is freezing cold, the water barely tepid, and there are terrible queues'.[75] In icy apartments and hostels people went without washing for weeks or months.[76] They slept fully dressed, trying not to get out of bed, hiding from the cold under piles of bedclothes. The sewage system was not functioning and apartments, staircases and courtyards were flooded with filth. Rats and lice became emblematic of the Time of Death.[77] Everyone was at risk of being infested with lice, which was more often than not the situation among orphans sent to the children's homes, but also among workers.[78] There was no electricity, no public transport, no mail or radio. You could not read, write, meet friends, or hear the news. You could not clean your room, wash your clothes or yourself.

When the use of electrical equipment was banned in September 1941 and paraffin was rationed to 2.5 litres per month, one Leningrader lamented that he would be unable to iron his linen.[79] Within a few weeks, people had ceased to worry about such trivia. They still suffered from the winter's cold even when covered with several blankets or coats. (Some who survived the winter of 1941–2 stressed that it was more of a trial than the hunger.) They carried on wearing felt boots and winter coats not only through the spring but even as late as July 1942.[80] Starving people found it more difficult to keep warm, and learned to overcome their embarrassment at piling on clothing which might be worn and dirty.[81] Everyone did it, both workers and intellectuals. When Alexander Fadeyev, the secretary of the Union of Writers, had a meeting with Leningrad writers, he immediately commanded in his customary masterful tone of voice: 'Clothes coupons! Clothes coupons for everybody! Writers need proper clothing.'[82]

6

'Eats the porridge slowly, spoon trembling in his bony little hand.' This is a starving child delivered to a children's home: his mother had been helping herself to his food ration. A 'little skeleton with a big skull above a tiny face the size of a fist'.[83] The slow speed of eating food was not just the result of exhaustion, but also of a determination to make the feeling of satiety last as long as humanly possible in order to stave off the obsessive, aching pangs of hunger. The body language of a person devouring bread betrays fear of being deprived of their tiny portion. There is a complete focusing on only this piece of bread, a detachment from the rest of the world and other people. There is a careful 'listening' to one's own organism, a concern to confirm that the hunger is going away. There is also a tormenting need to restrain oneself: what a powerful temptation it is to guzzle the whole piece in next to no time! The artistic performance which accompanied the actor Boris Babochkin's telling his friends about his trip to the besieged city conveyed these nuances starkly: 'He mimicked the scene of someone in Leningrad eating bread: he covers the slice with his hand, looks around him, breaks off a piece the size of a fingernail, halves it, puts it in his mouth, leans back in his chair and impassively waits for it to melt, before returning to the next piece.'[84]

Maria Mashkova wrote disdainfully about someone she knew who divided his bread into fifty tiny pieces, put them in two boxes, and apportioned minuscule amounts of sugar and other food between them: 'He does not simply eat the bread, but lays it out first, piece by piece, in a chequer or some other pattern.' When he was told about this, Mashkova's husband himself stopped dividing the bread even into small pieces.[85] One can see why, but such actions can hardly be considered pathological.

Everyone was trying to survive. Some divided their ration, and then ate part in the morning, part during the day and part in the evening. Some found a 4-hour wait for lunch or dinner unendurable. By dividing the ration into fifty pieces, they had only to hold out for 15 to 20 minutes.

Although the portions were microscopic and could hardly satisfy any-body's hunger, there was at least some prospect that they might alleviate the pangs. Apportioning them between two boxes was an aid to self-restraint, and perhaps even a form of reassurance: watching the rapid disappearance of the pieces in one box, there was the consolation that the other was still untouched. Arranging the bread in patterns can be seen as a way of overcoming the temptation to eat all of it at once. There was no doubt a danger that these manipulations might become obsessional. While they could provide a sense of structure, they might be seen by others as bizarre rituals on the road to degeneration.

'You fear that now you will never feel full. That is a bad, even fright-ening, feeling: frightening because the worst thing imaginable is that the hunger may become even more intense', we read in one diary.[86] That fear not only drove people to divide their bread into dozens of tiny pieces and hide pinches of sugar away in boxes. Some Leningraders, despite severe malnutrition, decided to hoard bread and other food from their already meagre rations. They also hoarded money in order, at some future time, to be able to supplement their diet on the black market. When one worker died, he was found to have saved up 3,000 rubles and hoarded a kilo-gram of sugar. Another had saved up 1,500 rubles. An employee at the Public Library who starved to death in December 1941 was found to have hoarded food at home. This behaviour was considered not just aberrant, but despicable, especially given that one of them 'had begged with tears in his eyes for help with food', while another had been 'begging for crumbs'.[87]

'The most terrible thing about hunger is that it can deform good people.' Such was the conclusion of the librarian's colleague, but these dead people had had no time for observing the proprieties.[88] They were probably aware that their behaviour was disgraceful, that they might die as a result of it, but found even more monstrous the hunger that could turn a person's life upside down and reduce them to a howling animal with no prospect of respite. Perhaps, too, they found life unendurable without the knowledge that they had a secret stash of food and money to fall back on if the suffering became intolerable.

7

The way people ate also started to change. This was particularly notice-able in the canteens, where plates would be licked clean. Nobody was embarrassed, because those next to them were doing the same.[89] People would eat in public with grimy, unwashed hands; water was in short supply and difficult to heat. As early as September 1941, some canteens ran out of spoons and forks. Maria Konoplyova complained to her diary about how quickly they had reverted to the level of 1919 and the 1920s: 'the same dried roach as then, the same lack of cutlery, the same angry, greedy mobs'.[90] She had to eat standing up because there was nowhere to sit: 'There was no fork to be found. I had to drink the soup and eat the dried fish with a spoon and, of course, some help from the bread and my hand.'[91] This later became commonplace. One report mentions the Primorsky 'Eating Centre' and Primorsky District Canteen No. 1, where 'some of the diners eat their food immediately, without the benefit of spoons or forks'.[92] Hungry people could not wait. On 18 January 1942, I. I. Zhilinsky noted in his diary that, owing to the lack of spoons, 'many of them slurp their soup over the rim of the plate, or lap it up like cats'.[93]

The information bulletin of the Staff Training Department of Leningrad City Party Committee on 26 March 1942 reported on restaurants which were clean and welcoming, and where the waiting staff treated diners with courtesy. It had rather more to say, however, about other outlets. The report notes that, in the two halls of the Kirov Eating Centre, 'the conditions are chaotic, disorderly and unhygienic'; 'Meals are frequently served on dirty crockery brought in by the customers themselves, who dine standing at dirty tables. The halls are cold and dirty, and the staff serving the food are in grimy work clothes. Some have hands and necks black with dirt.'[94] Things looked no better in the canteens of the Kuibyshev and October districts: 'The Metropol, at one time a high-quality restaurant, has been turned into a squalid dive. The staff wear dirty coats, the head cook excelling in this respect, with a dirty rag hanging from his belt instead of a towel.' In Canteen No. 12, also in Kuibyshev district, 'aspic and cheese are dispensed with dirty hands, and soup is poured into dirty tin cans directly over the cauldron'. In Canteen No. 18 of the October Canteen Group, 'the premises are unbelievably smoky (defective hob) and water is literally dripping from the ceiling and down the walls, while there is a rubbish tip immediately outside the window where food is being served'.[95]

Fastidiousness, something which mitigates the animal side of man, was doomed during the siege, because otherwise no one would have survived. This was much written about: there is a great fund of reminiscences, unromanticized and unapologetic. Izrail Metter recalled a hospital cook who, lacking crockery, poured porridge for his brother, who was a cleaner, into a galosh.[96] Rita Malkova recalled some herring heads she received from a kitchen, covered in soot and ash. There was no water with which to wash them but, 'We were so hungry, we just ate them as they were.'[97] A. P. Bondarenko recalled soldiers allowing her to take a crate of peelings mixed with cigarette stubs and used matches.[98] Such instances may not have been common, but it is clear that nobody turned up their nose at bread because it had fallen in the mud, or porridge because there was no bowl for it.

All sorts of items were used as food: wood and wallpaper glue; linseed oil; oilcake (more traditionally used as animal fodder); bran; belts made of pigskin; rotten, black cabbage leaves; acorns. People ate the leaves of houseplants, and candles.[99] Leaching nutrients out of 'sweet' soil from the site of the Badaev warehouses became routine: people dug the burnt-out soil out themselves or bought it at the market.[100] The top layer of this soil, to a depth of 1 metre, was most saturated with sugar and fetched 100 rubles a kilo: soil beneath that fetched 50 rubles.[101]

Fastidiousness disappeared rapidly. People became inured to the smell and taste of engine oil, buttons made of bone, glue, and petroleum jelly lubricant: 'I obtained axle grease. It is dirty and smelly, but now I am very glad of it. It helps.' That was the main point, not only for V. F. Chekrizov who wrote that diary entry, but for hundreds of other citizens.[102] When, in June 1942, a strict prohibition was introduced on issuing industrial raw materials as food surrogates, it caused major difficulties at the Zhdanov factory, where 'the workers had become so used to them'.[103]

'No matter how much they ate, it was never enough', commented one factory manager.[104] It was in spring 1942, despite an increase in the food ration, that the pangs of hunger became unbearable for many Leningraders. Months of undereating finally hit home. Some were now prepared to eat anything, no matter how disgusting, and scenes were played out that would have seemed unbelievable even in December 1941. In May 1942, Anna Umanskaya noticed a woman leaving a food shop who could not resist gnawing at a herring she had just been issued.[105] There were, however, considerably more startling incidents in spring 1942. Here is the story of a factory worker sent to clear a rubbish tip in March 1942: 'We took off two or three dead bodies, a layer of filth, and underneath it all found some pre-war potato peelings frozen into the ice. We shared it out among ourselves and promptly ate it.'[106]

This incident might seem incredible, but it is corroborated by other descriptions featuring corpses in courtyards and on rubbish tips covered in muck,[107] and the same irresistible urge to eat instantly anything remotely edible. In an entry in Esfir Levina's diary, dated April 1942, we find even more dispiriting testimony to the humiliation suffered by starving people who would stop at nothing to quell the pangs of hunger.[108] There is a detailed and frank description of this in the memoirs also of 12-year-old Rita Malkova. Her tale of how she used to hang around outside the hospital canteen is one of the most harrowing testimonies of the siege. She and her mother added the peelings thrown out by the kitchen staff to their soya yogurt and black cabbage leaves: 'but when there is nothing, I just sit with my mother and go hungry. If they throw everything out before my mother gets there, I don't go to meet her, I sit and collect whatever scraps there are.'[109]

On her way home from work, her mother would first head for the rubbish tip, and that is how they survived the first winter of the war. Other people came, who were just as hungry, and 'When a container or crate of cabbage leaves was brought out from the canteen, everybody would start fighting and swearing and wanting it.'[110] Memory selects from the past fragments of the stories from the siege. It edits them in unexpected ways and greatly simplifies them. Although unrelated to each other, the one thing they always have in common is the sense of hopelessness. There are digressions, but that is what is so valuable. Only by learning all the details of life during the siege can we reconstruct the experience of this terrible time, and the suffering of those stuck at the bottom of the pile.

Severely debilitated and with no expectation of help from anyone, they had no choices and would to go to any lengths to survive. 'But then, one Sunday my mum had the day off and was at home, tidying everything up. I was waiting around at the canteen, to be there for the container because it was on Sundays they threw out the best stuff. Anyway, they brought out the container and I grabbed it, but it was very heavy. I was dragging it along the ground but then just had no more strength and started shouting through the window to my mum. She came running.'

Sixty years later, Rita Malkova amended her story: 'No, what I wrote back then was wrong. Of course my mother couldn't run; she could barely walk. She was holding on to the wall of our building, sometimes falling. I remember one time she fell in a puddle and I wasn't strong enough to lift her. "Please, mister . . . missus, help me lift my mum", I asked passers-by.'[111]

8

People waiting outside kitchens in the hope of leftovers were to be seen in other places. G. Yurmin was in hospital and describes the queue by the canteen of the Voentorg army store there. Civilians servicing the army, from plumbers to cleaning staff, were completely emaciated and all stood with plates in their hands. They were wearing white coats, perhaps afraid of being thrown out as having no connection with the hospital. Yurmin writes that all of them had swollen, dropsical family members at home. They probably talked here about their family misfortunes in the hope of eliciting a compassionate response. They had no time for propriety and no cause to be embarrassed in front of others who were just as hungry. Everyone waited patiently, 'all of them trusting some small mercy would come their way. None of them dared hope for a proper serving, but all were hoping for leftovers.'[112]

Some of the starving abased themselves and managed to beg scraps at an army, factory, institutional or academic canteen. Others were out of luck. Unable to bear the hunger, and giving up hope of managing to beg anything, they were reduced to the even greater humiliation of licking used plates in full view of everyone.

Irina Zelenskaya, working at the canteen of a power station, witnessed such scenes of degradation every day. A distinctive feature of these people was a kind of resignation which characterized the dying. They never took offence, blamed nobody, did not complain, and accepted death as inevitable. Their efforts to resist it seemed more instinctive than deliberate. 'What a terrible procession of the dead passes before my eyes', she recalled in July 1942; 'That boy, Zelenkov. How he clung to the canteen partition, unable to tear himself away from the sight of food that was not for him. Old Frolov, begging for a second "wee soup".'[113]

She writes about another worker who behaved very imperiously in the canteen, until he lost his ration coupons and documents. She came across him then, 'so dejected, stooped, politely expressing gratitude for a single plate of coupon-free soup and a spare crust of bread'.[114] Zelenskaya seems to see him as having mended his ways, but the impression conveyed is that he had been broken.

After many days of starvation, some Leningraders became meek, unnaturally sweet-tempered, humbly listening to criticism. N. V. Frolov, a time-and-motion specialist, wrote of what he endured in early February 1942:

> I can't walk back on my own, of course. Kitty will pull me on the sledge. It's very demeaning but can't be helped. If you want to live you have to put up with it. Kitty won't let me do anything, so as not to use up my remaining strength. I find that very dispiriting, but there's nothing I can do about it. I am in her power. She knows how to treat me and what's for the best.[115]

When M. K. Tikhonova, the wife of poet Nikolai Tikhonov, saw people crying in April 1942 at the sight of the first tram, and giving way to their fellow passengers in it, she felt there was something 'dystrophic' about it.[116] They no longer had the energy to fight for anything or stand up for themselves. They could only pin their hopes on other people's kindness, hope they would not be refused a crust of bread or a log for the fire, not be pushed away from the stove, deprived of their ration coupons or kicked out of their home. So malnourished that they could now barely move, they tried not to appear useless, to find some way of showing gratitude. There are many mentions at this time of people eager to attach themselves to any source of support, not even asking for anything. N. I. Yerokhina described one person who, despite being the weakest, would not allow anyone else to take out the slop buckets: 'He has become an old man, with the feverish eyes of someone completely worn out, very thin. He speaks very nasally. So submissive, apologetic . . . he has become so sensitive and sentimental. Several times he was on the verge of tears.'[117]

It is difficult to see this as moral growth. These people often talked only about food and were no longer battling. The more intently other Leningraders observed such people, and the more unsentimentally they scrutinized their behaviour, the more clearly they felt they were showing signs of degeneration: 'This meekness, as we later came to understand, was an intimation of death. It was a state in which a person started constantly using sentimental diminutives and qualifiers, talking about "maybe a little piece of bread" or "perhaps just a wee drop of water", and became boundlessly polite and docile.' This insight comes from Olga Berggolts, one of the most insightful and objective witnesses of the siege.[118]

This is how all the old customs came to change. The undermining of one led to the loss of others. By no means everybody withstood this process. There is an inevitability, a relentless logic, about the pattern of deterioration of individuals in the Time of Death.[119] Who was capable of sharing bread and porridge? Someone who would endure any humiliation in order to obtain them? Someone who hoarded food while begging it from others? Someone who broke their ties with family and friends, withdrew into themselves and became indifferent to the suffering of others? Someone who let go, lost their sense of dignity and shame, and gave in to purely animal instincts?

This did not happen in the early months but, when we examine the course taken by any death during the siege, we cannot fail to notice certain markers of decline which apply to everyone, even the most steadfast. Once the process began, people might succumb gradually, barely perceptibly, or with extraordinary rapidity. Everything depended on their circumstances, which often changed, and their inner ability to withstand adversity.

The breakdown of moral standards

1

The most widespread manifestations of a breakdown of moral standards in the Time of Death were fraud, theft, robbery and looting. Fraud was most common in the markets. The techniques were familiar: fakes resembling authentic items were offered for sale or exchange. Instead of sweets, there would be putty; instead of cooking oil, industrial oil; instead of semolina, powder for making glue. 'Chemical compounds', according to one contemporary, were the mainstay of these fraudulent transactions, but there were more original approaches, which even found their way into a report of the *Sicherheitsdienst*, the security service of the German SS, compiled in spring 1942.[120]

There were more intricate and outrageous episodes. Vera Inber relates a case in which a swindler singled out a mother and daughter in a queue, got talking to them, 'wormed her way into their confidence', and promised to arrange a job for the daughter washing dishes in a military hospital: 'She took from the girl both their ration cards for the entire month, the girl's and her mother's, plus some money the mother had borrowed, supposedly to buy food for them, and promptly vanished in the darkness.'[121] This was evidently everything they had,[122] as the swindler must have known as she cheated them out of their last 45 rubles, a pathetic amount in terms of market prices at that time.

There were more conventional deception techniques, such as giving short measure in shops and bakeries. It was easiest, and least obvious, for sales assistants to cheat customers when bread was being sold against several people's coupons. Valentina Bazanova, who several times details the dishonest practices of sales assistants in her diary, highlights the fact that even her maid, who was entitled to just 125 grams of bread a day, was 'constantly being cheated'. She was usually buying bread for the whole family.[123] Owing to dim lighting in the shops, and the fact that many siege victims were barely able to stand on their feet, salespeople could surreptitiously tear too many coupons out of the cards. It was difficult to catch them red-handed.[124]

There are similarities in how ration cards were misused in civilian and military hospitals. The fraud was equally straightforward. When Varvara Vraskaya collected her daughter from hospital 'almost starved to death' on 6 November 1941, she found the child's ration card, which she had entrusted to the hospital while the girl was in their care, had been clipped of its special coupon for children for the 7 November holiday. She got the matter rectified only after pursuing it all the way to the hospital director.[125] Theft was not infrequent in the hospital service. It is no wonder so many people wanted a job of any description there, and made no secret of the advantages they expected that to confer. During an inspection in February 1943, it was found that between six and eight healthcare workers in the Nakhimson and Karl Liebknecht hospitals were regularly dining in the canteen without handing over the necessary ration coupons, and were effectively eating the patients' food.[126] This had probably been going on well before February 1943. The inspection documents for Hospital No. 109 show this was not a matter of the odd crust of bread or a few leftovers. In December 1942, patients had been cheated out of 22.7% of fats, 49% of potato mix, 9% of vegetables and 50% of their tea.[127]

There were attempts to steal food even in children's home and reception and reallocation centres, although these may have been isolated cases. There is almost no direct evidence, and such indirect evidence as exists is not always reliable.[128] Controls here were evidently more stringent. As Lazar Ratner recalled, the children had only to start yelling when they saw the old care assistant helping herself 'with the sleight of hand of a magician spooning something off every plate' for her to be dismissed, in short order, without fuss, without threats to send her to the tribunal, and without articles in the newspaper demanding she should be shot.[129] In another children's home, they decided to dismiss an assistant hired just three days previously. Prior to that, the woman had evidently been starving, and could not contain herself and behave like the other teachers: 'While she was taking their meal to the children, she scooped some porridge off the tray and ate it in a corner.'[130] In all these cases, the whistle-blowers were the children themselves.

Pilfering in public and institutional canteens became legendary.[131] The city's leaders seem to have become partly resigned to it. Noting that there was a flood of people applying to work in public catering, Alexey Kuznetsov recommended using the situation to advantage by selecting only the best to work there, apparently unaware of the ambiguity of his phrase: 'because the food issue is very serious'. Even in the Writers Union restaurant, in September 1941, before starvation became really acute, they discovered what E. Gollerbakh described as 'a Panama situation':[132] 'Each diner was entitled to 100 grams of bread as well as meat dishes without deduction from their ration cards, but the restaurant was taking bread and meat coupons off them.'[133] There was thieving also in school canteens. In September, representatives of the Lenin District Prosecutor's Office tested churns of soup in the kitchen of one school. They found that a churn with watery soup was destined for the pupils, one with 'standard' soup was for teachers, while a third churn contained 'soup as thick as porridge'. They were unable to discover who that was for.[134] In the canteen serving pupils of Vocational School No. 62 they also noted 'a number of instances of short measure and fraudulent weighing of bread'.[135]

Something which facilitated cheating in canteens was the fact that the official instruction governing rations of cooked food and how it was to be served were complex and confusing. The techniques to be employed in kitchens are described in a report by the team inspecting the work of the Main Directorate of Leningrad Canteens and Cafes: 'Porridge of a stiff consistency should have a ratio of water to solids of 350%; semi-liquid should have 510%. The addition of surplus water, particularly where production is on a large scale, goes completely unnoticed and enables catering workers to misappropriate foodstuffs by the kilogram, without resorting to giving short measure.'[136] Instances of giving short measure were more difficult to conceal, but they were nothing out of the ordinary, particularly in the canteens of schools and kindergartens, to say nothing of nurseries. Official inspections probably only uncovered the tip of the iceberg. They were not carried out every day, were not always performed scrupulously, and did not extend to all catering outlets. The inspectors were themselves sometimes being fed at the kitchens they were inspecting. Combating the evil was all the more difficult because many – including some who complained vehemently about pilfering – were prepared to help out others who were in dire straits, and could not always themselves resist the temptation to obtain an extra helping of food. One person who was trying to get something to eat by working on a canteen employee noted, 'Yesterday I was very much in luck. I am quite a diplomat. Not a Litvinov, perhaps, but still . . .'[137] Another Leningrader was appointed manager of a clinic where severely malnourished people were treated as inpatients. 'I may be able to do something in terms of getting extra rations', she writes in her diary.[138] A family of teachers discussed how to hold out in lean times: 'Our plan was for my mother to work, perhaps, in a children's home if that could be arranged.'[139] It was the same everywhere. Almost everyone had been beholden on at least one occasion to army personnel, to someone working in canteens, military or civilian hospitals, Party and Komsomol committees or other government agencies, institutions caring for children, warehouses, bakeries, bread shops, confectionery or tobacco factories. They took the food without asking where it had come from, feeling justified on the grounds that it was needed for their starving children or family, or needing no more justification than that their hunger had become unbearable.

2

Burgling and looting of apartments became more common. Many of these were empty, their owners either evacuated or all dead. Looting, as Z. S. Livshits testifies, assumed 'monstrous proportions'.

It was not only other people's apartments which were robbed. There was theft within hostels and institutes; one worker cleaning a bomb shelter even stole the emergency ration of biscuits for a local kindergarten from a safe.[140] Olga Grechina recalls a doctor writing a prescription, for a sick mother in the next room, and stealing nearly all the children's lollipops.[141] The inventory of what was stolen reflects the misery of life during the siege. Valuables were stolen, of course, and clothes, but most often it was firewood.[142] Personal libraries were plundered, sometimes from the ruins of buildings which had just been bombed. The books were used not only for fuelling stoves, but also to be profitably sold: books continued to be in demand. During a fire at the Gostiny Dvor shopping arcade, dozens of people were arrested as they attempted to make off with cologne, soap and tooth powder.[143] People sent to clear rubble also engaged in looting, especially 'vocational' schoolboys. 'After digging, one boy came back with a pair of galoshes', V. P. Bylinsky, the deputy political instructor of a vocational school, reported.[144] That occurred in full view of everyone, so there will have been many more incidents where people were not under close supervision.

Housing managers and caretakers were often suspected of being major looters. It was their job to seal up the apartments not only of evacuees (which offered quite a few lucrative opportunities), but also of the dead, which really did offer rich pickings.[145] Vladislav Glinka told, with his customary eloquence, the tale of one such housing manager:

> This formidable woman with the manners and vocabulary of the tavern, at this terrible time, February 1942, lost no weight at all, acquired an even more imperious tone and, fearing no man, took to swearing like a trooper. One time, when I happened to witness her lugging out of a neighbouring apartment, all of whose occupants had died, suitcases and a bundle, she informed me, evidently just to be on the safe side, 'I'm taking them to the storeroom to hand in to social welfare.' The apartment was duly sealed. By that time no social welfare department was operational.[146]

Where it was difficult to conceal their thieving from other people's apartments, housing managers would share some of the booty with other residents, to ensure they would not report the matter to the authorities. Sometimes neighbours robbed apartments with the connivance of the housing manager, which doubtless came at a price.[147]

A useful perk for housing managers and caretakers was withholding information about the death or evacuation of residents, thus enabling them to use their ration books to obtain food for themselves. They would also use ration books, which relatives of the dead returned to them to avoid getting into trouble with the authorities. Housing managers would sometimes conspire with caretakers to obtain ration books for fictitious residents.

3

Theft of food ration cards also became commonplace. Getting replacements involved cumbersome bureaucratic rituals, which were often too much for starving people to cope with. There were humiliating checks, carried out incredibly slowly, and there was no question of obtaining full compensation for lost cards. In any case, few people survived long enough, unless they had some alternative access to food.

Cards were most often stolen when citizens were in a crowd, usually at bread shops, stores or stalls. Some had their cards stolen more than once, probably because the thieves preyed on the most vulnerable people in a crowd. One siege victim was robbed when he fainted in a bread shop. The thieves could be very brazen. E. S. Kots recalled, 'They pickpocketed, almost in full view, all our cards, mine, my mother's, and all our canteen coupons.'[148] Food too was stolen, especially in trams, or during evacuation when people were boarding the train and unable in the stampede to keep a close eye on all their bags.

Frail people were also a target and could have their cards and food stolen.[149] This usually occurred in bakeries and bread shops if a customer was seen to be confused when taking food off the counter to put in their bag, or putting their card or gloves back in their pockets.[150] Thieves would also attack people just outside shops. Not infrequently, hungry citizens would be coming out holding their bread, totally absorbed in breaking small pieces off it and not looking out for possible danger. Often the thief would steal only the makeweight bread, which could be eaten faster. Children were also likely to be attacked, because it was easier to take food off them.[151]

Robberies were sometimes so well organized, the thieves appearing so suddenly and disappearing so rapidly, that it is hard to believe they were suffering from starvation at all. It seems highly unlikely that all the large-scale robberies were spontaneous. A motley crowd needed to be assembled, at least temporarily, its actions coordinated, and it needed to be imbued with resolve and audacity.

'Bread was being taken out of the bakery in our truck at six in the morning. As it came out of the gate, five people jumped in the back. Grigoriev stopped and, he says, a crowd of about fifty people appeared 'as if out of nowhere' and fell upon the delivery. They made off with about 100 kg of bread', Irina Zelenskaya notes in her diary on 20 January 1942.[152] Other large-scale attacks followed much the same pattern.[153] The driver would hardly have had time to count the number of attackers accurately, and may also have been under pressure to explain himself, but the coordinated nature of the raid was plain to see. Looting of bread shops was usually more spontaneous. That almost all these incidents occurred towards the end of January 1942 is readily explicable. At that time a succession of burst pipes, as was entirely predictable, cut the water supply to bakeries and they ceased functioning. During this period, from 27 to 29 January, 'senior comrades' disappeared from view, applying themselves to saving the lives of Leningrad's citizens only to the extent necessary for their inaction not to look completely outrageous, as mortality rose to unprecedented levels.

'Some of the bread was trampled underfoot.' This happened during the looting by a mob of Shop No. 8 of the Primorsky District Food Trust, when 50 kg of bread was stolen. Twenty-four people were arrested.[154] How can anyone talk about this having been 'organized'? The bread trampled underfoot is the most eloquent testimony to the fact that this was an anarchic, emotional, impulsive outburst by starving people reduced to desperation by standing in endless queues and, perhaps for the first time in several months, now having a whole loaf of bread in their hands. The spontaneity of the looting of Shop No. 97 of the Krasnogvardeisky Trust and of Shop No. 12 of the Lenin Trust in January 1942 is obvious from the sequence of the angry mob's actions: they smashed the counter, threw bricks, and broke into the storeroom.[155] These people are very unlike the robbers who attacked the bread delivery truck and instantly vanished into the darkness. They were people who, having queued for several hours in severe frost, were outraged to find the bread shop empty, demanded that the managers should come out to speak to them, and drowned their explanations in curses. They wanted to see for themselves whether these people were lying, and broke into the rest of the buildings looking for bread.

4

It was not difficult to see the faces of many of those who attacked customers in bakeries and shops. Themselves starving, they could not run far, and were usually children and teenagers.[156] Their families had either died or were not able to take care of them, and the bread ration for children was tantamount to a slow death by starvation unless they could sell or barter something, or beg. Nobody had any use for them, and they had no option but to hang around the shops and bakeries. Some asked for charity; others, despairing of that and unable to bear the hunger any longer, attacked equally malnourished passers-by.

Having stolen the bread, not all managed to get away. Lev Razumovsky describes how 'both of them ran unsteadily, a boy of fifteen and an elderly woman he had robbed'.[157] Varvara Vraskaya witnessed a slightly different scene: 'I was walking down Liteyny Prospekt and saw a young man seize some bread a woman was holding.' Vraskaya realized he was in such a hurry to eat it because 'he was in no condition to escape a beating'.[158]

Stolen bread was usually eaten immediately.[159] In December 1941, Boris Kapranov wrote in his diary about a girl who snatched some bread in a shop: 'She started eating it voraciously. The sales assistant began cursing and beating her but she just said, "I'm hungry, I want something to eat."'[160] Others who witnessed the rough justice meted out make no mention of any excuses the food-snatchers may have made. In one appalling scene, when an attempt was made to extract a piece of bread from a bloody mouth, no one was interested in explanations or excuses. They describe only the shrieking of the robbed and the wailing of those being beaten. 'Boys particularly suffered from hunger. They rushed at the bread and immediately began eating it. They made no attempt to escape: they just wanted to eat as much as they could before it was taken from them. They would turn up their collars in anticipation of the beating, fall upon the bread, and eat and eat', Dmitry Likhachev recalls.'[161] Many such scenes are described, and involved not only teenagers but people of other ages.[162]

Here is a typical scene. Someone receiving their ration dithered. A puny, haggard-looking 12-year-old girl was standing nearby. She, 'literally like a vulture, flew over to the counter, swooped on the bread and raced outside. The girl seemed to be clutching it in talons, ripping pieces off and, without chewing them, swallowing them whole. The crowd tore her shawl off and hit her frenziedly with anything that came to hand.'[163]

She managed to devour all the bread. No one could stop her.[164] She seemed unaware of the beating, concentrating on not letting anyone take the bread away and ripping off one piece after another. Perhaps the pain, the humiliation, and the beating would register later, when the murderous pangs of hunger were stilled for a time. 'The girl fell to the wet pavement, a little bundle, and began sobbing inconsolably.'[165] Curled up in a ball, she was less vulnerable to further beating, and perhaps her tears might arouse pity in those beating her.

'The crowd dispersed.' These final terse words are dry, as if everything ended in silence. Perhaps some felt shame and remorse. There had been people in the crowd who tried to stop the 'useless, ugly beating'.[166] We have no evidence about this kind of rough justice leading to a fatal outcome. Order was quickly restored and, where possible, the raiders were handed over to the police. The beating of the culprit was not only an act of retribution: people genuinely wanted to get back at least part of the bread which had been snatched, and were not fussy about how they went about it, or about keeping within civilized bounds.[167]

Lives were at stake. Behaving in any other way, you risked finding yourself without a crumb of even chewed and blood-soaked bread. The women in a nearby beer queue pelted a teenage boy who was making off with someone's bread with jars and canisters. In such fights, they grabbed anything that came to hand.[168]

Even in cases like this, however, there were some who tried to intercede. While others were yelling, 'Beat him so he knows not to do it another time', someone would say, 'No, stop it.'[169] There may have been few of them, but it took courage to stand up, and especially when the woman who had been robbed was wailing nearby. Feelings of compassion are more evident in later writing about the siege than in the diaries of the war years, and yet there was no doubt a basis in reality for the signs of mercy which people later recalled.[170] They could do nothing to help, they could not bear to look, and they could not excuse the behaviour:

How they beat that poor girl for taking the bread. I felt sorry. I did not know how I could help her. They were beating her for helping herself to someone else's scrap of bread. How they beat and kicked her. I couldn't watch. But she did not let go of the bread until she had eaten it, no matter how they beat her.[171]

5

The fact remains that there is precious little sympathy in the accounts of beatings of those who stole bread. They are usually restrained, although hardly anyone witnessing the incidents fails to mention the emaciation of those reduced to thieving. One can understand why they did it, but what of their victims? They too had debilitated children constantly asking for food at home, family members and dependants without the strength to get up from their beds. Take any diary of the siege and you will read how eagerly people waited for someone to come back from the bakery with bread. They worked out how many little pieces it needed to be divided into for them all to survive until the next day, how to eke it out with rotten cabbage leaves, jelly made from glue or leather belts, and how to make it more filling; how to barter a piece of bread for vitamins for dropsical people toothless from scurvy, how best to exchange it for a tiny piece of butter or a glass of milk for an expiring child.

M. P. Pelevin recalled the Klevanichev family in which only Alla had a ration above 125 grams of bread a day, and did what she could to sustain her little sisters: 'When Alla gets up in the morning, her footsteps, though barely audible, have all of them agitated. All of them wake up and their thoughts silently go with her. From the moment the door closes behind her they are waiting in eager anticipation.'[172]

If someone snatches her bread, who can she turn to, where can she beg, what can she say to those who trusted her with their ration cards, how can she comfort the crying children? 'Me, me, me!' One woman who survived the siege could never afterwards forget these words of a sick, hungry little girl as she waited to be brought her kindergarten ration. 'There was something so terrible in her eyes.' The little girl did not survive.[173]

6

One further deplorable aspect of life during the siege was robbery from the dead. Such looting was to be observed not only in obscure courtyards but even in the streets of the city centre. 'They strip the dead of their hats and boots, go through their pockets, steal their food ration cards and all their valuables.' This excerpt from a letter written by V. A. Zavetnovsky to his daughter provides a comprehensive list of what looters got up to.[174]

Most prized at this time were the food ration cards. Eyewitnesses regularly noticed the unnatural position of the arms of the dead, outstretched or brought together. Possibly the looters had searched through their clothing while they were still alive and their bodies froze later. Georgiy Kulagin noticed that, even at their factory's collection point, to which the dead were brought, their arms were twisted behind their backs and their pockets had been turned out.[175]

'They were nearly all barefoot', he concludes his description.[176] The same was noted by other Leningraders.[177] Felt boots were usually stolen, as were hats and coats. These were highly prized by people living for months in freezing houses.[178] In spring 1942, when boots were less in use, shoes too would be taken.[179] The dead were stripped of their clothes, and even of the coverings in which they were taken out (or, rather, thrown out) into the street.

This was done not only furtively, under cover of darkness. M. G. Alexandrov, chief of staff of Kuibyshev District Air Defence Unit, reported that the clothing, blankets and sheets they were required to remove before corpses were sent to the cemetery lay heaped near the mortuary. He was shocked to find 'several people wandering among them, chosing rags which were still more or less usable'.[180] This kind of sight became familiar and the disgust reduced accordingly; hunger and cold did the rest. Grechina emphasized that, as far as taking footwear from the dead was concerned, 'no one regarded it as looting, and even grudgingly admired the boldness of people who did not let good boots and shoes go to waste'.[181] It is difficult to find corroborative evidence, but, frankly, it seems unlikely that looting would have become as widespread as it did if everybody had vehemently opposed it. The dead were robbed, not only in the streets or at the evacuation centre, but often at factories and institutions where one might have expected higher standards.[182]

What was most striking was the alacrity with which the looters often went about their business. "One time I registered my place in the bread queue. The delivery was late and I went back home to warm up. There was a dead woman near the path. At first she was fully dressed, with a warm shawl, a coat and felt boots, but while I was walking back and forth she was slowly undressed. First, her boots were removed, then the coat and skirt', recalls M. I. Vorobiova.[183] M. N. Kotlyarova records a similar episode.[184] In other areas, in other streets, the same script was played out. 'Under the archway there is a dead woman, barefoot. In the morning she was lying there wearing felt boots', Esfir Levina wrote in her diary on 23 February 1942.[185] Alexandra N. Mironova, on her way into the City Education Department, saw the bodies of two young women who had been killed during shelling. Returning two hours later, she noticed someone had removed their boots and coats.[186] We find similar testimony in the memoirs of A. V. Smolovik, secretary of the Party organization at the Stalin Factory: 'You are on your way to the Party Committee and see a corpse lying there. You ring the old fellow in charge of corpse removal, but while he is on his way you notice it has been stripped of its footwear and outer clothing.'[187]

The readiness to start looting so promptly, so unhesitatingly, so shamelessly tells us a lot. It is doubtful that this gradual stripping of a body was the work of only one person who was having to hide each time someone came by. If that had been the case, the looter would have done everything very rapidly in one go.

It is not easy to discover who the looters were, and they were rarely caught. There was talk sometimes that they were groups of vocational schoolboys, and this seems plausible, given the straits they were in and their ruthless determination to survive.[188] Zhilinskii noticed that caretakers, who normally chased away passers-by who paused to rest on the porch of a building (which often indicated imminent death and meant they would have to bury them), were much more leniently inclined towards those who were better dressed, 'even offering them a stool to sit on'.[189] He suspected this was less than altruistic, 'because [if the visitor died] he will be able to strip him'. He witnessed no such scenes himself, as he makes clear, so this is probably surmise. He had observed that bodies always went 'naked from the mortuary to the cemetery'.[190] The theory is all the more credible given the reputation of caretakers, who often had items to barter or sell which plainly did not belong to them. Few people would have been in a position to know whether these had been taken from the dead, or stolen from apartments whose occupants had all been evacuated or died, but everyone knew that disposing of bodies was a job for the caretaker.

It is not always clear whether those stripped were dead, in their death agony, or had just briefly fainted from hunger. Looters, not wanting to be caught in the act, would have had little time to establish whether someone who had collapsed was actually dead and, given the urgency of the situation, would probably not have been overly concerned. Vladislav Glinka, walking along the Arsenal Embankment in December 1941, saw a man in front of him fall to the ground. 'Another man, coming towards him, stopped, kneeled down, began unbuttoning his coat and slipped his hand inside. The dying man tried feebly to push the thief's hands away.'[191]

A Red Army soldier walking behind Glinka overtook him and pushed the thief away. The robber and his victim lay in the snow, barely moving. When, having walked on 'twenty paces', Glinka looked back, he saw the thief had again 'fallen upon the dying man like a spider and was rummaging through his pockets'.[192]

The most secluded place for looting was the cemeteries, but not everyone had access to those. 'The cemeteries have become dumps for many thousands of corpses, all of which have been robbed', Irina Zelenskaya wrote in her diary on 1 March 1942.[193] She would hardly have been in a position to inspect each of these thousands of corpses, but the lack of respect for the bodies of the dead could lead one to expect that looting would thrive there. It is not beyond the bounds of possibility that members of the burial squads, who soon got used to anything, were among those doing the robbing. From such testimony as there is, it is unclear whether what they were doing was regarded as looting or merely as standard preparation of bodies for burial. They would have been unable to systematically rob the dead because the cemeteries employed hundreds of people of different ages and professions, and any all-encompassing conspiracy is out of the question. Most probably, the robbing began before the deceased reached the cemetery. This would not have been difficult, as there was no security even at sites within the city limits where corpses accumulated in large numbers.

Not all stripping of the dead can be ascribed solely to the struggle for survival. No one can doubt the motive as far as ration cards and money are concerned, but did anyone really need their shrouds and blankets? Some items were, of course, taken to be exchanged in the markets, but how much bread could you expect in return for a pair of socks? One has the impression that all this was fuelled, not so much by wartime as by pre-war attitudes. There is testimony about people's extreme reluctance during the siege to part with clothes, mindful as they were of how long they had had to save up before they could buy a coat or a dress. There was no ignoring that memory of penury in the past. By no means everyone had it in them to strip the shawl from a dead woman, but the temptation would have been there for many people, and there is no denying that there were excuses which these people were not slow to find. They did not need to worry too much about what other people might think, as so many of them were no less preoccupied with brute physical survival and had, in many cases, considerably fewer scruples.

By no means all citizens resorted to robbery, theft, fraud and looting. These were nothing new and, with the exception of looting and the raiding of bread deliveries, were to be found in both pre-war and post-war Leningrad. In peacetime, greed and covetousness could be kept within bounds by threats and repression, but what sanctions could stop looting when people were dying in their thousands? Fear of being put to death, when that was what they already faced? They hoped to get away with it if they were stronger and more agile than their victims, but knew for certain that they would die unless they could find ways of supplementing their officially authorized rations, which were sufficient only to send them more slowly to the grave.

These crimes were possible only during a period of unprecedented human suffering. Not only was bread being stolen, but those stealing it must have known that the person they were robbing would shortly die as a result of their action. To reach any bakery, you had to step over corpses. They well knew the state their victims were in as they came out of the bread shop, nibbling pieces off their tiny bread ration, because without that they might not make it back home. They knew that almost everyone they robbed had starving family members. They also knew that the pallid child sent to the bread shop because its parents were too ill to go themselves could offer no resistance.

No less deplorable were the consequences of their behaviour. The more people stripped the dead of their clothes, the easier it became to flout other moral prohibitions. Perhaps someone had found it hard to be the first, but the sight of ubiquitous looting going unpunished doubtless made it seem more acceptable and less morally repugnant. Not everyone joined in beating up bread thieves, but many came to accept it. They saw starving children and teenagers on their knees, covered in blood, without the strength to stand up: how could that not desensitize them to the point of callousness?

Neither was the desire to profit from a national calamity initially the primary motive of sales staff: that was to look after themselves and their dependants. This, however, was a slippery slope; they became greedy, and soon people who had only wanted to survive began in a more sophisticated, 'civilized', way to cheat those less fortunate than themselves, the enfeebled, those at the bottom of the pile, and to rob them in order to enrich themselves. If now terrible crimes were being committed which would have seemed unimaginable only a short time ago, was it not just common sense to take a more relaxed view of pettier violations of decent behaviour? Was it really so wrong, when others were looting, to turn away from someone who had fallen in the snow, or to ignore a plea for help? People absorbed these attitudes, perhaps unconsciously. They became part of a familiar reality which, after all, was not affecting everyone equally, and did not really require any emotional response. The change did not occur suddenly, but gradually came to determine people's reactions: some things you just have to accept; it is pointless to waste your breath discussing them; some things you do not need to be surprised about, or get angry about, make promises about or, indeed, think about too closely.

2

Moral commandments

The concept of honesty

1

The study of 'siege ethics' is difficult for several reasons. Firstly, because it can be difficult to peel away later assessments of events by those who witnessed them from those which were widespread in the Time of Death. Survivors, inserting themselves as protagonists in their stories of the siege, were bound to explain their actions in ways that did not seem cruel. They were expected by officialdom not to justify deviations from morality, which at the time were encountered at every step, but to give a dramatic retelling of the most striking episodes which would confirm the significance of their heroism.

Secondly, we cannot judge the firmness of the moral code of Leningraders in late 1941 and early 1942 when it was changing just as rapidly as the everyday reality of the siege. We can only competently assess it after studying the major texts, lengthy diaries and voluminous notes packed with detail. Such documents are, however, something of a rarity. All too often our source for establishing the moral standards commonly accepted at a particular moment are brief comments – sometimes, indeed, a single comment – where motivations are not always clear. We have difficulty deciding whether what we are looking at is a widespread attitude or the outcome of a moment of weakness, a custom or an isolated incident, an exception to the rule or a deeply held principle. The same person can be capable of performing both honourable and dishonourable actions almost simultaneously.

From fragmentary accounts, we can only outline the portrait of someone who would have been considered decent and honest. In documents conveying the details of the nightmare of the siege, it is difficult to find a balance of negative and positive assessments, let alone carefully weighed judgements. Quite often one single action which made a big impression on a person can completely erase all that had been troubling and hurtful in their relations with another.

For Izrail Metter, the writer Alexander Kron was the epitome of integrity. We detect in the way he writes about Kron the skill of a professional author, the use of literary language and an avoidance of cliché: 'I was struck by his natural humanity and dependability, the dependability of a person with dignity, of someone invariably decent and honourable.'[1] Metter gives an example of his kindness: 'He would bring me some of his own food, saved from meals on his ship.' This was all the more impressive because Kron was himself suffering from scurvy.[2] Here it is not only details which have an impact. In order to convey his admiration forcefully, Metter feels the need to generalize and give an appreciation of various humane and compassionate actions, in short sentences whose clear, emotional tone seems ideally suited to what he has to say.

Vladimir Maltsev was a teenager rather than a writer like Metter, so his language is more straightforward and his value judgements more direct. 'He is the first of all the army people I have met at the checkpoints or the enlistment centre who has made a big impression', Vladimir wrote to his father about Major Nikiforov, who was giving military training to schoolchildren.[3]

Vladimir Maltsev gives a specific, practical reason for admiring the major. In this he is unlike Metter who veiled his reasons behind a cascade of emotional phrases. Vladimir admires the major because he is honest. If his men have to dig trenches, he digs with them. He crawls through the snow on tactical exercises, the same as the schoolchildren he is teaching. He is experienced, straightforward and does not go out of his way to find fault. He expects an answer only after he has explained everything in detail and checked it has been understood. This selection of examples of what Vladimir Maltsev regarded as exemplary behaviour tells us what he regarded as the most important characteristics of an honest person: someone who does not use other people as a means to an end, is not indifferent towards them, but helps and understands them.

2

During the siege, such detailed characterization of virtue is rare. Typically, we have to infer it from briefly outlined responses to actions considered particularly deserving of note. It would be problematical to try to piece together a coherent composite portrait of ideal behaviour, but these responses give us a better idea of the moral standards of the time.

How did Leningraders envisage a decent, honest person during the siege? It was someone who was not prepared to live at the expense of others. Educator Ksenia Polzikova-Rubets tried to persuade children that, for as long as they were healthy, they should not let their parents give them 'their share of the food'.[4] Teenagers looking for a job explain that they want to help their family and not be a liability to them.[5] 'I get terribly tired', we read in Anna Umanskaya's diary, 'but at least with my worker's card I can feed myself without eating into my mother's ration, (she has become terribly thin), and share my rations with my dad (who has also changed out of all recognition).'[6] Of course, by taking on factory work these young people were looking also to increase their own rations, but the mention of the emaciated appearance of her parents is telling.

Some of those caught in the siege go to considerable lengths to stress that they are embarrassed to accept bread as a gift. Vladislav Daev recalls a distant relative who, having lost her job, had no money with which to buy bread and could not bring herself to ask her sisters, who had many children, to give her any.[7] The actor, F. A. Gryaznov, relating his brother's account of how well he was being fed eating in the canteen of the Red Army Club ('several meatballs of good size and quality, with boiled cabbage and nutritious soup'), writes that he and his wife found their mouths watering: they had no coupons themselves. When, however, his brother offered to let them have one of his meatballs between the two of them, they declined: 'He had lamentably little food himself.'[8] We can hardly claim this kind of behaviour was widespread, but the episode is illuminating.

'How low a person can sink', Alexandra Borovikova wrote in her diary. She had not even asked if she could have the bowl of soup left on her friends' table but only caught herself thinking she would not say 'no' if offered it.[9] A friend was able to persuade Yelena Mukhina to accept a piece of bread only after assuring her it was from the ration of her mother who had recently died.[10]

Not everyone could bring themselves to take advantage of the privileged rations they were entitled to, when they knew how many people near them were starving. In their notes about this there is a suggestion of histrionics, a sure sign of how highly they valued their human dignity even in the siege. 'Outwardly I appear to be a loser. (I really do look quite pathetic)', Arkadiy Lepkovich noted in his diary on 16 December 1941; 'I get a lot of sympathy, even pity, which I really do not deserve, but I would be ashamed to claim the privileges of a sick "invalid". I'm far too young to sink to that level.'[11] Another Leningrader, Georgiy Kulagin, was asked by the doctor why he was not eating at the 'enhanced diet' canteen. He replied, 'I would be embarrassed to sit down to a meal next to someone who had barely managed to hobble in with a walking stick.'[12] The doctor's response is also noteworthy: 'She nodded enthusiastically: "I do understand you, I do understand."'[13]

The daily reality of the siege ironed out any predilection for heroic gestures and, needless to say, when times were hard, even people who had publicly spoken out against privileges had little option but to avail themselves of them. There could be confused situations where it was not clear who was entitled to what, but the sense of digrace was scarcely diminished. Boris Kross recalled how embarrassed he felt in front of his comrades over his entitlement to a 'privileged' ration after a spell on duty as an air-raid warden. He could not share it with them because he was starving himself, but ate his potato 'in nearby lecture theatres'.[14]

F. A. Gryaznov agreed to work in the hospital as a reader for the patients, and the political instructor promised him a meal in the canteen.

The reading session came to an end but there was no sign of the instructor. The nurse, as she saw him to the door, wished him all the best. It was awkward, but he could not just leave. Very politely, 'timidly', not demanding, only requesting, he explained, 'Forgive me, I believe we were promised some tea.'[15] We can feel how excruciating every word was, but what is the alternative if you have nothing to eat, and why should you be ashamed?

Izrail Metter recalled that, after giving a lecture at a district committee of the Komsomol, he and another writer were supposed to be 'invited to dinner'. Evidently, these dinners were becoming a tradition. They were a kind of perk, enjoyed not only by lecturers but also by delegations of sponsors travelling to the front with gifts, by actors and many other 'performers'. They could not demand payment, but were rarely sent on their way without a meal. They knew they were being treated to 'charity', but, given the famine, could not afford to be choosy. Someone in the district committee had fouled up, and the lecturers were asked to come back for lunch the next day without having to give any more lectures. They had to settle for that. 'We were so hungry, we just didn't care', but they felt humiliated; 'It was extraordinarily embarrassing. What was particularly disagreeable was that we were led straight to the kitchen, nobody talked to us, and we were fed like yard-sweepers allowed in on a feast day.'[16] The guest speakers had, admittedly, little idea of how they should have been received. Perhaps just a little more gently, more civilly, but at least not as cynically as they felt they were treated: 'We would have liked just rather better manners, to be treated as guests, as if there had been no misunderstanding.'[17]

Not everyone in the siege managed to stick to their principles. We can compare two entries in V. F. Chekrizov's diary made on 14 October 1941 and 29 January 1942. In October, his moral rules have not yet been eroded by hunger. He disdainfully describes the customers in the factory canteen. 'They try to eat as much as they can, and to take with them whatever they can't. All they think about is food. They look as if they have never had anything to eat before. How petty these old members of the intelligentsia are. All their cultural trappings are cast aside and all that remains is the urge to pig themselves.'[18] The second entry does not call for comment. It comes after three months of fighting to survive, when, day by day, people had no option but to become petty, to strike deals, grovel, beg and, step by step, to lose face: 'I try to miss no opportunity to eat as much as possible. If you hold back and make a point of keeping up appearances, you'll soon pop your clogs. You can't afford not to beg, and sometimes to be pushy. It's the only way to stay alive.'[19]

I. I. Zhilinsky, a bluff, honest man, when he saw the shelves of the shop he was supposed to buy food at were empty, had to try to trick the sales assistants at another shop to let him redeem his coupons, which were for food other than bread. In another cultured family, the father, a school headmaster, tried not to hand in his coupons at the hospital where he was being treated in the hope that no one would notice. His family managed to acquire 2 kg of starch from molasses waste: 'The general conclusion was that it was inedible. It would need to be mixed in with something else and we could gradually shift it, especially to people who had not come across this kind of flour before.'[20]

Even declining an offer of food, people were sometimes hoping they would be offered it a second time. Old ways died hard.[21] Sometimes people had no choice but to ask for help. 'Today I scrounged a second bowl of soup', Yelena Mukhina writes in her diary on 8 January 1942; 'My mother and I are in a really bad situation. There are still two days to go until the end of the first ten-day period, and in our canteens they won't give us anything more against my mother's ration card or mine.'[22] 'So for those two days we are supposed to survive on that one bowl of soup I was entitled to.'[23] Even in a situation where two hungry people have to survive all day on only a helping of off-white 'empty' soup (Yelena even counted the number of pieces of macaroni in it and entered it in her diary), even then, she writes that she is embarrassed 'to be scrounging like this every day'.[24] It was not just because it was a humiliation. She was hypersensitive to unfairness and hated asking for an extra helping of soup when she could see how terribly thin her fellow pupils were.

Yelena Skryabina wrote irritably that, cajoling and pleading for food, she felt 'like a pitiful beggar'.[25] 'It's like being on the receiving end of charity' was how Anna Ostroumova-Lebedeva reacted to gifts from friends.[26] 'It is really unpleasant', Vladimir G. Kulyabko noted in his diary after asking a waitress to put four spoonfuls of sugar in his glass of tea.[27] The most excruciating embarrassment was when children had to 'lick the plate clean' for other children. Inna Balashova's memories have survived about how children were fed in school canteens. Not all of them were starving, and they would 'offer to let hungry children finish off their helpings'.[28] This was done in full view of the others, and there was no possibility of concealment: 'The whole class knew which children were reduced to eating up the leftovers.'[29] The girls were perhaps even more sensitive about this: 'I was one of them. The shame and humiliation brought my whole face out in blotches.'[30] Not everyone, of course, was so fastidious. 'Someone would say, "Who wants some leftovers?" and immediately there would be a chorus of children saying, "I do. Give it to me"', G. N. Ignatova recalled.[31]

3

In the various tales of life during the siege, the portrait of the individual who behaves in an ideal way is added to very personally, sometimes with a single brushstroke. A decent person was someone who would share their last bowl of soup with you. For Marina Durnovo, the wife of writer Daniil Kharms, such was her friend, the philosopher Yakov Druskin. She decided he was the only person she could entrust with her deceased husband's archive.[32] A decent person is someone who returns food ration cards he has found to their rightful owners. Relating the events of a day in December 1941 with exceptional scrupulousness, T. K. Valter and Olga

Peto reconstruct the ritual of returning found items. They took someone who had collapsed in the street to the first aid station, where he died almost immediately. His pockets contained money, his passport and food ration cards for the whole of his family: 'a nurse is sent to the address in the passport and returns a couple of hours later with the wife of the deceased. All the valuables are returned to her.'[33]

Such episodes, however few, particularly appealed to Leningraders. The times Valter and Peto recorded in their diary as precisely as in a police report, literally hour by hour, are proof enough of that. Everybody has behaved honestly, all the valuables have been returned, everything was done to track down the relatives of the deceased, and no one grudged the time it took. We sense the emotion attached to returning someone's ration cards also in the memoirs of Tatiana Kudryavtseva. The impact of her story is all the greater when we learn that her mother, who survived the siege, never talked about it. It only slipped out when her daughter was emotionally telling the story of a woman who had found cards, returned them, and thereby saved another person's family. 'We had the same experience', her mother mentioned; 'We returned cards ourselves, and people returned ours to us when we lost them. That is just normal behaviour, what you expect.'[34]

Without for a moment doubting the truth of these stories, their emotional subject matter often caused them to be phrased in categorical rather than nuanced terms. One tale which had a particular resonance in the city concerned two children who bartered a donkey jacket in the market, only to find when they got back home that it had had their ration cards in one of the pockets. In the morning, these were returned by the buyer, who read the address on them. There are two versions of this story. One was related to the writers Daniil Granin and Ales Adamovich by Ivan A. Andreyenko, the former deputy chairman of Leningrad City Council's executive committee. It is embellished with many details missing from the account of teenager Alexey Glushkov, who was one of the children involved in the incident. It was recorded by Dmitry V. Pavlov, the representative of the State Defence Committee responsible for food supplies to Leningrad.[35] Andreyenko did not give a straight answer when asked about the source of his information: 'We received reports on these matters. In Leningrad positive and negative phenomena were constantly being brought to our attention.'[36] In the secret NKVD reports on the situation in Leningrad published by Nikita Lomagin, we find no such example.[37] It seems in any case unlikely that the authors of these reports would have been interested in how many grams of bread the children obtained, where their father was serving in the army, or what kind of beard the person who bought the jacket had. Most likely, Andreyenko heard the story as an urban legend, which suggests such incidents can hardly have been regarded as commonplace. The very impact that the story had is, alas, a sure indication that it was uncommon. In almost every document of the siege, we encounter reports of the loss and theft of ration cards, but even the most voluminous diaries offer precious little evidence to suggest that anyone ever returned them.

Although it was difficult in purely practical terms, and often impossible, returning the precious ration cards to people who had lost them is invariably mentioned as a criterion of personal honesty by Leningraders who experienced the siege. Needless to say, not everyone had it in them to behave so altruistically. They were aware, however, that such things did happen, and could see how admiringly people talked about them, and understood what a person must feel who had returned to them some hope of survival. Evidently, the man who bartered bread for a jacket was not as hungry as other people, and it would have been less of a trial for him to return the ration cards. That was not what usually happened. No doubt, hoping for sympathy, the children might have told a stranger about their troubles. There is no reason to suppose the deal would have been done in silence. The sight of these debilitated children, who had brought their last possession to a street market, whose mother had just died of hunger and whose father was far away at the front, might have tipped the scales, made another human being take pity, and embodied as unquestionable reality the concept of honesty just when it was beginning to seem totally illusory.

4

Another characteristic of an honest person as envisaged by Leningraders during the siege was how scrupulous they were about bartering the possessions of relatives who had left the city. It was not always possibly to notify them and obtain their consent in good time. The post was unreliable and a decision had often to be taken as a matter of urgency, especially if they were watching someone die and could only help them by bartering for bread such valuables as the family still possessed. Reporting this in their letters, those in the siege tend to explain the extremity of the need and to assure their correspondent they are taking other people's possessions only to obtain the most basic necessities.

When you see the length at which the Leningraders apologize to their nearest and dearest, it is clear how difficult they have found the decision. N. P. Zavetnovskaya wrote to her daughter on 9 February 1942 that she would barter her dress only 'if father and I have a crisis with food, of which bread is the main concern'.[38] She is evidently having trouble finding the right words for an awkward request. Her daughter was a musician, could not appear on stage in rags, and this was an expensive dress, bought at the exclusive Torgsin store for foreign currency or valuables.

Her mother's excuses seem endless. She explains about father's ill-health: 'I am very worried about his weakness, and I am no stronger.' She reports on how long it has been since they were able to eat properly: 'Yesterday we finally obtained food against January's ration card. Until then we had nothing.' She continues listing their misfortunes: the apartment is cold, rumours about an increase in ration allowances have proved empty chatter. It is difficult to imagine what further justification could be needed, but she seems to find even these reasons insufficient. As if apologizing, she explains that the reason she needs to survive is 'to see you again' and that, if she does, she will entertain her royally. 'If we have any sort of provisions I will do everything it takes to feed you well.'[39] It is difficult to know whether she herself believed what she was writing (she had not much longer to live), but she evidently felt the need to further sweeten the unpalatable news for her daughter. The letter runs to only a few lines, but packs very many excuses, apologies, complaints and promises into them.

N. P. Zavetnovskaya's letter is not dissimilar to a letter B. P. Gorodetsky sent his wife and daughters on 20 February 1942.[40] He is discreetly explaining how unavoidable it was to sell certain things. His letter too refers to ill-health: he is 'malnourished', uninterested in anything, unable to walk, and has become very thin. He admits he has 'had to exchange a few things'. He puts it no more clearly than that, and in the following lines tries rather hastily, without going into details, to reassure those he is writing to: 'Do not worry, we have not exchanged anything that we particularly value or need.' He immediately adds, 'We really did have to do something to set the situation to rights.' He elaborates: 'My concern for you greatly slowed my recovery.'[41]

The sequence and substance of the excuses are logical and entirely typical. There is no weak link in the chain of explanations. The main thrust is dramatization of episodes in the Time of Death, eliciting sympathy, undertaking to compensate for the loss, and a desire to reassure.

5

An honest person is also someone who resists the temptation to help themselves to other people's bread. Tatiana Maximova reports how shocked she and her mother were when their guest, seeing the bread divided into equal portions on a dish 'helped himself to the lot with a sweep of his hand'.[42] Esfir Levina noted in her diary something an acquaintance told her: 'He was walking down the street and saw someone collapse. He went over, saw the man was unconscious, took his ration cards and walked on. "He was going to die anyway, and I could certainly use them."'[43] She refused to let him into her house after that. Not everyone was well brought up and highly sensitive to the plight of others, not everyone owned up to immoral actions, not everyone faced condemnation from their friends and family but, even in the abyss of the siege, not everybody lost their understanding of common decency. Levina's mother tried to find excuses for the thief: perhaps he was ill, perhaps he was afraid of starving to death . . . but she was having none of it: 'So, going into a mortally dangerous battle, according to your theory, it's all right to run away or steal from your fellow soldiers.'[44]

Assertions of this kind of moral decency were sometimes more straightforward and less ostentatious, but no less categorical. The doctors asked one of the nurses in their hospital to fetch their bread ration from the bakery, and she valued their trust: 'They weighed out the bread and would put another crust on top. I could have eaten the makeweight on my way back, but never did.'[45] A worker from the Nevgvozd factory was invited to receive an award, and given a meal before the ceremony. Not knowing the rules, he ate three rolls instead of two, 'but then went to a lot of trouble to make sure the roll was replaced'.[46] These were people who, in their inconspicuous way and with their straightforward assessments – sometimes not all that articulate – had a very precise understanding of what was the right way to behave.

6

At that time, when greed, cruelty and the urge to survive at the expense of others were only too much in evidence, what was appreciated above all else was the ability to endure uncomplainingly and stoically all the trials of life in the siege. This is particularly evident in the diary of G. A. Knyazev, director of the archive of the Academy of Sciences. On 7 January 1942, he wrote of Sofia Shakhmatovo-Koplan, a member of the archive staff and a Christian, who endured every ordeal: 'She never said much about herself, never opened up, but I detected that the only thing that sustained her was her faith.'[47] In another entry, on 1 February 1942, Knyazev records a few words with her: 'When I asked her how she was feeling, she replied, "What do I matter? It's other people you need to take care of."'[48]

'She was all alone, withered, asked for nothing, and even now is not complaining', Georgiy Kulagin wrote of one of the factory cleaners.[49] It is very striking that, when those in the siege talk of stoicism, the last thing to be found in their stories is talk of iron willpower, fanatical faith, unconquerable determination, asceticism and passionate self-sacrifice. Their stories are not usually trimmed to fit in with the clichés of the propaganda of the time. They record the endurance of good, caring people.

Not everyone was guided by considerations of morality. Those who were not stoical were the ones who 'guzzle anything edible without a second thought', never think about tomorrow, and are incapable of restraining themselves.[50] Those who were not stoical submitted to the inexorable power of hunger and adopted a 'plaintive, deferential tone in conversation'.[51] They were terrified of the shelling, and prepared to endure any humiliation for the sake of a piece of bread.[52] They would cheat and steal in order to survive.

Hostility towards people who had lost their sense of honesty is extreme and emotional. In the almost 'hagiographic' descriptions of the saints of the siege, we find an absence of rigour. Much of what is related about the situation in the city is hyperbole: everybody has become coarse, unkind, everybody is stealing, everybody is unwashed.[53] Such accusatory comments are a common means of intensifying the expression of emotion in any conversation, but this kind of categorical utterance became customary because it helped to demarcate very clearly the line between what was acceptable and what was taboo.

This is seen very emotionally in N. P. Zavetnovskaya's letters to her daughter. The mother has a friend who is a kind, helpful young woman. She misses her when she is not there. 'But the rest of the young people living here are completely useless, think only of themselves, don't help, and would steal from you given half a chance. They use my china, and have dealings with speculators.'[54] There is another description of dishonest people in an earlier letter to her daughter, sent on 27 December 1941. Here we see the same contrasting of kind people without whom she couldn't survive, and others who affect to despise moral behaviour: 'Lelya is a nasty piece of work. She could at least offer to help sometimes. She never buys bread for me. Off she goes to buy it for herself but never offers to do it for me, even though she can see I'm lying here.'[55] This unforgiving division of people into 'them' and 'us' is also evident in a letter from G. Kabanova to her aunt, M. Kharitonova. 'Us' includes Uncle Vasiliy, who came immediately he heard about 'these horrors' and brought her food: only a little, but it was a great help. 'Them' are people who abandoned her in her time of need: 'There is no sign of my family or friends. All the people who knew Mother and Father have vanished: some have been evacuated, and some keep well out of the way. So I have no one who really feels sorry for me or helps me.'[56]

Particularly disgusting are those who profit from the nation's plight. For many, they are the truly dishonourable ones. Their services are sometimes essential, but these vultures, as Irina Zelenskaya describes them, are openly shunned and despised. A man who takes bribes from starving Leningraders is considered totally immoral. This kind of bribe-taking is described by Vladimir G. Kulyabko, who encountered it during his evacuation across Lake Ladoga.

He, a frail old man barely able to stand, did not get a place in one of the covered trucks for transporting those most enfeebled by the siege. Kulyabko's notes relate not only the story of the humiliation he was subjected to: almost every page of his diary is seething with anger at thieves who fleece people in their hour of need:

An hour later we heard there was going to be a truck for the sick. I came out and joined the queue so as to be in with a good chance of getting on board. A covered truck arrived, and with it some boss with his own group of passengers who, under a hail of abuse from the sick people who were queueing, gave them priority for getting on. While this was happening, some fellow approached me and said he could get me on my way. I could see what he had in mind, and decided to give him a bribe. He asked if I had any tobacco. I told him straight away that if he could get me on to the next truck I would give him a 100-gram pack of top-quality tobacco. He immediately picked up my bags and off we went. He sat me down near a post and told me to be sure not to move away from there. About forty minutes later this boss turns up, looks around, sees me in that special place, comes over and tells me to go over to wait for the truck. I took my things and went over. I fell, not for the first time that day. The car arrived, someone else on the orders of the boss took my things and said, 'Give me the pack of tobacco.' I told him he would get it when I and my belongings were in the car. A minute later the chief himself opened the door for me, the man put my belongings in. I was finally settled and handed over the pack of tobacco to the bag-carrier.[57]

These corrupt officials were impervious to morality. They watched a frail old man fall, they heard all the curses directed at them, and carried right on, ripping people off, unashamed, unmoved by what they were seeing. They robbed people just like looters, taking their last possessions, totally unscrupulous, and there was nothing anyone could do about it, no one they could complain to. One of the siege victims rushed at them with his fists flailing. They beat him up and he was promptly arrested. Kulyabko continues with growing outrage and resentment:

It was only then I realized that all the earlier cars had been leaving with people who had paid a bribe in one way or another. And this was the sort of person who had been put in charge of supervising such a huge, important operation, which was a matter of life or death for all these people, a man who was subjecting sick old men, women and children to such an ordeal for days at a time just because they had nothing to bribe him with.[58]

7

Dishonourable people were usually condemned unreservedly. Little account would be taken of their frailty, the distress of their family, or the symptoms of starvation. If it had been, all moral principle would have collapsed, because an excuse could have been found for anything. Irina Zelenskaya was indignant that young, healthy workers should be afraid to go up onto the roofs for firefighting duty. She has no interest in their feelings: 'inexcusable cowardice is crawling out of every crevice'.[59] The father of a boy who was a fellow apprentice of Valentina Bazanova, died. She feels no sympathy for him: he took the body straight to the mortuary and did not even ask how much bread he would need to give to have a proper grave dug, despite obtaining food on his father's ration card. In addition, he managed to gain the sympathy of his master, who gave him an extra lunch and dinner.[60] She feels no sympathy for someone who has just been orphaned, and feels she knows quite enough. As far as she is concerned, there are no mitigating circumstances. Her diary entry reads like an indictment of shameful behaviour.

Yelena Mukhina noted in her diary on 21 November 1941 the misfortune which befell an elderly woman who lived with their family. She had been queueing for pasta but 'came back tired, frozen and empty-handed'. Another relative who had been closer to the counter had had better luck. 'What a bitch! Fancy not moving the old lady in front of herself.'[61] She overlooks the possibility that those in front of the old lady might then not have got their own pasta. In people's accounts of dishonourable behaviour, we constantly come across *non sequiturs* of this kind. They do not always pay much attention to what they themselves have had to do under the pressure of reality.

Nevertheless, censuring the actions of other people encouraged Leningraders to demarcate their own moral precepts all the more strictly. The unforgiving nature of their judgements signals a claim that they have every right to do so. Feeling hostility towards people judged immoral proclaims tacitly or explicitly: 'I would never behave like that.' The corollary of detecting in others sometimes very minor deviations from propriety was that they drew a red line for themselves which they were then under an obligation to observe.

After Yelena Mukhina's mother died, she was looked after by a friend. Trying somehow to repay her, she looked after the friend's ailing father. For dinner, she would have 'empty' soup: 'It was impossible to make my bread last until evening.'[62] There was a lot of bread beside her on the table and a sugar bowl. Her friend took 'big, thick slices of bread and sprinkled them with sugar'. The hungry girl took in every detail, but the food was not shared with her: 'I know it is not good to be jealous, but I do think Galya could give me a small piece of bread each day and never even notice it.'[63] She meticulously adds up how much bread her friend is getting: her own ration, the ration of her mother who died recently, and that of her father who is too ill to eat anything. 1,200 grams a day. Is her friend really capable of eating that much? She hardly ever dries bread so she must just be putting it away in the cupboard to go stale. She does not know that for a fact, but the cupboard is locked, and that can only mean that food is being hoarded there. 'It really is not nice at all.' Every day she is growing weaker from starvation, while there is bread going stale in the cupboard. She talks about that now as an established fact and, as she becomes increasingly indignant, dismisses out of hand anything that could excuse her friend's behaviour. Of course, the bread belongs to someone else, and she is not a member of Galya's family, but, 'In Galya's place I would not grudge a piece of bread. My heart would not let me behave like that.' Why should her friend not understand that if a person does not ask for bread, that does not mean that they are not hungry? 'I will never ask first. I have too much pride and self-respect to be a beggar.' Her friend knows perfectly well how hungry she is after being left an orphan, because 300 grams of bread a day is very little. She too would like to eat; she is starving, perpetually suffering pangs of hunger when 'your stomach aches constantly'. Her one wish is to get a response, some sympathy, some help: 'Dear God, please hear me. Lord, when will this ever end?'[64]

8

Yelena Mukhina's diary entries reveal her understanding of honesty very clearly. She would not say 'no' to an extra helping of soup in the school canteen, but would not ask for bread from friends: she would only accept it if it was offered. She is not wanting much, just a small piece. She would not accept bread from people who were themselves starving, only from someone who could afford to part with it. Her view of 'decent' behaviour is a direct response to immoral actions, and the more offensive they are, the greater is the need to reassert that moral precepts are sacrosanct. This was important, because they often provided the only prospect of survival. It was no good hoping for a miracle in the bakery, where you might have your bread snatched from you or be cheated by the sales assistants. The rigour of her principles is undimmed by the fact that she does not actually know the motives behind her friend's behaviour. It is more straightforward to set up the unambiguous image of an unfeeling miser against which to pit your own right to regard yourself as a decent human being. Her high self-esteem is encapsulated by that emotional exclamation, 'My heart would not let me behave like that.' That response to unworthy behaviour, if sometimes clumsy or uncertain, reaffirms a sense of human dignity.

Fairness

1

The concept of fairness, to an even greater degree than the concept of honesty, was consolidated by a captious, and sometimes biased, scrutiny of how other people were behaving. Personal impressions and rumours were relied on in almost equal measure, rumours often being trusted implicitly. Lessons in morality were only infrequently learned from examples of selfless or generous behaviour, which were encountered infrequently and often viewed with scepticism.

'Here we are starving to death like flies, and yesterday Stalin in Moscow gave another dinner in honour of Anthony Eden. It's a disgrace. They are gorging themselves there while we can't buy a piece of bread like normal human beings. They're organizing dazzling receptions there, while we live like cavemen', Yelena Mukhina wrote.[65] The vehemence of her reaction is all the more striking for the fact that she knew nothing about the dinner itself, how 'dazzling' or otherwise it might have been. It is not, of course, based on the official communiqués but on how they were perceived, and the contrast that suggested between the situation of the well-fed and of the starving. The sense of unfairness built up gradually. Such condemnation was not a sudden outburst but something that had accumulated over less dramatic but too frequent instances where those caught in the siege felt they were being treated unfairly. The process is very noticeable in Yelena's diary.

Examples of unfairness are not just briefly noted. The charges are brought emotionally, expressed eloquently, with metaphors to give them an extra sting. There is an entry in Lev Kogan's diary observing that, if you are ill, you have to produce a sick note before you can be paid your wages. He emphasizes the absurdity of this requirement at considerable length: 'Someone who is ill gets their wages only after they have recovered,

but a person who is ill needs money much more than a person who is well.'
He gives vent to his indignation with considerable sarcasm.[66] Vladimir
G. Kulyabko deploys the same techniques upon hearing that white bread
is only to be sold 'commercially'. He thinks this would be acceptable if
white bread could also be obtained using ration cards but, if that is not the
case, he thinks the implications 'stink'.[67] He is very indignant: 'If you've
got plenty of money, you can eat white bread; but if you haven't, think
yourself lucky to have black. The same old division into the haves and
have-nots.'[68] His polemical tone is evidently not for his own benefit but for
others who may some day read his diary, as Kulyabko made no secret that
he hoped they would. Accordingly, he tries to make his moral principles
as logical and convincing as he can. They are the support structure of his
message and he does not want them airily dismissed. His reference to have-
nots shows his concept of fairness draws on the promotion of egalitarianism in earlier years. There is no mention of 'revolutionary asceticism',
but the more alarming the times became, the more readily did categorical
moral judgements draw on the vocabulary of yesteryear.

2

The first, and perhaps most important, indication of fairness is the absence
of privileges. There should be none: that is the implication of many of the
diary entries. Those caught in the siege reacted not only to injustices which
affected them directly, but also to those which concerned others. This
enabled them to denounce an individual who had offended them all the
more effectively, by showing they were part of a larger problem, and hence
all the more to be condemned.

Muttering about privileges was evidently so rife that even Alexander
Fadeyev found himself obliged to mention it in a book about the siege,
which was generally upbeat and heroic in tone. This was something writers
who 'dropped in' on Leningrad found no difficulty in producing. Writing
about the family of a cousin who had lived through the Time of Death,
he commented that they 'had no connections or contacts which would
have enabled them to obtain things'.[69] He managed to get that published
in 1942.

Talk of privileges was often exaggerated, and clearly pointed in just
one direction. 'Rumour had it that officials were living well', was how
Alexandra Zmitrichenko succinctly summarized the main topic of quiet,
private conversations she heard in Leningrad.[70] Rumours require no
proof, since otherwise they would cease to be rumours; more significant is
the mindset they reflect.[71]

Indignation was most vocal where inequalities were less discreet, and
plain for all to see, especially when bonuses and awards were being allocated.[72] It would have been impossible to keep everybody happy, and it is
by no means certain that was ever the intention. The criteria for rewards
were not transparent, and practices from before the siege gave little guidance. The malcontents saw deceit and nepotism at every turn and, most of

all, corruption on the part of those in charge. It could hardly have been otherwise, since everybody knew that 'awards' varied greatly in value.

No fewer complaints related to catering privileges. Georgiy Knyazev noted great resentment among staff at the Archive of the Academy of Sciences who had to stand in a long queue to get into the canteen. Most were issued yellow tickets, while a select few received red tickets entitling them to eat in an elite restaurant section with few diners.[73]

It was considered unseemly to divide those suffering in the siege into persons of particular value, who should be fed as a priority, and those of less value. The offence caused to people considered of lower priority became manifest immediately. Dmitry Likhachev recalled his friend, the literary critic Vasiliy Komarovich, who was starving and dropsical, being refused permission to dine in the academicians' restaurant, where he had been allowed to eat in the past: 'After being refused admission, he came to me (I was eating at a table with an oil lamp burning on it) and, in terrible indignation, almost shouted, "Dmitry Sergeyevich, give me some bread or I won't have the strength to get back home!"'[74]

It is not difficult to imagine the context of this dramatic episode. However much those present might have sympathized with the unfortunate man, they themselves needed to survive. From Likhachev's description, we gather that those in the restaurant section kept quiet and tried not to notice Komarovich, aware that any one of them might easily be subjected to the same treatment. They could not fail to see that he was swollen from malnutrition, but nobody moved, nobody offered a word of support. If they had, they would have had to find a way to help him, and how could they do that when the select academicians' dining room was their own last hope of surviving? If he had asked for bread discreetly, he would not have been denied: Likhachev had helped him out in the past, helped him out on this occasion, and would share food with him in the future. His shouting was an outburst of animosity towards those who were receiving privileged rations. Why were they entitled to that when he was not? His outburst was also an attempt to intimidate the authorities, who would hardly want a scholar, who had not the strength to get back home, to die on their doorstep, into relaying what he had said to those responsible for granting passes to the reserved section.

Why were those categorized as 'dependants' not entitled to a butter ration, Nikolai Gorshkov wondered.[75] They were conscripted to do hard work, clearing away waste, cleaning the streets and courtyards, and the category included children over 12 years of age, who desperately needed butter in their diet. How else were they supposed to get it, when enterprises would not take on anyone under 16?[76] Butter was not being distributed fairly, and Gorshkov was so incensed that he wrote indignantly about it in a diary which otherwise reads more like an objective record of bombardments and weather conditions.

'Rations are being allocated as a matter of priority to manual workers and those with desk jobs', Maria Konoplyova noted in July 1942. 'They are evidently trying to give priority to those considered essential to the functioning of the city', she notes in a neutral tone.[77] In the next sentence, however, her judgement is categorical: 'Dependants have the option of being evacuated or dying.'[78] Georgiy Knyazev also writes about this: 'We are starving and freezing to death. Some people survive by being legally allocated a special ration, but the rest of us are second-class citizens.'[79]

No one disputed the need for rations to be dependent on a person's age, how physically demanding their work was, or how essential they were to the defence of the city. No matter how reasonable the criteria may have been, however, those enduring the siege never stopped feeling they were being treated badly. No matter how much it might be argued that all the measures being taken were unavoidable during a calamity on this scale, who, even if they agreed with that, would not feel aggrieved? Who would accept they were of no consequence, of no use, deserving only of what they were given?

A sense of unfairness was constantly arising over unequal sharing of the hardship among Leningraders, when they were being sent out to clean the streets, over the allocation of rooms in bombed buildings, during evacuation; over the special levels of nutrition for 'senior comrades'. This, like the dividing of people into 'essential' and, by implication, 'inessential', again touched on the thorny issue of the privileges of those in power. A doctor called to attend the director of the Institute of Russian Literature (Pushkin House) who ate constantly and so, unsurprisingly, had stomach problems, complained bitterly that he, on the verge of starvation, was being called out to see 'some director who has stuffed his face'.[80] Irina Zelenskaya noted in her diary on 9 October 1942 that all those living cosily at the power station and enjoying heat, light and hot water were being expelled. Whether the intention was to save money by visiting this disaster on them, or whether it was just some official instruction being implemented, was of no interest to her. One of those who suffered was a woman who worked there and whose home was a damp room unfit for habitation, who would now 'be obliged to spend two hours travelling in each direction, taking her young child with her and having to change trams'.[81]

'It is completely wrong to treat her so badly. It is unforgivable.' No amount of explanation from the bosses cut any ice, not least because these 'necessary measures' did not apply to them: 'All the families [of the bosses] are still living here, out of reach of the misfortunes afflicting us lesser beings.'[82] She was not alone in making that observation. Vasiliy Chekrizov wrote irritably about the foremen of workshops who were nicely set up in their offices.[83] A shop assistant even shared her grievances with people in the queue: 'On 30 December all the managers of the departments in the shop fried meat and drank wine behind a partition, and didn't let us sales assistants anywhere near it.'[84]

During evacuation too, people took careful note of who was getting priority in boarding the train and ignoring the strict baggage limits. General confusion over 'boarding passes' played a large part in this. Thus, Vladimir

G. Kulyabko, looking for his reserved place in the carriage, found it occupied by 'all sorts of "important comrades", mostly of a certain type, each of whom had not the regulation 30 kg of baggage but vastly more'.[85] This was evidently no rarity: Pyotr Kubatkin, Head of the Leningrad Province NKVD, in a secret report of 10 December 1941 to Andrey Zhdanov and Mikhail Khozin, relayed rumours that were circulating that 'priority for evacuation from Leningrad will be given to senior officials, their families, and Red Army units, and that there will be no evacuation for the rest of the population'.[86] Many people were aware there was a list of those entitled to evacuation from Leningrad and made every effort to be on it. They could have had no doubt that others were doing exactly the same. Dmitry Likhachev several times refers in his memoirs to the indecent haste with which, in full public view, directors and heads of institutions scrambled to leave Leningrad.

The evacuation in autumn 1941 of the Bolshevik factory caused particular outrage: only the families of the factory management were evacuated. The proposal was to send them off on a barge 'comfortably furnished and supplied with a vast quantity of food (chocolate, sweets, flour and so on) at the expense of the factory'.[87] The public protest was so great that the Party committee opposed the vessel's departure.

3

The concept of fairness included an expectation of due gratitude for a kindly deed. This did not have to be a material gift, and there was, of course, no clearly defined tariff of exchange. People did their best to thank others in whatever way they could, without any sense of compulsion. On the other hand, there was often an expectation on the part of the giver, and offence could be taken if nothing was received in return.

The firmly established tradition of exchanges of gratitude underlies Vladimir G. Kulyabko's tale of his own evacuation from Leningrad. As he was leaving, he gave the key to his apartment to friends, the Kuznetsov family. This was probably wiser than following the regulations by handing in the keys to the housing manager, and also benefited the Kuznetsovs. Eager to show gratitude, the husband offered to take Kulyabko's belongings to the railway station on a children's sledge. Kulyabko, in turn, decided to show his gratitude:

> As the Kuznetsovs had little enough to eat, I decided to cook a good-sized helping of macaroni for Nikolai Ivanovich to compensate him for the energy he would use up on his way to the station and back. For a long time he was reluctant to take it, but I put the pan on the table and said firmly that I would not take it back. The day before leaving, I gave them my last bottle of sunflower oil.[88]

Failure to observe these proprieties was judged harshly. People took offence, and confided it to their diaries and in letters. The description of gifts given is often much lengthier than that of those received. N. P. Zavetnovskaya fumed about her neighbour: 'She didn't once visit us, didn't warn us. What a pig! Father helped her, kept her room warm, arranged her mother's funeral, found the people for that. Then we got up at 7 in the morning, put the samovar on for her, gave her something to drink every morning and evening, and all the time, when she could see we needed to go together to draw water, she was nowhere to be seen.'[89]

The less educated and sophisticated people were, the greater the emphasis on reciprocating with material gifts. The most down-to-earth situations, the stark revelation of people's thinking, the almost childish way hurts are listed: none of it prevented the besieged Leningraders from considering major matters of principle. The situations calling for moral choice were stark, not veiled by cultural dogmas, and they feel there is only one possible answer to issues which they see in unambiguous clarity. 'She has 2 buckets of fermented cabbage, but when I took a piece of my bread and went to the market to barter, she didn't give me any to take along. When she came to visit me, I used to give her everything I had', A. I. Kochetova lamented about the grievance she felt against her grandmother.[90]

4

Kochetova was unkindly treated by other people too, and this elicits the same bewildered cascade of simple-minded grumbles in letters to her mother. Kochetova was staying with her friend Zhenya, whose daughter, Galya, took a particular dislike to her: 'She said they were tired of me and I should go away and her mum couldn't stand the sight of me and so on.'[91] Why was she being treated like this? It was not fair. 'She helped herself to some of my bread and sweets. But I've helped Zhenya lots. When she lost her ration card, she and Galya lived on my rations, and ate my rations when I wasn't at home.'[92]

Personal dislike is mixed here with a naive hope that gifts given will be properly appreciated. Kochetova was living with a friend because it was warm there, and recognized that there was a price to pay and that she just had to put up with it when someone was furtively pilfering her bread. Her friend evidently saw nothing wrong with the arrangement. When Kochetova later found herself in very dire straits and had nothing to offer in return, the reason for allowing her to share their heat disappeared. Children, who had not yet mastered the rules of life, were better able to articulate the situation. They took offence very directly if they felt they were not being given a fair exchange.

Unfairness could turn up anywhere: there was not enough bread in Leningrad for everyone to survive, and everyone wanted to do so. But there was another feeling of unfairness about the losses people suffered in the maelstrom of the calamity. Why did one particular person survive when another did not? Why was it the finest, most honest and honourable people who died? Why was it those who were most loved who died? Why had there not been that vital extra piece of bread, bottle of milk, those few grams of butter, that handful of millet? We do not find sober judiciousness in these exclamations, and it would be absurd to expect it. Sometimes what is said is cruel, unjust, not melancholy reflection but a cry of anguish. Olga Berggolts in 'Daytime Stars' describes in naturalistic and repulsive detail the wizened, skeletal body of an old woman in a bathhouse during the siege.[93] The woman next to Berggolts glanced at the woman and whispered, 'My husband has died. He was so young and handsome, and look at who has survived.' In a sudden access of hatred, she suddenly went on, 'He has died and that has survived. Perhaps those are the only ones who will be left! Why did he have to die?' She was trembling all over, unable to hold herself back. 'So that the likes of that one could survive!'[94]

We hear the same refrain in Maria Mashkova's diary. On 18 February 1942, she remembers N. Molchanov, a friend who died from malnutrition: 'He took with him the brightest, most joyful and selfless part of my life. I lost someone who was perhaps one in a million and a half, a bright humanist, a thinker with such a human smile. He was just so clever!'[95] The stronger the sense of irreparable loss, the greater the hostility in descriptions of those who managed to survive in that nightmare. We can expect no objectivity here. The passing of someone she loved only reveals the more starkly her alienation from other people who are remote and feel nothing for her. Her unremitting pain can only intensify that: 'The people who are left and who are going to survive are just so dreadful. What sort of future is that?'[96]

'The good people are dying, and the scum are flourishing', Vladimir Lyublinsky observed when he met a literary critic of his acquaintance wearing 'a very sumptuous fur coat and hat'. He had eaten three cats, did no work, and saw no reason to leave the city. Lyublinsky's characterization of scum is succinct: someone who is prepared, without compunction and insensitive to humiliation, to do whatever it takes to survive, who does not want to do so through honest toil, and is now so used to everything that he sees no reason to try to change his situation. He has other, more terrible, criteria. He continues the entry with a story about cannibalism: 'I have just, with the help of a policeman, arrested someone on Nevsky Prospekt who was transporting a dismembered corpse and openly admitted it was for making into jellied meat.'[97]

5

The siege physically disfigured people, something that is very obvious if you compare pre- and post-war photographs of the same citizens. It is not the haggard look, which soon disappears when diet improves. Many people's features became irreversibly deformed, their physical proportions affected, their muscles twisted. This was particularly hard for women. Prolonged starvation caused hormonal disorders and they began to grow moustaches and beards. Scurvy made their teeth fall out. The coarse skin on their faces, 'cured' by the smoke from iron *burzhuika* stoves, attacked by the frost during a severe winter, was a permanent stigma left by the siege. There was no way to bring back their earlier beauty and allure. They commonly looked ten to fifteen years older than they really were.[98] 'We saw skeletons with skin stretched over them, and all of them with "tails"', Zoya Travkina recalled of a visit to the baths.[99]

Beside them sat women who had escaped that tribulation. They had either been working in jobs with access to food, or had arrived in Leningrad after the Time of Death. These were cheerful, attractive girls who turned heads, whom men wanted to meet, who got invited all over the place. Those same men steered clear of scrawny women who had lost their figures, their suppleness and charm, women who were clumsy, bloated, wearing grimy fur coats or padded winter jackets.

Why? Were they to blame for having lived through that hell? Why should they be the ones who had to suffer such humiliation when those others had been spared? Why had their youth been so suddenly cut short here in the obsessive search for a crust of bread, as they gnawed tablets of wood glue, surrounded by the moaning and cries of the dying, unburied corpses, lice and rats? These questions, implicit or explicit, are often to be heard in the bitter writings of the women of Leningrad who had been through the war. It explains their resentment of those who did not look like the survivors of the siege, were not interested in hearing about what had happened, or who these other, disfigured, women were.

'Anyone who does not look starved is a scoundrel', Izrail Metter summarized the attitude.[100] At times, it could be manifested very aggressively. A rosy-cheeked, plump young woman was driven out of the baths by an emaciated woman with the words, 'Oy, my pretty one, don't come here again or we'll eat you', to the laughter of the rest of the clientele.[101] In Georgiy Kulagin's diary, this contrast between the healthy and the starved is almost artistically depicted. On the one hand, there were women cleaning the premises, very poorly dressed, and on the other there were the girls working in the canteen, laughing, dressed in spring clothes with short skirts and brightly coloured jumpers, fluttering past like butterflies. 'The cleaners look after the girls with animosity. A woman with ashen cheeks and a burning, hungry look in her eyes remarks angrily and loudly, "Oh, if I had my way . . ." The whole grimy line of them laugh and hiss and curse.'[102] The girls ran off, but it was some time before the 'disturbed anthill of hungry women calmed down again'.[103]

The plot of the story is simple, although its characters seem exaggerated. There is no obvious motivation behind such incidents. It is not easy to represent them as reflecting only a conflict based on age and social status. It seems rather to be a form of protest against forms of unfairness which are not entirely clear. Where women were lucky enough to escape the horror, whether in another city or by proximity to the kitchen, does not particularly matter. The indignation is caused by the fact that someone resorted to means not available to other people, and hence unquestionably underhand. From this position, it could logically be argued that not to be suffering during the siege was in itself immoral. A corollary is that those more fortunate are deserving of censure, which should make them more respectful towards those who were suffering.[104] Those disinclined to regard themselves as losers found it more satisfactory to explain their predicament as due to their strict adherence to moral precepts.

6

People became less restrained, and did not observe purely cosmetic proprieties. Everything was out in the open, visible to and checked by everybody else. The evidence is scattered and fragmentary, but reveals certain widespread approaches to ensuring that justice was seen to be done. Food was shared out publicly and meticulously.

Bread was divided in the family in full view of everyone, and sometimes with the aid of a ruler.[105] Dmitry Likhachev recalls how, when they sat down at mealtimes, his children 'jealously ensured that everyone was treated equally.'[106] In bakeries, shops and other places where food was distributed, monitoring by the customers was even more strict and demanding, and for that there were good grounds. In the bakery M. P. Pelevin went to, 'the bread was weighed out down to the last crumb in front of hungry, watchful customers'.[107] We hear the same from other eyewitnesses. Dmitry Likhachev recalls, 'People jealously kept an eye on the scales by the light of oil lamps.'[108] Hostile attention was paid to this because of the widespread dishonesty of those issuing the bread.

Customers in canteens were particularly suspicious. They carefully checked the weight of portions, concerned that their porridge or soup might contain fewer grams of grains than their food coupons entitled them to. They checked up in whatever manner they could, unembarrassed by anything or anyone. It could appear rude, but that was just too bad: lives were at stake. 'Porridge was weighed on the scales on a plate and then transferred to another plate, and we watched greedily to make sure everything was scraped off', 14-year-old V. Soloviova, who worked in a factory, recalls.[109] Other schoolchildren in the canteen checked their portions on scales. Vladislav G. Grigoriev justified this by pointing out that they had been going hungry for a long time.[110] In the canteen of the Red Army Club, the soup was measured out by the spoonful,[111] and a 'hungry and jealous eye' was kept on the cook dishing out 'offal meatballs in the restaurant of the Artists Union'.[112]

This far from tactful monitoring, which witnesses of the siege constantly remark on, did ensure that standards were maintained. There was a lot of intransigence about notions of equality and fairness, and the accusations made sometimes seem arbitrary and baseless. There was bias, but it would have been difficult to maintain moral rigorousness without great outcries and no-holds-barred censure.

What other force was there to constrain the urge to benefit oneself at the expense of others, to roughly elbow people aside, to get food for yourself which was not available to the many? The police? They were rarely seen on the streets during the Time of Death. The Party and Komsomol

committees? They hardly had the resources to keep every residential building and every family under surveillance.

It would be an exaggeration to suggest that the sense of fairness was
a sufficient defence against degeneration in that first winter of the war.
There was plenty in the egalitarianism of the siege that was unfair, but a
considerably greater threat was the trend towards dividing of people into
those who were of greater value and those who were not considered very
valuable at all. The fear of yourself being placed in the latter category was
fully enough to undermine traditions of mutual support and compassion.
When people detected that in this nightmare some were arrogating to
themselves the right to live better and look better, insistence on equality
became crucial. It was much more than an appeal for good manners: it
became a prerequisite for survival. What else could you appeal to if not to
the honesty and decency of other people?

Meticulous calculation of benefits and privileges did not, in fact, super-
sede compassion. To consider yourself fair, you had to be able to consider
yourself principled, and could not just ignore others in distress. Fairness is
inseparable from charity. Someone who had been offended against would
speak out not only for himself but also on behalf of everyone else. There
were many complex situations in which people came to the rescue without
first deciding what was fair or unfair. The understanding of fairness could
not be reduced merely to equitable sharing out of bread, allocation of
duties and designation of responsibilities. It was deeper than mere pedantic
egalitarianism. It required an understanding that you could not demand
from those who were starving the same level of effort that others might be
able to make; that you could not high-handedly divide Leningraders into
those were putting up a fight and those who had lost their will to resist, but
that you were obliged to give support also to the weakest; and not lecture
those crushed by the siege, but show compassion for them.

Charity

1

One of the main manifestations of charitable feeling is sympathy for the
afflicted: the weak, the helpless, those unable to fend for themselves. That,
above all, means compassion for children and teenagers. Of course, there
were limits, but this was a red line which, on the whole, was not crossed.
'This bread is for children.' That was the most telling argument when it
was necessary to deflect someone's self-seeking. This was how the teen-
aged L. P. Vlasova managed to halt a policeman 'checking her bag' and
keen to help himself to her bread. The exchange was brief. 'I yelled at him,
"I've got my mum at home and my little sister!" He said, "Okay, okay.
Fine."'[113] Perhaps he was just deterred by her determination, but it is significant that that was the argument she chose to defend herself with.

'Bread for children'. The expression could invoke earlier social traditions. On one occasion, a sledge with New Year's gifts for a children's home overturned by the Narva Gate and soya sweets spilled out of their containers. It was an unusual sight in the siege and passers-by were soon stopping. The woman transporting the gifts started gathering them up and, fearing the worst, waved her arms in the hope of shooing people away. 'They're for orphans in the children's home', she exclaimed. She could have asked them to go away, threatened them with the law, perhaps even asked for help, but those were the words which came to mind. And they worked: 'Suddenly, the people at the front surrounded the sledge, stood shoulder to shoulder, held hands, and stood like that until everything had been gathered up and packed away again.'[114]

The story may be exaggerated, but there are telling details. 'They held hands': a gesture indicating not only determination not to let anyone deprive the children of their gifts, but also awareness of how many people were entirely capable of doing so.

Newly orphaned children in the recently established children's reception and reallocation centres and children's homes did get robbed, and could be left without bed linen or even beds. That happened more than once. But, at that time, almost the worst accusation that could be thrown at anyone was that they were stealing bread from a child. From diaries and letters, we can see that this was more hurtful than anything else. Such behaviour was immediately noted, and brought down indignation and contempt on those responsible.

In the testimony of children and teenagers who found themselves facing death, there is one detail, which they seem not to regard as particularly significant, but which recurs constantly. That is the responsiveness of strangers when they learn of the tragedy that has befallen them. Their first impulse is always strikingly altruistic, although it may not be sustained. Thus, one girl who had lost almost all her relatives, in order not to die of hunger, took her remaining belongings to the market. She probably managed to barter them profitably, but also noted the kindness of other people there. Perhaps she told them about her predicament.[115] Maria Mashkova's tale about meeting a boy she knew ends with her remarking that he was starving. Later we learn that her family gave him a meal.[116]

We find children and teenagers who had been orphaned or whose parents had abandoned them being taken in by other families, and sometimes specially given bread and meat. People tried to comfort them in their distress and look after them, although this often lasted only for the first few days after their catastrophe. We encounter this sympathy for a suffering child regularly. In the diary of Lev Khodorkov, an engineer, we find him returning again and again to the topic of the death of children. He is pursued by the horror of it: 'If the child was tall, his legs are drawn up with rope to his thighs so that the body can fit on to a small sledge.'[117] One man exchanged his food for a book of Lermontov's poetry, held out to him by a boy begging for a bread ration: 'I felt so sorry for him. He looked so hungry and I decided just to suffer for a day.'[118] It is only one episode, but then, is not the whole story of the siege a collection of untypical tales in which, despite the muddled incidents and outcomes, one clearly senses that there have been instances of genuine human kindness?

'"Are you hungry?" "Yes!" He took me to the army commanders' dining room and gave me his meal. He sat there, crying. Later I was told two of his children were in occupied territory.' That is how G. N. Ignatova, a schoolgirl at the time, recalled the day when she unexpectedly had an extra meal.[119] E. Tiys, a 6-year-old, was even less hopeful. There was a yeast factory next to where she lived and every day treacle would be brought from it. At the gate, children waited for the truck in the hope of getting some. It happened rarely, but sometimes the workers would take pity, 'scoop treacle out of the barrel and share it out among the mugs held out towards them'. The little girl was also standing there with her mug, but to one side. She and her mother were saved by a stranger, one of the drivers. She never knew his name and never met him later. People often feel particularly sympathetic towards those who are not begging aggressively, who are not outspoken but look shy and timid:

> He asked me why I was not running after the treacle. I told him about my mother who could not get out of bed. He gave me treacle, and the next day brought a little pine tree and explained how I should boil the pine needles and give the water to my mother to drink. A few days later he brought a small pot of cabbage soup and told me to give it little by little to Mother.[120]

Undernourished children were often forgiven what was usually severely punished in the Time of Death. One little girl told the story of how her mother sat her at a table where soldiers were eating, hoping that someone would take pity and feed her daughter. Nobody did. Perhaps they thought the food for her was on its way, or perhaps they could see the situation but did not feel like helping. One of the diners had two cereal coupons and exchanged them for two helpings of pasta. He paid no attention to the little girl. After sitting there hungrily while people ate several helpings, she could bear it no longer. Saying nothing, she quietly moved the second plate of pasta towards her and began eating. The soldier may have thought it was her plate, and shortly afterwards asked the waitress for his second portion. 'Is the girl not with you?' the waitress asked. He evidently understood the situation, got up and left without a word.[121]

Despite its uniqueness, this incident reveals one recurrent feature. People might be reluctant to share, or refuse to share, with strangers in need, but if it was forced on them, they acknowledged, if only tacitly and probably with a degree of irritation, the other person's moral right to be helped. If the girl had been surrounded by other starving victims of the siege, the story might have ended differently: there would have been shouting, cursing and tears. Here, however, there were seated at the same table one person entitled to two helpings of his main course and someone else for whom that was beyond her wildest dreams. The moral imperative may have been acknowledged reluctantly, but acknowledged it was, both because here was a hungry child, and because someone was being allowed to eat more than a starving little girl. The moral imperative, presented as starkly as that and when there is no getting away from it, has to be obeyed.

2

Of course, even those who spoke of how sorry they felt for the children did not always resist temptation to deprive them. In the diary of the head doctor of a clinic and director of a district health department, we read a lot about the innocent victims of the siege. 'How old the children are beyond their years! How much suffering they have endured! They are passing their childhood in such a depressing state. Their minds will never be free from this trauma: it will be with them for the rest of their lives.'[122]

But then we read his diary entries from the Time of Death. They tell us he was sent out to inspect a nursery. This was a well-provisioned place and nobody would have wanted to lose their job there. It had plenty of shortcomings. The inspector was taken to the dining room, but appears blithely unaware of anything untoward about this: 'I had a good meal. It was marvellous! Set me up for the rest of the day.'[123]

This is not a greedy or callous person. He often takes care of his mother and shares his rations with her. He is not one of those who were flourishing, and was probably pained by the sight of unhappy, undernourished children. He just was not very good at resisting temptation. On 1 February 1942, he notes, 'I need to find a new place to live. I'm tired of these conditions. It's filthy here. The rest area has been turned into a byre. Perhaps I can get a job in a nursery.'[124] On 6 February 1942, he notes, 'Registered for meals at a nursery. The first few days have shown it is a considerable improvement on the food at the District Committee's canteen. I'm getting my strength back.'[125]

It is difficult to comment on these lines. Let us take just one more entry, written on 2 March 1942: 'People are dying in their hundreds, in their thousands every day. What can be done to help, to save lives?'[126]

He could not have been unaware that the hospitality he was receiving was taking bread from the mouths of hungry children, that even though he surrendered food coupons in return for the meal, he, as a boss with whom people were seeking to curry favour, would receive a larger helping at their expense, and that the privileged conditions in the nursery were there for those who were not getting enough bread, rather than to supplement the diet of an official.[127]

Even someone who kept a close eye on their own behaviour could, as we see from the documents of the siege, either deliberately or unconsciously, segregate their emotions from their actions without admitting there was any contradiction between them.

We note how tersely, soberly, without emotion or attempts at

self-justification, people who incline to heroics register their own infringe-
ments of morality.

Moral rules often changed if they were a hindrance to survival, but they
did not disappear. They did at least make more 'civilized', acts which were
manifestly selfish. Few were able to resist the temptation of getting an
extra piece of bread, but at the same time they tried to maintain at least
a semblance of propriety. No one was likely unashamedly and brutally,
ignoring everyone around them, to wrench bread out of the hands of the
enfeebled. But no one was watching as bread was denied to crying infants,
no one said openly and reproachfully whose food had been pilfered to
provide hospitality for a government inspector. That being so, perhaps it
was just best not to ask where the food came from, to keep quiet, to persuade yourself this was just how things were done. That way everything
was so much easier and more peaceful.

3

One of the ways charity could be shown was by recognizing that you could
not demand too much of malnourished people, that you could and should
disregard official instructions when it was a matter of life and death. The
conventional wisdom was that people who were thoroughly demoralized
could be made socially useful again only through the exercise of rigid discipline and being forced to work. Decisions were often taken, however, on a
more humane basis. Account was taken of the predicament of people who
could not do work beyond their strength, and who would die if deprived
of their entitlement to rations.

If a worker was seen to be collapsing from malnutrition, he would be
sent to hospital or given a holiday; school hours were reduced and pupils
were asked less demanding questions in recognition of the fact that they
were starving. Attempts were made to excuse those with small children
from frequent involvement in public work projects.[128] The secretary of
the Party bureau of a cooperative delegated its members to look in at the
homes of workers who had not been seen for several weeks: 'I tried to
choose addresses which were on their way home, because the girls were
themselves starving and we needed to conserve their strength and not send
them out of their way.'[129]

We can even speak of a kind of 'compulsory charity'. How, Irina
Zelenskaya wonders, are you supposed to demand 'supreme heroism'
from the workers 'if they are working with one hand while holding their
4-year-old daughter with the other?' The little girl was traumatized, terrified by the alarms, and never left her mother's side. Another worker,
instead of going on fire watch duty during an air raid, took her team to
the safety of a 'nook' (shelter), and she had a 10-year-old daughter tagging
along everywhere behind her. At one of the many meetings, it was proposed that 'notorious cowards' should be sacked, but that was tantamount
to 'a guarantee of unemployment and starvation'.[130]

Maria Konoplyova was the secretary of an occupational health inspec-

tion commission and saw how afraid those in the siege were of being categorized as Class 1 or Class 2 invalids. The reason was obvious. Invalids
were issued the ration card of a 'dependant', which was effectively a slow
death sentence. Konoplyova crossed those words out in her manuscript,
but it was probably the truth of the matter.

Invalidity could be certified without any detailed medical examination.
Everybody was suffering from dystrophy, vitamin deficiency and 'aggra-
vation on that basis of chronic illnesses'. If people categorized as Class 2
invalids could not be employed, doctors transferred them to Class 3. There
is no doubting the element of subjectivity in this decision: not all who were
eligible were reclassified, but only those who 'wanted to and still could be
put back on their feet'.[131] Others evidently got short shrift. As so often
during the siege, compassion and calculation were closely related, but
we have also to take account of a growing callousness and ill-concealed
antipathy towards 'dystrophics'. Clearly, not everybody could be classified healthy, and there was no option but to devise criteria for 'selection'.
Though an attempt was made to do this in a humane manner, it was
unavoidably cruel, because one person was being helped to survive, while
others were being condemned to death. This kind of selection became
routine in Leningrad, and not only in Konoplyova's commission and
the children's homes. For evacuation or admission to hospital, the very
weakest were often discarded, although not invariably. But what was the
option, if there were not enough places in the train carriages for everyone,
and there was a ban on admission to hospital of those unable to walk
unaided? The weakest were abandoned, often without even subsistence
rations, and only a few miraculously survived.

4

Charity was manifested during the siege in a variety of ways. People tried
to shield their loved ones from things that would upset them, and concealed a lot. When she saw her father's temperature was 34.5° and realized he had only a few days left to live, one Leningrader later wrote that
she 'took great care not to tell him that'. In turn, her mother, when she
was taking care of her daughter in hospital, tried not to mention that she
herself had a very high temperature. 'In the notes she wrote, she presented
a completely different picture.'[132]

Engineer Vladimir G. Kulyabko's letters to his son are a perfect example
of sensitivity when touching on a grievous topic with one's family. Every
word is chosen with care. Anticipating the worst, he advises his son on
how best to broach the subject with his mother: 'Indirectly, if anything
should occur, prepare her for the possibility that something might happen
to me, so that it does not come as a surprise to her.'[133] The ornateness
of the phrasing with its disjointed syntax is quite untypical of his diary
entries, which are dry to the point of being brusque. The circumlocutions
are clearly excessive. Nothing is said directly about the possibility he will
die. He chooses other words which might baffle anybody not in the know:

'if anything should occur', 'the possibility that something might happen'. Even to his son he only hints, evidently not wanting to upset him more than is unavoidable.

Admonitions and well-meant advice were a feature of life during the siege, and were most commonly to be found in letters. They arrived from relatives living in evacuation, in which case they were sure to contain the hope (and sometimes demands) that they should survive, not lose heart and take good care of themselves and other relatives. These exhortations were sometimes intended both to give reassurance to the recipient and in the expectation that he or she would in turn encourage others who were themselves in even greater difficulties. Those who were actually in the siege, when they urged others to be charitable, or exhorted and encouraged waverers or those who had lost their willpower, were also reminding themselves of the ethical guidelines. This was so because they were searching for words which were natural and emotive and did not jar with what they were saying but gave it a familiar, down-to-earth tone. The moral precepts being reinforced were artless and commonplace, without commentary or rhetorical flourishes.

5

Deviations from charitable behaviour were invariably registered. People did not always know exactly what had happened, and added extraneous detail themselves. Sometimes rumours about an occurrence were passed on in terms of familiar, oversimplified clichés, and evoked an equally unambiguous and damning reaction. Examples of uncharitable behaviour were the action of the NKVD investigator who called in Olga Berggolts's father for interrogation, his vigilance activated by the Germanic surname: 'Evidently expecting an early end to the siege with consequent awards for service, that esteemed institution is making haste to provide itself with evidence of how amazingly active it was, in order to justify the award of medals. They are such irredeemable scum.'[134] N. P. Zavetnovskaya deplored the uncharitable behaviour of a policeman who 'roams through the markets, picking on unfortunate people and confiscating every scrap of bread from them if they have bought it for cash or, in his opinion, have bought too much'.[135] She has the same opinion of one of her neighbour's relatives: 'Ill-mannered and very cold and insensitive.'[136] Alexander Nikolsky, a member of the Academy of Architecture, considered the behaviour of the senior officials of its Leningrad branch immoral. When he appealed to them for help, they advised him to buy food in the market.[137] A. I. Vinokurov, a geography teacher, decided a geologist he knew was 'a scoundrel' when the man was pleased to discover his own house had been hit by a shell. He was looking forward to being able to pick up firewood conveniently among the ruins.[138]

'He didn't offer us even a cup of tea, though he knew people here were starving', is how Vladislav Grigoriev recalls meeting someone in the army who was passing on 'a modest parcel' from his father.[139] I. I. Zhilinsky

wrote down what his wife told him about trying to exchange their belongings for oilcake at a Soviet farm. Everywhere, she was sent packing. They
had no need now of the property of siege victims, which they were being
offered for next to nothing: they already had more than enough. There
were just too many uninvited people turning up, timidly hoping something might come their way. His wife was crying: 'Even the children drive
unwanted visitors away. They throw logs at them.' She was appalled by
'this attitude of well-fed peasants to starving people'.[140]

There is comment too on the uncharitableness of those who took
advantage of others' misfortune. In an interview, we find L. P. Vlasova
expressing resentment, in a rather muddled manner, that nurses, who had
more bread than they could use, bought up people's belongings for next to
nothing: 'Well, like there was this one I knew. She was all, "Oh, I helped
the wounded, really put my heart and soul into it . . ." Well, I went there
myself, carting my clothes to those nurses to swap. And there she is, going
on. Well, I don't like liars.'[141]

V. A. Alexeyeva's mother cleaned a factory director's apartment 'just
to get something to eat'.[142] She also worked in a canteen cleaning the pans
'for nothing, just so as to be able to collect the scrapings of burnt porridge
from them'.[143] G. Glukhova's mother took a job unloading vans of flour:
'Some of it spilled from the sacks on to their clothes. They were allowed
afterwards to shake that off and take it home.'[144]

Starving people had no options, as well-fed people who did not want to
do dirty jobs themselves, and did not want to pay fairly for someone else
to do them, were fully aware. Why should they? Starving Leningraders
would work for next to nothing in order to save the lives of their children
and themselves, and there was a long queue of people just like them only
too prepared to take on any job. Or humbly waiting to be 'thanked'. 'At
the hospital one nurse said to me, "Clean this office. Take out the rubbish,
and I'll give you some porridge." I went back to her: "I've done everything
in that office you asked me to clean." "Oh, good." Silence. I said, "You
were going to give me some porridge." "Ah, yes, of course. I'll just get you
your porridge." She gave me two spoonfuls. She gave me it. I ate it. Of
course I did.'[145]

The protest against this heartless behaviour is implicit in the tone of the
story, in what is omitted, and in barely noticeable details. Lev Khodorkov
describes in his diary a production meeting taking place with a boilerman
dying in the next room. A request went to the canteen to do something
to help him. Khodorkov is succinct: 'A waitress arrives, her face bursting
with fat. She says with a snigger, "Where's the man who's dying? Here's
some soup for him before he dies."'[146]

The waitress is unfeeling. Perhaps she regularly saw humiliated people
begging for an extra helping of porridge or soup. We can imagine that they
too might have talked about shortly dying of starvation. She was evidently
tired of all that, and clearly not suffering from hunger herself. There is no
explicit condemnation by Khodorkov, but a hint of disgust in the laconic

way we are told how she looked, what she said, and about whom. There is no comment on her face 'bursting with fat' or her 'snigger', but the choice of words makes clear what he thinks of this repugnant episode. There are no evident grounds for condemning the waitress. She is not rude, she does not turn down the request for food, but her lack of charity is clear to everyone from her tone of voice. At this time it was not unusual for such a request to be refused, often in a foul-mouthed manner, but her derision was unusual, with its admixture of obnoxious condescension and primitive theatricality.

In the account of M. Kashtelyan, recorded by Lev Razumovsky, there is also no explicit judgement. A girl, who in March 1942 lost both her mother and father, evidently had nowhere to go. She was given shelter by a 'friend': 'For this she helped herself to 100 grams of bread from my mother's ration cards.'[147] The details of the orphaned girl's life during the siege are only too eloquent: 'I lost a lot of my strength. I became really thin. When my father was still alive we boiled hide belts. We ate two cats.'[148] The 'friend' who was robbing her must have known this. People at that time spoke about their hardships often and to anyone who would listen, either in the hope of receiving help or just because they needed to tell someone about them. There is no explicit comment about the 100 grams stolen from the starving girl, but there is a pointed description of how emaciated she was. Perhaps there were mitigating circumstances to explain the behaviour of the 'friend', but, if so, there is no mention of them.

Charity made people exceptionally sharp-sighted. They became indignant not only about acts of cruelty they had actually seen: sometimes mere suspicion was enough to release an avalanche of denunciation, with surmised misconduct treated as reality.

'His mother did not look after him very well', A. V. Sirotova later reminisced about a 5-year-old boy who lived next door. Her account clearly demonstrates how charitable feelings could cause a person to add 'finishing touches' to the story of someone's life and jump to very categorical conclusions. Sirotova noticed the boy turning inside out the bag they used for bringing bread home and trying to 'pick crumbs out of the seams'. She was rarely at home herself and can hardly have known the details of what went on in someone else's family. She passed judgement on the basis of a single incident which caught her eye. 'What kind of state must he have been in to resort to looking for food like that?' she later wrote,[149] but, after all, there could be several explanations. A. P. Bondarenko recalls that her children were allowed to collect the crumbs from a cart delivering bread from the bakery, and in her family the food was shared equally. People 'resorted to looking for food' not only because they were being denied their fair share or because someone was not looking after them well. Both adults and children resorted to such tactics, when they checked to see whether a packet of noodles, or mustard, salt or sugar bought last year, or some biscuit crumbs or sweets had slipped down under a sideboard or into a hole in the floor. They moved the furniture, shook everything out, and checked every last pocket of their old clothes. More than once, and always hoping against hope.

This predisposition to see cheating everywhere, greed, attempts to profit at the expense of other people, is deserving of note. It helped to create a shield against immorality. The details of an incident might be unclear, or even unknown. They were, however, bolstered by a whole raft of edifying moral considerations, where the details were deliberately exaggerated and evidence of malfeasance thrown into stark relief.

6

Nazism was seen as the embodiment of violence and brutality. The immorality of bombing a city, killing children, the elderly and women was particularly condemned. 'Twelve-year-old Galya Smirnova was brought to the reception area. Her leg was amputated at the thigh. She was conscious, crying for her mum.' That was the kind of thing people saw and remembered in those days.[150] 'You felt most sorry for the children: how were they to blame for having been brought into the world at a time like this?', Arkadiy Lepkovich asked in his diary on 12 December 1941.[151]

It was particularly objectionable that not only military targets were bombed but also hospitals, residential housing and facilities for children.[152] Those caught in the siege saw this as totally evil. What was the purpose of bombing if not to hit military targets? The only answer they could find was: for the pleasure of causing other people to suffer, in order to maim indiscriminately the frail, the defenceless, the vulnerable, and for no other reason than the sadistic satisfaction of crippling people. That seemed so outlandish that one girl asked in school, 'Do the fascists know how many of us are dying here?'[153]

The word that came to their minds might seem peculiar, coming from people who were suffering monstrous hardship, but it precisely reflects the limited range of the Leningraders' conventional moral values. They called the behaviour of the German army 'hooliganism'. 'This is complete hooliganism on the part of the Germans. They miss the military facilities and only hit people's homes and kill ordinary citizens', N. P. Zavetnovskaya wrote to her daughter on 5 February 1942.[154] We meet the same word and the same sentiments in Nikolai Gorshkov's diary: 'The shelling of civilians is blatant hooliganism on the part of the enemy because it is of no military advantage whatsoever.'[155]

Most importantly, the starvation wiping out so many Leningraders exposes the Nazis' immorality. 'Is it humane or any way for people to live when there are eleven families in my building, of which only one has a modest supply of food and is not starving, while the other ten, one after the other, have swollen up from hunger and many, including myself, can't walk outside without a stick?', Arkadiy Lepkovich asked.[156] Alexandra Borovikova describes the different stages of her life before and during the war, in an account which is not without literary merit: not virtuoso but profoundly sincere, which enables her to relive and convey more vividly how she has changed. She had a past in which she lived 'like a bird'. She loved singing and joking. Now she has a present in which she has become sad and says little. 'What a bastard that Hitler is. Look what he is putting us through.'[157]

Emaciated faces ravaged by the frosts, the yawning emptiness of ruined buildings, the furniture and meagre household goods thrown or spilling out of them into the street, the insatiable hunger and the suffering of people, family or not, and much else that became characteristic of the Time of Death, all gave rise to an enduring feeling of hatred. Although not always expressed vehemently or at great length, it comes through clearly in dozens of documents from the siege. It was not muffled by the daily struggle for survival, or irritation at disgraceful things happening in full view, or anger at the casual negligence of well-fed officials, at thieves and black marketeers. 'I was never bad-tempered. I wanted to do something good for other people', V. Peterson, a schoolgirl, wrote in her diary on 20 October 1941. Now, though, she hated those 'fiends' and 'animals': 'They have mangled our lives and disfigured our city.'[158]

7

No scrap of bread donated to the starving was forgotten by those who witnessed the siege. Many Leningrad tales, promptly written down in diaries, mentioned in letters or preserved in later memoirs are little more than a listing of gifts. When they saw someone else trying to help others, people wanted to support others themselves. They felt shamed when they compared themselves with a person capable of giving away all they possessed even though they themselves were in need. Helping someone else entailed testing once more your own moral qualities. Were you greedy? Were you capable of extended self-sacrifice? Had you a tendency to excuse doing things that were wrong?

Ksenia Polzikova-Rubets gave the following verdict on the act of a schoolmistress who heard the physics teacher had fainted from hunger and promised to bring him food: 'Where was she to find coffee and sugar? She would have to sacrifice it herself. That is real caring for a colleague.'[159]

Polzikova-Rubets's stories generally have a didactic purpose and emotive conclusion, but the same approach is found in other documents that are relating something particularly dramatic or unusual, even by the standards of the siege. This inclination to endow those who were self-sacrificing with every virtue is present to an even greater extent in an interview with another survivor of the siege. At the beginning of the war, he was 9 years old. He was not yet capable of understanding and judging everything, and, as was often the case, a child's experiences were incorporated in adult reminiscences which had a deeper understanding of situations.

Vavila (a boy of his own age) went to the bakery but never came back. His body was found in the spring, when the city was being cleared of snowdrifts. In the string bag he had taken, they found bread, still complete with the makeweight. This detail made a great impression on people at the time. Evidence for this is the emotional charge of the account, still discernible decades later, with its repetitions and emotion.

It could be argued that this has been written later and that back then, as a child during the siege, he might not have had such an understanding of what he had witnessed. But why then had he remembered this story so particularly? Why did it so stand out for him among the hundreds of other episodes of the siege? Why was he still not able to talk about it dispassionately? The story is related very emotionally: 'He knew that when he brought the bread back home it would be divided into three parts, and so would that makeweight. So if he ate it, he would be cheating his mother and sister out of it, and that was something that, even though he was starving and dying, Vavila could not bring himself to do.'[160]

Vladislav Daev witnessed a woman bartering 250 grams of butter for a kilogram of oilcake. He did not know the woman, what her circumstances were or why she did it. What he did know was that this was not a fair bargain: the butter was worth more than she was receiving in return. At this point he begins joining up the dots, when every action is seen as a manifestation of all the best qualities to be found in a human being. As the woman had butter, she must have children, because butter was only issued against a child's ration card. Then vague surmise rapidly turns into unshakable certainty: 'It was obviously important to the woman that her children should not be hungry. She was working out how many dishes of hot porridge she could make out of that piece of oilcake.'[161]

'She only drinks the soup, and leaves the main course', F. A. Gryaznov observed of one of those eating in his canteen. Kissel fruit jelly was served without the need for a coupon and the woman poured it into a canister. 'Perhaps you could ask the waiter for another helping and give it to me. He won't give me any more. I've taken three cups already', she said.[162] Gryaznov was an actor, and particularly alive to this kind of scene. He has no doubt that this is a mother, stinting herself, willing herself not to eat a main course in order to save coupons for her son. Her grovelling for the glasses of jelly is doubtless also for her son's benefit. Two others in the canteen are a mother and her son. He sees her give the boy half her main course and does not doubt she too is hungry. In fact, everybody in there is hungry. 'Her son declines, but only halfheartedly, before taking and eating it.'[163]

Another story is recorded, not half a century later but in May 1942, in a letter from T. I. Antonovich, who worked at the Public Library and served in the local air defence unit. It is a typical story. In March 1942, Antonovich fell ill with severe malnutrition. She was helped ('selflessly cared for', as she stresses in the letter) by her friends in the unit. She writes that she did a lot of rethinking during this difficult time, when other people were giving her so much support. They did not just take her off to hospital, which would have been far easier for them. She keenly appreciated that kind of detail, as any vulnerable person in distressing circumstances tends to. Her evaluation of the kindness of her friends and colleagues is unconditional and unequivocal, and expressed very directly: 'They worried only about me, and did everything they could to support my failing spirits and hopes of survival.'[164]

On other occasions too, the eye of those caught in the siege often picks out minute instances of altruism, sometimes with emotional commentary, sometimes laconically and without further remarks. Vera Inber wrote about one firefighter who had distinguished himself but declined an award saying, 'The only bonus I need is 100 grams of cod-liver oil for my wife.'[165] A. V. Sirotova noticed a little boy dragging a piece of wood four times the size of himself. 'My mum is not well, it's cold and we haven't got anything to cook soup with', he told her.[166] R. Belevskaya, a doctor, left a bar of chocolate for her little daughter when she came to visit from the front line. 'It brings tears to my eyes to remember how, each time I visited, they would give me a report on how much my daughter had been given and how much was still left.'[167]

Charity was something noticed by those who were themselves charitable, who could talk about it emotionally, with tears in their eyes, and who were able to see an ambiguous action as irreproachable. The instances of charity they observed made them look again at themselves and rehabilitate, as far as circumstances allowed, any moral principles which might have been compromised by the siege.

8

Every person had their own threshold of charity. M. N. Abrosimova told the tale of a worker to whom she gave bread, and the factory director standing next to her gave oilcake. Why? He had been 'brought in from a rubbish tip where he was eating a dead cat'[168] and the horror forced them to hand over what they had been preparing for lunch. He was brought in 'terribly ill and weak' and it was impossible not to help him. He was 'brought in', and it is not difficult to imagine how embarrassed and frightened the man must have been, not knowing what to expect, and evoking the compassion of everybody who saw him. That rubbish dump was compelling evidence of what he had been reduced to, and prompted them to offer him support without more ado.

This sort of thing happened regularly. A mother died, her children surrendered her ration card in order for her to be buried. Their food ran out and they went to the shop to beg. At the door, the boy noticed his sister 'began suddenly to wilt and her eyes glazed over'. They were saved by a woman who came out of the shop. 'She asked what had happened, broke off from her bread ration a piece of bread half the size of a matchbox and put it in his sister's mouth. She swallowed the bread, opened her eyes and came back to life.'[169]

G. I. Kozlova lost her ration cards and tried to survive by making a disgusting concoction from silage. The farm's Party organizer saw and gave her oilcake.[170] V. P. Kondratiev tells the very emotional story of how, when he worked on a soviet farm, victims of the siege would come hoping to be fed: 'An old woman came, stooped, haggard, her face pale and heavily wrinkled. She asked in a shaky voice to be given work.' At that time of year, there was no need for casual labour on the farm and there were no spare ration cards available for them. He felt sorry for her, but there was nothing he could do to help. 'Grandma, we just don't have any extra work now. Come back in the spring', he said.[171] At this point he discovered that the 'grandmother' was just 16 years old. Tears came to the eyes of the shocked office worker and, despite the fact that an artillery bombardment began, the girl did not move and once again asked him to help her. Her father had died at the front, her mother and sister had starved to death, and her aunt had been killed during an air raid. Her ration cards had been lost during the shelling, she was hungry and had no one to turn to. The only thing left for her was to beg. Despite their own situation, they rescued her: 'We took the girl, fed her with what we could find, and managed somehow to get her a worker's ration card.'[172]

Understanding what starving people were going through, help would be offered with great delicacy, without condescension, without any rudeness, because a person in desperate need would have no option but to put up with any humiliation. Vladimir Admoni describes how, in the restaurant of the Writers Club, one member, a translator of Proust's novels, 'was trying to pour a handful of sugar from a plate into a paper cone and spilled it'. He passed through all the circles of hell, and we can just imagine his slow, awkward movements, his trembling hands. It must have been embarrassing and difficult for an unsteady, elderly man to crawl about on the floor, but he had no choice: 'After a moment, without a word, he began slowly sweeping up the grains of sugar.' The literary critic Naum Berkovsky and Admoni were sitting at the same table as the translator and, no doubt not only to relieve his physical discomfort but also to dissipate his embarrassment, 'we did our best to make sure he got back every single grain'.[173]

9

Another form of charity was collecting gifts for soldiers, and taking on patronage of hospitals and children's homes. Donors bought practical items, warm clothing, mittens and towels. They provided crockery, sewed uniforms and warm jackets, washed and mended greatcoats, tunics and underwear.[174] At the Bolshevik factory, there were collections to buy accordions and board games.[175] Much depended on what the enterprise did, so that gifts to the Red Army from the Svetoch ('Beacon') factory included envelopes, paper and notebooks.[176] Later, predictably, there was increasing emphasis on equipping children's homes, and people donated clothing, footwear, cots and toys. Institutional patrons of children's homes helped bring them water, clothed the children, and even taught them.[177]

There were clearly defined rituals attending the collection of gifts, and improvisation was rare. In one school, pupils in the junior classes mended socks and stockings for a hospital and a children's home, the initiative and guidance coming, of course, from the teachers.[178] The 'attaching' of enterprises and institutions to hospitals was commonplace and undoubtedly valuable. We have no grounds to suppose this kind of charity was unduly 'organized', let alone compulsory. Very substantial quantities of gifts were collected for soldiers at the front and for hospitals.[179] This would hardly have been the case if people had not chosen voluntarily to donate, aware of what soldiers (including members of their own families) must be going through as they froze in the trenches, how sad the plight of orphaned children was, and how the wounded must be suffering.[180] There were no quotas, and whatever was freely given was gratefully accepted. Some people donated large sums of money and valuables, some a single saucer; how onerous the donation might be was entirely up to the individual. Getting people to subscribe to war loans was less straightforward. Here the voluntary nature of the giving was more questionable, and some did so reluctantly, even though money meant little during the Time of Death.

There is a special warmth and humanity in memoirs of the siege relating to the donation of items.[181] Particularly touching are the accounts of people who organized children's homes at their enterprises, as they describe how they prepared to receive the orphans and sewed little shirts for them.

It would be an overstatement to claim that this noble impulse was universal and unconditional. Not everybody could help, whether because of poverty, lack of time (which had to be spent scouting for food), malnutrition or illness. 'In spite of all the hyperbole in the newspapers, it is so difficult to get people involved. People do not want to know and say they are too busy. I just have to mandate some jobs to get them done', Irina Zelenskaya complained.[182]

'Sponsors' also visited army units.[183] Much of this was, necessarily, organized from above, and people were even give instructions by the district Party committee on how to conduct themselves with the army.[184] It seems unlikely anyone paid much attention to that. Simple humanity, so emotionally present at such meetings, overrode any pre-planned scenarios and instructions couched in officialese. The charity of the besieged Leningraders, themselves suffering privation yet bringing gifts to the front, and the charity they themselves encountered from soldiers who knew their guests were starving and did their best to feed them, was hardly the result of orders from 'senior comrades' eager to stage-manage a display of patriotism. 'One of the soldiers cut my hair. In the evening, we organized a bathhouse and were able to wash with hot water', A. P. Zagorskaya, the head of a sponsorship delegation from the Krasny Futlyarshchik [Red Casemaker] cooperative, noted in her diary.[185]

As described by Alexandra Borovikova, her visit to the front in early November 1941 seems to have resembled nothing so much as a pageant. Someone long unaccustomed to hearing kind words, she seems to have been in a state of euphoria. At rallies there were appeals to the soldiers, and speeches by the sponsors, but, reading what Borovikova wrote subsequently, the biggest impression seems to have been made by the fact that she was invited from one table to the next, heard all sorts of stories, and was fed amazingly well. Deeply troubled in later days when she was on the verge of starvation, she was to remember that with great nostalgia.[186]

10

Of course, things could be less idyllic. In one place, the sponsors might get a casual reception; in another they were not given a meal and people seemed just to want to be rid of them as soon as possible. That was very hurtful, even if there were extenuating circumstances. The director of the State Institute of Applied Chemistry, P. P. Trofimov, remembered a team of workers (which included women) being sent to a military unit 'to persuade soldiers of the Red Army not to desert the battlefield'. The trip was not a success: 'They told me there was such a panic it was impossible to find anyone to arrange the meeting. Unable to address the men, they had to talk to commanders individually.'[187] Such incidents were rare, however, and usually care was taken to leave the sponsors with the best possible impression. Not everything that might go wrong could, however, be foreseen.

It was also no easy matter to keep correspondence going between those in the siege and soldiers at the front.[188] This was not a grassroots initiative. 'They called us out, the girls, and said, "Write a letter to the front, to such-and-such a soldier. Say 'Fight the enemy. We will defend Leningrad. We will help you'"', M. Vasilieva recalls. She received an answer from a soldier she did not know asking her to send him mittens, wool socks and a scarf. 'Where was I supposed to get those? I had nothing.' She had to stop writing. Her friend was also sent a letter from a Red Army soldier. He was being treated at a Leningrad hospital and asked her to visit him. She was too afraid to go on her own and went with Vasilieva. 'Somebody told us, "You need to take a present." What did we have to take? "Let's take him some cigarettes or something."' At the hospital, it was dreadfully crowded and the girls retreated in alarm. A nurse reproachfully stopped them. 'We went in. "Hello." "Hello." "Here, we've brought you some cigarettes." "Thanks."'

Many had terrible wounds. A soldier whose stomach had not yet been stitched up was keen to make their acquaintance. 'Hey, girls, can I have your addresses?' It was like nothing they had ever seen. 'And he wanted our addresses! For heaven's sake!' Pity, fear, awkwardness: it was only natural they should feel that way, surrounded by people they did not know, in a hospital where other people soon became inured to pain and suffering. The episode does, though, show up the difference between genuine charity, shy and private, and the later glossy images of it which appeared. A longing to escape loneliness was probably also present. Vasilieva did again visit the soldier who wanted to meet them. 'He sent me a note: "Come and see me!" I did. I didn't go into the ward, though; I stood by a window, behind a drainpipe. He said, "Wash my handkerchiefs." I said, "Okay", and I did.

I brought them back to him, but then I was moved to another place and that was the end of that.'[189]

Correspondence is a very personal matter, not an exchange of morale-boosting propaganda. How are you to share something private with a stranger? How were you to go beyond the official instructions and tell him, without becoming emotional, about the ordeal of your life in the siege? This was not the same as an exchange of letters with your mother or your sister. There was none of that pre-existing family warmth to build on. You needed to find appropriate words, and there were not that many of those to keep a meaningful correspondence going. Those who were writing letters, to a soldier they did not know, already had friends and loved ones, and that too was a constraint. One Red Army soldier wrote to the actress N. L. Valter, 'I and my comrades warmly thank you, loyal daughter of the Motherland, for your patriotic feelings.'[190] How could you reply to that, sincerely, without lapsing into cliché? As soon as correspondence became organized, it tended to turn into an exchange of expressions of gratitude and a listing of duties. Of course, some 'pen-friend romances' were kindled, partly out of pity. 'I received a letter today from a Sergey Ivanovich Belyaev, whom I don't know, thanking me for the gloves. I am replying to him by return, sending him a long, long letter as if we are friends. Let him have the hope that we will meet some day', Alexandra Borovikova wrote in her diary.[191] Probably other women did the same. The ice of official phraseology would melt and letters become confessional, declarations of love, an outpouring of people's innermost feelings, but very often the correspondence terminated suddenly and brutally, when someone was killed at the front, or evacuated, or died in the Time of Death.

Attitudes to theft

1

During the siege, even a simple comparison of the faces of those who were starving with those who were well fed was enough to generate profound hostility. 'You could not imagine more inequality than we have now: it is clearly written on people's faces, when you see side-by-side the terrible brown mask of a malnourished employee being fed in accordance with that wretched second category, and the florid face of some person in authority or "girl from the canteen".'[192]

From this entry, we can see that the faces are not so much being compared as deliberately contrasted and their features exaggerated. One face is a terrible mask, the ration category is 'wretched': there is no attempt at a neutral sketching of the portraits of those besieged in Leningrad and their way of life. The girl is not just a girl but a 'girl from the canteen', hinting that her good looks come at the expense of others during the Time of Death.

Vladimir Lyublinsky also noticed the well-fed, well-dressed young women with their 'healthy faces and way of moving': 'Where have they been all winter and early spring? Who are they? Women working in the state catering industry, or the mistresses of army people, or spouses of top directors and specialists of enterprises which were not evacuated, who have been sitting it out in their apartments over the winter?'[193] Reading these comments, we see that those suffering in the siege could not pass by a healthy-looking (by the standards of the time) person without speculating indignantly about how they came to be looking so well.[194] They do not entertain the idea that, for example, a valuable specialist might justifiably be well paid, or that someone in the post of a director might bear a heavy workload, or that people who looked healthy might have been sent from outside into the city on business. There is suspicion of a colleague who treats someone to three spiced buns:[195] where had those come from, and how can he afford to be so generous when the person receiving the treat is starving? Another Leningrader, passing on rumours about the fire at the Badaev warehouses, supposes that 'they had stolen everything they could from there and then set the place on fire.'[196]

Anyone who did not bear the scars of the horrors of the siege could be suspected of the most heinous misconduct. This is strikingly evident in a scene Olga Berggolts describes. A blooming young woman appeared in the bathhouse in the midst of skeletal Leningraders, to be greeted by

> a quiet hiss of disgust, contempt and indignation. Almost every woman present took a look at her and started whispering, 'Whore . . . whore . . . whore . . .'
> 'She's been sleeping with some thieving manager . . .'
> 'She'll have been in there stealing and thieving herself . . .'
> 'Robbing the children . . . and us.'[197]

Here we see not only an escalation of the accusations: we see also an almost instantaneous transition from vague suspicions to categorical assertions, of which the most emphatic is the most shameful and repugnant way of profiteering: at the expense of children. Lower than that you cannot fall, and the humiliation is comparable to that felt by women who had lost the last glimmer of their earlier feminine attractiveness. It is unclear where this torrent of accusations could end. It seems to be a form of emotional release: the women could not stop until they had neutralized all the hurt they had unwittingly been caused, by bringing it home to the perpetrator that she had no right to be proud of her beauty and flaunt it among women so disfigured by the war.

Z. S. Livshits, visiting the Leningrad Philharmonia, saw nobody 'swollen and dystrophic' there. She goes on to comment that the starving have no time for such frivolities. This is her first shot across the bows of the music lovers she came across at the concert. These had managed to fix themselves up nicely 'on everyone else's troubles': that is her second shot. How had they managed that? By profiting from 'shrinkage', by giving short measure and, quite simply, by stealing. She has no doubt that all those in the concert hall are 'the traders, the cooperative trades people, and the breadmakers' who have accumulated their capital by criminal means.[198]

We find the same hostility to the well fed, accused by default of theft, also in the diary entries of Maria Mashkova. On 23 March 1942, she observed ticket touts at work at the entrance to the Theatre of Musical Comedy. Black marketeers were always despised, and particularly so during the siege.[199] From other sources, we know that tickets were acquired in exchange for bread, and this at a time when Leningraders were continuing to die from starvation.[200] That on its own was enough to cause animosity towards theatre-goers: 'The public going to the theatre are obnoxious, suspect.' Why? 'Rosy-cheeked girls, pen-pushers, fatted-up military types' – those are the people who exasperate her.[201] There is an obvious lack of clear, evidence-based charges, but why would she need them when, alongside these people, she can see others, ashen-faced and haggard: 'Two women diligently rummage through a pile of refuse by the rear wall of the Alexandrinsky Theatre.' The scene is recorded in a rather earlier diary entry by Vladimir Lyublinsky, on 27 December 1941, but who can deny it is symbolic?[202]

A. I. Vinokurov also feels no need for evidence. Meeting women among the audience at the Theatre of Musical Comedy on 9 March 1942, he immediately deduces they are waitresses from the canteens or sales assistants in food shops. The criterion is again the theatre-goers' external appearance. His note is hardly as neutral as it might seem: it is a moral judgement. He bolsters it with examples he considers it unnecessary to prove. These people, he tells us, have not only enough bread but much else besides. And when is all this going on? 'In these terrible days', – he writes.[203] His distaste is palpable.

Neither does Professor Lev Kogan require evidence when reporting that girls have been arrested for forging bread ration cards. He has no doubt that 'this sort of thing would be impossible without the connivance of the sales personnel'. Seeing whole loaves of bread on sale in the market, he asks: 'Where is it coming from?' but clearly considers the question rhetorical.[204]

Yu. Bodunov, a teenager, discovers that someone he knows is playing truant from school and spending most of her time with her mother, who is a hospital nurse, and that is proof enough: 'She's better off there: she gets fed.'[205] Every time Dmitry Likhachev went into the office of his institute's deputy estate officer, he found the man nibbling bread dipped in sunflower oil: 'Evidently there have been ration cards left behind by those flown out or evacuated along the Road of Death.'[206] Leningraders suffering in the siege noticed that the arms and hands of salesgirls in bakeries and cooks in the canteens were festooned with bracelets and gold rings, and wrote in their letters that 'there are people unaffected by the starvation.'[207] G. A. Knyazev was unpleasantly surprised when the chief of the fire service told him he had set up a 'food hall': 'How much will he manage to steal before he gets caught?'[208] What alerted him? It was enough to take one look at the 'repulsive, sly smirk' on the ugly face of the new 'food hall manager'.[209]

It was always the same. 'The only people who are not hungry are those whose jobs give them access to food', A. F. Yevdokimov wrote in his diary on 7 September 1942, expressing, no doubt, a consensus view among starving Leningraders.[210] In a letter to T. A. Konoplyova, G. I. Kazanina described how plump a woman they knew had become ('You would hardly recognize her now') after getting a job in a restaurant. The explanation seemed so obvious that no further comment was needed.[211] Even so, they were probably unaware that, of 713 people working in the Krupskaya patisserie at the beginning of 1942, not one died of starvation.[212] The scene at other enterprises, with corpses stacked outside them, told a different story. In the winter of 1941–2, at the State Institute of Applied Chemistry four people a day were dying; in the Sevkabel ['Northern Cable'] factory, up to five.[213] At the Molotov factory, while food ration cards were being issued on 31 December 1941, eight people died in the queue.[214] About one third of the staff at the Petrograd Communications Office died, as did 20–25% of those working at the Lenenergo electricity company, and 14% of those at the Frunze factory.[215] At the Baltic railway hub, 70% of train conductors and 60% of the track workers died.[216] In the boiler house of the Kirov factory, which was used as a mortuary, there were around 180 corpses.[217] At Bread Factory No. 4, however, the director recalled that 'during that hard winter, three people died, but not of starvation, from other illnesses.'[218]

2

The way hatred of thieving and fraud developed was that, without needing to actually see the pilfering, you just knew, from the appearance of someone who did not look like a victim of the siege, that they were crooked. Anyone who could get theatre tickets without having to queue must be dishonest and resorting to the black market. A rosy-cheeked, elegant woman was clearly the mistress of thieves. Anyone too lively by comparison with the majority of Leningraders, who were barely able still to stagger along, must obviously have helped herself to someone else's bread. A woman with gold jewellery was clearly not starving and must also be stealing from somewhere. If someone who worked in a canteen put on weight, hungry customers were plainly being cheated.

Anyone who began to look a little more attractive would soon find themselves eyed with suspicion by others in the siege, who were unlikely to confine themselves to sarcastic remarks. Whole stories were concocted, all with the same script and the same accusations. The entries in Boris Kapranov's diary may serve as an example. He is certain that not everybody is going hungry: sales assistants are 'skimming' several kilograms of bread a day.[219] He mentions no source, and we might doubt how he could have come into possession of such precise information, but each of his successive entries follows logically.

As they are skimming off so much bread, clearly they are 'making a fortune'. How could they not? If you can steal whole kilograms of bread every day, you can make a lot of money in a famished city. He provides a list of those who are pigging themselves: 'Army officers and the police, people who work in the military commissariats, and others who have access to everything they need in special shops.' Did he really know people in this situation, and did they unabashedly recount the details of their privileges to him? If their shops were special, then they would assuredly be getting more than you got in ordinary shops and, that being so, such customers were undoubtedly eating 'the way we did before the war'. He continues his list of those who are living well: cooks, canteen managers, waiters and 'anyone who could remotely be described as occupying an important position'.[220] None of this was in need of proof, and he was not alone in thinking this way. 'If we were getting our full ration, we would not be starving, ill and malnourished', the women working in one factory complained in a letter to Andrey Zhdanov, first secretary of the Leningrad City and Province Party Committees.[221] They have no irrefutable evidence, but ask him just to 'look at all the canteen staff. They're so sturdy you could harness them up and set them to plough.'[222]

The unusual intrusion of earthy speech into the officialese obligatory when addressing the top brass is indicative of the strength of hostility the women feel towards those they are close to regarding as personal enemies. Here too there is that 'filling-out' of accusations which enables them to express their feelings more forcefully, vividly and unforgivingly. A cumbersome, conscientious marshalling of arguments would probably only have got in the way. We find similar sentiments in other letters, not actually addressed to Zhdanov, but which, nevertheless, thanks to the exertions of those intercepting them, also ended up on his desk: those who work in close proximity to food are living well, while other people 'have to spend long hours to get hold of a pathetic amount of food'.[223] The contrast here may be deliberately exaggerated: another method of condemning the immorality of those seeking to profit at the expense of others.

3

Let us now turn to descriptions of people who did manage to do well during the siege of Leningrad.

The stories have much in common. What is primarily noted as characterizing thieves and speculators is uncouthness, boorishness and a lordly condescension towards starving Leningraders who now find themselves dependent on them. The diary entries of highly educated intellectuals show clear evidence of the influence of traditional literary stereotypes, where the personality of newly rich *parvenus* is characterized particularly vividly and graphically. Their least endearing traits are identified and emphasized without admitting of any excuses or explanations. For Vladislav Glinka, what makes him particularly hostile towards the housing manager is not so much suspecting him of theft as his vulgarity and contempt for those most disadvantaged by the siege.[224]

Lev Razumovsky has left us a more literary and artistic tale of a *nouveau-riche* bakery assistant. The narrative is based on an almost polar antithesis: her obscurity in peacetime, and her 'elevation' during the war: 'People seek her favour, fawn before her, cultivate her friendship.' It is noticeable how the disdain for this thief rises to a crescendo. From a dark room she has moved into a bright apartment, buying up furniture and even acquiring a piano. The baker woman's sudden interest in music is particularly emphasized.[225]

Another tale, but with the same trajectory: 'Before the war she was a scrawny woman always in need, but now Lena has blossomed. She is a rejuvenated, red-cheeked, woman dressed in clean, smart clothes! Lena has many friends, and even admirers. She has moved from an attic room within the courtyard to a first-floor apartment with views out to the street. Lena works at a distribution centre!'[226]

Descriptions of the sudden change in the fortunes of people whose jobs gave them access to food are not without sarcastic exaggeration. People do not change so quickly, and perhaps not everything in their lives was so transformed, but the build-up of animosity makes it impossible to paint a more nuanced picture. The path to their ill-gotten gains is invariably represented as smooth, predictable and replete with lurid detail, enabling the diarist to give vent to their indignation.

'Some very common women turned up', is how Sofia Gotkhart remembers exchanging her possessions for bread.[227] The word 'common' here is the key: even an educated speaker cannot settle for a less insulting word at the sight of people who had food to spare. 'We do not know where they were from. I think they must have been storekeepers or sales assistants of some sort.'[228] Nearly everyone thought along the same lines.[229] They had no choice but to run to these black marketeers, these thieves, for bread, to grovel, and they hated them with a vengeance.

'Oh, these swindlers, these wretches! They build their well-being on the misfortune of others!' A. T. Kedrov opined when he thought of those who, with 100 or 200 grams of bread to barter, could leave the market 'dressed to the nines'.[230] Leonid Galko was obliged to buy bread on the black market at 35 rubles for 100 grams, while tobacco was 100 rubles for 100 grams. The state price for tobacco was 12 rubles. He bursts out, in a diary entry that reads like a set of accounts, 'These black-market parasites cashing in on our national tragedy! They are no less enemies than the fascists, only the fascists come at us with guns in their hands while these warm their hands on this icy famine.'[231]

No doubt that is why people had no qualms about making complaints about sales assistants and canteen staff, even without solid evidence, to the city's top officials, all the way to Zhdanov. A worker from Confectionery

Factory No. 3 literally dragged a policeman by the arm to come and arrest a black marketeer in the market who was selling a box of matches for 8 rubles: 'The policeman said it was none of my business, everyone could sell whatever they wanted for as much as they liked. A policeman like that is a godsend for a speculator.' Women standing in a queue outside a shop, according to an informer, complained, 'The public and the police should find out where people selling whole loaves at a time are getting them from.'[232]

This hostility came through in hundreds of everyday conversations, in which those who were living too well were condemned and the prosperity of thieves was contrasted with the poverty of the speaker. In the Time of Death, this became the criterion for moral judgement. People refused to believe there could be any justification. A woman who brought home people on the verge of collapse and warmed them with tea was accused of only wanting to steal their ration cards. Olga Berggolts, reporting this on the radio, urged Leningraders to be more tolerant and encourage every glimmer of altruism, but it has to be admitted that, during the siege, the woman's behaviour was bound to arouse suspicion.

Of course, a lot of this inflexibility, distrust of other people, and insistence on seeing cheating everywhere was unfair. It was, however, the only way to uphold the rules of morality: by insisting that there could be no bending of them and that they must be complied with implicitly. If you start being too understanding and finding excuses, what will happen to these constant denunciations and the proud awareness that you have endured to the end, have not faltered like others, have not stolen?

Often it made no difference how someone looked, or how long he had been starving. N. P. Zavetnovskaya told her daughter in a letter about a professor who took some of her belongings, promising to barter them for food, and then disappeared: 'That's the kind of professors there are nowadays, thieves and frauds. I've known him thirty years and did not expect him to be so low and mean.'[233] Even from her angry, one-sided letters, we can guess what sort of state the man must have been in: he had given up, thought nothing of humiliation, ate cats . . . She feels no pity, however; from one letter to the next her judgements become more stinging and derisive. Everybody is suffering privation, but some people put up with it, while others stoop to deceit. The professor died soon afterwards, but she could not and would not forgive him: 'He's said to have died, but I don't believe it. A right bastard he turned out to be.'[234] It was the only possible verdict: he had not only contrived to get extra bread from some canteen, he had robbed her personally, someone just as starving and needy as himself. He knew how hungry she was, but robbed her anyway. In order to give full vent to her animosity, his portrait must be unremittingly repulsive. The uncertain report of his death must not be allowed to detract from her uncompromisingly harsh judgement of his behaviour.

A girl who stole ration cards in a student hostel at Leningrad State University was undoubtedly very hungry, but when the others found out they refused to let her stay in the same room with them.[235] A. I. Kochetova complained to her mother that her grandmother had flown into a rage when she saw her wearing a scarf she had taken from her aunt's wardrobe: 'How she scolded me! She saw me wearing the scarf in the street and made me take it off right there in the cold. She called me a thief.'[236]

By no means everybody in the Time of Death ceased to believe it was wrong to help yourself to other people's property. Vladimir Lyublinsky had to urge his maid not to be embarrassed to exchange his belongings for bread, pointing out that if they were to die their bits and pieces would be pilfered anyway, and, moreover (one argument evidently not sufficing), his wife, who had been evacuated, would never forgive him if she heard he had been miserly. Olga Berggolts noticed how proud her father was that in the hospital where he worked no one was stealing,[237] the implication being that this was not always the case elsewhere. Many people were principled enough to resist the temptation to burgle apartments whose occupants had all left or died – and not only from fear of being caught red-handed.

Many, but not all. Thousands did find themselves in circumstances where they felt they had no option but to steal. This was particularly the case when searching for fuel. The authorities did not at first even try to supply firewood to private homes which had no central heating, leaving it to the residents to find their own salvation. 'And that is how we lived for half the winter, finding a plank here and a log there', Harry Aesop noted. He saw people breaking into sheds to steal firewood, but then making off with the doors and walls as well: 'It is not seen as theft or anything disgraceful.'[238] People tried by fair means and foul to get fuel for themselves, and were paid to get it for others. They even helped themselves to the furniture of neighbours who had left. 'Houses bombed yesterday are today being taken apart for firewood. People are swarming there like ants', I. I. Zhilinsky wrote.[239] He was too late to follow suit, as he remarks ruefully, because guards were posted there later.

4

It was all the more difficult to resist temptation if you could claim it was not for your personal benefit but to help your family or friends to survive. 'Uncle Vanya would want you to have it', said a mother to her 6-year-old daughter as she took a spoonful of noodles from supplies intended for their relative in hospital.[240] People expected to be reproached for not taking full advantage of a stroke of luck. A sales assistant at the bakery, issuing bread to Tatiana Maximova, gave her the ration for two days but mistakenly tore off only the coupon for one day. Should she hand over the second coupon, or go to another bakery and get extra bread with it? She says frankly that it was not an easy decision. It was the most terrible period, in December 1941, and at home her mother and son had taken to their beds from starvation. She could have used the excuse that sales assistants were better fed than other people, but did not do so. She said nothing to her mother or son, knowing that not everyone would agree with her decision to be honest.[241]

Valentina Bazanova recalled her mother hesitating over whether or not to give official notification of her husband's death to their housing management office,[242] suspecting they would only use his ration card themselves. After a few days, she decided nevertheless to do so. It was more usual to leave reporting a death longer than that. If a body was found during inspection of apartments, then, as A. P. Borisov, in charge of one of the city's districts, noted, 'they will not admit the person died two weeks ago, but say it happened today or yesterday'.[243]

When P. M. Samarin found out that the wife of a worker had kept quiet about his death and come to the factory to collect the dead man's ration cards, he called her a bitch.[244] Such misdemeanours were, however, usually overlooked.

'A mother conceals the death of her infant son. Gets milk (condensed or soya) at the clinic, sells it for 100 rubles a litre. With the money she buys bread to feed her husband', Vera Inber noted, expressing neither surprise nor indignation.[245] The abundance of details passed on without comment leaves no room for moralizing and exhortation. Survival, not morality, is given priority.

There were more dramatic incidents. Maria Gusarova told of a neighbour whose baby died: 'She wrapped it in a blanket and got ration cards for him.' There is no emotional outburst, as if this is entirely a matter of course: 'Nobody blamed her. She survived.'[246]

That condemnation of theft was often gentler in the case of family. Alexey Yevdokimov did not blame his relative who agreed to collect his rations for him and kept some for herself. This was undoubtedly a serious matter for him, which is why he so meticulously calculated the amount of food she had misappropriated: 0.5 kg of meat, 1.5 kg of grains, 350 g of butter, beer, wine . . . 'She has behaved shamefully towards me.' Should he condemn her? No. 'On the other hand she has prolonged the lives of her children and herself.'[247]

Quite how serious this was for him, we have no way of telling. A diary was not only a means of self-analysis but also a way of telling others how stoical and humane you have been. Not everyone was as forgiving as Yevdokimov. Quarrelling and disregard of mitigating circumstances were more usual, but that only makes the more remarkable those instances where charity is in evidence, and understanding of the lengths starving people have been driven to. Many would never have picked a pocket or shamelessly stolen from someone in the same dire predicament as themselves, but could not bring themselves to refuse a share of the property from defunct ('escheated') apartments. They excused themselves by reasoning that all the tenants had died anyway, and an extra piece of bread gave someone dying of starvation a chance of survival.

Here is a typical scene, described by a teenage girl. Her neighbour died, and when the house manager was sealing her apartment, she found a lot of food. It was awkward. The neighbours knew about it, having been the first to report the death. She would have to share it with them. 'Granny Dunya came with a pan full of peas and said, "The manager gave me this."'[248] We find no suggestion in the story that anyone might have rejected such a 'present'. They were not themselves taking someone else's property: it was being offered to them. The haul included jam, and that too needed to be shared. 'The housing manager came and said, "Little one, here is a whole jar of jam. Share it out into these two jars." I was a bit naughty [laughs]. Here one spoonful for us, here two [laughs].' She has no second thoughts. She is even quite proud of getting away with short-changing the manager. After all, the jam does not belong to her, and the girl does not particularly like her. Besides, she seems much better fed than other people, so why not?

This besieged family, tottering like many others on the brink of starvation, would hardly have risked looting someone else's room, but their neighbour, when he left, gave them his key: 'When we had nothing to eat, Granny Dunya said, "Olya, let's go into the room. Perhaps we can sell something of theirs."'[249] They are ashamed when they remember this, and their account is perfunctory. We sense it is disjointed and that things are being left out. It would not be easy to claim they had right on their side, but excessive contrition would also have been unconvincing.

The girl's mother bartered a pair of kid gloves for a small glass of sunflower oil, 'because I was with her'. They were hardly profiteering. There was no alternative, and they had not taken much, and anyway the neighbour did not need them, and her mother had a hungry child with her. This is how the threshold of the permissible was gradually lowered, and once you had started, there was no stopping. For a moment, the pangs of hunger receded, and you wanted that to be repeated more and more often. 'Granny Dunya said, "Here's some material. Take that to the market," and Mum swapped it for bread.'[250] They sold the neighbour's shoes, his dishes, a cup and some saucers they found: 'In the end, we had stolen all their things.' She obviously finds it hard to admit that, and immediately softens it: 'At least, people regard that as stealing.'

They can't bring themselves to say they were thieves. They are not lying: they are being honest, not denying their guilt. They promise to give everything back, no matter how difficult that is: 'Our neighbour came back after the war and came to ask my mother what had been going on. She told him, "We sold all your belongings for food. I admit it. Let it all be taken out of my pay."'[251] And even though the neighbour, when he saw the poverty they were living in, said he was glad they had managed to survive, that still did not make them thieves. Of course not.

Lev Druskin's family too would never have helped themselves to someone else's property, but one day their relative unexpectedly found a purse in their communal apartment with a large sum of money in it. It had been dumped by their black marketeer neighbour when he was being arrested. Nobody felt the least bit sorry for their profiteering neighbour, and the main thing was that 'now evacuation was possible'.[252]

People who disapproved of others who had an unfair advantage by working with access to food considered it no great sin to want to get extra food there if they or their families were involved. A relative of G. A. Gelfer told him the hospital for victims of starvation where she worked was going to be closed. His response was, 'So our good life will shortly be over.'[253] Vladimir G. Kulyabko, who regularly denounces bribe-takers, described the following scene: 'The waitress came up to me in the canteen after I'd finished and asked, "How was the porridge?" "Very good." "Would you like some more?" "Of course, only without coupons." She nodded and brought it ten minutes later. I gave her 2 rubles instead of 1 ruble 45.' No outpourings or doubts: 'She was happy and so was I.' He mentions that this was not the first time he had done that.[254] Vladimir Lyublinsky talks in a letter to his wife, not without understanding, about a woman he knows who works in a food shop. She has discovered 'there is no prospect of supplementing her diet there'.[255]

Alexandra Borovikova's diary is particularly interesting. She collected gifts for the front, went to the military units and made emotional speeches. She liked being there: she was given a lot of attention and looked after. She writes about how grateful she is to the soldiers. By February 1942, however, she has less time for the proprieties. There is no longer any question of altruistically giving moral support. She hopes she may be able to do something for soldiers who wanted to come to their bathhouse. Her factory was supposed to be sponsoring that unit and helping them with some home comforts. That was all true but, 'I think I may ask them for bread.' It will be embarrassing, but, if you do nothing, well – 'If you want the cart to move you have to grease it.'[256]

5

The new ethic was reflected even in the Leningraders' dreams. They usually dreamed of having the opportunity of a good meal, but it did not always work out and often there was a last-minute hitch.[257] Getting plenty to eat usually means being somewhere privileged people are fed: 'I would like to describe two dreams', Natalia Yerofeyeva (Klishevich) writes on 4 November 1941 in a bomb shelter:

1. Mine. I dream we are being allowed into the canteen of the Hospital Workers Club if we show our student identity card. I get millet soup with a ration coupon, but suddenly they bring me a meat course without tearing off any coupons. They give me a nudge and say, 'Keep it quiet.' Of course, I eat it up quickly and make myself scarce. 2. Irina's. She and Tanya B. manage to get into the NKVD shop without a pass, but then, horror of horrors, there's a check. They desperately try to come up with something and say they are some sort of work brigade.[258]

These dreams almost perfectly mirror life during the siege. Everything is typical: the suspicions about where food is being stored up, and the desire to save oneself and others at all costs. Traditional moral standards were respected only if they did not endanger life, as the fate of the siege family described below shows vividly. The father of a 12-year-old girl was sent in the spring of 1942 to Lake Ladoga. Her mother was seriously ill and bedridden. On 10 April, her little brother died. They were doomed, but suddenly there was hope: the girl met, as she said, 'a kind lady' in the street. The woman said she had a lot of bread ration cards. The girl needed food for her mother and herself. She gave the woman a pair of shoes for the cards, but when she got back home and her mother examined them, they were found to be forgeries.[259]

Where could she go? The shoes had evidently been the last thing they had to exchange. She would have to go somewhere and try to use the cards. There was nothing else for it. She would have to try to cheat someone else, because her mother was dying in front of her, and she herself could expect no help from anywhere else.

'16 April 1942. Vera did all the same go with the cards to a shop but never came back.'[260] Perhaps she was thrown out of the shop and, in her state of starvation, fainted and had not the strength to get up again. There is no point in guessing, but we can assume that her last hour was far from happy.

6

As we read the dozens of accounts by eyewitnesses of how they were forced in the grip of famine to take things which did not belong to them, we find they all offer much the same excuse. A thief is not someone who has got hold of an extra piece of bread by devious means. Theft is when a piece of bread is exploited as a means to profit, when people who are hungry are humiliated and robbed. They themselves are not the thieves. The thieves are those who thrive by exploiting a national calamity, who buy a piano with a loaf of bread, who take bribes to give help with evacuation, who manage to hoard butter, grain and sugar by the kilogram in the Time of Death, when so many houses were full of corpses. Those are the thieves, not people who occasionally manage to get a crumb from someone else's well-provisioned table. There is no need to query whether food was obtained through legal or illegal channels. What matters is who got it and what they used it for. We can question the validity of these standards, but formal logic and Jesuitical hair-splitting have no place in siege ethics. Someone would share food with a hungry teenager without debating whether or not it was right that he or she had officially been deemed worthy of only a starvation ration of 125 grams of bread. And who would dare condemn a teenager who, despite the prohibition, sneaked a ration-free plate of porridge past the checkpoint to his mother. It was actually here, as in other instances, that by resorting to what seemed like trivial infractions, fundamental moral values were preserved.

3

The shifting boundaries of ethics

Infringement of ethical standards:
arguments used in self-justification

1

Justification of immoral behaviour during the siege was not always accompanied by long-winded deliberations. Seeing the rules of morality broken at every turn, people ceased to consider it as reprehensible as they used to.

Looking for excuses is more common when memoirs are being written later and moral standards are again more clear-cut than in wartime. Later accounts were intended for readers who had not witnessed the siege, so excuses are accompanied by more detailed explanation of actions, but also by detailed exposition of the realities of the siege.

Methods of self-justification depend largely on how cultured an individual is, how deeply rooted their moral precepts are, how emotional and responsive they are to others. The most common excuse for bad behaviour is that people were simply not in a position to help.[1] In many cases, the main excuse is accompanied by several others, making clear the obstacles in the way of responding to a plea. The more dramatic the appeal for support, the more vehement is the irritation both with the supplicant and with oneself for having had to push away an outstretched hand, and the more passionately the attempt is made to show no other course of action was possible. Refusal was inevitably emotionally coloured. It was difficult to reject a desperate cry for help on purely logical grounds.

Alexandra Borovikova received a letter from a worker who was in hospital. He asked her to let him have 200 grams of bread and some 'thick porridge'. Indeed, he did not just ask, he implored, trying to move her with piteous and touching words. That made the usual excuse seem rather lame ('How was I supposed to help him when I was myself sitting there staring at the ceiling?'), so it is supplemented by a further argument: 'Bread today is a kind of mixture that gives you indigestion.'[2] That might seem to be excuse enough, but she recognizes that the worker is even hungrier than she is, so she resorts to a further argument. She is not going to say that her own situation is hopeless, but she does very much emphasize that it too is tragic.

Arkadiy Lepkovich received a similar letter from someone he knew. His first reaction was perplexity, almost indignation. His disjointed and repetitive response indicates the awkwardness of someone thrown off balance by an unexpected question and not immediately able to come up with a satisfactory answer: 'Odd. He is an actor too, an eccentric, not like everybody else. How much can a beggar expect who begs from a beggar?'[3] Perhaps feeling, nevertheless, rather ashamed, he softens his tone: 'In my opinion, he is a decent sort, but a loser. Not unlike myself.' The last words are interesting. This too is an excuse: how could a loser have bread to spare? 'As I am writing, the hunger is making its presence felt.' How can he be asked for help? 'I try not to think about food, but still, I would so like some bread, and a little porridge.' His own situation is as unenviable as that of his acquaintance: 'I've had no porridge to eat for three months, and have not eaten my fill for the same time.'[4] He is not guilty of anything, but comes up with excuses again and again. It is hard for him, having denounced unfairness and heartlessness, to think that his readers may suspect him of being uncaring himself.

And it was hard for people who prided themselves on their fortitude and unshakable moral principles to be on the receiving end of reproaches. What did all their self-sacrifice count for if they refused to help? Would they still be considered good, honourable people? The manageress of the canteen at the power station saw herself in this light, but found herself every day having to refuse a bowl of soup or porridge to someone who needed it. People begged her with tears in their eyes, spoke of their illness, and she had to say 'no', she could give them nothing: 'We never received our full quota of rations.'[5] She could have left it at that, but she goes on to provide statistics to prove she is in the right: for 250, people she is sent 200 servings of soup; of the main course, she gets enough only for 80–100 people, and that not every day.[6] She is not refusing people for no reason: it is completely impossible to help them.

It was a straight, hard-hitting question to oneself. There was no wriggling out of it: the answer had to be equally direct. As they struggled to find it, they seem to be probing the robustness of their excuses, although discovering weaknesses tends to prompt a search for new arguments.

Here are the efforts at self-justification of an actor who was hesitating to help his mother-in-law, who was in difficulties. Her ration cards had been stolen and he knew she had nothing to eat but cocoa. His diary entry for 11 December 1941 is typical of that period: 'How can I help them out with my own bread and rations? I am hungry myself.'[7] He could, of course, go one day without eating and give them the bread, but the mother-in-law is living with a sister- in-law and needs continuing help, not a single act of charity. Is he capable of that? He is, after all, a blood donor so needs to eat properly, otherwise he will be too weak. He goes through all the arguments, and probably feels they are still not sufficient to justify doing nothing.

'I would give them a piece of my bread, but I don't have any today.' On that note he concludes his soul-searching, perhaps hoping mother-in-law will find her own way of coping. He makes no further mention of it, as if nothing had happened.

A few days later, however, he visits his sister and meets with a frosty reception. Irritation soon comes to the surface, and his sister, her son and her husband accuse him of being uncaring. The complaints rain down: mother-in-law has been starving for eight days; his sister-in-law has visited his sister with 'her nose sticking out of her face' and begging for food of any description to make soup with. That is the state the relatives he is so reluctant to share with are in. His sister has at least donated something ('a few scraps, two bits of oilcake and a 40-gram piece of bread'), but he is giving nothing.[8]

What arguments could he find to defend himself? 'Unfortunately, I've been starving myself since the eighth of the month', he repeats. Anyway, what right have they to be laying into him like this? His sister's son recently stole from him and was eating her rations too. 'It's only now, when he saw what his mother looks like, all skin and bones, and when he's been able to help her out a bit, he's getting above himself. He's feeling relatively well fed because he gets breakfast, lunch and dinner at home and then again at his vocational school, and he's decided I must be just as full as he is', he adds, his hostility gradually increasing.[9] He is reluctant to acknowledge that during the siege almost everyone did at some point help themselves to other people's rations, and that otherwise no one would have survived. Nevertheless, he cannot overcome a sense of shame and the next day sacrifices his bread ration to his mother-in-law, keeping back only 50 grams for himself. He still feels the need to justify his actions in the light of their unfair response. There had been no let-up in their reproaches. His relatives, representing themselves as the honourable people, continued to criticize him, and did not even thank him for the donation. 'There was no "thank you" and plenty of complaining. They seemed to think giving it was only to be expected, that it was an obvious obligation.'[10]

2

People found themselves having to explain why what they could give was so little. More excuses. Refusing to help is clearly perceived as an offence against morality, no matter how difficult a person's situation, since otherwise a single argument would suffice and there would be no need for further self-justification. Accordingly, there is little mention of how one is feeling or the size of one's own ration, and more of unforeseen circumstances which prevent an obligation from being met.

Boris Gorodetsky was unable to send a parcel to his family and, in a letter to his wife and daughters, emphasizes that it had been returned to him because it would be impossible to deliver. He confesses he has eaten the returned sweets and biscuits himself, but adds, 'As I ate them, I was saying to myself, "Let my little daughters be well, and forgive me for eating their sweets and biscuits, because I came back completely frozen, starving hungry, and was rather ill at the time." Your sweets and biscuits helped me to recover more rapidly.'[11]

These few lines have it all: an attempt to elicit sympathy, great appreciation of the family's sacrifice. Paradoxically, it is being thanked for something in which it had no part. For Boris Gorodetsky, the sweets and biscuits he bought are not an undeliverable gift but something that belongs to his family and to which he has no right to help himself. We note his additional self-inculpation: he was eating their sweets and biscuits: 'Your sweets and biscuits'. It emphasizes his decency and humility: he presents his voluntary act of giving as something which was his duty.

The argument that 'I ate the food not just for my own good but for the good of those I did not share it with' is extremely common. It is used when refusing to give food to children, sick relatives, and anyone else who, conventional morality suggested, should have been helped as a first priority. The line of argument in, for example, the diary of engineer G. A. Gelfer, is on the whole typical of other documents of the time. His wife was in dire straits in evacuation and waiting for financial support. He was intending to send her money on International Women's Day, 9 March 1942, but then writes in his diary on 16 March 1942, 'I am buying anything that can in any way make my life more bearable. By doing so I am being unfair to Gitka, but my death would be worse for her. She will just have to get by for 1–2 months with no money from me, but that way I will keep myself safe for her and our happy life in the future.'[12]

3

If the excuses are being made in public, they are more laconic. Enumerating them in undue detail might elicit a rejoinder from those in need, possibly well-founded. That would only protract a disagreeable dialogue whose outcome had already been decided. Not all the reasons people came up with for withholding assistance bore scrutiny. The pangs of conscience in the wake of such excuses could result in yielding to entreaties after much wrangling and categorical objections, when someone else's counterarguments could not be effectively opposed, or when the excuses in diaries and letters were perfunctory.

4

We not infrequently find inconsistencies, and deliberate omissions, in the explanations of those who have refused to help. Their excuses are not just a way of salving their conscience but a means of self-defence. There is an abundance of long-winded arguments, the serious side-by-side with the trivial. As we read descriptions – artless, not carefully thought through – of people's actions, we can trace a process of self-incrimination.

A girl looking for her sailor brother was treated to porridge on one ship. She was evidently invited to join the sailors at their meal, and they were doubtless looking to get better acquainted. She could not bring herself to ask them to feed not her but her starving parents by giving her some porridge out of the communal bowl. It is fairly certain that they would then have fed her too, but it would look as though, in response to their generous gesture of sharing the porridge with her, she had improperly obliged them to give her a further helping. Nevertheless, she could not stop feeling ashamed that she had not shared the food with her family: 'I was unhappy that I had eaten the porridge alone and my mother had had none, but what was done was done.'[13] She has been unable to end the story any more elegantly than that. Writing 'what was done was done' might have seemed an admission of not being bothered to help her mother, which, of course, was not the case at all. She needs to soften the ending, if only with something vague and unverifiable, so she rounds the story off with: 'And in any case, there was no way I could have carried it to them.'[14] Plainly, her self-justification would have had more force if she had said that earlier, but more important is that she did add it in the end.

The entry in Leonid Galko's diary seems not to have been intended for anyone else to read, but here too an abundance of supplementary excuses is in evidence. The episode is straightforward: he was intending to take bread to someone else (probably his wife), but ate it himself. At first, he seems not even to be seeking to excuse his behaviour. Quite simply, he ate the bread because he was hungry. Nevertheless, he clearly had meant to give it to someone, and if there was no problem he would not have been mentioning it. It is not his fault, he goes on, that he gave in to the temptation. He writes, 'I could not help myself', so he had tried. He goes into details: he was very hungry, and the bread he was setting aside was only a small piece, and it did look very tasty, and that made it all the more difficult to resist the temptation to eat it himself. In any case, the bread was 85 per cent oilcake, a food substitute.[15] So perhaps it is not such a big deal, no great loss, that the other person did not get it. He is unaware of any inconsistencies in his explanations. The main aim is to justify his action.

5

Where someone was reluctant to admit they felt they had done something unethical, the excuse might be that they had not asked someone for food but had given in to entreaties to take it. Atta Asknaziy relates that, when her ration cards were stolen, a neighbour came to her rescue by giving her half her rations. She tried to make it up to her, but clearly could not offer enough: grains for bread. In self-justification, Asknaziy quotes her neighbour's assurance that she preferred grains to bread.[16]

Another theme is that, while it would be unworthy to accept food from someone who was starving, it was all right if it was in recompense for efforts (often considerable) to help the person survive. Irina Zelenskaya visited one of the power station's technicians in hospital. 'He often gratefully offered me bread, and sometimes even money. Of course, I absolutely refused, but one day when I was really hungry I gave in, and when he offered me dried bread, I accepted it.'

This is written by someone who, in her diary, constantly stresses her qualities of endurance and altruism, and is quick to notice their absence in others. She cannot simply say she was hungry: other excuses are needed: 'Of course, that day I had spent two hours formalizing his discharge from hospital, then gave him the last of my rice and citric acid.' The justification cannot be faulted, but she still feels ashamed: 'It feels like having been paid for my services, which in my view is unacceptable.' But what can she do, when the ten-day ration period is ending and there will not be enough supplementary meals for everybody, and it is impossible to go on, and 'all your innards are begging for porridge'? Tomorrow she will have to borrow coupons from him for a meal. No, she will not ask him to give her them, only to borrow them, but still it is a bitter blow: 'So much for my principles!' That is why she needs to find further justification. It can only be the dreadful excuse which, in those days, Zelenskaya was not alone in using, because it was ultimately very convincing: 'To tell the truth, I do not feel all that bad about his coupons because, in spite of all the efforts, it will hardly be possible to save him and the card will be wasted.'[17]

The excuses are not just an attempt to persuade oneself and others that, even in desperate circumstances, you remain a kind and compassionate person. More important is the fact that constant repetition and reaffirmation of ethical rules does not allow them to be cast aside, even when they are increasingly being broken. Attempts to excuse or mitigate one's own behaviour have important consequences. We can see them, paradoxically, as reflecting a desire to uphold moral principles while, needless to say, adapting them to the everyday realities of the siege. Having been guilty of questionable behaviour, a person's first priority is to find an explanation. Is it ethical to expect gratitude for giving support? Is it permissible to take bread from another person, if he cannot or does not want to eat it? Everywhere, even in selfish actions and motives, we see people continuing to heed moral precepts.

On 21 November 1941, one Leningrader wrote in her diary that she had not managed to get food for her mother. Her first excuse is typical of the time: 'I expect she can find something there to eat.'[18] It is not really an excuse, so perhaps she should try a different approach – for example, writing about her feelings for her mother. Then no one will suspect her of being callous. Only, she should speak from the heart, emotionally, so there can be absolutely no doubt about how much her mother matters to her: 'My dear, wonderful Mummy will come here hungry. I will hug her tight and tell her about all the misfortune we have suffered, and I do not think she will be angry.'[19]

The same person was given a jelly at school and brought it home: 'I hid the jelly and now I am not sure what to do, whether to eat it myself or share it.' She has been hungry for a long time and is probably reluctant to relinquish her treat, but does not want to admit that and comes up with the following line of argument: 'It isn't much, only enough to make them lick their lips', so it is better not to tease them with it. 'I'll eat it myself this time', she concludes but, as a decent person, will definitely share with them next time: 'I will always take an empty jar, and if they give us any more jelly I will ask for three servings and give them a treat.'[20] That way, she will not tease them, they will be happy to have so much to eat, and now nobody can say she has been hard-hearted.

Was this always the motivation behind excuses? People could, after all, just keep quiet about what they did, but again and again we find them reproaching themselves, and often going to great lengths to seek vindication, to apologize and promise. Analysing each of these stories is itself a lesson in morality.

Olga Melnikovskaya worked in a hospital and noticed one of the patients had 'not finished his bread at dinner time'. The temptation was very great. 'I was tormented all night just looking at it.' Melnikovskaya may not have included all the mitigating circumstances in her diary, but does list many details. The patient is in a ward for officers, so he has an enhanced diet. He is hardly starving! He looks healthy. 'He spends all day in the city and comes back well fed', while she is starving. She hesitates long before deciding to eat what he has left. She reminds herself it is wrong to take what belongs to someone else, and surely that mitigates her wickedness: 'He has plenty to eat while I am dying of hunger.' That is the thought that finally sweeps away all her doubts. In the morning, she is aware that the patient has noticed, but again finds an excuse: 'Perhaps he did it deliberately to tempt me.'[21]

You need to find excuses if you are only too aware of the need of those you have failed to help. A factory engineer wrote in his diary that he had eaten 400 grams of sweets he had been keeping for his daughter, who had left Leningrad and 'had had nothing sweet' for a year. His verdict on himself was damning: 'It was criminal', and no way to behave. He feels he must make amends. 'To replace them, I bought 300 grams of sweets for 300 rubles and hid them.'[22] That did not, of course, fully make up for the 400 grams he had eaten, but was not far off. Those 300 rubles were a lot of money: for some people they would have been a month's salary. He mentions the amount pointedly, but still reproaches himself. 'Of course, the sweets I ate would also have been very welcome', but he no longer feels guilty: he has passed the test and shown he has not lost his sense of compassion.

'In 2–2.5 hours I ate the 300 grams of sweets I had bought just like the last lot. It is a crime against my family! What a bastard I am!' He wrote that entry in his diary the very next day. For the 7 November holiday, they were issued sweets, and he ate those too, cursing himself but lacking the willpower to stop. By this time, there was, in any case, no longer any reason to restrain himself. 'In the past few days my hopes of getting out on a professional trip have been dashed', but that did nothing to salve his feelings of annoyance and remorse.[23]

6

Justifying ambiguous actions, people could refer to obstacles of various kinds. These were usually:

(a) I could not help because that was impossible;
(b) I could have helped but had to make a choice whether to give priority to myself or others in the siege;
(c) not helping would make no difference to the person's fate: either they were doomed anyway, or there was someone else who could help them.

Awareness of the horror of life during the siege does not always seem to come through in public apologies, or the internal monologues of self-exculpation. Even where they are reflected in diary entries, there is little real representation of the appalling conditions in which other people are living. Of course, the writers of diaries and letters knew those in need were suffering; they knew they had been going hungry for many days, but often that did not stop them responding to the plight of the starving with what, at this time, was a wholly inappropriate casual brush-off.

Something else, though, is noteworthy. Nobody is confident they are in the right when they refuse to give assistance, even when they have solid grounds for doing so. People feel they are to blame, or that they need at least to anticipate reproaches. Self-justification is not a simple calculation of pros and cons to determine with mathematical precision whether extra grams of bread could have been found and whether, if so, they should have been given to someone with only a few hours more to live. Self-justification is an act in which the foundations of one's own morality are revealed. There is always evident a desire to comfort, to reassure, to hold out the promise of something better in the future, even when that seems highly improbable. There is always a sense of shame at not having been able to act in accordance with normal decent human behaviour. The hope is always expressed that they will be able to help more tomorrow, even if it has proved impossible today.

Self-justification almost always takes the form of a welter of arguments, where any one of them might have sufficed. Of course, much depends on the style of whoever is writing the letters, diaries or memoirs. When every explanation is packed with information and minute detail, it can be difficult to tell whether this represents chaotic exposition, or a desire to communicate the story as fully as possible, or is a deliberate device to explain why unkindness has been necessary.

Their occasional long-windedness was serving a purpose. Their narrators felt a need to come up with a plethora of excuses, which may not always seem logical, or adequate, or sincerely repentant, but which do seem to have been necessary. Their primary function was not to explain to others, but to comfort the writer. If it was not self-excoriation, it is, nevertheless, further compelling evidence of the rootedness of moral values.

The present narrative, intended to be read by succeeding generations unfamiliar with the war and likely to be repelled by many brute facts, has called for a scrupulous and rigorous analysis of these tales of life during the siege.

Compulsory ethical standards: coercion as a means of ensuring survival

1

Compulsion was inevitable in a situation where people had become so weak that they could not always work, look after themselves properly, battle against the temptation to live one day at a time, or voluntarily help others. The first and fundamental argument in favour of harsh measures was the war. The main thing was to win it, whatever the cost. Moral taboos could be observed only to the extent that they did not hamper efforts to achieve that goal. Early in October 1941, women teachers in Moscow district wanted to stop work during shelling and bombing but were forced to continue digging trenches.[24] The primary objective was what mattered, not the interests of the individual. Those who forced the women out during bombing no doubt feared reprisals against themselves if they failed to complete their tasks, but their motivation can also be seen as perfectly logical. A couple of people might get killed, but thousands of others would be protected: that is the 'ethical' calculation in any war.

Maria Konoplyova, reporting the incident in her diary, was at first not prepared to accept that logic, but this was her first lesson in the new ethics. 'A naive entry', she wrote in a note attached later to the diary. 'I was so indignant!' She reproaches herself for failing to understand a simple truth: 'Danger is no longer a consideration for someone who has been mobilized.'[25] She may be passing on the viewpoint of some pitiless and inflexible individual who was directing the works, but her note is significant. In order to come to terms with that rule in the new circumstances, people had to overcome many existing attitudes.

The postmen of Leningrad too were forced to work during bombardment. The rationale was that shelling occurred frequently, there would be long delays, and the work rate would be too slow.[26] They tried to find a compromise, delivering the post if it was 'not our walk' currently being shelled. Was a letter worth a human life? No, but there were work quotas for processing the mail which were inviolable if you did not want to be deprived of your worker's ration card.

Ye. A. Skobeleva remembered her family's firewood being requisitioned for a hospital. Her father 'begged, implored, pointed out that without heating we would all die'. His pleading fell on deaf ears.[27] Those confiscating it had no hesitation. They probably found it easier than going to all the trouble of preparing logs themselves. In any case, where else were they to find firewood which was urgently required for the severely wounded and

patients so weak they could not get out of their beds? Who was supposed
to chop the firewood? The medical staff? There were not enough of them,
and not enough rations to put an orderly by every bed. The hospital no
doubt had its own view of the matter. If they sent their staff to look for
firewood by conventional methods, there would be no one to respond to
the cries and groans of the ill, to treat people and save them from death.

Alexander Sokolov, the head of a section at the Mekhanichesky
[Machinery] factory, went to the apartment of a worker who was irreplace-
able: 'He crawled towards me on all fours, like a dog. He was too weak to
walk.' There was no alternative: 'The driver and I took him by the arms
and put him in the car. We brought him to the factory and put him in the
sickbay.'[28]

Compassion was evidently not the main motive here. In his reminiscences, Sokolov describes taking a starved skilled worker by the arms to
his machine, lifting workers into the car because they were 'so weak they
could not get in by themselves.'[29] They resided in the sickbay and they
worked, falling down, holding on to others. People undoubtedly felt sorry
for them (as is evident from the tone of Sokolov's recollections), but they
accepted that there would be casualties. Those in charge were fearful of
the draconian penalties for failing to deliver military supplies on time,
and some hoped to be awarded a better ration category for meeting their
targets. There were many pressures.

There was some justification for this harshness. If they did not do
their duty, they would open the way to the enemy, to those fiends for
whom nothing was sacred, who burned and destroyed. Who but the
Leningraders themselves must protect their vulnerable old men, women
and children? Could they really expect to shuffle that responsibility on to
others while they themselves hid away?

The argument was incontrovertible and people did not object. It was
difficult to decide which was more moral: to take pity on a starving person
who could hardly stand and might die today, or on defenceless people
who might die tomorrow unless people who had one foot in the grave were
forced to work today.

We find a detailed justification of this harshness in the memoirs of M. P.
Ivashkevich, a teacher working with schoolchildren on a soviet farm. Her
discipline was exceptionally strict and rigid. Her colleagues reproached her
for being so hard on the children but there was no convincing her: 'I shall
continue to require the pupils to carry out my instructions.'

Ivashkevich was convinced she was right. Were they trying to suggest
she did not love the children? That was untrue. It was for their sake she
had stayed behind in the besieged city. You could, of course, allow the
children out half an hour before the end of their work to feed in a nearby
field where swede was being grown. (This reference was barbed.) You
could let them eat this far from delicious vegetable or wrest it from their
enfeebled hands. That was the acid test of the kind of pity you felt for
hungry adolescents. Her rejoinder must be vehement and emotional, to

emphasize how acutely painful it was for her to have to do that. It must also be compelling: let those others hear something they could not argue against: 'We are driven by a different kind of pity. We do not want our young girls and boys transported to Hitler's Germany to be sold in slave markets, for them to be starved and have dogs set on them on German farms. In the name of that pity we must be and will be demanding.'[30]

She has the same choice to make: to take pity now and create a threat to life in the future, or be harsh and ultimately save them all. Her thinking must be inflexible and her rhetoric grandiloquent if the spirit of stoicism for which she is calling is not to be diluted. She has learned to use this harsh language in her day-to-day teaching, admonishing and punishing the delinquent. Orders cannot be accompanied by complicated explanations: they must be terse, precise and unambiguous. The more vividly and starkly she talks of the yoke the invaders would bring, the less likely you are to hear sceptical rejoinders and counsels of moderation.

2

'Compulsory work detail to clean up the city – in 20° below freezing', Esfir Levina noted in her diary on 28 February 1942.[31] Feel sorry for people? Well, someone has to clear the city of snow. Instructions have been received from the Party district committee to clear several streets of rubbish. 'For this a total of 200 able-bodied persons were conscripted, but they were weak, barely able to stand on their feet, swollen with hunger', G. Ya. Sokolov recalls.[32] Replace them? Who with? If they do not clear the streets of filth and corpses frozen into the ice, there will be an epidemic in the spring when the ice melts.

The first 'voluntary' working Saturday, scheduled for 8 March 1942, was not a success. Few people wanted to join in. Emergency measures were quickly put in place. The ranks of the political organizers in house management committees were, as A. Blatin tactfully put it in *Leningradskaya Pravda*, 'augmented and renewed'. A number of house managers were fired, and senior comrades went round checking apartments.[33] All citizens were obliged to assist in cleaning the city for at least 2 hours a week. On the streets, the police stopped Leningraders and checked their conscription cards, which indicated how much time they had put in. 'Anyone who cannot produce their card is handed a shovel. Our cashier went to the bank and left her card in the Architectural and Planning Administration. She was forced to chop ice for two hours', Esfir Levina noted in her diary.[34] Of course, sometimes officialdom took into consideration medical certificates and whether there were young children in the family. The mother of Yekaterina Lentsman (Ivanova), however, was made to clean the streets. Already as she was going down the stairs, she felt poorly: 'My mother became ill and never got back on her feet.'[35] She had young children too: 'The boys had not been able to walk for a long time. They kept trying to find pieces of food in their mouths with their tongues.'[36]

This coercion became commonplace. You were not allowed to pretend there were not other citizens even more malnourished than you. You were not allowed to claim they could just get on with it. Everybody was to learn the lesson that, if you could not control yourself, you would be controlled by others, even if you had dozens of excuses. Such was the mechanism for strengthening the moral rules: not admonition but prohibition; not a request but an order; not an attempt to understand the point someone else was making, but abrupt refusal. Of course, there were pragmatic arguments to justify the coercion, often accompanied by sentimental propaganda and stinging reprimands (which were probably completely unnecessary). An emotive rebuke to the vacillating did not require fault-less logical argumentation. It had the whole personality of the individual imposing the coercion behind it, with his sometimes unpleasant habits, groundless suspicions and petty grievances. It was one way of enforcing moral principles, powerfully and categorically, and it was not based only on rational argumentation. If you snatch a piece of swede from the hands of half-starved children, if you force a woman whose children are dying and who is reeling from weakness to break ice with an iron bar, or compel a worker crawling on his hands and knees to work relentlessly, something is destroyed in the taskmaster who stops at nothing.

The quality of compassion is not a tool that can be put away and taken out of its box again when circumstances change. Everything has consequences. Any choice, just or unjust, can cause moral degeneration. A teenager heard the doctors talking during their inspection of children: 'Oh, and this one needs an enhanced diet, but we can't go putting them all on enhanced diets.'[37] After saying something like that, whether justified or not, has the speaker not already forfeited his humanity? Will someone pronouncing that kind of sentence on starving children not also be cruel in less extreme cases?

'The idea is beginning to take root that those who are still viable should be supported, and not endangered by feeding the dying', we read in Irina Zelenskaya's diary entry for 19 March 1942.[38] Are we not hearing an echo of that same inexorable 'iron logic' which was used to justify choosing between those equally in need of sustenance? 'It is brutal. The logic is acceptable as long as you yourself are still healthy, don't stumble and collapse, but it is very frightening to know that if you fall no one will help you back to your feet', she adds. For those who approved of brutality as a survival technique, putting themselves in another person's shoes would have been impossible even if they had wanted to. 'What's the point of giving her that? She's going to die anyway', said a doctor in response to a request for a white bread coupon for a sick woman, not embarrassed to be staring straight at her.[39] 'This tragedy simplifies my task of cutting back on staff', we read in an engineer's diary when he hears that one of his workers has been killed in the shelling.[40] It is an example of the same bean-counting mentality, expressed with stark, imperturbable clarity. He probably was not as callous about the man's death as he might seem, but that is exactly what he wrote.

When a choice was made or a verdict pronounced, often enough no attention was paid to the difficulties people faced. They were given short shrift, their explanations ignored, and there was a refusal to acknowledge that those explanations might completely change the picture. But, referring to the reason for tough measures, those justifying them could not get by without referring to moral precepts. In his memoirs, Izrail Metter relates the story of his brother, a professor with a Ph.D. working in a hospital kitchen. This was saving him and his family from starvation. When the clinic's political officer found out who he was, he fired him. 'With your academic knowledge it is required you work in accordance with it', the commissar announced. 'Instead you are occupying a job intended for the workforce who have no additional opportunities being as they lack special education. It is intended for a working man, ensuring his survival.'[41]

The political officer's reprimand is incisive, perhaps even impassioned. He is not drily reciting some regulation framed in officialese. The style seems uniquely his own. Behind every word there is an unwavering certainty that he is doing the right thing, honestly and, most importantly, justly. Where a scholar is to find work in his speciality in a besieged city does not concern him, any more than whether the man will be able to survive without his present access to food in an army kitchen. The main source of his confidence is the clichéd nature of his pronouncement. He restricts his logic to the most obvious, striking, seemingly irrefutable points. He repeats what has become a standard slogan of the time, and in the same sloganeering format. 'I didn't want to leave my younger brother on his own', is another reason for working in the kitchen. The political officer has a ready answer to that: 'The issue of your brother is no issue at all in the circumstances of the siege. The fate of Leningrad is the only issue for all of us.'[42]

3

This was a commonly heard excuse. In summer 1942 it was decided to evacuate as many 'dependants' as possible from the city. Anybody with more than one child must leave. Concern that the starving children or their parents might not survive the journey in carriages not adapted for evacuating people, that there would be no one to look after them when they arrived and they would die from epidemics, that here in Leningrad their apartments would be looted when they left, that they would have nowhere to live at their destination, that they would have to accept the humiliation of being a millstone round somebody's neck and have trouble finding work . . . no account was taken of any of it. They must leave. If anybody refused, they were stripped of their food ration cards,[43] and nobody worried how they would survive after that. If someone could not understand the argument and see that the besieged city could not be burdened with the weak and vulnerable, they would be made to see; and that would be done without considering their feelings, without paying attention to the wailing of starving children. It would be done in the firm conviction that this was the humane thing to do, and that it would have been the only way to have saved the hundreds of thousands of people who died in the first winter of the siege.

In December 1941, a number of kindergartens were closed. Food continued to be issued to children from them, but only orphans could still actually live there.[44] It would have made sense to take pity also on children whose parents were alive but freezing in icy houses, suffering from lice and rats, and unable to reach a bomb shelter quickly; to take pity on those who had to step over dead bodies on the stairs and in the courtyards. But no, only orphans were allowed to stay (and by now there were a great many of them). The top priority must be saving the most vulnerable. S. I. Maletsky recalled (or rather, passed on the recollections of his parents) that children were admitted to the kindergarten only on condition that they brought their food ration cards with them. If there was no card, they were sent back home. 'No, that was not cruel', he insists. In 1941, he was very little, and possibly his judgements have been influenced by what his family told him of the siege. But there is something else he cannot pass over in silence, and which causes him to contradict himself: 'The teachers in the kindergarten were aware the child would go hungry at home, until the card was brought.'[45] Pleading would get you nowhere. These children were not to be helped, because otherwise they would be getting food at the expense of other hungry children. Not everybody, desperate to save their child from starving by whatever means they could, accepted these arguments, and in that case, they had to be forced to. Analogously, an emaciated doctor, declining to re-examine a woman who had already been diagnosed and treatment prescribed, in response to reproaches, pointed out that if he could not make it to the clinic, other patients he was obliged to help would suffer.[46]

Prudent pragmatism and moral rules went hand in hand, together with justification of coercion as a means of saving lives. Forcing a person to do something against his will, something which caused him pain, forcing him in spite of all his complaints, cries and supplication, in order to save his life was, in spite of everything, considered moral.

The corollary came to be that cruelty should be shown to everyone, to other people and to those closest to you. If you showed clemency towards family and friends, if you gave in and let them have what they wanted, you would be condemning them to death.

Callousness must be practised in everything: in how the bread was shared, and in the allocation of hospital places for the 'dystrophic'. This was inevitable where bread was being divided into equal portions, irrespective of the age and state of health of family members.[47]

Callousness must be manifest everywhere, because you cannot allow yourself to be deceived by rumours of a possible improvement in the food situation or assume that the worst is over. What jubilation there was over the increase in bread rations on 25 December 1941 – but then several thousand people a day died in January.

4

Coercion became one of the main ways of ensuring the observance of moral precepts, even as it eroded them. Olga Melnikovskaya witnessed the hospital director ordering that the dead should be dressed in 'whatever was most ragged' before burial. It was done in a hall full of dirty uniforms crawling with lice.[48] It was difficult to object: clean clothing was more necessary for the living.

In the vocational school, teachers hid letters in which parents were urging the students to come back home, where it was light, warm and food was plentiful.[49] Possibly the staff were concerned that their students might die on the journey. Perhaps, though, they were afraid of being punished for failing to prevent 'desertion'. They had no qualms about acting callously, knowing very well how much a letter means to a child.

M. P. Fyodorov, the secretary of the Party bureau of Bakery No. 14, encountered hungry women and children begging for alms on the stairs every day. 'It is impossible to just pass on by when I see the children's little hands stretched out towards me, begging for bread.' Should she help them? At whose cost, when every piece of bread had to be accounted for and 'it was impossible to feed them all'?[50] People who knew what went on in the bakeries might have argued with that, but the arguments are logical. Thousands of Leningraders passed through this school of callousness during the siege. Reading their testimony, you see how attitudes even towards those closest to them changed.

There must be no pity: that people took firmly to heart. The argument was simple. T. Kulikova's mother forbade her to share bread with her own son: 'What will become of him if you are gone?'[51] L. Reikhert recalled that his mother 'soon stopped giving everything to the children. People warned her, "If you die, where will they be?"'[52] Often, even the attitude towards one's parents became pragmatic. S. Magaeva visited her mother in hospital every day. When the doctor saw that, she told her off and forbade her to bring food any more, fearing for her health. She did not agree, and felt that the crumbs she was bringing really did not amount to much, but here is how she continues: 'When I went back to the children's home I found lunch waiting for me, and then there was dinner. I ate it all myself and kept nothing for Mummy, because it was important to build up my strength for the next day.'[53]

If that change was taking place within the family, what must be happening in respect of other people? Cruelty as a survival skill was not only practised on strangers, but it was often easier to be uncompromising when dealing with people you hardly knew, or did not know at all. Of course, even in these cases, there was a need for excuses. These were most strikingly expressed by more educated people who valued their self-respect.

'One of my duties was to make sure that the schoolchildren ate their soup in the canteen, rather than pouring it into jars and mugs to take home', Ksenia Polzikova-Rubets, a teacher, writes in her diary. Does she understand why they are doing that? Yes. 'At home mother, father and the younger children do not have any soup.' Can she do anything to help them? No. 'My job is to stop Nadya taking soup home. There is no alternative. The bodies of children and adolescents are weaker than those of adults.' How can you stop one moral imperative, to help the weak, cancelling another which bids you to be kind, sensitive and generous? If you are forced to make a choice, that does not necessarily mean what you choose will be the good: 'Do I have a right to behave like this? I, who have always tried to instil in the children that they must be considerate towards their families', Polzikova-Rubets agonized.[54]

Children are not adults; they do not burden themselves with long-winded questions and answers, or understand casuistical tergiversation, or how tangled situations can be. They see things more simply: he did not help, although he should have; he gave nothing, although he could have. The education of children is always visual: they learn through seeing rather than from rational explanation. So, if a teacher confiscates from a girl a jar of soup she is taking home for her starving mother, what can we say? Who needs that sort of instructor? Teaching a child to coolly watch her family dying from malnutrition and hope that will give her a chance to survive. Is that what needs to be taught?

Efforts to resolve these moral conflicts were not usually particularly original, as is only too evident from Ksenia Polzikova-Rubets's diary. One could not change the rules, but excuses, often legalistic, made it possible to get round them without challenging them. 'Could not Nadya, a schoolgirl who asked for soup for her mother and sister, be given a third bowl for herself?', Polzikova-Rubets wondered for a moment. After all, they had given a bowlful to a boy for his brother, who could not come to school because he had swollen legs. But no: that boy was supposed to be attending their school, while Nadya's mother and sister were complete outsiders.[55] It confirmed the rule that no one's life could be saved unless you compromised your principles. Although, then again, it was questionable whether these were principles at all, since you could hardly claim that dividing people into 'them' and 'us' is particularly moral.

5

'A few days ago I went to see the city prosecutor. He told me he had recently arrived from Moscow, and the next day insisted on having the floor washed. Then he organized a "self-inspection" of the staff. Many were sent off to wash themselves and brush their teeth.' This entry was made on 28 February 1942 in her diary by Esfir Levina, who worked at the Architecture and Planning Board. That this 'self-inspection' was a humiliation is obvious, but the prosecutor is not given to sentimentality. He has no doubt he is right. 'Never mind, they're getting used to it.'[56] It was not only the prosecutor who considered it unnecessary to spare the feelings of Leningraders demoralized by the siege: there were many others. A doctor refused to see one citizen referred to a day clinic in early February 1942 'on the grounds of louse infestation and cardiac insufficiency.'[57] Who can blame him? No one with a contagious condition should ever be allowed into a clinic, and its staff clearly have far too many other duties to attend to someone in need of medical care!

If a person does not want to take care of themselves, they must be forced to do so. All attendant circumstances must be ignored and pleas must not be listened to. Here is how Ye. P. Pavlova compelled her mother to get washed in the morning: 'I brought the water: it had ice floating on it. I said, "Wash yourself and then I'll give you soup." She was having none of it. She didn't want to get off the warm stove. I threatened to wash her myself. She started crying, and said, "Why are you being so rude to your mother?" She did get off the range though, and washed herself.' The icy water and her mother's tears are mentioned deliberately. The daughter knows she is upsetting her mother, so casts around for an excuse. Her mother was silent after washing herself, and Pavlova would like to believe that is a sign of approval of her actions: 'She realized I was not just being rude. She knows perfectly well it is for the best.'[58]

If something is for a person's good, there is no need to stand on ceremony. Those who behaved in this way were convinced that they knew best what a desperate Leningrader who had lost everything in the siege really needed. To allow them to lead you by the nose would be very bad – it meant you did not really love and pity them. Maria Konoplyova witnessed just such a scene: 'An old woman was literally dragging her grandson, a pale boy of about twelve as thin as a reed. The boy kept stopping every ten steps. He was crying and complaining that he could not move his legs.'[59] She was not listening, trying to lead him to a 'heap of sand in the sun'. Another woman came to help the old woman, and she evidently had no doubt that the saving of the boy could be accomplished only by *force majeure*. The fact that he was totally run-down ('he collapsed against the wall and immediately shut his eyes') was neither here nor there. Precisely because he could not walk, he must be forced to. Then, perhaps, he would not be so weak.

'I was staying in bed. We all were because, living like that, we had lost all sensation', Veronika A. Opakhova recalled. This was recognized by a doctor who came to her home. 'How she scolded me. Ouch!'[60] Do you need to spare someone's feelings, to try gentle persuasion, coaxing, encouragement? No, the only way is to rain unbridled curses on them and let them know how worthless they are! The following story is related by Nikolai Tikhonov in his remarkable book, *In Those Days*. It has none of the bombast of his optimistic Leningrad essays. This truth about the siege, oddly enough, was deemed suitable for publication only in a book for children:

A small woman wrapped in three shawls, stumbling through deep snow, was pulling along an emaciated man on a child's sledge. He was sitting on the sledge with his eyes closed, and every three paces he fell backwards. The woman freed herself from the ropes with which she was dragging the sledge, walked back to him, lifted him back on, and he sat there, looking as grim as Kashchey the Miser, with his eyes closed.

She walked on, and he fell off again. There was no end to it in sight, and the distraught woman kept looking around, hoping someone might help. Meanwhile the man fell off again, and again, and again. 'Then a tall, bony woman with a stubborn look in her deep blue eyes stepped off the pavement, went over to where he was lying, heaved him up roughly and yelled loudly in his ear three times, "Citizen, sit or die! Sit or die! Sit or die!" He opened his eyes, blinked and sat himself on the sledge. He did not fall off again.'[61] It is the only way: shriek in someone's ear! Do not spare their feelings! It is the only way: heave them up abruptly without worrying whether you are hurting them. The only way is to put the fear of death in them, and never mind the psychological state of a person half-starved to death, their characteristic disorientation, timorousness and nervous trembling.

The woman's boniness is not confined to her appearance but probably reflects the very core of her being. Someone bony has clearly lived through the most terrible days of the siege, has no doubt witnessed many scenes like this one, and her senses have been coarsened. She is the kind of person who would know how to bring a man back to life, having no pity for him. It is the only way: take a reckless swing and punch as hard as you can.

Did she, or others like her, have any qualms about behaving like this? It hardly seems likely. They were confronted by people who were not only weakened and ready to acknowledge the right of others to order them to pull themselves together. They saw despairing people who had lost their willpower, who were unsure of where they were or how they should behave; who, like little children, were not even capable of looking after themselves. What point could there be in speaking reasonably to them? The women workers in one of the domestic squads, as they were going round the defunct apartments, found an intellectual half out of his mind, who would not get out of bed. They didn't find him to be suffering from any diseases: he had simply given up.[62] Another educated man, working in a laboratory, also lapsed into depression and stopped looking after himself properly. The laboratory technicians decided he needed help. Despite his embarrassment and protests, they warmed some water, washed him and dressed him in clean clothes. He wept and kissed their hands. Why would you stand on ceremony if you encountered someone in that state?[63]

Should you be polite to a cleaner who had come to terms with the fact that she was close to death, a typical dystrophic whose eyes were 'puffy with oedema', and who had a 4-year-old child 'no less malnourished'. When Irina Zelenskaya saw her, she had no hesitation: 'I gave her a right dressing down. I really put my heart into it.' The woman started making excuses: 'My legs aren't right.' She could not get to the district soviet and enrol the little girl at a kindergarten. Zelenskaya rolled up her sleeves and got the little girl registered for food rations: 'Literally within a week the woman changed out of all recognition. The swelling on her face went down, her depression lifted, she began moving around normally, working, smiling. Every day she was telling me how much happier and calmer she was, how well her baby girl was recovering in the kindergarten, what a good lunch she got there.'[64] Why would you waste time on gentle persuasion if you came upon somebody disorientated and confused?

6

Frailty during the Time of Death was often mistaken for a lack of will-power. Those caught in the siege very soon, and rather inflexibly, identified a fatal sequence of stages of degeneration. To an extent, they based this on personal experience, but it was based also on what they heard from other people. Observing that someone who had become demoralized could be spectacularly resurrected, they came to believe that you needed only to compel someone to pull themselves together to effect a transfiguration. There were a whole set of features characteristic of a severely starved victim of the siege who was no longer strong enough to get out of their room: their clothes were torn and ragged, their hands unwashed, their hair in clumps. In reality, whether they washed themselves or combed their hair made little difference to their prospects of recovery, but the illusion that the rot could be stopped without addressing its root causes is unsurprising when we bear in mind the widespread Soviet belief at the time that changing external circumstances could effect internal change.

It was also believed that one of the most effective remedies for spiritual decay was work. 'I gave no jelly to anyone who did not want to work', A. S. Ganzha, head of the air defence unit at the Sudomekh [Shipbuilding equipment] factory admitted. He was evidently immediately aware of making a gaff, and corrected himself: 'That is, in respect of those who were strong enough, only lazy.'[65] He, of all people, would have been well aware of just how many people at that time were strong, and what the cause of their 'laziness' was. Andrey Zhdanov was particularly exercised over the problem of 'laziness', but evidently did not himself have sufficient strength to address a single public meeting during the Time of Death. 'Comrade Zhdanov said then, "Find everyone a job," and immediately we began to find work for everybody', the chairman of Vyborg District Executive Committee, A. Ya. Tikhonov, recalled.[66] Factories and plants were idle at the time, and mostly people were needed to work in the funeral details. Why was it necessary to set to work starving people who froze on their way to the factory and were killed by the shelling, who collapsed from exhaustion and died at their workbench, or crawled about on their hands and knees? Zhdanov's explanation is so cynical that the only way to convey it is by direct quotation: 'It was necessary in order to stop the workers from thinking all the time only that they had nothing to eat and were feeling cold.'[67]

Ye. F. Yegorenkova, director of the Public Library, in December 1941 found her own original way 'to occupy the library staff and thereby distract them from their gastric problems'. This was a great work plan for

1942, a panacea for hunger and reliable way of stopping everyone from endless, dispiriting talk about bread. When you read such pronouncements, you understand who this was all being addressed to – it was certainly not for the benefit of the siege victims who had just been through the horrors of the Time of Death: 'You should have seen how the ashen, blue, yellow and green faces of my colleagues lit up. For a whole month nobody thought about anything other than the Plan.' There is something nihilistic about this degree of cynicism from a person who is totally shameless and can sink to a level unthinkable, even for someone professionally engaged in generating optimism, who had not lived through the siege and whose face was accordingly now neither blue nor green. 'How many creative discussions flared up spontaneously. People who were tired and hungry had no time for sleep for several nights.'[68] What matters here is not what is claimed (which we are entitled to disbelieve), but the confidence that this is how things should be done.

Zhdanov's call to arms was rapidly put into effect. Pyotro Murashko, chairman of the Kuibyshev District Executive Committee, readily talked later about putting dystrophics to work to clean up the city. The logic was the same: 'When someone is lying in bed and not doing anything, he only thinks about food and that he is going to die.' Of course, he added quickly, no one was going to work them to death: 'We explained to people that we were doing this in their own best interests.'[69] If a dystrophic got too tired, he could go home to rest, although there is no mention of how long it might take someone who could hardly walk to stagger back to bed when the lift was not working and the stairs were iced over. Why work should be so therapeutic nobody particularly enquired. Irina Zelenskaya notes that the hospitals' practice of admitting relatively healthy people and putting them in bed 'did a lot of people no favours at all'.[70] That is open to question, and there is no shortage of testimony from citizens whose lives were saved in the hospitals. There were, however, grounds in support of such thinking, and the enthusiasm for getting people back to work for their own benefit was not prompted solely by the clarion calls from 'above'.

Alexander Fadeyev's sketches, *Leningraders During the Siege*, has a section dedicated to the story of Vocational School No. 15. In the first winter of the war, almost all its pupils survived. 'They did not die because they worked hard', the headmaster, V. I. Anashkin, explained. Encouragement alone was not enough to make adolescents work during this period, and Anashkin makes no secret of his methods: 'They worked hard because I instilled a sense of discipline into the boys' minds. I instilled it not only by persuasion but also by employing the most rigorous compulsion.' Does he have any qualms about that? No. 'It was the only way to enable them to survive.' His story is not an atttempt to justify his actions. He sees no need for that. Rather, it is a list of actions to be proud of. Many headmasters of vocational schools, when they found themselves unable to feed their students, sent them home. Anashkin did not. He was not afraid of bearing responsibility for them. The winter was severe, the water supply and sewerage no longer functioning, but he did not back down. His resistance to the nightmare of the siege is noted almost pedantically, down to the last detail. He will try anything, and simulates the way life was before the war: 'I ensured that the dining room was spotlessly clean, that there were posies of paper flowers wrapped in dazzlingly white paper on the tables, and that an accordionist played at lunchtime.'[71]

He was hardly responding to pressure from above, and was evidently not the sort of person who needed official instructions. He feels he is not only organized, but also an artist. He recreates the details, mostly crude and 'bourgeois', of an unreal world of comfort, cleanliness, harmony and tranquillity. This is not some bureaucratic requirement but rather an artistic improvization. He has no doubt that this is the only way to survive, and has no hesitation in compelling others to go along with this brittle world of orderliness which defies the chaos of everyday life in the siege. Only order ultimately creates freedom: chaos creates slavery. It is unlikely he knew this aphorism from Charles Péguy, but the spirit behind his exhortations is the same. One has the feeling that the main thing here was less the work itself than the deliberate, stable and mechanical nature of the community's actions:

> I tried to ensure that the boys got up only at the specified time, that they invariably washed, drank tea and then went to the workshop. Some were so weak they could not work, but nonetheless busied themselves at their lathes and that helped to keep them in good spirits. When there was no electricity and the workshop was at a standstill, we went out to clear the yard or did military drill. I always tried to ensure that from the minute they woke up until they went to bed the boys had something to keep them busy.[72]

It is unclear how the teenagers felt about this, but their registration at the school canteen gave them at least a prospect of survival. Fadeyev was evidently little interested in how they felt, and any note of scepticism would have been out of place in the climate of bombastic optimism which informs his story. (His publishers would have expected nothing less from him.) To prove his rightness, Anashkin quotes a girl as saying 'It's boring with no school', 'There's nothing to do', but that hardly seems conclusive. He does admit that some, because of their physical weakness, can only 'busy themselves' at their bench, but does not delve into their feelings. To instil such discipline, and inexorably maintain it, requires a particular kind of personality. It would call for ruthlessness, self-assuredness and insensitivity to the suffering of others if more humane feelings were not to prevail and the entire system of coercion for the sake of survival were not to collapse overnight. Moreover, the more systematically this approach was implemented, the sooner the understanding of its objectives began to go off course. Action to help people survive was supplanted by the sum of the techniques of micromanagement and control, which became an end in themselves. More began to be demanded, more than was necessary. People were forced to overstrain their last resources, unintentionally propelling them on their way to the grave. Rituals were devised to demonstrate the outward signs of vitality. None of those forcing others to show 'optimism' were psychologists or physicians capable of demonstrating credibly what role labour played in enabling a dystrophic on a diet of 125 grams of bread a day to survive. But just try to undermine their faith!

7

Taking work as a universal duty which all must perform at such a time naturally justified coercive measures against those who refused. An attempt to realize this ideal of work as an unchallengeable duty, irrespective of whether it was really necessary and worth the superhuman effort being called for, was undertaken with egregious enthusiasm by Georgiy Knyazev, director of the Archive of the Academy of Sciences. Almost every entry in his diary is divided into two parts. The first is an emotive introduction, emphasizing the difficulties of the present situation and the need for fortitude and self-sacrifice. The second is a succession of stories, episodes and scenes, in which he excoriates the unrighteous, reassures the vacillating, and gives heart to those in danger of losing faith. There is only black and white: modest, unpretentious people who uncomplainingly bear with dignity and in silence the burdens of the war; and their opposites: the thieves, hypocrites, liars, loudmouths and cowards. In the centre is the figure of the diary's author, unshakably convinced of his own righteousness and in possession of a set of clear, simple ideas about how one ought to behave.

His staff, whom he pulls up every day, are, as a rule, weak. They spend more of their time thinking about bread than about their work; they can hardly walk and are happy when they get to warm themselves by the stove. They do not respond well to passionate exhortation: 'They were sitting by the stove, none of them doing anything. I informed them that in March we would need to prepare a study room. They growled at me. Salaries still have not come. They are all cold and hungry.'

That was written in February 1942, when the number of people dying each week of starvation was in the tens of thousands. A month later, he is again complaining, 'none of the archive staff are showing the necessary concern [for the archive – S. Ya.]. They come in to work, but they work only for their ration card as a member of staff.' He is hungry himself. Well, maybe not as hungry as other people, but he's certainly not living in luxury. Why does he not give up? Why do other people look so defeated? One of the staff came to him. He saw how old and haggard the man was looking, but he was still on his feet and there could be no indulging his weakness: 'He asked to be excused from duty. I did not consent.' It was unpleasant that this fellow, a Doctor of Sciences, there and then, in front of him, deliberately began doing lowly work, emptying water out of the sink. Was the director ashamed? No. That job should be delegated to others, but the

Doctor of Sciences had to do his share of the duties. After all, he could still walk. In late February 1942, Knyazev observed the staff crowding round the stove 'for a full two and a half hours, talking about nothing but food'. What sort of way was that to behave? Who would do the work? 'When I suggested there was work to be done, they apprehensively referred to objective difficulties and that they were weak from malnutrition.'

They 'apprehensively referred'. There was no shouting, but 'growling'. They did not express indignation loudly; there were no overt accusations. People were probably afraid of being made redundant and downgraded to the rations of a mere 'dependant'. So they staggered on, constantly terribly cold, and baffled as to why anyone in this nightmare might need the folders in an archive. They did not miss an opportunity to find some way of registering a protest, but a silent protest. So a Doctor of Science wordlessly obeys orders, deliberately humiliating himself, but in silence, always in silence.

In this instance, the sight of powerless, starving people moves the observer not to pity but to an awareness of his own uniqueness and powers of endurance. For Georgiy Knyazev too, this is an ordeal: to go against the consensus, and not to feel pity when that is your natural inclination. Otherwise, he will look just as malleable and lacking in principle as those he is rebuking. This is what gives him the right to decide how generously to reward key staff who are not shirking their work, at the expense, of course, of those who are not pulling their weight. He is only too aware of the consequences: 'I compile a list of the order in which they are to die.' He does not lose too much sleep over that, 'because I myself am somewhere on that list'.

Many of his staff did not survive the siege. Nameless caretakers and cleaners died, and single people who had nobody to support them. He does not so much mourn them as celebrate them: 'These are the people with whom I live, and will perhaps die.'[73]

In Knyazev's notes, there is little mention of why anyone would need to browse the archive's files. It would be a disquieting discussion, and the conclusions might not be to his liking. The top priority is to do your duty. If everybody does that, then victory will be assured and there will be hope of survival. A number of moral principles are implied, but are not made explicit. You should not expect to be paid for doing nothing: that is tantamount to theft. You should not set a bad example to those who are wavering, because it will prompt them to sink even lower. You should not expect someone else to do your work for you, because that is tantamount to living at the expense of others just as malnourished as you are yourself. And you should not disdain whatever work is assigned to you, however repellent.

As always, having to determine the odds of survival for other people faced the person making that calculation with a moral problem. Determining who should be helped and how, or when you should compel someone to do something they did not want to, obliged the person in authority to re-examine closely his notions of morality.

But there is something else we need to note. Coercing a person, inexorably and ruthlessly, even if for the sake of his own survival, was against morality. Push aside someone plaintively begging alms and, no matter how intelligently, irreproachably and irrefutably you may argue that it is for his own good, you can no longer hold moral principles to be unshakable. Those were extraordinary and merciless times, but that wormhole of callousness had only to open up and a slippery slope could lead to the fatal conclusion that 'all is permitted'. If to cause pain was allowed, and subsequently excused, where was the red line which could not be crossed when what was at stake was something other than survival. Repetition establishes a rule. The tragedy is that there really was no alternative. Coercion was a prerequisite for people to survive, even as it undermined the morality which sanctified the act of saving them. The medicine proved to be, at one and the same time, both antidote and poison.

4

The influence of moral standards on people's behaviour

Appealing for help

1

Moral rules were undermined in many respects during the siege of Leningrad, but it did not happen overnight. Asking for help in the Time of Death demanded determination, even ruthlessness and disregard of moral standards, since those being asked for bread were themselves starving. Those who came to them for help could not have been unaware of the price of the alms they were asking for.

Many accordingly could not bring themselves to ask for help directly, hoping that those who knew of their misfortune would offer it of their own accord. They understood that not everyone had the strength and time to visit their family and friends in need of support, so they themselves came to pay a 'visit', making no demands, but hoping that just their outward appearance would evoke pity. They were relying too on the long-established custom that you cannot refuse hospitality to anyone who comes to your door. 'It is difficult to get used to the idea that a guest is someone to whom you should not offer even a cup of unsugared tea', Izrail Metter wrote,[1] and the custom of offering hospitality – if not, of course, as generously as in the past – was honoured even during the first winter of the siege.

At first, half-starved people who came to visit showed fortitude and would not always ask for bread, but nobody was fooled: everyone understood the need that had brought them into another person's home. 'To be completely honest, if you go to visit somebody now you're just waiting for them to give you at least something to eat', A. Kochetova told her mother.[2] Her story is only too common for that time, although what makes it stand out is the naive honesty with which she tells it, leaving nothing out and making no attempt to show herself in a good light. By the end of December 1941, she was extremely thin and past caring where she went, whether to a closer or to a more distant relative, in search of help. Someone shared an oilcake with her. She had no one else to turn to, and came to visit him a second time. Again he treated her to oilcake. Then she visited him for a third time. She knew that was unfair, that she had no right to abuse someone's hospitality. 'I knew it was awkward, but then I decided just to swallow my pride. There, Mummy, that's the kind of person I've become, what has happened to all my pride.'[3] But she cannot stop herself. If someone helped her out once, perhaps he'll help her again, and again. Her hunger sweeps all before it, her modesty and her pride. She begins to feel the generosity is almost owed to her, and it is hard for her to describe, with barely concealed resentment, how it felt to be refused: 'But then I suppose he saw he couldn't get anything out of me so he didn't give me any more food and I stopped going to see him.'[4]

When people visited relatives and friends or met up with their neighbours, they usually talked about their troubles, described in detail the most tragic episodes of their life under the siege, and spoke about their sufferings. Nobody asked anybody for anything; they just needed somebody to talk to. Tatiana Kononova recorded in her diary on 29 January 1942:

> In the morning Anya Kiprushkina came to warm up after standing in the bread queue, and couldn't stop crying. Valya and Andrey Ivanovich are all swollen. It's just awful. Then Kira and Anastasia Nikolaevna came to warm up and were going to go and enquire about evacuation, but after they'd been sitting for a while decided not to go anywhere. They are living on a ration, i.e., 250 grams of bread and practically nothing else, because at the shop for the whole of January dependants got only 50 grams of butter and 100 grams of meat.[5]

Often, shocked by the stories of others caught in the siege, people would be more generous than usual. Partly because of that, visitors would do their best to supplement dreadful siege stories with further details: not made up, true, but with enumeration of the most appalling realia of the Time of Death. And seeing others 'feasting', they would not wholly accidentally elaborate on their own troubles.[6] When one woman's brother came to see her, 'all swollen and looking much older', and then 'licked the kitchen table', she could hardly have asked for more eloquent testimony of how severely starved he was.[7]

'By evening, I was so upset I was crying and couldn't do anything properly', Kononova ends her diary entry for 29 January 1942.[8] Perhaps that was why people came to her to 'warm up': they knew she would at least give them a drink of hot water, if she had nothing else. 'Visitors' came to see kind, caring people in the expectation of help, and did not always take full account of the fact that they themselves were in great hardship. They came because they knew they would get nothing from others, because they no longer had any shame, and were at the end of their tether, even if their own diet was better than that of their hosts. They came and came. N. L. Mikhaleva describes a whole succession of such visitors in her diary. Moreover, they would come on more than one occasion, always in the hope of being given something. One was 'a skeleton with a terrible look in his eyes'; another came 'literally crawling'.[9] They had no one else to turn to, Leningraders marginalized by the siege, only to her, a deeply religious woman who would not drive them away, or purse her lips as she heard of their need. She was living in poverty herself and a note of despair constantly comes through in her diary entries. 'He is expecting to be fed, but I have nothing more to give. I feel sorry for all of them and give what I can, but now all our own reserves have gone', she writes on 18 December 1941. ' I feed them all, giving away my own food, but it is becoming unbearable', she notes on 7 January 1942. 'I gave him what I could, 50 grams of bread, and mended his mittens', she writes in her diary on 5 April 1942.[10] Perhaps she complained of her troubles not only to her diary but directly to her 'visitors', but why did they keep coming to her, in December and January and April?

2

When having to ask for help, the supplicant often apologetically emphasized that it was not for themselves but for others. Lev Razumovsky tells of his nurse who fell ill and asked him to see whether their neighbours could spare a 'bowl of soup'. He stood outside the apartment for a long time 'hesitating, shifting from one foot to the other', trying to work up the courage to knock on the door, and it was only the thought that he was doing this for someone else that enabled him to do it. When, instead of soup, he was given a glass of soya milk, he stressed, 'for a third time', that it was not for him but for the nurse: 'Thank you so much. It is for Ksenia. If it had been for myself I would not have asked.'

Note the excuses. It could have been for himself, and for the person giving the gift it might not have been particularly significant, but interceding for others is respected more.

Direct requests for support are always accompanied by explanations which bring out the humility of the supplicant, how awkward they feel at having to trouble other people with their complaints. If you have to beg, you ask only for the absolute minimum, only what is essential and can be given ungrudgingly. If you are begging, then it is only as a last resort, in extremity, when you are faced with death. That is the common theme of such appeals.

Let us look at just a few personal letters asking for help and see how similar they all are. In a letter from Alfred Kube, who worked at the Hermitage, it is immediately made clear that he is asking for very little. He is in good health and even 'full of energy'. All he needs is some warm socks: his feet 'get terribly cold during the night watch'. He makes the request with the utmost delicacy: 'I wonder whether by any chance there might be a pair of woollen socks left after our Stepan Petrovich?!' He understands it may be inconvenient to give him these leftovers but is very flexible: 'If they have holes in them, I can darn them.' The tone of the letter is apologetic, as if he is afraid of appearing pushy. 'I know there is little chance because, if I remember, he did not wear wool', but this is followed by a direct request: 'But if there is, perhaps you could, after all, let me have them?!!'[11] Here he more clearly shows his persistence, but it is framed with impeccable politeness, and for good reason. He cannot afford to cause offence, or demand, or complain. Everything must be presented as an act of purest charity. His qualifying phrases firmly indicate that he knows his place as a supplicant with no rights.

The same mood is present in a letter he sent in late February 1942, but all optimism is gone: 'I am in hospital in an awful situation with terrible colitis. Things are very bad.'[12] Again he is asking for very little: 'Might you by any chance have even just a little red wine?' It is nowhere to be found, and he is presuming to ask this favour only because he is in desperate need. He does not feel he can just list everything he needs for fear of appearing presumptuous. Every subsequent request is made in the same self-deprecating tone and accompanied by the obligatory assurances that he is entirely willing to accept tiny portions. If there is no red wine, then perhaps something else 'of good quality' could be sent? Also, if there is any, 'a little vodka'. And then there come the apologies, all in the same tone of supplication: 'Do be so kind. Forgive me. I feel quite wretched. I suddenly have this disgusting pain in my bones.'[13]

The same delicacy is present in a letter from K. M. Ananyan sent to his wife on 7 March 1942. 'Food is a constant problem', his request begins. There follow several lines inked out by the censor. It is not difficult to guess that he referred in them to details about life under the siege. He then again apologizes to his wife for asking her to 'regularly send comestibles'. He is not asking for anything fancy: 'Dried bread would be fine, or crusts of bread, potatoes.'[14] That will cheer him a lot and in return he will send her money.

He might seem to have said all that needed to be said, but everyone was living in hardship. He is certainly aware of that, and may also be concerned that his appeal may be dismissed as a momentary weakness. He writes some more about how hungry he is and makes sure he will be believed: 'I must confess that I have never experienced such difficult days in my whole life. As you know, we have faced many troubles, but never on the present scale.'[15] He does not have high expectations of delicacies and will content himself with whatever food they send: 'Do not put yourself out. Don't go looking for special food. For example, butter. It does not necessarily have to be from cow's milk. Butter from ewe's milk would be fine.'[16]

A. V. Nemilov, writing to ask a friend to send him a parcel, is concerned that he may be misled by rumours that the siege will shortly be lifted. Even if it is, it will be quite some time before normal food supplies are restored for everyone, and there has been a big build-up of refugees in the city. He needs sugar, dried fruit, dried root vegetables . . . but here he pulls himself up and, not wanting to appear too demanding, writes flatteringly to his friend that, of course, he does not need a lot of detailed advice because he is well versed in 'such domestic and culinary matters'.[17] And, of course, he will repay the cost. He is happy to send books in return.

By not being demanding, people had more reason to hope for help. If they got the wrong tone, if they said too little about the situation in Leningrad, if they asked for more than was reasonably to be expected, they could expect nothing. The appeal itself should be informed by humility, tact, an understanding of the situation being faced by other people, and contain a promise of recompense at a later date. With its pragmatic aims, the plea for help strengthened the commonly accepted moral rules. If anyone chose to ignore them, the supplicant's efforts to improve his situation would fail. Accordingly, he had to comply with them.

In 'begging' private letters we easily discern a common pattern: first, a (usually brief) description of the writer's troubles; then, the request; next a more detailed account of their suffering, dramatic and sometimes hyperbolic. The tone of some is emotional and vivid; that of others, more unassuming and simply expressed. At first you notice only that distinction, but as you read on, the letters become increasingly chaotic. Each writer gets caught up in the flow of emotion and begins improvising, relating their misfortunes to the best of their ability. Some fight against them, others give way, and the epistolary transcript of their days and doings during the siege becomes like a play, each with its individual plot and dénouement. Their main feature, however, is the unassuming tone of these pleas for help.

In a letter sent by A. Konnov's mother on 30 March 1942 to her son at the front line (he was on the Nevsky Bridgehead, 50 kilometres east of Leningrad), this unpretentiousness comes through very clearly. The letter's content is typical: 'I feel ill. I can't use my legs and don't go outside', her letter begins. She must be sure to say how much she appreciates the parcels he has already sent. It is an expression of gratitude, and something she hopes will continue: 'Thank you, Leshenka, for everything.' And then the request: 'Leshenka, if you can, send me a wee loaf.' The affectionate diminutive she uses for the bread foregrounds the modesty of the supplicant. Note also that 'if you can'. And heaven forbid that he should think she is expecting anything else: 'That is all I need.'[18]

She could have ended the letter there, but she goes on. We sense that she wants not only to move her son to pity, but also to open her heart and receive sympathy: 'I've bartered all I had for bread and have nothing left to exchange. I live in the kitchen. I've burned everything up. Send me a letter at least. I hope for one every day. Are you keeping well? I worried about you a lot. Perhaps we'll never see each other again. Waiting for your letter.'[19]

3

'Don't go hungry', she ends her appeal, a strange wish to address to someone you are asking to send you bread: perhaps she is letting him off the hook in case he cannot help. We see how the anxiety and fear of causing trouble change the tone of a letter from a grumble into a confession. There is much less constraint in appeals for support to people not personally known but professionally obliged to show concern for the weak and those in need of care. 'Sometimes when you went into a hospital the patients would turn to you and beg you with tears in their eyes to save them: "Don't let me die!"', recalled Alexey N. Kubasov, chief of staff of the Kuibyshev District Air Defence Unit.[20] Leningraders caught in the siege were not always sure who was who in the cumbersome hierarchy of authorities, but knew from hearsay who to appeal to and who had more than a word of encouragement to offer them. They looked for help to the management of enterprises and institutions, those working in the air defence units, Komsomol and domestic hygiene squads.

How often and how insistently people appealed depended primarily on where they were. You would rarely miss an opportunity to ask the management for something if you came across them in hospitals or factory workshops. What sort of state you were in also played a role and, if you were starving, you might ignore all the proprieties. This also happened where rights and privileges were being ignored: claiming them was considered natural and no disgrace.[21] Even those who had no privileges of their own would mention the merits and awards of their relatives, and expect better treatment. Vladimir G. Kulyabko, when asking the head of the evacuation centre to put him in a covered vehicle, told him, 'I'm going to see my son: he's in the army and has won a medal.'[22]

Letters asking for support and addressed to official institutions often took the form of a brief application with a businesslike statement of the request. Rhetorical embellishment was not necessary: all that was needed was information about the problem. Here are the texts of some, preserved in the archive of the Primorsky district committee of the Komsomol. T. I. Ivanova wrote, 'I request your assistance to provide firewood as I am in a cold room with two children. The room has no window frames after bombing. My husband lived at the barracks but died of starvation. I hope you will not refuse. Thank you in advance.'[23]

Another application was written by 13-year-old V. Shustarovich, apparently under dictation from her mother:

> We request that you help us to be placed in a children's home because our father is at the front defending Leningrad, leaving us four children behind. On 8 January our house was hit by a shell. We were moved to another room. Here too the windows were soon blown out. Our mother is ill with scurvy and cannot walk, and neither can Tatiana or Leonora too. We have no windows and no one to saw up wood. We are sitting in the cold, hungry because we have nothing to cook with. We request that you send a youth commission to find somewhere for our mother and us to stay as children of a Red Army soldier.[24]

These statements closely resemble each other, but not all of them are couched in bureaucratic language. The similarity of their contents was due, of course, not to the canons of some ritual but to the fact that people's troubles were much the same. On the whole they are succinct, very specific, and without spontaneity or wordiness. Possibly they were written while Komsomol household squads were doing their rounds of apartments, and following their advice. One detects an implicit bureaucratic template in them. These are not personal letters with diverse intonations, hints, apologies and excuses. The most telling argument is a reference to family members being in the Red Army, something which counts for more than tales of how unbearable life is under the siege. There is also no mention in these applications of what the families would undoubtedly like to receive but which the 'youth commission' had no power to give: medicines, vitamins and milk for children. The requests are very limited, as if the applicants have already been informed about the limited resources of the donor, as if someone was standing beside them and advising them on the wording. Asking for more or hoping for generosity was pointless without the additional support of 'influential' people.

'The old man was sitting in my office and cried as he told me about his wife. She was sixty-six, ill, and using up what remained of her failing strength to provide him some rudiments of comfort and care. Recently, their diet had consisted of jasmine leaves from their houseplants. They were so old and helpless that they were somehow managing not even to collect their rations', Irina Zelenskaya noted in her diary on 25 November 1941.[25] There was probably a reason why they were telling her about their troubles: she was the manageress of a canteen, and they may have been hoping for special treatment, perhaps an extra bowl of coupon-free soup or porridge. Not a few Leningraders wrote about the power of tears to soften the hearts of those in a position to help. They could sometimes prove the most effective argument.[26] We notice a tendency everywhere to try to make the request for support as informal as possible. Sometimes this was because the petitioner did not know the bureaucratic rules, but people hoped that by appealing directly to the person, to their charity, and not forcing their pleas onto the Procrustean bed of bureaucratic phraseology, they might find a more direct route to the help they needed. The architect Alexander Nikolsky, when he turned to the Academy of Architecture, insisted that he was 'not making a formal request for assistance but asking for help'.[27] The point was that he was asking for a personal favour. That same style of a very personal appeal for help is evident in a request engineer I. L. Andreyev directed to the deputy director of the Marty factory, G. I. Nikiforov: "My very dear Nikiforov, help! This is the second day I have had nothing to eat. My wife is in hospital. There is nothing to cook. Please send at least some oilcake or take me away from here to the factory. Here, I will die.'[28] Even shorter was a note from the head of a workshop at the Molotov factory to the chairman of the Cultural and Educational Propaganda Section: 'Turkov, I am dying. Save me!'[29]

M. M. Tolkachyova, a school teacher, lost her ration cards. 'My dear Valentina Fyodorovna', her letter to the headmistress begins. It is not even an official request; she is just hoping her superior will take pity on her when she hears of her predicament. The words she chooses are personal, intimate, plaintive: 'What can I do? I have almost a month ahead of me and we will not even have 125 grams. We will surely die. My sister is so malnourished she is bedridden, and I myself can barely move around. Forgive me if I have done anything wrong. Sincerely loving you, M. Tolkachyova.'[30] There are no bureaucratic clichés, no references to laws, regulations or privileges. In one factory archive, there are several such appeals, entirely free of the taint of official language. Each has something the petitioner clearly hopes will reinforce their message and soften the management's hearts. One, a communist, mentions in passing that he has given his membership card to the Party committee for safekeeping, to be sure it will 'not fall into the hands of the enemy'. He evidently hopes this will be suitably appreciated. Another communist asked for his wife to be admitted to hospital, and attached a medical certificate to the effect that she was in need of an enhanced diet.[31]

4

Children appealed for help, and adolescents. Left without support by their parents or having lost them, they tried to survive as best they could, and they were not very good at it. G. S. Yegorov came across a 2-year-old girl sitting on the porch with a doll she was offering to those who passed: 'This is my doll, I love her but I want to sell her. My Mummy is ill, I have nothing to eat. I'm hungry. I will sell you my doll for 100 grams of bread.'[32] If a doll is your favourite doll, that makes it expensive. People won't buy something cheap, and the hungry little girl knew that.

Turning to anyone, whether or not they were from your family, knowing nothing about rules and customs, just crying and begging someone to take pity: what else could these abandoned, starving children do? P. P. Trofimov, the director of the State Institute of Industrial Chemistry, saw one child in the street. People were walking by, paying no attention, and the little girl, freezing in the icy cold, was 'not even sobbing but wailing monotonously'.[33] He went over and started questioning her: 'Almost without ceasing to cry, whining piteously, she said, "I'm hungry."'

Completely bewildered, not knowing where to look for bread or how to live on their tiny rations, children chose the most obvious thing to do and went to beg at the bakeries. These, of course, were only the older children. Not every writer of memoirs could bring themselves to describe the state of little 2- or 3-year-olds, helpless, starving, looking for food next to their dead mother's body. 'They say that swarms of starving people are begging from people coming out of the bakeries for a piece of bread', Anna Ostroumova-Lebedeva noted in her diary in 1941.[34] Charity was not uncommon then, and people even gave money. It was there, by the bread-shop counters, that the starving hoped to get a crust of bread. Zarya Milyutina writes very emotionally about a girl holding out her hand for alms in a shop.[35] Boris Mikhailov recalls how, as a teenager, he was taken for a thief and kicked out of a bread shop he had gone into to get warm:

'A soft-hearted old woman (maybe not so old, but wrapped up in rags) quickly came to me and put a makeweight in my hand. It was five or ten grams of bread: alms.'[36] That did not happen very often, however; there were just too many beggars, and those they were begging from were too hungry themselves.

'He begged at bread shops but rarely got anything', Olga Peto writes of the life of one of these boys. The only place he could get 'leftover soup' at the end of the day was a canteen.[37] The people who worked there had more to eat and it was easier for them to share food.

Two young girls who frequented the bread shop on Dzerzhinsky Street evidently had little luck. They would come before closing time and, with the permission of the sales assistant, gather up the crumbs of bread. Kind, sensitive Olga Peto went looking for homeless children and arranged for them to be looked after in children's homes. She tried to speak to one of the girls who was about 5: 'She shied away and hid in the nearest courtyard.'[38] This was not uncommon. Abandoned, feral children who had long been unloved, timorously anticipated danger at every turn and knew only fear: fear of being deprived of even the pitiful crumbs they collected, fear of being driven out into the frost, fear of being taken away to unfamiliar homes and unfamiliar people who would mistreat them. Often, they could not say why they thought they would be mistreated, but instinctively anticipated it.

'I came to an agreement with the assistant. The next day at about 9.00 pm, I was in the shop and the girl was there. There were no customers. The door was locked. The child rushed to the door but could not get out. I showed her a piece of bread and some Croquette sweets I had been given that day. She came over timidly. Barely audibly, she said "My name is Manya." She was so thin. After much persuasion, she agreed to come and have some hot soup and porridge.'

The other hungry child hiding there heard everything, about the sweets she had not seen for so long, the soup and porridge which were beyond her wildest dreams as she scrabbled about on the floor looking for crumbs: 'From a dark corner (the store was lit by just one candle on the counter) emerged a girl of about ten. Her jacket was dirty, her face severely swollen, her lips blue. "Auntie, take me too. I'm going to die here."'[39]

5

Children would endure terrible things, living for weeks in deserted houses from force of habit, clinging to the past, hoping that what was familiar and dear to them would somehow save them. Only when their strength was finally running out, when their hunger overwhelmed everything else, when they realized there was no longer any hope for them, would they appeal for help, usually from the children's homes or district committees of the Komsomol. As reported by the staff there, the children's requests assume an uncharacteristically brisk, official tone. Starving, frostbitten, muddling the names of institutions, living on rumours, they would hardly have been able to talk coherently about their sorrows. 'She wandered in.'

Such was the condition of a 10-year-old girl. She came to the Komsomol district committee and related how she had been living for several months since her mother died, with her sister and two other girls aged between 5 and 7.[40] The stories of children and teenagers are all remarkably similar: no mother, because she had either died or become bedridden, nothing to eat, no fuel for the stove.

From what children offered by way of explanation, it is often difficult to understand what had actually happened. Two 7-year-old boys who asked to be admitted to a children's home told the district committee how hard their life was: 'They were alone at home. No fuel. Very cold and hungry',[41] because, they said, their mothers had been conscripted to construct military installations. Almost anything was possible in the days of the siege, although it seems unlikely that parents would agree to leave their children to starve to death while they went off digging trenches. Probably some of what the children said had been articulated for them by someone else,[42] and the bit about labour mobilization added because it was thought inconceivable the committee would refuse to provide for them in those circumstances. Despairing of being able to feed them, not having the strength to care for them, their families had probably recognized that continuing to share out their meagre rations could only lead to the child dying.[43] Families went to great lengths, trying to ensure no one would dare refuse admission to a children's home or reception and reallocation centre. As a last resort, if unable to get them into a children's home, they would look for a foster parent or, more often, just abandon them outside someone's door. A. T. Kedrov, deputy director of Factory No. 224, discovered a 'foundling' in the hallway of his apartment. The 4-year-old girl had been respectably dressed, perhaps in the hope that would get her treated better. She sat there 'quietly, saying nothing', but then began crying loudly: 'I asked her, "Where is your mummy?" She said, "Mummy gone to get powwidge."' They fed the little girl and, two days later, managed to track down her mother. The woman was unapologetic and came out with the usual excuse: '"Well, what am I supposed to do? I'm starving to death. Is that what's to happen to her too?"'[44]

The children and adolescents themselves tended to look for help not to children's homes but to other relatives. For them, the main thing was to be with their families and not among unfamiliar, sometimes rough people with precious little sympathy for them. They did not know anyone beyond their immediate family or more distant relatives who might help them, and clung to them.

Those whose entire family in Leningrad had died sought help from friends and family who lived farther away. It is painful to read their letters. They try to convey, as vividly and touchingly as they can, their loneliness, vulnerability and ill health. Each does their best, often with childish directness, hoping for an immediate response, sure that help cannot be refused once people know how they are suffering.

Galya Kabanova, whose mother and father died during the Time of Death, pinned all her hopes on her aunt Natalia Kharitonova. From

16 February, the day her mother died, she writes constantly to her, sending two telegrams and four letters. There is no reply. She worries that she may have failed to get through to her aunt; perhaps her younger brother, Slava, will be more successful. He is not so good at grammar and spelling but, who knows, perhaps his artless appeal will work. Here is his letter: 'Oh Aunt Natasha how much Galya and me have gone through in this war. Bombing hunger and then the dirt and epidemics. If I wrote it you probly won't believe it all. On 24 November it was Daddy's funeral. On 15 January it was Granny's and Aunt Liza's funeral. On 28 January it was Mummy's funeral. Me and Galya are together with no family oh it is horrid Aunt Natasha you are our only hope please come soon.'[45]

Natalia Kharitonova posted a letter on 1 March, which Galya received at the end of March or beginning of April. Her aunt knew nothing about the fate of the family and, in the hope that when she did she would surely help, Galya again related their tragic fate: 'So, then, on 16 February Mother died. On 16 November Father died. On 10 January Grandmother died and on 15 January Aunt Liza died.'[46] The last name in this heart-breaking list is that of her brother, Slava, who died in hospital after a bombardment of the city. She writes to her aunt about the conditions she is living in. 'All my things are dirty. All covered in cement dust. It is the kind of dirt you can only clean off with water, but there is no water. You have to bring it from far away, and queue for an hour for a bucketful, and it is not easy to take the used water to the cesspit.'

She needed to conclude with something personal, to express openly all she was feeling: 'Dear Aunt Natasha you are my only hope and I am waiting for you like my guardian angel. I do not think you will abandon me I am all alone.'[47]

After her mother died, Yelena Mukhina, a schoolgirl, just wanted to get out of Leningrad. She had no family left and was hungry almost every day. She could not work and was afraid that if she was categorized as an 'unemployed dependant' she would be forced to do all the dirtiest jobs: 'When it gets warmer, all the filth will thaw out, there will be a lot of work and they may even send me to the cemetery to bury dead bodies. No, I'd much rather move to Zhenya.'[48]

Zhenya is her aunt. She has had no news from her, but the image of this woman is painted in her diary in glowing colours. She is kind, responsive, closer to her than anyone else. Yelena loves her and it will be wonderful to stay with her. She will feed and never abandon her. She is a symbol of hope. Zhenya's name first appeared in the diary when her mother died.

Almost at the same time as her mother, another woman who lived with the family, and whom everyone called Aka, died. Aka is mentioned several times in Yelena's telegrams: she needed to make it clear that she had been left completely alone. Her first telegram to Zhenya was sent on 4 February 1942: 'Mother and Aka died. Telegraph answer.'[49] There was no answer. She waited for a little over two weeks before deciding to appeal to her aunt again.

She did not know why there had been no answer, and her telegrams clearly reflect her worries and surmises. The first version she wrote runs, 'I am alone. Aka and Mother died. Can I come to you. Reply soon.' Yelena probably felt that was too categorical and pressing and, fastidious in matters of courtesy, she is reluctant to demand help openly. Perhaps her Aunt will herself invite her to come, and all that is needed is to let her know what has happened. Here is the second version: 'Only I am still alive. Aka and Mother have died. I am very weak.'[50]

That might be better, but she cannot afford to wait. It would, of course, be more honourable, but perhaps she should make it more specific, more dramatic? After all, why should she not just ask her aunt directly? Of course, she should justify her directness by describing the horrors she has been through. She needs to make it clear what killed her family, and that she could be next. Then, surely, she would be pitied! The third version reads, 'Aka and Mother died of starvation. I am very weak. Zhenya, may I stay with you?'[51]

6

Appeals for help were addressed not only to the directors of enterprises and institutions, or to family and friends. Christians and members of religious communities asked for support from the parishioners of the few churches still open at the time. Here is a typically tragic letter from one such supplicant, I. V. Lebedev, deputy choirmaster of the Cathedral of the Transfiguration. He wrote on 28 December 1941:

> I have to say I am slowly dying. My strength has been undermined. I am just skin and bones. For several days we have had nothing to eat but bread. Of course, everybody is in the same situation now, but we want to live. Save our lives. Also starving alongside me are my wife, daughter and 9-year-old grandson whose father is at the front. We have no food and no money. Save our lives![52]

The themes in parishioners' appeals were very similar. What is distinctive about their letters is a more rapturous tone, greater intensity, a heightened sense of drama. The main theme is a simple desire not to die, without any emotive assurances that this is because of a desire to live to see a better future, to survive to see the darkness vanquished, or to contribute to the common cause. It is expressed with a frankness rare in 'secular' appeals. Twice in Lebedev's letter, he repeats the plea, 'Save our lives!' There are other examples. 'I beg you, do not let me die. Help me to get out of this terrible situation' – such is the request addressed to the Cathedral of the Transfiguration in October 1941 by A. Galuzin.[53] The letter from another parishioner, I. P. Bolshev, sent on 10 January 1942, is a real cry for help: 'My situation is appalling. Help! I want to go on living.'[54] Perhaps they felt these were the most compelling grounds on which to appeal to the Church, which rejected despondency as a sin and valued human life above all else.

People on the brink of the grave often had no more strength to endure their suffering. Nothing held them back: they had no interest in manners, and made no attempt to mask what they wanted. 'I want soup! Soup, soup! Desperately!', her uncle told Olga Grechina when he came to help at her mother's funeral.[55] 'I am terribly hungry', P. M. Samarin told a relative. He asked her to send him potato peelings.[56] Someone visiting N. L. Mikhaleva blatantly 'asked me to give him food because he was so starved he could hardly walk'.[57]

In the Molotov factory canteen, one of the workers cried, 'wanting to be given more soup.'[58] Many heard people crying like that. M. P. Pelevin noticed starving Leningraders in queues who bought their bread and promptly ate the entire daily ration and hoped to buy the same again using the next day's coupons: 'They asked the assistants to give them bread on credit one last time, and cried quietly, begging the assistant to be kind to them.'[59]

People facing death had no interest in good manners. They had no strength left to wait for people to take pity on them, and no hope. All that was left was to beg, no matter what, to beg in the face of every imaginable humiliation. They might know that life was very bad for other people, but still beg for a crumb at least. 'Vera Nikolaevna, my dear friend, help me. I can't stand it any longer. Give me something, anything! I am dying, dying, even just a sip of hot water', Vera Nikolskaya's weeping neighbour begged her.[60] She had no hot water. 'Well, even just give me a cigarette.' He was given a cigarette but could not restrain himself. If someone was kind, if they shared once, you could ask them again, because no one else was going to help: 'Give me a piece of bread, for God's sake.' He cannot believe it when only a small piece is broken off for him:'Well, even that I can eat !!!' He carries on complaining, 'Never a penny left, never a log of firewood.'[61]

'His hands were black as soot, his face dirty, less a face than a skull with dirty skin stretched over it, and terrible, pleading, hungry eyes.'[62] That is Nikolskaya's portrait of this man, starving, ready to do anything, because otherwise he is finished, no longer able to resist, doomed. Lev Razumovsky describes a similar case. His neighbour came into his apartment too. The man had changed so much he did not at first recognize him. And another only too familiar picture: 'Tatiana Maximovna, perhaps a piece of bread? I've had nothing to eat for three days.' She has no bread to spare. 'Tatiana Maximovna, maybe a bowl of soup? A little one? Maybe some peelings?' His neighbours too have nothing, but who knows? Perhaps they will take pity and give him something. He relates a terrible tale. His wife has taken his bread away from him, an old man without the strength to stand up for himself: 'They took everything, all my ration cards, all the bread. Everything. They haven't given me a piece of bread for three days.' The old man cried: 'I'm so weak now. I can't go out for the bread myself. Three days they haven't given me a piece. They beat me. They beat me every day.' His speech is slurred, not speech but exclamations: 'They're out for now. I've come down to you. I have no one else to turn to. Tatiana Maximovna, my dear . . .'[63]

7

Something broke irreparably. If the starving and helpless were spurned, they would come back anyway and again ask those selfsame people. They were pushed away, sometimes roughly but, as if unaware of the humiliation, remained just as ready to beg and pour out their hearts. If a kindergarten refused to take a child, they would abandon it at the door.[64] Dmitry Likhachev told the story of a relative who begged him on his knees for bread.[65] One of P. M. Samarin's colleagues all but snatched a piece of bread out of his hands: 'He wouldn't give up – give it to me, give it to me!'[66] You had only to light up a cigarette outside and, as A. I. Vinokurov noted, 'you could be sure someone would come up and start tearfully begging you to let him finish smoking it'.[67]

People would turn in desperation, on the threshold between life and death, to anyone, without bothering to see who they were talking to.[68] And yet, even then they would try to comply with moral precepts, although perhaps not always and perhaps not completely. In appealing for help, they observed the proprieties of normal, everyday requests, with their characteristic apologies, explanations and promises. They did, however, acquire a particular 'siege' spin.

First and foremost, we note their emotionality. Even the most trivial request was often accompanied by a flood of emotive effusions. They were typically full of vivid outpourings of the heart. The ubiquity of appeals was down to the realities of life under siege. You needed support to do anything: where before you could do something on your own, you now most definitely needed the involvement of others. Accordingly, the language of appeals was refined and adapted, and acquired certain nuances. The language mirrored survival techniques which would have been unusual in the past.

Appeals took on a persistence which it would be difficult to discover before the siege. People were not prepared, as they often were in the past, to oblige someone else with supplementary explanations and excuses. They became more finicky than in the past. There was a desire to shift responsibility for your fate on to the shoulders of others, without particularly concerning yourself about whether it was a burden they could be expected to bear. And yet, seeing the generosity in others, and being conscious of how much they owed to others, people were still capable not only of asking, but also of giving help. Charity became more deep-rooted, because neglecting it made survival impossible. Why would people have appealed for help if they had not known that others might feel ashamed to refuse support to someone even more malnourished than themselves?

Expressing gratitude for help

1

Like anybody else, victims of the siege did all they could to thank those
to whom they were indebted. Nobody, of course, would ask for a gift in
return, but reciprocity was expected, and a refusal to share, especially in a
time of difficulty, caused resentment.

Lyudmila Ronchevskaya, a copyist at the Russian Museum, recalled
having been able to 'feed up a little' a girl who had once been taught by her
mother. Being very hungry, the girl could not restrain herself and gobbled
up a three-day ration of bread, which 'at that time was lethal'. With some
ceremony, the girl she had rescued came back a few days later and insisted
she should come home with her. She had been sent a parcel. This ceremo-
niousness is a human characteristic, a desire to surprise, to amaze, to see
someone delighted at receiving something completely unexpected, to turn
the act of giving into a little performance. It survived in Leningrad during
the siege. They shared the contents of the parcel, but that was not all: 'She
would not let me go back home, and set herself the task of getting me back
on my feet.'[69] In April 1942, as a valued specialist, Ronchevskaya received
'very generous rations', and makes a point of stressing how happy she was
to share them with her new friend.[70]

We see this pendulum of good deeds at work also in the diary of
Alexandra Borovikova. When a friend gave her two packs of cigarettes
and a box of matches, she sent her some potatoes and noted in her diary,
'I might go and buy something and send her another parcel.'[71] The degree
of gratitude was measured not only by the size of the gift, but also by how
unexpected it was, and the delight with which it was received. People tried
to show their gratitude immediately with whatever was to hand. 'Come
with me. I'll give you all I have left. I still have a wardrobe with a mirror.
Take it!', a tearful woman exclaimed. She was wrapped in a filthy shawl
and her face was thin, dark and ravaged by hunger. She asked a Red
Army servicewoman for bread, and had unexpectedly been given half a
loaf.[72]

Dmitry Likhachev remembered a relative he had regaled with dried
black bread bringing dolls for his daughter, and not forgetting to emphasize that they were worth a lot of money.[73] Boris Gorodetsky, a professor
at the Library Institute, had no food to offer a student who brought him a
loaf of bread to help him get well again, so gave her a book.[74]

Normally, the recipient of a gift would promise to give at least something in return, even though nothing was asked for. When A. A. Gryaznov
was in the canteen, he saw a girl 'staring at the diners with eyes greedy with
hunger'.[75] Noticing his 'compassionate gaze', she sat down beside him and
told him her doleful story, which was only too common: she lived outside
the city but had come in to bury her mother. He gave her 25 grams of
cereal, a piece of bread and offered her some soup. She immediately under-

took to repay him tomorrow by guiding him through the 'prohibited zone' in Koltushi where there were stores of potatoes, horsemeat and more.[76] He even believed her, although he could not help noticing how avidly she had wolfed her meal. He had not, after all, asked for anything; she could simply have left without promising anything in return, but there is something noteworthy about her impulse not to go away without offering at least the prospect of help.

It would be entirely mistaken to suggest there is any thought-through calculation here, but it is entirely typical for the first, almost instinctive, response to a gift to be a desire to reward someone for their kindness.[77] Where they were unable immediately to repay one good deed with another, people would do so weeks or months later, invariably making reference to what their act was in return for. It is, admittedly, often difficult to separate a return gift from more general support for the vulnerable which would have been offered in any case. A gift could induce a person hardened by the chaos of the siege to return to the moral standards they had upheld in the past, if within certain limits. In deciding to thank someone who, through all the troubles, managed to remain generous, people in their debt were conscious that that person too was suffering hardship. This impulse had a knock-on effect, often bringing together citizens who until then had been strangers.

Vladislav Grigoriev recalled his grandmother bringing on a sledge a special ration in the form of a sack of grain, a rarity in those times. She was never going to be able to carry it up to the fourth floor where she lived, but was afraid to shout for her grandson, not wanting to attract attention. Neither, however, did she want to leave the sack down in the yard. A woman was passing by carrying a bundle of firewood, and she appealed to her. 'Could you help me lift this sledge? It's too heavy for me.'[78] According to Grigoriev, what followed came as a surprise to the woman, although it would have been unusual for a starving person to agree to carry a heavy sack up so many flights of stairs without anticipating anything in return. His grandmother poured her out some of the grain and some sugar.[79]

The woman was taken aback. She might well have been hoping for something, but evidently was not expecting such a generous gift. As usual in such cases, her first, almost reflex, response was to want to give something in return: 'She was so pleased. She left my grandmother the bundle of firewood.'[80] She came back later on more than one occasion, probably hoping for something to eat, but invariably brought in return a bundle of firewood. The warmth of human generosity kept the pendulum of good deeds swinging.

2

Alexander Fadeyev noted what an elderly woman said to a Red Army soldier who helped her up onto the platform of a tram: 'Thank you, son. For that you will stay alive. No bullet shall find you.'[81] Those who had nothing to give in return for a kindness would instead try to cheer those who helped them by saying something pleasant to them.

Yu. Tsimbalin, to whom N. L. Mikhaleva gave half a bowl of meatless soup with some pieces of bread, told her that the authorities would shortly be issuing 'sanatorium rations', that the siege had been raised, and that commercial shops would reopen.[82] 'I imagine the poor chap will die', she noted in her diary.[83] He had nothing and the only person sharing food with him was this good Christian woman. He did his best to thank her by giving her hope with these rumours.

People overcame their embarrassment, suppressed their vanity, and showed no pride. 'He bows at the feet of the girl who has helped him', Z. V. Vinogradova, secretary of the Dzerzhinsky district Party committee, reported of a starvation victim picked up in the street by staff of the Russian Red Cross.[84] Boris Bernstein was clearly stunned when he met up with a colleague he had got into hospital: 'How he thanked me. He kissed my hand and said "You are the person nearest and dearest to me."'[85] The man had been starving for a long time and knew the value of the help he had been given: 'He ate greedily, with one hand under his chin to make sure not a crumb of bread was lost.'[86]

Enjoying the hospitality of someone else's apartment, living in warmth, people would do their utmost to make themselves useful. Irina Zelenskaya's daughter, in her fifth month of pregnancy, brought water from the Neva ('a fair distance') in icy temperatures.[87] The relatives she and her husband were living with were far from overjoyed about taking in their new guests. Her mother felt that and so, no doubt, did the daughter: 'She does everything she can to compensate for her presence in someone else's family.'[88]

This feeling is expressed very emotionally and naively by A. I. Kochetova. In that terrible winter she found herself having to warm herself at other people's hearths. All alone, the only person she had to complain to was her mother: 'For ten days I went without any bread at all and drank only one bowl of soup each day. Someone had stolen my bread ration card. I had eaten all my food and lived only on grain. Then, in the last two days of November, there wasn't even any grain, so I had to go and visit Alla Alexandrovna.'

It was shaming, but there was nothing to be done about it: 'When I'm on my way to work I slip over five or six times because I have no strength left.'

She was welcomed warmly. Nobody tried to send her away, or insulted or reproached her. She writes in a state of euphoria: 'She welcomed me very, very kindly, poured me three cups of cocoa and gave me an oilcake. I am treated well and always allowed to stay overnight when I visit.' She would certainly like to go back, but she feels shy and embarrassed: 'It's awkward, but perhaps I'll visit them again tomorrow.'

She did go to see her again: 'We even eat together. Oh, Mummy, I'm so pleased. I feel very happy. I sleep on the couch in her room.' She will find ways to thank her. She cannot give her any bread, but is willing to fetch water, to tend the stove and walk to the shop: 'Today I dusted the room. I do everything I can.' Alla's husband, Spiridon Moiseyevich, 'likes to talk', so of course she makes conversation with him. How could she not? They have come to the rescue: 'It is warm in the room, and for me that is the main thing. Spiridon Moiseyevich gave me a pair of felt boots. Altogether, I have been given refuge by kind people.'[89]

To warm themselves by a stove, with people who had retained their sense of charity, to tell them all your woes, to feel their care and affection, that was absolutely the most these victims of the siege needed when they were accepted into someone else's home. Lonely and bewildered, tossed about by the storms of wartime, they will listen to any advice, and take it. They will carry out any request, and are always ready to tell their story, even to people they barely know. N. P. Zavetnovskaya tells the tale of one girl who had lost all her family. She says, 'Lelya helps me very often. She is a funny person, but a good girl and kind-hearted. She is lonely, asks me to be kind and to help her. She cannot really cope with life.'[90]

The ritual of expressing gratitude was inevitable, and not only because it was traditional. People who were rude and did not observe the rules of courtesy were usually shunned. Few people in these hungry times would risk seeming ungrateful. Expressing gratitude, whether with eloquent verbosity or by awkward, angular gestures, was a custom universally honoured. Even children, engulfed by the nightmare of the siege, understood how important it was to respond to the kindness of those coming to their aid. Olga Peto encountered a hungry boy in the street and took him to the children's reception centre. He was fed and when, after a few days, he cheered up a bit, he began asking to be given some work 'so as to help'.[91] Rita Malkova, handed in at a children's home, was taken along with other inmates to hospital: 'Their bodies were covered in festering sores.' The doctors and nurses heard that the children gave performances and asked them to put one on for them: 'We gave them a concert, dancing and singing, right there in the ward.'[92] What other way could there be for the children and orphans from a children's home to repay the miracle of bread and warmth, other than by dancing on their stick-like legs, bent by malnutrition?

3

Not everyone had something of value to offer their saviours. The best they could do was promise something in the future. There is a lot that is naive and touching in this. People hoped to give their friends a slap-up meal when the siege was raised, and a dying girl, whose friends had clubbed together to get her food, promised that, after the war, she would present them with a bouquet, 'not an ordinary one, but one of young branches with sticky leaves'.[93] The special feeling after receiving an unexpected gift often encouraged the recipient to express their gratitude in a clear and far from trivial manner. Those branches with their green leaves could hardly be dismissed as a conventionally romantic gesture. Like the endless talk about bread, it stood in for the warmth that seemed so unattainable in the icy chill of frozen houses.

Further evidence of the gratitude people felt obliged to express is found in letters sent to various state and public organizations.[94] Their contents are very similar, although they come from different people. Usually they follow a standard pattern: a description of the plight the person was in, then gratitude (to named individuals), or thanking the youth group members who helped, and the Party or Komsomol committees charged with taking care of Leningraders.[95] There were departures from that overall scheme, depending on the individual style of the writer, but as a whole it remained fixed. Nearly always, those writing the letters were motivated solely by gratitude.[96] Possibly they had at the back of their mind that the testimonial might lead to preferment of those who had helped them, but the letters are primarily an expression of gratitude addressed personally to whoever had assisted them, and are evidence of a sincere, spontaneous impulse not organized from above.

In the language of letters sent to the committees of the Komsomol and Red Cross, the bureaucratese is palpable. Of course, these are not personal, family letters with all the diversity of mood and directness, emotion and incisiveness typical of that genre. It is not always clear how far the writers are trying to tailor their language to official stereotypes. Even in the most stunted appeals, they are noticeably trying to break out of the fetters of cliché and rhetoric. Here, in full, is one such document:

To the Lenin District Committee of the All-Union Leninist Young Communist League

Scurvy (scorbutus) cut down myself and my wife at the same time. We had become two helpless, bedridden patients. Then we wrote a letter to the Lenin District Committee of the Komsomol asking for help. We were given it almost without delay. Every day Komsomol comrades came to help us as best they could. We would like, however, to single out deservedly and thank individually Tamara Tarasovna Tuzanskaya thanks to whose care and help my wife is back on her feet and I am on the mend.

T. T. Tuzanskaya cared for us as if we were her own parents (calling the doctor several times, receiving money on our behalf, fetching meals from the canteen, bringing water and cleaning our apartment). Thanks to her my wife was granted an enhanced diet.

In addition to the above-mentioned assistance, T. T. Tuzanskaya extended moral support to us like nobody else over the fact that our son was at the front. Moreover, although now she has been transferred to other work in the District Committee, she continues to help us in every way in her spare time, and all this selflessly and voluntarily.

Allow me to convey our deep and heartfelt thanks to the Lenin District Committee of the Komsomol in the person of T. T. Tuzanskaya for your concern and care for us.

T. T. Tuzanskaya is a worthy daughter of the Leninist Young Communist League, honest, decent and responsive to the suffering of

others. She has saved my wife from death and got me back on my feet
to be of further service to the country.
Mikhail Grigorievich Andreyev.[97]

The repetition is obtrusive, and there is a particular quality in the letter's long-windedness. We can feel the live, emotional language forcing its
way through the thickets of cliché about moral support, being of service
to the country, and 'the above-mentioned assistance'. You cannot say in
officialese, 'cared for us as if we were her own parents', 'saved my wife
from death and got me back on my feet', 'decent and responsive to the
suffering of others'. The repetition may signal an access of emotion when
you cannot, as is customary in bureaucratic dealings, make do with two or
three hackneyed words, when what you want is to thank someone again
and again for all they have given you.

In other letters we know about, these deviations from convention are
even more apparent. There is good reason why they were selected by those
who published them, because the most striking aspects of life during the
siege are depicted here not only in great detail but also with great emotion.
'We lonely, ill people were helpless, but at the centre we were met with
a level of concern which was quite unexpected', some hospital patients
wrote to the district committee of the Russian Red Cross.[98] A letter to
L. A. Peshcherskaya seems to kick over all the traces expected in a letter
to an official: 'There are three of them, Nina, Tosya and Panya. They
treated me like a dear, close friend. I am weeping tears of joy. How grateful I am to these comrades. I feel I have nobody closer to me.'[99] From a
reading of A. N. Loktionova's letter, it is difficult to decide to whom it is
actually addressed. Although sent to the Primorsky District Committee of
the Komsomol, it contains lines like, 'This wonderful girl even took the
trouble to bring the note admitting me to hospital to my own home. It was
like something out of a fairy tale! Thank you, my dears, for your marvellous, heartfelt work. I am completely alone, and your concern and sympathy have made me feel that in our great, beautiful city I have a family.'[100]

In these letters, we find an assemblage of all the most distressing aspects
of the siege, an abyss from which it could be impossible to escape unaided.
This only served to emphasize how crucial the help extended had been. It
was presented as a heroic act, and to describe it in a fitting manner, suitably solemn words were looked for, even a touch of poetry.

It was often the case that people who were given support believed the
volunteers were not simply doing their duty, but had been sent to help
them by someone very high up, who evidently considered it especially
important that they in particular should survive. Anna Ostroumova-
Lebedeva was certain that a valuable gift of food had been sent to her by
Andrey Zhdanov personally. This explains the frequent expressions of
gratitude to the Party, the Komsomol and the Soviet regime. It is unlikely
that they were insincere, although the rhetoric may prompt the historian
to question them.

Letters can become very detailed and comprehensive when describing a painful loss. Quite possibly they were another way of unburdening oneself, continuing to dwell sorrowfully on the endless hardships of the siege. Letters of thanks are very conscientious in detailing how meals were brought, floors washed, wood chopped, bread rations collected. There is a marked tendency to present a normal action as something incomparable and to represent the helpers as paragons of virtue.

Letters of thanks to family, friends and acquaintances differ in content and tone from those to the world of officialdom, but here too judgements sometimes seem exaggerated. One can hardly believe that a tiny piece of food is enough to resurrect someone, but that is the kind of thing the writers insist on. 'Thank you for the 150 rubles and piece of bread you sent. You have saved my life. I am feeling better', Ye. Radeyev, a member of the choir, writes to parishioners of the Cathedral of the Transfiguration.[101] His letter ends, 'I used your money to buy firewood in the market.'[102] This is simultaneously an expression of gratitude, an acknowledgement of how sorely needed the gift was, and evidence that he spent the money wisely, so that continuing to help him will not be a waste of time.

4

We know little about the gestures, phrases and exclamations people used to express their appreciation during this time. The evidence is fragmentary and reflects only some of the most memorable incidents. 'I thanked him with great feeling', Vladimir G. Kulyabko writes after the director of his institute told him he was to be evacuated.[103] There are no further details and we can only guess at the scene.

'I kissed my mother-in-law, who was also weeping with joy.'[104] In this diary entry by P. M. Samarin, who had received an unexpected gift, there are again no further details.

In the diaries, there are often long lists of food people have been given. Enumerating the details of who ate how much of what was an extension of the endless discussion of food by those trapped in the siege. This was evidently needed by starving people as a displacement technique. This feature of the Time of Death comes through particularly clearly in Anna Ostroumova-Lebedeva's diary entry: 'Pyotr Yevgenievich came round today. He brought me a tiny piece of meat, four dried wild mushrooms and four frozen potatoes. I was extremely grateful to him for that, because all I have had to eat for the past week has been kelp soup and black bread.'[105]

Maria Mashkova, the librarian of the Public Library, describes the presents she received from Olga Berggolts (she was given 'a loaf of bread, a jar of rice, several packs of vitamin C, some Kapitansky pipe tobacco, a pack of Belomorkanal (White Sea Canal) cigarettes, a biscuit each for the children, a bar of compressed cocoa, some vodka with a bite (pieces of sausage) to go with it, and some lumps of dried pea soup and buckwheat porridge'). She feels an apology is necessary: 'I list this in such detail because it is all such a rarity, a miracle, an unbelievable delight.'[106] Yelena

Mukhina mentions similar rarities in her diary: 'We need to say thank you to England. They send us quite a few things, like cocoa, chocolate, real coffee, and sugar. It's all from England.'[107]

This listing of gifts was also a way of acknowledging the self-sacrifice other people have been capable of, their compassion expressed not only in words but in the form of a tiny piece of bread or cake.[108] For starving people, a small piece of cake was worth its weight in gold. For every scrap of food, they give thanks again and again.[109]

5

The more severe the hardships became for those caught in the siege, the more they noted acts of kindness towards themselves.

One of these was Vladimir G. Kulyabko, an engineer at an institute which was evacuated from Leningrad. On the journey he had to endure many insults and humiliations. He was travelling with young engineers, and they went out of their way to harass and even rob him. The old man was not strong and suffered in silence, but his hostility towards his 'bandit travelling companions' accumulated steadily: 'They fired up the stove and were determined not to let me warm myself by it. Only when I persisted in asking them several times to make room a little so that I could sit closer and warm myself up did they reluctantly make way, making it very clear how much they disliked having me as a fellow-passenger.'

He belongs to a different generation and speaks its language. He talks only very timidly about their 'cruel and completely unjustified complaints about me, who anybody else might have treated as a senior colleague'. Every word here betrays an intellectual, wounded by such brazen disregard for elementary good manners. It seemed no one would come to his aid, but someone did, and the entry describing it reveals just how moved he was. This is not his usual kind of entry, jotted down in haste, cursorily listing the sorrows of the Time of Death. The pace is more leisurely. We sense how much he would like this tale of a miracle of humane compassion to go on and on as he draws out the smallest details:

> My arms and legs became extremely swollen; it was very painful . . . I asked a rather young Red Army soldier who I thought seemed pleasant to help me remove my boots. He replied, 'Sit down, Pa, and I'll help. I can see you're finding it hard to stand.' I took off my felt boots and two pairs of socks and looked sadly at the blocks of wood I now have instead of feet. I put the boots on over a single pair of socks and that was easier, but it was still painful. I thanked him and hobbled off towards the exit.

Then we have a very detailed description of how the episode ended:

> The same Red Army soldier came after me and could see how hard I was finding it. I stopped and began rolling a cigarette. He came up

to me. 'Son', I said, 'here, have some good tobacco.' 'No', he said, 'thank you. I don't smoke.' He asked what was wrong with me and I asked him who he was and where he came from. When I had lit the cigarette, I carried on towards the exit. He came after me again and said, 'Pa, you're finding it difficult to walk, and it's dark outside. Let me take you back.' He took my arm, carefully brought me back to my carriage, and there we said goodbye.

After all the sneering and rudeness and cynicism, at last he had met someone kind. He bursts out, 'I was so pleased to have met someone who behaved decently towards a sick, suffering old man.' He was even more moved when later another Red Army soldier helped carry his things to where he was to stay: 'I was so touched that tears came to my eyes. My reaction was so strong after travelling for five days in the company of cruel, heartless young swine.'[110]

The impressionable Yelena Mukhina also felt intense gratitude after all the disasters which had so undermined her. She had still had no answer from the aunt she was hoping would take her in. She was cold, hungry, lonely, depressed, and with nowhere to turn for pity or help. In desperation, she went to some people she knew. How suddenly the whole tone of her diary changes: 'I have been welcomed here as if I were one of the family. Everybody was so glad to see me. Galya hugged and kissed me. She and her father have warmly invited me to move here and stay with them. They promise to help me in every way they can.'[111]

She had not expected to be received so kindly, and is sure they have been brought together by their shared misfortune: her friend's mother has died too. She now identifies with all their concerns, as if this is her own family. When they are evacuated, they will, of course, go together: 'They will take me as their daughter.' She takes very personally the suffering of these people and, together with Galya, fears for the health of the father. She tells Galya she is sure he will recover. And she cannot contain her emotion, which almost makes her shout with joy: 'I'm suddenly alive again. I'm not alone. I have friends now. What a joy, what happiness!'[112]

6

It is an ineradicable memory left by the siege. Years later, one might expect to find some gifts less valued, on the grounds that they had been very small, or just against the background of other more dramatic matters. But no! Even the meanest gift is firmly lodged in the mind, and mentioned in stories detailed or brief, but always emotive. The strength of feeling experienced in that first moment continues undiminished, decades later.

When they recall those who helped to save their lives, survivors of the siege will invariably remind those listening of how difficult it was to remain a decent human being at that time. N. Shubarkina wrote about the 13-year-old sister who 'could barely move around because of the starvation and scurvy', but who kept feeding her: 'I am so grateful to her.

Throughout my life she has served me as a role model.'[113] K. Chikhacheva told the story of R. Itse, a student who gave her his coupons when, at death's door and with two children to care for, she lost her ration cards: 'I still remember that day with deep emotion and gratitude.'[114] Evelina Soloviova remembered a gift from her husband, who was being treated for a wound and was himself emaciated and hungry, of a bar of chocolate, several pieces of dried bread and pieces of sugar: 'That has stayed in my memory for a whole lifetime.'[115] 'He will live on in my heart forever', was A. Samulenkova's reaction to the act of the head of her local air defence unit who, 'although he too was starving', gave her his ration cards when she lost hers.[116] 'Remember a kindness for the rest of your life', was the advice of Ye. Krivobodrova's father, which she recalled many years later. He had been fed by a not especially close friend, 'even though he was starving himself'.[117]

In memoirs, tales of kindness, where even a tiny gift is recollected, where every act of charity is recounted with exclamations of admiration, the desire to see, unconditionally, only the very best in people, is highly noticeable. R. Yakovleva, who collapsed from hunger in the street, was lifted up and taken to her home by a passing driver. She tried to repay him with a piece of bread, but he 'angrily' refused. His anger in this context is such an attractive reaction. It tells us he would not dream of taking advantage of another person's misfortune. His swollen face tells her that he too was starving, which makes his refusal of recompense even more impressive. We find everything in Yakovleva's gratitude – empathy, and the desire to express her unqualified appreciation of the action of this unknown driver: 'I was saved from imminent disaster by a truly good, selfless person. It was incredibly difficult at that time to turn down the offer of a piece of bread. I will always remember the young, swollen face and first name of that man who saved my life.'[118]

Mina Bochaver had in the Time of Death, like everybody else, to divide her bread into three pieces and stretch them out to last the whole day. It was all the more surprising, therefore, when a friend gave her a gift of real cocoa (without milk) and real sugar (not saccharin). As usual, she details this meticulously. Mina is sure her friend 'filched the sugar from her son's ration'. It is not clear whether someone told her this, which seems unlikely, or whether she was guessing, but she sees the episode as unambiguously heroic: 'I have remembered it all through my life, and to this day it brings tears of gratitude to my eyes to think about it. No words of mine can do justice to such human goodness and generosity in such a deadly situation.'[119]

People not only wrote in memoirs and diaries about gifts which saved their lives. They told their family and friends about them, and many other people they knew or did not know. S. Kuzmenko often walked back home past an army unit. She probably talked sometimes to the soldiers and, when she took to her bed (she was receiving only the rations for a 'dependant'), they noticed. Her life was saved by a pot of porridge one of the soldiers brought her: 'I did not see him again. I have a family, a husband, a daughter and son. I have told them about that soldier many times, but now it has occurred to me he may still be alive. If by chance he reads this letter, I would like him to know he has family living in Leningrad.'[120]

Ye. Bokaryova lost her purse with her ration cards outside the bakery. When she went back, she found a thin man (no memoirist ever fails to mention if someone was thin) waiting for her by the door. He returned the purse to her. She can write of him only using the best, most heartfelt, most elevated words: 'This man saved my life. All that I am able to write today is thanks to this great, amazingly honest man. My children know all about him, my grandchildren, of course, my sister and her family, and, of course, all my friends too . . .'. She cannot hold back the torrent of emotion, listing again and again the people she has told how honourable he was.[121]

The shock endured by those caught in the siege was so powerful that they carried on for years afterwards trying to find those who had saved their lives. Forty years later, R. Ozhogova was still looking for those who picked her off the street, took her to a children's home, and sent her to be treated at the hospital. She has searched in the archives, but to no avail: 'It distresses me that for all these years I have not been able to say thank you to the people who saved me in those dark, terrible years of starvation. If only I could find them! I never stop thinking about that.'[122]

Vladislav Glinka, who worked at the Hermitage, had similar feelings. In the Time of Death, when all their resources had been exhausted and his starving family were bedridden, he decided to sell his books. The dealer in rare books found them of no interest, but he met two sailors at his stall who were looking for foreign novels. He had some in his library at home, and invited them back.

The first thing that concerned them when they came into the apartment was not the books but Glinka's terribly emaciated daughter. They asked why she had been left behind in the city and how old she was. '"Nine," Lyalya told them herself, her deathly pale face peeping out from under a blanket.'

'The sailors looked at each other.' One took out of his bag a loaf of bread, some sugar and other food. The scene is clearly being described by a hungry man: 'One, two, three tins of meat.' When he offered them books in return, they replied shortly, 'That's all right', and left. He did not see them again.

'When I went back to our room, the three of us were crying. Lyalya was standing by the table counting the sugar lumps.'

He looked for them for many years. After the war, he asked friends, who were rear admirals, to help him find the officer whose name he remembered. They had no success. He did not give up. He appealed to yet another friend who was a vice-admiral, but he too could find no trace. He wrote to the archivist at the Ministry of Defence, searching tirelessly. He just could not find closure: 'At that terrible time when all around there seemed to be only death, cheating, greed and looting, for a quarter of an hour two complete strangers came into our lives, and left in them forever the pure light of immaculate compassion.'[123]

Part II

The Ethical Dimension

5

The family: compassion, consolation, love

Relations with one's nearest and dearest are rarely idyllic. The dramatic circumstances of the terrible first winter of the siege put these under particular strain, leaving even less room than usual for compromise, and starkly exposing emotions and intentions. Families quarrelled and made up, blamed and forgave. There is nothing consistent about their joys and grievances. Not everyone was able to share out their piece of bread, and not only because it was tiny. Not everyone was prepared to give comfort to the weakened, to give shelter to those in need, or to resist the temptation to help themselves to what belonged to others. All that is true, but it is not what matters most.

Sympathy for the sick and the hungry is often expressed in the tone of the story told about them and the episodes a witness chose to record. Compassion is noticeable even in the descriptions of loved ones whose appearance had changed out of all recognition. 'My poor Mummy, so skinny, her head often spinning from exhaustion and malnutrition'; 'Dad, pale and as thin as a skeleton.'[1] 'A terrifying skull with dirty skin stretched over it.'[2] 'Her arms are in a terrible state.'[3] 'He is frightening, his face all swollen.'[4] The way people on the brink of the abyss were relentlessly undermined evoked a whole range of emotions, sometimes contradictory, in those who saw them, and which it could be difficult to control in that first minute, when they needed to be concealed. There was fear and horror, and other things people might later be ashamed of, but one thing we do not find in their descriptions is uncaring scrutiny. Family members try to turn away, to avert their gaze from gaunt faces suddenly aged. We are not given a snapshot of a face now monstrously distorted, but something retouched. Our witnesses try to find words which will not be cruel.

Often in their letters, diaries and memoirs, Leningraders express dismay that they were so powerless to help those near and dear to them, especially children. They are dismayed and ashamed. We can read in their words the anguish, and the desire to try to explain what they did – sometimes more articulately, sometimes less, but somehow always in broken sentences. Dmitry Pavlov heard the testimony of a woman working in a factory:

'To watch my children starving – I have three of them – and feel helpless, there could be nothing worse. They are waiting for bread, but where am I to get it?'[5] Veronika Opakhova expresses the same feeling more briefly, but perhaps even more tellingly: 'My children had been taught not to ask for things, but their eyes, their beseeching eyes! I just can't tell you how that felt.'[6]

The eyes of starving children inflicted the most searing pain of all. Lyudmila Volkova recalled days when they were unable to obtain their ration of bread: 'How our mother suffered then at having nothing she could give us to eat.'[7] Varvara Vraskaya had no option but to take biscuits instead of bread (of which the bread shop had none). She sent them in meagre portions, two per day, to her 6-year-old daughter in hospital. The little girl had just learned to write and passed notes to her mother which all had the same message: 'Do not send two biscuits, send the packet.' 'That upset me more than anything else', she recalled.[8]

One can cite many such stories, each more tragic than the last: brief stories without literary pretensions, and all the more telling for that. When parents look at their children, they see everything: the dreaded symptoms of decline or signs of convalescence, touching deeds and the inexorable approach of disaster. How someone looks at a child, what they notice, what they dwell on and what they try to pass over, enables us to assess the degree to which they are charitable. 'My nephew has a disproportionately large head and tiny body. He looks like a toothless little gnome. In his eyes you see a degree of suffering and dismay intolerable in one so young. I brought two biscuits. Little Yury, trembling with impatience, grabbed them and clutched them in his wrinkled, almost chicken-like little hands', recalls Pyotr Kapitsa.[9] This portrait of a failing child, which softens the naturalistic details as far as possible, is accompanied by a description of his behaviour. He may have done many things, but only those actions which really make us feel for him are mentioned (he 'grabbed', he was 'trembling with impatience', he 'devoured them avidly').

The eye of the memoirist does not skate over the surface of a scene, neutrally communicating details. It picks out what is most terrible and grievous. 'Suffering intolerable in one so young' is a value judgement, not a detail in a portrait. It speaks of a profound empathy with another person, an effort to convey the measure of what they have endured.

Artist Anna Ostroumova-Lebedeva's description of children during the siege gradually fills up with details. We can see from her lengthy diary entry for 16 November 1941 how she brings out the tragedy of the situation: 'It pains me to look at my nephews: they are as pale and thin as paper. Day by day they become increasingly apathetic and dejected.' Soon, one of them died. In the following entries about the survivor, Petya, the sense of how close he is to death predominates. We find everything in Ostroumova-Lebedeva's diary: the starvation, the cold, the bombing, the inconsolable grief, but her writing about Petyunechka, as she calls him, is suffused with heart-rending emotion. The entries become increasingly anxious: he 'looks as pale as a corpse, he is impossibly thin' (24 May 1942); he is 'very weak and lethargic; his eyes are pale and sad' (27 May 1942); he is 'weak and walks very slowly, barely moving his feet' (30 May 1942). Her pity for the doomed boy is not confined to the descriptions of his appearance. It is manifest in other lines where it intensifies the sense of his misery: 'He sat by the open window, looking at the beauty of the sky, the springtime clouds and the leaves coming out on the trees and said quietly, "How wonderful!"'

This desperately emaciated 15-year-old boy, who leans on a walking stick in order not to fall, is sensitive, talented and capable of appreciating beauty. He sketches well and is gentle and caring. The artist takes in every detail of his personality, the intensity of her vision a sure sign of her acute awareness of what she is experiencing. On 24 May 1942, Petya was unable to get to the tram without assistance, but just three days later Ostroumova-Lebedeva is writing optimistically, 'To a tiny, quite microscopic, extent he is better.'[10] She does not tell us she was sharing food with her nephew, but it is reasonable to assume he was not only being taught how to paint on his visits, but also hoping to be fed. For the artist, who was a kind and sensitive woman, that was only to be expected, but to have to watch the way a starving child eats . . .

2

The heartbreak caused by the sight of children's suffering is particularly evident in the diary of Maria Mashkova. Her children, Galya and Vadim, are just as emaciated as their mother and father. The boy tries his utmost to be strong: his little sister finds it more of a struggle. It is impossible to explain to her all that is happening, and she has not the strength to cope with everything. She knows she should not ask for bread, but cannot help it. All this is noticed by her mother's eye. How painful it is for her to record, on 20 February 1942, 'Galya asked Vadik, in a whisper, for some dried bread.' Her pain only worsens: 'The children in the gloomy room, hungry, huddle in the corners.' 'In the evenings, Galya gazes imploringly at Vadik, silently begging for a piece of his bread', she writes in her diary the next day.

Her eye picks out in minutest detail all the good that is in her daughter: 'Galya is sweet, with her twittering, her little, hungry eyes, her dreams of food and her curiosity about everything around her.' Here is how she describes her daughter receiving a May Day gift at a Children's Hearth day centre: 'She was afraid to let go of the bag, and time and time again took out and put back the few sweets, two biscuits, raisins and small spiced honey bun.'[11] The role of a miser seems unnatural and even comical for a little girl, but for her this was no game, a hungry child afraid of losing a few raisins and fingering them again and again, like a priceless treasure.

'The life of my children is distorted, terrible, even, but they are touchingly good', Mashkova writes in her diary on 25 February 1942.[12] Through all the entries about rations, grumbles and tears, and shame at not being able to give her children more than their share, her admiration for them and her pity shine through, sometimes not explicit, but there to be felt in even the briefest descriptions.

In a letter sent by S. A. Pavlova in January 1942, we find the same loving watchfulness over her children, chilled and dressed in shabby clothes as they are. Her daughter Nadya wears a little flannel dress and knitted blouse under an Orenburg shawl. It is not enough: 'Her little arms are swollen, her cheeks and nose are purple and blue.'[13] The children are emaciated, and the first pitiful words the mother hears from the little girl as she comes into the room are: 'Give bread.' How can that not evoke compassion? And how can Pavlova's heart not bleed at the sight of her 12-year-old son, no better dressed, with his 'little, waxen face' and dark rings under his eyes, indifferent to everything, his eyes fixed only on his mother's bag?

'My children's distorted life', but a mother's eye cannot always dwell on what is crippling her children. Compassion is incompatible with the endless listing of signs of catastrophe imprinted like a stigma on their faces. The diarist cannot, in the end, continue and abandons this painful enumeration. She will write only about goodness and kindness.

In the diary of Professor Lev Kogan of the Library Institute, we read constantly about how hungry his children are: 'There is nothing to eat. It is hard to hear the children asking for food'; 'First thing in the morning the children eagerly fell upon the butter. It pains you to look at them. Now they dream of sugar and chocolate.'[14] This builds up, repeats day after day and becomes unbearable. The entries become increasingly crestfallen, extreme, bordering on desperate. 'We will have to transfer the children to a Hearth. They can feed them much better there than we can', he notes in his diary on 2 March 1942. This was not decided on in haste: he has concerns about epidemics, and has to work out whether they have enough money, but eventually makes up his mind. On 6 March 1942, the children 'received food from the Hearth'. He lists what they received and finds it difficult to stop: 'Today they were given a tasty, if small, meat patty, bread, and sugar for tea; for lunch there was delicious soup with dumplings, a decent helping of semolina with sweet milk and bread; in the afternoon, sugar for tea, and bread; and for dinner a sweet compote of dried fruit with dumplings and bread.'[15] Such listing of food received is nothing out of the ordinary: it takes up dozens of pages in siege diaries. In Professor Kogan's, it is unusual: he writes far more frequently about books, the state of his health and the situation in the city. As you read on, you begin to understand that this is not an account of the past day jotted down in haste, but something more. Every gram, every grain, every diminutive patty issued to the children and enumerated in excessive detail is enabling him to drive out, if only drop by drop, gram by gram, the torment he has been witnessing: 'For the first time, the children are well fed. We looked at them and rejoiced.'[16]

Compassion can be measured also by the concern shown for the lives of their children by those already dying. The advice passed on by the dying varied considerably, from requests not to waste money on a coffin to the conventional admonitions to take good care of themselves. One survivor of the siege recalled her father, when he was close to death, urging his family to take care of themselves, not 'waste their time' on him, and in particular asking his wife to make sure their daughter survived.[17] Was that the usual pattern in the besieged city? No. Far more frequently, we hear of people begging to be allowed to eat their fill before they die, of incoherent rambling, the cries and groans of those in their agony, and even accusations that their families are hiding bread from them. Nevertheless, fear for the future of their children often tormented the dying until the last, breaking through their loss of emotion, weakness and lapses of consciousness: 'The mother could not get up. Those of her children who were still alive were crawling over her. Everything was louse-ridden. The mother said to the Komsomol household squad, "Take them, take them. When I die, I will know my children are being cared for."'[18]

That was the final thing desperate people would agree to.[19] Ye. Skobeleva remembered how, after her father's death, her mother became increasingly worried about her, fearing that she herself would die soon and her daughter would be taken to an orphanage: 'If you don't do as you are told there, they make you kneel on peas and beat you cruelly.'[20] Her mother may not have known anything about conditions there, but had heard as a child about orphanages, or remembered something from her lessons in school. Orphanages were for children with no family, and what could be more terrible than that? The girl tried to catch her mother's eye, afraid of losing her and wondering who she could run to after she died if strangers would have no time for her.

She tried to argue with her mother that, during the shelling, she had taken refuge in a children's home and people had been kind to her and even given her a meal. The children there had seemed sad and thin, but that was true of everywhere in Leningrad: 'My mother listened attentively, hugged me even more tightly, and said nothing.'[21]

3

When he received news that his son, who had been evacuated from Leningrad, was dying, Alexey Yevdokimov wrote in his diary on 19 December 1941, 'Why can't I help? Or at least see him. I can't write. I can't keep myself from crying.'[22] Two days later, he writes, 'I can't get that terrible news out of my head.' It was several months later that he had a letter from his wife to say the boy was recovering. He read it in a daze, almost fainting: 'I wept.'[23] He describes his feelings with tremendous emotion, which testifies to the anguish he has endured. He tries to express it intensely and with originality, because only that, he feels, can convey it adequately.

A. V. Sirotova worked in a hospital and saw what her parents were eating: 'Soya meal cake (horrible, disgusting!), jelly made from wood glue!' She saw how swollen her father was, and that he could hardly stand. She was starving herself but drank only her soup, storing away her porridge in a glass jar: 'When father came home, he was so pleased with his "present".'[24] How often diarists try to convey as fully as they can the joy of starving people. Natalia Zavetnovskaya tried to support her husband: 'He was beginning to weaken.'[25] She went to a distant market. 'It was very difficult getting there. I was weak and my legs were swollen. I almost didn't make it', she reported in a letter to her daughter. She went there nevertheless, and in spite of the bitter cold, because she needed 'at all costs' to get food for her husband. She could not stay at the market for long and was able only to barter some belongings for bread. It was not enough, so the next day she again went out there, and 'barely managed' to drag herself back home, but she had achieved her goal and her husband 'ate properly for two days'.[26] Behind all the details is concealed what made her prepared to follow this Via dolorosa. There is not a word about love, but that is what her description of the episode is really about: how unbearable it was to see her husband suffering from being unable to eat 'properly', and we know from the notes about the siege just how terrible that could be. There is no way we can experience it ourselves, but the irresistible urge to let nothing get in the way of supporting and protecting loved ones tells us just how strong the ties of family were. Of course, much had changed, but there was a degree of pain which could make you cry out loud, as we know from the diary of Rita Malkova, one of the most tragic documents of the entire siege.

It is dreadful to read the descriptions of starving people who had the lowest priority during the siege. The infinite loneliness of the dying is the background to this sorrowful tale. Rita, a teenager, helped her skeletal mother, who constantly slipped and fell in the street, to get to a clinic where she faced an unpleasant and painful procedure. 'When she went in to the doctor's surgery I stayed outside the door', Rita recalls; 'I suddenly heard my mother cry out in pain, and I burst into tears.'[27] Finally, the procedure was finished, but she had barely taken her mother out of the clinic before they had to go back to have the same operation repeated. This time she refused to leave her mother alone in the doctor's surgery, and went in with her: 'My mother cried out again and so did I: "Doctor, don't do that!"'[28]

4

The wailing, groans, screams and entreaties of their family members could move even a starved, stumbling relative suffering blackouts to summon up the strength to do something effective. Not everyone was capable of helping, but there is a lot of evidence that something could explode in people at times of extreme emotional stress. The phenomenon is clearly registered in Izrail Nazimov's diary. On the day his father died, 8 February 1942, he decided not to leave his mother alone and took her home with him. He was very upset at the bereavement, but what he found hardest to bear was the sight of of his mother's suffering: 'How unhappy she was! She was weeping quietly to herself.'[29]

Everything is intense: his weeping mother, the bitterness of his loss, the memory of all the privation they have had to endure. It all, like a great wave, lifts a person, gives him no rest, forces out of him categorical, deeply personal, deeply felt expressions of emotion. At such a time it does not matter that the words may be hackneyed. Profound grief calls for strong, solemn, dramatic words. There is no place for banalities, and no sense of artificiality in such pathos. It would be strange indeed to encounter artifice at such a time. That day his grief was inconsolable: 'I am in tears as I write.'[30]

Comforting people calls for empathy. There was nothing different about condolence in the days of the siege, but great tact was called for. Words of comfort were being offered by people who were themselves in need of them, but saw that others were in a state of even greater despair and dejection. Everyone was only too familiar with the seemingly endless misery of daily life in Leningrad. What comfort could you expect from someone who had themselves passed through all the circles of hell? But people did want to hear words of comfort, just as they were willing to believe all the optimistic rumours. Few family members, finding themselves beside someone in tears, could not find words of sympathy which were so much needed, even if little practical help could be offered.

The language of condolence varied, depending on the degree of kinship, how much sympathy relatives had for each other, the psychological state they were in, and the extremity of their grief. Words of comfort for children were different again: simple, affectionate, sometimes in the terms of a fairy tale.[31]

We find the most precious testimony on sensitivity in letters. Here the individual voice is not mediated or overlaid by later accretions. Most letters, of course, were being sent outside the city, often to addressees who had experienced no horrors comparable to those of the letter writer. The contents of the letters are by and large quite similar, with injunctions to take care of yourself, to take care of your health, and not to worry about those still left in Leningrad. The writers are often very cautious and economical with information about the actual conditions they are living in, and this is probably not because of fear of the censor. Letters whose writers had reason to suppose they would be read by others besides the addressee are instantly recognizable by their unnatural optimism and spoof enthusiasm.

There is not usually anything very dramatic in the admonitions and exhortations. There are no grandiloquent phrases, and possibly the writers could not have come up with any even if they had wanted to. There are ordinary, straightforward expressions: 'don't worry', 'let's hope', 'don't be concerned', 'don't let it get you down', 'keep your spirits up', 'eat whenever you can', 'try to eat a good diet'. Almost every letter contains that latter injunction. From Natalia Zavetnovskaya's letter to her daughter, we see how shocked she was after visiting a relative: 'She is in a bad way, swollen from malnutrition.' Her advice is very specific: 'Do not grudge money for food. That is very important. Spend as much as you can afford. This worries me a great deal. If you have a chance to buy something in the bazaar, do.'[32]

Vladimir Zavetnovsky, immediately after giving a detailed account of the hell of the siege, says in a letter to his daughter, 'I am very concerned that the food situation in Perm [where she lived – S. Ya.] may be bad.'[33] 'You may be in dire need and, perhaps, swollen from hunger', Vladimir Lyublinsky wrote to his wife.[34]

The same concerns were shared by A. I. Kochetova, whose mother had been evacuated. Here she describes how she celebrated the New Year of 1942: 'I wolfed 350 grams of bread and felt a bit better.'[35] Eating her entire daily ration of bread without dividing it up into several portions, as was more usual, indicates extreme hunger. 'I felt a bit better', is a very exact diagnosis. She could not stop herself, and went on to drink a 'small bowl' of soup made with oats ('like they feed to horses'), to drink coffee without sugar, then coffee with salt, then to eat some 'small pancakes without butter' made from the remains of the oats. Everything was in tiny portions, without seasoning. Even after eating it she was hungry. She supposed her mother was probably just as hungry, and kept coming back to the subject:

Mummy, how are you getting along with your pension, and in general how are you doing for money? I've been waking up at four in the morning, unable to sleep any longer. So I was lying there and today had the idea of selling my bread – I'm hardly going to die of hunger in two days – and send you some money, if only a little. At work they still don't pay me much, and altogether I'm a bit short. That's the only way I'll be able to do it.[36]

Something quite remarkable is that, even as they report the horrors of the siege, Leningraders were offering help, in money and materially, to their families living far away. They could not send parcels, of course: it would have been well-nigh impossible to put one together, although occasionally even that was managed. F. L. Shuffer-Popova, when she received a parcel from a relative in Leningrad in early June 1942, was touched by the 'pharmaceutical doses of everything sent'. She realized immediately they must have 'sacrificed it from their own rations'.[37] Usually, what was sent was money. Vasiliy Chekrizov, transferring money to his family, was glad they had left the city: he could not imagine how he would have looked his son in the eye 'seeing him hungry'.[38] V. N. Dvoretskaya regularly sent 200–400 rubles to her eldest daughter, who had gone to Siberia together with her younger sisters and brother. She was particularly worried about her youngest daughter in the Siberian winter 'because the little girl will freeze in her short coat.'[39] She even wanted to send shoes with a friend who was being evacuated from Leningrad, but was embarrassed to ask, because the woman would have had to walk 120 km to deliver them. Nevertheless, she could not conceal her anxiety: 'I really do not know how you will get through the winter without boots.'[40] All this was taking place, not when life had become easier, but when the hunger was at its worst: 'Father gets 400 grams of bread a day and I get 200.'[41]

There are not many such letters (indeed, few letters from the siege have been preserved), but they do exist. Their writers could not help but mention their own predicament, because it was awful and they needed to get it off their chest and feel others' sympathy for them. Everything was talked about in a natural, direct way, without any ulterior motive. They were writing to their own families and people who were dear to them.

5

People did not, though, necessarily talk about everything or to everyone: 'I was pulled to the kindergarten on a sledge, and on the way always wondered why people were sleeping on the street.' A child had somehow to be shielded from the horrors of the siege, distracted, not told about some things, not given answers to every question.[42]

These attempts to mitigate the bitter realities of the siege were not always successful. One mother gave extra food to her daughters, pretending she had been given an additional ration. Although she said nothing herself, the girls 'understood it was her bread they were eating'.[43] People admitted the truth when they could endure it no longer, and perhaps desperately needed support and sympathy, even if from their children. Why tell your children they had just eaten a cat? But when the 'hunger became relentless', their mother did come clean, and admitted that now she would be prepared to eat it herself.[44]

Why tell the children their mother was donating blood, literally in an attempt to save the lives of her own loved ones? The mother of one Leningrader did go, without a word to anyone, to donate. She was barely able to stand afterwards and feared she would collapse.[45] She kept quiet about how she had come by that extra ration: 'She said it was a gift from where she worked, or that it had been brought from somewhere on a plane and they had all been given presents.' She too, however, found it impossible to keep the secret for long. She wanted to talk about it and told them everything. After a repeat blood donation, she had had to walk for two hours and 'more than anything was afraid she would not be able to bring the ration home to them'. She could not keep this up for long: due to extreme emaciation, 'the blood no longer came'. The doctor tried to help by asking the nurse to give her sweet tea to drink. That did not work, 'so in March my mother did not bring anything home'.[46]

Even little children would offer words of consolation to their families. There are few records of this, but each is worth its weight in gold. They would comfort anyone who was crying, or when they saw someone was sad or ill. When they spoke to grown-ups, children repeated words that had

been used to comfort or calm them. They did not, of course, understand
fully, and were in any case not told everything to spare their feelings. In
their words, there is always something very direct, artless and, just because
of that, endearing. They make promises and offer encouragement without
considering what justification there might be for hope, but just because
someone is in need of comfort. 'Our ration cards had not been honoured.
The two of us were lying alone in bed and I was crying, wailing, even, and
my daughter, who is just four, reassured me: "We'll have something to
eat later and it will all be fine", Evelina Soloviova recalled.[47] Alexey N.
Kubasov, who was clearing the debris after the Gostiny Dvor arcade was
bombed, remembered the words of a girl they managed to free, together
with her mother, from the rubble: 'You see? I told you someone would
come to rescue us and now they have.'[48]

'"Mummy, I think you must get very tired." "Why?" I ask. "Well, I go
to bed but you are still busy, and then you go to bed late, and tomorrow
you will get up early, so I think you must get very tired."'[49] Probably only
V. M. Ivleva is fully aware of the nuances of this conversation between
her and her son, but that it meant a lot to her we can tell from the way
she reports it word-for-word in her diary. There is comfort for her in the
intent, far from child-like, attention with which her son is watching his
weary mother. There is comfort in the touching naivety of his guesses, and
perhaps also just in the straightforward directness and ordinariness of the
conversation, which are such a rarity in the nightmare of the siege.

B. Prusov expressed the sympathy he felt for his mother in a poem. He
saw her going out in a snowstorm to walk to the Hermitage canteen and
wrote his simple, unsophisticated, rather awkward verse. The result, as it
often is when children write poems, is a rhymed retelling of what he saw
in front of him, without the complication of metaphors or hyperbole. The
story is slightly elevated by emotive phrases from the language of politics
and poetry:

> You battle through the blizzards and the snow,
> Through bombing by the foe and all the shelling,
> Along an icy pavement onward go.
> A canister for food, for hunger quelling.
> You think of bread, a stove's warm glow
> For me and Nadya. Love so telling.

'Mother liked the poem and immediately wrote it down in her diary.'[50]
Perhaps the main thing that made people decide to record these incidents
is their unusualness. They were used to children being the ones in need
of consolation, and here they were doing the comforting. In addition to
the touching, naive purity of children, though, we detect something more
grown-up, something coming from what Maria Mashkova so aptly called
their 'distorted' lives. This grown-up quality is not just the usual desire
of children to seem older, but a legacy from bombs exploding in front

of them and the suffering they witnessed in people dying next to them. They were judicious, sensitive to other people's misfortune, and gentle in the encouragement they gave far beyond their years. The adolescent Ilya Glazunov was evacuated from Leningrad in an extremely emaciated condition in early 1942, leaving his mother behind in the city. The sense of shame that he had been saved while her health was deteriorating day by day gave him no peace, and lent an unbalanced tone to his letters.[51]

The guilt feelings were inevitable. There can be no end to them, because no one is, in reality, guilty. The boy's evacuation was predetermined, because it was the only way his life could be saved. The policy was to give priority to the very young and the weakest. No one could have known how tragically his parents' life would end. He does not, cannot, take any of this into account. His family's misfortune causes him to restructure the whole history, as if his departure had been voluntary, something that could have been avoided. He looks for grounds to believe this, expresses the hope that some miraculous means can be found when, in reality, there is nothing anyone could do. The only comfort he can find is to claim his guilt and, without for a moment excusing himself, write emotionally about how keenly his mother's letters are awaited, allowing himself to cry out with pain, and not denying himself emotional outbursts.

6

The letters exchanged between loved ones inside and outside the ring of encirclement are not only an exchange of news and advice, and not always just a list of requests. They are also an outpouring of a person's innermost thoughts to someone still capable of hearing them. Thus, the modest, unassuming, not very literate letters of A. I. Kochetova to her mother and brother are remarkable testimony to human endurance and love.

They were written by a shy, rather gawky, poorly educated girl who was left behind in Leningrad when her mother and brother went off on distant wanderings. Her life was hard: 'I am completely abandoned and have no one to share my thoughts with.'[52] She is living with another girl, whom she is trying to help. She has more troubles than she can express: 'We have to just sit here feeling hungry for days at a time, and she eats my food on the quiet.' She has no one to turn to: 'I just say nothing, and at night cry my heart out and then it's sort of okay again.' The situation is hopeless: 'There is nothing to buy in the shops, you only get 250 grams of bread, and water to drink, and that's it. People collapse in the street. Really, Mum, I can't tell you what it's like here in Leningrad.'

This comes from a letter to her mother and brother of 24 December 1941, the first she had been able to send for several months, as soon as she had an address for them. It begins by reproaching them for their long silence: 'I have been so upset that I just keep crying. I'm sure you have no idea how much I have missed you and more importantly how worried I was and am about you.' She is bubbling with delight, and that shows in the breathless style of writing with its telltale jerkiness. Before she has finished one sentence, she is interrupting herself, and repeating the same idea, only differently phrased: 'Mum, I am writing so messily because I'm very stirred up. I'm just so glad to hear you have found somewhere to stay and that now I can stop feeling I'm completely alone.'

She wants to get away, to go and join her mother, and right now, at all costs. That is what is really important:

> When I heard you wanted to stay in Perm I kept wanting to *walk* the 300 km there. Or maybe get a lift on a train without a ticket, and then just find you one way or another. It's one thing to think about it, but the cold has been so severe here, and I only have ordinary shoes and galoshes. I was thinking about it night and day, going around, finding things out. I had a plan to sell things.

She began to realize this was just not feasible, but how could she escape from her foul situation and get away from the boredom: 'In the apartment they were all being really beastly to me. I was crying all the time and felt so stirred up. It was so hard.'

Her confidences are without guile. Everything is ordinary, straightforward and open. Her surmises about her mother's life are a mirror image of her own life in the siege. She is hungry, so her mother must be hungry. She is lonely, so her mother, living among strangers, will be pleased if she comes to join her. Many of those trapped in the siege did not know what conditions their relatives were living in, but were inclined to believe the worst. They imagined the most dramatic scenes, one more lurid than another.[53] They put in something of their own experience in the siege, and supposed their families must be swollen from hunger and living on minuscule rations.

Testimony of concern for loved ones is varied. People tried, however they could, to alleviate the plight of their families, not disdaining heavy labour and risking their lives and health. It could be objected that the actions we nowadays describe as heroic were involuntary, because there was no other way to survive. Perhaps so, but it took strength, tenacity and willpower not to give in to despondency, not to allow yourself to be broken, not to eat someone else's bread and to share your own: to act, in other words, against the instinct of self-preservation. A person could have declined to give blood on the grounds of fatigue, weakness or the cold, but, in an attempt to save their family, went ahead anyway.[54] Zinaida Moykovskaya, seeing that a bottle of soya milk had not satisfied her baby's hunger, soaked a piece of bread in boiling water. 'Pieces of sawdust floated up and those I ate myself; the rest I gave to my son.'[55] Anna Nalegatskaya did much the same: 'I cooked the peeled potato for my child and cooked the peelings for myself.'[56] Evelina Soloviova came by chance upon a packet of dried mustard and tried to bake a patty out of it. It turned into a completely inedible mess which burned her insides. She could not offer it to her daughter, but felt very sorry for her: 'She could not take her eyes off my efforts.'[57] She shared some of her portion of bread with the little girl to mollify her.

Alexey Ptitsyn said of his mother, 'I remember an episode which made me shudder. Walking across the tracks at some station, she carried a child with her teeth because she could not hold it in her frostbitten arms.'[58] Even more desperate was the situation of M. A. Galaktionova, evacuated from Leningrad with her family. They were all emaciated. On the journey, her brother died of starvation. She herself was travelling with feet black from frostbite. She began to suffer from dystrophy and the doctors proposed amputating her feet: 'My mother managed to protect me and get me better, but for that she had to exchange absolutely everything she had with her. She bartered a silk dress for one egg. [The doctors] themselves were digging leftover frozen potatoes out of the ground and eating grass.'[59] One hesitates to say what else they were eating, overcoming their shame and disgust.

7

There is another topic, rarely mentioned by those writing about the war, and that is the topic of love.

Love letters written during the siege invariably have strands of patriotism woven into them, but they were not being sent to a lover in order to paraphrase the latest Informbyuro bulletins. Even when their writers cannot avoid pathos, they express their feelings in a special, warm tone:

> Today I received two letters from you. I couldn't get to sleep after reading them! Now I will think about you even more, and wait for your letters even more impatiently. I will wait for you twice over, because you will not come back until the war is over, and for me the war will not be over until you return. Do you remember I told you I could not live without you? I am certain you will come back, it cannot be otherwise. If you do not, you know that half my life will be for nothing.

So wrote a university student, Liya Levitan, to her friend, who died at the front in the winter of 1941–2.[60]

The same intimacy is present in the tale of a lovers' meeting described in the diary of A. L. Yanovich. In previous entries, she refers to bombing and starvation, but when you read these lines, it is as if the sound has been turned off. There is not one detail of the horrors of the siege, which would jar with the purity of her experience and only drown out the feelings of happiness she finds so restorative. She has no need of resounding declarations, no wish to declaim like an actress on stage. The words she chooses are simple and ordinary, but deeply affecting: 'Now more than ever, there is such depth in his love, such intimacy, so much mutual care and understanding. In our home I suddenly felt such calm, such a stillness. The stove was burning, it was so warm and pure. There was good music on the wire-less. No alarm. It was peaceful.'[61]

In the letters and diaries, where people are writing about their love, there is a special language. It can be elevated, even solemn. Sometimes letters are exchanged in verse.[62] Raptures are usually avoided, but a vehement quality resulting from life in the siege is clearly present. In Olga Berggolts's entries, there are many lines devoted to her husband, Nikolai Molchanov. An exceptionally talented man, gentle, generous and high-minded, he volunteered for the front and suffered concussion. Its consequences, as well as malnutrition, aggravated a severe, incurable illness. His fits became more frequent and Berggolts's entries become increasingly frantic: 'I will never, ever leave him, never replace him with anyone else.'[63] His end came swiftly, inevitable and terrible. He had no chance of survival. He was delirious, and in lucid moments did his best to comfort his wife, before again relapsing into delirium, groaning from unendurable suffering. The more obvious it became how the tragedy must unfold, the closer the diary entries become to a conjuration: 'Don't give up. I will get you out of this. I will beg for food from all and sundry, buy it from black marketeers, and work insanely hard to get money.'[64]

There is some correlation between the rapidity of someone's decline and death and the lamentation of those who witnessed it. Here there is more desperation than confidence, more illusion than sober calculation. 'Begging from all and sundry' was futile, because even if they were able to give food it would be too little to restore a seriously ill person to health. Her friends helped to the best of their ability, but everybody was on the verge of starvation. She could hardly work 'insanely hard', because she herself was beginning to waste away. All that remained was, as always, to sacrifice a portion of her own meagre rations regardless, as if she were herself already living her last days.

Alexey Yevdokimov's love for his wife is vividly expressed in his diary. She has been evacuated and he looks forward impatiently to letters. Indeed, this is the only reason he goes back home from his factory.[65] His entries on his wife are reticent and not very lengthy, but they are numer-ous. Almost every day his thoughts turn to her as he wonders how she is getting on, whether she is suffering hardship, and whether he will soon be getting her reply. She is the only person he has whom he can talk to. There are dead bodies in the streets, in the basements, on the stairs, in apart-ments. There is a limit to everything, including human endurance: 'I feel dizzy. It is difficult to walk, and I cannot stand upright for more than three minutes.'[66] Death might come at any moment, as he knew. How many people who had no one to help them collapsed in the street or in a deserted house? How could they ease their last moments? 'If I am destined to fall, *forward this note to my wife.* She should know that in my last minutes I was with them in spirit. I am theirs.'[67]

Diaries were kept by very different people, but, during this time of severe, emotional stress, they all have a similar writing style. For V. M.

Ivleva, her husband is the only person who makes life worth living: 'I don't want to die. I want to come through all this and be with Pavel again.'[68] Her diary entries are at one moment an impromptu monologue, at another a hymn, and sometimes a confessing of her soul: 'Pavel, I want only one thing: to see you again. It would be so dreadful to die alone. I want to look into your eyes before I die, to hear your voice and hold your hand.'[69]

Emotion disrupts the usual diary format. We find not a story about loved ones, but that they are being directly addressed. There are promises like sympathetic magic, a recollecting in memory of the personal traits of someone greatly loved which best convey their uniqueness, their charm, their attractiveness. These are the bedrock of the entries. Repetition of words echoes the violence of the shocks they have endured, disjointed sentences reflect overwhelming emotions, and reveal the loneliness, wretchedness and inexpressible grief linking them.

8

Tales of how people witnessed the death of their family and friends are the most difficult to read. They are usually terse. The first, and often the only, thing mentioned is groans and tears.

'You are walking at night-time and hear a wail, "Mummy, don't die. Don't leave me all alone." You see a woman lying there, glassy-eyed. Beside her, a little girl of eight or nine, so thin, starving, shaking her mother and begging her not to die. You see so many incidents like that', recalled the director of the evacuation centre in Kobona.[70] Yekaterina Lentsman hoped her mother would not die if she did not let her fall asleep: 'When my mother closed her eyes, I shouted loudly, she opened them again and I stopped shouting. That happened several times but then it was all over. She was gone. Daddy thought Mummy was still alive and kept calling her, "Tanya, Tanechka," but she was silent. We all cried.'[71]

Everywhere there are signs of the terrible blow people had felt. They said they could not go on living; many years later they did not want to believe their children were dead. The writing in diaries, letters and memoirs is often laconic, but even in those few lines you detect incredible stress.

All the letters describing death, although written by different people, have much in common. They say how difficult it is to write, that they cannot find the words to express fully all that is in their heart, or that they have not the strength to find words at all.

Their descriptions sometimes break off abruptly, and not because they are choosing between episodes they see as being of greater or lesser significance. As you read the documents of those years, you realize there are sometimes accesses of such pain that all coherent narrative is out of the question. The writing becomes jerky and the writer's thought seems constantly to circle back to the same thing. In these texts about the death of someone loved, you find clusters of associations, one image giving rise to another. They are permeated by the bitterness of bereavement, the fear of losing those they love, the horror of a way of life which has become routine. They are simultaneously the description of an event, a protest, a baring of souls, and a cry of inexpressible grief, all jostling each other, uttered in a feverish torrent and a rush of overwhelming emotion:

> It is hard to write this. It is difficult and distressing, but I have to tell you all the truth so that you know the difficult and horrible situation we are in now. Our dear, sweet, beloved mother has died. Her death was very peaceful, but she had been seriously and painfully ill for some time. Three days before Mother, little Misha died, and on the same day Fedya, so I have only three left now, and two of them have also taken to their beds. Their fate will be the same as Mother's. They are very weak and ill. You know yourself what kind of times these are and the kind of situation we have in Leningrad. To make matters worse, I have not had my welfare paid for the past five months. It is so hard without Mother, losing her I have lost everything, I am now a lone orphan, no use to anybody. I cry day and night, I have all swollen up myself, my legs are like barrels, my face is puffy. It turns out I have trouble with my kidneys and all that is on top of the malnutrition so that I can hardly move my feet and have already become an old woman. I am so sad about Misha and Fedya, they should not have died, it is all because of the Germans. If you knew and saw all we have experienced and are experiencing, it would make your hair stand on end. I miss Mother so much, it is really getting me down, I feel very sad without her. I don't know how I will live without her, but I need to somehow. When I have calmed down I will write to you again, but now I can't go on. I can't lift anything, I see Mother standing in front of me all the time. Write to us orphans.[72]

9

Reading the diaries and letters which contain responses to the death of loved ones, you do notice one feature. People often describe the details of the day-to-day life of the departed, phrases they used, their gestures and actions. They seem to be trying to bring them back to life for a moment, and sometimes to converse with them. The present, with its rows of anonymous graves, is unbearable and you need, if only for a moment, to escape back into the past, to soften the blow if only temporarily. 'Poor Tanya just cries all the time and cannot bear the loneliness. She keeps remembering all sorts of little details from their short life together', G. A. Gelfer wrote of a relative who had just lost her husband.[73]

The most impressive document in which we observe the psychology of this 'modelling' is the diary of schoolgirl Yelena Mukhina. On 8 February 1942, we read in her diary only a few lines: 'Mother died yesterday morning. Now I am alone.'[74] She avoids writing anything associated with this tragedy: '10 February. I fuelled up the stove until it was really warm. Now on average the room is 12°. I'll write more tomorrow.' What she writes about in detail, however, is other things: the caretaker helping her take the body to the mortuary (she paid her in bread). She seems afraid to mention her mother, and writes only about herself and her predicament: 'How hard it is to be alone. All the people around me are strangers. Nobody is the slightest bit interested. They all have worries of their own.'[75] Her mother is no more. What a frightening thought. It is better to think about who might be able to look after her now. There is always Aunt Zhenya, although she lives far away, but at a time like this she is bound to support her: 'She will help me. Definitely.'[76]

Still no entries about her mother. She writes about having to cook food, chop firewood, other routine matters, without emotion, in a kind of daze. On 13 February, the pain suddenly bursts out uncontrollably: 'Mother is not there! Mother is dead. I am alone. At times I suddenly feel so furious. I want to howl and scream and bang my head against the wall and bite!'[77]

The wound has not been healing. Perhaps it would be better to write about something good, something comforting to cheer herself up. 'I'm really rich! In one jar I have millet and in another barley porridge. Today's bread at 1 ruble 25 is delicious: firm, very good. This is the third day I have been listening to the radio. It's great. I don't feel lonely at all. I have money. I have firewood and food. What more could I need? I'm entirely content', she writes in her diary on 17 February 1942.[78]

The pain did not and could not go away. Sooner or later she was bound to write about her mother again, and there was no possibility of deluding herself that life had become better. That was not going to happen. The siege had not been raised. Yesterday she had bread, today there was not a crumb. She had eaten it all at once, in feverish haste and with a vague hope that tomorrow might be a lucky day, or perhaps without that hope, just because she could not stop. 'I am so hungry! And so fed up of dragging out this half-starved existence', she writes on 5 March 1942.[79]

She needs to find a way to alleviate the grief. Cheerful auto-suggestion does not work: the hunger is still there, and the cold, and the loneliness. Maybe try something different: 'I keep thinking Mother has only gone off on business for a short time and will soon be back.'

Nothing helps. She remembers everything: how hard it became in those last few days for her mother to talk, how she looked: 'Her legs were like a doll's bones, and she had what looked like rags instead of muscles.' She tries to keep the pain at bay by writing in a more orderly, even literary, way – but then starts screaming again: 'Mummy, Mamusya, you could not take any more. You died. Mamulya, dearest Mamonchik, my darling friend . . .'[80]

There was only one way to dull the pain: to feel that your mother was near you again, to hear her voice, to write a long story to keep her image in your memory, her every word, her every gesture. The more of these details you can write down, the more alive the loved person seems and you can hope, at least for a moment, to elude the searing anguish. Yelena's description of her mother's last days dates from 5 March 1942, and often turns into a dialogue between mother and daughter. Their closeness seems less than convincing:

> 'Come on, take the blanket off. Right, now move your left leg; now your right. Good.' 'Oops-a-daisy!' she said joyfully, trying to get up herself. 'Oops-a-daisy, and now lift me this way.' We hugged one another and both of us were crying. 'My dear, dear Mummy!' 'Lena, why do you and I have to be so out of luck?'[81]

10

Much has been written abut the feelings of people who lost family members during the siege. Some wrote from hearsay, hastily; some wrote cautiously, with an eye on the censor. Alexander Fadeyev, who visited Leningrad in late spring 1942, noticed no signs of the Time of Death. A clean, well-scrubbed city, no corpses in the streets, sunshine, children basking in the sun. The Leningraders are still very thin, but determined to defend their city. The workers face some difficulties, but are ready for new feats of productivity. Everything is awakening: hope, determination, optimism. Fadeyev was not the only person writing about Leningrad in this vein. This was the line of editorials in the city's newspapers, and it was followed also in Nikolai Tikhonov's articles, whose titles mirrored those of Tolstoy's *Sebastopol Stories*: 'Leningrad in May', 'Leningrad in June'. They lack, however, the graphic detail of Tolstoy's work. It is difficult to say whether Alexander Fadeyev knew the whole truth: there was a lot about which it was impossible to speak openly. The uncensored sketches of city life in his notebook are surprisingly sparse,[82] and some of them were transferred almost verbatim into his *Leningrad During the Siege*, published in late 1942. He interviewed eyewitnesses, including Tikhonov, and something of the terrible scenes of the past winter breaks through in his diary. He even ventures to say, 'The sight of someone dying of hunger in a snowbound street was not uncommon in Leningrad.'[83] The way this note continues shows how much he knew: 'People passing by would doff their hats or offer a couple of words of sympathy, and sometimes not pause at all.' Perhaps he was lied to, or perhaps he invented that, but, as we know, hats were not doffed, words of sympathy were not offered, and this happened not 'sometimes' but very frequently.

Fadeyev does, however, have one chapter in his book, where the smug, confident tone disappears, where everything so firmly averred in his wartime journalism judders to a halt.

It is his account of children who had lost their parents and were living in children's homes. They do not need to be kitted out with a heroic halo because they are too little to need one: hunched, sad, 'they all as one clustered round the stove, crying and fighting for their place'.[84] They are taciturn, disobedient, and all of them bear the mark of a misfortune too great and terrible for them to bear, which everyday language is inadequate to describe. Fadeyev wrote everything down as it was told to him by the carers, and something of the gentle instructiveness of their way of speaking is transferred to him. In some instances, he simply copied out their reports.

In these notes, we see a whole succession of children with 'distorted' lives, sad, suffering, still affected by malnutrition. Only later (and then very rapidly) will what they remember of life with their mothers be erased, but for now they cling to everything that still links them with that past.[85] Take Lorik, a little boy trying to hide a powder compact with a portrait of his mother from prying eyes:

> He was terribly embarrassed when he saw me watching him. 'I have my Mummy, I am keeping her safe', he told me in a whisper. 'I made it myself. I tied the ribbon on it.' That day, he told me all about the death of his mother and of his auntie, and why he did not want anyone else to see the portrait. 'I wanted it only for me, only for me.' He couldn't think how else to explain.

The 7-year-old Lenya did not want to be parted from his cap, which had become misshapen, because it was a much-loved memento of his brother. When he was brought to the home, 6-year-old Zhenya wanted to show everyone photos of his mother: 'At night, he asked the nurse to bring a light so he could look at her. When the nurse asked why he was not asleep, Zhenya said, "I'm still thinking about my Mummy. I don't want to myself, but I think and think."'

'She clings obsessively to anything that even remotely reminds her of her mother and her life back at home.' It is all they had left to salve the unbearable pain. Life had not been all that great for them there, and you could hardly say they had enough to eat. There was no forgetting the realities of their earlier life, cutting up bread into tiny pieces. 'They drank their soup in two goes. They spread their porridge or fruit jelly on bread. The bread they tore into microscopic pieces and enjoyed making it last for hours.'[86] Fadeyev was not able to see everything, but there is information indicating that the children in these homes were not paragons of virtue. Children there were maltreated, and the stronger would take food from the weaker. There were fights.[87]

They no longer had, and never again would have, someone who would always protect them, who would sacrifice their own ration for them, whom they could trust. They were among strangers. The carers, themselves half-starved, did their best to think of ways to lighten up the children's joyless lives, but they had too many cares of their own to be able to stand in for the mother of every child. Other children could be completely out of control, indifferent to everything, and would sometimes tell anyone who would listen how their families had died. 'I remember our mother dying. I felt sorry for her. I pulled her to the bed. She was very heavy, and then the neighbours said she was dead. I was so scared, but I didn't cry then but now I miss her so much. I feel so sorry for her', one of the carers heard. She mentioned that the orphaned boy then 'pulled the blanket over his head and cried silently'.[88]

They all were suffering the same pain, and shielded themselves from it as best they could: with tears, or silence, by trying to screen off the past, with a toy given by their mother, by telling a story choked with emotion, and with poetry, heartbroken and uneven.

6

The family: ethics

Continuity and disintegration

1

In the writings of Leningraders caught in the siege, we often find the notion that, by doing their duty by the family, people were attempting to insure themselves against the future, knowing that nobody could survive on their own.[1] For all that, people did give all they could to young children, old people who were dying, and many others who would be in no position to repay them. They supported not only brothers and sisters, but distant relatives, even those they had not seen for years.

The most ordinary everyday actions performed by family members, shopping for food, calling the doctor, finding firewood, nursing the sick, acquired a different significance in 1941–2: they made the difference between life and death. 'For as long as one person in the family could walk and go to buy bread, others who were confined to their beds stayed alive', Dmitry Likhachev recalled.[2]

This involved standing for hours in endless queues, in severe cold, often with little prospect of success. Family members usually tried to take turns in the queue, but that was not always possible.[3] After Likhachev himself became too weak to walk, the whole family was dependent on his wife: 'She would queue from two in the morning in the entrance to our building to redeem our ration cards.'[4] This was a common situation. 'I had to go for bread because my sister, who was swollen with hunger, was no longer allowed out', Vera Lisovskaya recalled.[5] You did, nevertheless, see people dropsical and barely able to stand, and outside the bakeries were the bodies of those who had collapsed and been unable to get up again.

Redeeming ration cards was no simple matter. It was easiest to buy bread, but extremely difficult to get such other products as meat, grains, butter and sugar, no matter how wretchedly small the rations were. Enormous queues formed outside shops to which they were delivered. There was not enough food for everyone and, until December 1941, Leningraders had no option but to go round dozens of shops. Ration cards expired at the end of the month and could not usually be extended. Anyone who had not managed to redeem them by then just lost their entitlement.

There was no pattern to how family members cooperated. Everything depended on the circumstances. Account had to be taken of work hours, how many people there were in the family, their state of health, and who was able to make arrangements for very young children to be looked after. Not least, the extent to which someone was malnourished mattered, because 'dystrophics' were more easily robbed and liable to have bread stolen from them. Not everyone trusted their relatives: some were suspected, and not without reason, of giving in to hunger and eating others' rations on the way home.[6]

Erosion of pre-siege morality was also evident in how people behaved during shelling and bombing. Yelena Mukhina witnessed the first of these episodes, and wrote in her diary on 8 September 1941, 'People spilled down the stairs like dried peas, some carrying children under their arms or hauling old ladies.'[7] At times when the lives of their family were in danger, many people showed real heroism, among them the grandmother who fell to the ground and shielded her 3-year-old granddaughter with her own body, and the mother who sheltered her 6-year-old with her coat.[8] Even young children would run during shelling to help the clean-up brigades trying to rescue their brothers and sisters from fallen rubble.[9] Anna Ostroumova-Lebedeva recalled her nephew pulling her by the hand to a shelter during bombing and looking after her, bringing a chair and finding her somewhere to sit in the midst of the overcrowding.[10]

With time, however, people became used to bombardment and were reluctant to use the bomb shelters. Many did not even take their children there. There were sundry excuses: exhausted people would not have time to crawl to the shelter before the all-clear, and in any case were not safe there and just as likely to be buried under rubble. There was a grain of truth in that. In families where already no allowance was being made for the age and condition of relatives, where people could not ask for an extra helping of porridge because they were ill, and where people could drink a bowl of soup in front of a hungry child and not share it with them, this behaviour during bombardment did not seem shocking. The more the rules were flouted, the less unacceptable that seemed.

2

The psychology of moral deterioration is starkly revealed in Maria Mashkova's diary entry for 20 February 1942. The day before, she had left behind 'the gloom of starvation and wretchedness', had got away from her home and her hungry children and dying mother-in-law. She went to visit her close friend, a poetess, in her home where it was 'warm and light' and where, she knew for sure, there would be bread to eat. She loves her children and tries her best to make life easier for them; she looks after her mother-in-law, but something snaps. She knows the rule of the new ethics:

if you want your loved ones to live, first make sure you yourself survive. She has to eat her own rations under the watchful gaze of her hungry son, and make sure that caring for her mother-in-law does not undermine her own health. Such behaviour had become customary and unavoidable, but everything has consequences. Perhaps moral breakdown occurs so easily because people do not notice it happening.

In her friend's house everything was different: 'I so enjoyed the food, and could not leave my plate until everything in front of me had been demolished.' It was so cosy, people were reciting poetry, and not openly counting every crumb. Drunk with a sense of satiety, she began at last to thaw out: 'It was a strange evening, and lots of different feelings went through me. Slices of toasted bread paralyzed my will and fettered me to that warm, bright room. I had such a melancholy feeling that I would not survive, a terrible urge to live at all costs, and a clear awareness that much was already irretrievably lost. It all somehow became absurdly mixed up together.'[11]

Just at that moment, the air raid warning sounded: 'At home my children were alone with their dying grandmother: I must get up and go to them.' But she really did not want to. It was warm, and there was the smell of bread, which was being shared generously. Out there it was fiendishly cold, with an iced-up staircase, filth, the cries of the dying, the wailing of frightened children: the whole nightmare of the siege, the rats, the lice, the hungry glances of her son and daughter, the humiliating sharing out of the bread; in the streets and courtyards, corpses stripped, robbed, their flesh cut off. Everywhere death, death, death!

'I stayed.' And immediately, the excuse: 'It made no sense to run there and try to do something. Anyway, where would I take them? To a freezing bomb shelter? What would be the point?'

This sounds less than convincing after the vivid description of the sudden, sensuous euphoria from the comfort and satiety. Her siege diary entries contain much bitter reproof of people who have given in, whose will has broken, who have gone to seed, and she shows little interest in understanding what broke them. Has she the right to find excuses for herself when she is so hard on others? Listing all the reasons for behaving as she did, and no doubt there could have been many, is not the same as being honest with herself. The honest thing would have been to identify her main motive. It is difficult for her to put a name to it, but in the end she does. She says openly, not hiding behind the excuse of the cold and hunger or how nothing could change anything: 'To tell the truth, I could not bring myself to leave.' They were about to serve coffee, there was still bread on the table, waiting to be eaten. She could not bring herself to leave.

On 1 March 1942, her family prepared a 'proper funeral tea' for the lately deceased mother-in-law. They scraped together their meagre reserves and were hoping for the first time in weeks to have a proper meal. At just that moment, the shelling began. It is hard to tell whether Mashkova would have taken them to the shelter, but her little daughter started screaming: 'It was the first time she had been so scared and begged us to run.' She had to take them down: 'I was tired, in a foul mood and very hungry, but had to carry Galya downstairs. I felt there would be no end to this. I fell into such a state of mindless despair, not from fear of being killed, but because I had not even been able to drink a glass of hot tea and eat a piece of toast. We had been dreaming about it for two days.'[12] And that is all. No words about protecting lives, or about how it feels to know her family will be safe. In the entry for 7 March 1942, the same arguments are repeated: 'What is the point of running with the children to a cold, frosty bomb shelter where every empty place on a bunk reminds you of people who only recently were still alive? In any case, it is physically impossible to run.'[13]

The arguments are questionable. It was frosty in the apartments too, and there too, just a short time ago, people were living. And did she not have to overcome her weakness and get to work in the Public Library, and stand in queues? Without that she would be unable to feed her family and would of a certainty condemn them to death. Whether she was about to be killed during a bombardment nobody could know, so she could just hope for the best. That is undoubtedly true, but for one detail. She could perfectly well just have written about her troubles without coming up with excuses. Why does she produce them every time there is a bombardment? She has an explanation for everything, but just can't forgive herself for everything.

3

Those whose houses were destroyed by the bombing and shelling were issued permits entitling them to other rooms, but many preferred to move in with relatives. Here, they got a mixed reception. New residents could mean new hardship, of which most people already had more than enough. Many who had lost their property moved the whole family, relying on help not everyone was in a position to give. Irina Zelenskaya visited the apartment of the family of her brother-in-law, where the newly married couple had found temporary refuge. She noted in her diary: 'All the talk revolves delicately around when they will be moving out. Their invasion is clearly unwelcome.'[14]

Quite often, however, relatives and friends were invited to move in even if their accommodation had not suffered. This support was especially valuable in the winter of 1941–2, when the water supply and sanitation were not working. Lazar Ratner remembered his mother inviting her sister to come and stay because, after her husband died, it was difficult for her to carry water and firewood up to the sixth floor, and five of them had to live in one room.[15]

It was, of course, more usual to live with family members than with strangers, and the hope was that it would be easier to endure the hunger and cold together. Somebody might have a larger room, or might still have their window panes, which meant the room could be heated with a conventional stove rather than a smoky cast-iron *burzhuika*, and that could be enough to tip the scales in favour of moving. Otherwise, the commonest reasons for relocating were that the plumbing was still working in the new place, that it had electricity or easier access to food, or that there were more goods or possessions which could be exchanged for bread. Living in a kind of family commune, relatives helped each other with such tasks as washing clothes, looking after children, going to collect rations, and sharing bread.

Links between family members who lived apart or far away became more tenuous. The trams stopped running, the shelling became more frequent, and everybody was seriously weakened by hunger.[16] People did, however, go to see those who were in need, who had been affected by the bombing, had lost their ration cards, could no longer walk due to malnutrition, were ill, or were trying to save their young children from starvation.[17] Sometimes visitors were able to bring gifts, if only tiny. Everything went into the family 'pot', which was small, but everyone could expect access to it. Resentments and suspicions were inevitable; people might be overoptimistic and not realize how meagre a gift was likely to be, and then grumble when they were disappointed. Any unfairness was noticed, and it was not always accepted that little could reasonably be expected from someone who was starving.

The grudges, though, are not what is remarkable about communal living during the war. Support given was evaluated by different rules during the siege. What mattered was not how much or how little people gave, but whether it was all they had left. It might be their last piece of bread, so that sharing it doomed the giver to suffering. It might be the last steps of someone on their way to help loved ones but who died during bombing or collapsed and froze to death. The small gift they had prepared, which could hardly have saved a life, was accorded a much higher value.

4

Help for ill and starving family members was crucial during the first winter of the siege. Because supporting them was so difficult, people tried to get them into sickbays or hospitals. This was not easy, because all the hospitals were already overcrowded. There were different approaches. Some could be got in with the connivance of relatives who worked there or had connections in the right places. A more extreme measure was simply to dump the would-be patient at the hospital door and hope they would not be rejected. That did not always work. In Boris Mikhailov's memoirs, he tells of one woman who brought her dying child to the hospital and tried to run away: 'She was caught, given bread, porridge, and her child back, but in parting they promised to give them extra rations.'[18] The comment of Mikhailov's mother, who told him the tale ('She was very lucky') suggests that such stories did not always end so fortunately. During the Time of Death, frail people were sometimes shooed out of factory gatehouses, shops, pharmacies and institutions where they had gone to get warm, for fear they might die there. It seems unlikely that the reception given to starving people in the overcrowded hospitals would always have been benign, although A. Neishtadt recalled: 'I never heard of doctors failing to help people in that situation.'[19] Recourse to this technique was, in fact, usually a last resort. It was feared that the ill person was more likely to be treated in an offhand, even insulting, manner than given timely support and the necessary treatment. What chance had a helpless, dying person of standing up for their rights?

Often the ill were incapable of walking to a hospital, and would be pulled there on a sledge by two or three family members, themselves starving and frozen. It could be a long way and not everybody even had a sledge. Valya Tikhomirova recalled how her aunt transported her mother when she became very weak: 'She put her on a rug, slid her down the stairs, and then dragged her on the rug all the way to the hospital.'[20]

Hospital was the last hope for desperate people, and they had few illusions about the fate of anyone staying there unattended by relatives. There was not enough medicine to go round, the meagre rations were insufficient to provide an enhanced diet, the doctors and nurses were too rushed to give even essential care to everyone, and sometimes chose not to. It was impossible to find a place in the wards or a separate bed for everyone, and there was no way to muffle the terrible groaning and crying out of the dying. The traditional expectation that family and friends would visit the sick became, during the siege, essential if they were to survive. They did their best to help, despite weakness, hunger, cold and fear of the shelling. 'It was so difficult to walk. I often slipped and lay on the ground for a long time. I would fall down, get up, fall down again, get up again . . .' and that was the way Svetlana Magaeva made her way to the hospital to visit her mother.[21]

Where it proved impossible to get the sick into a hospital, they were looked after at home by their relatives. There were many obstacles to overcome: fear, greed, irascibility, fatigue and, not to mince words, revulsion. Lyudmila Alexandrova remembered her dying grandmother calling for help when the children were all alone in the apartment and they were afraid to go near her.[22] Rita Malkova could not bring herself to help her grandmother unless her mother shouted at her: 'I was horrified: you cannot imagine how many lice there were.'[23] Such instances were, however, unusual and families generally fought for the life of their members to the end. They washed those who were ill, fed and, if need be, spoon-fed them, changed their clothes, made up infusions and decoctions to order, and looked in the shops and markets for products they particularly needed. Getting the doctor to come for a home visit called for extraordinary efforts. They had to stand in long queues in the clinics, and going even a short distance was difficult. If a family was reduced to helplessness, with both the parents and children bedridden, relatives would, if possible, take them into their own home. When parents died, relatives would help to get their children into an orphanage, or add them to their own family. Instances of the dying warming frozen children with their bodies are described by dozens of witnesses.[24]

The relationships between family members were not always unclouded. Squabbles and grudges had often marred them long before the siege. They resurfaced during the Time of Death, although it is impossible to separate pre-existing animosities from the effects of starvation. Even during the siege, though, compassion and pain at the sight of the misery of their family members overcame whatever feelings of alienation, malice and contempt they might once have harboured, if not always immediately or fully. 'Late one evening', Lazar Ratner recalled, 'my little brother Grisha began to cry with hunger, but there was not a crumb in the house, nothing. Then my mother said, "Go and ask them [her sister – S. Ya.] to lend us a crust of bread until tomorrow." In response to my request, Auntie Ira shrieked, "She's been scrounging off me all her life! I have no bread. Go away!"'[25]

This may have been the discharge of some long-standing animosity caused by his mother's poverty, which the siege had aggravated. There follows the only too familiar pattern of the death of a Leningrad family. They had their ration cards stolen, the mother became bedridden: 'I myself had just hot water with salt to drink and gave her that.'[26] It could only be a matter of time before the swelling up, when the dent left by a finger pressing on the body would remain visible for several hours. His mother's brother came to see them: 'He stood for a time without saying a word, looked at us and, obviously shocked, left.' Two days later, his mother's sister, Ira, came and took away 2-year-old Grisha. Then she came and took Lazar to a children's home. The woman in charge refused to admit him, saying that he would die soon anyway, and his aunt replied, no less rudely than when she had refused her sister's request for bread, 'Well what do you think I'm going to do with him? It's bad enough I'm having to take in his mother.' Ratner met her again in June 1942. 'I asked, "Where's Grisha?" She said, "Your Grisha died." "How is Mummy?" She burst into tears and walked away.'[27]

Here is another story, about an old lady who was picked up after collapsing in the street. At the warming-up station she was given a drink of hot water. It was obvious nobody was looking after her, and that she was in no state to look after herself. They managed to find out her address but nobody in the building knew anything about her: 'Finally, one of the women, after hearing my description of the old lady's appearance, exclaimed, "Why, that's my mother-in-law! How did she get there? She lives with her daughter. Why did she give my address?"'[28]

Taking a sledge, the daughter-in-law went to the warming-up station. She could not contain her anger and already on the way there gave vent to it in front of a complete stranger. 'She has a daughter here, but evidently they no longer have a use for her. While she had her own home in Vyritsa, while she was bringing them jam by the kilo, they treated her decently, but now she's in deep trouble and has suddenly remembered she has a daughter-in-law. Of course, her daughter has a lot of children and I'm on my own now, so perhaps that's why they've sent her to me.'

The old lady could not walk, so three of them 'loaded her' on to the sledge. She tried to say something but the daughter-in-law interrupted, perhaps not even having noticed: 'Okay, Mother, just keep quiet. I'll put you up in memory of Stepan [her husband who had died at the front – S. Ya.].[29] This declaration was rather overdone. She was clearly not making it for the benefit of the old lady, who had collapsed in exhaustion and was probably not even aware of where she was. The daughter-in-law was getting something off her chest in front of people who might sympathize and even, perhaps, be willing to listen to the story of all her troubles. The old lady may not have had much of a life to look foward to, helpless and miserable, in an unfamiliar house, berated by the same daughter-in-law who had given her shelter, but at least she had not been abandoned in the icy cold. She might have been rescued by people who turned up their nose at her, and given refuge by a woman who had no time for her, but in coming to the rescue, stripped of all the phoney gilding found in moralizing accounts, we see, limpidly displayed, the Leningraders' sense of common cause. We see, not the gaudy heroes of the propaganda machine, but real people, irate, resentful, but still imbued with a sense of compassion.

5

The help given to family members during evacuation is a topic in its own right. It was not easy to get away. Special lists were compiled, certain quotas decided. In the overcrowded trains there was insufficient room even for those granted permission to leave Leningrad. Many who were trapped in the siege were able to leave if they had relatives working in factories, children's homes, schools, colleges or other institutions that were being evacuated.[30] Others who did not have that kind of pull could only get out as a result of the persistence of family members who did not want to be parted from them. One of the most upsetting chapters of the siege was the attempt of desperate Leningraders to escape on their own initiative across the frozen Lake Ladoga. They had no choice: their families were starving to death before their eyes, and there was no immediate prospect of getting transport across the lake. They lived in the hope that, on the far side, they would find bread to eat and warmth, and every hour they delayed seemed a missed opportunity to save the lives of the dying. 'They were not allowed onto the ice. It was patiently explained that they would never make it to the other side. In desperation they would contrive to set off on their own, but within an hour or two would freeze to death', writes Georgiy Makogonenko.[31] That was the situation in December 1941, and it was unchanged in February 1942: 'They pull little sledges along behind them with small children riding on them. The children soon freeze to death, and their mother carries on pulling them until she herself collapses or someone rescues her.'[32]

Those leaving in the crowded railway carriages or icy trucks were seriously malnourished and in need of medical care. They could not stand up for themselves, get food, find a warm place by the stove, or get off the train unaided at stops. Many of the trains were not designed for transporting human beings. The loaf of bread issued to the evacuees caused many tragedies. People were so hungry they could not stop themselves from wolfing the entire loaf, and often died on the spot in great suffering and in the midst of filth. Those who survived almost all say it was the help of family members that saved them from certain death.

There is also testimony of people refusing evacuation because they were not prepared to abandon their loved ones, or giving up their place on a train to other family members. There could be different reasons for this. Many were reluctant to leave their homes and apartments because they feared looting. Some were afraid of journeying into the unknown, to sponge off distant relatives and burden them with their problems. Nobody ever believed they might be next in the queue for the grim reaper, and just hoped to survive the calamity. All this is true, but the signs of impending disaster were no secret. Anybody turning down the opportunity to be evacuated must surely have understood that not everyone would survive the nightmare. By putting on a show of optimism, those remaining behind tried to encourage those hesitating or ashamed, to leave. In their later writings, Leningraders who got out invariably emphasize how insistently they were urged to do so.

We cannot, however, omit to mention those who, when they left the city, were abandoning family members, often frail, lonely, ill people who now had no one to whom they could turn for help. It is one of the most painful pages in the history of the siege. In his memoirs, Dmitry Likhachev recalls only too many instances of relatives being abandoned and left to their fate.[33] He finds this inexcusable – and there can be few excuses – but in fairness we should add that the decision to abandon relatives in their hour of need can scarcely have been taken lightly or cynically.

As we read the documents of those years, we can see that family members were abandoned only in extreme situations: when an evacuation deadline was imminent and an answer was required in a matter of hours, when no other option could be found. At the very least, people would try to convince themselves and others that their family would be fine,[34] that they would receive medical treatment and be well fed and warm. It was rare for anyone simply to be abandoned without a second thought.[35] Attempts would be made to find them a hospital bed, or acquaintances would be asked to keep an eye on them. Perhaps people knew that was not going to save any lives, but wanted not to lose their self-respect. Likhachev was particularly appalled by an incident in which people he knew abandoned their helpless mother, tied to a sledge, as they were leaving from the Finland Station ('The Sanitary Inspectorate refused to let her through'). Perhaps, though, they have some excuse in that they were at least not dumping her in a deserted, icy street but at a busy railway station, possibly hoping someone would show compassion and take her in. Others of Likhachev's acquaintance abandoned their little daughter who was dying in hospital. They evidently felt that by doing so 'they were saving the lives of their other children'.

There was a widespread view during the Time of Death that the most talented, the most viable should be saved, and one individual could be sacrificed if that would mean two others would survive. Evacuation was the moment of truth, when just a few minutes could be enough to discover who was prepared to sacrifice their mother for the sake of their own survival. No matter how unpredictable the decision, it always gave a stark insight into someone's personal morality.

Dmitry Likhachev describes in great detail the tragic fate of language and literature specialist Vasiliy Komarovich. His daughter studied at the Theatre Institute, and it was decided to evacuate her along with the other students. Her mother decided she would leave too: 'Her father was in no state to travel, so they decided to abandon him.' Of course, they wanted their departure to have some semblance of decency by arranging for him to go to a hospital for dystrophics which was due to be opened at the Writers Club. They needed to leave immediately, but the hospital opening was being delayed and their efforts to get him admitted ahead of time were unsuccessful. They tied him to a sledge, took him across the Neva, and dumped him in the semi-basement of the Writers Club. He died a few weeks later.

An aspect of this tale of depravity which particularly disgusted Likhachev was that, after Komarovich's wife and daughter had left him, they crept back and 'surreptitiously watched, spying on him'. Likhachev makes no comment on this episode, but from his tone it is clear that he saw it as a manifestation of moral degeneracy. That was also how Komarovich saw it: 'Those monsters hid from me.'[36] But then, they could just have hastened from the scene to avoid being caught in the middle of such an unsavoury act. Instead, they left, but then came back, hid and observed. To give them the benefit of the doubt, perhaps they still had some humanity, some sense of shame which kept them from just running away, some modicum of pity which made them want to check whether a frail old man left on his own was going to be all right.[37]

In situations where an instant decision was called for, everything could be very confused, and depend on the smallest detail. There could be no time to reflect on what was happening and be sure of not doing something unwise. There could be a frantic rush, chaos, and pressure from other people. Often those making the decisions were siege victims, sick and starved and barely able to consider the consequences of their actions rationally. We find a dramatic and unusually vivid illustration of the chaos in Irina Zelenskaya's diary, which describes the would-be evacuation of her pregnant daughter and her son-in-law. I will quote as fully as possible from this section of her diary. Detailed commentary would be superfluous:

The process of getting dressed was very difficult for Boris. It took a good hour for him to slowly put on one item of clothing after another. I bandaged his poor legs. They were swollen and looked like tree trunks. All the skin on his heels had peeled oddly and was hanging down in pouches. We had no proper footwear for him. I had to try to pull on the ragged felt boots he walked about in, but it was so difficult and painful that at one moment it seemed to me I would not be able to pull even them on to his swollen feet and we would be unable to leave. We managed in the end, but it greatly weakened him. We set off at 4 o'clock. He got down the stairs but, outside, took only a dozen steps before his legs packed in. Natasha and I put him on the sledge, on top of all the baggage, and we got under way. It was far from easy, not least because he was afraid of falling off, and kept braking the sledge by dragging his feet along the ground. All the same, we managed to haul everything to the station. I got them and their belongings into the crammed waiting room rather than outside, but Boris was weakening. If he sat down he could not get up without help. They were supposed to be boarding at 6.00, but instead had to wait until 10.00. On the platform it was like a crowd of nomads, with sledges and great bundles of belongings, and in places, like a terrible omen, great blockages of people. One person collapsed from exhaustion. When we were only going in the station entrance we met two men dragging a woman by her arms. She had a face like a skull with wrinkled skin on it. She was bent at the knees and her legs were trailing behind her like sacks. We did not want to risk piling into the crush with a sick man, so let most of them go through before we went on to the platform. By then Boris could hardly walk. I sent Natasha ahead with the heavy bags to 'save a place', as we naively imagined, and decided I would come slowly along to the carriage with Boris. At this point he had his first fall. I barely managed to get him back on his feet, and step by step, with much coaxing and encouragement, got him to some sort of bollard. By now he could not walk. I stopped a lad who was passing, who agreed in return for enough tobacco for a roll-your-own to take him on a sledge to the carriage which, inevitably, was right at the front of the train. One way or another we got him there and found Natasha in a completely hopeless situation: besides us there were thirty or so people milling around, all with boarding passes for the same carriage, which was already packed to capacity with people and baggage right up to the entry platforms. It was 11 o'clock by this time, freezing and windy. The cold was seriously affecting Boris and, when Natasha went to sort out the boarding, he could not even keep himself on the sledge. One time he fell face down and I just could not lift him back up. Three policemen arrived and roughly pulled him back up the steps on to the platform. He could hardly move his tongue, and kept repeating over and over again, 'Wanna get in.' Natasha came back, having sorted out the boarding, but when she saw the state Boris was in, she panicked: should she go or should she stay with him? She came rushing to me and said, 'Mum, who should I save, Boris or the baby?' Somebody from her institute's management came up, took one look at Boris and said, 'Go and take your place immediately. It's obvious he's not going to live till morning.' I shouted at Natasha, 'Go on. I'll stay behind and look after him.' By this time Boris seemed to have lost consciousness. Natasha got some girls from the medical team to bring a stretcher and take him to the medical centre. While we were busy with him, somebody stole Natasha's suitcase with the food and all the things she needed for the journey – more, probably, than everything else put together. I was so cold I was only semi-conscious myself. My felt boots were sodden and my hands were soaking. Two fingers seem to be frostbitten. I have only a vague recollection of Natasha getting into the carriage, and have no idea who helped her with the luggage. I only memorized the number of the carriage and went to look for Boris at the medical point. I found him unconscious and without a pulse, his pupils not reacting to light. I injected him with camphor, but nothing happened. He lay in that state for two and a half hours before the 'emergency ambulance' arrived.[38]

The paramedics, when they arrived, roughly shoved him into the ambulance, and that was the last Irina saw of him. She could not locate him in either the mortuaries or the hospitals, and even suspected the paramedics had gone through his pockets and then just thrown him out of the ambulance. Her daughter failed to save the baby, and the whole sad story encapsulates the destruction, but also the tenacity with which those trapped in the siege fought death to the last.

6

The main measure of a person's charity was their preparedness to share bread. No Leningrader had any to spare, so the gift meant they were donating a portion of an already meagre ration. They shared everything with their families: food, firewood, hot water. The gifts were often minuscule: 'a small sugar lump', 'some crumbs of bread', 'a sliver of butter', 'the crumbs from his ration', 'a piece of biscuit'.[39] But those receiving them understood they were being given all that someone had to give. Belongings were sold, sometimes even the most precious, for next to nothing, to help loved ones. Food surrogates were shared: jelly made from wood glue, fritters of wallpaper paste, cattle feed, skins, oilcake – whatever anyone had to spare.

Not everyone was generous, however. Relatives stole the ration cards from starving people too weak to defend themselves, thereby condemning them to death. Concealing it from their starving family members, and sometimes robbing them outright, there were some who obtained food and did not share it, or who could not resist eating another person's ration. 'There were cases where old people were given no food at all. "You're going to die anyway", they would be told, "so it is better for you to save your grandchildren"', V. E. Skorobogatenko, the Central Committee Party administrator at the Elektrosila [Electric Power] factory, noted.[40] There were instances of violence, sometimes between the most closely related people: husbands, wives, children, parents, brothers, sisters.[41] 'Even at home I was afraid that someone in the family would steal my bread', recalls Alexandra Zmitrichenko.[42] Few people would have been surprised at the time by the admission of one Leningrader that she took her grandmother's bread, even though the old lady was hungry and crying: 'As for me, offer me everything and I'd eat it. I had no pity for anyone. All those feelings got blunted.'[43]

Families with members serving in the army in the vicinity of Leningrad stood a better chance of support. Many service personnel did not immediately discover just how badly their families were suffering. The censors firmly deleted from letters all mention of starvation. Those fighting on more distant fronts were likely to know even less about the calamity which had befallen Leningrad, and their families also appealed to them for help. The soldiers shared everything, from bread to horse meat; sometimes they even handed over their military food entitlement certificate. There was a kind of redistribution of food, from the less hungry to those on the verge of starvation, from those who were embarrassed to receive a larger piece of bread than their friends to Leningraders whom nobody else would help.

There is something particularly touching about the concern for their families of soldiers who were being treated in the Leningrad hospitals. They were cold, suffering from wounds, barely able to walk. They themselves were hardly being overfed, but they did their best to help out. They were glad to escape the groaning and screams of the dying. One Leningrader recalled her father coming from hospital to visit his family: 'He saw that mother was confined to bed, and began bringing her food from hospital: a piece of sugar, and ever such a small eau-de-cologne bottle he would pour jelly into for her.'[44] Another Leningrader describes his mother going to see his father in hospital: 'I tried to guess what Dad would send this time: a piece of butter or, like last time, a rissole?'[45] His father would give the family pipe tobacco to exchange for food.[46] When it was time for him to leave Leningrad, he gave his son and daughter pieces of cake with apple jam.

Over time, this custom began to be seen not only as a moral duty, but as an obligation. Families sometimes went to relatives in hospital in the expectation that they would be fed, or given food to take home.[47] If they found they were out of luck, they could not hide their disappointment. For example, Evelina Soloviova often brought food to share with her husband when visiting him in hospital with her daughter. During the Time of Death she had nothing to take him, and at just that time he was transferred to another hospital. 'It was really hard for me to visit him there. I could barely drag my feet along, and didn't take our daughter', she recalled; 'It was a very sad visit. He could give me no help and I had nothing to take him. I told him, "Don't expect me. If I don't come it will be because I have died."[48]

This same custom of donating part of your hospital ration to others was practised by other patients whose 'enhanced diet' was even less generous than that of those in the army. Many were admitted as 'dystrophic', but even they tried to share with their families the bread, soup, porridge and whatever else might come their way. 'Hospital' food was either taken home (sometimes in the form of a packed ration) or given to those visiting relatives. Sometimes patients would feed a visitor from their own dish, and the food might be something quite delicious and completely unexpected at that time. 'Mother treated me to her serving of buckwheat soup, and what an amazing fragrance that cherry had which I tried', Anna Nalegatskaya remembers.[49]

People also often shared the food they were issued in enterprises, schools and institutions. The system for redeeming ration cards was extremely complex and at times confused, despite attempts to reform it. You could be issued bread in a bread shop, a school canteen, or from a stall in a factory. Coupons for cereals and meat were taken as payment for meals; you might be given, instead of sugar, sweets and jam; butter was interchangeable with cheese and soya milk. Arms factories were able to feed their workers better. It was easier to obtain rationed foods from the factory shop, which other people might be unable to buy even after queueing for many hours. Sometimes meals were provided without the need to sacrifice coupons, and there could even be more than one helping, although the nutritional value was not high. The same was available, although infrequently, to 'particularly valuable' staff: professors and lecturers in institutes, scholars, artists, actors, writers and architects. They were entitled to more generous rations, and were sometimes issued 'assortments' of food products.

This system was exploited to support other family members who lacked such privileges. 'The only thing that saves father and me is the Scholars Club. Father gets dinner there and brings it back to me in boxes, we add some food here, and dine', Natalia Zavetnovskaya reported in a letter of December 1941.[50] Translator Vladimir Admoni brought his family porridge in a jar, and sugar in an envelope, from the Writers Club.[51] The actress, A. S. Belyaeva, gave concerts for the army, and brought home soup and porridge in jars, and even chunks of bread she had been given.[52]

Eyewitnesses independently mention people barely able to walk and often falling down as they carried a jar or pot of soup out of their factory canteen. On 14 January 1942, Pyotr Kapitsa witnessed one such scene. He noticed a lot of women at the gatehouse into his institute with sledges and food containers. They had come to collect the meal for staff who were ill and unable to work.[53] At this time, it was common for families to help their relatives to get to their workplace, or even to transport them there on a sledge, since otherwise they would lose their ration cards.[54]

It was easier for those who worked in civilian or military hospitals. Supervision there could be more lax because of the vagaries of medical histories. Someone might die before receiving their ration; it might not be possible to feed someone promptly because of bureaucratic delays; someone else might be unable to eat because they were hovering between life and death. Many of the stories of chicanery in hospitals – and they were widespread – were wildly overstated, but certainly those working there had little difficulty getting hold of an extra piece of bread. They could often eat together with the patients, receiving an enhanced diet and reserving part of their own meals, which of course were more modest, for their families. They could not absent themselves from the hospital every day, and often had to squirrel away what they took from their bread ration or porridge in jars, and this at a time when many found it difficult not to devour their entire ration in one go. Witnesses speak about how they stinted themselves to save up food for their families. 'We had this girl there working as a nurse, and she would always try to take anything extra she got home to her mother', a Leningrader who worked at the hospital recalled in an interview.[55] Another nurse 'used to bring her mother there every morning, take her own breakfast out to her and just drank tea herself'.[56]

It was not uncommon during the Time of Death for relatives to starve to death because they gave their bread to other members of their family. They understood they might die, and that if they did their children would be doomed with no one to look after them, but still they gave away their last crust. Who could tell? Perhaps they might not die, and that child was hungry here and now, begging for food; he was thin and pale and wasting away in front of them. He was only a child, after all.

In some families, they had to keep an eye open to stop relatives giving away the last of their rations.[57] 'Her sister told my mum she should eat some of the grounds too, but Mum said Ira [her daughter – S. Ya.] was weakest and mustn't be allowed to die.'[58] A young girl could not control herself and ate up all the bread her mother had prudently divided into several portions: 'I was crying because I had gobbled it all, and Granny Dunya quietly gave me a piece. She was crying. Mum said, "Why did you do that? You'll starve." She said, "Olga, it's nothing. Don't fuss." We all three sat there weeping!'[59]

Children saved other children. If they lost their mother, brothers and sisters did their best to help each other. Zarya Milyutina came across a 7-year-old girl by a bread shop: 'She was very thin and pale, with dark circles under her eyes. She was leaning against the wall in order not to fall over.' People were giving her bread, but she did not eat any of it: she was keeping it for her sister.[60]

A brother and sister, aged 5 and 12, were brought in to one of the children's homes: 'The girl gave her entire, meagre ration to her slowly fading brother.' She had no one, no family. Her mother had starved to death and all she had left was her brother, who seemed as transparent as glass, indifferent to everything, and slowly dying. He was the one connection she still had with the world she had known, where there was love and caring, where her mother was alive, and she was determined to keep him from dying at all costs. Her efforts were in vain. The little boy died, and then so did his sister.[61]

Children and teenagers would bring their only too meagre rations back home. Probably at any other time people would have felt unable to take bread from a hungry child, but it was accepted because there was no alternative. People could stand the hunger no longer, and had not the strength to refuse the gift, even though they knew what it was costing. V. A. Alexeyeva told how, as a 7-year-old, she was taken to a care home for dystrophics. Her mother did not leave, and through the glass door could see her daughter being fed. The children were forbidden to take bread out of the dining room, but she felt sorry for her mother: 'Well, naturally, knowing the conditions we were living in and how hungry my Mum was, I put a couple of pieces of bread in her pocket, secretly.'[62] Her mother knew this bread was for her dystrophic daughter, but took it: 'She was so happy . . . She said when she got back home she would drink some tea and eat those two pieces of bread, but of course she didn't. She ate them in the tram.'[63]

7

This kind of behaviour did not immediately become commonplace, but the siege was to undermine much stronger traditions than that. As it continued, the process gained pace. To start with, people were ashamed; they looked for excuses and were apologetic: 'Because, by the end of September, food was in very short supply, I would eat the leftovers on my daughter's plate. When she fell ill she lost her appetite.'[64] By the Time of Death, such explanations are extremely rare. We find that everywhere the soup and porridge given to children in kindergartens, schools and colleges are being brought, often smuggled, back home.[65] Nobody in the family objected: the food was shared out without ado. Children did not just understand that they ought to help their family out: they knew it was expected. Their parents made no secret of it.[66] They knew they had to do their bit if everyone was to live to see the next ten-day ration period.

The servings of this watery soup and porridge without butter or season-ings were so small that it was sometimes necessary to spoon it into cups a teaspoonful at a time.[67] The children were even ashamed that the presents they could give were so pathetically small.[68] They rarely spoke about finding it difficult to share their food, but the surviving testimony speaks volumes. One child had promised to keep a piece of bread from the kin-dergarten for his mother. He nipped off one tiny piece after another, until all that was left by evening was the crust.[69]

There are many entries about helping his mother in the diary of V. Vladimirov, a teenager working in a factory. 'I got two sausages and took them home. I gave one to Mum, and one to myself and a little bit to everyone else to try', he notes on 28 February 1942.[70]

That phrase 'a little bit to everyone else to try' tells us more eloquently than any direct admission just how hungry he was. On 3 March 1942, he brought home 'four porridges', but on 5 March his willpower failed: 'I drank the *rassolnik* soup with pickled cucumbers without bread, and I meant to take three portions of pease pudding home, only I tried some, couldn't resist it, and ate the lot.' 'I feel weak', he writes in the diary that same day, as if in explanation.[71]

Yelena Mukhina was intending to take her mother the meal she had received at a New Year's party: 'I drank up all the liquid and started putting the food into a jar. Just then there was a power cut, but in the darkness, I managed to scrape in all the pudding.' But then, as she was surreptitiously preparing this present for her mother, 'I used the darkness to empty the whole jar, licking the pudding off my fingers.'[72]

People passed food on to their families, despite all the prohibitions from the managements of hospitals, child care centres, schools, army hospitals and factories. The official logic was clear and simple: the extra rations were being issued so that a patient would recover more rapidly, a victim of starvation would get better, children would be able to learn properly, and workers to work without collapsing at their machines. This would seem to have provided all the justification needed for not sharing food with your family, but people generally devised ever more ingenious ways of smuggling it out.

One Leningrader who worked at a large bakery was given bread but told 'You must eat it yourself. You mustn't take it outside the bakery.' There was even talk of criminal prosecution if he did; but he managed, nevertheless, to smuggle 'some crusts' for his family out through the gate-bouse.[73] Ye. P. Bokaryova recalls that, when her mother, who worked at the Svetlana works, was forbidden to take away ration-free soup in a can, 'My poor mother would drink the liquid out of it and put a spoonful of the solid matter remaining into a handkerchief, which she then folded and brought home.'[74] V. Vladimirov was stopped at the factory entrance smuggling out porridge: 'I had wrapped it in paper and tucked it away.'[75] Vera Churilova and her sister had a pass to the meal after a holiday theatre performance on 6 November 1941. They 'ate the porridge and fruit compote, but wrapped the patty and bread in a handkerchief and hid it on our chests under our coats'.[76]

Children and teenagers did not have to be asked to smuggle food out for their families; they understood themselves why it was important. Schoolchildren who were caught offered a variety of explanations, seeking to soften the hearts of those supervising them. Ksenia Polzikova-Rubets recorded in her diary the dialogue between a boy and his kindergarten carer who had noticed that at lunchtime he 'had a glass jar with him and was decanting soup into it. "You mustn't do that. You know it's not allowed." "Let me, please! The soup is for Volodya [his brother – S. Ya.]. His legs have started swelling."'[77]

Bread and other food tended to be shared out equally in the family, regardless of how much each contributed. It was unusual for people to eat separately. Sometimes that happened if a member of the family had lost their ration cards. At that point, a starving family's cup of suffering could overflow, and the suspicion that they were 'being eaten out of house and home' (which might already have been nagging them) could become unbearable. Stealing within a family was also not unknown. That could put its members on the alert, and suspicions would very soon arise when they saw the meagreness of the porridge and soup being cooked for everyone in the communal pot. Close attention was paid to anyone helping themselves to more soup too frequently, or who had a bigger spoon. Quarrelling was inevitable. Esfir Levina wrote about a legal adviser at a bank who received treble rations, and left his family on the grounds that they were 'eating all his food'. She related a story about a professor whose wife had only a dependant's ration card: 'For dinner they had sausage stewed in soup and he thought the amount of sausage was too little. He took it out, weighed it and demanded extra.' His wife assured him it was just that the sausage had boiled down a bit in the cooking but he did not believe her. He took part of hers and ordered her in future to cook without tasting the food: 'You'll taste it so often I shall end up hungry. Never mind if it doesn't have enough salt in it.'[78] From this bare narrative, it is difficult to imagine what prehistory the incident might have had. The couple might long have been at daggers drawn, and a part might have been played by the 'siege lethargy' so familiar to all Leningraders, which prevented people from responding vigorously to even the most obvious offences against common morality.

To prevent others from helping themselves to your grams of bread, even children would go to great lengths. 'Mummy, Mummy, separate 200-gram portions', two little girls shouted in a bread shop when they saw the assistant was weighing out a loaf of bread on the basis of the whole family's entitlement. The assistant refused to divide the bread into equal portions and 'the girls were in tears.' I.I. Zhilinsky, who witnessed this scene, suspected there was more to it than met the eye: 'Evidently they were hungry, they wanted to eat, and it seemed to them that their mother was not treating them fairly.'[79]

Boris Bernstein reports that a girl denounced her mother: 'She told us the mother had taken her ration cards and was feeding her on something that did not taste nice, bad-tasting meat.' The mother was arrested: 'At that time people like that were tried very swiftly.'[80]

For some people, these communal family rituals became customary and marked a red line which could not be crossed. Some, however, did cross the line, and the next step after businesslike calculations on the principle of 'contribute to the pot and eat' was misappropriation by parents of their children's bread. This did not happen immediately. It needed a whole set of preceding circumstances. Few people were capable in the early days of snatching bread out of the hands of a child. Where it became easier to conceal what was going on, many could not resist the temptation. 'There have been instances where a mother collects a child's ration and, barely out of the kindergarten, on the stairs, eats it all, while the child is dying at home', the head of a kindergarten told Evelina Soloviova.[81]

After that there could be no restraint, no hesitancy, no pity: the hunger had broken them. Irina Zelenskaya remembers taking a 3-year-old girl to the children's home, who never smiled and whose face was swollen: 'Her mother was not feeding her and eating all the food. When the woman fell ill, she screamed at the neighbours looking after her every time they gave food to the child.'[82] When deciding which of the children to feed and which not to, a family member might, of course, be taking account of their own chances of survival. It is difficult to assess this from the available testimony. To misappropriate a child's bread was a crime, so talking about it would be risky. A child might sincerely believe they were being unfairly treated, and it would be difficult to explain to them why, as children, they were entitled to such minimal rations.

Here is the testimony of 15-year-old Valentina Ryzhkova: 'I saw a mother in our apartment, to save her two older children, giving no bread at all to the two younger ones and sharing out their rations. I saw, and I cried together with those little ones, and they were crying, "Mummy! Bread!" They were two and four, and they had such big, pleading eyes full of tears, but their mother was in the kitchen eating their rations with the two older children. The younger ones died, then so did their mother.'[83]

The increasing emotion evident in this entry keeps its author from communicating the detail of the episode. We do not know where it happened, why it was not concealed; we do not see how other neighbours, the mother, her older children reacted to the cries of the little ones. Everything is generalized, but Valentina's undisguised hostility excludes any possibility of understatement. Years later, the incident cannot be reconstructed but this response to it remains, expressed more vividly than we might expect from a teenager. The same is true of how the story ends, where what we detect is not vengefulness but an elusive, yet palpable, sense of revulsion: 'The older children, who were seven and twelve, froze to death somewhere in the streets. I saw them one time in a bread shop. Their clothes were in tatters and their faces swollen and disfigured. They were begging for bread, and were beaten if they tried to snatch it.'[84]

Other testimony is less emotional, but the story is essentially the same: a mother helping herself to bread; a swollen, morose child who does not understand what is going on; then ever more dreadful images of degeneration with pathological details. There are many episodes of this kind in Maria Mashkova's book, with a boundless, overstated concern for the child and appalling finale: 'She died not like a human being but like an animal, screaming at the child, "You little bastard, you get more than me to eat and still keep looking at my food."'[85]

Lev Khodorkov's diary entries are more reserved, but even there we can see how difficult it is to talk coolly and coherently about such episodes, to elucidate the circumstances and apportion blame. On 8 April 1942, Khodorkov describes some 'wayside scenes' he witnessed while walking along the embankment with 'a commanding officer of the Red Fleet'. 'Scene 4. A husband and wife are pulling along the incredibly thin body of a child. In their family they have only children and "dependants". They decide who is to die and underfeed that child in order for the others to survive.'[86]

What is this? The confession of strangers? The account of an eyewitness with later compassionate reflection? Or something else? Evidently, there has been a conversation and, as is usual at such dramatic moments, people have poured their hearts out, not sparing themselves, heartbroken, wanting to be heard. The entry continues: 'How dreadful! A child is doomed. He wants to live, he picks up every crumb, wailing.'[87]

This is less a story than the emotional response of a Leningrader caught in the siege at the sight of the distress of others. He has probably embellished the scene, which he had not witnessed, with details familiar to him from other tales, and this has made his upset at the sight particularly acute.

This dreadful scene is created with individual brushstrokes, from those talking about themselves, and from the person recreating, from what he been told, the image of a child starving to death. He recreates it, adding poignant and tragic details of the nightmare which he infers. We do not know why these people told their story without apprehension to people they had just met in the street. Perhaps they were at the end of their tether and did not care what they revealed; perhaps, seeing a naval officer, they had hopes of support, since those in the forces were better fed. We can only surmise. The fact is that we do not know and have no way of confirming anything. Documents from the siege are difficult to interpret because what they relate has been written when people were severely traumatized, and that results in different rules of construction and logic. People are trying to avoid further anguish and are reluctant to peer once again down into the abyss. Their discourse is feverish and chaotic, and how could it not be when they are in such emotional turmoil and their imagination is magnifying the details of degeneration?

8

Some children were left at the door of children's homes and hospitals in the hope that they might survive. In February 1942, nine foundlings aged from 18 months to 3 years were discovered at the door of one children's home. 'They have taken my husband, so let them now feed my children', was how one Leningrader explained her decision.[88] Not infrequently, children were left at evacuation centres, where not every face was known and there was general chaos and confusion. At the Borisova Griva evacuation centre, they discovered a 4–month-old baby 'in a bag', as well as other foundlings.[89] People were motivated by wanting to save not only their children, but also themselves. 'There were instances where a mother left her baby and her own aged mother, took their ration cards, and went off to live in a completely different district', A. D. Yakunina, chairwoman of the Lenin District Red Cross, recalled.[90]

A 'freezing' of emotion, starvation, fatigue, desperation, all made people act in ways they would not have dreamed of even a short time before. Small wonder that we so often find mention in diaries and memoirs of people's 'stony' expressions and heartlessness after losing loved ones. 'A complete absence of grief for the man they were taking to the mortuary', Izrail Nazimov wrote in his diary, after seeing two swollen teenagers hauling a sledge with the corpse of their father.[91]

Lyudmila Eliasheva met a woman taking a body to the cemetery. Someone pointed out to her that the person lying on the sledge was still alive and moving his hand. 'Yes', she replied, 'he's moving a bit, but by the time I get there he'll have stopped. Anyway, tomorrow I might not be able to bury him.'[92]

We observe the collapse of morality within the family in several stories. One is the tale of a girl who was robbed of food by her stepfather. He was not a cruel man, but weak-willed. He sincerely wanted to be a substitute father but was broken by the siege. She was disgusted, and reproached him and tried to make him ashamed of himself. He bore it all without complaint, all the accusations and the insults, but then robbed again and could not control himself. The mother was visibly failing, but he carried on stealing her food. On 25 December 1941, the size of rations was increased, but the euphoria soon passed. He ate his own rations, then those of the mother and finally, unable to restrain himself, the daughter's rations too: 'I hate him. How can anybody be so mean!? For heaven's sake, I'm hungry too!' The girl finds it difficult to control her emotion. Her hostility increasingly envelops her until, on 29 December 1941, the stepfather dies and all the bile she has been trying to hold back bursts out: 'I'm so glad! This is the moment I have been waiting for. He died and I laughed out loud! I could have jumped for joy!'[93]

Another Leningrader had supposed his family life was idyllic. He felt his wife cared for him, and he reciprocated in full measure. Then he took to his bed and could see he was thought to be dying and was just 'a hateful burden': 'She began misappropriating those pathetic crumbs of mine, and concealing them in order to fortify herself to the detriment of my already poor health.' He has no doubt about it: 'I made scales, began checking all the food she brought, and my suspicions proved well founded.'[94] His irritation becomes increasingly obvious, until he no longer doubts she has always deceived and robbed him – not only now, during the siege.

Another diary can justly be described as a record of the disintegration of family ties, in this case between a wife and her considerably older husband. This is not a steady process. Anger is succeeded by remorse, and it is notable that the damage done to the family is not always proportionate to the strength of the blows to which it is subjected. The entries are self-explanatory.

7 December 1941. In the evening we quarrelled over sugar and sweets. They needed to be apportioned to last for the whole of the

ten-day ration period. Lidusya became very angry. She is quite unable to understand our situation. She considers that I am being greedy, but this is not a time for good manners and behaving like a gentleman. It is a matter of rationally sharing food in the interests of self-preservation.

21 December 1941. Lidusya gave me a book. Her attentiveness is very pleasant. I am attached to my Lidusya. I love her. I have nobody dearer and closer to me or whom I love more, but what a pity we have to squabble over every little thing.

22 December 1941. In the evening Lidusya brought me dinner. She fed me well and was particularly attentive and caring. She brought me vitamins made from pine needles. That was so touching of her. Very, very pleasant. It is a long time since I have been shown so much concern and I do very much need her. It is pleasant.

25 December 1941. Barely able to crawl to the office. Lidusya cursed and swore, as if it is my fault I am starving.

2 January 1942. Instead of sugar and sweets she brought jam. She said it was 500 grams but it was probably closer to 150. It was a lie. I no longer trust her. Her whole attitude has changed. No friendliness, no warm, attentive, caring behaviour at all. Everything she does is evidently only out of self-interest, although she keeps saying, 'I do it all for you.' She blames me for everything, swears at me, mimics me. I shall have to leave. I've really landed in it in my old age.

3 January 1942. I am very hungry. Came home with Lidia. Asked for a piece of my dried bread. She swore at me. We had an unbeliev-able quarrel and only then did she make me three oilcake patties. I told her I can no longer live with her and asked her to return my ration cards. She did not do so.

4 January 1942. I feel incredibly hungry. I asked her endlessly to hand over my food ration cards. She threw down an envelope without saying a word. I looked, and saw that she has been helping herself to meals, grains, meat and butter from my cards. She left me without a meal for one day. That is how she has been caring for me. Completely disgraceful! Unbelievable. Daylight robbery! Now I can see why she was in such a hurry to get me to sign my life insurance over to her, give her an engagement ring and so on.

5 January 1942. More quarrelling about food. Again accusing me of eating too much, that I am the only one getting fed and should be ashamed of myself. We had a flaming row and stopped talking.[95]

9

Often, even the death of relatives and friends came to be regarded differ-ently. During their death agony, when personality changed abruptly, their behaviour seemed disgraceful, inconsiderate and selfish. People would ask themselves what right this person thought they had to demand such special attention. Life was hardly a bed of roses for anyone! Here they were, greedily demanding good bread, meat, butter and sausage: where was that supposed to come from? And who did they think they were, anyway? Distant relatives you rarely met even before the war, and had never particularly liked?

Few people would admit to the sense of relief sometimes felt when people finally died. Few would confide that even to a diary, but it was difficult not to see it. Watching funeral processions in the city, Maria Konoplyova felt 'a concealed wish just to get it all over with as quickly as possible.' She had no doubt about the reason: 'The dead were just an added complication in an already difficult life.'[96] Even the death of a mother, the person closest to you of all, did not always cause great grief. It was only later that the sense of irrevocable loss would be felt, but while she was alive people were more conscious of her frailty – which only added to the burdens of life under the siege – her lack of stoicism and irritating grumbles. A mother is expected to be a source of kind words first heard in childhood, her face is expected to have its dear, familiar features, but now instead there was a ravaged face, a changed personality, someone estranged from her children, unable to recognize them in starvation-induced hallucinations, snatching the bread from their hands, a complete stranger. 'One morning in early April, my mother could not get out of bed. I tugged at her hands and saw a cold dislike in her eyes. She no longer had any feelings for us', one Leningrader recalled.[97] A brother and sister were afraid to stay at home for long and preferred to go outside: 'After our father died, Mother changed somehow. She was not working and could hardly walk. She began having terrible fits and started to cry frequently.'[98]

The mother of A. G. Usanova was dying of dysentery, and her daughter could not bring herself to warm or hug her. Her son was dying next to her; he had long been too weak to get out of bed. Everything seems ghastly and unreal in this terrible scene: 'I said, "Mum, my brother is dying." She said, "Don't trouble him. Don't frighten him away."'[99] Soon, her mother could not even speak and her daughter was afraid to go closer to her. She wanted to go out but her godmother stopped her: 'Don't go to bed. Your mother will die tonight.' The girl stayed up: 'I sat down and waited for my mother to die.' When it was all over, her godmother took her away: 'She washed me and put me in a soft, warm bed. I still remember two feelings struggling in me. On the one hand, now I was all alone, but on the other hand, I was warm and clean and everything was behind me.'[100]

The dozens of everyday trials which Leningraders were burdened with kept them from feeling pain at the inevitable outcome. While they were waiting for it, they often thought about the rations that would remain, and were not embarrassed to talk about that. 'I'm in luck. There's a couple of kilos of grains left on her card. I'll get a boost', a worker remarked à propos of his wife's death.[101] Some considered themselves fortunate if relatives died at the beginning of the ten-day ration period: the bread issued against their cards could be used to pay for a funeral or they could eat it themselves.[102] There were not only ration cards to be considered, but also the possessions of the deceased. I. I. Zhilinsky, obtaining his mother's death certificate from the registry office, could not restrain himself and ate 175 grams of bread and 50 grams of butter before he left. He had immediately sold her felt boots.[103]

Children were the worst at concealing the fact that they were looking forward to getting bread when someone died. One Leningrader tells of the day her younger sister, Lyuba, went out and never came back home: 'Her ration was lying there all this time and still she had not come back . . .'. She just could not banish unworthy thoughts about her sister's bread. Her 3-year-old sister, Vera, was beside her and perhaps afraid she would not get any of it. It was such a temptation to see it sitting there: 'Vera whispered to me, "I hope Lyuba doesn't come back, then we'll be able to eat that bread."' It was only later that her older sister felt bad about this, but at the time she unhesitatingly replied, 'That's true. Better if she doesn't come back. We'll be able to eat that bread.'[104]

'Oh, you're dying, but you've still got some bread left over.' This thought tormented another girl who witnessed her grandmother's death. It was difficult to hide what she was thinking, and her mother saw right through her. The girl was in tears for her grandmother, but she really did want the bread: 'It was all I could think about. Oh, dear!' (She cries.) 'I've felt so bad about that all my life. I was just thinking, "She's dying, and that's her bread lying there."' (She cries.) 'Then my mother said, "All right. It's over." And, of course, the next thing she said was, "Go and eat the bread."' (She cries.)[105]

Funerals

1

The stages in the deterioration of moral standards during the Time of Death were most fully reflected in families' funeral rites. Leningraders began dying in their masses in December 1941, but until mid-January 1942 people did all they could to take coffins to the cemetery themselves. That became more difficult by the day. People were starving, there was no public transport, the roads were not being cleared of snow, and unprecedentedly low temperatures became a major feature of the siege. Funerals had to be held at cemeteries out on the outskirts of the city. The younger members of a family would be harnessed to pull the sledge, but later that was just done by whoever was still on their feet.[106] From many of the descriptions, we can see this was a real Via dolorosa for grief-stricken family members, frozen and starving, and often exposed to artillery bombardment. Maria Konoplyova describes an emaciated 16-year-old taking his grandfather for burial: 'He had to pull the body there on a sledge in 20° below zero. He came back from the cemetery almost delirious and could hardly answer our questions.'[107]

Everywhere in these descriptions we come across the same words: 'harnessed', 'dragged', 'fell', 'staggered'. As early as 16 November 1941, Anna Ostroumova-Lebedeva noted how few mourners there were in the funeral processions, 'only occasionally one or two people'.[108] Later it became more common for the family to ask strangers to deal with their dead. These were often the caretakers and, of course, they were paid, at first with money, but later only with bread. The family and friends of the deceased could not accompany them on their last journey, some because they were ill, some because they could hardly walk, and others because they were so swollen they could not get out of bed.[109]

In the early days, people tried to bury their dead in coffins, but that soon became the exception. In Leningrad, in the grip of icy cold, every wooden plank was precious, and supplies were running low. Requests for a coffin were granted reluctantly, and later regarded as eccentric.[110]

From mid-December 1941, many Leningraders ceased to use coffins, which no doubt prompted others to do the same and cut back on funeral ritual. But not all. The very sight of the cemetery and mortuaries, with corpses stacked one on top of the other, or often flung in a heap or scattered along the roadside, robbed, stripped, motivated others to protect their relatives' remains from desecration and maintain the traditional rites. When Maria Mashkova brought the body of her mother-in-law to a mortuary, she encountered 'a terrible scene of cynicism and horror. Black faces which seemed to have been cured with smoke, corpses with sprawling limbs, in filthy rags, their legs exposed. I felt sick and appalled at having to tip her on to a pile of other people.'[111]

This all became commonplace in the Time of Death, but initially the sight of corpses desecrated during the process of burial made families all the more determined to adhere to the old rituals: 'You know, I was horrified when I saw on both sides of the Serafimovskoye Cemetery what I at first thought was firewood but then realized were dead bodies. They had just piled them up like logs. Well, we asked them not to take Father out of his coffin, although they were just laying the dead straight into the trenches.'[112]

Abandoned corpses fell prey not only to looters. 'In the morning, by the statue of the Bronze Horseman, someone had laid the body of a child who was of angelic beauty', the artist Vlasov recalled. Later, he saw that all the flesh had been cut off the corpse.[113] There are many such stories.[114] Alexandra Grigorieva, who lived in the city centre near Gorky Prospekt, mentions how often she saw corpses, shrouded in sheets, abandoned by someone in the street. If they were not removed, the next day the shroud would have been ripped off and the naked bodies desecrated.[115] A coffin seemed at least a rudimentary protection, whose ephemerality people refused to acknowledge. Perhaps the fear that the same fate might await the remains of their loved ones forced people, in spite of all evidence to the contrary, to seek out a coffin, or make one themselves, and insist that it, or something approximating to a coffin, should be used for the burial.

Vera Inber saw an emaciated young woman pulling along on a sledge 'an art nouveau wardrobe she had bought in an antique shop to use as a coffin'.[116] People used the drawer from a wardrobe, a baby's pram, or rented a coffin. When even that was not possible, they would try to construct something that served as a symbolic coffin. 'I recently saw a corpse with no coffin which had wood shavings interwined on its chest with the strips of the winding sheet, evidently to make it respectable. It had all the appearance of the work of an expert, far from amateurish hand', Vera Inber wrote, surmising that the services of the 'hand' would not have come cheap.[117]

The high cost of coffins is mentioned in a report of the Leningrad Department of Communal Service Enterprises, which notes that it was not deterring relatives from buying them.[118] By mid-January 1942, however, funerals complete with coffins had all but ceased.[119] Coffins were no longer being sold, and people lacked the strength to make their own or to take them to the cemetery. They had to be paid for with bread, and people had to decide whether their priority was caring for the dead or for the living.

The burial team at Serafimovskoye cemetery 'arrived with a homemade coffin, hastily laid the body in a trench and threw the plywood coffin on the fire', we are told. 'A good-looking but very thin girl calmly told us, "Don't be upset that we bury them without coffins. It's all the same to the dead, and we get very cold out here in the open. The fire barely warms us as it is, and we have no firewood allocation. If it goes out they'll be putting us in that grave too."'[120] Nikolai Baranov was struck by how confident the girl seemed. She evidently was used to having to explain herself. A gravedigger had no interest in observing proprieties, and no time to worry about other people's feelings. They came here to bury the corpses because that qualified them for enhanced rations. They were here because they wanted to survive,[121] and aimed to do so, come what may. They had no hesitation about adding false names to the burial lists, incentivized by the extra rations they received for exceeding their quota. It made no odds to them whether they pitched a body out of its coffin in full view of the family or after they had left.

2

People also refused to pay for coffins because they knew they would only be re-sold at the cemeteries and mortuaries. Because of the shortage, there was good money to be made that way. At the mortuary, Varvara Vraskaya's family were 'advised by people who had brought their dead to take the body out of its coffin and hand it in as it was because, they said, the body would in any case not be left in its coffin, which would be exchanged for bread.'[122] N. V. Shirkova, who went to bury her father, noted that 'if a coffin was good it would be sold on'.[123]

In the early days, it was up to the family and friends to dig the grave in the rock-hard frozen ground, but that ritual was superseded even sooner than the use of coffins. Those who could not dig a grave paid in money or valuables to have it done for them, although later, from December 1941, only bread was accepted in payment.[124] The stages in which burial rituals changed were common to all: instead of a coffin, there were winding sheets (for 'swaddling'); instead of burial at a cemetery, there were strictly defined collection points for corpses within the city;[125] at first there was burial in separate graves, but then in a common grave, or even no burial. These changes applied to nearly everyone. Many were unable to object because this was not a purely personal choice: they had to go along with what everybody else in the siege was doing. The narrowing of choices open to a large group of people subsumed those of the individual, who was integrated into the community's way of life and obligations.

The custom of burial in mass graves became universal from January 1942.[126] People may have felt it was shameful, but there was no alternative. Letters have survived which were sent from Leningrad by people who buried their loved ones in mass graves. They are apologetic. Let us quote two from quite different people: N. Makarova, an obscure victim of the siege, and the poetess Olga Berggolts. Although the style is different, both are primarily an attempt at self-justification. Makarova's letter telling her sister that their mother has died is written more prosaically.

> We buried her yesterday, but not separately like used to be our way but in a communal grave, that's how everyone gets buried now (more than 3 million people are dying) and there is no possibility of doing it separately because in the first place there are no coffins for any money, only for bread, and we only get 300 grams, but now they won't even make a coffin for bread, there are no planks and no men to make them.[127]

She emphasizes the 'objective' reasons. There is no suggestion that it might be possible to get back to the old traditions, only further considerations:

> I do not think you will think ill of us and will understand how bad we all feel about it, but there was no other way, we did everything we could for Mother. I do not know if we will stay alive or not but our life here is horrible, there has never been anything like this. We have no water, no electricity, no firewood, we are almost starving and every day there is the shelling. My children will probably all die soon and I will probably be dead soon when the tumor gets to the heart and that is the end.[128]

She is obviously feeling some guilt, and that she has to explain herself to people who do not know how nightmarish life is in Leningrad by referring to horrors she is powerless to prevent.

This feeling of guilt is even more evident in Olga Berggolts's letter, sent to her sister early in 1942 after the death of her husband, Nikolai

Molchanov. In the main, the tone is briskly practical and has something in common with N. Makarova's self-justification:

> I did not even try to bury him myself. I could not drag him, wrapped in a blanket, the whole way across the city as nearly everybody here now does. I simply could not get my hands on enough bread for a coffin and a separate grave. I decided to consent to having him buried by the hospital in a communal grave.[129]

This evidently strikes her as insufficient to explain why she did that, and her letter takes on a more solemn tone: 'He lived like a soldier on the front line, so let him be buried as a soldier would be at the front. He would approve of that.'

Evidently, however, this pathos, grated with her and she introduces more personal and intimate notes: 'We agreed between ourselves that whichever of us outlived the other must try to survive until the end of the present tragedy. I shall try to live. It is hard to do that, my sister, more difficult than ceasing to live, but I will try.'[130] She had nothing to reproach herself with: she was dystrophic herself, but sacrificed her tiny rations in the hope of saving her husband. How typical, though, these explanations are, so various in such a short letter. There are too many excuses, but that is not something we would be finding if people had become insensitive to moral imperatives.

We need to keep this evidence in mind when we talk about how rapidly the funeral ritual changed. We often see only what happened, and have little idea of the emotions it evoked. Eyewitnesses either shy away, or consider it superfluous to talk about a new ritual they are already accustomed to. Certainly, many families were unable to take a body, not only to a distant cemetery, but even to the nearest mortuary. Zinaida Ignatovich, however, witnessed a 'shivering, stooped, almost withered old lady' giving valuables to two men and 'tearfully imploring them to take her husband to the mortuary'.[131] A family which arrived at the Georgievskoye cemetery 'asked the gravediggers to bury a body carefully because "she was a good woman"'.[132] At another cemetery, a mother who had lost her 6-year-old son asked them to 'lay him down gently, my own sweet boy'.[133] N. Makarova, when her son and mother were buried in a common grave, paid the workmen to 'bury her in the corner', so that later it would be easier to identify where she was buried.[134]

3

Symptoms of moral depravity did not take root immediately, and attempts were made to resist them. What was achieved was not a victory against them, but a demonstration of determination not to accept them. 'When we arrived at the mortuary, we were ordered to strip him and put him outside the mortuary gate, in the street, where there were stacks of naked bodies. At that, we broke down and refused to undress him', recalls Tamara

Ivanova, who helped a friend when her father died.[135] The everyday realities of the siege did not, however, defeat only the weak. The same picture of abandonment of the old obsequies is seen where families would bring a body to the cemetery and, lacking the strength to dig a grave, just leave it there. They would take it to a stack of corpses at the cemetery, and depart, abandoning the sledge with their dead on the path.

'There were corpses in the streets, on the stairs, in apartments, at the gates of a hospital, beside fences, in the courtyards', I. K. Stadnik recalls, quoting his wartime diary.[136] The hellish chasm of the siege widened inexorably, and by New Year 1941–2 the dead were being dealt with unceremoniously – as indeed, not infrequently, were the living. 'Early in the morning, they always found several dead bodies in the snowdrifts by the walls of our hospital', wrote Valentina Gapova.[137] Sometimes bodies were left in the basement of someone's own home, or taken in secret to a hospital.[138] Soon corpses were simply being dumped in the streets, and not only in back alleys but right in the city centre.[139] Ye. Mironova recalled a friend who, not having the strength to bury her sister properly, just put her 'outside the gate in a snowdrift'.[140] When people abandoned dead bodies in the street, they were usually hoping they would be collected by the police, according to several testimonies.[141]

By the end of 1942, funeral ritual had been severely curtailed. The form was now determined not only by moral considerations and what families were capable of, but also by official instructions. Conforming with these was compulsory, and perhaps that facilitated the switch to the new system, as well as the speed and ease of disposal they provided for: bodies were to be taken to collection points established in all districts of the city, and from there were taken away on trucks.[142] No longer did you have to try to hack out a grave in the frozen earth of a cemetery; no longer did you have to worry about what other people might think; no longer did starving people have to sacrifice their bread rations to gravediggers; no longer did people on the verge of collapse have to drag swaddlings to the outskirts of the city. Everything was now done for you: you just put the body on a sledge, pulled it a few streets, left it at the approved collection point, and went home.

Even this ritual was not always observed. This was particularly the case when people were being evacuated. One evacuee left his brother's body in his apartment: he had little time and could only hope someone else might bury him.[143] There were yet more dramatic episodes. N. Kartofelnikov, a student at a vocational school, recalled:

My friend Tolya came to see me and said, 'Come over to my place and help me bury my Mum. She died three days ago, and we're being evacuated tomorrow.' I and another comrade went to his apartment on the Fontanka canal. We dragged the body from the third floor. We just hauled it down. When we got outside, we began wondering what to do with it. Tolya said, 'Let's just slide it down over the snow straight into the canal.' And that is the funeral we gave Tolya's mother.[144]

That was unusual, and it is worth saying that Tolya was barely able to stand on his feet. A few days later, he died from malnutrition on the train taking him away from Leningrad. His own body was thrown off the train in the countryside by his classmates. Dumping a corpse in the street was not actually that straightforward. You had to look out for the police, the neighbours, the housing manager, and just people passing by. It was usually done at night.

People steadily, if not without hesitation, became reconciled to the new rituals. Some found that more difficult than others. In February 1942, one person would still manage to get a coffin, while another, in December 1942, would be dumping a body without taking it to the cemetery. There were many factors contributing to how a person behaved: how great the affection was for the family member, their strength of personal morality, their cultural level, the level of public scrutiny, their state of health, their ability to find additional resources and, by no means least, religious faith. There were too many other factors for us to be able to list them all. They were personal to each individual.

The pace at which funeral rituals changed seems hectic only if judged by ordinary standards. We need to apply different criteria to days during the siege. If Leningraders for even a few extra weeks went on searching for a coffin, burying someone in a drawer, dragging a body through frozen, uncleared streets at constant risk of fainting from hunger and themselves dying, setting aside, when starving, a portion of their bread ration in order to give someone at least 'a half-decent funeral', we can only say that they held out for too long, because in these circumstances a week was equivalent to a year.

What happened next was also inevitable. It did not come as a shock, both because people were becoming used to the new approach to burial and because of the rapid deterioration of morals during the Time of Death.

People began hiding corpses in their apartments in order to continue using their food ration cards. Nearly every memoirist mentions this as if it were nothing out of the ordinary. Their descriptions even lack the excessive emotion commonplace in tales of life during the siege. Ration cards were usually issued for a ten-day period. By not reporting a death to the housing manager promptly, which necessitated surrendering unused coupons, they could continue buying food until the start of the next period. Initially, when arranging disposal of the dead, calculations of this kind were not usual, but even when, in January 1942, the rules were changed to allow families to retain the leftover ration cards of the dead, corpses in a state of rigor mortis continued to be kept in the icy apartments. It seems clear that the temptation to obtain an extra ration did influence the behaviour of people who, at first, would not have dreamed of breaking with centuries-old traditions.

4

Such funeral rituals as burial in a coffin, formal leave-taking, laying flowers, wrapping in a cerecloth, and holding a wake were not mere needless tradition. Each part of the ritual is a means of expressing respect and love for the departed. Downgrading the funeral to simple interment, often undertaken by strangers, deprived family relationships of their inherent warmth.

This marked a shift in perceptions of civilized behaviour, and with it inevitably came a decline of moral standards. What kind of civilized behaviour can you talk of if you are lugging the dead around in an apartment like so much baggage, constantly hauling them from one place to another? If children, parents, husbands and wives are eating and sleeping in the same room? What kind of respect could there be if the deceased was being used as a handy means of scrounging extra food rations? What sort of moral values could you impart to your children if all the members of the family were having to conceal their misconduct from the neighbours, the housing manager and the caretaker, and trying to convince themselves they were not committing fraud? What kind of love for the dead could you speak of if every day you were seeing their contorted face and body, and apprehensively waiting for even more visible signs of decomposition? People could only live like that if their senses had been dulled, and then it was only a matter of time before you could slide the no longer useful body of your mother into a canal.

The funeral rituals suffered the same fate as other family customs during the Time of Death. They could not remain unchanged, not only because everyday life had become more primitive. People themselves had changed, as had their attitude towards values which, until recently, had been considered almost sacred. Caught up in a monstrous tempest, people tried their best to hold on to something, even if it was illusory, which at least endowed their actions with a sense of humanity. Their resistance could not last long or be too intransigent, and we cannot judge it by conventional standards. It had its own coordinates, with callous notions of what was acceptable and unacceptable, and its own siege logic.

Friends

1

Relationships between friends inevitably changed during the siege, but there is no direct correlation between the breakdown of friendships and increasing starvation. Much depended on how close people were, their personalities and moods.

'No gunfire to be heard. We took advantage of the lull to visit friends. The opportunities for that are increasingly limited, because during the day everyone is busy, and in the short autumn evenings everyone stays at home', Maria Konoplyova noted in her diary in September 1941.[145] With every week that passed, that became more evident.[146] The old ways died out, and even the intelligentsia made no great effort to prevent that. The writer Anatoly Tarasenkov recalled his friend who 'used to share bread with me, but then started taking bits back for his wife'.[147] Even the histrionic Ksenia Polzikova-Rubets, who tried so hard to set an example for everyone to follow, confessed to her diary on 15 December 1941, 'If somebody comes, I give them coffee, but cannot offer them bread.'[148]

If people no longer exchanged gifts, that did not mean that their friends had no sympathy for the misfortunes befalling them. It may be objected that expressions of sympathy did not require any special sacrifice, but a word of comfort was important in itself. Expressing sympathy was not just empty words, because they were offered by people who were themselves in need of sympathy. They would try to reassure their friends, and perhaps themselves, with rumours that the siege would be lifted any day now. They showed concern, when there were precious few grounds for optimism. People told their friends about their bereavements and shared their sorrows. Yekaterina Lentsman recalled that, when she met a friend, they would ask each other about which members of their family had died, until the time came when her friend no longer came to the door when she knocked: 'We had first met in a children's home.'[149]

In many cases, the bonds of friendship proved indestructible. You can always feel that in the few lines of a letter which stands out for its unusual warmth and the greater receptiveness towards tales of quite ordinary everyday occurrences. 'Whenever she has time off work, she drops in on us, saying, "I just wanted to see your dear faces again." Every time she says goodbye, it's as if it's for the last time', the artist Yelena Danko recalled of her friend.[150] When Alfred Kube, a member of the Hermitage staff, heard that his friend was at death's door, he rushed through the pouring rain to see to him: 'I stayed for a long time and got very cold, because it was freezing in the room. I talked, and told him things, and asked him questions.' Nevertheless, he felt dissatisfied about something: 'I left satisfied, well, partly.' The entry is rather unclear, but perhaps he felt he had not managed to support and encourage his friend as much as he had hoped: 'It is not surprising, because I had set myself unrealistic goals.' He excuses himself, commenting that Ivan Mikhailovich looked better than he had expected.[151] Doubts, reflections, a degree of pedantic self-analysis. Some people live for their friends. 'He phoned me at the office to see how I had fared in the bombing', Vladimir G. Kulyabko recalled of his friend.[152] It is worth mentioning that these, sometimes very minor, indications of friendship are highlighted all the time: fleetingly, in passing, just by the way, or specially and in detail, with a warm expression of gratitude, or just a short note.

'You have no idea how upset I am by her death', Natalia Zavetnovskaya wrote to her daughter when a friend died.[153] The same intense emotion is found in other testimonies. People write of how their friends suffered before dying, and were bereft when they remembered how gifted, kind and trusting, witty and enchanting they had been. Only the very best is remembered in these sorrowful reminiscences. So much is recalled, down to the last detail: nuances of the way they spoke, their external characteristics. They try to bring back, if for only a moment, to recreate as fully as may be, every aspect of the fading memory of those they have loved.

2

Meeting up with friends became a rarity in 1941–2. Starvation fettered Leningraders to their beds. Some had difficulty walking even 100 metres. Public transport was not functioning, and to go out walking, swaying from weakness in icy cold conditions during the blackout and under fire, was a prospect few people relished. They did their utmost to adhere to the good old ways, and were reluctant ever to turn up empty-handed. They also did not want it to be thought they were trying to scrounge. Neither did they want to humiliate their hosts, who also would have nothing to offer in the way of hospitality.

People did not even write letters. There were plenty of excuses: that there was no electricity, no paper, no ink, the post was unreliable . . . but everyone knew that was not the reason. If nobody writes, nobody has to answer, and, in any case, nobody wanted to.

Some did nevertheless do their best to visit friends even in December 1941 and January 1942, especially if they did not live too far away. We often read how they dropped in on friends on the way home from work. They emphasize that; it is their alibi. They do not want people to think they have only come in the hope of scrounging food.

Great efforts were, nevertheless, made to give visitors some sort of hospitality, if only coffee made from acorns, or fritters made from barley bulked out with soil. Some visitors brought their own hospitality: if they could not share it, then at least they could try not to impose on their hosts. A. B. Ptitsyn told the tale of one guest who came with a piece of bread and the tail of a herring tucked away in a cigarette case: 'Armed with this snack, he went round several friends.' This was evidently not too exceptional: 'As a rule, when people visited they brought their own bread.'[154]

Sometimes people moved in with friends for the long term – and not always by invitation, but on their own initiative. They had no choice but to move out of bombed and icy houses with broken windows.[155] Not everyone wanted to move in, on the strength of an official 'order', with strangers, who might be less than happy to make room for uninvited refugees, but people were often reluctant to turn down a friend in need, and it can be difficult to judge whether they were accepted out of sympathy, a sense of duty and decency, or because people were just glad of someone to relieve their loneliness.

The help extended to friends varied. It depended largely on the contacts and opportunities of those providing the support – largely, but not exclusively. They could, after all, have turned away, pretended not to notice; they could have lied, made excuses; they could simply have declined to help – but compassion usually proved stronger. It is difficult to tell whether people did all they might have for their friends. Those whose lives they were saving were naturally grateful for any largesse, especially if it was unexpected. To ask for more, to complain about someone who was sharing what they had with you, to suspect them of being miserly, would look ungrateful. That was something nobody wanted.

It was not just a matter of sharing bread. You might help someone on the verge of collapse to get home or to a canteen, although this usually occurred as the result of a chance meeting in the street or where people were going in the same direction. You might get someone admitted to hospital, or entered on the list of those to be evacuated, or fix them up with a job with access to food. Children whose parents had starved to death might be taken to the children's home. You might bring a coupon-free meal from work, or help someone to receive the food their ration cards entitled them to; you might help to carry heavy items or water, give advice on available welfare benefits, write a complaint, or invite someone for a wash in an apartment which still had hot water. At the request of a friend, one Leningrader, an engineer, inspected the basement of his house and advised that during bombing the safest place to stand would be next to the stairs.[156] Almost every story has something unique about it.

Leningraders even gave friends the most valuable gift of all: food. It might be dried black bread, sugar, or such delicacies as cheese and wine. Children too shared food with their friends, and these stories are particularly touching.[157] This was a demonstration of the finest human qualities. Of course, no matter how generous a person might be, they could not take bread from their children to give it to someone dying of hunger. The food involved naturally varied greatly, depending on the opportunities available to each friend.

'I was visited today by my friend, Pyotr Yevgenievich. He brought a handful of oatmeal to make thin porridge, and Ivan Petrovich brought three sprats', Anna Ostroumova-Lebedeva notes in her list of New Year gifts.[158] Most often, gifts really were that small: an onion, a bowl of soup ('Water, with blackened cabbage leaves floating in it').[159] Lyubov Tikhonova remembered the father of one of her school friends presenting her with some broken bone buttons he had been given at his factory, to make soup with.[160] He had nothing else to give, and died of starvation a week later.

3

The bone buttons were a gift after the father heard that she, her sisters and little brother were starving after their mother's death. All sorts of things were going on in that first winter of the siege: there was cruelty, and greed, but how remarkable that primal, instinctive, noble impulse is. Everybody is suffering, but there are some whose anguish is intolerable, and not to comfort them is unthinkable. That principle did not disappear even in the Time of Death. People well understood that not all friends could bring themselves to ask for support. They gave help without waiting to be asked: perhaps not very lavishly, but the gesture deserves to be appreciated.

'If I had not met him in the street I would never have recognized him: thin, dirty, hungry, his coat hanging on him like a smock.' That is how Alexandra Borovikova describes a friend in her diary. There was no need to ask him anything: 'I brought him to the canteen, where he was given soup, without bread.' She was not surprised when he 'gulped down two bowlfuls'.[161]

'Olga! I'll get you bread and some other things', a friend informed Olga Berggolts at a time when, pregnant, she was emaciated and on the brink of collapse.[162] Somebody shared a handful of barley with Leonid Galko when they saw how terribly his wife had changed: she was swollen 'from head to toe'.[163] T. Nezhintseva's husband died in April 1942: 'At that bitter time I was visited by Vsevolod Azarov, who brought a loaf of bread.'[164] A friend of the actress Alexandra Smirnova was being treated for malnutrition in hospital. She took her 'a little tobacco and some food'.[165]

None of these thoroughly decent people were working in jobs which gave them ready access to food. They were taking food from what they had managed to store up. As one, they say apologetically that their gift was meagre, although they could easily have presented their actions as heroic. They could not pass by on the other side when they saw a fellow human being in trouble, even though that would have been the easiest thing in the world. Knowing that everybody was starving, friends were sometimes hesitant about accepting gifts, no matter how tiny. Tamara Rigina wrote that her friend 'categorically refused' all help, although there were compelling reasons to share with her. The friend had herself described how she 'brewed "aspic" from glue and sucked Sen Sen tablets she had once bought at a chemist's shop'.[166] Despite that, she preferred to starve than be a burden to others. Zinaida Moykovskaya's friend 'tried at great length to persuade me' to accept a piece of bread and margarine. She probably looked terrible. The friend even wrote to Moykovskaya's husband, urging him to come as quickly as possible if he wanted to see her alive.[167]

When offering food, friends would often come up with subterfuges to avoid embarrassment. 'Dunya came, and brought a piece of oilcake. She did not eat any herself: she is suffering from gastroenteritis', N. V. Shirkova noted.[168] Oilcake was highly prized. Her friend is unlikely to have considered her gastroenteritis so incurable as to be certain she would never need the oilcake herself in the future; she could, after all, have exchanged it for bread and butter. The variety of expressions used between friends in such situations, with their exhortations to 'Go ahead – help yourself!', 'Don't worry, I've got more where that came from!', 'I don't need it – I can't eat that', were heard throughout the war, although with every day the siege continued, the number of those willing to share unselfishly diminished. No excuses or explanations are needed. People did what they could. Everybody had their own set of standards, which departed in varying degrees from what was generally regarded as the norm. Nobody had any way of judging whether help being offered was too much or too little, although tallies of good deeds were often kept in diaries. At times, a few grains of sugar might save a life.

Gifts were expected to be reciprocated, although it was unusual for hints to be dropped. More often the bonds between friends made it natural for them to support each other. This is not always made explicit, but can be inferred from the documents. An actress describes a friend, also an actor, helping her to bring home a bag of food because she was very weak.[169] It is unlikely he was not hoping to be given at least some small recompense. Nobody was demanding an exactly equivalent gift in return, but friends who came visiting empty-handed, especially if they did so repeatedly, were likely to get a dustier welcome than they might have hoped for in the past. They would be tactfully made aware that their visits were proving burdensome and unhelpful, although it was accepted that there were no real grounds for reproach.

Presents were exchanged as a matter of course, each person giving what they could. Vladimir Lyublinsky asked his housekeeper to do the laundry, and gave her a log and 80 grams of bread; in return, she treated him to a glass of tea with two sugar lumps.[170] When he went for a consultation with a doctor friend, he took her 'a roll-your-own made up from cigarette stubs'.[171] The mother of I. Zapadalov, who suffered burns while putting out incendiary bombs, gave a doctor she knew 10 rubles, not a very substantial sum.[172] The notes written by Evelina Soloviova include detailed description of occasions when friends tried to thank her for gifts. She helped a family she was friendly with to haul firewood out of the basement, and even gave them cigarettes she had 'accumulated'. That was considered a valuable gift: they would usually be exchanged for bread. Her friends went out of their way to help her 'in every possible way', and gave her sunflower husk cake and oilcake.[173]

The tradition of sharing gifts proved ineradicable. All that changed was the size of the gifts, which also became increasingly exotic. The stories are varied and ambiguous and, paradoxically, each is typical in its own way. The tales of intellectuals, with their literary polish, point out more clearly, with restrained gratitude and without fuss or undue prolixity, the fastidiousness of their friends. We see this in the memoirs of the Nekrasov specialist, S. A. Reiser, about his friend Vladimir Gippius, a connoisseur of Gogol. Together they dined on oilcake with dolphin fat in the canteen of the Scholars Club; together they boiled water in Reiser's apartment. They fuelled the stove with books, and Gippius pointed out which ones he did not have in his own library.

Reiser decided to give some of them to his friend. He wrote later that at the time he was completely indifferent to what happened to them, and no doubt that is what he told Gippius, who hesitated to accept such a valuable gift. He would have been finding a form of words to mitigate his friend's sense of awkwardness, but Gippius was not to be outdone.

He 'refused to take them for nothing, and offered money and a certain amount of something relatively edible'.[174]

Taking food from a starving man? Selfishly exploiting his love of books? No, he would need to accept something less vital. He agreed to take the money. 'It was virtually impossible to buy anything with it', Reiser points out, and that was the simple truth. In any case, they would hardly have been talking about a large sum. Here they were, two friends at death's door (Vladimir Gippius was to die only a few weeks later), looking for a tactful way of effecting this exchange without hurting anybody's feelings.

4

Not infrequently, in extreme necessity, people would appeal to friends for help directly.[175] In the process they would say, unapologetically, that they were starving, and wait for a positive response. Sometimes they just bluntly demanded to be fed. They would turn to strangers, but begging from friends was no less awkward, knowing perfectly well the circumstances in which everybody was living. It was humiliating, and they knew it was no way to behave, but they could not control themselves, and ate anything they were offered. Few were optimistic enough to hope for bread, and they would ask even for cat, perhaps explaining that they had starving children to feed.[176] They must have been aware of how such requests would be viewed, and no one wanted to seem, in the eyes of their friends, to have let themselves degenerate.

Although such visitors were sometimes considered an annoyance, they were not always refused. Usually they would be fobbed off with surrogates, and if they were given 'natural' food, it was almost invariably emphasized how little of it there was.[177] It would he unusual for anyone to leave their friends entirely without assistance, although there could be no fully adequate support. Responding to pleas helped people to overcome their lethargy, and look more closely at others who were on their last legs. They might later chide themselves for misplaced generosity, and even think of stopping it, but nevertheless they continued to help. There is something understated, something matter-of-fact, in the stubbornness with which people fought to save the lives of their friends: what it always demonstrates is high-mindedness and the power of compassion. We find a striking example of this in Lev Khodorkov's diary.

> Sasha phoned and asked for help. Then he rang to say he could not come; his legs would not do as he told them. I visited him on 28 December, took some food. In another two or three days he would have been dead. How can I save him? He looks terrible.
>
> 4 Jan 42. Went to see Sasha this evening. Took him some food. Dark. Difficult walking. Got soaking wet. Rested there for an hour. No strength to go to the station. Think I can save him.
>
> 7 Jan 42. Got a passing car and took Sasha porridge, bread,

horsemeat patties. He is much better. Even tried to go outside. Did not manage it.

10 Jan 42. Visited Sasha today. Took him some food. Came under artillery fire. Sasha very weak.

18 Jan 42. Visited Sasha. Took him something to eat. Came home worn out. Barely made it.

29 Jan 42. Visited Sasha today. Took him some food. He is very weak.

9 Feb 42. Today Sasha left Leningrad. Glad I shared my food with him.[178]

Thus, without pathos, even brusquely and rather monotonously, we are given a description of human charity at its most altruistic.

Neighbours

1

Life under the siege encouraged solidarity, bringing people together who, before the war, kept themselves to themselves even in a communal apartment. It was bound to happen. Most often they would meet up in the kitchen, around the stove where, because of the cold, they might sit for hours. The situation was not always idyllic. There were never enough warm places; people tried to occupy them early on, and were unwilling to allow in others who had not squeezed close to the stove at the outset.

This was where long discussions were held, where people heard the news, found out who had died and who was surviving, where you could buy or barter what. There were endless conversations about what had been eaten in years gone by, with a listing of all manner of mouth-watering comestibles. That united the people in the kitchen as firmly as the shared heat. During shelling, the residents tried to leave their rooms and assemble in the corridors and on the stairs which, for some reason, was believed to be safer. Here they comforted, encouraged and advised each other, and even read stories to the neighbours' children. The obligatory air raid duties also brought Leningraders together. 'Everyone in the house got to know everybody else while on duty, and talked about where to get food. While I was on duty, I met a woman who offered to let me and the children sleep in a room on the ground floor which faced in to the courtyard', recalls Zinaida Likhacheva.[179]

Sometimes people even moved in to live with their neighbours. There could be many reasons: hunger, cold, loneliness, or the desire to get out of a room with the dead bodies of family members in it. It is not always clear why people agreed to share their homes. Nobody mentions selfish motives for doing so, although, of course, it was more difficult to survive in isolation. Moral standards were maintained between people, some of whom already more or less knew each other while others did not, but who had a common interest in surviving.

Fetching bread for the neighbours was both a way of maintaining moral standards and a means of survival. Help was given to those who were ill or bedridden, or too weak to walk far. Neighbours would take turns standing for ages in the queues.[180] This also strengthened a sense of compassion and solidarity with the starving. The human urge to impress other people, to hear their expressions of gratitude or delight, would be satisfied when someone who had been queueing came back after managing to buy bread for everyone, or had some good news to impart. 'A knock on the door and she comes straight into our room, even before going to her own', recalled L. Reykhert of one neighbour who had struck it lucky at the bread shop.[181] The mother of another siege victim, when she noticed the ration had been increased, rushed back not to her own children but to the neighbours, exclaiming, 'Get up, quick! Go to the bread shop, they're issuing extra bread.'[182]

Taking care of orphans was another burden neighbours often had to shoulder. It was too much to expect them to maintain children after their parents died, but often they did not abandon them, and cared for them as best they could.[183] They would try to get them into children's homes, either taking them there themselves or forwarding a note to the district committee of the Komsomol. There were other good deeds too. In December 1941, Lyubov Tikhonova's mother died and the ration cards for Lyubov, her younger sisters and brother were lost. 'When the neighbours sent in an application, a commission came and restored the cards', she recalls.[184]

Neighbours would alert the Komsomol household squads if other residents weakened to the point where they could no longer take care of themselves.[185] Help from neighbours was sometimes the last hope of the dying. Tamara Loginova, who went to stay with her aunt after her mother died, said, 'We ran out of food completely. We would dip our fingers in salt and wash it down with warm water. Then my aunt fell ill and told us to go home, to the neighbours.'[186]

Needless to say, it fell to neighbours to bury residents who died in their building. This was heavy work even for someone in good health, so it was not always possible. Usually, the only other people you could call on for help were the caretakers, and they expected to be paid. It was officially their duty, but everybody was fully aware there were many ways for them not to discharge it. It would in any case have offended against tradition to abdicate all responsibility for the burial of a family member to someone else without giving them something in return. There were instances where relatives or friends simply had nothing for paying a caretaker, and then the only option was to appeal to the neighbours. Svetlana Magaeva, when she was trying to get her music teacher buried, wrote about the ordeal: 'It was impossible to collect a kilogram of bread. We gave some bits to the caretaker, and added various belongings of the deceased.'[187]

Attempts to collect that amount of bread were rare. Everybody was starving and had to be self-reliant. Often the caretaker would be paid with the bread left over on a dead person's ration card,[188] but that would usually be done by the family. Neighbours tended to give short shrift to the corpses of those who had no surviving family members. Bodies were thrown out into the street, or surreptitiously moved into other people's buildings and yards. Many neighbours were too weak to behave like that, or afraid of being caught and punished – but not all. They had no intention of paying to dispose of corpses for other people, but were repelled and frightened by the sight of dead bodies and feared epidemics. Ivan Ilyin relates how he brought gifts from a battalion commander for his wife and daughter who had been stranded in Leningrad. 'I opened the top window in there, so they would be lying in the cold', a weeping neighbour told him, but many must have been tempted to get rid of the horror as quickly as possible.[189]

2

During the blockade, there was a decline in the small favours people who were barely acquainted used to do for each other. Neighbours were not family, and were rarely given presents of bread, the most precious commodity during the Time of Death. Water was also precious. One Leningrader makes particular mention in her notes of a neighbour, 'a quiet, modest accountant', who was in need: 'He ventured to come and ask us for hot water.'[190] They obliged, but that was not always the case. Here, from a carer at a children's home, is what she heard from a 6-year-old orphan. He saw his mother come home and fall to the floor: 'I was frightened and ran to ask the neighbours for water. They did not give me any. It was a lot of trouble to fetch water.'[191] V. N. Nikolskaya wrote about her aunt who lived in appalling conditions: 'The room temperature is minus two. No bread for one and a half days, not a sip of water or other food for a long time. No water for ten days.' Even that was not enough to soften everyone's heart: 'She has to beg for a cup or two of water every day from the neighbours. They grudge it.'[192] She was, of course, not just asking for water once or twice, but every day, and people had become hardened. They had worries of their own.

Exchanges between neighbours could be so various that it is difficult to tell how far they were even-handed. P. M. Samarin gave milk to his neighbour, who made him coffee.[193] Lazar Ratner's family was given a tumblerful of millet in return for a suitcase their neighbours needed when they were evacuated.[194] L. Reykhert's mother shared food with the woman who swept the yard, who was able to get all her ration cards redeemed in full, which was a great achievement.[195] Ye. A. Kondakov recalled making soup from potato peelings his neighbour gave him for himself and her daughter, whom he looked after while the mother was away at work.[196]

Nina Soboleva's neighbour asked her to go with her son to a New Year party, for which she had managed to get two tickets. There was evidently an agreement that she would bring back some of the food, if there was any. Nina succeeded in drinking just one glass of tea and eating a biscuit.[197] The neighbour of Allan Kargin and his grandmother regaled them with patties made from flour mixed with baby powder: 'In return, we gave her an infusion of garlic.'[198] Another family succeeded in buying a fir tree for New Year, and a neighbour, who worked at the port, offered to swap a box of 'fabulous American dried apricots' for it.[199] 'We agreed the deal. Those apricots saved our lives.'[200]

We cannot tell whether other exchanges had equally momentous consequences, but there is no doubt they helped people to survive. This solidarity between Leningraders living alongside each other, and aware that they could not survive on their own in this nightmare, was not restricted to sharing food. The testimony is fragmentary, but it is enough to tell us that neighbours were helped to evacuate, their rooms were warmed, their letters collected for them. Customs changed, morals became more brutish, but even the ritual of extending hospitality to the neigbours did not entirely disappear. This mostly involved surrogates of one kind or another and 'waste' like potato peelings, soya products, wood glue, coffee ground fritters and glue sauce, but not always. Nothing was thrown away. Neighbours often sat down together to drink what was called gruel. Here too people did their best to find some way of showing their appreciation.

3

Relations were not always warm and neighbourly. Even before the siege, quarrelling in communal apartments was an everyday occurrence. The war did not neutralize neighbours' hostility to other residents, and sometimes made it worse. There was stealing,[201] and there were attempts to survive by trampling on others.[202]

Everybody warmed themselves in the kitchen, and could see who was eating what. How could that not lead to bad feeling? There were small children present. They too were starving, as they watched other people feed. Not everything could be explained to them, and sometimes they did not understand what was allowed and what was not. They watched, hoping something might come their way. Much else besides, unseemly and shameful, went on in those communal kitchens during the siege. A girl who survived the war recalled that they were making soup in a pot with a tumblerful of peas her mother had brought: 'A neighbour smelled it upstairs and came running down. "Girls, the peas are ready."' She came in several times, expecting them to share it with her. Probably this neighbour had shared with them in the past, or was someone they knew well, but people were suffering such hunger that by now they could not give food away: 'When Nadya had gone, we fell upon it.'[203]

The very nastiest stories concern neighbours robbing orphans who had become dependent on them, and thereby condemning them to death. It was probably not always premeditated, but the logic of self-interest, when people took in children only because they had ration cards, inevitably led to this outcome. 'The neighbours took everything out of our house they could carry. They took me to stay with them too, but in the spring stopped giving me food and I had to eat all sorts of herbs in their vegetable plot.

One time I overheard the man telling his wife not to give me any food because, "He needs to die"', one child later related in an orphanage.[204] It was a miracle he survived. He left and went to other neighbours, and they sent him to the children's home. Another saga is described in Maria Mashkova's notes. A 6-month-old baby boy sat for several days by the body of his grandmother and was taken in as a 'dependant' by the family of the caretaker. They decided they could profit from the tragedy. They found the ration cards of the baby's dead family, and so 'were in no hurry to report the deaths and get them buried'. They evidently had little interest in the baby: 'He was infested with lice, dehydrated, and had severe bedsores.'[205]

The fact that orphaned babies found themselves in such circumstances does not always indicate cruel intentions. Where were people to find the milk needed to feed a baby? How were they to get rid of lice, which had become a scourge for all Leningraders? How were they to wash nappies when there was no water or firewood? It was shrugged off as part of life under the siege, an unavoidable evil, just as people reconciled themselves to other, previously unacceptable, departures from conventional morality. Indifference and apathy were integral to the Time of Death. There are few witnesses to such episodes, but they were more than isolated cases. People were prepared to do anything for a piece of bread, and that was not the case only where children were involved. Children are trusting and vulnerable, and the temptation to take advantage of their naivety, when hunger was turning a person inside out, was very great. If you steal a baby's food behind closed doors, who will he be able to tell?

4

With every month that passed, there were more weak, penurious people: how were they to be helped? The mark of the siege became imprinted even on the faces of caretakers, whose jobs were considered lucrative, because not all of them were thieves. Ilya Glazunov related that members of his family, trying to get his grandmother buried, asked the caretaker, a woman who had been 'fat before the war, but was now skeletal and unrecognizable, kind Auntie Shura, to accept 200 instead of 350 grams of bread'. To that they added 100 rubles in cash, but it was 'only after much persuasion that she agreed'.[206] Dmitry Likhachev recalled that the caretaker, who had helped him in the past, began refusing to carry firewood.[207] They too, although regarded as relatively well off, were buckling under the burden of the siege.

Did the Time of Death erase all trace of companionship among those living in close proximity? No. In the dull monotony of the siege, it was not always in evidence, but when someone was on the verge of death, there were sometimes acts of charity which shone through the widespread callousness and calculating self-interest.

The first impulse was the most admirable. People at the end of their tether would overcome their shame, knock on any door, beg, weep, implore. Their startled neighbours, no less haggard, not always willing to share with others, would try to find something, even if very little, to give them. Often, indeed, they offered help without waiting to be asked, unable to turn away or pass by on the other side. Vladimir G. Kulyabko's neighbour, when she heard he did not have enough food, brought him 300 grams of bread and a packet of broken rice. 'She is not very bright but has a good heart', he wrote in his diary on 17 September 1941.[208]

So much depended on these 'not very bright' people, compassionate, incapable of adroitly avoiding an imploring gaze, and immediately looking around to see what they could do to help! It may be objected that in September 1941 nobody was yet starving, but we find just the same thing later on. 'There was all sorts. People would share their dried bread, half their last bit, and if a person was really bad they would give them the lot', Raisa Mashukova recalled.[209] This is not the standard heroics of a survivor looking back at the past and eager to present it in a more positive light. Then there is the story of the defunct apartment, where a woman had died and her husband, lying next to her, was so weakened by starvation that he could not move away. The description by the neighbour who helped him is awkward and disjointed, an indication of how upset and emotional she felt: 'And mother made sure he had light and that he was lying comfortably, and heated up hot water for him and gave him it so he had something hot to drink.'[210] We can see the feeling of pity behind the actions of another Leningrader. She had a woman with two children moved into her apartment after their building was bombed. From her rambling story we can understand why the charitable urge proved so indestructible:

> Three, the little boy was, and his lovely little sister, well she was just so, so little . . . Anyway, so I start baking these things, you know [oatcakes – S. Ya.] and he comes into the kitchen and he's looking, and he says, 'Patty, patty', that's what he called it, the flatbread I was baking, and anyway, so I gave him the cakes and that, and the little lad had something to eat. It just wouldn't have been right . . .[211]

5

A. A. Vostrova told the tale of a neighbour who no longer had the strength to get out of bed. How could they just leave her? She would die. 'We bought bread and took it to her; we looked after her.'[212] Another Leningrader bought a kilogram of white flour 'for my neighbours, who were dying'.[213] They had once saved her life themselves, but that was not the point. Who during the siege kept accounts, neatly recording the debits and credits? When T. I. Sakharova fainted from malnutrition at school, a classmate, told his/her mother, who was the caretaker, about it: 'She came and invited me to her home. She gave me a whole bowlful of cabbage leaf soup.'[214]

Not all neighbours who initially felt a great sense of compassion proved capable of sustaining it. But some did. Almost all Klavdia Fyodorova's family died. She could not even do her own laundry: 'I was a dystrophic.' Clearly this must have been known to a neighbour, who had a job as a waiter in a restaurant which had been converted during the war into a canteen. He was probably suffering less than others, and something moved him: 'He called to us one day and said, "Are you hungry?" He took us with him to his canteen.' Of course, they were not being offered a proper meal: 'He threw us the leftovers.' She could have used different words, but those were the ones she chose. And why take exception to his directness, when he was saving them from the pangs of hunger? 'I would eat my fill and even got to take something with me. That is how I survived.'[215]

G. Petrov heard that the mother and grandmother of Ye. Tikhomirova, his neighbour, had fallen ill. He was a driver on the Road of Life across Lake Ladoga and, when he came home, would bring firewood and even branches of spruce fir which were believed to cure scurvy. When Tikhomorova's mother became very ill, Petrov drove her to the hospital and, when she died, saved her daughter by taking her to the centre for reception and reallocation of children.[216]

People shared the pain of those who had lost loved ones. Neighbours tried to comfort and take care of them, at least in the days immediately after their bereavement. Yelena Mukhina records asking her neighbour if she could 'borrow a teaspoonful of sugar'.[217] This was a few days after her mother died. Sugar was very precious and there could be no certainty that an orphaned schoolgirl would be able to repay the loan, but they chose not to turn their backs on her misery. After the death of her mother in January 1942, Ye. Krivobodrova's neighbour, R. Ya. Kozlova, took her in, 'warmed me, and gave me a drink of hot water and a spoonful of oilcake porridge.' She continued to help her later.[218]

Let us not overlook these gifts. Everything is small-scale, but has been obtained with great effort and was probably difficult to part with. But part with it they did. Was that 'crumb or two' given to an orphan something easily spared by a person who was eating wood glue? We keep encountering these tales of a few grains of sugar or wheat, or crumbs of bread when people are talking about help given during the siege. Why not embellish the story? But no, people readily admit that was all the support they could give. Everything is related hastily and inexpertly, and we often have no idea how people felt about sharing food. Who could tell us? Those delighted to have received an unexpected gift, who would not have dreamed of imputing an ulterior motive to the benefactor who had saved their life? Or others, trapped in the siege, who often noted in their stories only the best and noblest behaviour they encountered during this time of inhumanity? And, indeed, compassion for the destitute was not limited only to sharing food with them. It was manifest in many other ways. Klavdia Dubrovina took her neighbour in to live with her: 'I felt so sorry for her.'[219] We see in the following entry what it is that gives rise to that sense of pity which motivates her to do a kindly deed: 'This poor old woman could not even . . ., that is how ill she was. She asked me if I could first bring her some water, and boil some for her to drink.'[220]

Maria Mashkova took in the daughter of a dead neighbour, whose body they were unable to bury for a long time. The girl 'was frightened of the cold and hunger, and by the dead body'.[221] Evelina Soloviova, suffering from the cold, appealed to her neighbours who had a cooker in their apartment. She was not asking for much: only if they would allow her to sleep on the floor in their kitchen if she brought a mattress. They agreed, and her little daughter slept beside her.[222] The 15-year-old boy from one of the siege families was an outsider. All his family had died, and he came to his neighbours: 'He could hardly walk either. "Aunt Dunya", he asked, "do you think you could let me have a lump of sugar?" Grandmother gave him a piece, barely the size of a fingernail. He said, "Oh, thank you so much." He took the sugar lump, and died during the night.'[223] And just as people blamed themselves if they had failed to help someone back to their feet, so that family were very relieved not to feel responsible for the death of that teenage boy: 'Grandmother Dunya said, "I'm so glad I did not refuse him that." I remember it very clearly, and that we all felt the same: "How glad we are that we did not refuse him!"'[224]

'They themselves could hardly move.' That is a detail which says a lot, like the portrait Ye. Sharypina paints of a neighbour who took in an orphan girl. 'She looked less like a woman than the relics of a saint. Her cheek bones jutted out on a face with the skin drawn taut over it. Her eyes shone feverishly.'[225] A person like that could be forgiven for refusing to help, on the grounds of their own frailty, but people did not refuse. As we read through these repetitive stories with their listing of the same limited range of foods and good deeds, it is not always easy to understand what motivated people. We know for a fact, however, that it was not fear, or greed, or vanity, or any wish to elevate themselves in the estimation of others, or any hope that those whose life they saved might some day save theirs. Somebody gives a few crumbs to starving children who are soon to die: where is the profit in that? There is something else, not always palpable, in these lists of minuscule donations, something that came from the distant past and could not be dispelled by the present. Why should a caretaker bother about people who had been evacuated from Leningrad? But he did respond to their request to write about what befell them:

> Olga, you ask about your mother, and Cecilia and Kolya. I can tell you you are right, they left to make their way to your brother-in-law, and then they were going to go to you, ill and very weak, but wherever they meant to go I do not think they will get there alive, they were so ill, they cannot move, they hired a car to cross Lake Ladoga. Olga, I really beg you send me a letter to my address, I will really look forward to it, perhaps in the future we will know each other better.[226]

'This man struck me as a person of great sensitivity, humanity and decency', someone who read that letter later recalled. It is a short letter, but what kindly and affecting words he found. It seems unlikely he was particularly close to this family, but we can feel how much he wants to alleviate another person's pain, and his own loneliness, and to find a human warmth that had long since fled the icy buildings of besieged Leningrad.

There is no call for us to idealize the relationship between neighbours. It was not a time for great neighbourliness. Neighbours were not invariably friends, but the life under siege which was common to all did bring them together. Your neighbours were near you and could not go away, having nowhere to go to. They would see everything: the misery and death, the joys and hopes, the suffering and despair. They had to feel for you, to help you, to behave decently towards you. There was no escaping it.

Colleagues

1

Colleagues might not be particularly close, but people working in the same place were sure to share their troubles. Everybody wanted to survive, and they talked constantly about everyday matters. Leningrad's tribulations brought them together. In places, they pooled their efforts to celebrate the New Year, saving up bread and confectionery.[227] 'There was animated discussion of matters relating to food, and the differing opinion of doctors as to whether it was better to stretch the rations of sugar and fats over the whole ten days or eat them in one or two days', Maria Sadova recalls of the hot topics among colleagues at the Public Library.[228]

It was the same everywhere: arguments, indignation, pity. The hardship of others met with a sympathetic response, although there the matter often ended. The old traditions of mutual support were not completely swept away, and at all times support was given to colleagues if their lives seemed threatened. People rarely appealed for help if they had nothing to give in return. 'One of the staff boasted she had stocked up 20 kilograms of rice and I brazenly asked her for a couple of tablespoons of it for my child. She refused', we read in Evelina Soloviova's notes;[229] no matter how proud people might be of such achievements, the fear that they might find themselves starving again tomorrow often stopped charity in its tracks.

Mostly people applied to the management and trade union committees in the hope of obtaining coupon-free food, although whether that was possible depended on where in Leningrad they worked. If they could help out from sources other than their own meagre supplies, people could be more generous. 'My mother fell ill. She wrote a note for me to take to the bakery where she worked as a confectioner, asking them to let me have something. I handed the note over at the gatehouse and was given a loaf, but told to hide it under my jacket', Valya Tikhomirova recalls.[230] Alexey Yevdokimov wrote in his diary on 10 February 1942: 'The timekeepers toss me an extra lunch coupon', but of course that was no great sacrifice for those with responsibility for allocating rations.[231] It was less easy for other people.

'Save us! We are dying', read a note from a member of staff at the archive of the Academy of Sciences a few days before she died. She was considered a 'wonderful, dedicated' worker, noted for her stoicism and never complaining, but they could do nothing to help: 'The chairwoman of the local trade union branch took them meals from the canteen which consisted of little more than water.'[232]

2

Colleagues, when it was possible, often did what they could for starving fellow workers without waiting to be asked. Their gifts were not very varied. They would share surrogate food,[233] but also often donated portions of 'civilized' food, if only in small quantities. These gifts included bread, milk, sausage, sugar, cereals and cigarettes. Zarya Milyutina wrote about her aunt, whose colleagues brought her frozen potatoes found in a field after shelling.[234] Possibly their delight at an unexpected find caused this exceptional, if short-lived, generosity.

It probably cost them an effort, but let us note the circumstances under which help was most likely to be extended to colleagues.[235] A. Samulenkova lost her food ration cards for twenty days. Her life was saved by Pimenov, chief of the local air defence unit.[236] Dmitry Likhachev gave the librarian a box of dried bread: 'Her husband had died of starvation and her (two) children were also dying.'[237] When she reached the outskirts of Leningrad, the colleagues of starving Olga Berggolts, who was setting out on a long journey to see her father, 'poured her some thin, barely sweetened tea' and gave her several cigarettes.[238]

Ye. Krivobodrova recalls that her father, 'almost collapsing from exhaustion, was walking home and met the headmaster of the boarding school'. The headmaster was probably not a particularly close friend ('They knew each other from work', she writes), but he did not just pass by: 'He gave my father hot water to drink, some food and even a handful of a mixture of different grains, lentils and peas for my mother and me.' Reading this list of meagre donations, we can fully believe her other testimony that 'he was emaciated himself, starving'.[239]

It was not easy to share, but people did when they saw someone had only a short time left to live, when they saw the pleading eyes and clumsy gestures of a person trying to find a way to be helpful in response to their charity. There was every opportunity to do nothing, to say nothing, to refuse help, and yet people shared. It is one of the great features of the siege. That is how friends behaved, and neighbours, colleagues and other people who hardly knew you, or even did not know you at all. It may be objected that people would naturally be ashamed to turn their back in full public view on someone asking for help, with whom they had worked for years, but that did happen in the Time of Death. Here is the story of Susanna Kazakevich, a librarian who received rations of 50 grams of butter for the staff at the Public Library. Marauding boys from the vocational school stole one portion.[240] It is not difficult to imagine the scene when the food was being distributed: the delight and excitement of the staff, and the dismay and hunger in the eyes of the person who had brought them the butter: 'At the library I made no mention of it, but they noticed and shared with me. How sensitive and compassionate these people showed themselves to be, by responding like that, despite their own predicament, to the predicament of another.'

Maria Chernyakova, who also worked at the library, served in the joint HQ of local air defence centres. She had her ration cards stolen. This was not a matter of 50 grams of butter, but of life and death. She began a woeful round: 'The first time the girls at the joint command shared with me.' They were all hungry, though, and she needed to look for someone else: 'The next time my sister fed me.' She had to go to friends, acquaintances and relatives asking for food. Then she collapsed and it seemed she was doomed: 'I went for three days without bread, just lying motionless.' She was saved by a colleague who 'baked me some flatbread'.[241]

Anna Nalegatskaya remembers that an assistant professor at the Medical Institute 'went out every morning with his son to catch a cat or dog'. His colleagues evidently knew all about this if it was being done openly and not kept secret, but how could they help? The man failed to catch any at all; his wife and son died, but he had a daughter still alive and here charity came to the rescue: 'The members of the department sustained her with their few crumbs.' When her father in turn died, it might seem there was now no longer any connection between the family and those helping her. We will never see that hungry girl waiting for her piece of bread, never know what words she found to thank them, but they did not abandon her: 'They carried on supporting her, and she lived.'[242]

3

It is difficult to tell what was voluntary and what was obligatory in the actions of people who worked together. On instructions from the Party committee, communists were sought out and taken care of. Notes to the Party committee from bedridden workers were responded to. The team spirit, generated by work of any kind, encouraged people to take more of an interest in the welfare of those alongside whom they worked. There were no walls dividing them. Hundreds of victims of the siege fell in the streets and people walked impassively past them, but one can hardly imagine a similar indifference to someone who collapsed at their workbench.

'He was sent 200 grams of mustard oil and 150 grams of butter, taken against his ration cards in the canteen', wrote Vladimir G. Kulyabko after visiting a sick colleague.[243] He would not have been able to obtain these, however, without permission from the institute's senior management. Like other 'non-staple' foodstuffs, these could be bought only by standing for hours in a queue, and not always even then.

'Those who were still on their feet looked after those who were bedridden, bringing them food from the canteen', Maria Konoplyova recalls of life at the Hermitage.[244] This too would have been impossible without the approval of the museum's management: a close eye was kept on the distribution of 'institutional' meals. When Galina Ozerova, the chief librarian of the Public Library, was taking firewood round the city outskirts to staff members who 'had decided to sit it out at home', it is quite likely that she was being assisted by the director's office.[245] How else could she have obtained the firewood, which was in short supply and highly valuable, for not one but many of her colleagues? How could staff have moved in to live in the factories, institutes and museums where it was still warm and light if they were not being given support from 'upstairs'?

Senior management were in a better position to help, and were under an obligation to take care of the health of their staff. Indeed, their staffs would not have been willing to undertake every job without rewards or compulsion. 'We were exhausted, and played tricks, sometimes leaving a dead body half way, in the entrance', wrote T. Dorofeyeva, who was compelled by her factory to take corpses from the mortuary to the cemetery.[246] There was an incident where a worker doing this job collapsed and died while digging a grave.[247]

It is not always clear whether food was given in return for this sort of work. Few people write about that. One of the staff at the Academy archive agreed to take the body of Academician Alexey Shakhmatov's daughter, who had worked there, to the cemetery, in return for a loaf of bread. It evidently proved difficult to procure this, and it was several weeks before the body could be buried. The few lines in Georgiy Knyazev's diary give us a clear enough sense of what this entailed: 'He had to drag the coffin on his own from the apartment down to the sledge. Needless to say, this was beyond his strength, so he had to slide the coffin down the stairs and drag it along on the ground. He had no one to help him.'[248]

A terrible, repulsive job, draining all the man's physical and spiritual resources. He could hardly have been expected to do it without some kind of incentive. 'We stopped sewing them into shrouds. We transported them piled up in trucks and buried them in mass graves in stacks. There were just too many. We had no time, and were short of petrol and vehicles', recalls the deputy director of the André Marty shipbuilding factory, where more than 3,000 workers died during the siege.[249] But if it was not a matter of moving a corpse to a distant cemetery in the suburbs, colleagues were willing to help in this time of sorrow. When Alexandra Smirnova lost her husband, her colleagues helped tear boards off theatre scenery, knocked together a coffin and brought it to her home.[250] N. Ya. Komarov's colleagues did their best to support his family when his stepfather died: 'They helped us swaddle the body in sheets, lay it on the sledge, secure it with belts and rope, and even helped us to drag the sledge with his body for part of the way.'[251]

4

Not everyone could be given what they asked for, and evidence of
grievances – not always aired openly, often groundless – is to be found
in the documentation of the siege. Substantial efforts were made to
support workers and state employees with hospitals and canteens, and
by providing assistance with their living conditions. Not everyone who
was ill, however, could be admitted to a hospital if they were not essential
workers or valued specialists. Not everyone could be fed just because they
were weak. Harsh selection was not uncommon. 'I did not discharge such
specialists as plumbers or accountants from the hospital, with a view to
retaining the essential workers. I took charge of this issue personally in
order to save the basic, essential workers, and did so at the expense of such
less valuable workers as caretakers etc.', the director of Dairy No. 1 later
reported.[252]

One is embarrassed to read that, but this sort of approach was common.
Managers talked often and openly at this time about ensuring the survival in hospitals of 'valuable' individuals. The chief energy engineer of
Hydroelectric Power Station No. 7 was not ashamed to talk about this
later, and indeed boasted of his firmness and strong will: 'I gave to those
who, in my estimation, would pull through if supported. I withheld from
those in whose eyes I could see death, who I reckoned would be dead
within two or three days anyway. I got good at telling that from their eyes
and spotting a dead man standing in front of me when I saw one. I got
good at spotting the difference.'[253]

That certainly went on, but here is a story told by an engineer.
Completely exhausted, he collapsed on a sofa: 'People came running in.
One offered me valerian drops. The director arrived and asked what was
up. I told him, lying down, it was weakness. "Hang on", he says, "I'm
going to brew you a cup of real coffee." Sure enough, twenty minutes
later back he comes, invites me in to his office.' No doubt the engineer
was considered a valuable employee, but is this reflecting only utilitarian
considerations?

The director let him rest as often as he wished (and kept him on full
salary). He gave him brewer's yeast, and his deputy gave him 'a vial of cod
liver oil and some vitamins from pine needles'.[254] Where is the calculation
in that? The engineer is old and frail, but on more than one occasion he
sees the norms of 'institutional' behaviour disappearing in the good deeds
his colleagues do him.

From their first spontaneous gesture, we can see that not everything
in the way people behaved can be reduced to cold calculation. Of course,
quite apart from compassion, there could be other reasons for helping
people who were 'not valuable'. Many decisions had to be taken almost
instantly: how could they be preceded by rigorous analysis of the arguments for and against? When someone helped a worker who had collapsed
at his workplace back to his feet and offered him a glass of hot water, he
would hardly be calculating whether or not the worker was useful. No

matter how dire the times, ineradicable moral commandments broke through the mentality of accountancy which tallied up profits and losses and rated every person on the basis of how 'valuable' they were. Someone shared their own coffee rather than that of the enterprise, gave their own food rations rather than those of the sickbay. It can be objected that directors were better fed than others, but we have only to consider what was happening in the 'senior management' dining rooms, to read of the head of one of the academic institutions endlessly chewing his bread without the least inhibition, or the mother of the secretary of the district committee of the Komsomol boiling up leather belts to make jelly, to understand one truth: outside the walls of the Communist Party's Smolny Institute, no one living through the winter of the siege had any bread to spare, whatever 'academic' or 'enhanced' ration category they came into and no matter who they were, be they the director of the Hermitage or the last academician left in Leningrad.[255]

The head of a laboratory every day fed her employees modest portions of nutrient powder, without categorizing them as essential or non-essential.[256] When a hungry member of staff asked, after it had been distributed, if he might lick the spoon used to measure it out, no one stopped to wonder whether he was worth saving. He asked, and he received. S. M. Glazovitskaya, the secretary of the Party committee in the Rabochiy [Worker] factory, records in her diary how the weakest workers were transported to hospital: 'They were put into a car on a stretcher.'[257] Did they really believe these people would shortly be back at their workbenches? Ryzheyeva, the chairwoman of a factory committee, moved one of the workers to the sickbay when she was 'about to die'.[258] Georgiy Knyazev, director of the archive of the Academy of Sciences, tried to get a colleague into hospital precisely because 'his days are numbered', as he writes explicitly in his diary.

The issuing to workers of industrial manufacturing ingredients to use as food deserves a special word. During the Time of Death, that saved many lives. At the Zhdanov factory, raw materials were even awarded as bonuses: 1 kilogram of drying oil or 100 grams of wood glue for carrying explosive shells.[259] It is interesting that A. A. Kuskov, the chairman of the Vasileostrovsky District Executive Committee, saw them as extremely helpful. His comments about them are crossed out in the transcript of his report: the truth about the siege was considered inconvenient even before the war was over:

> Our people in the Kozhevenny tanning factory survived, and that was helped by the fact that during the period of starvation they were able to eat the skins. The Red October factory had a lot of glue, from which they made soup and aspic, and the people there also survived. The Mekhovaya fur factory also kept people alive because they were able to use the skins as food.[260]

At the Ordzhonikidze shipyard, they issued wood glue for use as food, as well as treacle, which was essential for casting shells, and pork fat intended for lubricating slipways when launching ships.[261] At the Molotov factory, they issued industrial-grade linseed oil, and 'people fell upon it in a frenzy of delight'.[262] The workers at the Leningrad Optical Glass factory were issued alcohol used for cleaning the glass. At the Svetoch factory, they were given potato flour used for making sizing for paper.[263] At a textile enterprise, the management even allowed the workers to use pigskin rollers from the machinery as food.[264] A factory making turret drilling machines, in the words of its director, 'did not have large quantities of edible industrial resources at its disposal', but even there they were able to give out 'a certain amount' of starch and wood glue.[265]

People are usually well aware when they are being exploited for commercial purposes, and have no trouble distinguishing genuine from officially prescribed compassion. When there is an undisguised deal, with a commensurate response expected in return for a good deed, expressions of gratitude tend to be carefully weighed. It was quite a different situation when those trapped in the siege knew there was nothing they could offer their benefactors in return, and that, moreover, nothing was expected. Vladimir G. Kulyabko, weak and seemingly completely 'non-essential', responds when someone shows concern for him, with words of gratitude to his director which are evidently the most emotional his innate reticence will permit: 'I will never forget his words and his concern for me.'[266] The director of a clinic helped one Leningrader to get a job as a nurse: 'It was one more example of her sensitivity and kindness. In the course of doing her work, she was concerned to make sure we survived.'[267] The emphatic nature of these words conveys the strength of feeling behind them. Many people, only too aware of their powerlessness and of how 'non-essential' they were during the siege, write selectively only about instances of this kind, and had every right to do so.

It is not always possible to tell whether colleagues were friends or just 'close acquaintances'. Were they just people moved by charitable impulses to do what they could to help? Relations with other people did change in the Time of Death, but colleagues were likely to be visited if they had been absent from work, or it was known they were not well or confined to their beds. That called for a considerable effort. Zinaida Ignatovich recalled a member of staff who had not been seen at the institute and was visited only two days later, even though she lived nearby: 'Everybody was starving, and moving about unnecessarily caused an inordinate amount of stress.'[268]

Colleagues on the verge of collapse would be taken back home from their workplace on a sledge; those who fell in the streets would be helped back up, and no instructions to perform these acts of kindness were needed from the director's office. Ksenia Polzikova-Rubets wrote in her diary that a lecturer in physics collapsed from weakness in the queue outside a bread shop. Would people turn their backs on him, on the grounds that everyone was similarly suffering the effects of cold and hunger? 'I saw Marusya, one of our technical staff, mustering the cleaners to take a sledge to the bread shop.' The man was too weak to get back on his feet, and had no family to care for him. Was he abandoned? 'Comrades brought him food and stoked the stove in his room.'[269]

We see compassion everywhere. People helped their colleagues with the practicalities of living, interceded for them, did their work for them, encouraged them when they were exhausted, without expecting praise or any return. It was noticeable that they took particular care of those who had children.

Here is a sad story told by M. N. Abrosimova, secretary of the Party committee of the Bolshevik factory. The family of a worker who had gone to the front, six children, had been left behind in the care of his disabled wife. They were doomed. It was rare for families with many children, all classed as 'dependants', to survive:

> We found his adolescent daughter a job at the factory and gave the family material support. During the winter, despite all the support from our side, his family almost died out. His wife and two of the children died. Another two we placed in a children's home organized at the factory. It has to be said the children were very frail when we took them, unable to stand. We fed them up and then got them evacuated. After that we evacuated a daughter who was ill.[270]

There is a great sense of charity to be felt in every word here, not masked by the monotonous language and dry exposition typical of an official report.

How many kind words of condolence, how much tact and sensitivity people showed when they heard of the death of the family or friends of those with whom they worked. They took care, they kept a close eye on their colleague, they comforted them just as they would have in peacetime. People left on their own held on to every word of sympathy and noticed every caring gesture. The acknowledgement by one Leningrader who had lost her husband can stand for all of them: 'It brings tears to my eyes when I recall the love and care our comrades surrounded us with.'[271]

Of course, relations between colleagues were not always cordial, even if they saw someone was in need of help. A first generous impulse was not always sustained. One Leningrader felt sorry for a colleague who was suffering from dysentery: 'The local Party committee said, "Take her into your own home, or she will die."' She soon realized this was too much. Her husband was ill, 'and on top of that, the woman was tall and heavily built'. She had to give up: 'In the morning, I went to the committee and told them, "I can't cope with her. Come and take her away."' She was asked, in that case, to take the woman back to her own home. Perhaps hoping to soften her heart, the woman warned her not to take her back there: 'After the bombing the apartment has no glass in the windows and no doors.' She dumped the woman on a carpenter who lived nearby, in spite of his objections, but felt guilty and did later go to visit her.[272] She may just have been afraid she would be accused of callousness if something bad happened, but more probably still had a modicum of compassion left in her.

Colleagues quarrelled, even over hot water, jealously watching to make sure they were not cheated in the canteen. They tried to get out of the exhausting duty rosters by lumbering other people with their stint. When it came to sharing out gifts from the management, there were plenty of squabbles. Factory foremen compelled workers who could hardly stand to carry on working at their places, and watched like eagles to make sure no one took coupon-free soup out of the factories or institutes to their families who were dying of hunger. That all happened.

But it was not universal. There were some places in the city where traditional decencies were still observed, if less rigorously than in the past. In a defunct building, where there were almost no residents left, neighbour might refuse to give water to neighbour. On deserted, ill-lit, icy streets, people might callously walk past the living and the dead. Where, however, people were working and always in full view of other people, where they were entitled to expect to be looked after, moral behaviour was slower to die out. The force of established work practices and communal pressures ensured that people did, however reluctantly, continue to behave in a civilized manner.

7

Party and government

Rules of behaviour

1

The siege of Leningrad was bound to highlight the ethics of the Party and state authorities. A person elevated to the ranks of the heavenly host of senior administrators was inclined often and articulately to declare his responsibility for the fate of Leningrad. The purpose of this was to justify his actions, which would sometimes be unsavoury. It is difficult to argue with him. It is not easy to decide in which cases he was just following harsh guidelines and in which he was improvising, mitigating or exacerbating orders. He could readily deploy entirely sound arguments about the need for drastic measures. If you pointed out to him the predicament of those who were not enjoying the support of the authorities, the desperate extremity of their situation, he could airily refer to the harsh realities of wartime which leave little room for humaneness.

This is clearly visible in the policy documents issued to government and social organizations. The Decree on Evacuation Procedures from the Military Soviet of the Northern Front on 28 June 1941 states:

> Top priority for evacuation is to be given to:
> a) the most important industrial assets . . ., non-ferrous metals, grain
> . . .
> b) skilled workers, engineers and administrators accompanying enterprises being evacuated from the front, the population, especially young people fit for military service, officials and Party workers.[1]

This is not a proposal floated at a meeting: it is the law of the land. There is not a word here about what is to happen to everyone else: women, the elderly, children, unskilled workers. Are they to be left to the mercies of the enemy, to atrocities and starvation? It is in any case clear: metal takes priority over people, Party workers over children. No matter what justifications one might come up with for this document, there is no escaping that conclusion.

It may be objected that this was the only way to win the war, that the ultimate goal of these harsh measures was to save people's lives. The actual experience of those days unfortunately showed only too clearly a tendency not to extend help even where that was possible. A typical example is the replacement of lost ration cards. Of course, there were false claims made by dishonest people, as well as by others desperate at any price to save themselves and their family from starvation; but what about all the others? A more lenient approach to those trapped in the siege could have been adopted, but in Leningrad the authorities chose the most draconian option. 'One hears of the terrible suffering of those who have lost their cards or had them stolen. Some have been going to the centre where the cards are issued since 5 January. They have sold or bartered everything they possessed and now face imminent death ... An inspector came to investigate. Was our staff member a black marketeer? He questioned her neighbours', Georgiy Knyazev noted on 20 January 1942.[2]

Alexey Kuznetsov, secretary of the Leningrad Province Party Committee, and Dmitry V. Pavlov, representative of the State Defence Committee, spoke against any replacement of ration cards. Neither of them went hungry in the course of the siege, and are unlikely ever to have crossed the threshold of a defunct apartment. The reasoning was that the stolen ration documents would also be redeemed, and accordingly additional food supplies would be needed in a situation where they were in extremely high demand. They would hardly have had the audacity to say the weak, the helpless, those unable to stand up for themselves, those who collapsed from hunger and were preyed upon by thieves had only themselves to blame, but it was these vulnerable people, and only they, who bore the brunt of that policy. The system for investigating applications was cumbersome in the extreme, humiliating and, frankly, inhumane. Few people lived long enough to receive their new cards, unless they had been able to fall back on the support of family members. Those who were 'lucky' enough to have their cards restored were henceforth entitled to much-reduced rations.[3]

There was, of course, no covert aim to reduce the number of surplus Leningraders. When thieves trying to steal the ration cards of a factory worker succeeded only in tearing them, she was able to have them replaced promptly with new ones.[4] There was nothing to check, everything was very clear. It was a different matter though, if the situation was confused and there was a lack of evidence. What is obvious, however, is that in deciding whether it was more important to check thoroughly or to save a life by processing a claim swiftly, thoroughness came first. Slow, scrupulous checking took priority, and it was useless to protest. Everyone was under suspicion: everyone was starving, and even a stoic might turn to theft. Anyone might cheat when they saw their child suffering.

Not all officials saw rejecting people's pleas as an unpleasant but routine part of the job. Some acted out the role of righteous souls called upon to instruct lesser brethren without embarrassment – indeed, with gusto, with dramatic intonations and theatrical gestures. They needed no prompting and improvised only too readily, showily, malevolently. In her notebooks, Lydia Ginzburg presents a gallery of types who creatively embellished this humiliating bureaucratic scenario:

> Quite widespread among administrative staff is the outright sadist, the evil secretary. She talks with practised intonations, slightly under-stating her sense of triumphant administrative superiority.
>
> Then there is the languishing secretary. She looks at you with the sole desire of getting rid of this hindrance to her day as quickly as possible, and turns your request down lethargically, even rather plaintively. Finally, there is the businesslike woman. She refuses you majestically and circumstantially, with accompanying homilies.[5]

2

Before we direct too many reproaches at those in positions of power, we need to remember that often they had no say in the matter of how they behaved. They were required to implement decisions taken at 'the top' unquestioningly, as precisely as possible, and with no show of sentimental-ity. It would be quite pointless to ask them whether or not they approved of procedures for renewing lost ration cards which condemned hundreds of people to death. Their job was to say the 'correct' thing, whether or not they believed it. They had to implement harsh measures and could not, like others, avoid responsibility. Often, they delayed, afraid of showing initiative. Doing their job was a higher priority than showing compassion.

Even among representatives of the authorities, though, there were more than a few who tried, without perverse formalism, to alleviate the lot of those at the back of the queue during the siege. Always, however, there is a clear limit to their sympathy and, in that, fear of taking responsibility is an important factor. It demarcated a boundary beyond which they would not go, even if Leningraders were themselves eager to assist the authorities by making sacrifices. The authorities knew best when they needed the help of the public and when they did not, and nobody should think they could impose their assistance where it was not wanted. No matter how absurd that might seem, it was a firmly established principle which no one dared to challenge.[6] This fear of taking responsibility was particularly evident when deciding whether or not to leave the ration cards of a dead person with their family. It would have been contrary to a nationwide law and none of the city's leaders wanted to take that risk. A memorandum from the chairman of the Board of the Workers'and Peasants' Militia of Leningrad, issued on 7 February 1942, makes no reference, as would have been usual, to any decision by superior bodies.[7] In the event of trouble, the blame could be shifted from the chairman of the Leningrad City Executive Committee to other, lower-ranking officials. Until then, officials had been going from door to door, confiscating ration cards if they found anyone had died. They

were obviously aware that this made it necessary to do the rounds more frequently, but orders were orders. Officials came from the rental cooperative
to inspect Veronika A. Opakhova, who lived with two completely emaciated daughters. There is a famous photograph of these girls, one of whom
is leaning on a stick, while the knees and shins of the other look like canes
with knobs on them. The officials had no interest in the girls' health and
only wanted to make sure the mother was not able to use the daughter's
ration card when, as they evidently anticipated, the girl died.

This cruelty infected everyone who held the fate of others in their hands.
There is no shortage of examples from the history of the Public Library. A
library has hardly the strategic importance of a local air defence unit or an
arms factory. There could have been no harm to anyone if requests from
staff were given sympathetic consideration, even if they were contrary to
instructions. But no, there was a set procedure and it was going to be followed, come what may. It had been decided once and for all that there
were to be no holidays, not even unpaid, during the war, and that was to
be observed meticulously, even if it was impossible to stay on the premises
for more than two or three hours a day, because not only your hands froze
but so did the ink. Heads of departments were obliged to monitor the time
people left and report it at precisely the hour appointed to the director.[8]
There were no new accessions and few readers, so perhaps some relaxation of the rules might have been in order. But no, there was to be no rest:
the rooms were to be cleaned and the grounds swept. People should not
expect to get a ration of 200 grams of bread for nothing. V. A Gusev, an
electrician, had not come to work for more than two months. Perhaps he
was ill, no longer able to walk because of starvation? No concessions! He
was struck off the list of staff and thereby deprived of his ration card status
as a worker.[9]

It may be objected that it was not Yelena Yegorenkova, the director
of the Public Library, who made the regulations. That is undeniable but,
for example, the director of the institute where Vladimir G. Kulyabko
worked, recognizing that he was completely worn out, gave him indefinite
leave. There are many similar examples. 'Burn furniture to keep warm',
Alexander Voznesensky, the rector of Leningrad University told his students as they shivered in their lecture rooms.[10] That was probably also
against the rules, but was there a secret police informer in every room
of the Public Library reporting back to the Smolny Institute how many
minutes late a librarian was who could barely move their legs? It was
always possible to extend help, without fuss and without putting yourself
at risk, but how many people did?

T. I. Antonovich wrote to a friend on 16 May 1942: 'One night a truck
came to our library for corpses. I was the duty commander and had to
hand them over. We saw a completely horrible sight: people sprawled in
all sorts of poses.'[11]

At precisely that ghoulish moment, the director found a job for herself
and others: 'In the ice-cold halls several people, led by the director, were

illuminating the cabinets with lighted spills and removing books from the shelves.' What were they looking for so urgently in the night that they had to get out unsteady, malnourished people, knowing that they might share the fate of those being loaded at that instant onto the truck? 'They were meeting a rush order from Smolny.'[12] That is obscure: were these perhaps books on hydrography, medicine, ballistics? Another member of the staff lets the cat out of the bag: 'On more than one occasion, at the request of Smolny, we selected "interesting reading": albums, books, for the moments of relaxation of Andrey Zhdanov and other top Party officials.'[13] The director had good reason to busy herself: she stood to gain an advantageous reputation in the eyes of Party bosses as an efficient and dependable comrade. Nobody would be asking her at whose expense the result had been achieved. The librarians dependent on her would know better than to argue, fearing they might be dismissed, be moved to a lower ration category, or not sent to the sickbay when they needed it. Their director would have no pity, and would not be looking to curry favour with them. They were not in the same category as Zhdanov and his cronies.[14] She had no time for tales of the sufferings of those trapped in the siege. After the war, she talked about a meeting she had with foreign guests who had come to Leningrad: 'Straight away they were asking about the victims, the horrors of the war, looking for sensations. I did not care for visits of that sort.'[15]

3

Reluctance to tell the truth about the siege is a distinguishing feature of many 'senior comrades'. This aberration undoubtedly came from the top. 'Zhdanov was silent, Popkov was silent, and none of the whole gaggle of provincial and city Party committee officials would come anywhere near the microphones of the Radio Committee to say anything to the people', Izrail Metter commented in his notes about the siege.[16] The excuse offered was not entirely without foundation. Information about the destruction, the food situation of the population, the number of victims and location of bombing might be of value to the enemy. There was certainly plenty to hide. Kira Mikhailova, who scrutinized Leningraders' correspondence in the military censorship department of the Main Post Office, wrote that her duty was to 'read the letters meticulously, in order not to let through any information about how hard life was in besieged Leningrad'.[17]

It was impossible to find out anything about the death of thousands of people or the consequences of bombing from the newspapers or radio. Maria Mashkova was relieved to see that there were far fewer funeral processions in February than there had been in January, and assumed that showed the food situation had improved. Her joy was premature: it had just been forbidden to move dead bodies during the hours of daylight.[18] 'There is no denying the fact that a certain proportion of the population of Leningrad died of cold and hunger'; these lines from a book on the siege by Alexander Fadeyev, which was published in 1942, are highly typical.[19] 'There is no denying . . .' was, in fact, a phrase which usually introduced stories which stood little chance of publication. The cold was more commonly mentioned as a cause of death of Leningraders than was starvation. There is no mention in the book of bombardment as a cause of death. The expression 'a certain proportion' was traditionally used to conceal information about casualties. This tradition of 'vigilance' sometimes assumed exotic forms.

There was, however, another reason to conceal the situation in Leningrad. Too much detailed evidence would have highlighted the Soviet authorities' indifference to the fate of their citizens and their inability to deal adequately with the emergency:

> They have no concern for the people. They hide and keep silent about what is going on here. The starvation is terrible, people are dying. They are walking in the street, collapse and die. Men's corpses were left lying at the chemist's for two days and nobody came to take them. The body of a woman wearing only trousers (she had been robbed) lay for several days in the yard. To read the newspapers you'd think everything was fine. They even wanted to film an orchestra, as if there was a concert, but couldn't get the electricity. There is no electricity anywhere, no water. Starving, feeble residents bring buckets on sledges to the Neva. The courtyards and streets are covered in filth.

Natalia Zavetnovskaya poured out these complaints in a letter to her daughter.[20]

Reading the minutes of a discussion at the Smolny Institute of the film *The Defence of Leningrad*, you have the impression that those in the audience are more concerned about the 'decency' of the panorama of the siege presented in the film than in recreating historical truth. Their main objection is that the film does not give an injection of optimism and enthusiasm, or summon the workers to accomplish new feats of labour heroism.

Life in Leningrad was already dreadful enough, and the demand not to rub salt in the wounds cannot be regarded only as hypocrisy. German leaflets calling on the besieged citizens to abandon resistance painted their lives in exclusively dark colours. It would have been odd to repeat that message when seeking every opportunity to bolster the fortitude of those in the siege. Leningraders themselves were doing their best to forget the nightmare of their lives by talking about food and life in the past, reading books, visiting the theatre, concerts and libraries, writing poetry and 'celebrating' holidays.

Alexey Kuznetsov insistently demanded more emphasis on optimism in the film. He was irritated by the mournful music, and that it did not show 'the struggle of people' and that 'there seem to be too many difficulties'.[21] He was supported by Andrey Zhdanov, who probably also regarded himself as something of a connoisseur of bracing tunes. Alexander Fadeyev noted his reaction to the monotonous clicking of the metronome: 'Are you trying to discourage everyone or what? You ought to play some music there.'[22] Here we find a familiar attitude. Zhdanov's eye clearly identifies all divergence from the propaganda line. His remarks are trenchant: cut out the gloomy music. Why? It is unnecessary: 'Cut out all the mourning stuff.'[23] The New Soviet woman is nowhere to be seen. That is bad. What is shown is an old woman sitting in a park. She was probably a far from cheerful sight. He did not like that clip: 'The old woman needs to be cut.'

The more you read of these criticisms from the 'highest level', the more you detect that it was not only the mournful tone of the film which was causing such official disfavour. 'The negative is overdone', says Zhdanov. From the report of Pyotr Popkov's speech you see that was the real problem. Popkov evidently considered himself a remarkably well-qualified film editor. The film shows a string of dead bodies. Cut that! 'The impression is too depressing. Some of the episodes with coffins need to be cut.' He saw a vehicle frozen into the snow. Why show that? 'That could be seen as due to a lack of good order.' He is outraged that the work of the factories is missing, and keeps quiet about the obvious fact that most of them were not functioning during the first winter of the siege. The film shows a Leningrader collapsing from exhaustion. Cut! 'Who knows why he is staggering like that. Perhaps he was drunk.'[24]

There we have the idyllic life of Leningraders during the siege, as presented by Pyotr Popkov. No coffins. No dead people. No wrecked vehicles. No frozen factories at a standstill. No people staggering about in the streets. Probably all he would have shown in the film would have been joyful workers happily beavering away at their machines, but surely there needed to be some narration of the harsh realities of the situation to contrast with their heroism? 'Where are they being taken?' Popkov demanded when he saw an endless succession of corpses in the film. That was a fairly extraordinary question, coming from someone whose job it was to be better informed than anyone else about the tragedy of Leningrad.

These attempts to shield themselves from criticism could also be disguised as stemming from concern to safeguard military secrets. Later, there would have seemed to be no call to meticulously conceal information about the numbers of victims, but Popkov's approach changed not one iota. Vladislav Glinka attended a press conference given by the chairman of the Leningrad Executive Committee for foreign journalists. What he heard struck him as the height of cynicism:

When, in the course of the discussion, one of the British journalists asked if it was true that over 500,000 people had died in Leningrad, Popkov, with his typical twisted smirk, unhesitatingly replied,

'That figure is greatly exaggerated. It is a complete journalistic invention.'

A minute later, he replied with the same smirk to a question about provision of public services during the siege.

'The provision of electricity and operation of the water supply in Leningrad were not interrupted for a single hour.'[25]

4

Faking it was a characteristic of those who ruled Leningrad during the Time of Death – faking cheerfulness, efficiency, activity. Much could not be done, but it was dangerous to let it be detected that anyone was failing to do their duty. Visits to the theatre by senior comrades can be taken as an example of this kind of fakery. One such visit is described by Dmitry Pavlov, the representative of the State Defence Committee responsible for Leningrad's food supplies. He attended a performance at the Musical Comedy Theatre, along with Popkov and Pyotr Lazutin. The temperature outside was –25 °. The artists' faces were, as was to be expected, grey, pale, haggard. They were wearing light costumes. During the interval, some of them fainted from hunger. Those who could still walk went up to the government box to ask for a coupon-free helping of yeast soup, a brew which tasted disgusting.

What a disgraceful episode: it is not well-fed people who go down to offer bread and ask about the welfare of starving actors, but emaciated people climb up to them and humbly explain: 'Please excuse us for this intrusion.'[26] They had not removed their make-up and were still in their costumes. Perhaps they were in a hurry, afraid that their visitors would leave, or were too weak to change, or thought that in costume they might arouse more sympathy from people who would not give that kind of soup a second glance. That there might be something obscene about three well-fed men sitting there to watch people who were on the verge of collapse from starvation dancing for their benefit seems never to have occurred to them. One can only wonder what satisfaction they got from it. 'It was less entertaining than sad', was Arkadiy Gordin's comment as he looked at the actors.[27] That, however, was not what the senior comrades were interested in. For them, what mattered was to demonstrate that they were capable of inspiring confidence in the hearts of the besieged Leningraders. The main thing was for that to be noted elsewhere: 'It was a victory of the will: they got up and acted.'[28] They needed to show that those in charge of the city were side by side with ordinary people, sharing their joys and anxieties, together with them in the theatre or under fire, concerned.

They got into acting the role of steadfast champions, urging others on to ever greater feats on a daily basis, counselling the waverer, threatening those in retreat. They worked out a script of how to behave and memorized cut-and-dried rules for defining what constituted heroism.

It is not difficult to see what they were modelling themselves on, but less obvious how much energy they put into it. Yemelian Lagutkin reported how often Popkov risked his life to visit the site of disasters. He 'took an active part in eliminating the consequences of enemy air raids and shelling.'[29] The dull officialese of this statement can be partly explained by the fact that often the only literary endeavour officials engaged in was the writing of reports. What does raise an eyebrow is the marked lack not only of vivid description, but of any detail whatsoever. An eyewitness told the story many years after the lifting of the siege of how the rector of Leningrad State University, Alexander Voznesensky, would talk to people still trapped in rubble, bringing them warm clothes and chocolate.[30] People vividly remembered the deputy chairman of the Council of People's Commissars, Alexey Kosygin, 'going round the feeding stations and speaking to evacuees'.[31] What kept Lagutkin from bringing his story to life by describing Popkov helping to put out fires, aiding the injured and freeing them from the rubble? Instead we have that bland assertion of the 'active part' Popkov took, a catch-all phrase if ever there was one.

The book containing Lagutkin's assertion was compiled by one of Popkov's subordinates, which doubtless should be borne in mind. In the hundreds of siege documents I have studied, I have found no evidence that anyone ever saw Popkov in the ruins of a bombed building. It would certainly have been remembered, but there is no mention of any such thing from eyewitnesses. After September 1941, there were no sightings among the ruins of Zhdanov or Kuznetsov. It would be surprising if Pyotr Popkov had suddenly decided to court popularity by displaying compassion when it was so conspicuously absent in the other 'leaders'.

The apocryphal stories about Andrey Zhdanov are no more deserving of trust. Their hagiographical tendencies are all the more glaring when they are included in official documents. 'The Leningrad city administration and Comrade Zhdanov personally paid extraordinarily close attention to the needs of schoolchildren', we read in a report by the education department of the Leningrad Executive Committee.[32] Only a few paragraphs below that, we read an admission that: 'In School No. 369 in Moscow district during the first inspection after their arriving at the school it was found that 96% of children were suffering from acute malnutrition and scurvy.'[33] The authors of the report seem blithely unaware of how self-contradictory their report has become.

Where eyewitness accounts are more detailed, we find the faking of hectic activity characteristic of the bureaucracy. The inspection tours of apartments attended by secretaries of the district and Party committees of the Primorsky and Petrograd districts were considered to exemplify this concern for the people of Leningrad. This too was one of the all-too-familiar 'campaigns'. The first visits were also the last: there is no evidence of any others.

We should not deny the contribution the government and Party authorities did make towards saving the lives of Leningraders. It would be irrelevant to ask them whether they were prompted by humane feelings. They did the job they were obliged to. No doubt the authorities did genuinely want to relieve the suffering of citizens, and did a lot to achieve that. No matter how well these senior comrades were fed, it was painful for them too to see every day the intolerable suffering of the starving, and the frozen and stripped corpses in the streets.

There is reliable evidence that Andrey Zhdanov and Kliment Voroshilov did go after the first bombing raid to Millionnaya Street to see a child who had miraculously survived.[34] We can tell in a message from the secretary of the Vyborg district Party committee who supervised distribution of surrogate foods to those in need that he was often pleased to have been able to help someone.[35] Alexey Kuznetsov was emotional in one speech when he talked about the high mortality rate in the city, despite an increase in rations: 'That is a big worry for us and, in particular, for Andrey Zhdanov.'[36] This is not a hackneyed expression. He spoke with unusual frankness about how edgy Zhdanov was, and how outraged that nobody, not even the doctors, wanted to explain to him what the reasons for that were. When the redoubtable Popkov, calling for household squads to be set up, told the tale of a helpless old lady trying to keep two little children warm in her bed, we know that story had affected him. It is, however, one thing to help people while conforming to rigid discipline, and quite another to do so without waiting for orders from 'upstairs', when you are having to overstep the limits of your authority and be held accountable for your actions. Did many people prove capable of that? No.

Popkov, responding to a request from rock climbers – who were being asked to conceal tall spires with coverings – that they should be issued with special-category ration cards, replied, 'Why? You are getting exercise in the fresh air.'[37] That gives a very precise indication of the level of their morality. 'Do you think the district soviet is a milk cow?' the chairman of a District Executive Committee yelled at one of the women who had come to ask for furniture for a children's home.[38] There was no shortage of furniture left over from the 'hearths', which had been closed after a significant proportion of children had been evacuated from Leningrad. The real reason for the refusal may have been that the official was tired, scared to take responsibility, or just selfish. It is not really of any interest what pretexts he came up with.

Privileges

1

The system of privileges in Leningrad during the siege was no secret. The principles on which it was based were not new. Priority went to people in the Party and government bureaucracies, and to 'essential' specialists: the directors of factories and institutions, highly qualified engineers and workers, and academics. The value of specialists was relative and 'situational': the value of government and Party workers was absolute. We know that during the siege the level of mortality among communists was half that of the population at large.[39] That gap would increase disproportionately if we included not all Party members but only those in senior positions. 'The workers in the district committee also began to feel the harshness of the situation, even though they were relatively privileged. None of those working for the district committee or its plenum and none of the secretaries of local Party committees died. We managed to look after our people', recalled A. M. Grigoriev, the first secretary of the Lenin district Party committee.[40] Rank-and-file communists, like any other residents of Leningrad, had no reliable sources of food. Did the senior comrades feel guilty about that?

Before we answer that question, let us look at the arguments used to justify the existence of privileges. If they were granted only to a restricted group, there would seem to be a clear injustice, but in fact they were extended, although on a much reduced scale, to several other categories of citizens, not least to the weakest and most vulnerable. Many did not find the principle of privileges abhorrent. There was irritable talk about the rations enjoyed by those in the Smolny Institute, but an acceptance that there was no equivalence between working in 'hot' workshops and sweeping the floors in factories where production had stopped. Every day there had to be discrimination over who should be considered more and who less valuable, who should be awarded rations and who should be denied them. Moreover, there was little scope for favouritism because there were instructions to be followed, which meant that the system was seen not as arbitrary, but as a matter of national importance. And once it was accepted that discriminating between people was warranted and not simply disgraceful, the privileges of the ruling elite were less likely to be viewed negatively. The greater rewards could also be justified on the grounds that those managing the city had to work all hours, and had heavier duties and responsibilities. In any case, there is no hiding the fact that thousands of Leningraders were compromised by hoping, by a variety of means (usually 'contacts'), to gain access themselves to food supplies not available to the majority of the population.

2

A sense of shame was felt more strongly (but even then, not always) only when the difference between rations for senior comrades and ordinary victims of the siege was excessive by any standards. The vicissitudes of N. A. Ribkovsky stand out. Released from 'senior' work in the autumn of 1941, he experienced in full the horrors of the Time of Death alongside his fellow citizens. He managed to survive because, in December 1941, he was appointed as an instructor in the personnel department of the Leningrad City Party Committee. In March 1942, he was sent to the City Committee's nursing home in the village of Melnichny Ruchey. Like any other Leningrader who experienced the rigours of starvation, he cannot help dwelling in his diary on a comprehensive list of food he received:

The food here is like what you found in peacetime in a good resort: high-quality, varied and delicious. Every day there is a meat course: mutton, ham, chicken, goose, then sausage, fish (bream, herring, smelt), fried, boiled or jellied; caviar, sturgeon, cheese, pies and black bread every day; 30 grams of butter and, to cap it all, 50 grams of good fortified wine for lunch and dinner. I and two other comrades get an additional snack between breakfast and dinner: a couple of open sandwiches or a bun, and a glass of sweet tea.[41]

'The best stuff got thrown out on Sundays', a starving girl wrote in her diary. She and her mother lived off whatever was thrown on the rubbish tip. 'The best' – that tells us something about the criteria of people who did not enjoy privileges. Ribkovsky had been one of them, and it was no wonder he needed feeding up in his nursing home. He is clearly uneasy. He is looking for excuses. He would like to believe it is not only here you can live 'like in a good resort': 'The comrades tell us that the district sick-bays are in no way inferior to the City Committee's nursing home, and that some factories have sickbays that put our amenities in the shade.'[42] Information has in fact survived about the food ration standards in the sickbay at the steel mill. Even the bread ration there was less, not to mention the variety of food on offer. The meat allocation was 40 grams a day, and the grain ration was also 40 grams. Ribkovsky and his colleagues may well not have known about that, and, even if they had, they would hardly have renounced their privileges: not only because of the hunger, but also because they would not have been allowed to do so. What is notewor-thy here is their sense of shame: they really did feel they had to find excuses for themselves. Does that mean they considered the privileges immoral? No. The best they could do was to make themselves feel better by sharing their 'senior comrade rations' with other people, and reassure themselves that there was plenty of food in other, similar facilities. Their belief that discriminating between people was appropriate never faltered.

When you read the transcripts of reports from directors of factories, one detail leaps out. If they found anything in their stores that was edible, they had no choice but to hand over some of it to the Party and Soviet workers. A. P. Alexeyeva, the director of the Svetoch factory, did her best to protect the potato flour found in their warehouses, but officialdom found out about it and she had no option but to surrender some to 'our comrades in the district committee and the government bureaucracy'.[43] The deputy head of the commercial port of Leningrad, Boris Bernstein, when men-tioning that fresh fish was not only distributed to the port workers but also 'sent into the city', manages only to name one recipient: 'in particular, it went to the Party district committee'.[44]

The same was noticed in other instances. The city's bomb shelters had been constructed in a hurry. Could the staff of the Prosecutor's Office really be expected to sit, like thousands of Leningraders, in these 'stone coffins', in the crush, with no benches, fearing at any moment to be be buried under rubble? Of course not. 'We are designing a comfortable bomb shelter for the Prosecutor's Office', a member of the Architectural and Planning Administration wrote in his diary.[45]

Because of the shortage of transport, it was possible to leave Leningrad only if you had an official order, and many people died before it was their turn. The wife of the first secretary of one of the Komsomol provincial committees in the Urals decided to return to see her husband, confident that evacuation orders were needed only by ordinary people. She did not even show any identity documents to the head of a group of workers who were being evacuated. He included her in the list of evacuees 'as his wife'.[46] He felt unable to refuse, for fear of getting into trouble, although he suspected she was a fraud. That was the only thing that worried him. That, if genuine, she would have a right to jump the queue, he had no doubt. Another Leningrader was lucky enough to meet a provincial committee official she knew, who helped her to be evacuated along with the Krasny Vyborzhets [Red Vyborger] factory, and he too, in all probability, did not doubt he had the right to decide who was worthy of being allowed to leave.[47]

One young woman survived only because she managed to get herself authorized to eat at a district committee canteen where 'you could have a good meal once a day'.[48] These canteens for senior comrades were an improvement – if not always a big improvement – on factory canteens.[49] If factory directors were entitled to a coupon-free lunch, the leaders of Party, Komsomol and government organizations were entitled also to a coupon-free dinner.[50] At the Smolny Institute, only coupons for bread were torn off to the full value. Only 50 per cent of the meat coupons were torn off in respect of meat dishes, while dishes made with grains or pasta were coupon-free.[51] Precise information on the consumption of food in the Smolny canteen has not been made available to this day, which says it all.

Among the few tales about the meals eaten at Smolny, in most of which rumour is mixed with pure invention, there are some which seem reasonably trustworthy. In spring 1942, Olga Grechina's brother brought her two 1-litre jars: 'One had cabbage, which had once been sour but was now just rotten, and the other had similarly rotten red tomatoes.' He explained that they were clearing out the Smolny basements, removing barrels of rotten vegetables.[52] One cleaner got to see the Smolny banqueting hall when she was invited to wait at table. Her friends were envious, but she came back in tears: nobody had given her anything to eat, even though 'You would never believe the kind of food they had on the tables.'[53]

Izrail Metter told the tale of an actress at the Baltic Fleet Theatre who received, as a mark of favour from Alexey Kuznetsov, a member of the Military Soviet of the Leningrad Front, a 'chocolate cake specially baked at the Samoilova confectionery factory'.[54] It was enough to feed fifteen people, who included Metter. There was no ulterior motive; it was just that Alexey Kuznetsov had no doubt that, in a city littered with the bodies of people who had starved to death, he had a perfect right to give an extravagant gift at other people's expense to an actress he had taken a fancy to. These people behaved as if they were still living in peacetime, when you need have no qualms about relaxing in the theatre, sending cakes to actresses, and obliging librarians to find books to fill your 'moments of leisure'.

3

The discrimination between people who were essential and those who were inessential had far-reaching consequences. It was deemed necessary to differentiate further the rations of those in power themselves.

In the semi-secret shop for 'generals' in the courtyard of the Leningrad Military District's headquarters, as early as September 1941, there was nothing but champagne on the shelves, while in the cafeteria of *Leningrad Pravda*, even in late autumn, they had coupon-free, luxury items which not everyone would ever have set eyes on before the war: top-quality tinned crab, excellent grainy sturgeon caviar . . . although there was no bread.[55]

An instructor in the political department of the Police Directorate was disciplined for obtaining food for herself using the ration card of a dependant who had been evacuated. She was issued a Party reprimand and dismissed from the directorate, but they then took pity and moved her to the Institute of Party History, warning that until the reprimand expired she would have to act as manageress of the facilities there.[56]

'All our reserves had been used up by this time and I was reduced to looking for anything to chew on. I found a tallow candle and chewed that', recalled B. P. Fyodorov, first secretary of the October district committee of the Komsomol. His mother fed him with dandelion roots and boiled up aspic from leather belts. He had to coax his deputy to walk to the Party's utility management meeting by feeding him another piece of bread every kilometre or so.[57] M. I. Gorbachev, the secretary of the Moscow district committee of the Komsomol, was keen to emphasize that 'Workers of the Komsomol District Committee enjoyed no privileges.'[58]

All these statements were made to shorthand typists during the war, when the experiences were still in everybody's minds, and there were people alive who could confirm or dispute them. District Komsomol workers were arguably on the lowest rung of the regime's ladder. It is glaringly apparent that we find no such statements in the recollections of the heads of Party district or executive committees.

In the transcript of a communication from the Vasileostrovsky District Executive Committee chairman, we detect a certain amount of embarrassment as soon as he starts talking about privileges. The style is chaotic and jerky, and there is a sense that some information is being deliberately withheld. He says the committee's secretary was 'dystrophic', would fall asleep in her office and be impossible to wake. The Party's district committee issued him tinned fruit, but there is not a word about what else he ate. 'We too had a ration of 125 grams of bread', he claims.[59] That makes one cringe.

On 17 December 1941, the Executive Committee of the Leningrad City Council resolved to grant secretaries of Party district committees, chairmen of District Executive Committees and their deputies an evening meal without deduction of food coupons. The picture of how these senior comrades viewed their privileges would be incomplete if we did not note how they reacted to requests to give support to others. Here their 'statesmanlike' approach is most starkly evident. It was, of course, impossible to help everybody, but it is striking how parsimonious they were in dispensing concessions to others suffering in the siege. A directive of the Executive Committee of the Leningrad City Council of 31 December 1941, on the organization of New Year's parties for children, permits the 'issuance of free tickets to children in the families of privates and junior officers in the Workers' and Peasants' Red Army and Red Navy, pensioners and families in acute need, but not exceeding 30% of the total number of tickets'.[60] A ticket cost 5 rubles. Even here, where money had almost lost its meaning, the penny-pinchers were in control.

We see the same scenario repeated, where seemingly rational argument fails to conceal indifference to the fate of those not granted access to the feeding trough and unable to fight their own corner. Those most often denied were citizens whose work was classified as not important to Leningrad and survival of the population. One cannot take exception to that: those at the 'top' were guided by a logic which, although harsh, is not unjustifiable. We need to look, however, at how refusals were presented. Georgiy Knyazev writes of the zeal with which a woman he knew tried to extract a first-category ration card for him: 'At every turn her efforts foundered on the cold, empty stage of the bureaucracy.' We might dismiss this as the rhetoric of a man with a grudge if we did not have more detail of this saga.

Knyazev's applications kept getting 'lost', and when it was suggested there should be an increase in rations not only for the director, but for all those with a higher degree, the instant reply was a resounding 'No!' Trying to soften the relevant trade union officials, the question was asked, 'So what are they supposed to do – die?'[61] 'Maybe so', the woman interceding was told. Perhaps, when every day these officials were deciding who should live and who could be left to die, concealing what they were doing behind a smokescreen of bureaucratic formulations, they became desensitized to the cynicism of such an answer. They became dulled; they wearied of the never-ending petitions, of repeating the same clichés and gestures, and just wanted to put a stop as quickly as possible to an endless and futile conversation, harshly, brutally, shamelessly.

The tale of Academician Ignatiy Krachkovsky's letters to the authorities is replete with this kind of bureaucratic brush-off. He was the only academician left in Leningrad, and probably hoped his status, age, talent and achievements would gain him better treatment. He dared to ask for help only when close to death, and even then only indirectly. He wrote to friends, academicians in Kazakhstan, and they telegraphed a request to the Leningrad City Council, having first secured the support of Vladimir Komarov, president of the Academy of Sciences of the USSR. Their request caught Pyotr Popkov on the hop: it had evidently never occurred to anyone at the Smolny that they might take an interest in the fate of a scholar. A telegram from the president of the Academy of Sciences could not, like a plea from some obscure victim of the siege, be dismissed out of hand. There might be consequences, and who knows who might be appealed to next and start asking awkward questions about the real situation in the city. Bureaucratic games are convoluted. In late February 1942, the chairman of the Board of Administration and Management of Academic Institutions, M. Ye. Fedoseyev, received a phone call from Popkov's office (they did not deign to respond directly to Krachkovsky). It was explained they could not simply ignore an appeal from the president of the Academy of Sciences and would need to come up with some sort of an answer. They asked Fedoseyev whether the academician was still alive and, learning that he was, rang off. Nobody offered him any help and, indeed, they probably thought none was needed. Nobody had died, there was nothing to worry about, and that was what they could tell President Komarov. The official in Popkov's office was told that the academician had a telephone and they could call him, but nobody bothered. At this point, Fedoseyev himself called Popkov's secretariat, and was informed no telegrams had ever been received.[62]

Here all the characteristic bureaucratic ploys are on display. It is decided who has clout and who can be ignored. Not a foot has been put wrong: the practised moves of brush-off and concealment are deployed with virtuosity. No one can be caught out and accused of callousness, and, if need be, everything can be put down to attendant circumstances.

In March 1942, Ignatiy Krachkovsky felt so acutely hungry that, setting aside all pride and self-esteem, he appealed directly to Popkov. He asked him to send doctors and talked of medicines and vitamins. No response. He humiliated himself again. It was a waste of time hoping for compassion: he could see that. What bureaucrats most fear is culpability: should he work on that? Krachkovsky, with exquisite tact, ostensibly determined to avoid again offending an official or getting himself branded a troublemaker, tries to explain to Popkov that this inaction may be potentially awkward for the chairman of the Leningrad Executive Committee personally: 'It would be undesirable if the information, of which I have no knowledge and which, without my involvement, reached the Presidium of the Academy of Sciences in Sverdlovsk, were to spread more widely here or abroad, giving a false excuse to misinterpret the attitude towards scholars who are continuing to work at their posts in Leningrad.'[63] No response. Academician Krachkovsky was not a person who had to be feared or whose hints had to be taken seriously. The wrath of Andrey Zhdanov, however, was to be feared, and when Krachkovsky appealed to him, something unexpected happened. The academician was suddenly visited by staff from the department of health, supplied not only with medicine and vitamins, but also with fresh meat, white bread, grains, butter, dried apricots, flour, biscuits and chocolate. Everything, it seemed, was possible after all, if you just persistently and resourcefully, using first one approach then another, intelligently selected the optimal levers to pull. Even with one foot in the grave, it was possible to get the bureaucracy to acknowledge your right to be fed no less adequately than the senior comrades.

This was just one case, and in the course of studying it, one seems to hear the clanking of that rusty bureaucratic machine. This was not a case of somebody trying to obtain undeserved privileges. They were deserved, but what efforts it cost to assert them. Meanwhile, what about all the other Leningraders who had no influential intercessors and who perished unmourned? It is possible, of course, to refer to the trials of wartime when attempting to justify the zeal with which senior comrades sought to whittle down the numbers of those entitled to privileges. Only, why then were they not equally selective when it came to themselves?

Their decision to feed themselves better than others is understandable, and there might seem little cause for condemnation in that. When, however, they were in a position to decide how abundantly and at whose expense to eat more, we see their morals most starkly. If the need for enhanced feeding was dictated only by the laws of national survival, we could see some justification, brutal but appropriate in the conditions of the siege, for the idea that senior comrades should enjoy privileges. But we know how lavishly many of those with access to power and hence to food, lived. The notion that you may not sumptuously indulge yourself, albeit by the standards of the siege, in front of people without so much as a crust of bread, somehow did not catch on with certain of the senior comrades. They violated moral prohibitions, as they had in the past, and often only too readily.

8

Strangers

Parentless children

1

Helping parentless children assumed a special urgency from the second half of December 1941, when the death toll among the city's residents began rising steadily and rapidly. Leningrad's children's homes were over-crowded, and the traditional way of providing care became increasingly ineffective. Restructuring did not begin immediately, or with the urgency required by the calamity of the siege, whose scale was not immediately appreciated. Leningrad City Council's directive of 13 February 1942, which proposed providing children's homes with fuel, beds and bedding, was belated. This should all have been taken care of before. According to eyewitnesses, nappies were freezing to mattresses and children sleeping five to a bed. The customary rituals of decision-making were even now strictly adhered to. The directive of the USSR Council of People's Commissars 'On arrangements for children left without parents' elicited a bye-law from city officials only one month later, by which time several thousand bodies a day were being buried in Leningrad. Reading the directive of the secretariat of the Leningrad City Committee of the Komsomol dated 16 March 1942, 'On the responsibility of Komsomol organizations to identify and resettle parentless children and adolescents', it is difficult not to feel that this is primarily a tool in the campaign, begun at the time, to clean up the city because of fear of epidemics. It proposed that Komsomol leaders, together with representatives of the regional department of education, should, by 20 March 1942, conduct a 'comprehensive inspection of apart-ments in order to identify unsupervised children and adolescents'. The extraordinarily short period of three days allowed for carrying this out in a large city suggests that those issuing the directive were fully aware of how many children and adolescents had actually survived and would be in need of sending to children's homes.

Bureaucratic documents, of course, often bear little relation to the reali-ties on the ground. Receiving no coherent, timely instructions from the top, and unable to waste any more time waiting for them, local leaders were not afraid to improvise. Much was decided on the spur of the moment.

Pyotr Popkov had delivered an important and businesslike speech at a meeting of the Leningrad City Party Committee on 9 January 1942 in which, giving examples of support for children, he stressed that 'this humane concern, this attention on the part of our organizations, needs to be put on a firm footing. A great deal depends on it.'[1] One must also acknowledge the justice of his rebuke at a meeting of the Leningrad Province Soviet on 24 February 1942 that, in a number of districts, the task of supplying children's homes was 'completely unplanned', and that this was 'a disorderly outrage which cannot be blamed on the war'.[2]

The standard recommendations at sundry meetings did not have the force of an official harangue from the top. They were not accompanied by detailed implementation plans, were unclear, set no deadlines, pinned no responsibility on anyone, and contained no provision for reporting back on progress. Indeed, there was no programme, only the usual exhortation.

The main way in which children's lives were saved was inspection of apartments. The documents relating to this make distressing reading. They describe the bodies of dead parents, next to which feral children tried to keep warm and gnawed at the corpses. There are descriptions of the lice covering them and of swarms of rats, gnawing at the children themselves. Prior to the beginning of January 1942, it would seem the city authorities had not concerned themselves with the conditions in which Leningraders too weak to get out of their apartments were living.

Many different kinds of people helped with saving the children. They were teachers, the staff in schools, kindergartens and children's homes, officials from the city and district education departments, doctors, the Komsomol household and hygiene squads, housing managers, factory workers, senior schoolchildren, young 'Timur' volunteers, and housewives. It was not exceptional for starving children to be brought to the children's homes by their brothers and sisters, distant relatives or neighbours; babies were cared for in paediatric clinics.

Until late January 1942, there were far fewer people inspecting apartments than there were later. Certainly, there was no suggestion at the time of a large-scale campaign to save citizens' lives. It may be objected that many did not yet know the whole truth about the scale of the deaths, but from the end of December 1941 an endless succession of sledges with swaddlings became an everyday sight in the streets of Leningrad. In the documents dating from December 1941 to January 1942, there is a lot of testimony about how moral principles were breaking down, even in the relationships between close family members, so what could be expected in the way of help for strangers? The only people being satisfactorily fed were the household and hygiene squads. For many, this was just a job, and they were not always conscientious about carrying it out. In any case, inspecting apartments required permission from the authorities, even if those

wanting to assist were charitably minded people sensitive to other people's
misery. In Leningrad, there was also no shortage of looters, robbing frail
citizens in the streets and in their homes, sometimes disguising their villainy as support for the vulnerable.

Urging – and sometimes obliging – citizens to give help, the authorities were primarily pursuing the practical aim of saving as many lives as
possible, but those caring for the weak found themselves in an immensely
stressful situation. Many had never seen anything like this chasm of
unspeakable misfortune. Even those accustomed to such scenes encountered situations which shocked them so profoundly that they were still
affected many years later.

M. N. Abrosimova was the secretary of a factory Party bureau and
could have been seen as a model Party activist: 'Work has been conducted
on popularization of the progressive vanguard role of the party. I rebuffed
incorrect rumours to ensure the people did not have an incorrect percep-
tion of the present moment. In order to prepare the masses it was necessary to establish a foundation . . .' Her words are confident, her gestures
energetic. Everything is her concern; she jollies along the waverers and
scolds the laggards. She has been instructed to go to the children's home
on Podolskaya Street to collect the children from it. She will be up to the
task.

What she found there was horror:

> The little children were in the second and third stages of dystrophy.
> They could not stand up and were almost all suffering from bloody
> diarrhoea. They were lying in heaps of five or six, doubled up, filthy,
> covered in lice, frozen. They did not get up. They excreted where they
> lay. It was a hideous sight. The room temperature was 5–6 ° above
> zero. The children were between three and five years old.

She cannot stop: 'They were dressed in whatever had been found. The feet
of some were wrapped in rags, some had holed shoes on their bare feet,
others had felt boots. None had stockings. One had a sun hat. Whatever
had been available.'[3]

All those practised, repressed, 'correct' words vanish in an instant. She
seems to be shuddering. Her writing is disjointed, repetitive, full of exclamations. What matters is to take these unhappy children in her arms, to
wrap them up warmly, hug them to herself and get them out to the van:
'They were literally dripping over you as you carried them.' People were
overcome with pity, and brought toys and crockery to the factory's children's home. How much charitable feeling there is in these prosaic stories:
'The women in their spare time sewed and altered pants and dresses for
these children. They sewed them new little suits and dresses, and made
them little shoes out of greatcoat material. They heated tanks of hot water.
They dressed them in clean clothes, brought them to a clean room, put
them in beds, and gave them hot food and drinks.' They watched lovingly

as the children recovered, as they began to run around and laugh: 'We even thought that when they came back, grown up, we would find them jobs in our factory.'[4]

M. P. Prokhorova, the secretary of the Primorsky district committee of the Komsomol, recalled conducting inspections of defunct apartments. The tone of her note is wholly businesslike, the language close to official-ese. It is a standard progress report: 'In the apartment a boy was sitting among the bodies of three adults. We were unable to establish how long he had been sitting like that, but evidently three days.' She continues her report in the expected format: 'This confirmed to us how greatly our assistance was needed.' But she cannot remain unemotional and just leave it at that. She returns to the child they have rescued: 'The boy was three years old, just a baby, and there he was sitting among dead bodies.' As she continues, it is clear she is trying to move on from the horror. 'We went round, checking the work of the team', but again a few lines later, she returns to a description of the same scene: 'I cannot get the sight of that boy out my mind. He was so chilled, his lips were blue. It seemed that in a few more minutes he might die. He looked like an old man. He clearly wanted to express his joy at seeing living people.' What shocked Prokhorova most of all was his ghastly senile smile .[5]

There is something unexpected in her repetition of the same numbers: the 3-year-old boy, alone for three days with three corpses. Perhaps that first detail of the three corpses made such a searing impression that she unconsciously repeated it as she speculates about things she could not have known for sure: the age of the child, and how long he had been starving in there. In these artless, rhetorically almost identical stories, we sense a rigid framework. In the successive layers of imagery of the unfortunate little boy, from which she cannot free herself, we detect a changing of perspective as her vision becomes almost microscopic. As we follow this sequence, we can identify clearly her growing sense of compassion. A cursory glance at a scene of horror yields to a closer look at the boy, and then to extreme concentration on the symptoms of his decline. She focuses attention on his lips, his skin, his smile, the incongruous combination of early childhood and old age, and cannot tear herself away or blanket it with crude bombast.

As we read the inspection reports about defunct apartments, we generally find that the businesslike tone with its bureaucratic clichés, the listing of facts and figures, cannot be kept up. It is disrupted by emotional exclamations, and details which nobody has required but which the writer cannot pass over in silence.

The entry for 28 January 1942 in the diary of Alexandra Mironova, the director of a children's home, begins with the dispassionate recording of information about an orphan discovered in such-and-such street, building number, apartment number, name, surname, age. Here she might have stopped, but cannot: 'His mother died waiting in a queue. The boy lay night and day beside her, "Only, Mummy made me cold." Yura did not want to come with me, and cried and screamed. His farewell to his mummy was very moving. "Mummy, what have they done to you? What have you done to me? I don't want to go to the children's home."[6] The brisk beginning of the entry is replaced by an emotional story and concludes almost with a scream, until, increasingly upset, the diarist has got the pain out of her system.

2

A scream, a whisper, a story broken off, the selection of episodes from the siege, affectionate words – everywhere you feel a tide of emotion when people reminisce about saving children: 'You might open an apartment door and see a little baby pressed to its mother's breast; it is hungry, but its mother is cold. You wrap the little waif in something warm and take it just as quickly as you can to the hospital.'[7] A 'little baby', a 'little waif', 'pressed to its mother's breast': the emotion attached to these scenes is undiminished, decades later.

The emotion to be found in official reports tells us how highly the task of saving children's lives was rated. Coming into contact with them made a profound impression on all who did. The children are touchingly grateful, they cry, they complain. They cling to the body of their dead mother, they talk about how happy they were with her. They are so vulnerable and so winning: who could not be deeply moved? All children have their own, unexpected questions and answers, for each their grief is very personal; they ask for some special thing which is terribly important to them, talk about deeply personal things. Who could be callous towards them? 'I'm back to living!', said a rescued boy after he had warmed up and been given a glass of tea to drink.[8] His words were remembered many years later. How could that not affect people permanently?

It was not only a matter of going round inspecting apartments. In the Time of Death, when nothing was as cheap as life, a firm determination arose never to be indifferent, whatever the circumstances, to the plight of dying children. The hygiene teams heard words of gratitude from bedridden mothers who hoped that their children at least would escape death. How could anyone write an impersonal report after that? They were saving children's lives, but they could see others doing the same, often sacrificing themselves in the process, and that common cause brought them close together. It was not enough just to find orphans. They had to be carefully brought to the hospital, washed, warmed, comforted, fed, rescued, while shells were exploding all around.[9] The systematic implementation of this mission contributed powerfully to consolidating siege ethics.

Great efforts were put into making life easier for orphans. There were collections of presents, linen and clothing, footwear and crockery. Children's homes were set up at factories. Hundreds of people became involved in helping, including some whose situation was much less dire and who had not suffered anything like their terrible misfortune. Appeals were made to people's better nature and to their compassion; they were reminded of the obligations of common humanity, and these appeals were answered. At the same time as the lives of children were saved, civilized values were being rehabilitated in an uncivilized environment. A whole torrent of emotions, sorrow, love for the children, pride, charity, a great willingness to help, burst forth to confront the heartlessness, the cruelty and cynicism.

The outrage people felt at the abuses which went on in children's homes was also a sign that they had not lost their humanity. Placing orphans and vulnerable children in homes was not easy. Decades later, people whose lives had been saved by their admission to these homes were inclined to idealize them, as is only to be expected. When you read their gratitude for how well, for the first time, they were fed in a home, you can well believe it, knowing what they had been through. Ye. G. Bronnikova remembered two children who were cared for:

> I remember a case. They brought in the two little Filippovs: a girl of ten and a boy, her little brother, who was seven. First we heard terrible crying, and then we saw these two children with swollen arms, their hair all matted, and very frail. I was particularly shocked by the girl, who was thin and whose face too was swollen. The children were so weak they could not climb the stairs. We began removing their felt boots and they cried terribly. Their feet were frostbitten and extremely painful. Their legs were terribly dirty, and quite blue with bruising.[10]

In documents relating to the siege we read a lot about the efforts made to rescue unfortunate children. There were, however, other aspects which should not be covered up. Until January 1942, the policy was to admit to children's homes only young people up to the age of 14. This regulation, introduced before the war, had some justification then, but during the siege it was absurd. The same regulations required that, for a child to be admitted to a home, it must be clean and its clothes must have been laundered. Under normal circumstances, one could hardly object to that, but, in the winter of 1941–2, when there was virtually no heating, many children were covered in soot because they had been trying to keep warm by staying as close as possible to the smoky *burzhuika* stoves. There was a shortage of firewood even for cooking, the temperature in apartments was just a few degrees above zero, the bathhouses were rarely functioning . . . was an enfeebled, emaciated child to be scrubbed in an icy room in a tub of freezing cold water?

This indifference to the fate of unfortunate children, this fear of showing initiative, the reluctance no matter what the circumstances to do anything that broke bureaucratic rules, the fear of losing a job which gave access to food (as many children's homes did) is only too evident in an episode described by Lazar Ratner, when the attempt was being made to have him admitted to a home. He was suffering from severe malnutrition, barely able to move, and seemed more likely than not to die within a few hours. The director of the home gave orders that he was not to be admitted because she did not want to see the commendable statistics of the survival rate of children at her home spoiled. They left him lying on a couch and waited for him to die. They waited one hour, then another, but he failed to do so. He was left there on the couch when the woman went home. In the absence of witnesses, she was untroubled about leaving a boy to die. A few hours later he was, nevertheless, fed and taken in to the other children. Evidently, fear of the responsibility for his death outweighed concern for their statistics. Having now admitted him, they continued to take care of their statistics. 'For the first few days I was seemingly the most emaciated inmate in the home, because once for dinner I was the only child brought a glass of sweet red wine', Ratner recalled.[11]

Such cases were rare, but they are symptomatic. Rigid state monitoring of the mortality statistics in children's homes could produce such unexpected and perverse results. Some of those working in the homes were not averse to making a profit out of other people's distress. There was scope for this: the children's homes and centres for reception and reallocation were over full and could not cope with all those in need of help. The 12-year-old Ira Sinelnikova was taken by her sister to a reception centre. She wrote later, 'The director of the centre told us to bring valuables from home, as they would need to be sold to buy food for us. Faina and I handed in silverware and an expensive Chinese tea set. Other children brought what they could.'[12]

There was always a plausible story, but we find no evidence in the siege documents that any of the hundreds of children maintained in the reallocation centres were paid for not by the state but by individuals using funds generated by selling silverware and tea sets. Those familiar with the dealings in the semi-legal markets of Leningrad are more likely to explain this as monstrously cynical exploitation. Plain-clothes police officers tended to overlook those trying to exchange 200–300 grams of bread, but arrested anyone trying to sell a whole loaf, having no doubt that they were apprehending a thief. Ira Sinelnikova also reports that, at first, they did not want to admit her to the reallocation centre (she was shortly to turn 14), but 'then they said they would, as I was dystrophic'.[13] Probably the expert determining who was or was not 'dystrophic' was the same director as was showing so much concern over how to fund feeding the children.

The dark side of life in the children's homes was no secret from Leningraders, and indeed it would have been impossible to hide it.[14] Maria Mashkova wrote bitterly in her diary that, in one family where everyone had died or was bedridden, 'we managed by a miracle to find a place in a boarding school for the daughter. She had been sitting, crawling with lice, on a bed under a blanket.'[15] There is little doubt how much venom she put into that word, 'miracle', when relating the sorry details of this episode. A. I. Vinokurov visited a children's home on 6 April 1942 and, without making any accusations, but with the same sense of outrage, describes what he saw: 'They feed the children very badly They get 300 grams of bread a day, and a meagre lunch consisting of watery soup and a very small serving of porridge. The children are completely emaciated.'

That many of them were wrapped in threadbare rags is clearly visible from surviving photographs. Reception documents of children evacuated across Lake Ladoga record how poorly clothed and emaciated they were.

There was more. The children's feelings were not always taken into account, and they could be treated in a very offhand manner. Perhaps because they were aware of this, some children hid, and a great deal of effort could be needed to get them to the reallocation centres: 'We ended up in a children's reception centre. They shaved our heads and forced us to carry buckets of sewage.'[16] Gone forever was a world in which their mother was alive, where there was comfort, care and affection. In a directive from the secretariat of the Leningrad Province and City Committees of the Komsomol on 16 March 1942 it was, entirely reasonably, decreed that children should be required 'to care for the weaker and younger children', but how far was this implemented in a manner which did not offend against the dignity and self-esteem of the children?

The sight of unfortunate, wronged children deprived of proper care provoked strong emotional responses. As would be expected, only the most appalling instances and the most terrible torments suffered by children are recorded. As N. G. Gorbunova noted in her diary, 'Children were brought in filthy, covered in lice, barely clothed, so emaciated that you were afraid to take them in your arms.' In the diary of Alexandra Mironova, the director of a children's home, we read, 'I admitted a girl, born 1931, father at the front, mother dead. The mother's body was lying in the kitchen. The girl was filthy. Scabies on her arms. Found her in a pile of dirty clothes under a mattress. Ration cards stolen.' An even more appalling picture emerges in the transcript of a communication by A. Ya. Trifonova:

In a building on Vatenina I found a mother lying on the bed and little children crawling around her. The filth was unbelievable! They were covered in soot. Unbearable stench in the room. Appalling scene. No electricity. A little girl grabs her dead mother's hand and whines weakly, 'Mummy, I'm hungry.' Another child is staring mindlessly, his swollen face that of an old man, and saying nothing.

A no less horrifying scene is described by A. D. Yakunina:

We found a second bed, where two toddlers (aged two years or less) were stirring about. In the same bed we found the gnawed corpse of a woman. Her face and breasts had been eaten. It was difficult to tell whether the children had done that or rats. The children, though, had not been touched but the dead body had been. One of the woman's feet was sticking out in a sock, the other without a sock. The children's hair was literally threaded, as if with beads, with lice and nits.[17]

It is no good those who were in the siege, and who saw the suffering of these children, saying everyone was starving, it was unavoidable, it was better to rescue those who were most likely to survive. To that there can be only one answer: it was unforgivable. That is a clear, unambigous answer, unencumbered with attempts to see the other person's point of view or listen to their ponderous explanations.

'How can you do that? It is unforgivable!' is what the officials from one executive committee said to the staff of a children's home when they saw how they were selecting children for evacuation.[18] Only the strongest would be evacuated. These children were orphans, and the very thought that some of them were worthy of being saved while others were not was so immoral that the explanations offered by those 'caring' for them became charged with emotion, with all the predictable interjections and false pathos: 'What was wrong about it! That is just the kind of time it was!' We are looking at a confession from the years after the siege was raised, when more sensitivity was called for towards the moral rules expected in peacetime, and that affects its style. It is probably due to an unresolved guilt about a quandary from long ago, and the conversation has been brought up reluctantly but deliberately. It would have been perfectly possible to hush it up, but the woman returns to it again and again, emphatically and heatedly. All her replies could provoke unflattering comments from anyone who knew the realities of life during the siege, exposing the nonsensicality of her excuses. Here is her argument in favour of leaving children behind in Leningrad: 'When we were brought to the Finland Station, just as we were getting to the carriage, the siren sounded! Bombing! And we had twenty children to deal with! We all ran to the bomb shelter with them. What would have happened if we had taken the weak ones with us? We would not have been able to save them, and others would have been lost too.'[19]

In her excuses, we repeatedly hear this appeal to others in the hope that they will not condemn but understand her. It seems she is well aware of the questionable nature of her assertions. She speaks as if conscious that she may be about to face awkward questions. Was life in a bombed city really safer than in evacuation where the children would be spared air raids and shelling? Were the very weak children who would be unable to reach the shelter in time really better left in Leningrad? Was that truly where they would be safer?

3

We should look more closely at how their carers selected the children to be evacuated:

We set them the best test we could under those conditions: we stood the child at one wall of the room and asked them to walk across to the other wall. If they walked over normally, we considered they had passed the test and kept them on the list for evacuation. If they fell down several times or could not reach the other wall at all, we left them behind in the home, to be patched up and got ready in time for the next departure.[20]

That expression 'patched up' tells us a lot. One could have said 'given plenty of nourishment', but they knew that would only be possible after evacuation. In Leningrad in the summer of 1942, everyone was terrified of what the coming winter might bring. The expression might have been 'for medical treatment', but that would have been laughed at, as everybody knew how little was to be found in the chemist's shops by that time in the siege. So the woman came up with her bizarre 'patched up', a catch-all which avoided having to give an answer about where, in besieged Leningrad, the food and medicine essential if the children were to be saved, could be found.

There were plenty of instances of severely weakened people being evacuated even if they were in need of care. Many Leningraders were probably not fit to be evacuated, but people still interceded for them, they were cared for, taken to the station, literally lifted into the carriages and spoon-fed. That was a lot more trouble than devising a test for selection, but a lot more honest than talking about the possibility of 'patching up' their health with siege rations and under artillery bombardment.

The women who chided the 'selectors' merely irritated them: 'Two old bats turned up from the executive committee and started kicking up a fuss.' They were put in their place by what seemed like irrefutable logic: 'Give us someone to accompany each child, then there won't be a problem.'[21] It might seem difficult to counter that, if you overlooked the fact that this arithmetic was dooming children to death. The 'old bats' from the executive committee, hamstrung in their actions by bureaucratic regulations, proved a good deal more humane than those entrusted with looking after the children. We recall the instance where, because her arms were frostbitten, a woman carried a child to be evacuated in her teeth. She seemed to get by without anyone to accompany her. The siege was a time when not every starving person had a loaf of bread, not everybody who was ill had a bed, not every dead person had a coffin, and not every child facing death had a mother to take care of them. No lives would have been saved if everyone had demanded ideal conditions, complained about difficulties, or found excuses for the inexcusable. You could find an excuse for just about anything: in the baby clinic, 'it was so cold the little ones froze to their nappies'.[22] The District Executive Committee gave permission for beer stalls and fences to be broken up for firewood only after an appeal from those working at the clinic, and who knows who had been finding excuses up till then for failing to notice the state the children were in.

But nothing went unnoticed. A special kind of cross-check appeared, which left an ineradicable moral legacy. This was a check, by idealists who had not lost their sense of compassion, on bureaucratic pragmatists; a check by people still shocked by the sight of abandoned children, on those supposed to be looking after them but who had become inured by seeing that sight every day; and finally, a check by the state, on all who tried to shirk their duty. It was a revival of self-respect, common decency and a sense of human dignity by those who were still anguished by the suffering of children, still horrified by the sight of the conditions they lived in, still outraged by the attitude of those who did not care what happened to them. These were people who grieved for their dying parents, and rejoiced when the lives of children were saved.

People collapsing in the streets

1

In the Time of Death, indifference to those who were worn out was evident not only in the streets. The failing of one moral principle did not necessarily undermine others, but it could facilitate that. What complaint could there be at failure to help strangers during the siege when people were not sharing food even within their own family, and that was regarded as nothing out of the ordinary? Nevertheless, the loss of the custom of lending a helping hand to someone who had fallen in the street was particularly significant. Meanness, unwillingness to share with others were not uncommon even in more normal times, but few in the past would have walked by someone weeping and begging for help to get back to their feet.

We read briefly, but tellingly, about such scenes in Maria Mashkova's diary:

> Early on, people were acutely aware of the need to help someone who slipped and fell. You would try to help them back up and support them, but as time went by you came to see that the most you could do was prop them up against a wall. With every passing day more people were falling, in the roadway, on the pavements, the boardwalk, in bakeries and shops. I no longer had the strength to help them up and lean them against a wall, and began to walk on by.[23]

That it was impossible to support everyone in need of help is pointed out in almost every tragic narrative about the siege. It is difficult, nonetheless, to imagine that even the most exhausted person would pass by their parents, their children or other members of their family without helping them back to their feet. It seems more a case of indifference towards strangers. Someone who was starving, barely able to stagger along semi-conscious, unaware of other people, was primarily focused on getting back home, making it to the shop, or to their workplace. All else was a distraction, and the first impulse was to wonder how to make it go away. Even the less exhausted began ignoring citizens who had fallen down. There were so many people suffering from exhaustion that anyone willing to help one would despair at the sight of a dozen others, also hoping to be helped.

There was no sense of shame about walking on: others nearby were doing the same.

'I walked through a city which appeared to have fallen sick. It had no time for passers-by', Yevgeny Shvarts recalls of the Time of Death.[24] This insensitivity was soon to be felt everywhere.[25] Neither the groans of the dying nor cries for help could make people stop. '4 January 1942. On my way home. Corner of Nekrasov Street. A 10- or 11-year-old girl lying on her back in the snow. Dying, groaning in her agony. By the Red Army Club a poorly dressed boy of eight is freezing to death. He is sobbing, crying out, "Mum, Mum!" Nobody pays any attention', Lev Khodorkov noted in his diary.[26]

Writing about scenes of tragedy, people usually try to present themselves in a good light, or at least to keep silent about facts that shame them. In stories about people who had fallen in the street, eyewitnesses, with rare exceptions, make no attempt to offer excuses. They have just been observers, usually impassive, of deplorable episodes, and write frankly in their diaries about scenes which do not show them in a good light.

Vladislav Glinka helped a fallen man to his feet, but after taking a few steps, turned round to see he had sunk back into the snow; Glinka could not bring himself to go back.[27] 'Opposite our house, in the middle of the road, a woman was on her knees, almost squatting, and crying out, "Help me, help me, citizens. Don't leave me to die." People walked silently past, and so did I. I had no strength, and still had to climb the stairs to the fourth floor', we read in the diary of another Leningrader.[28]

'We have become as hard as stone', T. Zhdanova-Stepunina noted in her diary on 2 January 1941.[29] Not only did they not help people to get up, they did not think twice about stepping over them, alive or dead.[30] Many things were looked at pragmatically, without feelings of shame or distress: 'A dying man crawled into our entrance. The gatekeeper pushed him back outside.' The explanation for this scene, described by Lev Khodorkov, is simply that the factory would have had to pay to have him buried, and nearby the bodies of workers were piled up in a stack. 'In the morning there will be one more corpse', the entry concludes.[31]

People felt that the dying could, in any case, not be saved, and helping them could undermine the already precarious health of others. 'So what if he has fallen down? In an hour's time it will probably be your own turn', is how Sofia Gotkhart recalls January–February 1942.[32]

It would not just be a matter of helping an enfeebled citizen to their feet. Sometimes the person who had fallen could not even give their name and address coherently. Where were you to take them, particularly at a time before warming-up stations had been set up in the streets? To one of the overcrowded hospitals, where few were being admitted?[33] Who was going to spend time and effort on this, when there was no certainty of success and you had to worry about your own survival? So people were left in the street. Someone might raise them, sit them on a snowdrift or some steps, and move on, without looking back.

A tale told by the writer Vsevolod Kochetov shows the details of this sorry state of affairs. Walking down the street, he and his wife found an old man lying on the pavement. They could not lift him: he fell back down again and again. An 'old woman with an empty basket warned as she walked by, "You can't pick them all up. Over in that entrance there's a woman has collapsed."' There was a chemist's shop nearby, and they went in to call an ambulance: 'The sales assistant came out from behind the counter, raised her skirt up to her knees, and showed us her horrifyingly swollen legs. "Do you think you can call an ambulance for all of us? Your old man collapsed from hunger, and here I am, swelling more and more every day, and maybe tomorrow or the day after it'll be me collapsing. What can we do about it?"'

He turned to a policeman on duty and said it would be quite wrong to leave someone in a helpless state like that. '"Quite wrong, quite wrong," the policeman agreed, and I could see from his eyes that he too was starving.'

When he got back, the old man was already dead. The people they had asked to help had a kind of lifeless tranquillity. Nobody was agitated or angry or resentful. They explained gently, agreed without arguing, and were sorry for the old man, as they tacitly condemned him to death. The old man himself understood everything. 'Barely opening his lips, he said, "Please do not trouble yourselves. There's no need."'[34] The end was inevitable, and everyone knew what it would be.

2

How many people, moved by compassion, at first went to the aid of exhausted siege victims, only to find that the person was already dead. Later, however, without looking too closely, they would tell themselves that the person who had just collapsed near them had also died or, if they had not, very shortly would. Even if they wanted to help, on their own they would hardly have the strength, and who else could they ask to help when the streets were so deserted? In any case, could you really feel you had done your duty if, next to the one you had saved, there were several more whom people were just walking past?

It is in the stories of people who came to Leningrad from afar, and not for long, that we read in great detail of these attempts to save citizens' lives. Those who encountered such scenes every day describe them in much less detail. Edit Postnikova arrived in Leningrad in early 1942 and this sort of sight was very new to her. Walking down Bolshoy Prospekt, she heard the groans of a man freezing to death. He was incredibly emaciated. She hurried over: 'On the steps of a front entrance I found a young man doubled up. I leaned over and asked him what was wrong. In a croaking voice he said very slowly, "My ration cards were stolen. I am dying."'

Her first, generous impulse was to help him. She may have thought this was where the boy lived and that she could find his apartment and call his family and neighbours to come. It was dark in the entrance hall. She got no answer from the first apartment where she knocked. Groping in the darkness, she knocked on a second and third door but nobody opened up: 'I went back out of the building. The boy was silent now and I went on my way.'[35] She tried to find excuses for herself. She had no strength to continue up the staircase, and other siege victims would hardly be able to save him. She probably found it easier to leave now that he was silent, not groaning, no longer asking for anything.

Go away, just walk away as quickly as you can, not looking back, comforting yourself with the thought that the boy would probably rest a little longer and then get up by himself. Go away before he could start crying again and your last vestige of humanity would force you to return. And if someone collapsed right in front of your eyes, you could raise them up again and again, if only to convince yourself you had done something at least to help.

V. Semenova and her sister helped a woman up three times: 'Then we sat her on the steps at the front of a building. When we came back some time later, we saw she was dead.'[36] Vladislav Glinka, going outside for the first time after a long illness, tried to help everyone he saw lying in the street. At first, he tried to help them up: 'Two I managed somehow to put on the steps of nearby entrances.' He moved on, but when he looked back he saw what had already become a familiar scene: 'One had fallen, slid down the doorpost and was lying on the pavement.'[37]

That was not uncommon, but claiming that someone had not fallen but had just sat down or fainted and, when he came to, would be able to continue on his way, was often merely an excuse. Such things did happen, however. The educationalist A. P. Serebryannikov fell nine times while bringing his archive on a sledge to the Public Library, but still made it.[38] Pyotr Kapitsa describes workers going into a factory walking round a fallen worker: 'He was lying there silently in the hope that, after a rest, he would be able to get to the gatehouse on his own.'[39]

In order to conserve their strength, some Leningraders would crawl part of the way, explaining that this was easier than picking themselves up each time after constantly falling. Perhaps, then, there is no need to get too upset at the sight of yet another person crawling, and no need to ask if they are all right. If they are trying to move, not asking for help, not crying out, presumably they are confident they can cope on their own. So why worry? Perhaps that mentality explains a scene painted by Boris Mikhailov, one of the siege's most emotional eyewitnesses: 'A man falls in the street. He is not going to be able to get back up. He tries to shout but cannot, and produces only a wretched silence. He claws with stiffening fingers at whatever is still alive in people as he tries to pull himself up. Nobody comes to help. They are all on their way to work.'[40]

No matter how unconvincing some of the excuses people found, they do at least suggest that moral principles have not been eroded completely, even in the Time of Death. They could, after all, have walked past those who fell without a qualm, but do try to do something to help, and feel guilty enough to need to look for excuses.

The mother of one young Leningrader did not react to a suggestion she should help to lift someone who had collapsed. She had seemingly irrefutable arguments in favour of not helping, but she returned again and again to the incident: 'When we got back home she was telling everybody about it and crying. "A sin? I expect it was. But there, what can you do?"'[41] In interviews, the stress when people are talking about times when they did not help shows very clearly, because what they are saying is unscripted and sometimes barely coherent. When they make excuses later, the endless repetitions which signal remorse and shame are particularly noticeable. They have said all they have to say, but need again and again to make their confession, even if merely by recycling the same words, because they are too agitated to stop:

> But then, apart from all the fear, the horrors and cruelty, there was also kindness; kindness and a human attitude towards each other. There was that too, and if anyone says there wasn't, they are lying, because there was. You see, there was, and there was kindness and a human attitiude towards each other, there was. It is . . . You know, it was good and it was, and the human relationship to each other before. There was all that, see? There was all that.[42]

3

People avoided looking too closely into the haggard faces of people who fell, avoided taking too much interest in their actions and gestures. There was shame at not being able to help meaningfully. They could not convince themselves, no matter how obvious and straightforward the logic was. Yes, everybody was exhausted; everybody had to remember their duty to children waiting for them at home; everybody wanted to survive; everybody was aware that a dystrophic did not have long to live; but also, as Lyudmila Eliasheva so precisely puts it, 'we knew we should not look'.[43] This was something many people knew, including some who had a duty to come to the rescue. 'We had to keep walking past neighbours who collapsed from hunger, to turn away from former colleagues for fear of hearing a cry for help', recalled the Party administrator from the Central Committee at the Elektrosila factory, V. E. Skorobogatenko.[44] It is a characteristic of many notes and diaries that, when exhausted people in the streets are being described, the narrative becomes less detailed. We rarely hear how they behaved or what they said. It is as if people were afraid to take a second look at them and tried to skirt round, afraid of hearing a plea for help.

V. G. Daev observed that, when a man in front of him in the queue began to sink to the floor, nobody tried to support him: 'It was odd, but they tried not to touch people who were falling, as if they were infectious.' Perhaps, as he suggests, this was because everybody was worn out and afraid that anyone coming to the rescue might overtax their strength and themselves end up collapsing. Recalling the incident later, however, he tries to find a different explanation: 'Most probably, in fact, people tried not to touch them because that first touch imposed a moral obligation to continue to provide assistance. Nobody could do so without prejudice to themselves: they might lose their place in the queue, or be late getting back home to their hungry children.'[45]

Some might object,[46] but these records carry weight. An eyewitness is better placed to evaluate gestures and glances than we are, and to compare them with his own. Seeing people who are suddenly, for some reason, inhibited, who are looking aside, unexpectedly struck dumb, he may ascribe to them the same motives he has himself. It quite often happened that siege victims, when they were helped back to their feet, would ask to be helped back home, or assisted in other ways. They might beg: they might even demand.[47] There was no point expecting tact and delicacy when it was a matter of life and death. There was no other way: few people were willing to help, so it was a rare stroke of luck to find someone who would. And who could tell when you might find another?

There was another reason for this reticence: 'Somebody taking care of a vulnerable person might be suspected of having an ulterior motive, more specifically, of planning to steal their food ration cards.'[48] Given that even Olga Berggolts mentioned such suspicions in a radio broadcast, they cannot have been uncommon.

4

Vladislav Daev's notes make one important observation relating to moral obligations. Nobody could be forced to fulfil them, but they existed. They influenced the behaviour of Leningraders, and explain where the fear came from of being mistaken for a marauder looking to rob frail citizens. None of these excuses would have been necessary if people did not have a sense of moral obligation, which they could not simply abandon. Even when they repudiated it, they felt the need to find excuses. Why? Even in the darkest days of the siege, the attempt was made to support the weak, to some extent at least.

When this topic is discussed, there is sometimes no distinction drawn between the actions of ordinary citizens and the actions of the various social services: the police, the ambulance teams, the Russian Red Cross, the hygiene teams and the warming-up stations. The distinction is, however, crucial. The latter had material resources allocated to them: rations, premises, sometimes transport. Much depended on them, and an exhausted policeman could also indifferently walk past someone who had fallen, or waste time wrangling with the staff of warming-up stations about whose job it was to pick them up.[49] It would be difficult to overstate the role of these stations, but they were set up absurdly late. Apart from drinks of hot water, the warming-up stations had nothing to offer, ambulances usually arrived very belatedly, and those who collapsed in the street had to be taken on a sledge, or more often on a stretcher, to hospitals which did not always agree to admit them.

Most of the Leningraders who helped the exhausted in the streets had neither assistants, extra rations, stoves, hot water nor sledges. People most often helped if they witnessed some dramatic episode, or saw citizens who were exceptionally frail and helpless. 'My mother was taken very ill on the bridge', Boris Mikhailov recalled. At that point, a young woman came up to her and gave her a piece of bread.[50] People warned others if they showed signs of developing frostbite, or pointed out the deadly danger of walking too slowly in the freezing cold.[51] They would help pregnant women back to their feet,[52] and in general tried to assist anybody in the street with children.[53]

Help was usually given to policemen who collapsed, and better care was taken of young people and well-dressed people, perhaps because they were thought more likely to get proper care afterwards and survive.

Among those who came to the rescue were disproportionate numbers of Red Army soldiers. Boris Mikhailov had the impression that the woman who shared her bread with his mother was a doctor.[54] The desire to live up to your reputation, as a member of the intelligentsia, an actor, doctor, teacher, scholar or communist, encouraged citizens to go to the assistance of those who collapsed. They not only gave help themselves, but called on others to behave charitably who had been hardened and grown accustomed to regarding the wretched symptoms of the siege as normal, even after the stupor of the Time of Death began to recede.

On 13 March 1942, Professor Lev Kogan of the Library Institute saw an old man who fell in the street and was unable to get to his feet again. 'All around people were walking past or standing and watching his efforts to get up and nobody made the slightest effort to help' as the familiar ritual of the siege in that first winter was played out. Kogan went over and, with considerable effort, managed to help him up. The person he had taken to be an old man proved to be just 40 years old. He was staggering about, unable at first to come to his senses. He had lost his hat and his mittens and seemed disorientated, unable quite to believe that one person at least had come to his aid. Then Kogan exploded.

'I yelled at the crowd.' The bystanders seemed suddenly to remember where they were. One women picked up the man's hat for him, and a man gave him his mittens. A policeman came to see what the shouting was about, promised to take the 'old man' home, and 'led him off attentively and courteously'.[55]

Of course, this was more likely to happen in the spring of 1942. During the Time of Death the story would have ended less happily. People took time to 'thaw out', and the increase in rations would hardly be sufficient on its own to break through the inertia and indifference. Yet this episode is remarkable. No matter how immersed the victims of the siege were in the struggle for survival, no matter how emaciated, no matter how inured they had become to the realities of life under the siege, it took just one slight gesture of charity for their humanity to re-emerge, which no spiritual crisis could wholly eclipse.

'Dystrophics'

1

The term 'dystrophic' was widely used in Leningrad in the winter of 1941–2.[56] Any citizen could be classified as dystrophic who did not have access to abundant food supplies provided through connections or by theft. Later, the word came to be applied to a particular category of people, emaciated in the extreme, on the verge of physical and spiritual disintegration, and ceasing to appear fully human. 'How greatly, in just six months, not only the intonation but the very meaning of the term "dystrophic" has changed', Vladimir Lyublinsky wrote to his wife in July 1942:

Initially (in January–February) it carried an overtone of acute pity and denoted a victim of hunger and called for help and compassion, or at least the granting of ration privileges of some sort; then it began to acquire an increasingly ironical tone, and one began to hear talk of 'moral' and 'moderate' dystrophics, not only referring to those who had degenerated or, on entirely genuine grounds of physical exhaustion, were neglecting their obligations (even to themselves). Finally, in recent months, when there are ever fewer bipedal dystrophics left, the word has begun to acquire purely pejorative connotations and sounds increasingly contemptuous.[57]

The same was noted by other Leningraders, sometimes more categorically but usually less extensively. Their notes are more impressions, jotted down with almost no attempt to explain the strange phenomenon. Boris Babochkin visited Leningrad and reported, 'They hate dystrophics, the starving. In the railway carriage you hear them swearing, "Oh, you pathetic dystrophic!"'[58]

Babochkin was in the city for only a few days and may have overgeneralized from a single incident, but the same is reported by survivors of the siege, and very emphatically. 'A few years ago, if you wanted to insult someone, you called them a collective farm worker, but now we have a new term of abuse, "dystrophic"', A. I. Vinokurov wrote in his diary.[59] The usage was taken over by children, with the same intonations and gestures as those of adults.[60]

'The first wounded soldier depletes our reserves of charity, and we treat all the others with indifference', as Pushkin once said. Lyublinsky's letter clearly charts the atrophy of humane feelings and the behaviour that accompanied it. The initial shock soon fades, and later, when people saw not just one dystrophic but hundreds, they wanted nothing to do with them. Everyone was just trying to survive themselves. They also had to do the work of the feeble dystrophics, which was an irritant, and compassion began to give way to disgust as symptoms of loss of human dignity became more extreme.

They looked repulsive, with 'flaking skin, a bluish complexion, and a very particular odour of decay which emanated from them even while they were still alive'.[61] Many tried to look the other way and get past them as quickly as possible. The dystrophics' emotional ties, even with their families, weakened.[62] They thought only about themselves and would not share with others. They usually talked about nothing but food, and would go to any lengths to get it. Nina Ivanova remembered one dystrophic who agreed to help her escape from the children's home in return for two sweets.[63]

M. P. Pelevin witnessed the following scene. In the hospital where he was being treated there was a dystrophic who never got off his bed. When a patient who had a habit of hiding bread in his clothes died, the dystrophic on 'almost buckled legs all but crawled over to the dead body. Slipping his hand under the blanket, he began fumbling about.'[64] What happened next is unprintable, but he did it in full view of everybody and without embarrassment. A lack of shame or feelings of disgust, and a reluctance to take care of themselves and observe the rules of hygiene, were 'characteristic of the way dystrophics lived their lives'. The doctors noted that other characteristics which made them unpleasant to deal with were such psychological peculiarities as 'lacrimosity, importunateness, permanent dissatisfaction with those around them, constant complaining and whining'.[65] They often talked incessantly: the 'awful, rushed prolixity of dystrophics' immediately struck Vitaliy Bianki when he visited the city for a few days.[66]

Not everybody was prepared to excuse, endure and forgive. Georgiy Kulagin noted that when he came into contact with the starving and the sick he found himself becoming impatient, irritable, almost hostile.'[67] He behaved quite differently with healthy people. Maria Mashkova wrote in her diary, 'I find the dystrophics at the Public Library, who are putting in their hours of conscript labour alongside me, even more nauseating.'[68] Why? She does not give a direct answer, but we can deduce her reasons for feeling hostile towards them: 'They potter about uselessly in the yard moaning about being hungry, dreaming about food, and greedily clinging to life.'[69]

It was the very feebleness of these people that caused irritation, and no one was interested in why they in particular should have become dystrophics. No excuses were acceptable. Everybody was starving, but some people stood up to it while others were broken. Why should anyone feel sorry for them? Some people helped, while some took care only of themselves; some silently endured hardship, while others never stopped talking, begging, complaining, crying, explaining and imploring. Why should people who were able just to grin and bear it, while suffering no less from hunger, be treated less considerately than the dystrophics? Was that fair? And were other people really supposed just not to notice their greed, their voraciousness, when they tried to push everyone else aside, the children, the elderly, demanding food for themselves, always only for themselves?

On 10 December 1941, Irina Zelenskaya came across a dystrophic in the dining room, with that same 'senseless fixed grin' Bianki had noticed. She could not hear what he was saying, but she noticed the 'odd way he seemed to pounce on the person he was talking to, as if trying to attach himself to him'. She felt no pity, not only because she had witnessed scenes of this kind before and was used to them. There was another feeling, which she was perhaps even rather ashamed of: revulsion. She could not help herself: 'I hold fast to all the good I feel towards people who show even a modicum of fortitude, in whom I sense that the human spirit is alive, but these walking corpses . . . they are just the shadow of a human being and his appetite. No, I cannot help it. They frighten and disgust me.'[70]

2

People were afraid of becoming dystrophics themselves, instinctively feeling that anybody who was starving might turn into one. They kept an exaggerated watch on themselves, fearful of detecting the first signs. The dystrophic was the living embodiment of a state of mind against which one had constantly to battle, to squeeze it out of yourself drop by drop. But how, then, were you supposed to retain your respect for the sick and weak? Georgiy Kholopov told the story of one woman, a farm manager, who used to laugh at 'those rickety types' and said that was one fate she would never suffer: her father had been able to shoulder a burden of up to 250 kilograms.[71] She was proud that she was not as one of these. How was she supposed to feel compassion for 'those rickety types'?

The appearance of the dystrophics and their psychology were equally repellent to all who met them, but what could they, the despised and persecuted, do about it? They too wanted to survive, but ran up against a wall of indifference and disgust. It was easy to bully them: what resistance could they offer?[72] Given their weakness, they could be robbed, cheated or elbowed aside. So many dishonest people tried to take advantage of them, the dystrophics needed some way of defending themselves. Their blood-curdling shrieks, their incessant gabbling, their whining all came in useful, and how were they to get what they were fully entitled to without fuss, moaning and hysterical outbursts? Certainly, they were presumptuous, but how else were they to get their bread when, exploiting their condition, people took their cards from them? How were they to get themselves treated fairly when they could barely stand, talk articulately, or concentrate?

At Pushkin House, Dmitry Likhachev remembers the manager helping himself to the cards of staff members confined to their beds, anticipating that they would soon die. One managed to find the strength to come to the institute: 'He looked horrifying, with spittle dribbling from his mouth, his eyes and teeth protruding. He appeared in the doorway like a ghost, like a half-decomposed corpse, and mumbled just one word: "Cards, cards."'

As soon as he heard that, the manager 'became furious, swearing at him and pushing him'.[73]

The temptation to push aside a powerless person, stealing their food and cards, was evident only too often during the siege, in different ways, but all of them equally disgusting, cruel and cynical. The weak could be bullied and even beaten up, and this sort of immoral behaviour was most common among teenagers.[74] It would be wrong to think that dystrophics were never given medical care, looked after or fed, or that efforts were not made to save them. All that was done, and not only because of the obligation to follow the regulations. It is sometimes impossible, though, to separate charitable behaviour from straightforward fulfilment of professional duties. Undeniably, however, the unprepossessing appearance and behaviour of the dystrophics did often override all other feelings. Not everyone remembered their obligation to treat the sick with gentleness and consideration. The prevailing morality was that everyone should look after themselves and not complain about their circumstances. Not everyone allowed for the difference the war made, and that could see aversion defeat compassion.

3

Attitudes towards the dystrophics reflected the attitude towards all isolated people in need of support during the siege. While every effort was made to ensure the survival of other family members, to do what you could for friends, and to give neighbours at least a modicum of help, isolated people were extremely vulnerable. This was universal. 'Everyone is focused on saving only their own lives and those of their immediate family, and pays no attention to what is going on around them', A. I. Vinokurov wrote in his diary on 28 February 1942.[75] People living alone often had only the hygiene teams to rely on, and their help was often limited and usually too late.

Factories did not give much thought to single people and rarely took any interest in the conditions in the hostels where they lived. 'The residents' rooms are dirty and louse-ridden. There has been no attempt to keep the stairs and courtyards clean', an inspection report on the district's hostels, compiled by the Primorsky District Committee of the Komsomol, complained.[76] Official reports were circumspect in their language, but in eyewitnesses' notes the reality of life in a hostel is more startling. 'I went into our wooden hostel today', Irina Zelenskaya noted on 4 January 1942:

> It was horrible there too. Many laid-off loaders had been left to fend for themselves. Sitting round a hot, coal-fired stove, the lucky ones were frying oilcake. One half-dead woman was lying in bed and crying lifeless tears. The last of her bread had been stolen from her. Another dying woman was sitting with her head on the table. It was a scene of terrible dejection. Sharandova's child was screaming continuously. She had exchanged her last possessions, like her coat,

blankets and so on, in exchange for a few handfuls of oat chaff from which it was impossible to squeeze anything edible. She was sifting the chaff and crying over it.

Zelenskaya's entry concludes: 'And nobody takes any interest in them. Monstrous cruelty and lack of fellow-feeling.'[77]

The obsequies for lone people were often a bitter reflection of their last days, with no respect for the body and no rites to acknowledge their human dignity.[78]

Refugees and boys attending vocational schools were another group of isolated people in whom few took any interest. 'The refugees were the first to begin dying', recalls K. Ya. Anisimova, the director of an evacuation centre located in a school.[79] In another evacuation centre, Boris Kapranov found sixteen people living in a 30 m² room: 'Everyone completely depressed. Irritable, hungry, barely able to move their legs.'[80] Another story is told in Maria Konoplyova's diary. A young woman who had been working on the city's defences was brought in to the clinic but soon died: 'She was just a gawky skeleton covered with greyish-yellow skin.'[81] Her 7-year-old daughter, now an orphan, said they had been trapped in the city in the winter and had no relatives in Leningrad.

The woman was later found to have 1,600 rubles hidden away, and those savings raised suspicions of hoarding, but there was nothing pathological about them. They merely testified to the horror they had endured in the siege and the total isolation in which they found themselves. Who was going to help them if they could not help themselves? Today they might have a crust of bread, but tomorrow there might be none. Who would help them then?

A vocational student who died of starvation was found to have left 1,500 rubles. Reporting this, G. M. Kok, an engineer, was puzzled. He supposed they were fed quite well, given a hot meal three times a day. Kok thought he must have been operating on the black market and, hearing they were going to be evacuated, had begun saving up his ill-gotten gains from selling bread at an exorbitant price.[82] That might be plausible, if we did not know the reality of how these students were really fed and the kind of care that was taken of them in other respects. There are documents which make this clear, each one more dire than the last.[83]

4

Hundreds of vocational schoolboys and apprentices trapped in Leningrad endured the full gamut of suffering. The report on an inspection of Vocational School No. 62, conducted in January 1942, says it all: 'Gross overcrowding. The two-tier bunks are placed adjacent to each other, the heating is in a poor condition, the students are in a filthy state, not having been to the bathhouse for over six weeks. They are all dirty and covered in lice.' In the school canteen, the students were being cheated out of bread and their food was being prepared from substandard grain.[84]

They were very poorly dressed. When Vladislav Grigoriev saw a boy 'wrapped in rags and very dirty' in a shop, he immediately assumed he was a vocational schoolboy.[85] Vladislav Daev saw a 'vocational' slip off the icy buffer of an overcrowded tram. There was no sign of underwear on his severed leg and 'his rough shoe had newspaper sticking out of it, which the boy had evidently wrapped round his feet for warmth'.[86]

These children did everything they could to survive. Wanting to live, they would snatch food in bakeries and shops.[87] They did not always operate on their own. 'Vocationals' mounted a raid on a bakery and made off with a whole cartload of bread.[88] Those who did not have the strength for that, or who could not beg for alms, fed on substitutes like cats and dogs, or rubbish from the tip. The tragedy which played out within the walls of the hostel of a vocational school on Mokhovaya Street in December 1941 is unlikely to have been an isolated incident. According to a secret report from the Leningrad Province NKVD, up to twenty-five boys were living in the hostel: 'They had all been expelled for indiscipline and fired from their jobs for various reasons. They were left to their own devices, and not supplied with food ration cards for December. During December, they ate the meat of cats and dogs. On 24 December schoolboy Kh. died of malnutrition and part of his body was used by the schoolboys as food. On 27 December, a second pupil, V., died and his body was also used as food.'[89]

'Of the population being evacuated from Leningrad, students from the vocational and railway schools are in a particularly weak condition', Alexey Kosygin, deputy chairman of the USSR Council of People's Commissars, wrote to Andrey Zhdanov on 10 February 1942.[90] One survivor of the siege recalled that, in the winter of 1941–2, vocational school students disappeared off somewhere. He believed they had put on their winter coats and ceased to stand out among other Leningraders in their 'uniform'.[91] There could have been other reasons.

A member of staff at the Borisova Griva evacuation point saw vocationals in December 1941, when attempts were being made to transport them out across Lake Ladoga. The attempt failed, and they were left there without any provision of food. There was no solution: 'It came to the point where they were going out on to the lake to pick bones from the remains of dead horses and other trash, bring it back, cook it and eat it.' When the vocationals were sent back to the city, Ivanov, who carried them in his arms (of 200 young people, only 60–70 could still walk), had to wear a raincape, 'so the parasites they were crawling with didn't guzzle me and all'.[92] Later, the vocationals were transferred to Kobona, where their condition horrified the staff who had seen plenty of horrors in the Time of Death: 'They were all so wraith-like and withered. The boys fell on food greedily, pulling it out of each other's hands. If they travelled on public transport, the situation was equally terrible. They stole food from women and children, and had to be separated from the general public because their thieving was out of control.'[93]

Izrail Nazimov wrote down what he was told by a chief fire prevention officer about the hostel of one of the vocational schools: 'He passed on nightmarish details to me. A mortuary had, of necessity, been set up in two of the hostel rooms. There was a large number of corpses of boys, who had died in the oddest postures. There were a lot of them, piled up any old how.' A telling detail: a toilet for the students had been set up in this makeshift charnel house.[94] In another school, the mortuary was in the basement. In the spring of 1942, 'a large truck drew up, on to which the students' bodies from the basement were loaded'. It was filled to the top.[95]

They were marked out for death: starved, alone, robbed by those whose duty it was to care for them. Several starving vocationals were taken to hospital for treatment. They were given a bath and died almost immediately. All of them. One after the other.[96]

A daunting picture of the casualty rate among vocationals is to be found in the notes of Atta Asknaziy, a nurse. The college where she worked had mostly adolescents from Smolensk region, who had neither friends nor family in Leningrad. 'Several of them died every day. At first, in early December, not all the beds in the sickbay (intended for six pupils) were occupied, but then the number of rooms in use increased. The entire first floor was turned into an infirmary and the large assembly hall filled up with beds.' The bodies of the dead were dragged to the mortuary on plywood boards by the boys themselves, in return for an extra meal. It was a long way and the bodies were often dumped somewhere along the route: 'We guessed what was happening but, of course, kept quiet.'[97]

5

When we try to understand why isolated people were so neglected in besieged Leningrad, we should note that this was not only caused by the indifference of the state authorities or as a result of the shortages of grain and fuel. Not every initiative would have required a huge effort on the part of those whose duty it was to save lives. There were occasions when they proved unwilling to fulfil even a small part of what might have been expected of them.

Not all citizens were moved to compassion by the sight of the starving, of dystrophics begging for alms, of refugees, vocational schoolboys, or even of children. Support was sometimes denied even by Leningraders we know to have been good, generous people in their dealings with their family and friends.

People are often reluctant to help strangers without knowing anything of the details of their lives, their ideas and intentions. One might have expected that during the siege this hesitancy would have been mitigated, because everyone understood hunger. But were people prepared to share their bread with those who remained in the city and were in need of care? No. Did they always help the sick to get admitted to hospital? No. Did they always help to their feet those who had fallen in the snow and accompany them to their homes? No. Did people really not know the conditions the vocationals were living in, as they boiled up a dead dog in a pot? They saw, they were startled, frightened by what they saw, and passed by on the other side.

The line separating 'them' and 'us' has always existed, but it became particularly marked during the war. Isolated people were less likely to survive. We cannot blame anyone, when almost all were on the brink. They had nothing to share. Many could not contain their disgust when they saw someone's personality disintegrating. In any case, some things would not have been tolerated by the authorities: groups of Leningraders daring to come together to render assistance on their own would inevitably have aroused suspicion. They consoled themselves with the thought that there were officials to take care of the dystrophics. There were hospitals, warming-up stations, Komsomol teams, Red Cross units: they would pick up those who collapsed, warm them and care for them. And then, people just got used to the spectacle of unending catastrophe, just as they had become inured to much else that in the past would have seemed unthinkable, only then to become part of life during the siege.

Leningraders in the queue

1

Queues were emblematic of wartime Leningrad. All those who witnessed the Time of Death talk about them. They became particularly marked in September 1941, when the size of rations was reduced. Fear, intensified by rumours about the fire at the Badaev warehouses and bombing, had residents rushing to buy up such foods as were still commercially available. The shelves emptied. Ration cards for meat, sugar and grains could not be redeemed, even if you went round several districts. As the cards were time-delimited, citizens were prepared to stand for hours, even at empty counters and outside closed doors, 'keeping their place' and not letting anyone else in.[98] Queues at bakeries were less common, and when Maria Mashkova saw one in March 1942, she assumed it was because 'people had been waiting for and dreaming of the increase in rations, and had not collected their bread the previous day, waiting for it to come into force'.[99] The queues were no less gigantic at the city's canteens where, as late as October 1941, you could still get coupon-free meals. Large crowds gathered at the 'enhanced diet' canteens, opened in 1942. An acute shortage of paraffin made itself felt in late October 1941, and caused citizens to gather in their hundreds for even a glass of hot tea or coffee at a patisserie.

Silent queues were virtually unknown. Optimistic reports circulated about the 'victories' of Marshal Kulik and General Fedyuninsky and of an imminent raising of the siege, but mostly people talked about the usual everyday problems. There were rumours of an impending increase in the size of rations. People taught each other how to cook food surrogates. A. I. Vinokurov saw a woman in a queue who 'was assuring her neighbours that you could make the most marvellous aspic from wood glue'.[100] Those in a queue were always interested to hear where you could redeem the 'non-bread' coupons.

Conversations in the queue had their particular hot topics in every period:

> If in September, for example, all the talk was about our rocket troops, in October it was about the land round the Badaev warehouses being saturated with sugar, and about the police having orders to summarily execute black marketeers. In November, the topic was racketeers who were forging bread ration cards, and the extortionate price of bread. Gradually people completely stopped talking about the Germans: they were regarded as a kind of natural disaster which had already peaked.[101]

What people talked about was determined not only by what was topical: they 'burned out' certain topics and wearied of talking all the time about the same thing.

2

'I came across a stranger on Lev Tolstoy Square who was walking along, laughing, crying and clutching his head', one Leningrader reports of 25 December 1941, the day rations were increased.[102] Queues could be boisterous or restrained, but when something happened which caused a surge of joy, people were not shy about showing their feelings. Their sullenness and irascibility vanished. That was evident on 9 December 1941, when they learned about the liberation of Tikhvin. There was no quarrelling in the queues, as everyone looked forward to an increase in rations: 'People shared the news. Loud voices, animation in the streets.'[103]

The outburst of jubilation on 25 December 1941 was unlike anything else in the history of besieged Leningrad. It was not exceeded even when the siege was finally raised. 'How wonderful, how absolutely wonderful! I want to shout as loudly as I can. My God, how wonderful! They've increased the bread ration! It means we're going to live, and in recent days we all got so weak we could barely move our legs. Hurray, hurray, and hurray again. Long live life!', Yelena Mukhina writes in her diary.[104] Zinaida Ostrovskaya remembered a 'girl-mother' who lived in a bomb shelter with her three children: 'Her hands were shaking. With tears of joy she showed everyone a piece of a heavy, sticky loaf and kept repeating, "They've increased it; see, they've increased it. Now there will be enough for the children!"'[105] The Leningraders in the queues promised that now they would really go to work, and talked to everyone they met on their way. Everything was loud and uncontrolled, everyone was shouting: 'People hugged and congratulated each other on this great occasion, and in several bakeries people cheered and tossed the manageress in the air.'[106]

It was not only a time of general rejoicing that could break down the usual barriers in a queue and bring a sense of solidarity. There were certain topics people loved to talk about, and about which everyone had something to say. Often, stories would be told of unfairness, of swindlers, black marketeers, thieves, robbers and chancers. Indignation united the citizenry, in the process consolidating their moral values, and doing so every day. When one little girl cheerfully said that now her mother had died she would have more to eat because of the ration cards she had left, she found herself under the stony gaze of 'the haggard faces of the entire queue'.[107] Here, under the eyes of strangers, in an assembly of the people, a citizen was still obliged to honour moral precepts. Anyone refusing to do so promptly came up against a harsh reaction. The queue could impose its discipline, sometimes brutally, even sending someone to their death. It maintained order in places where no policeman had been seen for a long time, with a consensus of people of different ages, characters and customs.

3

The psychology of a queue: they envy those in front and wish all manner of misfortune on them to get them out of the queue. They despise those behind them. Alliances and enmities form. Tricks are played in support of 'us', and people keep a close eye on others to ensure they cannot do the same. There are systems of numbers, there are checks and surveillance. The public are restrained. If one woman says her husband has died at home and her children are lying, swollen, in bed, another will reply that her husband died long ago, and that of her three children, two have already died.

It is amazing that this could have been published in Leningrad in 1947.[108] The author, Esfir Levina, cannot have known the innermost thoughts of those in a queue, who would hardly have publicly called down misfortune on those standing ahead of them. Nevertheless, from the gestures and glances, casual remarks, comments, exclamations and interjections which she shrewdly selects, we can at least partly picture the aspirations of hungry citizens who have been freezing for hours in the street. She has obviously not sampled every queue, and yet some of the mores she picks out are highly typical.

The people in queues always warily scrutinized outsiders, suspecting them of all manner of malevolence: trying to snatch bread, to steal ration cards, jump the queue or cheat in other ways.[109] Cursing, disputatiousness and irascibility were mandatory. Olga Berggolts has a poem about a queue placing in front of the sales assistant the dead body of a customer who had been crushed. People had to hold on tightly to each other as they got closer to the scales. 'I kept right in there, clinging with both hands to the coat of the woman standing in front of me. We were buffeted like waves from side to side', recalls Yekaterina Lentsman.[110]

Queues devised their own codes of conduct. Not everyone had the strength to stand in the freezing cold for many hours, but there was no alternative. Thus, in order to obtain bread, Maiya Bubnova was obliged to queue from 3.30 am until 12.40 pm.[111] At the end of January 1942, there was a delay in issuing the bread and N. I. Yerokhina arrived at the bread shop at 4.00 am to find she was thirty-third in line.[112] Anybody who came later would have had little prospect of success. 'Yesterday I stood in the icy cold for five hours, from 12.00 noon until 5.00 pm. I was No. 2,354 in the queue for tomato juice but, of course, it ran out', N. L. Mikhaleva wrote in her diary.[113] Those who made it to the front of the queue were often those who had someone to stand in for them, but the queue reacted with great hostility to any attempt to let someone in: 'No one tries to sneak forward to the counter. They know the queue will not allow them through. The queue permits no favours to friends or neighbours.'[114] This was not always enough to prevent quarrels and altercations. It was inevitable that 'numbers' for your place in the queue would appear. Self-appointed organizers tried to impose their arrangements, but not everyone would go along with them. Arbitrarily issued numbers were sometimes ignored.[115]

It was not always possible to restore the original order of a queue after a period of shelling, during which the shops closed. After the all-clear, queues would re-form in the original order,[116] but that did not always happen, particularly in the first weeks of the siege before everyone was accustomed to the rules. 'After the alarm was over, we all ran ran back to the bakery. Of course, the queue got all mixed up and was now in the order in which people had run back. I found myself not first at the cash register but twentieth', Maria Konoplyova noted in her diary on 14 September 1941.[117] The morality changed rapidly, and from her entry on 1 November 1941 we learn that the re-forming of new 'irregular' queues 'brought housewives to engaging in fist fights'.[118]

Usually, in kilometre-long queues, people were well behaved, but, at the doors of shops, the crowd would become increasingly nervous. People feared that at the last minute someone might push in and they would not obtain the products they had been queueing for, frozen and exhausted, for so many long hours. N. P. Gorshkov reports in his diary on 6 February 1942 that, in the grocery shop on the corner of Razyezzhaya Street and Marat Street, where butter was being sold, 'there was a stampede in which six people were crushed to death and six others severely injured'.[119] Irina Zelenskaya also witnessed a crowd 'yelling and literally forcing its way into the shop'.[120] Natalia Zavetnovskaya, trying to get her ration card redeemed, adds, 'If you fell you had not the strength to get back up and would be crushed.'[121] Sofia Meyerson describes a similar scene: 'Only a few people could get through into the shop. There was turmoil at the door, a crush.'[122]

No numbers, no cries, no pleading helped. People wanted to live, and not a few, at the moment a shop opened, were tempted to push their way in, taking advantage of a gap in the crowd which appeared in the confusion at the entrance. Someone had only to stop for a moment, trying to decide which counter to go to, for someone else to push past and others, jostling, to follow. They drew in their wake other people who had been trying to stay in the queue, but were afraid of losing their place, and everyone got mixed up together. People fell on top of each other at the counters:

> The door opened and this whole avalanche of people, pushing and shoving each other, burst into the shop. I was clinging to the coat of the woman standing in front of me. The crowd, shoving from behind, squeezed me into the shop and separated me from her. The queue inside the shop bent under the pressure of the crowd, broke and there was pandemonium. Somewhere a child began to cry. I heard a frantic scream. 'Calm down! You'll crush the child!' Nobody paid any attention. From being at the front I found myself at the back. It was completely impossible to get to the cash desk. Everybody was trying to regain the place in the queue they had lost in the pile-up and get as close to the cash desk as they could. That caused chaos and brawling.[123]

4

Was this typical? It may be objected that the Leningraders tended to note down the most dramatic rather than commonplace episodes, and that queues where there was no crush and no fighting attracted no attention. There is some truth in this. We should compare the stories above with the testimony of Vera Lisovskaya: 'I can confirm that people never pushed to the front of the queue. Everybody stood there calmly, no one called anyone names. People just behaved normally. People are not the same in Leningrad nowadays. I was back there recently.'[124] When someone tries to compare the past with the present, they usually end up idealizing the old days: they seek and find more generosity in the way people behaved towards each other. It would be wrong to describe every queue as a place where people were constantly squabbling. We find hardly any citizens in the grip of animal passions, pushing others aside just because they are hungry and more nimble than the vulnerable. No matter how ugly the quarrels, they were caused mainly by unfair behaviour. It was not only a matter of morality. The insistence on fairness enabled the weak to survive in the struggle with the strong and to defend their right to life. This was the source of the wariness, the nervousness, the fear with which people reacted to any action by people suspected of trying to jump the queue. The fighting and the crushes occurred at the door of the shops. Overhastiness, ill-considered behaviour arising from anxiety not to lose your place but perceived as offensive, would lead to a barrage of accusations.

Georgiy Knyazev's wife was queueing at a shop and noticed that, 'at the slightest provocation, there was shouting, yelling and swearing'.[125] One young woman was shrieking more hysterically than anyone else. She spoke to her and discovered she had four children aged from 6 weeks to 4 years. Four children in a family during the siege meant death was only a matter of time. What had their mother to look forward to? The horror of knowing that outcome was approaching, a wailing baby failing before her eyes, which she could neither feed nor comfort. Herself hungry, it was no wonder she was going to scream at anyone trying to push in front of her. There were no goods in the shop, nobody was trying to move ahead of her, but she was ready instantly to sound off at anyone she believed might be thinking of trying to.

Everybody wanted fairness, and to ensure it, nobody could live by the law of the jungle. The moral law was being upheld in all these dismal episodes, when even a dystrophic would assert their right to avoid being trampled underfoot. We find other, more positive incidents in the bakeries and shops. Zinaida Ignatovich describes a woman in a queue solicitously questioning a boy who had no one to stand in for him.[126] The queue might be unmoved by the death of people in it,[127] but still showed compassion for the living. 'I saw an old lady with hideous purply-red, fingers clutching her string bag and sitting helplessly in the snow', N. L. Mikhaleva noted in her diary on 31 January 1942. Some compassionate person took her ration card to fetch the bread for her, saying, 'There, when she eats that she'll be able to get up again.'[128]

A. Tomashevskaya tells the tale of a woman she met in a queue. There was a rumour that there had been a delivery of round loaves at the Filippov bakery on Vvedenskaya Street. They agreed the woman would go there and try to buy bread on the girl's ration card. When other people in the queue heard this, they advised her to run after the would-be benefactor and get her coupons back. In great confusion, Tomashevskaya ran to the bakery but the woman was nowhere to be seen. She tried to go inside and encountered the usual reaction: the crowd were not going to let anybody go in front of them. She burst into tears and explained what had happened. There was no question of her trying to get ahead of other people to the counter because she did not even have a ration card. Everybody hated swindlers and thieves, and would go out of their way to help anyone who had fallen victim to them. People moved aside, and 'those at the back shouted to those at the front, "Let the girl through to find who she is looking for." "Go ahead, dear, look for her," people said, moving me forward.'

She did not find the woman and went back. When it was her turn to go to the scales, she had no ration card. She went outside and stopped by the door. She could not cry, she was just indifferent to everything: 'Women coming out of the bakery shook their heads and tut-tutted sympathetically. Some went off, but others stayed, sympathizing, feeling sorry for me, asking me questions.' All of them, no doubt, had concerns of their own, but how memorable that first impulse is: to comfort her, to feel indignant at what had been done. There is much that can be said about the harshness and intransigence of the crowds outside shops, the sullen, stony faces of people who are ready to throw a punch at anyone who tries to violate the discipline of the queue, but there is an epilogue to this story. The girl did get her bread restored to her and there was an immediate response from

people who might have seemed little concerned about her misfortune:
'They crowded round me, and I distinctly heard a general sigh of relief run
through the crowd.'[129]

Part III

Means of Reinforcing Morality

9

Concepts of civilization

Art, creativity, reading

1

Art, reading and creativity inhibit a descent into a barbarity which would exclude even the most basic morality. The impact of elevated human emotions, the sense of fairness, aversion to violence, humane impulses, appeals for compassion and concern, the preaching of goodness were almost certain to be assimilated, even by people who came to the theatre, cinema or concerts at the Leningrad Philharmonia for the most prosaic reasons.

The appeal of art was both diminished and enhanced during the siege. The struggle to survive, the overriding focus on finding bread, rarely left time for other interests,[1] but the habits of a lifetime and cultural needs could not be displaced instantly. That took time. Talking about bread, important as it was for Leningraders, as it went on endlessly, became unbearable. There would be impassioned outbursts, inveighing against a 'spiritual vacuum'.[2]

The diary of B. Zlotnikova chronicles the life and times of a person who battled, often unsuccessfully, against the destructive power of the siege, but who was drawn irresistibly to art, music and the theatre. 'No amount of toil and no person can extinguish that spark of nature in me which is the urge to create. How I long to listen to music: it would so restore my strength', she writes in her diary on 1 October 1941.[3] She finds her factory job 'barren and trivial'. She finds only one of her fellow workers intriguing, but is too shy to talk to him. For her, art is everything. She repeats that in almost every entry in her diary. Only a month later, however, the tone changes radically.

'I am hungry', she notes on 5 November 1941. She is ashamed of the feeling and reproaches herself: 'There is nothing worse than being able to think about nothing but food. It is the point at which you cease to resemble a human being.' She is not yet on that level, is still susceptible to beauty and capable of creating. In the entry for 7 November we find, besides self-recrimination, a poem on the siege of Leningrad (using standard poetic diction) and a well-known quotation from Nikolai Ostrovsky's novel *How the Steel Was Tempered*, to the effect that we are given only one life and must live it with dignity. The profundity and originality of the literary sources included in the entry may not be great, but they are undoubtedly edifying. She creatively misquotes Lermontov: 'Empty is the man who would fill the world with himself.'[4]

On 16 November, she notes that she is focusing on her own concerns, which is not good. 'After all, you should live for other people.'[5] Her entries become more edgy, and tend towards grandiloquence. 'After living five months without theatre, I can understand why the people at the factory are so dull and coarse. I can't live without it', she writes on 9 December.[6] What is going to prevail, the spirit or the flesh? She fights off all that is base and worldly, but prays for bread. It is like a pendulum: no sooner is she willing to give in, to repudiate the sublime, to acknowledge there is nothing more incontrovertibly precious than bread, than she thinks again about the theatre in a way that is so mechanical as to seem unnatural. Which will prevail?

I have this constant gnawing in the pit of my stomach. I thought this morning I might even eat the sheet. God, let me survive. I want to live and create, to create without end. The main thing in a person's life is food. God, let me survive! I want to eat and eat: bread, porridge, potatoes, on and on! I just want to survive. God, let there be an end to this! I so want to go to the theatre. I cannot believe I will ever get to see opera again.[7]

Later, something broke in her. The weariness and apathy increased as life became monotonous in the extreme: 'In the morning you get up with the aim of drinking soup with bread, after which you blunder about for the rest of the day before eating in the evening and going to bed as soon as you can. That's it, every day. You don't feel like doing anything or going anywhere.'[8] She was planning to go to the theatre but arrived too late, after meeting a friend and getting engrossed in conversation. How unlike her previous fanatical enthusiasm that was.

There is another change. After 25 July 1942, some of her entries take the form of homilies. At first these alternate with sketches of the life around her, but then begin to dominate. It would be straining a point to call them aphorisms, because their heavy-handed moralizing makes her attempts at word play and paradox seem merely out of place. Her fixation on the theatre is replaced by moralizing, although her cultural preoccupations do not fade, but morph. Possibly one of her sources is Tolstoy's *Calendar of Wisdom*, or something similar, with its moralistic language and preachiness. There is a logic to the monotonously repetitive didacticism. 'To love is to live the life of the one you love'; 'Without love, no project will prove beneficial, while any project undertaken with love, however seemingly small and insignificant, will yield abundant fruit'; 'You ask how

freedom is to be achieved? You must first learn to distinguish good from
evil for yourself, and not follow the crowd'; 'Doing good is perhaps the
only action that makes us blessed.'[9] In all these aphorisms, the underlying
theme is the need to rise above the primitive morality of vegetative existence and oppose it.

2

'Theatre attendance is naturally insignificant as the attention of the
Leningrad populace is mainly restricted to finding ways of obtaining essential nutrition', notes an intelligence report of the Nazi *Sicherheitsdienst*,
compiled in spring 1942.[10] The document is long on prejudice and ideology,
and reads like propaganda. It is hardly a source for any genuine insight into
the attitude of Leningraders to the theatre. Only the Theatre of Musical
Comedy was functioning, and it plainly could not cope with demand, even
if that genuinely had been 'insignificant'. The *Sicherheitsdienst*'s inform-
ant had obviously failed to spy the crush readily observable at the theatre
entrance.[11] Concerts at the Philharmonia were also sometimes sold out. It
continued to attract audiences even after starvation set in. In circles consisting mainly of members of the intelligentsia, new poems were read and
the works of painters discussed. It can be difficult to decide whether this
was due to habit, concerns about personal status, fear of deteriorating, or
a desire to show oneself still to be a cultivated individual. There may have
been more prosaic motivations: wanting to stay warm, to escape the loneliness of apartments lacking light and heating, to alleviate depression and
the sense of hopelessness. 'The people in the theatre were just like me, emaciated, wrapped in layers of clothing, awful', I. Z. Drozhzhina recalled,[12]
although, for the sake of accuracy, we should note that not all theatre-
goers were starving. In the hungry, deadening reality of the siege, having
access to culture was one way for people who were feeling humiliated and
depressed to reaffirm their distinctiveness from everybody else. Nobody
wanted to feel they were at the bottom of the heap, contemptible and
rejected. Yevgeny Shvarts describes how, in a train evacuating artists from
Leningrad, each was pulling documentary evidence out of their luggage
to show to the others and certify their cultural status: 'Avilov showed a
newspaper reprinting the order for his state award and a letter of praise
from Repin, written with great verve. I pulled out my play, *The Shadow*,
published by the Theatre of Comedy. Shervud stirred himself and showed
us a monograph written about him. We were showing these to each other
as if they were identification documents.'[13]

   If you have nothing to put on to conceal your rags, if you are desperately short of bread which might help to smooth your bony, withered,
dystrophic features, then at least cling on to the feeling that you are a
cultured human being, and make sure others see you in the same light.
The enthusiasm for music and the theatre during the siege has generally
been described in a one-sided, emotional and heroic key, but the reasons
for it are not always clear. Writing poetry was an affirmation not only of

poetic, but also ethical, norms. This can be seen from the choice of subjects (charity, optimism, mutual support) and in the poetic vocabulary, which recalls older moral values, and affirms them by bringing together the reader and a receptive audience. This act in itself is a symbolic release from the routine of vegetative existence. 'She sits in the dark every night, writing poetry', Georgiy Knyazev notes of one Leningrader, who evidently had found this an escape from self-centredness, greed and apathy.[14]

Reciting poetry was not only a means of manifesting your cultural level, and did not always guarantee exemplary personal behaviour. It was, however, seen as an affirmation of the uniqueness of the individual. That was proclaimed, it was appreciated, and talked about with other people. Reading the Russian classics and Soviet literature in the Time of Death strengthened morality. In it, vice was invariably put to shame, or at least condemned; its readers followed and empathized with the noble deeds of likable characters. As they tried to assess books critically, readers again exercised their ability to distinguish good from bad, virtue from vice. G. M. Kok, the foreman of a factory workshop, commented on a Soviet novel he read in December 1941 that its main strength was the 'psychological growth' of the hero: 'All the rest is just ballast.' He excoriates the author for including in the plot 'the whole paraphernalia of the period, Lomonosov, the year of war, all the court favourites, Bazhenov, without thinking about the structure of the novel'.[15] It would be an exaggeration to say that the practice of reading was a guarantee that moral rules would be respected, but there is no doubt that it could prevent complete disintegration of personality, at a time when there was not always observance of even the most basic morality.

3

During the siege, every instance of an interest in art and creativity contains at least a trace of a recognizable moral standard. We find that also in the expressing of thanks to artists and musicians. The burst of applause at the end of a performance brought people together, if only for a moment, in a single emotional impulse, and in a special way 'cleansed' them of the everyday realities of the siege. Olga Iordan recalled sharing a cigarette with the pianist V. V. Sofronitsky, who was a patient in the sickbay at the Astoria Hotel. He decided to express his gratitude, and her delight in that moment had not been dissipated many years later.: 'He played quietly and slowly, but with great skill and feeling. It is difficult to describe how moved I was. I almost burst into tears.'[16]

Some may find this exaggerated and its language too theatrical, but there are other examples. 'The lyrical, and especially the sentimental, moments in the play were particularly moving', wrote Esfir Levina, amazed that such a thing should still be possible after all the horrors of the siege.[17] The language of responses to concerts and performances is sometimes deliberately florid, reflecting the heightened emotions of the theatre. 'I want to experience everything, in the name of the wonderful future I believe in!'[18] It comes as no surprise that we find these lines in the diary of B. Zlotnikova, a token of her extravagant cult of the theatre. In the letters of M. D. Tushinsky to T. M. Vecheslova, we detect even a deliberate condensation of the emotional outpourings, expunging from them anything routine and earth-bound, although that did not help to make his writing any more original: 'At yesterday's concert we had ballet music without the ballet, and yet how wonderful it was. Life goes on. The orchestra plays, the stirring music of Serov rings out, and I so want to send to my favourite actress and honoured citizen, greetings from your own beloved city.'[19]

In this unique set of examples of high-register speech, a consolidation of ethical norms is taking place. The language, heavy with emotive formulations, is far from natural. It would be inappropriate in ordinary conversation. Elevated language is associated with elevated moral precepts. Using it, a person was simultaneously being given a moral lesson, although there is no telling the extent to which this would keep them from backsliding.

Browsing through postcards in late November 1941, Yelena Mukhina bemoaned the fact that 'nowadays they make them so badly, without any real effort, without taking proper care'.[20] One would have assumed that the trials she was to go through in the months that followed would cause her to lose all interest in them, but no. In March 1942, we find the interest rekindled, despite her hunger. On 18 March, she went to the market to sell a copper kettle. She was unsuccessful but saw some postcards: 'I couldn't resist, and bought them.' Hunger again drove her to the market: 'I collected up all my things. I was so hungry I decided to swap my aluminium canister for bread.'

This down-to-earth little story reveals the battle between the spirit and the flesh much more clearly and vividly than any amount of hair-splitting introspection larded with philosophical reflections. She again saw postcards, and again could not resist them: 'I could not stop myself. I started going through and choosing postcards nobody could have resisted. Coloured, with all different views and most of them foreign, so pretty, I couldn't tear myself away, and bought fifteen at a ruble each.' Was that any way for her to struggle to survive? 'If I were to tell anybody about my acquisition they would scold me for all they were worth, and with good cause.'[21] She has no defence to offer, but just could not pass up on these cards – the beauty, the views so unlike the streets of besieged Leningrad: the unconquerable sense of beauty cannot be suppressed by the unconquerable pangs of hunger. Her need for beautiful postcards proved just as compelling as her need for bread.

4

Operettas, foreign melodramas, Soviet comedy films needed to be entertaining and jolly, sentimental and funny. We find no trace of the horrors of the siege in them. That is what people liked. Watching the ups and downs of somebody else's life, where everyone always has plenty to eat, where life is carefree or chock full of intriguing adventures, people could live vicariously, in just the same way that they tried to drown out the nightmare of the present months of starvation with tales of how they had lived in peacetime. It was as if they were trying to relearn how to live with dignity, to remember how courteous and beautiful language should be, what comfort and tranquillity felt like, how vividly and artistically they could express their feelings.

'There is a lot of life, beauty and music in this film', Nikolai Ribkovsky noted in his diary on 23 February 1942. 'I found the music a delight, while admiring beautiful shots of the countryside of the leafy North and the high mountains of the Caucasus, with the streams of burgeoning springtime and the wild torrents of cascading waterfalls. I was carried away by the splendid acting.'[22] The language and the emotion here have been purified, as if we are reading a 'very good' essay by a schoolchild. The description seems to be keeping to the traditions of theatre criticism and travel writing customary in Soviet journalism. It is moderately emotional, limpid and devoid of challenging or provocative metaphors. What is of significance, though, is not the stereotypical language but a kind of symphony of the hallmarks of civilization, with its orderliness and serenity. The impressions are conveyed in emotive words, with never a hint that anyone could lose the will to live or find their personality disintegrating.

Yelena Mukhina watches an American film and cannot conceal her admiration: 'A wonderful picture. You suddenly so want to surround yourself, just like the characters in the movie, with the same brilliance and comfort. Just like them, to enjoy music, and dancing, parties and entertainment.'

Her description begins to speed up, and soon there is no stopping her. She seems to be in the grip of a fever. This is the life you need, free from hunger and cold, without hatred, without darkness, without hand-me-down clothes. She misses nothing, not even the most minor glossy detail in the film, and every detail is seen through the eyes of somebody who is very hungry:

> This is how life should be, with luxury, beautiful women dressed in accordance with the latest dictate of fashion, women in clinging dresses, sleek gentlemen, restaurants, entertainment, jazz, dancing, glitz, wine, wine and love, love, endless kisses and wine, loud, shriek-ing streets, dazzling, luxurious shops, dazzling automobiles every-where, endless advertising, advertisements everywhere, thunderous advertising, squeals, everything just such a whirlwind![23]

5

None of this has been hers in her life under siege. The past was her mother's agonizing death from starvation, inconsolable misery and tears. The present is immense suffering from that 'perpetual gnawing in the pit of my stomach'. She has no joy, no light, no bright advertisements, so let her, if only for a moment, exist in this fantasy world of comfort and affluence

– live anywhere, just as long as it is not in the daily nightmare of her real life. On one occasion, she made a list of all the dishes she would have on her table after the war. Its excess was spectacular. Here too, the scrupulous listing of all the most alluring features of life overseas, the very epitome of how life ought to be lived, helps to drive out the sense of despair.

Concerts served exactly the same purpose. Everything was appreciated: not only the content but also the actors' costumes, their outward appearance, their gestures full of dignity, their flowing speech. The 'concert entertainers' played in factory workshops, in schools, even (usually on the front line) in bathhouses. One could spend a lot of time questioning how appropriate it was to put on concerts in bomb shelters, in the dirt, in the midst of crying, frightened children and the noise of exploding bombs, but that would hardly deter the officials who had decided that this was the way to prevent panic, to cheer and reassure the citizenry.

In order to understand how Leningraders thawed out, how mistrust and hostility gave way, if not immediately, to other emotions, let us look at a few descriptions of concerts in which the actress Alexandra Smirnova (Iskander) took part. One of them started very unpromisingly. People crowding near the bomb shelter were being issued firewood, probably not without disputes: 'There were not many of them. Their faces were weary, and some were scowling in our direction. It was damp and chilly.'[24] Everybody was in a hurry to get their firewood before the next alarm, and may have been anxious that, before that had been completed, they might be herded in to watch a concert.

The concert programme was fairly standard. An actress began reading newspaper reports about 'how the husbands and sons of these women were fighting in order not to let the enemy get into Leningrad'. Putting it that way was appreciated. Everybody quietened down and, perhaps in response to a change in the mood, another actress began reading passages from the diary of the aviator, Marina Raskova. The reading was no doubt emotional, people began listening more carefully, and then asked them to 'read us something else'.

Their public moved closer. It was a moment when they felt something more emotional was needed to retain the audience's attention. They began reciting poetry by Pushkin: 'Women threw back their headscarves, smoothed their hair, and once again asked us to read. When it was time to say goodbye, warmer, friendly voices invited us to come again.'[25]

In another bomb shelter, the concert started no less dramatically. As usual, the surroundings were squalid. Officialdom's indifference to the fate of the besieged Leningraders was particularly obvious in the crypt-like bomb shelters: 'The place was full of rubbish. There was water on the floor. All around were dilapidated iron beds, benches and mangled chairs.' It was into this chaos that the actresses stepped. They were not expected and nobody could be bothered with them. One woman shouted in exasperation, 'What do we need a concert for? They'd do better to bring us some food.' Others were silent. The actresses began reading, as usual, reports on the situation at the front, but something else was needed to get the audience on their side. The reports were bleak and evasive. Some theatrical gesture was needed. The actress Valentina Borovik had also come with Alexandra Smirnova. She took off her fur coat and stepped out 'in an evening dress and patent leather shoes'.

'That made an impression.' Smirnova noted an instant change of mood among these people dressed in rags. They began to listen: 'At first the women were sitting away in the corners and the front bench was occupied by some boys. Then the grown-ups moved the boys aside and shifted their chairs and beds closer.' Not everybody when they left the concert had been enlightened: the reality of the siege was just too dismal and people could see too much misery around them. The idyll of the reading was disrupted when the manager arrived: 'The women looked askance at him but said nothing. When the recital was over, however, they cursed him for all the dirt in the shelter, for not having prepared properly for the winter, and the manager blamed them and asked them to help.'[26] This 'heated exchange' would probably have occurred anyway, even without the poetry reading, but perhaps the gulf between beauty and squalor, which it was impossible not to feel in a shelter which was more like a cowshed, reinforced the women's longing for a bit more 'civilization'.

6

Accounts of how creativity saved Leningraders are often neither detailed nor deeply insightful. Probing the darker corners of consciousness, doubts and musings, was perhaps thought too 'Hamlet-like', when a vivid portrayal of stoicism, without a lot of complicated baggage, should have a much higher priority. A typical example is the film footage depicting the work in Leningrad of the composers Dmitry Shostakovich and Boris Asafiev. The fact that this was for public consumption dictated a brisk depiction of their extraordinary achievements, without psychological subtlety, a purely superficial image of their heroism. The purpose of the film was not to delve into the composers' inner doubts and travails, but to display their endurance and integrity.

Asafiev's article, 'My creative work in Leningrad in the early years of the Great Patriotic War', is a rare exception to this rule. It is full of quick and poignant sketches of his life and work in the besieged city. The pace of the narrative slows when he is describing the Time of Death. There is no fuss or haste, but a prolonged, often agonizing self-scrutiny. There is also a clear understanding of the causes of disintegration of the personality and of how to oppose it with creativity.

The main cause of degeneration was hunger. It became unendurable. Eventually, Asafiev and his family had to exist on oilcakes: 'These proved to be our worst enemies.' The only solution was to go to bed and try to 'retain the warmth in yourself'. There was no electricity and his weakness was increasing. His thoughts about music occurred suddenly and naturally, themes and subject matter intermingling. There is no rhetorical dwelling on the greatness of his heroic creativity. He was trying to write songs which 'distracted me from disagreeable feelings', and thinking through a book on musical intonation: 'Whenever the electric light came on again, I immediately began writing down my thoughts on intonation, almost as aphorisms, rushing to catch them, like glowing specks in my brain.'[27]

There is here a chaotic collection of impressions, and there are disconnects. There is, no doubt, also an attempt to force his own text into the canonical pattern for tales of heroism, although that does not work. The complex, volatile, paradoxical thinking of Asafiev cannot be fitted into the Procrustean bed of moral didacticism, and instead illuminates the true story of his spiritual resistance. He wants to 'preserve the will', an odd collocation, but evidently one which expresses what he means. He has to beware of anything which might deprive him of stability and destroy the fragile inner world of a musician. Asafiev found slights and injustices hard to bear, and this fragility, his 'mimosa-like' hypersensitivity, came to dominate his personality. He could feel the silence in Leningrad, he saw the people dragging corpses on sledges through the streets. He needed to 'protect the will, only the will'.

He wants to sleep. In a state of semi-consciousness, he again focuses his thoughts on intonation: 'I had to recreate a lot of music in my memory.' He felt there was something ominous in the 'tide of sleep' which was beginning to engulf him. It was essential to find a way of halting it: 'I started to compose my music, at one time giving form in brief aphorisms and little pieces to impressions from radio reports from the front; at another, listening intently to the direction of choral voicing and revelling in the beauty of the imagined harmonic progression of the scores.'

Work on melody would be abruptly terminated by restoration of the electricity supply, when he would return feverishly to writing up his thoughts on musical intonation, trying to complete that before again being plunged into darkness. The conclusion of his book suddenly became clear to him: 'After writing it out, for a long time I could not recover my senses because of my weakness.' He was aware of cold and darkness and did not know how long that lasted. He thought he was dying: 'My heart began to fail.' It seemed like the end, and he had to make an incredible effort to break out of the stupor: 'Suddenly music arose in my brain and, completely unaware of whether we were living in daytime or night-time, I remember I began composing my symphony, *The Changing Seasons*, around the life of the Russian peasantry.'

How could he halt the unchecked flood of impressions, sounds and sensations which was obsessing him and threatening to destroy him? How could he bring under control the chaos of heterogeneous thoughts which suddenly came to mind and rapidly faded? He needed something commensurate, with a complex but not confused architectonics, something 'classical': 'My desperate attempt to compose in a strict, elegant form rescued my fading will.'[28]

We can see that constant artistic impulses gave him the balance he so needed. He was not always sure where they were coming from, but their fruits were clear to see. Certain feelings are quickly replaced by others, which often take up and develop them, or interrupt and fragment them, but without tearing the fabric. Asafiev is braced by this succession of incoming musical themes, reflections, obscure pictures and images. He tries to separate them out and understand them, to eliminate their inherent chaos and clarify them, and his sense of order and harmony returns to him.

7

Reflecting on how people survived during the siege, we would be hard pressed to claim a major role for the arts. Interest in creativity inevitably faded if there was no electric light, where the cold made fingers stiff, where people barely able to stand on their feet spent hours counting the minutes to their next meal, and where endless queues were the norm. The domestic and international response to the revelation of continuing artistic creativity in the besieged city was caused not by the quantity of it, but by its sheer unexpectedness in the context of war. Their continuing to attend concerts and visit the theatre, to write poetry and articles, to create musical works is rightly seen as the most striking illustration of the fortitude of the Leningraders.

The true significance of the arts, creativity and reading is that, during the siege, they offered Leningraders, immersed in the struggle for survival, stable moral support. They did not always prevent the collapse of morality, but retarded it. The perfection and immaculateness of artistic form reinforced the criteria for judging good and evil. The special uplift which comes from reading gave people a greater sense of their human dignity and uniqueness.

Tales of the siege

1

Tales told during the siege were more than an exchange of news. They highlighted the most appalling and pathological things revealed during those dark days. This was often in the hope of obtaining help from other citizens, and requests would be accompanied by dramatic descriptions of the nightmare.

This was not always possible in letters sent out of Leningrad to families and friends on the 'mainland', which were subject to scrutiny by the censors. Their work was no secret, and its influence can be felt in the palpable caution evident in letters: 'Neither you nor those in Moscow have a clear understanding of how things stand here. Unfortunately, I cannot tell you anything in a letter for reasons you will understand', Georgiy Lebedev, who worked at the Russian Museum, wrote to a colleague who had left the city.

'We all get little sleep', is the only negative detail about everyday life he gives. What is he allowed to say? We learn that also from his letter: 'In general, everything is fine and good so far. We are all in cheerful and optimistic spirits.'[29]

The lack of reliable information from Leningrad could give rise to extraordinary ideas about what was happening there. One citizen wrote to tell her family that she was now a dystrophic, and was asked in return, 'What's this new job you've got?'[30] Only later, when trains began arriving in the hinterland with Leningraders whose appearance spoke only too graphically about how cheerful and optimistic their spirits were, did it become much more difficult to conceal the true situation. In the process of dispelling the more absurd nonsense, Leningraders described the calamity which had befallen them in more detail. 'I haven't been in the city for a whole month now', M. M. Krakov noted in his diary in late January 1942. 'They say the place is a nightmare, with naked corpses left lying in the streets for several days.'[31]

Alexander Werth recalled that, when he arrived in Leningrad, people almost immediately started talking to him about the famine.[32] The human urge to amaze, shock, evoke sympathy, even in the absence of any other immediately apparent reason, added to the stock of these stories. For some, this was a way of unburdening themselves, and visitors to whom what was happening in the city was a shock were considered the best listeners. They were instantly recognizable from their clothes, their skin colour, and the absence of signs of oedema and facial swelling. Passing by, Leningraders sometimes lost patience and tried to engage them, if not in conversation, then at least with a comment. Vitaliy Bianki, who came to Leningrad for just a few days, saw a sledge with swaddlings on Liteyny Prospekt while he was waiting in a car for his friends: 'A stooped, grey-haired woman with a concrete-grey face and strands of faded hair suddenly paused by the car and said in a muffled, flat voice: "Surprised? We are all like that now. Many. We will all die." Without waiting for an answer, she waddled on her way.'[33]

'Everyone is talking about the same thing: food, death and the invisible prospects for our existence', G. A. Gelfer wrote in his diary.[34] Their tales became more and more depressing. Things considered unthinkable today, which made people shudder with horror when they talked about them, would seem minor tomorrow against the background of even more terrible happenings. 'Now all you hear people talking about is that a whole family has been wiped out, or that everybody in an entire apartment has died', wrote Sofia Meyerson in December 1941.[35]

Lev Razumovsky recalled that this was also what his friends talked about when they came together in his apartment in spring 1942: who had died where, who had survived what, which buildings had been bombed, cannibalism and gangsterism.[36] In what was now the normality of the siege, where the nightmarish was no longer any surprise, new information surfaced which could shock even the Leningraders. A particular detail could assume symbolic status and be remembered. Yekaterina Lentsman recalled what her father told her he had witnessed at the Piskaryovskoye cemetery: 'A man and a woman were placed in a single pit, and between them a boy, just like our Vova.'[37]

2

Tales of the siege are primarily tales of how people changed. Every stage of degeneration is noted in a keenly felt narrative, felt and meticulously studied in endless conversations. There was no escaping this interest in pathology. Why were people keeping diaries? It was not merely to record routine and unimportant details. Why did they meet to discuss events? They were not going to keep silent about the most dramatic news.

The pathological is something out of the ordinary, and always attracts attention, irrespective of its scale. When people talk about the pathological, they try to dissociate themselves from it, and do so emphatically, expressing anger, surprise and disgust. They always emphasize that they are not like that, but they are scarred by it. One person may see hundreds, if not thousands, of fellow citizens crushed by the siege, and all the more hastily and insistently will he try to differentiate himself from them, the healthy person from the sick, the civilized individual from others who have reverted to barbarism.

The more stories are told about the siege, the more prominent the concept of civilization becomes. 'To think we tried to eat that during the Time of Death!' Vitaliy Bianki heard in a conversation between a man and woman;[38] these people most certainly knew the difference between real food and surrogates. G. Kabanova admitted in a letter to her aunt that her room had become very dirty. She is aware that this is bad.[39] The artist Vlasov told the writer Vsevolod Ivanov about how a wardrobe drawer and a child's pram had been used as a coffin.[40] These are the particular details he remembered.

Tales of the siege were rarely dispassionate or rapid. Their emotional charge remains palpable in later memoirs: time did not erase all trace of the trauma. 'They seemed so quiet and timid', Ye. N. Sorokina wrote later of the children attending a New Year party. 'We were particularly affected when we remembered the bashful joy with which the children left the theatre, tightly clutching their little presents.'[41] These reports of the details of life under the siege, touching descriptions of the unfortunate children, and many tragic or joyful details of things happening during that time, no matter how used people became to their circumstances, still evoked a powerful reaction. M. K. Petrova wrote about 'how awful it was to hear from a doctor that in the building next to ours a hungry child, to still its hunger, had begun to gnaw and eat its mother shortly after she died.'[42] Things people had become inured to in earlier days were replaced now by further, yet more horrific, testimony which sickened even the most desensitized. When he learned of cannibalism in Leningrad, Nikolai Gorshkov was moved to write in his diary, 'I cannot pass over in silence another phenomenon resulting from the hunger, cruelty and greed, the most appalling brutishness which transgresses every boundary of what the human mind can accept.'[43] This is hardly the reaction of an impassive witness of events, such as Gorshkov appears to be in many pages of his diary, which otherwise reads like a dispassionate daily listing of the times and impacts of shelling.

3

'In came a little boy. He was seven', the secretary of the Primorsky District Committee of the Komsomol, Maria Prokhorova, begins her tale: '"Granny died", he said. "The manager and I couldn't take her to the cemetery, so we pulled her to the River Karpovka and threw her in, and Auntie died four or five days ago and she's lying in the apartment."'[44] He may have said other things besides, but this is what was selected, highlighted and magnified. What is brought out is the most dramatic, monstrous, uncivilized detail. That is what lies at the heart of all these tales, which always have a story line and are never just a collection of trivial details of the day's events. They are always histories, with a beginning, a middle and an end, with a crisis and a commentary by their authors. These are histories which their authors try to make particular and visual, and they are usually accompanied by moral judgement: '"The housing manager and I threw Granny into the river and left Auntie Tanya in the apartment." This was said by a 7-year-old boy with a little knapsack, totally emaciated, dirty, covered in soot, and with the wizened face of an old man.'[45]

Soot-blackened faces, tears, suffering, mud, uncleaned streets, dead bodies, burglary – it is all reflected in the tales of the siege. Every action is evaluated on the basis of what is understood by civilization. People imagined they had become accustomed to the realities of the siege, but by the next day there were more horrors and they had become even more appalling. The Leningraders did not immediately become accustomed to these. Talk about incidents, invariably emphasizing the deviations from traditional values, became endless, and the commandments of morality remained alive and relevant.

Tales about life in the past and future

1

Telling stories about life in the past and future became a habit during the siege. They accurately reflect the vicissitudes of life in the Time of Death, with its primitivization and the degradation of individuals. What people talked about most often and most readily was food, and that was true of everyone: writers, actors, schoolchildren, workers and housewives.

'It is easy to get a lively conversation going when you are visiting, because you have only to start talking about food', Izrail Metter commented.[46] Leningraders soon became aware of how pathological this talk was, going on at such length, discussed so passionately, so monotonously and repetitively.

A prohibition on talking about food was one way of maintaining self-control, although probably not very effective. It was difficult to find anything else to talk about in all the hours of enforced 'leisure' generated by illness, hunger, the lack of electric light and heat and, finally, the bombing and shelling. That was almost all that got talked about in the bomb shelters. There was something unreal about the ban, as if it were a game. In one of the hospitals there was a ban on talking about food on night duty, about yourself and your family, and even about the war. Breaking the rule got you fined.[47] Ksenia Polzikova-Rubets threatened to punish her school-children for talking about those topics, but it seems unlikely she would have carried out her threat to confiscate their crusts of bread.[48]

Life during the siege revolved around the search for bread, so it was inevitably going to be a topic of conversation. At first this took the form of exchanging information on where to buy it, but later there followed uncontrollable and interminable descriptions of food, delicious, filling, abundant, which were startling for their gastronomic excess. The talk became unstoppable. People would interrupt each other in order to give themselves that moment of illusory 'substitution' of bread they could not eat.

In all these stories, one feature stands out. People invariably talked about delicious and, importantly, 'civilized' food; not about wood glue or jelly boiled out of a belt, not about soya bean patties or nettle soup. This was not just any food, but a loving selection of only the most mouth-watering dishes. That gives away the function being served by what one Leningrader called 'these gastronomic fantasy narratives.'[49] Schoolchildren were the most unabashed practitioners. They found it easier, and were more used to, expressing their feelings without inhibition, and were always ready to compare different foods. They were particularly emphatic when it came to saying which was their favourite. 'What could be tastier than a rissole with lots and lots of macaroni?', Polzikova-Rubets heard one say in a bomb shelter.[50] In another bomb shelter, Valentina Bazanova, a schoolgirl, noted one pupil saying, 'I would like to eat, right now, sausages and mash, or fried macaroni with like a crust on it. If somebody offered me cake or 100 grams of bread, I would take the bread.'[51]

The way the food was cooked was also important, and this further underlines that the food is 'civilized'. How many notes we find at this time where someone is dreaming of food that is 'golden brown'. There was interest in cookery books, as encyclopaedias of real, not siege or surrogate, food.[52]

2

The main benchmark of civilization was how things were before the war. Food might not have been particularly plentiful and there might have been little prosperity, but that was what those trapped in the siege of Leningrad compared their present situation to.

Talking about delicious food was a first step towards distinguishing what was civilized from what was uncivilized. 'Nowadays we are not eating Siberian *pelmeni* dumplings and eggs but anything we can get our hands on, even soya soup, which is nauseating', wrote Alexandra Borovikova at a time when hunger had barely taken hold.[53] This clear distinction between good and bad was retained into the future. The contrasting was not only of 'delicious' food with nauseating food surrogates. We sometimes find the place of delicious food being taken by oilcake, cattle cake and milk substitutes, but even then awareness of the difference between appetizing and unappetizing food persists. At first, people were content with any piece of bread, but later dreamed of palatable bread instead of the raw black mess with sawdust which was issued in January 1942. On 27 February, Yelena Mukhina wrote in her diary, 'There is always appetizing bread in the bakery, but people are not satisfied with that. They keep complaining, and now wish there were buns and gingerbread.'[54]

The demand for appetizing food could be met by cheering up the siege food, and people attempted to do so everywhere. We can see the revulsion felt for surrogates as reflecting resistance to falling standards. What needed to be overcome was not only physiological, but also psychological, aversion. It was not impossible to produce a digestible (one can hardly put it more generously than that) aspic from leather belts, and even to cook up something edible out of wood glue. Even so, the mere thought that one was about to consume glue or belts caused almost overwhelming waves of nausea because of all the other non-culinary associations people had firmly fixed in their minds.

'We are eating wood glue', Anna Ostroumova-Lebedeva writes in her diary on 1 January 1942. 'Never mind. You may experience a first spasm of nausea, but I think the revulsion comes from an over-active imagination. This aspic is really not so disgusting if you add cinnamon or a few bay leaves.'[55] Even when faced with a surrogate mess, the old discrimination can be brought to bear. Some things are really not all that disgusting, and, if they are, they can be cheered up and made less disgusting. Other Leningraders show the same attitude. Irina Zelenskaya pondered the question of how to make the watery white yeast soup more palatable: 'You can make it drinkable if you add a lot of pepper and mustard.'[56] Another family added two slices of onion to, probably, the same soup: 'It was very tasty.'[57] M. M. Krakov tried to bake a patty made of rotten potatoes: 'It is terrible, but perhaps if you fry it in oil?'[58]

'Improving' food was just another way of retaining one's human dignity. Everything was derived from the past: the concept of good food; the distinguishing of taste from tastelessness; the recognition of the difference between good and bad. The memory of life before the war constantly helped people to recognize what was or was not 'proper' food. It was strengthened by endless conversations about who had chosen not to buy the food and medicines which had still been available in shops and chemist's shops before the siege, and what the circumstances had been.

Someone had not bothered to buy onions, someone else had walked past jars of jam. It was a source of enduring frustration. So much had been freely on sale, and everything had been relatively cheap. Anyone who, for some reason, had passed up on the opportunity when it was there of buying a packet of mustard, sugar, cereal, a bottle of vegetable oil, a tin of condensed milk, would kick themselves every time they recalled it. Lev Razumovsky daily heard people bemoaning the fact that 'a month and a half ago I could have bought such-and-such and I didn't'.[59] The wife of one writer bought a 3 kg tin of caviar but, on her husband's insistence, donated it to a children's home. Two years later, they both admitted to Alexander Werth that they had regretted that many times since.[60] Dismay that they had not bothered, while it was still possible, to buy food and vitamins which were desperately needed later can be detected in the memoirs of Dmitry Likhachev.

Similar to these are the stories of people who had turned up their noses at certain foods when they had plenty to eat in the past. These too are tales of nostalgia for the past, and equally darkened by suffering and unimaginable hunger pangs, remorse and self-reproach:

> I drink so much liquid I am all swollen up. I have nothing else to eat. So now I often remember when you told me, 'Eat, damn you!' I go to bed but can I sleep? I only think about food, and that is so wretched. I lie there and don't know what to think about, I want to remember the past but it's only food, food, food. I keep remembering when I would not eat my bread because I said it was too sour and now I dream of eating bread until I am full.[61]

3

The more dreadful conditions in the siege became, the more intently did people peer back to the past with all its details recalling its unique savour. They remembered all the more clearly everything that had been heart-warming, stomach-filling and cosy. That is how people resisted the nightmare: by getting out of it, if only for a moment – by escaping. 'Sometimes lovely thoughts come to mind, all of them from the past and what I have experienced.'[62] We find G. A. Gelfer's words mirrored in the notes of other Leningraders.

Talking about good food often helped to bring back memories of other details of life before the war: the warm, cosy room in which meals were eaten, and how generously bread had been shared. It lodged in the memory all the more strongly because that accommodation was so drastically different from the buildings of besieged Leningrad now, ruined by bombing, covered in filth and full of dead bodies. This helped to root the memory of civilized standards in people's minds, and those related not only to standards of food, but also to standards of normal human relationships not distorted by war, standards of domestic comfort and cleanliness, standards of beauty, and standards of calm not shattered by shelling.

This is graphically reflected in a letter from Vladimir Lyublinsky, the librarian of the Public Library, to his wife. He remembers an outing they had together in early summer 1941: 'And then we sat in a new delicatessen shop where we bought, if I remember, cakes, a bar of chocolate, and either some cheese or meringues. I saw this in my mind's eye down to the last detail, and how I wished I could take you out again, or take a boat with you back to the city, as we did a few days before the outbreak of war.'[63]

Not the sort of food you got in the siege but in a delicatessen, so unlike the points where you could get your ration cards redeemed; an outing unthinkable for malnourished people in the ice-bound streets with their abandoned corpses; a boat trip to admire beautiful scenery. Every detail of the nightmare of the siege is held at bay, cancelled out by a succession of peacetime scenes. This is not a series of unrelated impressions but one integral event, and it is the result of more than stream of consciousness. Because of its completeness, the way in which the parts are condensed, we perceive a perfectly happy day all the more vividly and powerfully. The memories revolve around food but are not limited to it. The action does not come to an end. The outing and the boat trip are associated with a sense of stillness, serenity and celebration.

Nikolai Ribkovsky, in his diary entries, also writes a lot about food, but his almost pastoral tale of a summer holiday in peacetime relegates it to the background. There is nothing naturalistic about his narrative:

Here, under the shady trees, in the dense grass, I often relaxed in my spare time with a book or the newspapers. Sometimes I would fall asleep. Seryozha, who was still very little, would come running up, wake me, and give me no chance of any more sleep. I stood at the very spot where I often rested beneath the windows of my little room, and I felt as if at any moment the window might open and my wife call, 'Kolya, come for dinner or we'll be late for the theatre.'[64]

What is remembered is the sense of comfort and quiet family happiness. It is an apotheosis of peace, of a sweet dream from which you are reluctant to wake. The protective shade of a tree, grass on which to sleep softly, a book, a newspaper, the theatre, a funny little boy, a caring wife calling you in for dinner. It is an idyll in which there is no hint of the monstrous circumstances of the siege or, indeed, of any of the worries of the pre-war era. Only the most endearing and only much idealized images of the past, with all its problems erased, could displace the grim reality of life under the siege.

Attempts to actually reintroduce this felicitous past in the present rarely succeeded. They were usually made at celebrations of the New Year or a birthday. A fir tree was bought, a suit brushed, a pretty dress donned, crusts of bread hoarded, a bottle of wine carefully put aside, delicacies acquired by some felicitous chance stored – but more often than not something would go wrong and the celebration be spoiled. Someone would fall ill, someone would fail to bring what they had promised, someone could not get off work, someone was being bombed, and all that remained was disappointment, tears that, even just this once, it had not proved possible to organize a half-decent holiday.

Atta Asknaziy tells of her attempt to celebrate her 7-year-old brother's birthday. She did her best to decorate the room, lit a lamp, and put a little toy ship and some chocolate on the table. Everything was clean and light; she had prepared – and perhaps not only for her brother but also for herself – a little spectacle which would let her share the surprised delight of a loved sibling. Her brother doubtless sensed that something wonderful was being prepared for him.

When he came into the room, he burst into tears. This was not what he had known in the past. There was no bread, just a ship he did not want and which was no substitute for bread, and a chocolate bar whose diminutive size only reminded him he could not eat it as he might have in the past: 'He did not eat the chocolate all at once, but just broke off a tiny piece.'[65] That tiny piece caused more sorrow than joy. Sorrow because it would all too soon be eaten, and also because he would have to make an incredible effort not to gobble all the chocolate up at once.

The past also determined how life was imagined after the siege had been raised and the war brought to an end. These scenes were composed on the basis of memories of all the most ideal features of life before the war, and not without exaggeration. Leningraders wanted not just to return to a bright and comfortable past, but to an extreme distillation of all that had been good in it. That applied particularly to food: there was to be a huge amount of it, and it was to be unprecedentedly varied, delicious, nutritious, and well cooked.

The most detailed account of what was to happen is found in the diary of 17-year-old Yelena Mukhina. Perhaps it is because of the emotional nature of someone on the verge of despair that the description is so dramatic, not to say frenzied:

When the war is over and everything is balanced once again and you can buy anything, I will buy a kilo of black bread, a kilo of gingerbread, and half a litre of cottonseed oil. I will crumble the bread and gingerbread, drown it in the oil and mix it all up, then I will take a tablespoon and pig myself to my heart's content. Then Mother and I will bake all sorts of pies, with meat and potatoes, cabbage and grated carrot. And then Mother and I will fry potatoes and eat them golden and sizzling straight out of the pan. And we'll eat croissants with sour cream and *pelmeni* dumplings, and macaroni with tomato and fried onions, and a hot, white, crusty loaf smothered in butter, with sausage or cheese, and it will be a very large piece of sausage so that your teeth sink into it when you bite. Mother and I will eat grainy buckwheat porridge with cold milk, and then take the leftover porridge and fry it in a pan with onion glittering with butter. Finally, we will eat hot, fatty crepes with jam and thick, plump griddle cakes. My God, we are going to eat so much we will scare the wits out of ourselves.[66]

4

Yelena had reached a stage of starvation where, for the act of displacement to be effective, she needed to imagine an extravagantly sumptuous banquet to pathological perfection. Everything is measured in kilograms and litres, everything is doused with oil; not only the smells but even the sounds associated with appetizing dishes are invoked. Everything is gleaming with fat, there is a lot of it, there is great variety. It is mouth-watering, fresh and it is all there for you to pig yourself on. The nightmare of the siege compels people to look into remote corners of times past, which may rarely have been given much thought before. It is as if all the known signs of a good life have been meticulously collected and ingeniously woven together. Civilized life is being reimagined in an unrealistically generous form to include all the features closest to one's heart. It is not only the present but also the past which must be excelled. Everything in the future must be unique, and better, much, much better, unlike anything there ever was before!

One Leningrader made a bet that, when peace came, 'after eating a three-course meal, he would drink a litre of vegetable oil with bread.'[67] Vladislav G. Grigoriev records his neighbour's remark that, 'When the war is over, I am going to buy a barrel of pickled cabbage, and once I start eating there is no way you will get me to stop, even if you try pulling me out by the legs.'[68] The hungrier someone is, the more extravagant the gastronomic excesses featured in their tales; the more extraordinary the variety of ingredients, unthinkable in an actual pre-siege meal; and the more vividly and colourfully will they imagine their post-war life of comfort and satiety.

Throughout her tale, Yelena Mukhina's joy comes from the fact that she will not be eating alone, but with her mother, who is no less hungry. It is as if she will only experience the happiness if she can share the feeling with her mother. This is not just an added detail but, when we look closely, a principal theme. Mother is to bake the pies, eat the buckwheat porridge, enjoy the griddle cakes and drink the milk. Everything that is tastiest but currently out of reach she must definitely get to try. This reflects the fact that the rivets of moral principle are still holding, that people are not fixated on their own troubles, not yet storing away their own rations in different drawers in the sideboard. Her 'baroque', almost fairy-tale story about a civilized meal almost unimaginable in the Time of Death has also that distinguishing feature of a civilized world: generosity.

She repeats these stories several times, perhaps less rapturously than before. On 3 January 1942, Yelena is again dreaming of how bright and well fed life will be after the raising of the siege:

We decided we would most definitely fry up lots and lots of pork scratchings, and be sure to dip bread straight into the hot fat, and we also decided to eat lots of onion. We would feed ourselves on the cheapest porridges livened up with large amounts of fried onion, golden, juicy, soaked in oil. We also decided to cook oat, and barley and lentil griddle cakes and much, much else.[69]

'Sufficient unto the day is the evil thereof.' Now, after a period of starvation, what is being written about is not particularly sophisticated food (which, even in the previous, gastronomic entry was not much in evidence), but what people eat every day, cheap, ordinary varieties of porridge. These are more convincing for 'displacement' of what is lacked; they are more tangible in the context of everyday reality. The core of discussions is still an abundance of food, but no longer that abundance of varieties remembered from the now already distant past, but food which has become the norm, the food that is now constantly being measured out and the lack of which was felt yesterday, is being felt today, and will be felt tomorrow. 'After victory we will be sure to cook lentil porridge and eat our fill', mother and daughter fantasized after receiving in a jar some of just that kind of porridge from a relative who worked at a hospital.[70] They had nothing more delicious, only this. They had been looking forward to it, and it would unquestionably be the centrepiece of future 'feasts'.[71]

It is difficult to say whether all talk about the future was limited to food, because we have little testimony. As a rule, Leningraders described the details of what they expected life after the siege to be like more laconically and less emotionally, sometimes in just one or two lines.[72] Yelena Mukhina's diary is quite unique, so let us make use of it again, as evidence of how people during the Time of Death pictured that better life.

Most often it involved travel, and journeys in general. That is how in the past they had escaped their routine, everyday concerns and hardships, so it was natural for them to think of that when they sought escape from the horrors of the siege. Their wretched rations were displaced by visions of gastronomic excess: the filthy storeys of their icy buildings were displaced by fantasies of a first-class railway carriage. Yelena and her mother had not managed to take the trip they had planned for the summer of 1941, and here the past encourages them to idealize the future:

My mother and I will have seats in first class, with little blue curtains, a lamp with a lampshade, and the moment arrives when our train pulls out from under the glass dome of the terminus and rushes out to freedom, and we will be sped far, far away. We will sit at a little table, eat something delicious, and know that ahead of us there will be interesting things to do, delicious things to eat, unfamiliar places, the countryside with blue skies, greenery and flowers. Ahead of us there will be delights, each one better than the last.[73]

The gulf between the present and the future is here particularly stark: blue skies in place of the gloom of Leningrad's winter nights; greenery and flowers in place of the murderous cold as 1941 yielded to 1942. Unimaginable comfort and peace. No starvation, no cold, no bombs, no furious quarrelling over bread, just pure, untrammelled enjoyment. The lampshade softening the light from the lamp contrasts with the blinding harshness of the searchlights. The glass dome no doubt is contrasting with the darkness of windows in the blackout and shards of glass blown out of windows by the bombing. To travel far away (as Yelena puts it, 'rushing out to freedom') will enable them all the sooner to leave behind the scars of past experiences. And, of course, there is food, and even other ill-defined delights. There is plenty in this tale to weaken the grip of the nightmare of the siege: 'We want to eat, and not only to eat but we want something else. I don't myself know what exactly. We want something good, and happy. We want to see a brightly lit New Year's tree.' Yelena wrote that in her diary in January 1942, when the hideous features of the Time of Death were revealing themselves most starkly.

'Life before the war was a different era, which you remember with affection, as you might a distant, carefree childhood. Life after the war is a beautiful dream about which everyone has their own ideas.'[74] Esfir Levina's brief diary entry succinctly summarizes the main motifs in 1941–2 of tales about the past and future life in Leningrad. It also explains why they were so prevalent: there was no other way to escape this hell. In their memories, dreams, aspirations and hopes, people returned once again to the civilized environment of which they had been deprived, and thereby had restored to them their sense of human dignity, of traditional values, of beauty, and manifestations of purity, tranquillity and harmony.

Diaries and letters

1

People kept diaries by force of habit, in order to adapt to new customs, on insistent advice and, finally, as a means of anaesthetizing their misery and hunger. Their entries were an attempt to tell others about their own self-sacrifice, about what they were having to endure in the hell of the siege, and thereby gain a measure of recognition beyond the circle of their friends and relatives. Diaries were sometimes used as a book for keeping the household accounts, listing rations and unexpected gifts received, and for making calculations to see whether there would be sufficient food to last them through the next ten days. The same can be said about letters. They, in addition, contained requests for support, and enabled people to keep alive the hope they might receive parcels, although their hopes often came to nothing.

Leningraders wrote very little about their motives for keeping a diary.[75] The dramatic period of the siege obliged them to dwell more fully on the realities of the period. Exercises in introspection were inevitably relegated to the background. Any deliberate choice of topics to be covered did, as

Eduard Shubin points out, have a major influence on the contents of the diary.

Few thought it worthwhile to set out with the intention of creating heroic stories of stout resistance to the enemy. The future was unclear, and degrees of heroism could only be properly assessed at a later date. Some diaries give the reader prior warning that there are more excuses than bombastic promises. Diarists apologized for tedious and unnecessary detail, for the chaotic and fragmentary nature of the impressions recorded; some also forgave themselves on the grounds that, if the entries were chaotic, they were at least honest.[76]

'Well, I'm now going to write down here everything that comes into my head', announces Tatiana Kononova.[77] Her words could be repeated by dozens of other diarists, who did not usually attempt to classify the events they described as important or insignificant. She says without guile that keeping the diary takes her mind off gloomy thoughts. Other Leningraders say the same.[78] Not the least important reason for keeping a diary, of course, was that it was seen as an aid to self-control. Speaking of her diary, which takes the form of letters to an imaginary friend, Esfir Levina noted: 'Talking to you provides a constant check on myself.'[79] Not everybody was prepared to admit that so openly, but in these seemingly very personal entries we should note how many self-critical admissions there are, how many apologies, promises, and analyses of everyday situations where a difficult choice has had to be made.

The rhetoric in which entries of this kind are couched helps, through its emotional expression, to reinforce moral principles. Rhetorical language is the language of civilization, not of degeneration: its clichés reflect established traditions and customs. The knowledge, repetition and memorizing of this language protects against a relapse into barbarity. Rhetorical passages are often set apart from the more purely factual text with its facts and figures and descriptions of real-life incidents. An element of rhetoric elevates a person, distancing them from the routine of life in the siege, where it is considerably more difficult to adhere to moral principle. Rhetoric is a means of fitting one's actions more definitely into the accepted canon of good behaviour. The architect Alexander Nikolsky deliberately showed someone else an entry in his diary for 22 January 1942 which read: 'All around people are weakening and dying, but we cannot surrender the city. I firmly believe the siege will soon be raised, and have started thinking about the design of triumphal arches to meet the heroic troops who will liberate Leningrad.'[80] All the entries in his diary are written in that key. There may be variations, raising or lowering the pathos, alternating them with harrowing details of the siege, but this does not affect the underlying integrity. There is nothing he need be ashamed to show to others. The entries are something to be proud of.

Who would he show them to? Intimates and friends who know him and would be in a position to compare his lofty ideals with the principles he genuinely lives by in his everyday life? What sense would it make to present himself in his diary as a decent person if all those around knew him to be a scoundrel? As a smokescreen? But even that could serve to hold base passions in check: some things he will refrain from doing; others he will do in a less provocative and unkind manner. The more a person talks of himself as a heroic Leningrader caught in the siege, the more he burns his bridges: even in a moment of weakness and despair he needs to apologize, not make excuses.

2

The more rhetorical and emotional passages in diaries and letters have different origins. A certain amount of rhetoric is invariably present in the preface to diaries, thereby setting the tone and predetermining the approach in many entries. It also appears in response to reports published in the newspapers about the heroism of Leningraders. It replicates the emotional rhetoric of the press. Diarists resort to rhetoric also when they wish to place themselves among the most steadfast citizens, when they feel they have earned – the hard way – the right to speak on behalf of others: 'The enemy is in retreat. Let us then continue, comrades, with fortitude. The time will not be long. Let the enemy know a Leningrader would rather die of hunger than surrender.' This is not a stirring call to boost morale at a meeting, but an entry in Anna Umanskaya's diary for 19 December 1941.[81] We find almost the same propaganda speech in the diary of Arkadiy Lepkovich, who was not drafted into the army for health reasons: 'We, the disabled and toilers on the home front, will endure all suffering, all ills. We will die, we will crawl on our hands and knees, but we will never surrender.'[82] That pronoun, 'we', confers great authority on his assertions. Being a hero proves to be not so much a right as a duty, and the inertial force of firm words spoken with conviction makes it difficult later to qualify them or retreat.

Any action which stands out and is intended to make clearer one's heroism and optimism has a primarily rhetorical aspect. Form subordinates content. The home newspaper, a kind of open diary, was not made by schoolboy Yura Zvezdin with any intention of sowing pessimism. Here is a note he published in it, with the resounding title of 'We are not downhearted': 'On 13 [November 1941] new quotas for the bread ration have been introduced. Despite the reduction, our whole family has taken the news in its stride. Mother says, "We shall not be downhearted. We shall overcome all difficulties with perseverance." These words are not at variance with real life: we are making the bread last for the whole day.'[83]

This is not a form of autosuggestion, but a fully conscious public demonstration of perseverance. All clutter, details, doubts, have been removed. The text clearly does not reflect the consternation at what has occurred, and neither should it. Fortitude is best expressed calmly, not by shouting.

The rhetoric in personal letters is usually more muffled. A letter cannot be propaganda: the epistolary genre has its own rules. There are exceptions, but they too follow rules. The rhetorical exclamations in a letter from Mikhail Tushinsky to Tatiana Vecheslova ('Our great Motherland, the State of a Great People which has created such values will stand her ground and rise again')[84] are couched in language peculiar to this ardent lover of the theatre, for whom elevated language is the norm: 'I am writing to the beloved leader of an astounding company.'[85] Even in more prosaic letters, rhetorical passages can feel less alien and artificial. In a letter from Maria Konisskaya to I. V. Shcheglova, the upbeat conclusion is preceded by a detailed list of the misfortunes which have befallen her, and hence the optimism seems perfectly natural. It is not inappropriately grandiloquent or over-emotional: 'As for myself, I can honestly say that I am not despondent and believe the future is bright.'[86]

Irrespective of how emotional the conclusions of letters are, their optimism must accord with moral values. Usually rhetoric comes as an ending, the conclusion of a story. A superfluity of minor details could confuse the addressee, and indeed the writers themselves, but the final conclusion must be stated clearly and unequivocally. It is a means of looking directly into oneself, rising above routine everyday matters. Rhetoric and elevated language are not garments the faint-hearted can wear. By presuming to don them, a correspondent was giving an undertaking. It could not always be fulfilled, but it was not something negligible.

3

In certain diaries and letters, we find a very condensed statement of everything that is officially approved. Value judgements, actions, self-characterization are as if written specifically to be seen by other people. Curiously enough, this kind of writing tended to come from the better-fed. The traditional sense of gratitude to the state authorities is more marked. Again and again, they try to demonstrate that they appreciate the care being taken of them and are boundlessly grateful for it. It is as if they are anticipating that some representative of the state will be glancing through their diary or reading their letter, and will see that the support given was deserved and has not been wasted. A sincere expression of political loyalty, even if only in a diary or private letter, gave a sense, possibly illusory, of security in the present and confidence in the future.

The rhetoric in documents of the siege, even if it seems spurious, had one undoubted merit. It enabled a person to derive guidelines for their behaviour based on the norms of communist morality, which were to a considerable extent based on traditional ethics. The director of the October District Enterprise Group titled his January 1942 diary: 'Bolsheviks are different. Brief notes from life in undefeated Leningrad, by A. P. Nikulin'.[87] This set a special tone for the narrative, which we see already on the following page: 'I am a soldier of the revolution who has given all his strength to serving our mother, our homeland, and our people. Finally, I am a steadfast Marxist-Leninist-Stalinist. I do not despair. I do not feel doomed. No, I am a fighter. I am a Bolshevik. I will not bend the knee. I will not surrender.'[88]

This was written at a time when thousands of people were starving to death, and the pointed detachment from the news of the day might seem surprising. The first entry in the diary was written on 10 January 1942, at the peak of the calamity, and this is probably no coincidence. There can be no condemnation of Nikulin's desire to make the most of rhetorical devices. He has chosen language which accurately reflects his mood and his determination not to retreat. It is language which implies a whole repertoire of behaviour. It is succinct and not diluted by long-winded argumentation which could only undermine the will to resist. The language is the essence of this man, and perhaps important to strengthening his resolve. Constant rhetorical flourishes are a means of maintaining mental strength: 'There is no despondency, no fear, no sense of doom. My gait is firm, my step confident and that of a master. The people of Leningrad are experiencing immense difficulties, but the city is alive, the city is fighting back. This city of heroes is undiminished.'[89] This register is typical of other entries, but even for this diary, the entry on 21 January 1942 stands out. It is not only an avowal of political loyalty, but also a means of testing his resilience. Will he prove up to it?

Today is the day that 'greatest of great men', V. I. Lenin, died. Lenin's cause lives on. Lenin's cause will be victorious. To be a Leninist means to love our socialist homeland, to fight for it without sparing one's own life. Now we are led by [the handwriting becomes difficult to read – S. Ya.] Stalin, under whose leadership we shall win. There is no light to write by.[90]

Nikulin made no other entries that day. He systematically creates the image of a rock-hard Bolshevik in the most exaggerated form imaginable. Knowledge of political education clichés facilitates this. In each diary entry, the selfsame clichés recur. The code of exemplary behaviour applied to his own actions becomes unchallengeable. He tries to reflect the most appalling episodes of the siege in the same language:

I myself saw a man first stagger and then fall. Malnutrition had undermined the redoubtable strength of a hero. As he fell, he extended his arm forward as if to say, 'Even in dying, I am falling not back, but headlong forwards! I die not as a coward, but as a fighter, but have not the strength to carry on fighting until complete victory over the enemy is won.[91]

This style can make other eyewitnesses of the siege wince,[92] but it is made up for by a deep sense of compassion, undimmed even when communicating in this sort of language. The fabric of the bureaucratese tears only when he comes to describe a frozen woman with her child in the mortuary: 'Her undermined strength as a mother and a citizen gave way.' That could be put more straightforwardly, but the sincerity of these crestfallen lines is beyond doubt. As he continues to stress the tragedy of the scene, he does manage to find other words, more affecting and touching: 'With the lowered head of a loving mother, she bent over her own dear child, but it too, like its mother, was immobile and cold.'[93]

Sheer emotion causes these tears in the fabric of officialese. Strong feeling cannot be completely contained by cold rhetoric; it prompts those writing to give more acute, immediate and vivid expression to their sense of pity, sorrow and pain. It is fair to comment on the one-sidedness of optimistic entries: the picture of the siege is not composed only of manifestations of fortitude. The diary of S. M. Glazovitskaya, Party secretary at the Rabochiy factory, much quoted by Mina Bochaver, is full of information about the labour successes, cheerfulness and resilience of Leningrad's citizens.[94] There are other examples. In the letters of A. G. Belyakov, assistant commandant of railway junctions, to his wife S. Belyakova there is much that would seem more at home in a propaganda article than in private correspondence. The selection of emotive exclamations is particularly notable, and few letters are devoid of them. Even the re-asphalting of an avenue testifies, in his view, to the 'great strength of the Russian people'. We encounter the expression, 'Great Warrior City', just like that, in title case.[95] This is, of course, written with an eye to the wartime censorship, but perhaps it did point up the moral undertakings contained in the letters.

Accentuating the heroic, and only the heroic, also had a moral sense. Out of hundreds of details of the siege, only those are selected which conform most fully to morality. This makes the thinking of the author rather one-dimensional, but enables him to skip everyday events in which he shows up less well, and relieves him of the need to stoop to humiliating excuses, which would only emphasize his weaknesses.

4

High rhetoric is, nevertheless, rare in the diaries. It required special skill and a considerable level of culture. Usually diaries were kept in order to record the trivia of life under siege, and where better to talk about something other than just your daily bread? Writing about a visit to the theatre or a concert, about books, and poetry, whether read in books or composed by the diarists themselves, we invariably find the entries accompanied by lyrical and emotional comments and digressions, some of them perhaps not without an element of posing. It is only about bread that you write in a prosaic manner. In recording a visit to the theatre or a concert, attention is drawn to how exceptional this was. It is separated out, and there is much emphasis on how much it meant to this member of the audience, and how severely, in the process, they were suffering from cold and hunger.

It comes as no surprise to find letters offering moral advice. There are not that many of them, but each can be seen not only as a lesson offered to others, but also as an injunction to oneself. A whole succession of edifying letters were written by Yu. Bodunov, a teenager who died of starvation in February 1942. One of these, sent from Leningrad to his family on 16 December 1941, is a combination of the standard exhortations (unusually detailed for a boy of his age) and heroic symbols attached by his school. Moral advice is invariably accompanied by reference to one's own example of endurance. Without that, there is no certainty that one's moral teaching will have any force, or one's more mundane advice be accepted. The writing radiates benevolence, tolerance and understanding:

> Lyusya, I advise you to study on your own at home. You have the books, so read them, make sure you understand them, make notes. Help Mother. And again I advise you not just to keep crying. It is very bad when someone finds difficulties in their way and backs down from them. Keep your spirits up! We here are not losing heart, and we have more hardships to put up with. You write in your letter that you are brought sour cream, potatoes and cabbage: that is all food we can eat only in our dreams. We just put up with it: nobody here has been crying. When all this is over, we'll live even better than before. Now we need to work, study, and not feel sorry for ourselves. You also write that you cried when Aunt Nyusha put those rustic bast shoes on your feet. That is not good. Of course, you made a mistake in not taking shoes with you, but you had to pack in such a hurry. I have to learn my lessons by candlelight because there is no glass left in the windows and they are boarded up with plywood, but I just get on with it.[96]

It may be objected that he is only passing on the elementary lessons he has been taught at home and school, but this is a personal interpretation. He is not just teaching, but choosing the words himself, deciding where his tone of voice should be instructive, insistent or emotional. He needs to be persuasive, and to do that his comments have to be intelligent, concerned and personal. He deploys the whole arsenal of simple words of comfort, and in the process conveys the basic principles of morality, defends them and emphasizes their importance.

5

Moral advice did not always take the form of premeditated rhetorical declamation. It often arose spontaneously as a response to adversity facing family members, which someone had learned about from letters, or as a means of reassuring them when news from the front was disturbing. Letters to children and teenagers could resemble parables. Yu. Bodunov's letters are not dissimilar to those which Vladimir Maltsev sent to his sister.[97] In many cases, though, the moral advice was little more than the usual expression of good wishes at the end of a letter.

People recorded in their diaries and letters how they had helped their family, friends and, indeed, people they did not know particularly well. Sometimes the price of a gift is mentioned. They emphasize how difficult it was for them, and how important the support was to the recipient. They also talk about how other people manage to help their fellow Leningraders who are in difficulties.

These are not mere lists of food and items donated. Every good deed is accompanied by details and discussed and evaluated as a manifestation of moral qualities. Writers seem sometimes to be consulting others over how best to support family members, not always disguising their despair. A diary or letter can chronicle the birth and maturing of charitable instincts. Such are the diary entries of Alexander Nikolsky, as he frantically tries to save his wife's life in the terrible days of January 1942: 'How am I to feed Vera? She sleeps all day. She has eaten all the dried bread and is afraid of eating fresh bread. She has weakened' (entry of 1 January 1942); 'Vera has been nibbling at a very thin bar of what is claimed to be chocolate. I fear this is mainly food for boosting morale. The one thing on my mind is where to get food, food and more food for Vera' (entry of 2 January 1942).[98]

A letter from Vladimir Lyublinsky to A. D. Lyublinskaya of 23 January 1942, describing his rescue of librarian V. E. Goronskaya, almost ranks as a novella: there are clearly delineated storylines, an exposition and a dénouement. Goronskaya did her best to help her relatives, and soon became ill herself. 'No longer having electricity, firewood or food, not even a single skirt and pair of shoes, she collapsed helpless, unrecognizable, blackened, no longer able to walk to the bakery', Lyublinsky writes. We feel him becoming more agitated with every line he writes: 'She had absolutely no one to help her.' Having discovered that, it was impossible for him not to assume responsibility for her. He details everything he has done for her. 'I embarked on a frenzied round of activity, shared my porridge and bread with her, several times pulled her back from despair, got her daughter into a nursery (no simple matter!).' He could not get her admitted to the sickbay and performed what he describes as 'a second miracle'; 'I dragged Vera Eforovna, who was in a very frail state, to the library on a sledge.'[99]

This tale was recorded vividly and touchingly in a letter, and must surely have left a mark in its narrator's heart. Perhaps it was met with approval by witnesses and his family: he did not give up, did not abandon the lady, was not discouraged by the difficulties. In notes where Leningraders list the good deeds done to them, we find much the same: they note the value of the gift and the joy it gave them.[100] Just rereading their own diaries could be a help to them: looking through the entries, people could trace the stages of the gradual deterioration they were trying to combat.[101]

Control

1

No matter how noble people's aspirations or how strong the habits of compassion instilled in them, not everyone was willing to sacrifice themselves for others, to help and care constantly for them.

The city's leaders evidently had no effective programme of support for hundreds of thousands of Leningraders before the beginning of January 1942. This was partly because the extent of the calamity was not immediately recognized, and when they could no longer simply conceal it, they became jittery about the possibility of recrimination. This led to improvisation, and reluctance to give too much scope to public initiative for fear of attracting closer attention from the upper echelons of the state to how the Leningrad authorities were coping. Appeals to the public, cautious and vague, are nevertheless to be heard in the speech Pyotr Popkov delivered at a meeting of the Bureau of the Leningrad City Party Committee on 9 January 1942: 'We need to develop the initiative of the public and involve them in this matter. This must be done in every district. If we successfully mobilize the public, the government, Party and trade union activists, the lives of many citizens caught in the siege will be saved.'[102] Ivan A. Andreyenko, the director of the trade department of the Leningrad executive committee, was even more emphatic, making clear the kind of 'mobilization' he envisaged: 'the public must be forced to work.'[103] It was not only a matter of saving lives: the authorities were afraid of chaos.

Methods of 'unfettering' the initiative of the masses had been tried out in numerous propaganda and industrial campaigns in the 1930s. The public were accorded the status of extras: when the order was given, they were to play the role of being active, and when so ordered, they were to stop. Any activities not approved by the authorities, especially collective action to save lives, was viewed with suspicion. It would be much safer to 'force' people to work, and better still to rely mainly on activists.

Support for Leningraders was scaled up largely ad hoc as the extent of the calamity increased, and often without the need for any prompting. M. S. Krasnov, the Party secretary of Dairy No. 1, recalled that the husband of one of their communists 'was at the front, she was in a very difficult situation, she became ill, she had three children. We resolved under the auspices of the Party bureau to bring her to the dairy with her children and accommodate them in the Komsomol committee room, where she lived for a period of one month. We allocated her two communists who cared for her and got her back on her feet.'[104] 'Caring' is different from carrying out a one-off mission. It calls for patience, compassion and kindness. Why was she allocated the Komsomol committee room? Probably because it was warmer there. Krasnov also reported that the communists assisting another frail woman and her two children brought them 'waste products' from the dairy.[105] This was also how thousands of people kept their families alive.

A. I. Kochetova wrote to her mother that the Komsomol organization had helped her get her job back in view of her difficult situation, and that this deserved to be remembered.

Evelina Soloviova, collecting supplementary food for her daughter from the kindergarten, recalled a conversation with its headteacher, who politely but firmly insisted on seeing her little girl, mentioning that many mothers were eating their children's rations.[106] Antenatal nurses visited newly born babies at home, not only to give instruction to inexperienced mothers, but also to make sure the baby had not fallen victim to hungry people.

Visiting Leningraders who were in need of support brought people together, stopped them from degenerating, and awakened honourable feelings in them, thereby also 'unfettering' them. This could lead to long conversations as people shared their troubles, or asked for and expressed gratitude for support. Bonds were forged, people became friends, and this led to ongoing care for the most vulnerable. There were, of course, quarrels, and people did not immediately cease to be suspicious. With time, however, Leningraders got to know each other better, and their acts of charity were remembered in appreciative reports, in diaries and letters, and in memoirs.

The advice freely given to Leningraders whose lives had been saved went beyond anything prescribed in official instructions, if only because of the diversity and unpredictability of their situations. The sight of starving orphans had a long-term effect on those who worked in the hygiene teams, which kept them from looking the other way when there was help they could give. Filled with compassion, they would go beyond the call of duty, sometimes sharing their own bread. They would tell other citizens about the plight of children, and the heartfelt response was a determination to do everything possible to alleviate the suffering. One member of a unit, V. Shchekina, rescued dozens of children, and wanted each of them to be given her surname. Certainly, she did not find the work a hateful burden.

2

By naming and shaming, those who did not immediately respond to the misfortune of others were prodded into giving help. Thousands of citizens were on the brink of starving to death. Not only could they not support others, they could not even support themselves. Other, more extensive measures were urgently needed to prevent massive loss of life. This was the origin of the Komsomol household squads. The enthusiasm for unreservedly extolling their heroic deeds has, however, prevented the full and accurate examination of their work which it deserves. The actions of the Komsomol have sometimes been presented as resulting purely from a noble impulse, but they would not have been able to do much if they had not had substantial backing from the state. Much can be said about their eagerness to rescue Leningraders in serious trouble, but for that resources were essential, without which no amount of humane concern could have succeeded. Food and firewood were needed, but more than that, people were needed who were capable of feeding and washing enfeebled Leningraders, taking them to hospital, cleaning their rooms, washing and cleaning their clothes.

The first Komsomol household squad was created in January 1942 in Primorsky district. There had been no direct orders from above, but

Popkov's speech at the meeting of the Bureau of the Leningrad City Party Committee on 9 January 1942 could be considered, in accordance with the traditions of the time, to be not advice but an official instruction. The decision was taken by the district committee of the Komsomol, and it is unclear whether it was the development of a grassroots initiative. Without official support, the good intentions of Komsomol committees to help the enfeebled would have resulted only in a few groups descending periodically on a few apartments. That would not have solved any problems, and would have amounted to little more than the only too familiar official 'campaigns' for this and that, with their subsequent falsified reports about corrective action carried out at improbable speed.

The squads were obliged to keep a journal of the state of the apartments and the families living in them, and of how they had completed their assignments. The detail required in these might seem puzzling, but does not seem to be targeted at preventing misreporting of the figures. It probably only reflects the standard bureaucratic practice of requiring a receipt or report for each and every action. The 'soldiers' of the squads were being maintained at state expense and were required, as in any other state enterprise, to report on their activities.

The experiment was a success, and by late February 1942 every district in the city was ordered to establish such units.[107] They operated through until 1 July 1942.[108] The 'Soldier's Checklist', a set of instructions for the Young Communists, deserves a few words to itself. First, at the heart of the document is a concern for people rather than any pragmatic or opportunistic considerations. 'Conducting political education work' is relegated to Point 8. The terrible first winter of the siege left no room for official claptrap. The tasks listed for the 'soldiers' are based on moral principle.

1. Assist the local activists and manager of the building to take account of weak and ill residents, particularly in the families of Red Army soldiers.
2. Organize delivery of water to these families for cooking and washing.
3. Help the sick to make tea and cook food, and obtain bread and other food from the shops. Help those in particular need to obtain firewood and deliver it to them. Organize cleaning of apartments.
4. Assist in calling a doctor to the sick, also in having them transported to and admitted to a hospital or sickbay.
5. Help, if need be, to bury the dead.
6. Ensure the sick receive money, wages from their workplace, or sickness benefit.
7. Arrange for admission of orphans to a children's home or nursery.[109]

3

Let us turn to other forms of state support. These were, first of all, the district and factory sickbays which existed until April–May 1942. Tens of thousands of people were fed there.[110]

The universal appreciation of these is understandable, but even here there were problems. The sickbays were poorly provisioned, and in some cases had soon to be closed owing to lack of food. Emphasis was on treating the most valuable specialists, with little concern for everyone else.

State and public institutions monitored the distribution of food in canteens and shops. Many people were drafted in to help with this in view of the scale of pilfering. Nina Mansvetova recalled a meeting of their district commission for inspection of canteens where the way staff were treating their customers was raised.[111] Their dignity as human beings was not being respected. In some places, the Komsomol even opened their own model bakeries and canteens in the hope of putting dishonest sales assistants and canteen staff to shame.[112]

Monitoring affected every aspect of daily life during the siege. Without it, the mortality rate in the city would have been much higher, and instances of human compassion which supported morality in the community would have been far fewer.

Even in the Time of Death there were inspections – although not always – of conditions in hostels, children's homes, 'hearths' and kindergartens. Particular attention was paid, because of fear of epidemics, to hygiene in apartments, buildings and courtyards, and threats were made and punishments meted out to those who were responsible for it. Appeals to observe good personal hygiene, however embarrassing, did also help to 'civilize' people. The issue of workers' personal hygiene even found its way onto the agenda of a meeting of secretaries of workshop Party bureaux at the Kirov factory in early January 1942. It was noted that many workers, effectively 'confined to barracks', had not been to the bathhouse for a wash for three months or more and were infested with lice. After the mains water supply ceased to function they had 'nowhere even to wash their faces'. It was proposed that the Party secretaries should 'keep an eye on hygiene on a daily basis',[113] although in many cases this could be no more than wishful thinking.

When you read the minutes of the grassroots Party and Komsomol organizations, they do seem to be spending a disproportionate amount of time on such matters as the scheduling of meetings, payment of membership dues, filing and record keeping, completing documentation, registering and deregistering members, and conducting propaganda. The big issues of the Time of Death are often completely absent from these documents, because of their brevity, but also because of the addiction of the committees to routine paperwork. It is, of course, possible to take a more positive view of this. All aspects of discipline, industrial, Party, domestic and ethical, were interlinked. Communists and Komsomol members were expected to maintain standards, help others, and keep up appearances.

'They were dropsical from malnutrition, hobbling with walking sticks, but still they turned up to the Party activists' meeting', Leonid Galko, instructor of the Kirov factory Party committee, observed of the behaviour of the factory's communists.[114] In just the same way, they went out to enterprises, carried out tasks, jollied along the demoralized and sorted out 'alarmists'. Their status as communists carried obligations. Any member of the Party or Komsomol who chose not to set a good example for others to follow was coerced, shamed and threatened.

In the railway workers' canteen, a communist disgraced himself in front of everybody. 'He will have to be called in for a firm talking to. The things people are allowing thermselves!', I. S. Namochilin, Head of the Party Propaganda and Agitation Department of the Baltic branch of the Leningrad railway fumes in his diary. The control room staff were also giving cause for concern: 'They too have let themselves go, and keep talking about food and evacuation. They will have to be called in.'[115] Calling people in and bawling them out is his solution for everything. He is trying, of course, to have all the most emaciated admitted to the sickbay, but there are not enough places for everyone.[116] There is nothing he can do to help them, but a communist is not allowed to let himself go.

If it is his duty, by virtue of his calling, to set an example for others to follow, how can he demand to be rewarded for doing so? Leonid Galko noted that seven of the workers in the tool workshop were dystrophic. Should this be taken into account? Should less be expected of them? No – he speaks of that cell of communists with growing irritation and without any allowance for circumstances: 'The work is not up to much, Party work in particular. The secretary of the Party bureau is inactive. Propaganda work is being neglected, professional work completely run down.'[117] This is not a reference for someone seeking admission to the sickbay, rather it is his notes for an all-too-familiar berating.

4

There is no doubt that propaganda, for all its faults (crudeness, suppression of the truth about the situation at the front and in the city, false optimism), helped to maintain the rule of morality. Of course, we should not overestimate its contribution. Radio was barely functioning in the first winter of the siege. From January 1942, almost nobody saw a newspaper. There were none to be bought in the news kiosks, and Dmitry Likhachev recalled: 'The first newspaper began to be pasted up on the fences in the spring, once in every two weeks, as I recall.'[118] People found this absence surprising, and Lev Kogan, who noted, on 3 February 1942, 'The radio is not broadcasting and no newspapers are being delivered', wondered whether the enemy was already operating in the city.[119] Even so, the radio and newspapers did contribute their mite to maintaining moral standards. This is evident from Leningraders' responses to their reports, usually of crimes committed by the Nazis.

The Soviet Information Bureau regularly reported on torture and abuse.

Hoardings throughout the city showed posters depicting the torment of civilians under the heel of the invaders.[120] In newspaper articles, depiction of outrages perpetrated against Red Army prisoners, defenceless women and children, were often accompanied by pathological details. 'Reports of German atrocities enrage the Leningraders. "Reptiles!" is all you hear around the newspaper display cases', Vsevolod Kochetov recalled.[121] In P. M. Samarin's diary we read of his reaction to a radio report of the desecration of the Tolstoy and Tchaikovsky museums: 'Those thugs! Words cannot express my indignation at such barbarity.'[122]

The very emotional Yelena Mukhina, with her keen sense of injustice, expresses her hatred of the oppressors vividly and categorically. Shocked by all the testimony of Nazi villainy, she reacts to each and every report, and her growing thirst for vengeance is striking:

> No, they will pay for all this, for the Leningraders, Muscovites, Kievans and many others killed by their bombing and bombardment; for the mutilated soldiers of the Red Army, for the women and children they have shot, crushed, and torn to pieces. How they are going to pay for the young women and even little girls they have raped; for the small children and women with babies in their arms they have shredded with their explosive bullets, sitting at the controls of their aircraft, hunting them for entertainment. For all this they are going to pay.[123]

All these angry, pitiless responses confirm the basic rules of ethics: you may not hurt people, torture children and those unable to defend themselves; you may not look on indifferently as crimes are committed. But no less striking is the reaction of Leningraders to the publication of a poem by Boris Likharyov which contains the lines, 'and cold-hearted German bitches no more give birth to German vermin'. Vera Inber, relaying the response of citizens to this poem ('They laugh at it') warned, although she expressed herself very diplomatically, that it 'does no credit to this subject'. In her view, 'some literary restraint is called for, some degree of common decency at least'.[124]

5

Another significant contribution to maintaining moral standards was made by radio reports about Leningraders' good deeds, compassion, readiness to help those dear to them. The sentimental tone only strengthened their impact. 'This evening there was a wireless broadcast which tugged at the heartstrings. It was about a little 5-year-old girl who asked her mother for a piece of chocolate and about how, in 1962, she would study the history of the Great Patriotic War', Alexandra Borovikova noted.[125] Helping children was something that featured in the broadcasts, often very emotionally. In V. Peterson's memoirs, we read of her family eagerly awaiting the promised increase in rations for the New Year of 1942:

'And at last, the long-awaited announcement: the bread ration was being increased, and something else besides. At the end of the announcement, the newsreader's voice became even more solemn as, with long pauses in between, he announced, "For the children . . . chocolate . . . 25 grams!"'[126]

Most often, talk of compassion, of love for other people and trying to help them, was heard in the broadcasts of Olga Berggolts. That truly made her the figurehead of Leningrad during the siege, ahead of the thunderously voiced Vsevolod Vishnevsky with his patriotic rhetoric, and Nikolai Tikhonov, whose speeches too artfully struck a balance between tragedy and optimism.

Berggolts leavened emotional speech, which from overuse had lost much of its power, with straightforward, human documents which were touching and sometimes naive. Her tales are, of course, often emotional, but she had a way of telling touching human stories in words with not a hint of officialese or floweriness. She never raises her voice, yet her words invariably strike home.

Such was her tale of a dying Leningrader, Zinaida Karyakina. She managed to survive with the help of others, living and dead, as was not uncommon during the siege. Someone in the army gave her food he had brought to Leningrad, before he was aware that all his family had died. Berggolts's story has a moral: 'She wondered whether she should eat it all herself, but decided that would not be right. It was tempting, of course . . . But that would be a bad thing to do, a sin, and she called through Anna Fyodorovna and a boy, an orphan, from the other room, and an old lady who had found refuge there too.'[127]

The tale may seem over-sentimental and its ending implausible, but there is nothing saccharin about it. The woman at death's door, the unfortunate orphan and the old lady abandoned by all – there is nothing saccharin about that. We have no way of knowing the motivations which led people to do good deeds. Nobody was going to ask their benefactors about that: they were only too happy to be given even a small piece of bread, and too many questions could have led to doubts, excuses and refusals. But such stories did happen, and are referred to in the diaries and memoirs. Olga Berggolts's talks were not without literary artifice, but they were based on the letters of Leningraders themselves. Her words were imbued with profound sympathy and compassion for those most in need, notable for the attention she paid to the minutest details, often devoid of ideological moralizing, and they brought her very close to her listeners. It was most often to her that people talked about their personal tragedies, and her they told about people they had helped.

The power of Berggolts came from the fact that she spoke quietly and sincerely about things everyone understood and had experienced. The morality she inculcated was equally unhysterical, straightforward and decent: 'And Zinaida Yepifanovna and Anna Fyodorovna and the boy survived. All through the winter they shared with each other, and they all survived.'[128]

Means of Reinforcing Morality

In her talks, there is no wordiness (in fact they can seem terse), but their precision and emotional power are extraordinary. This feature came to the fore later in 1943, when Leningrad was shaken by the most barbaric bombing. She tells the story of a boy, P. Diakov, who had both his arms blown off during the shelling. The doctors just managed to save him. In an attempt to take his mind off the pain, his mother took him to the cinema. There was an air raid: the boy lost a leg and his mother was killed.

Berggolts saw him in hospital. 'He tells the story in a strange, wooden voice, in detail, unemotionally.' Now he has nowhere to go: '"I am alone now," he said and turned to the wall, away from people, not crying.'[129]

And then, full force, like a slap in the face: 'One more victory for *Generaloberst* Lindemann.'

6

No amount of control would have been effective if it had been the only means of maintaining moral behaviour. People did not save the lives of children because they felt they were under scrutiny. They did not share their bread because they had read an editorial in *Leningradskaya Pravda*. They did not help back to their feet citizens who had fallen because anyone ordered them to.

Nevertheless, at a time of cataclysm, it was enough for a crack to appear in the edifice of human morality, which might have seemed built to stand for all time, for it to be on the verge of collapse. Control was the cement, if not of particularly high quality, which was used to fill those fractures. They were bound to appear, but compulsion and encouragement, punishment and praise, reduced their number. Thus did appeals to people, and uncompromising demands that they should do their duty, awaken noble sentiments in them, and the candle of charity was not snuffed out.

10

Self-control

Codes of behaviour

1

In a time of calamity, it was natural that people should wish to work out a firm code of conduct for themselves. The rules were not new. The main motive was usually the desire to 'remain human'. Live for others! This moral dictum has a long history. Measuring yourself against the ideal is a feature of many 1930s diaries, especially those of young people. During the war, the sense of disaster gave it particular poignancy. Both the ideal and its political ramifications were often starkly evident.

One incentive was a sense that one had to set an example, to be a person whose heroism was acknowledged, and who had, every day, to demonstrate high moral qualities: 'We are continuing to watch a great play and to act in it. It is going on rather too long. If we regard a month as the equivalent of an act, every structural rule of world drama has been broken.' Not everybody expressed themselves in terms as ornate as the author Anatoly Tarasenkov,[1] but awareness of the unprecedented nature of the epic of Leningrad is to be heard everywhere: 'Where else is the fighting and the privation for freedom endured so steadfastly and heroically?' Ksaveriy Seltser's diary entry is less dramatic, but more in keeping with other documents.[2] Devising a code of conduct is inseparable from this sense of outstanding stoicism, sometimes very deliberately displayed for the benefit of oneself and others. Other diaries, however, were clearly never intended to be exemplary, edifying reading. They endlessly list grams of foodstuffs successfully obtained, the dodges employed in the process, petty insults, rumours, and suspicions whose lack of foundation is later admitted. The same can be said of letters, sometimes only semi-literate, with down-to-earth requests and complaints.

Their writers had no intention of establishing any comprehensive code of good behaviour. For some, the need to 'keep a grip' was because these 'events are huge, unbelievable'.[3] How people behaved was usually dictated by their circumstances. Ye. K. Beletskaya told how she met an NKVD agent who had helped her in the past. He was skeletal, 'barely able to move his legs'. At the sight of him she was unable to hide her fright, the reason for which was only too obvious. It was embarrassing, and she reproached herself afterwards for having been so tactless. 'That meeting forced me to adopt a different, more sensitive, attitude to other people, and try to the best of my ability to help everyone', she wrote later.[4] Evidently it was not the only reason: an insensitive person might have experienced a whole succession of such encounters without becoming any kinder. It is difficult to judge the relative importance of all the elements which brought about her moral choice. What matters is not so much the precise succession of details as the sense of epiphany. The vivid, dramatic nature of the encounter evidently enabled her to feel real pity for a starving person, fixed it in her mind, and went on to provide a benchmark against which to assess her later actions.

For I. Z. Drozhzhina, the milestone in her moral renewal came with news of a fire which nearly killed her mother. Her family's fate was tragic. Almost simultaneously, she lost her baby, heard that her husband and brother had been killed at the front, and her daughter died in an air raid. She lost all interest in the world (how else could she have survived?) and took little care of her mother, until the fire: 'Then I felt pangs of conscience. I had been paying so little attention to Mother. She was 73 years old and I hardly ever visited her. I decided I would take better care of my mother. She was, after all, the only person I had left.'[5]

The strength of family ties is not something you can calculate: its determinants are too complex. The constant fear of being orphaned is only deepened by what is seen every day during the siege: incidents brief or protracted, blurred or only too distinct, but all of them bringing home the fragility of human life. Drozhzhina's tale is very brief, so her path to discovering (or rediscovering) moral truths appears more direct than it probably was, and we detect some of the stereotypes of self-edification. We see a number of the rules for moral behaviour within the family expressed very clearly in the form of a code of conduct: her mother must be protected because she is on her own; she needs to be taken care of and visited more often because of her advanced age.

2

Ethics, like so many other things during the siege, had to be selective. You needed to take care of your parents, but it was sometimes felt that was necessary only if nobody else was able to do so. You needed to help your children, but rations had to be divided equally if everyone was to survive. You should give bread to the hungry, but that usually extended only to those closest to you. Everywhere the time-honoured traditions of ethics had to be tempered by present circumstances. To fulfil every moral obligation to perfection was probably beyond the reach of anyone at this time.

Entries in diaries and confessions in letters presupposed some level of self-analysis, and that had inevitably to touch on the most appalling aspects of the siege. The judgement of a person's fortitude, kindness, self-denial was all based on quantities of bread, porridge and yeast soup. Someone would hear endless talk about food, and vow to take no part in it, never to succumb to the general mood of despondency. B. Zlotnikova wrote in her diary that she wanted to develop her tolerance. She was certain that was within her powers, only what was to be done about her stomach? 'Here, unfortunately, I have no answer to write', she said.[6] Others asked themselves the same question and tried to find a different approach.

'There are too many people whingeing and whining', Irina Zelenskaya notes on 7 December 1941.[7] Who would not want to emphasize their individuality, to let others know they were strong-willed and different in many ways from everybody else? It is a means of asserting yourself. Whingers get on your nerves, and who wants to be counted among the despised and rejected? It is too easy for people to let themselves go, so let them see that some people are capable of rising above that. It is a difficult role to play adequately. Irina Zelenskaya fears her own personality is deteriorating. She flies off the handle more frequently, and cannot overcome feelings of hunger. She finds it difficult to keep conversation about food to the minimum.[8] How is she to behave? What is the best defence against the attrition of life in the siege which eats away at both body and soul? The only solution is to resolve to be steadfast to the end. If you hear squabbling about bread, do not join in. If you feel like complaining, don't, and watch everything you do like a hawk, ascertaining where the temptation is coming from and slamming the door on it. That is the answer given in her 'positive' diary entries: 'Not one single word of dismay or capitulation.'[9]

She has to keep returning to the topic, however, in order to draw a clear line between what is worthy of a human being and what is not. Her entry on 22 November 1941 is a kind of stream of consciousness in which everything surfaces: determination to adhere to her ideals, awareness of all the troubles assailing her and, finally, a means of overcoming her 'animal nature'. The description is not very detailed, but clear enough. It is not original, but she avows it with her usual determination:

No, I am ever more profoundly convinced that one's inner energy is the only salvation, and I will not give up until the last, for as long as my body continues to obey my will. What of it if I too have that disgusting leaden feeling in my legs; if I am beginning to find it an effort to climb the stairs to the first or second floor, when until recently I had no difficulty making it up to the fifth? All this can be surmounted as long as you do not dwell on everything negative, as long as you force yourself to move faster, not to think about food, and especially never complain about anything, to yourself or others. That is the only way to hold on, and hold on I shall, and even help others who are able and wish to have the benefit of my experience.[10]

Alya, a schoolgirl whose notes Ksenia Polzikova-Rubets quotes, does not have the experience of life of Irina Zelenskaya, or her ability to identify the moral significance of her every action. Like most children, she repeats moral prescriptions based on what she has been told. 'We need to be tough and suppress the feeling of hunger by willpower', she notes in her diary on 15 December 1941. Alya is repeating what she has been taught in class, but it is difficult not to see that this too is a call to retain human dignity, even though she has a limited choice of ways of doing so. In teenagers' diaries, where they are formulating their code of conduct, we also find a determination to improve their performance in class, and here the influence of their teachers is even more obvious.

'We need to keep learning, and as well as possible', Alya writes in her diary.[11] In the diary of Yelena Mukhina, another schoolgirl, we find a whole set of rules. They are fairly straightforward, but she pins many hopes on them, and they are binding. 'If I carry out my plan exactly, I will be able to read a lot at home. I need to finish Dickens's *Great Expectations* and then start reading something else. I want to have a "Bolshevik's Bookshelf" and buy various booklets. Then I will need to buy a Russian grammar and repeat all the spelling rules so as not to ruin my essays on literature with grammar mistakes.'[12] We detect here something of a trend. Some things have undoubtedly been instilled in her at school, but much has been reworded in a personal way. The core is the same as in the other diary codes: be tough, do not lose heart, force yourself to work hard and become better. What she is parroting from school is immediately obvious. It differs from the other notes by its didacticism and value judgements, its clichéd language, and almost verbatim quotation from internal school rules and regulations. 'I want us to live as Lenin said. A Soviet school pupil should fight against copying other people's work, playing cards, cigarettes and many other things.'[13]

When schoolchildren are writing about the correct way to behave, they lack any more nuanced, colloquial language. They seem not to know it, and there are no grounds for supposing they deliberately chose to write formally. Of course, there were so many convoluted situations that everyone had of necessity to keep deciding what 'to live as Lenin said' might mean. Any open, detailed discussion of what you could or could not do at a time of such historic turmoil would have burst the banks of primitive school discourse.

3

The letters from Vladimir Maltsev to his father, M. D. Maltsev, are in the same genre of codifying good conduct as we see in the less sophisticated writing of schoolchildren. The topic is set by a letter from his father, wondering whether starvation can turn a man into a scoundrel. In their correspondence, both father and son deliberately avoid the mundane, which would be out of place when great matters are being debated: human dignity, the meaning of life, life and death. A more elevated tone is called for, and more philosophical vocabulary. The only domestic item mentioned is the mess of pottage for which one might betray oneself, a reference to Esau's selling of his birthright for a bowl of lentil stew. The question is: whether there is a price above which you could rightly betray your ideals and surrender your human dignity. It remains opaque which ideals are being discussed and who might be betraying whom. This is seemingly a purely abstract discussion of principles.

The son's reply might seem mannered at first sight, with an evident effort being made to hone the irony: 'I could not sell myself for that tempting bowl of pottage for two reasons. Firstly, it is not a recipe we are familiar with in Leningrad; and secondly, I am quite tight and wary of poor bargains.'[14] He has difficulty continuing in that register and there are lapses in his rhetorical phrasing, although the text is not without emotion and he is clearly attempting to give it a literary turn. Continuing to toy with the image of the stew, he does abandon the heavy-handed witticism and the discussion becomes more frank and open:

> You know, it is difficult, after you have guzzled that pot for free on the basis that you were a Soviet person, to give up that right, just in order to guzzle it again now because you are hungry. I would rather die than give up the hope that in maybe ten or fifteen years' time I may have it again in limitless quantities. The motto of the Guards is one I subscribe to: 'the Guards die before they surrender.' That I can promise you.

The logic here is difficult to follow (partly because of the attempt to play with abstract concepts), and perhaps it just is somewhat confused. The mess of pottage is both a symbol for surrender and a symbol of reward for fortitude. That already seems muddled, and one has the impression that something is only being hinted at. The thought, though, is clear that, if you stand firm today and do not show weakness, do not buckle, you will win the right to a good life in the future. The emotional charge of the son's reply determines the nature of his rhetoric. He is not going to deflate the theme of the unique heroism of the moment with some promise to keep the apartment tidy. Regardless of whether he is genuinely identifying himself with the Guards, he is conscious of his own distinction, and stresses that very clearly. Will he be up to the challenge? Well, he agrees, he is a bit short on fortitude. He is inclined to grumble about the hunger and the dreariness, but that is minor. Where it matters, he is indomitable: 'I will endure all I have to, to the bitter end. I still want to live, and if that means holding out for another six months, a year, five or ten years, so be it. I will endure to the end. However hungry or ill, I will not surrender the citadel. Unless together with my life.'[15]

A bookish register is detectable in this style, and in places its author locates his emotions within the familiar canon of narratives about heroes. He is writing an answer to his father, not just something for himself and, perhaps because of that, vague feelings are formulated more categorically. Although not a code of conduct based on the promise of the

Young Pioneers (it is much more generalized), the themes are the same: the more terrible the reality of the siege becomes, the more correctly a person must conduct themselves. Behave with dignity, always, siege or no siege.

4

Musicologist Yakov Druskin was prompted by some 'ugly scenes' which had occurred the previous day to set out a comprehensive code of conduct in his diary. 'It was my fault', Druskin insists, but it is difficult to guess what kind of 'scenes' these may have been.[16] His notes are not remotely similar to those of others, which often have gruesome tales about life during the siege. His diary is filled almost entirely with religious and ethical meditations. Life under the siege intrudes only rarely, and Druskin seems determined to avoid mentioning the grim reality around him. There is almost no denunciation of other people, and where he does allow that, it is usually mild and accompanied by acknowledgement of mitigating circumstances. He readily accepts blame, views his own actions hypercritically, and it is entirely possible that the scenes he mentions were 'ugly' only because of the mercilessness of his self-criticism.

'Today, 25 November, I am beginning a new life.' With these words he prefaces a set of ethical rules he has devised. The desire to change oneself and start a new life from a precisely identified date is something anyone might do. There comes a moment when the need to feel you are a new person, free from transgressions of the mind and heart, is particularly urgent. Given the uncertainty about what their future life should be like, other people contented themselves with two or three guidelines. For Yakov Druskin, however, given the length, persistence, profundity and radicalism of his preceding pondering of religious and ethical issues, this resulted in a meticulously thought-through code of ethics.

> Firstly, I shall try to cast aside all thoughts and speech relating to the satisfying of hunger, which I am currently experiencing regularly and very acutely.
>
> Secondly, I shall attempt to suppress the sensation of hunger within myself. To achieve that all that is needed is not to think about it before or after a meal, but to think about other people and demonstrate concern for them; or think about the *Treatise on Logic* [a philosophical work he was writing at this time – S. Ya.], or about God.
>
> Thirdly, I shall try always to be joyful, not to raise my voice, not to become angry.
>
> Fourthly, I shall not take offence and not consider it unfair to myself if others talk and act in ways I would not feel were correct. The more so as they may be right, and may understand my thoughts better than I do myself. If they condemn me, I shall agree with them, even if at first that may seem to me wrong and unjust.
>
> Fifthly, if I should not succeed in this, or if I am unjustly reviled,

or if it seems to me that I am unjustly reviled, I shall try to find joy in this and be glad, since this is one of the beatitudes.

Sixthly, I shall try to understand the thoughts and feelings of those close to me with whom I come into conflict, in order not to say or do anything they find disagreeable, providing only that that is not contrary to my conscience. I shall strive to develop sensitivity and tact in myself.

Seventhly, if I have some desire, or if some whim comes to mind, I shall not be upset if I have to renounce it, especially if that is done for the sake of others. That will signify, in the first place, an understanding that all is good, both the whim and the rejection of it; and in the second place, an understanding of the joy of sacrifice.[17]

The thoroughness – at first glance, pedantic – with which Druskin enumerates alternative moral acts is designed to stymie any temptation which may unforeseeably arise. What appears in these points to be repetition is, in fact, another attempt to predict or anticipate courses of action which would lead to a loss of moral orientation.

The everyday reality of the war is patently reflected only in the first points of the code. The rest may be considered more a continuation (or generalization) of Druskin's religious seeking, made more urgent by the circumstanes of the siege but intrinsic to his personality before the war. These are religious truths, but reworked individually and thus made more personal to him. They are supplemented by commentaries, meditations and questionings. He should not think about food, but does wonder whether 'While I am eating, I can nevertheless register its taste.' He is prepared to agree with those who revile him, but acknowledges that it is difficult. He views this ethical code as no more than the beginning of a new way, in which not all the issues have yet been resolved. His set of rules goes on to have new precepts added to it. There is no need for him to go out of the house, because it is possible to do battle with abominations while he is at home. Error must be sought not in others but in ourselves.

Furthermore:

If I feel that I cannot find the right solution, or start feeling offended or that I am being treated unfairly, it is better for me to keep quiet than to try to justify my position, to explain, to argue. In general I will try, when I do not definitely know how to express myself or what to say, just to remain silent; when I feel I am starting to become angry or offended, or when it seems to me I am unjustly reviled, or I can tell that a conversation is not going to lead anywhere, and in general, when there is no pressing obligation to talk, I should remain silent.[18]

Druskin's ideas take an upward spiral, within the circle of his established concepts, prohibitions and assumptions. This is only to be expected, as he extends the number of possible situations in which he may have to defend his choice, and shield himself from various temptations.

We can recognize in this codification of good conduct something predictable in diaries and letters. If they sometimes detail trivial emotions and impressions, we can only expect there will at times be an attempt to set out goals which are considered important. There may, however, be more to it than that. Writing out guidelines is a means of fixing them in the mind, giving additional strength to combat the temptation to infringe them. Using solemn, emotive words reinforces a categorical commitment to uphold the moral ideals accepted. It ensures that they will remain prominent and be remembered, crystallizing all that is best in mankind, and relegating to a less prominent position the more mundane elements of the code.

5

The image of the heroic Leningrader took some time to evolve. The nature of the phenomenon is detailed in Lydia Ginzburg's *Notebooks*. Those who lived through the siege gradually formed what she called a collective self-image:

> They retrospectively delete from their past behaviour all the vacillation, deviations and irritations, and leave only the stereotypical set of actions and results which will get them into the newspapers, the lists of recipients of official awards, and so on. They delete from their consciousness the fact that many remained behind in the city for pragmatic, random or personal reasons; that they were afraid and despaired; that for months their only interest was in food; that they were wicked and pitiless; and that they experienced the most humiliating and dark mental states.[19]

The image of the heroic Leningrader was churned out by the propaganda machine, in the press, on radio and in the cinema. It was trotted out whenever there was a need to thank and encourage citizens, to call upon them to endure hardship fearlessly and accomplish new acts of heroism. Anyone who had a high opinion of how they had behaved during the siege was offered a set of ideological stereotypes. 'It was difficult for people to feel subjectively that they were heroes until they had that explained to them, and were persuaded that they really were', she emphasized.[20]

She believed that, in 1941–2, 'people had other things to do than listen to such explanations',[21] although awareness that life during the siege was something extraordinary and heroic came, not after the Time of Death, but simultaneously with it. It became established in the course of the endless conversations about what people had had to endure during that terrible winter, about their bereavements and losses, the cold and the bombing. Everybody was conscious of the momentousness of what they were having to endure.

We can see from Georgiy Knyazev's diary how the image of a hero is created – someone who may not be particularly conspicuous or free of doubts and failings, but who is invariably steadfast.[22] A refusal to consider one's actions as heroic was also part of what Ginzburg calls the 'idealized image of oneself'. Of course, those actually attempting to survive in the most trying period reflected, to a greater extent than later, the 'unheroic' aspects, the indifference, callousness, deception and theft, but people understood their situation and knew what they had to do. They believed they were acting heroically, and that they should be suitably compensated. 'They say (and it is true) that everywhere, in Tikhvin, Volkhov and Murmansk, particularly in Murmansk, there are trains laden with food. The crates bear the inscription, "Only for Leningrad". We are told there is everything there, even bananas', we read in Vera Inber's diary on 3 January 1942.[23] Lev Livshits, quoting Zhdanov, reported Stalin as having said, 'Take good care of the Leningrad cadres';[24] and M. M. Krakov wrote in his diary on 2 January 1942, 'Stalin is being quoted as having said that, as soon as the blockade of Leningrad is broken, he will provide the residents with convalescent levels of care (in respect of food).'[25]

Heroic Leningraders were tougher, more organized, and did not panic like certain others.[26] These ideas were not only inculcated by propaganda. Those who had survived the first winter of the siege were keen to emphasize their own merit. Vsevolov Vishnevsky stressed in one of his letters that Leningrad 'had been *first* to show how to halt the enemy'.[27] Not everyone wanted to resort to full-blown bombast, but equally no one would have said it was inappropriate. There was sometimes irritation at the rhetoric, and a desire to emphasize modesty, but the terrible wounds of war were there for all to see. Would the mother who, herself on the brink of death, managed to save all her children at the cost of untold suffering have denied herself the accolade of heroism? To assert that she had done nothing out of the ordinary would have been taken as an insult in a Leningrad strewn with corpses. But acknowledging your own heroism (which included how you had coped with everyday living), taking pride in the fact that you were among those who had persevered and not been broken, and expressing that publicly, in conversations, arguments and counterarguments, also brought with it greater responsibility. 'This is an accolade which will persist', Lydia Ginzburg wrote:

because it will become a benchmark, it will be invoked. An unalterable average expectation of behaviour has been manufactured against which, as always, average people will subconsciously measure themselves. To fall short of this average would be to admit one's inferiority, which people cannot accept. This average does not mean, for example, you may not squabble, be greedy and haggle about rations, but it does mean that, not so long ago, you would not have said, 'I refuse to go where I have been sent because I am afraid of being killed by the shelling.' That statement would at best have been met with a

stony silence. Almost no one would have said it and, more importantly, almost no one behaved that way.[28]

6

In the early days of the siege, refusing to be evacuated was often considered an essential feature in a heroic Leningrader. Those caught in the
siege saw many things in terms of life on the front line. Leaving the city
was tantamount, in their opinion, to cowardice and baseness, and they
sometimes called those who left 'deserters'. They had no hesitation about
saying of them that they had 'made themselves scarce'. It would be inac-
curate to say that attitude came only from 'above'. The authorities were
in something of a quandary: while urging everyone to repel the advancing
enemy and defend their native city to the last, they were simultaneously
making a major effort to empty Leningrad of 'dependants', trying to force
them (sometimes with threats) to leave their homes. The reluctance of
Leningraders to leave the city may have been reinforced by contempt for
those who desperately wanted to leave,[29] especially if they had been at the
forefront of those calling for Leningraders to defend their city.[30]

'It is a very unpleasant sight', B. Zlotnikova wrote in her diary, after
watching departing Leningraders.[31] Others expressed themselves more
forthrightly. Their remarks have the tone of a stinging rebuke, as if they had
been personally insulted: 'What are these fugitives going to write after the
war? And how will they face Leningraders who stuck it out?' This was said
openly at a meeting of writers in the Baltic Fleet's Political Directorate in
February 1942.[32] Even where the need for evacuation was recognized, there
were times when no argument could neutralize the aversion to 'fugitives'.
Esfir Levina noted in her diary that evacuation was essential to save lives
in the besieged city, and that Leningrad was better off without people who
could not even stand. These people would find useful work in other regions.
All that might be true, but she did not want to meet those leaving 'in order
not to say something rude to them'.[33] People who did later return to the city
were conscious of hostility on the part of Leningraders who had remained.[34]

Explaining why he was refusing to leave, K. M. Ananyan said he had
no moral right to do so.[35] One's attitude to evacuation was a touchstone:
rejecting it was to repudiate cowardice, treachery, selfishness and indifference to the fate of your family. Instead, you were displaying courage,
steadfastness and self-sacrifice. To some extent, this was a recycling of the
basic concepts of official propaganda, and was expressed in the language
associated with it. Sometimes, the arguments shade into lyrical declarations of love for the city. People could also have mixed patriotic and more
worldly motives for staying.

Not all motivations, which could be quite prosaic, were acknowledged.
There was fear of the unknown, reluctance to be a burden to other people,
and fear that apartments would be looted in their absence. It is revealing,
nevertheless, that the moral arguments tended to be given greatest promi-
nence, thereby doggedly supporting moral standards. During the Time of

Death, when thousands of people were evacuated, these considerations lost nearly all their force, but in September–October 1941 they were first articulated very clearly, and helped to contain the threatened wholesale demoralization of the populace.

'The standard phrase you hear from men who are running away, flying away or otherwise departing is, "I'm only taking my family out and will be back soon." It is becoming increasingly exasperating to hear that', we read in Izrail Metter's notebooks.[36] Other excuses for leaving stressed how dear Leningrad was to the speaker, how sad they were to leave, how long they had hesitated before taking the decision, and what remorse they felt afterwards. It was particularly stressed that it was not fear which made them leave.[37]

The main thrust of all these excuses was that one felt superfluous in a city one was powerless to help. 'All I could have done would be freeze, die of starvation, be lost. I lay under a pile of rags, listened to Olga Berggolts's poetry on the radio, and wept', the poet Lev Druskin recalled.[38] This theme features in considerable detail in the later diaries of Yevgeny Shvarts, dated 1956–7. He destroyed his siege diaries when he left Leningrad in December 1941, and the later description has plainly been simplified. There are none of the unexpected twists, pointed silences and paradoxes typical of the rest of the prose in his diaries. Ornate flourishes are inappropriate in excuses, where the simplicity of the words needs to be in harmony with the simplicity of the explanation. How could he be of help to the city? 'It would somehow be embarrassing to go into a bomb shelter with women, children and the elderly, but neither could I just sit at home.'[39] He did not immediately decide to leave, and went to work at Broadcasting House in the hope of being of some use there. He did not, of course, leave Leningrad because he was afraid of being killed, but because staying in the city was so pointless.[40] He was hardly ever invited to broadcast, and acting as an air-raid warden on the roofs of houses was unnecessary, since the last heavy raid had taken place on 7 November 1941.

The shakiness of his excuses is obvious. When he left, he could hardly have been sure that air raids would not resume the following day, and he might have been called back to broadcast on the radio at any minute. No doubt there was work for all in besieged Leningrad. But these were not the main reasons. Deciding not to remain in the city was clearly perceived as something that needed to be explained away again and again. He was not afraid, but 'tormented by the pointlessness of the situation'. There were places where people could fight. 'There, on the front line, the duties of each person were plain.'[41] Here, however, he could only take cover with the sick and vulnerable, the old and the very young. Was that more moral? What else could he do – just endure?

Other people's excuses are less extended, but they are still excuses. 'He said he had been born here and that Leningrad was infinitely dear to him, but he had been deeply affected by the death of his son' – that was how the head of the building section explained his wish to be evacuated to Georgiy

Kulagin.[42] The writer Veniamin Kaverin explained that the main reason for his abrupt departure was because the state security police were trying to recruit him as an informer: the only way to avoid it was by accepting evacuation. Why were these explanations necessary? Because otherwise it would be difficult to seem a decent person, not only many years after these events, but also at the time, during the siege: 'Rumours were spread that I left on my own initiative, from cowardice, without the knowledge and permission of my superiors. Echoes of those rumours may well be found in letters written during the years of the siege.'[43] The decision was complicated in this case by the fact that honouring one moral precept might necessitate undermining another. Would it have been preferable to stay in the city and escape insinuations of cowardice, at the price of becoming a snoop for the secret police? What was more reprehensible, to leave Leningrad at a difficult time or to betray your friends? That is the choice as he presents it, but at least he made his choice with full acknowledgement of the demands of morality and honour.

There could be many reasons for seeking evacuation. Later, there was nothing to be discussed: everybody left who could, and there was accordingly no need to worry what other people might think and to offer excuses. The endless processions of swaddlings clearly justified the work of those who had been trying to empty the city of 'dependants'. But the very fact that people wanted to stay, and to find patriotic and moral arguments in favour of that, and, of course, the sense of shame felt by those who left, did maintain in people's minds respect for the precepts of morality, however difficult it might prove to live up to them in real life.

7

With status come obligations. On 6 December 1941, A. Berman was appointed controller of the issuing and auditing of ration cards for food, bread and manufactured goods. 'The district committee selected only the most steadfast and trustworthy people for this work.' She is clearly proud to have been chosen. She is hungry herself and understands what it means to be deprived of your last piece of bread. She will do her duty honourably: 'We have been put in charge of something supremely valuable. We have been entrusted with taking good care of every last gram of bread and distributing food ration cards.'[44] She knows some people are 'playing games with other people's cards and coupons and [are] on the brink of moral degeneracy'. That is something she would never do, and the district committee had good reason to select her as its most honest official.

Staff at the food office were shouting at visitors and this was going on 'in starving Leningrad'. She is outraged. She wrote a report about abuse of ration cards by a certain housing management team, but the head of the auditing office told her not to make a mountain out of a molehill. What molehill? 'I am fighting for every gram of bread, and when I detect a gram stolen from our starving population, I take it as seriously as looting at the front. I can and will do no other, even if some people do not like it.'[45]

Being malnourished herself, she finds it difficult to climb the stairs of the countless buildings to check on claims for lost ration cards. She is afraid to let go of the banisters and pauses on every landing. Perhaps she does not really need to be so meticulous? No! 'This is the only way. We have to account for every last gram of bread.'

What she confronted in the very first apartment she inspected, shocked her: 'All eight people, members of a family of workers, are dying from dystrophy. They have lost their cards.' They probably had plenty to tell her. What abysses of grief they would have to reveal to someone on whom their lives depended. Berman's charity was not for show, not something designed to impress those who had given her such a flattering assessment. The time has come to show in practice that she is worthy of their trust, and Berman's writing style is suddenly stripped of its usual emotion. The speed with which this happens is further evidence of her sincerity. The small domestic items she includes do not obscure or muddle the description. 'Form is content and content is form', said Hegel. The rhetoric of the form fits the pathos of the action. 'I went to the canteen and got them to give me three plates of soup against my coupons for the second ten days, which I brought back to the family in a jar. I had no bread, though, because they cannot issue that in advance, and I had already eaten my ration for today.'[46] Here is one of the most striking instances of human compassion, modestly expressed, without affectation and with touching apologies. Perhaps later on she was unable to be so generous, but here is her first instinctive response to disaster, without calculation, without commentary.

With status come obligations. Georgiy Knyazev (and he it usually is) wrote about the moral duty of the intelligentsia. Who, if not the intelligentsia, the guardian of moral commandments, must bear this ordeal with dignity? He, for his part, tries to maintain, when meeting people, 'courtesy and a gentle manner, to make life easier for everyone'.[47] People can dig up many instances of spiritual degeneracy among the intelligentsia, and some believe it was among them that the loss of willpower was most clearly identifiable. Against that, let us not overlook the fact that in hundreds of siege documents they have left us, a sense of their special obligations is conspicuously present. It would have been hard for any member of the intelligentsia not to have been conscious that their behaviour was under scrutiny by others who singled them out from the rest. They expected support from the intelligentsia, and passed on in perplexity and surprise rumours of their moral lapses. One person might help back to their feet someone who had fallen; another might share their bread, give comfort, help with moving items. There was no narcissism about this, but a firm belief that it was the only permissible way for an intellectual to behave.

Olga Peto met a boy in the street who was barely able to stagger along and had a fixed, distracted expression:

When I asked him his name he mumbled something unintelligible. 'I'm hungry.' Then, suddenly and angrily, 'Why ask? You won't feed me.' When she promised to give him food, he walked behind her. He obviously did not trust her, but had no alternative. He walked in silence, asking nothing. It was quite a long way, and he began to realize she was not just going to brush him off with an expression of sympathy or she would hardly be taking him so far.

'Suddenly he stopped and caught hold of me by the sleeve. "Wait, missus, I'll tell you everything. I'm called Vova."'

He was not a ragamuffin or a thief, and it was through no fault of his own that he had become so dirty and degraded, begging for a crust of bread. He was from a respectable family, and even showed her a photo of his family which he kept wrapped in several scraps of paper. Perhaps he kept it with him because at every step he encountered contempt for himself and did not want to reconcile himself to that. His father was at the front, his mother had starved to death, and his sister was in hospital. His ration cards had been stolen, his room burgled, and he had been refused new ration cards for the coming month.

'As he told me all this, Vova wiped away tears with his dirty sleeve. "Only believe me, missus, I've never stolen anything."' He could not stop talking, and she spent a long time trying to steady his nerves.[48]

8

You could not one day just discard your grimy jacket, find better clothes, get up, get washed and tidy your apartment, but even so people wanted others to know they were not like all the rest, they were better. They explained that however they could, mentioning their exemplary behaviour, that they were from a good family, that they had worked tirelessly until the last minute. They believed virtue should be properly recognized, and the expectation of support as a reward led to recognition of the value of moral behaviour.

Vera Inber met a worker in a hospital crammed with 'living corpses'. 'He could barely move his tongue, and kept repeating just one thing: "Seventeen years . . . seventeen years on the factory floor."'[49] Political organizer Ye. Sharypina, looking for debilitated workers, found a starving woman in an apartment who had lost her ration cards. Sharypina explained to her in detail how to get them restored and the woman, who had evidently given up all hope, suddenly revived: '"I worked as a seamstress at the Shveinik factory, making army tunics, I overfulfilled the quota."'[50] She had been working for the front, giving her all, and who could deserve help more than she? It was right that the political organizer had come to see her; it was right that she was being cared for. She had deserved that.

On 18 March 1942, members of the Komsomol household squad of October district found a man lying motionless in a room: 'We told him we had come to help him but he did not believe us. He watched us silently and mistrustfully.' The suspicion of a helpless siege victim was understandable: feeling incapable of standing up for himself, he probably saw any intrusion into his home as a threat. The 'soldiers' of the squad cleaned his room, washed him and bandaged his legs, and heated some tea for him. He seemed suddenly to come to his senses: 'The man started talking. He said he was a radio operator. He had worked and fought to the last, until he had no strength left at all.'[51]

Regarding yourself as a member of the political elite, as a communist or Komsomol member, also helped prevent Leningraders from offending against moral principles. They could not, even if they wanted to, completely shrug off the prescribed standards of behaviour. In the press, at meetings and rallies, and in conversations, it was persistently explained to them that the first duty of communists was to set an example for waverers. They were not allowed to behave differently, and must not dare to be found among the 'whingers', alarmists or the self-centred. One Leningrader recalled her communist father haranguing his wife. He was dissatisfied that she had become so disconsolate:

You are a communist. Why are you lying there? You may not. If you lie down what is going to happen to Tanya [their daughter – S. Ya.]? It will mean Tanya dies too. Who will look after her? You must get up. It is your duty. Only we, communists, must somehow find a way to fight on. It is our duty. We must help each other, we must raise . . .

The repetition is noteworthy. He evidently found these arguments effective and, by repeating them, was also persuading himself of them: 'In fact, he was always going on like that: "Communists, communists. Our duty, our duty." And my mother did get up.'[52]

'We are, after all, the leaders, and if we start whingeing, what are the workers going to say?', Alexandra Borovikova asked her diary during the Time of Death.[53] The secretary of the Lenin district Party committee compelled his wife to be among the first to accept evacuation in order to silence mutterings from other people: 'I told her we had to set an example.'[54] Of course, this demonstration of fortitude and self-sacrifice had a utilitarian purpose, but even that was of value. There was no insurmountable barrier separating the public from the private. It was impossible to be two-faced, continuously to serve two masters and two separate moralities. The entry in Party administrator Nikolai Ribkovsky's diary was hardly written in order, as people said in those days, 'to be shown to the authorities'. It is chaotic, with little in the way of rhetoric (it is more lyrical), and the image of the steadfast Soviet worker is diluted by scenes of hunger affecting everyday life and complaints about his infirmity. Ribkovsky very much needed to obtain some items in short supply to send to his wife and daughter, and this immediately placed him in a moral quandary. He is not unduly sensitive about his reputation, and sometimes writes without a blush about having access to food not available to others. This, however, is a different situation: it is not a matter of accepting help when it is offered, but of making an outright request, a demand, and playing an unseemly game in the process. This he is reluctant to do: 'Of course, I could buy them quickly, under the counter, through people I know, but that is something I really do not care for. It is unpleasant even to hear people saying, "Yes, he got hold of it, arranged it by pulling strings."' There is a red line he will not cross: 'It would be wrong, unfair.'[55]

With status come obligations. Joining the Komsomol brought obligations, as members were regularly reminded. 'When you were joining the Komsomol, you wrote that you wanted to replace your brother, but you are not performing as your brother did', a worker was told at a meeting of Komsomol members at Factory No. 5.[56]

Reading the minutes of Komsomol meetings, you notice that those members accused of misconduct always make excuses, but never protest when they are reprimanded for breaking the rules. They are willing to acknowledge their guilt and undertake to rectify shortcomings as quickly as possible. 'My absence from work was connected with the difficult period of January–March, when I had to rush home and did not feel very well. At the present time all these difficulties are behind us and we members of the Komsomol must return to work.'[57] Such was the apology of a member at a Komsomol meeting at the Red Bavaria factory, as if during that 'difficult period' there had not been corpses littering the streets and buildings, and people crawling about on the ground who lacked the strength to get back to their feet.

It is possible that these confessions were extracted under compulsion. To be expelled from the Komsomol left young people feeling inferior, and could mean trouble, sometimes very serious trouble. Komsomol discipline was seen as no less mandatory and unchallengeable than the discipline imposed at work, school and college.

We have ultimately no way of telling whether acceptance by Young Communists of their superior political and, by extension, moral status was voluntary or imposed. The documents that touch upon the subject do, to a greater extent than other sources, bear the impress of Soviet-era mythology. This acceptance did, nevertheless, have a real importance. It bolstered the code of moral behaviour during the disasters. It was not something you could think about, but something you were required to implement unquestioningly. It can hardly have been observed by all members, but diverging from the rules led to the need for subsequent repentance, apologies, explanations and promises, and in the circumstances of the siege that was no small matter.

Introspection

1

Introspection is a standard device for those who write diaries and letters; it is due to the generic peculiarities of these documents. Writing down a daily account of your actions inevitably culminates in an evaluation of them, without any need for a special effort or melodramatic gestures. But evaluation is a means of checking your behaviour. It prompts you to 'reread' yourself. How productive this is will depend on the degree of frankness, ability to consider your actions objectively, and willingness to look inside yourself constantly.

Several kinds of introspection can be identified, which are largely determined by a person's cultural level, bent for philosophical reflection, and ability to analyse, to play with concepts, and weave what Thomas Mann called 'living, spiritual, insignificant veracity' into the literary text of a memoir. Introspection as a systematic, self-conscious approach to self-improvement usually requires the elaborate structuring of autobiographical, moralizing stories such as we find in memoirs. People more commonly watch themselves without giving too much thought to why they are doing it or where it may lead. The morality is uncomplicated, the examples graphic, and the conclusions obvious.

More complex kinds of introspection are analysed by Boris Eikhenbaum in his famous study of the young Tolstoy.[58] Introspection, as reflected in Tolstoy's early diaries, is systematic and edifying; it is openly didactic, sometimes casuistically interweaving 'soul' into the minor details of the everyday life which sustains it. Tolstoy's codes of moral behaviour are polished so meticulously and pedantically as sometimes to become, in Eikhenbaum's view, comically over-simplified. There is a lot here which is shared with the methods of introspection practised by most of our diarists. There is speech addressed to oneself, dissatisfaction expressed at one's actions, emotional engagement and the search for a path to spiritual renewal.

The complex kinds of introspection found in the notes written by people who remained in Leningrad during the siege are most extensively studied in the literature devoted to Lydia Ginzburg's *Notes from the Blockade* [translated by Alan Myers, edited by Emily van Buskirk, London, 2016]. Referring to the adoption of memoir stereotypes by writers of diaries and memoirs, Irina Paperno quotes an aphorism from Michel de Certeau: 'This is a special kind of reading, where someone else's text is used for the projection of one's own life: the book is populated as one might someone else's apartment.'[59] Ginzburg's *Notes* is a multi-layered text whose origins are not always clear and the reasons for its creation have yet to be fully researched. The same is true of the devices Ginzburg uses. Many scholars are convinced that the primary influence was that of Alexander Herzen, to whose memoir-writing Ginzburg devoted a book.

Literary devices cannot, of course, always be seen as the property of any particular writer. Even open acknowledgement by authors who have been unusually influenced by the style of another rarely explains very much. Everything has invariably been reworked, complicated, sometimes intricately restructured, not as the paraphrase of a classical canon but as its antithesis, and the initial concept of a book cannot be isolated from later influences.

The structuring of introspection in accordance with a particular literary tradition changes its form and content. Here, there is a need for digressions; there, a need for moral maxims. Here, emotions are treated more freely; there, a more elevated tone is called for.[60] To maintain fully a narrative scheme based on generic stereotypes is something few are likely to manage: the scheme will be disrupted, if by nothing else, by the logic of chronological description of the stages of a life. It is nevertheless capable of distorting the image of the introspection of those caught in the siege.

I selected diaries and letters in which conscientiousness and duration of the introspection were most marked. Not many meet those criteria. In daily entries we more commonly find brief assessments of the writer's own behaviour, not particularly profound, often fragmentary, jotted down in passing and contributing little to the overall fabric of the narrative. In the diaries and letters I have studied – those of Maria Mashkova, Yakov Druskin, Yelena Mukhina, G. A. Gelfer, Vladimir Lyublinsky and Vladimir Maltsev – it is clear that they are less a vehicle for describing trivial details of everyday life during the siege than a means of self-education. We cannot give a straightforward answer to the question of whether they are typical of the thousands of other documents of 1941–2. We would only emphasize that the methods of introspection characteristic of the vast literature of siege memoirs and letters are here applied systematically, shown more clearly, and are often dominant when episodes in the history of Leningrad during the war are being illuminated. Introspection is integral to these writings. Its methods are the main structural principle maintaining system, consistency and emotional integrity in the presentation of events.

Tolstoy said: 'The cement which binds every work of art into a single unit and thereby creates the illusion of reflecting life is, not the fictional integrity of characters and situations, but the integrity of the distinctive moral attitude of the author to his topic.'[61] We can adapt this by saying that the integrity of these descriptions derives from the individual moral assessments of their authors, which are sometimes very uncompromising and unforgiving. Attention is often focused not on episodes which were the most important in the attempt to survive, but on stories in which morality is very prominent. Is your behaviour that of a good human being, or is it becoming mired in selfishness and callousness? Often this is the backbone of the tale. It is essential to be able to empathize with daily life during the Time of Death, with the interrelatedness of its constituent parts, and to be aware of the unique methods of introspection of each of the writers of these diaries and letters. If it seems that the exposition of this process of self-education has been fragmented by the present author, that is to some extent unavoidable: we cannot prescribe the direction in which our writers will move. Instead, we must follow them on their own tortuous path, sometimes coming to a standstill, sometimes moving backwards.

2

In everyday life, people naturally respond to everything that happens in their vicinity. Their eye notes both the unusual and the commonplace. The Time of Death was so full of dramatic episodes that powers of observation (and self-observation, which is related) were particularly acute. You could not take a step without seeing someone about to fall or who had already fallen, and had to decide whether to give them your hand, when you were afraid you might fall yourself. There was no escape from the pleading of family and friends, and of complete strangers. Should you share your bread with them when you yourself were suffering from hunger? And so it was at every turn: constant self-scrutiny, often accompanied by remorse and self-justification. The focus came to be on things which, before, you would hardly have given a second thought, which would have seemed self-evident.

Why was it considered an act of self-sacrifice to 'give your last plug of tobacco to a comrade, or allocate a sick member of your family 10–15 grams of your butter ration'? That was the question posed in a letter by Vladimir Lyublinsky, who worked at the Public Library. And why would you not just perform some feat of heroism easily, simply, as a matter of course? For him, that is a crucial question.

We detect in Lyublinsky's rhetorical question a determination to keep to the framework of the old morality, which had been undermined by the Time of Death but remained in the minds of Leningraders as the bench-mark for measuring degrees of moral deterioration.

If there is no set of standards, you cannot tell what is acceptable, and many were not yet prepared to switch to another, much harsher, 'siege' set of moral standards. It seems unlikely that by February 1942, after a terrible winter, Lyublinsky still could not see what was so special about those 'trivial' gifts and the logic of what he calls a 'dislodging of concepts'. The Time of Death really did demand, of those still prepared to help, an incredible effort and endless soul-searching. By then one could hardly say the choices were easy. Nevertheless, we must agree with his diagnosis that, 'ultimately, the much-needed spontaneity in people's behaviour was being replaced by heightened self-monitoring and pondering over every unshared piece of food'.[62]

Recording the results of one's introspection in diaries and letters could be undertaken for a number of reasons. The first, and probably most important, was fear of degenerating. The issue was not only preserving one's human dignity, but life itself. The stages by which siege victims died were obvious to everyone, because they were regularly repeated in the same sequence: domestic disorder, hunger, cold, bombing; leading to apathy, loss of interest in the outside world, a weakening of family and other social ties, indifference to one's appearance, to one's clothing; abandonment of civilized behaviour; a readiness to accept any humiliation to obtain a crust of bread, to endure insults, ridicule and contempt from other people; loss of the will to resist and, finally, death.

In their determination to avoid this fate, those caught in the siege often viewed moral standards not as an end in themselves but as a means of bolstering their fortitude. People clung with great tenacity to the view that those who survived were those who helped others and did not lose the will to live. The miracle of survival was explained in precisely this way: life was a gift awarded to those who saved the lives of others. If this was just the easiest way to interpret what happened, it was not seen as paradoxical at the time.

In introspection there could be no divorcing of body and soul, which explains the intense interest in the stages and forms of disintegration of personality. This is perhaps most convincingly expressed in a diary entry of 18 February 1942 by Public Library librarian Maria Mashkova: 'The worst of it is that, under the impact of severe starvation, friendly, intimate, family relations collapse. You cease to be quite human; how shamefully you tremble at the sight of a piece, even a minute piece, of bread, and how you grudge giving it to even the person closest and dearest to you.'[63]

The obvious causal link (hunger leads to degeneration) seems here to be deliberately ignored. It is not the poverty of everyday life which has the consequence that people cease to be quite human, but the other way round: the loss of human dignity expresses itself in a number of ignoble actions. The difference might seem insignificant, but it is crucial: if primacy is given to the cold and hunger, degeneration becomes straightforward and forgivable. You must be allowed no excuses; there can be no extenuating circumstances. Your account of yourself must be deliberately biased, and that is evident in the choice of words. You do not forgivably 'vacillate', but contemptibly 'tremble', and before the verb there is the adverb 'shamefully'. The first priority is your duty as a human being, irrespective of the circumstances, with no excuses. If today you begrudge giving a minute piece of bread, tomorrow everything will come to an end as you descend into callousness. That is Mashkova's logic in this entry, and characteristic of her diary as a whole.

3

Mashkova's diary entry remarks on only one of the signs of degeneration. In other diaries, we find a more extended and intent monitoring of the various stages. Commentary may be scattered all through the diary, covering a considerable period, but no less frequently it scrupulously depicts the rapid foundering of personality in a few short moments of crisis. Goethe once remarked that there is nothing more instructive about normality than pathology, so it is very important that diarists in their introspection are conscious of the horror of the situation in which they find themselves, peering again and again into the abysses surrounding them as if they are trying to anticipate which direction danger will come from.

The final entries in Yelena Mukhina's diary are of considerable interest. By May 1942, she was on the brink of a precipice. She now had no family left in Leningrad. The hopelessness, despair, the unremitting hunger began rapidly to undermine her spirits. She had been promised evacuation at the end of May and was looking forward to it impatiently, day by day, but now questioned whether there was any point in leaving. Her diary entry of 25 May 1942 paints a depressing picture of her mental state, the main symptoms of which are lethargy and weakness: 'I am so weak now that I no longer care. My brain does not react to anything. I feel half asleep.' She mentions her weakness again and again: it gives unity to the story of herself. It is described as something progressive and irreversible.

Are there other signs of extinction? She again gives a detailed description of her condition, restating, or rather intensifying, her earlier assessments, finding new words, emphasizing the increasingly alarming nature of what is happening to her 'Total lack of energy. Listless, tormented eyes. I walk like a category three invalid, barely able to hobble, climbing three steps with difficulty.'

Yes, she is failing, but she resists, perhaps not very firmly, perhaps not fully aware of the fact. She resists by going back to memories of life as it used to be, noticing how her appearance has changed. She is puzzled that, being now so accustomed to her meagre bread ration and no longer feeling hungry, she is continuing to weaken. She has a sense of the norm, and continually compares past and present, noting the gradual progression of signs of deterioration:

> With every passing day I am becoming weaker and weaker. What remains of my strength is drying up by the hour. Before, say, a month ago, I felt so hungry in the afternoon I would become determined to go out and find something to eat. I would go to the ends of the earth for an extra piece of bread or anything edible, but now I hardly feel the hunger. In fact, I do not feel anything at all.[64]

Her language is still metaphorical, and she is trying to preserve the integrity of her words and not lapse into gibberish. Her sentences remain complete and meaningful.

4

The same techniques of introspection are found in the diary of G. A. Gelfer, a foreman at the Stalin factory. There are grounds for comparing the content and development of the confessions of Gelfer and Yelena Mukhina, despite the differences of personality, experience, culture and age. Both diarists seems to be viewing themselves from outside, with the same metaphorical language and relentless emphasis of the most alarming features of their degeneration: 'I can paint my portrait in just a few words. Imagine a man with bleary eyes (hungry, grey, listless), whose clothes hang on him like a sack, with slow, senile movements, the soft, lethargic voice of a sick man, and total inner debility.'[65]

This depiction of his disintegration betrays considerable literary polishing. The bleary, hungry grey eyes are not a clinical diagnosis, but a focusing of his outward appearance to reflect his inner condition better. Irritation tends generally to be accompanied by exaggeration of the disagreeable, and that is what Gelfer chooses to emphasize. He not only sees his decline, but the whole tone of the passage is disparaging: 'Did I ever imagine myself looking like this? Did I ever dream I would be reduced to such a state?'[66]

This perpetual criticism of himself, despite its relentlessly self-pitying tone, is like a medicine, bitter but powerfully healing, capable of shaking a person out of their torpor and restoring their willpower. This intensely negative self-evaluation, the special emphasis on the most repugnant details and the vividness with which they are displayed, can be seen as a form of resistance. This person is not meekly submitting to his circumstances but railing against them, and again comparing the present with the past.

Dissatisfaction at one's appearance and with oneself, at one's symptoms of deterioration, is a prerequisite for the return of the will. We hear in it the ring of implacable determination and toughness. In an entry a few days later, on 23 January 1942, Gelfer continues his detailed description of life in the siege, paying less attention now to himself and more to the conditions in which he lives. 'For several months now I have been sleeping without undressing. I have not been to the bathhouse for two months.' This entry too ends with an emotional comment in which there is, not despair, but an unflinching assessment of himself: 'If I go on like this I will end up infested with lice. How low I have sunk. I cannot bear to look at myself.'[67]

5

The more merciless and unsentimental, even brutal, a description of supposed faults, the more robustly moral is the conclusion reached. Lurid representation of extreme degeneration is accompanied by an injunction to oneself which has the force of an order. 'I'm tired of myself. I've really gone to the dogs. Often in the morning I'm too lazy to wash. I just lead an animal existence. Eat and sleep, that's all I am capable of', 16-year-old Vladimir Maltsev writes, detailing his life in the siege in a letter to his mother and sister.[68] Does this signal acceptance that he has been defeated, that he is giving up all hope of regaining his human dignity?

Before us is a kind of confession, not without a degree of self-abasement. The analysis of his behaviour is one-sided, brief and oversimplified. Vladimir makes no attempt to delve deeply into its causes but, again, more important is the fact that he is thinking about the sources of degradation. It is not merely a measure of deterioration, but also a warning of dangers to be avoided: 'If it goes on like this for another couple of months I will turn into a caveman.'[69]

The value of taking a negative view of oneself can be seen in other documents. Maria Mashkova notes in her diary on 5 March 1942, 'I am living and behaving in full view of Vadik [her son – S. Ya.], who has grown up a lot. So what am I supposed to do with my bowl of soup with somebody hungry watching me? Vadik is getting a lesson he will remember all his days. He is learning how to live his life from me, and I am behaving like a harsh, callous, miserly person.'[70] Her judgements are so self-critical they prevent her taking an objective look at an obvious truth. She should drink the bowl of soup herself and not hand it to her son because, if his mother dies of hunger, so will he, as other victims of the siege look apathetically on. These were the only possible rules of survival in the nightmare of the siege, but observing them undermined the foundations of family ethics. The relentless system, and obligatory nature, of food distribution within families during the siege drove them apart and made relationships less emotional and coarser.

Such was the new siege ethics, which it was still difficult to accept, but whose rules had to be obeyed. Its aim was to save lives, just not by acting in what had previously been considered the only way possible: by giving away your last crust, sacrificing what you could not do without and giving no thought to tomorrow. The formula for saving lives was different: you must deny a person what he asked for, ignore his moans, pleas and cries, take no account of the age and health of those in need, not deprive yourself of what you could have given to someone weaker and, instead, not succumbing to entreaties, yourself take responsibility for deciding what was in the best interests of the person begging.

The transition to the new ethics was seen as trampling on moral boundaries which those caught in the siege had been brought up since childhood to respect and which were an integral part of their identity, the principles on which they based their behaviour. Maria Mashkova's distress was the anguish of a sincere and sensitive woman, resisting the transition but aware that it was inevitable.

The new ethics had to be recognized as a fact, but, as far as possible, people continued to measure their actions against the old ethics. Yes, an egalitarian sharing of food was unavoidable; but how were you supposed to raise a child to become a decent, moral adult if, when he asked for bread, he saw it being eaten in front of him, not even shared? That was the question. And what about your own morality? How easy it was to become callous if you looked away every time you made eye contact with your starving family members.

It seemed entirely possible not to notice any moral problem here. One could shelter oneself behind references to the inexorable laws of survival, to how this was in the best interests of those you loved. In Maria Mashkova's diary entry, we see the sense of guilt of those who have no cause to reproach themselves, but for whom reproaching themselves seems a more human response than justifying themselves. The moral position for Mashkova is not rejection of the rules of life during the siege. They are essential. It is impossible to live without them. They will wither away when the war is over. It is to continue, nevertheless, to protest about the downside of siege morality. That is never going to be forgotten, and people

will still be held relentlessly in thrall to its past wrongs and injustices long
after all trace of the siege is gone.

6

Maria Mashkova describes with horror the degeneration of people she
has known since before the war. In April 1942, she chanced to meet
12-year-old Igor, and his appearance astounded her: 'You feel not pity but
horror. He looks like an old man, barely able to shamble along. His face is
emaciated and he has bags under his eyes. Unshaven, dirty.' Demoralized,
and prepared to cling to anyone who might be able to help him, Igor told
her his bitter story: 'His mother is dying and he had crawled to the shop to
get 100 grams of butter.'[71] Perhaps Mashkova promised him something,
because the following day he visited her. 'Hungry and miserable. Cannot
walk without a stick. Lost his bread ration card, weakened by hunger.'
Mashkova writes that her son and husband were equally horrified to see
how this boy they had known had changed out of all recognition: 'Vadim
whispered to me, "Mum, give him my rissole." Vsevolod offered him his
bread, miraculously left over after lunch.'

'I fed him and we warmed him up. He is terribly weak, spoke uncontrollably, muddling events.' He was close to the turning point which led
to death: 'He does not complain about his mother.' This particularly
incensed Mashkova. Only someone completely on their own could be
in such a state, yet Igor still had family. Shortly afterwards, she went to
visit them and was profoundly shocked. The room was filthy and his sick
mother was lying in bed. That came as no surprise, as Mashkova notes.
What shocked her was something else: 'The woman was like a wolf, no
longer human because of the hunger. Her only concern was to seize Igor's
food, her only fear that he might snatch a crust of bread from her, or drink
a spoonful of soup made from her grain ration.'[72]

Of all the worries the dying mother of a young boy might have, Mashkova
concentrates on only one, which she finds particularly wretched. Her
description is so indignant there is no room for mitigation. Mashkova's
metaphor reveals the plenitude of her horror and revulsion. She concedes
nothing to the circumstances and has no inclination to put herself in the
other woman's situation. She feels only anger, contempt and anguish. This
could be seen as just one aspect of moral uprightness, but it has another
consequence. The woman hurling such accusations sees a lesson in them
for herself. Mashkova observes that she herself is often 'sucked into that
swamp', only she abruptly pulls herself up: 'It is good to live, but only as a
decent human being.' She is ashamed to give her children only tiny pieces
of bread while guzzling her own with uncontrollable greed in the morning,
'but I have not degenerated into an animal, and hope I never will'.

The continuation of Mashkova's tale clearly shows why she is so hostile.
She can see little attention is being paid to what she has to say and, more
to the point, that the main aim of Igor's mother is to avoid giving any
bread to her son. She says appalling and pitiless things, completely una-

bashed, and with real bitterness and hatred: "'I'm hungry, I want to live. I don't give a damn about Igor or whether he's hungry. He lost his ration card, let him get on with it." She is not going to give him anything. She is the one who must survive.' Not even the fact that Igor was present could hold her back. The final element in the picture Mashkova paints is Igor, voraciously eating a piece of bread he has been given by a compassionate neighbour, unspeaking, exhausted. It is a scene out of hell. 'Don't listen to his whining. Look at the size of that piece of bread he's just eaten, while I'm lying here starving and worn out', his mother shrieks.

Maria Mashkova just wanted to run away as fast as she could from that 'cesspit'. She makes no secret of her pressing need to put all this behind her and find an antidote as soon as she can. Perhaps she will suffer the same fate, but she, unlike Igor's mother, is not alone. She has someone close by to support her, her husband, Vsevolod: 'On the way back home I thought so warmly about him and the children. Vsevolod is a wonderful man, and after all the shit that had been thrown at me today, I couldn't wait to bring all my love and affection back home.'[73]

That was the antidote: having confronted a scene of human dishonour, the need was to find something to oppose to it. Mashkova had just left a filthy, neglected room: her own home must be an oasis of love and affection. She had left behind a woman mired in hatred, and was returning to a husband patiently waiting for her and who had lately started helping her cook the meals. She had witnessed a mother trying to steal the last piece of bread from her own child, while she would lighten the hungry routines of her children with a kindly word and a gift:

On the way, I heard children in the street saying they knew a shop which was selling children's scooters. Vadim had long been going round the shops unsuccessfully trying to find one, so I would look one out and give him a surprise. I wanted to get home to eat, but combated the urge and went round all the shops in the neighbourhood. I didn't in the end manage to find a scooter, but I did come home to Vsevolod in a joyful mood. We are kind people in our family, particularly Vsevolod. That makes me happy.[74]

7

Another reason for introspection might be religious and ascetic practices. These pay close attention to the symbolic value of particular actions, the extent to which they accord with the Ten Commandments, and refuse any attempt to seek to justify temptation. We have few sources which enable us to observe introspection imbued with the spirit of religion. In the extant documents, much which could elucidate a diarist's outlook is cryptic, implied, sometimes expressed in a single word, which makes it almost impossible to recreate fully the logic of moral and religious reflections and the extent of their influence on a person's behaviour.

The most extensive document with religious meditation is the diary of the Christian philosopher Yakov Druskin, who, 'in the world', taught mathematics at night school. It is highly original and has no parallel in the literature of the siege. Written from within a quite different tradition from the diaries of other eyewitnesses of the Time of Death, its terminology is unusual and it has a different logic connecting the component parts of the text. If in most texts attention is focused primarily on everyday life during the siege, Druskin's priority is analysis of an abstract dialectic of the soul far removed from the times. The notes he made during the war bear little relation to the reality of those terrible days. One can attempt to interpret them, elucidate their themes and context, and discover what prompted them by comparing the dates of his entries with the chronology of the drama of the siege. This approach, however, has little success in identifying any entry as a response to a particular incident, rather than as a link in a chain of increasingly arcane and profound meditations. Many seem an echo of events quite unrelated to the siege of Leningrad.

That said, it is not always clear where a particular assertion by Druskin fits in the overall chain of his thinking. Even the more down-to-earth entries, separate from his meditations and relating to things which happened to the author in 1941–2, tend to be laconic, vague and obscure. His conclusions are often surprising and do not seem to follow from the preceding detailed consideration of arguments and counterarguments. They more resemble epiphanies.

The first introspective entry to refer directly to the realities of the siege is dated 25 November 1941. It contains a detailed code for how to behave during the siege, rather pedantically divided into rules. The first, fourth and seventh of these demand that he should cease to think or talk about hunger; that he should not take offence if others speak or act in ways he considers wrong; that he should not be upset if he has to renounce things he considers desirable, especially if that is for the benefit of others.[75] He failed to observe his precepts that very day: 'That caused a certain amount of despondency to arise as a result of self-loathing. Perhaps that is the principal source of despondency. How is one to be cured of it?'[76] Later, Druskin writes about being taken to a sickbay, fed and cared for, but no vivid sensations attend these events, which take place in a kind of haze. All his impressions are fractured, cut short, and do not fit into a consistent whole.

A sense of desolation, silence of his inner voice, and inability to become involved in everyday life were aspects of his spiritual 'syncope' during the Time of Death. No troublesome anxieties, no vices, no passion: everything was 'purified'. Druskin uses words in a way that is difficult to decipher even by reference to other entries, though he tries to define them by analogy: 'Their specific nature departed from the links between people.' On 19 May 1942, he tries to relate his feelings to the Gospel, which is unsurprising, given the intensity and profundity of his reading of religious texts, evident throughout the diary. He finds an exact correspondence in Luke, chapter 8, verse 33: 'Then went the devils out of the man, and entered into the swine: and the herd ran violently down a steep place into the lake, and were choked'; 'During those four months, something departed from me, from all of us.'[77]

It is difficult to follow the logic of a person who deliberately chooses not to use 'ready-made', familiar words, but looks instead for unconventional words to mirror his condition more precisely. In his repudiation of easily accessible everyday speech, there is something close to lexical experimentation in the philosophical prose of Druskin's diary. Here too we find a palpable searching for new language unfettered by academic tradition, which will enable him to extract the meaning of phenomena from the detritus of familiar concepts obscuring it.

Druskin writes a further diary entry which integrates with the preceding segment to give a consistent, if all too brief, summary of the results of his introspection. The entry reveals that he has had a glimpse of the afterworld and that, after returning, he has retained the memory of what lies beyond the grave: 'The shades from that other world are here.' It is very concise, summarized, and yet there is a feeling that he is holding something back, as if fearing to again conjure these shades and re-experience the other-worldliness of the Time of Death. His impressions of the first winter of the siege are intentionally fragmented: 'When I stopped working, the greed intensified and I could feel desires and feelings wither.'[78] This, however, was also a means of monitoring himself, rather jejune in its identification of cause and effect, but clearly delineating the stages of deterioration.

8

What happened to him? Why did hunger so change him? To understand this, we need to recall the stages of degeneration: 'On the feeling of hunger. Three phases. A downward trend. Increasingly, involuntary thoughts about food, which are difficult to suppress. Until January, however, I did manage somehow to control that.'[79] In the evening Druskin would drink coffee, sleep for a short while:

> then write for about four hours. During these four hours I had absolutely no sensation of hunger. In January came a fall, the flesh triumphed, but having triumphed, failed, lost its dominion. This was the second phase. The sensation of hunger weakened: I did not even want to get out of bed to eat, only sometimes there would be a sudden disgusting lust for food, and then again indifference. And then, in the treatise, some shades and a sudden uplift.[80] The third phase. The sensation of hunger again increased during convalescence, but can be contained so that you no longer feel it. Hunger in the first phase sees a weakening of the spirit along with weakening of the flesh. Asceticism, in the third phase, is containment of the flesh. True asceticism is possible only when you have an understanding of the sanctity of food, and for that you must have passed through the first and second phases.[81]

The spirit, the flesh, asceticism, holiness, temptation, the sin of despondency: Druskin in his introspection uses mainly religious and psychological categories. They are clear and distinct, thanks to the centuries-old tradition behind them. They are incontrovertible, and demarcate clearly the boundaries of permissible compromise. From the agglomeration of hundreds of tiny details of life during the siege, ambiguous, leading into temptation, the significance of which it was difficult to assess immediately, there finally emerges the religious antithesis of the spirit and the flesh, and the meaning of, and means of resistance to, degeneration becomes clearer.

A year later, Druskin would again try to recreate the picture of what had happened to him during the Time of Death. His retrospective impressions, less acute but also less chaotic, become more considered and detailed. He reconstructs more carefully the sequence of events, establishes cause and effect, and describes the pendulum swing of his victories and defeats. 'In November–December 1941, *A Treatise on Thought*. Here clarity and purity were interrelated in a very complex manner. It too was not earthbound, but there were no temptations. In November–December I crossed a boundary. In January an error invaded the new world: I lost part of myself and became a prey to temptation.'[82]

Here too, as in an entry for 3 May 1942, the description seems to divide into two parts: diagnosis of a disease, and an effort to understand its causes: 'How did this happen? I saw my powers weakening, sound becoming muffled, the light fading, sensation dying, emotion failing. I saw the dead in the streets, death, including my own. I was on the brink and temptation arose. Ghosts appeared: ghostly people and ghostly worlds. They appeared in reality, with swollen or withered faces.'

The main thing is his description of temptations which have to be overcome – the emotive metaphors he uses help us to feel that all the more strongly: 'Greed, loss of feelings, the half-light of morning and the shades of people. I was an observer of the underworld and, in the darkness of evening, a participant in it.'[83]

In his periodization of degeneration, we notice the identification of 'intermediate' sensations. Distinguishing phases makes possible continuing objective self-evaluation, based as it is on an awareness of the boundaries between the normal and the pathological. Attention paid to detail facilitates distinguishing between and comparing different states. The comment that it is difficult to suppress thoughts of food points to the disciplinary value of self-monitoring. The judgement of greed as 'repugnant' facilitates differentiation of good from evil. On closer inspection, this proves to be a tale not of a fall but of resistance to falling.

9

In Druskin's introspection, a whole range of prohibitions, behavioural, domestic, philosophical and ideological, delineate the ethical realm far more clearly than enumeration of positive examples. Not encouragement, but censure, just as, at confession, what is noted is not virtues but transgressions: that is the major technique for improving the morality of behaviour.

Extreme severity – one might even say, malevolence – in how you view yourself naturally goes hand-in-hand with a negative attitude to the misdeeds of others. They are all judged by the same ideal standard and, moreover, it is only the misdeeds which are singled out.

It is difficult to say how important introspection was in strengthening ethical standards in the Time of Death. The person who today was emphasizing their fortitude might be broken tomorrow, quite independently of their will. In the nightmare of the siege, that was commonplace. A person might also be bragging about their fortitude and tranquillity solely in order to gain the approval of society. More importantly, in the monstrous maelstrom of this national calamity, people instinctively looked to protect themselves in any way possible from the ominous approach of death. Whether they realized it or not, introspection was a kind of seismograph, detecting tremors which could lead to disintegration of the personality. It was not a guarantee or a means of salvation, but enabled people to detect the mechanisms of degeneration, and thereby helped them find ways to defend themselves against it, in ways peculiar to each individual but which bolstered the steadfastness of all of them.

Leningraders in the Time of Death: human and superhuman

'The siege divided behaviour with terrible clarity into the humane and the inhumane', Vladislav Glinka noted.[1] Not all Leningraders caught in the siege were prepared to accept that, either trying not to think about the morality of what they were doing, or coming up with excuses intended to show that their actions were not immoral. Siege ethics was not a coherent system of rules which allowed clear and unambiguous judgements of behaviour, but a chaotic mix of the old moral rules with amendments designed to adapt them to the realities of wartime. The 'deterioration of morals' was neither consistent nor irreversible. For some it occurred quickly, for others more slowly, and that in itself prevented any sudden, total collapse of morality. The same person could be, at different times, generous and parsimonious, sentimental and callous, responsive and impassive. That was not explicable solely by fluctuations in the size of rations: a part was played also by the cultural level of an individual, how rooted moral standards were in them, their position in society, and their circle of friends, acquaintances and colleagues. Much depended on their state of health, how great the difficulties facing them were, and what shocks they had been subjected to.

Being well educated was no guarantee that a person would not let themselves go, become hard and insensitive, and disregard the basic values of civilized life. They could unashamedly cheat and rob those closest to them. Someone who gave away their last crust of bread to a child might, unable to stand the strain and having overestimated their strength, then break and help themselves to their children's rations.

A part was played also by the 'collective' nature of the ordeal people were experiencing. It was difficult to be the first to decide to behave immorally, but once that was being done by other citizens, immoral acts did not seem so terrible. They did not need to have become universal. The appearance of even a few unkempt people could be enough to prompt someone to go about in rags, not wash for months, or be unashamed of lapping food off a plate. Stealing, looting and cheating became acceptable to people who had previously prided themselves on their standards, not only when there was no other choice, but also if you could observe them wherever you turned, meaning you no longer had to be ashamed or wary of what other people might say.

There was a brutal pragmatism in siege ethics: those should survive who were capable of doing so, who were more valuable and more talented. That attitude was to be observed everywhere: in kindergartens and vocational schools, enterprises and evacuation centres, in civilian and military hospitals. Thousands of people were complicit in this 'selection', and it could not but inform their behaviour and ethics as a whole. It was often claimed to be sanctified by time-honoured moral principles: was it not fair to support the best? Not to give rations to ten, none of whom would survive, rather than to one whose life that would save? Moral standards which best contributed to ensuring survival proved the most enduring. They were subjected to a kind of grinding down to adapt them to the realities of the siege, but often supported at grassroots level.

Completely disregarding traditional morality was not a good idea. If you gave nothing in return, you risked being left to die: nobody would share with you in a real emergency. Anyone who was boorish, who openly despised and humiliated others, could not expect to be given a helping hand when it was needed. A person who let themselves go, stopped taking care of themselves, whose very appearance was repulsive, could not expect anyone to take their hand if they reached out to them. You needed to be aware that people should harbour feelings of pity and compassion, since otherwise how would you even know you could turn to them for charity? If victims of the siege could not survive on their own, they needed to abide by the code of conduct generally accepted in society.

Talking about the reasons for the persistence of moral precepts during the Leningrad calamity, we need to note one feature. Something we might expect to undermine them did, at the same time, strengthen them. The endless talk about food, which was considered a sign of degeneration, in fact conspired to perpetuate the memory of a civilized way of life, with vivid, expressive details magnified by hindsight, and nostalgic descriptions of feasting. Reporting these conversations and 'gastronomic' dreams of the future in their diaries and letters, Leningraders chided themselves for falling so low as to have lost interest in literature and art, science and creativity, but that also unobtrusively confirmed the importance of moral rules. Hatred, irritation and the urge to punish are not the noblest human qualities, but they helped to drive home lessons in morality, intolerance of stealing, cheating, unfairness and callousness. Defending their place in the queue with angry shrieking, arguing with the sales assistant over ration coupons, mistrustfully checking the weight of porridge received in the canteen, Leningraders corralled themselves all the more firmly within the confines of fairness, which is an essential feature of a civilized person.

The sorrowing and mournful diaries and letters of those who registered the nightmare of the siege have brought down to us one aspect of the great, collective achievement of the people of Leningrad. Few chose to talk about their feelings as they extended help to others. An unknown, mute multitude who uncomplainingly did their duty will never now tell us anything, and neither will those whose lives they tried to save. All of them perished.

As the abyss of the hell of the siege deepened, something was undermined in people themselves: not everyone was prepared to sacrifice themselves. Even the most steadfast could be broken. The instinct of self-preservation suggested only a few ways which might conduce to survival, and those left little room for compassion and solace. Consolation was predicated on having something to share, and where was that to come from when rations were measured in grams? Those who showed the best qualities of selflessness, generosity and kindness might, on another occasion, have no choice but to compromise their moral principles. When we talk of the tragedy of Leningrad, perhaps what mattered was not whether people were always able to show compassion, but whether they had the strength to show it at least once.

These people had, after all, nothing more than a handful of millet and a tattered shawl in which to wrap themselves against the cold. No amount of bombardment was able to destroy the citadel of the human spirit for as long as there was even one person who, themselves on the verge of starvation, raised the fallen to their feet and gave comfort to the despairing. Leningrad saved itself through redeeming actions great and small: the dedication of hundreds of people who sought out orphans, or took a glass of hot water to a helpless neighbour. The baton of human goodness was passed on by the strong and the weak, by relatives and strangers, through encouragement and censure, through hatred and gratitude. Leningraders knew they were more likely to survive by not sharing with anyone, but share they did. They knew they could never be repaid, but gave what they could. Themselves starving, they found the strength to give food to others. The price they paid to enable others to live was sacrosanct, life itself. There can be no greater love than that.

Now, through the testimony of these eyewitnesses, we have looked into the very depths of the hell that was Leningrad during the siege. Every day, not one or two but thousands of human beings were dying from starvation and illness. Their deaths were protracted and terrible: they died in delirium, often begging for bread, and they died among others who had none, who were as malnourished and suffering as they were themselves. They died one after another, the closest, dearest family members, forcing citizens to become accustomed to something no one should ever get used to. Every day seeing the suffering, every day subdividing a tiny piece of bread, every day standing hopelessly in long queues, every day seeing the tears and hearing the pleading of starving children. That was the abyss they lived in.

Every detail of life under the siege, like a leaden weight, pounded people down into the mire. How then were they to be open to compassion, charity and love? And yet, there was compassion. We see gathered round the bed of the dying those of their family and friends who were still alive. And there was charity: bread one was keeping for oneself which found its way into a child's outstretched hand.

But there was another emotion, which anyone who reads these writings from the siege feels, and that is anguish. There can be no plainer evidence of human compassion. Anguish from start to finish. Anguish in the diaries and letters; the anguish of the dying and of those seeking to save them; the anguish of yesterday and today. Everywhere, anguish.

Notes

Preface

1 D. S. Likhachev, *Vospominaniia*, *SPb.* [St Petersburg], 1995. Translated by Bernard Adams as Dmitry S. Likhachev, *Reflections on the Russian Soul: A Memoir*, New York and Budapest, 2000; V. M. Glinka, 'Blokada', *Zvezda*, No. 1, 2005.
2 Interview with S. P. Sukhorukova, *Nestor*, No. 6, 2003, p. 177.
3 M. S. Konopleva, 'V blokirovannom Leningrade. Dnevnik', 8 September 1941, *Otdel rukopisei Rossiiskoi natsional'noi biblioteki* (*OR RNB*, Manuscript Department of the National Library of Russia), *fond* 368, *delo* 1, *list* 66.
4 L. Shul'kin, 'Vospominaniia balovnia sud'by', *Neva*, No. 1, 1999, p. 153.

1 The tragedy of Leningrad

1 V. V. Bianki, *Likholet'e*, *SPb.*: BLITS, 2005, p. 180.
2 Valentina Kabytova notes, 'In July the cards provided quite decent rations: workers were entitled to 800 grams of bread a day and non-manual workers to 600 grams. That was actually more than you could eat. Workers were entitled to 2.2 kilos of meat per month and non-manual workers to 1.2 kilos. Moreover, commercial restaurants and cafes were functioning without any need for ration cards at all. There was plenty of ice cream, beer and pies' (V. I. Kabytova, 'Ob odnoi leningradskoi blokadnoi sem'e', *Neva*, No. 10, 2005, p. 147). 'You could be issued your food rations for the whole of the coming month, and did not need coupons for meals in the canteens' (ibid.).
3 'There were no pies or ice cream. The shops were emptied in a single day: everybody took their rations in advance' (ibid., p. 148).
4 A. M. Sokolov, *Bitva za Leningrad i ee znachenie v Velikoi Otechestvennoi voine*, *SPb*: Asterion, 2005, p. 98.
5 V. A. Baikov, *Pamiat' blokadnogo podrostka*, *Lg.* [Leningrad], 1989, p. 39.
6 V. G. Daev, 'Printsipial'nye leningradtsy', *OR RNB*, *fond* 1273, *list* 102.
7 Compare G. I. Kozlova's memoirs where she describes how, at the end of 1941, she managed to buy horsemeat: 'Someone told me a worker had been brought a horse's leg. I found her. She exchanged the very lowest part of the leg, with the hoof and a horseshoe, for a pair of shoes and an old sweater.

The horseshoe was heavy and nobody at work could get it off for me. I had to carry the whole thing home. My mother boiled the leg for almost a month before the hoof softened and became rubbery. At least it was a broth, not just water' (G. I. Kozlova, 'Moi studencheskie gody (Stranitsy iz vospominanii byvshei studentki priema 1940 g.', *'My znaem, chto znachit voina . . .' Vospominaniia, pis'ma, dnevniki universantov voennykh let*, SPb., 2010, p. 202).

8 Konopleva, 'V blokirovannom Leningrade. Dnevnik', *listy* 125–6.

9 K. I. Sel'tser, *Dnevnik*, 12 October 1941, quoted from S. Glezerov, *Ot nenavisti k primireniiu*, SPb., 2006, p. 44; compare with L. El'iasheva's notes: 'In October, the desire to eat, the gnawing feeling in your stomach, was becoming ever more insistent. It drove you away from interesting lectures to canteens and restaurants in search of food' (L. El'iasheva, *Odnim by glazom uvidet' pobedu*, p. 252). See also the entry in E. Mukhina's diary from October 1941: '150 grams of bread is obviously not enough for us. I eat it all at night before going to school, and then have to sit through the day with no bread. All the time something is gnawing away inside me. How I long for something to eat' (E. Mukhina, 'Dnevnik', *Tsentral'nyi Gosudarstvennyi Arkhiv Istoriko-politicheskikh Dokumentov Sankt-Peterburga [TsGAIPD SPb.*, Central State Archive of Historical and Political Documents of St Petersburg], *fond* 4000, *opis'* 11, *delo* 72, *list* 51).

10 D. N. Lazarev, 'Leningrad v blokade', *Trudy Gosudarstvennogo muzeia istorii Sankt-Peterburga*, vyp. 5 (*SPb.*, 2000), p. 198; V. I. Ravdonikas to L. A. Ravdonikas, 8 April 1942, *'My znaem, chto znachit voina . . .'*, p. 537.

11 I. D. Zelenskaia, 'Dnevnik', 9 January 1942, *TsGAIPD SPb, fond* 4000, *opis'* 11, *delo* 35, *list* 50 verso.

12 V. Garshin, 'V dni blokady', *Zvezda*, No. 7, 1945, p. 118.

13 On the causes and manifestations of apathy, see N. N. Erokhina (Klishevich), 'Dnevnik', 15 June 1942, *Rukopisno-dokumental'nyi fond Gosudarstvennogo memorial'nogo muzeia oborony i blokady Leningrada* (*RDF GMMOBL*, Manuscript and Documentary Department of the State Memorial Museum of the Defence and Siege of Leningrad), *opis'* 1, *delo* 490, *list* 34; M. A. Bochaver, 'Eto – bylo (Priadil'no-tkatskaia fabrika "Rabochii" v gody voennoi blokady. 1941/IX-1944/I. Byt i nravy blokadnykh let)', *OR RNB, fond* 1273, *delo* 7, *listy* 18, 33; Nina D. Khudiakova, *Za zhizn' leningradtsev. Pomoshch' komsomol'tsev naseleniiu Leningrada v blokadnuiu zimu. 1941/1942 god*, Lg., 1948; N. Glukhova, 'I byl sluchai . . .', *Neva*, No. 1, 1999, p. 221; A. Vert, *Rossiia v voine 1941–1945 gg.*, M., 1963, pp. 251–2; Alexander Werth, *Russia at War 1941–1945*, London, 1964; N. Frantskevich, 'Kruzhka moloka', *Neva*, No. 5, 2002, p. 221; E. S. Kots, 'Epizody, vstrechi, chelovecheskie sud'by', *Publichnaia biblioteka v gody voiny*, SPb, 2005, p. 192; E. Kapustina, 'Iz blokadnykh zapisei studentki', *Neva*, No. 1, 2006, p. 220; M. I. Khivilitskaia, 'Simptomatologiia', *Alimentarnaia distrofiia v blokirovannom Leningrade*, Lg., 1947, p. 164.

14 V. Admoni recalls, 'One of our former . . . companions described seeing me in the middle of the first January of the siege standing immobile on the corner of Mokhovaya Street blankly staring straight ahead. She waited almost a quarter of an hour to see whether I would stir, but there was no change' (T. Sil'man and V. Admoni, *My vspominaem*, SPb., 1993. p. 250). See also E. P. Vitenburg, *Pavel Vitenburg: geolog, poliarnik, uznik GULAGa. (Vospominania docheri)*, SPb., 2003, p. 250; N. V. Bazhenov, 'O tom, kak oni umirali (Iz zapisnoi knizhki)', 15 January 1942, *Otdel pis'mennykh istochnikov*

Novgorodskogo gosudarstvennogo muzeia (*OPI NGM*, Department of manuscript sources of the Novgorod State Museum), *opis'* 2, *delo* 440, *list* 12; F. A. Vitushkin to V. Kh. Vainshtein, quoted from S. L. Sivokhina, 'O zhizni v blokadnom Leningrade. (Po materialam arkhiva V. Kh. Vainshteina v sobranii OPI NGOMZ)', *Ezhegodnik Novgorodskogo gosudarstvennogo ob''edinennogo muzeia-zapovednika*, Novgorod, 2009, p. 97.

15 A. F. Evdokimov, 'Dnevnik', 26 October 1941, *RDF GMMOBL*, *opis'* 1, *rukopis'noe delo* 30, *list* 10.

16 A. P. Bondarenko, 'O blokade', P. K. Bondarenko family archive.

17 Transcript of a communication from Z. V. Vinogradova, *Nauchno-istoricheskii arkhiv Sankt-Peterburgskogo instituta istorii RAN [NIA SPbII RAN*, Historical research archive of the St Petersburg Institute of History of the Russian Academy of Sciences], *fond* 332, *opis'* 1, *delo* 24, *list* 11.

18 I. I. Zhilinskii, 'Blokadnyi dnevnik', 10 March 1941, *Voprosy istorii*, No. 8, 1996, p. 12.

19 Ibid.

20 *Otkuda beretsia muzhestvo. Vospominania petrozavodchan, perezhivshikh blokadu i zashchishchavshikh Leningrad*, Petrozavodsk, 2005, p. 73.

21 O. Solov'eva, 'Vospominaniia o perezhitoi blokade . . . iunoi zashchitnitsy goroda Leningrada. (1941–1945 gody)', *OR RNB, fond* 1273, *delo* 25, *list* 5.

22 'A continuous flow of people walking, ravaged, hideous, their faces swollen and disfigured. Everybody has suddenly become old, clumsy, a continuous stream who do not give way and bump into others' (Z. V. Ianushevich, *Sluchainye zapiski*, *SPb.*, 2007, p. 62); 'This is how it is nowadays. If, before, people avoided the traffic, now those buses still running have to give way to them. Pedestrians no longer hear or care. If you swear at them they say "Thank you"' (A. N. Borovikova, *Dnevnik*, 7 January 1942, *TsGAIPD SPb.*, *fond* 4000, *opis'* 11, *delo* 15, *list* 98).

23 Savelii Shul'kin, 'Vospominaniia balovnia sud'by', *Neva*, No. 1, 1999, p. 151. Z. S. Travkina described the eyes of those in the siege as 'lifeless' ('Vospominaniia Zoi Sergeevny Travkinoi o blokadnom Leningrade', *NIA SPbII RAN, fond* 332, *opis'* 1, *delo* 149, *list* 4). Iu. P. Marugina speaks of a 'dead, lifeless expression on their faces and in their eyes' (transcript of a statement by Iu. P. Marugina, *NIA SPbII RAN, fond* 332, *opis'* 1, *delo* 85, *list* 23).

24 Evgenii Shvarts, *Zhivu bespokoino. Iz dnevnikov*, Leningrad, 1990, p. 659. See also the description in war correspondent Nikolai Mikhailovskii's diary of the family of an engineer: Rokhlin 'was completely emaciated. His lifeless, glassy eyes stared into space.' The engineer's wife told him, 'in a completely uninterested tone', that her legs were swelling. Their daughter 'was lying there, just as sad and uninvolved in anything' (N. Mikhailovskii, 'Na Baltike. Iz dnevnika voennogo korrespondenta', *Deviat'sot dnei. Literaturno-khudozhestvennyi i dokumental'nyi sbornik, posviashchennyi geroicheskoi oborone Leningrada v gody Velikoi Otechestvennoi voiny*, Lg., 1962, pp. 99–100).

25 I. S. Glazunov, *Rossiia raspiataia*, vol. 1, book 2, *M.* [Moscow], 2008, p. 98.

26 L. El'iasheva, 'My ukhodim . . . My ostaemsia . . .', *Neva*, No. 1, 2004, p. 205.

27 M. V. Mashkova, 'Iz blokadnykh zapisei', 17 February 1942, *Publichnaia biblioteka v gody voiny*, p. 15.

28 According to P. M. Toksubaev, on 8 September 1941 during the first attack on the city the police even had to 'hold back the crowds of people curious

to see the ruins' (transcript of a communication by P. M. Toksubaev), *NIA SPbII RAN, fond* 332, *opis'* 1, *delo* 124, *list* 4 verso.

29 V. G. Kuliabko, 'Blokadnyi dnevnik', 6 October 1941, *Neva*, No. 2, 2004, p. 237; see also V. Mal'tsev's letter to M. D. Mal'tseva of 15 December 1941: 'There was a radio announcement that an artillery bombardment was imminent. It's all so familiar now it produces no reaction. It's routine. Even a ruined building you walk past seems routine' (*Deviat'sot dnei*, p. 268).

30 L. Ginzburg, *Zapisnye knizhki. Vospominaniia. Esse*, SPb., 2000, p. 742; *Pamiat' o blokade. Svidetel'stva ochevidtsev i istoricheskoe soznanie obshchestva*, SPb., 2005, p. 115; Bianki, *Likholet'e*, 29 September 1941, p. 58; A. F. Evdokimov, 'Materialy blokadnykh zapisei', 5 October 1941, *RDF GMMOBL*, *opis'* 1–r, *delo* 30, *list* 69; L. El'iasheva, *Odnim by glazom uvidet' pobedu*, entry for 8 October 1941, p. 252; 'Vospominaniia o blokade Leningrada Aleksandry Ivanovny Uzikovoi (Kostinoi)', *Ispytanie. Vospominaniia nastoiatelia i prikhozhan Kniaz'-Vladimirskogo sobora v Sankt-Peterburge o Velikoi Otechestvennoi voine i blokade Leningrada*, SPb., 2010, p. 32; 'Vystuplenie po leningradskomu radio V. Ketlinskoi 29 oktiabria 1941', *900 geroicheskikh dnei. Sbornik dokumentov i materialov o geroicheskoi bor'be trudiashchikhsia Leningrada v 1941–1944 gg.*, M., Lg., 1966, p. 234; I. A. Brodskii, 'V dni blokady', *Il'ia Iakovlevich Bilibin. Stat'i. Pis'ma. Vospominaniia o khudozhnike*, Lg., 1970, p. 283.

31 See V. Bianki's notes about Leningrad in spring 1942: 'Humour of the doomed. "When leaving the hotel, kindly extinguish any incendiary bombs." "Exchange: One high-explosive for two incendiary bombs in different districts"' (Bianki, *Likholet'e*, p. 171).

32 Ibid., p. 173.

33 V. F. Chekrizov, 'Dnevnik blokadnogo vremeni', 25 November 1941, *Trudy Gosudarstvennogo muzeia istorii Sankt-Peterburga, vyp.* 8, SPb., 2004, p. 34.

34 Bianki, *Likholet'e*, p. 173.

35 Ibid. See also the notes of N. Tikhonov: 'The shelling was at night. "That's in the next quarter", the host told his guest and continued their conversation' (N. Tikhonov, *Leningrad prinimaet boi*, Lg., 1943, p. 307).

36 'Shells exploded in the crowded market area. A woman who was there told me that a shell hit a bread stall; when someone ordered everyone to lie down, loaves of bread landed on top of them. Some people rushed to grab them, while others fought to take them off them' (Konopleva, 'V blokirovannom Leningrade. Dnevnik', 19 December 1941, *delo* 2, *list* 10).

37 Transcript of a communication by A. Ia. Tikhonov, *NIA SPbII RAN, fond* 332, *opis'* 1, *delo* 123, *list* 17.

38 D. S. Likhachev wrote that a woman's body was left lying at Birzhevoi [Stock Exchange] Bridge, near the Institute of Literature, for around two months, although that was unusual (D. S. Likhachev, *Vospominaniia*, SPb., 1999, p. 477).

39 See I. Il'in's memoirs: 'I was afraid of tripping over the body of someone who had starved to death, which lay for a week in our entrance hall at the foot of the stairs' (I. Il'in, 'Ot blokady do pobedy', *Neva*, No. 5, 2005, p. 178); A. I. Vinokurov, 'I saw three naked corpses outside the Peter and Paul Hospital. They had fallen off a truck transporting dead bodies and just lay there all day in the street. No one paid any attention' ('Blokadnyi dnevnik A. I. Vinokurova', *Blokadnye dnevniki i dokumenty*, SPb., 2004. p. 245). See

also V. Inber, *Pochti tri goda*, 2 February 1942, in Inber, *Sobranie sochinenii*, vol. III, *M.*, 1965, p. 193; 'Blokadnyi dnevnik N. P. Gorshkova', 6 January 1942, *Blokadnye dnevniki i dokumenty*, p. 57; an account of V. V. Lishev's story in K. Ardentov, 'O leningradskikh skul'ptorakh', *Khudozhniki goroda-frontu. Vospominaniia i dnevniki leningradskikh khudozhnikov, Lg.*, 1973, p. 104.

40 L. S. Ronchevskaia, 'Vospominaniia o blokade Leningrada', *OR RNB, fond* 1249, *delo* 14, *list* 3.

41 See I. D. Zelenskaia: 'Chistiakov's father died early this morning, in the bed in his study. Left lying there all day. Son working alongside, eating, taking a rest on the same bed. A lot of people coming in – nobody bothered about the body. His mother died about ten days ago. Still lying there in a room in the hostel' (I. D. Zelenskaia, 'Dnevnik', *listy* 61 verso, 62); A. M. Sokolov's memories of an evacuation point in Zhikharevo: 'The dead were lying all over the place. People sat on them, ate and slept on them' (A. M. Sokolov, *Evakuatsiia iz Leningrada, SPb.*, 2000, p. 122).

42 Sof'ia Gotkhart, 'Leningrad. Blokada', *Dve sud'by v velikoi Otechestvennoi voine, SPb.*, 2006, p. 43; V. A. Muranova, 'Tsentral'nyi gosudarstvennyi arkhiv rabotal vsiu blokadu', *Vystoiali i pobedili. Vospominaniia uchastnikov oborony Leningrada, voinov i truzhenikov Oktiabr'skogo raiona, SPb.*, 1993, p. 168.

43 V. I. Nikol'skaia, 'V ocherediakh', *OR RNB, fond* 1037, *delo* 907, *list* 13. See also an interview with A. V. Andreev: 'My father and I went for water to the Obvodny Canal. Its banks were strewn with dead bodies' (*Chelovek v blokade: Novye svidetel'stva, SPb.*, 2008, p. 263); memoirs of Tat'iana Maksimova: 'One time a woman fell into a well. The people who had come to fetch water had not the strength to pull her out, but could not go back home without water, so they scooped it out, pushing aside the icy strands of the dead woman's hair'(T. Maksimova, *Vospominaniia o leningradskoi blokade, SPb.*, 2002, p. 41); a letter from Z. Fomberg to V. Kh. Vainshtein: 'People frequently fell into the hole cut in the ice and it was not always possible to rescue them. The body would be pushed to one side with a boathook and people would immediately go back to drawing water' (quoted from Sivokhina, 'O zhizni v blokadnom Leningrade', p. 97).

44 Bianki, *Likholet'e*, p. 181.

45 'This is the kind of sight we have all become used to. A child's sledge with ragged bundles on it has become commonplace' (Dmitrii Moldavskii, 'Stranitsy o zime 1941–42 godov', in O. B. Shestinskii, *Golosa iz blokady. Leningradskie pisateli v osazhdennom gorode. (1941–1944), SPb.*, 1996, p. 356); 'Hundreds of people are lying all over the place, but nobody is looking after them, let alone paying attention to dead bodies' (G. A. Gel'fer, *Dnevnik*, 19 January 1942, *TsGAIPD SPb, fond* 4000, *opis* 11, *delo* 24, *list* 4); 'Death is now an everyday matter. We are used to it. The bodies of those who have died or frozen to death are to be found almost every 100 metres in the street. Everyone is so used to it now that they just walk past' ('Blokadnyi dnevnik A. I Vinokurova', 8 January 1942, pp. 240–1); 'Our battalion impassively marches in line past the ravaged body of a young woman near the Okhtinsky Bridge' (V. A. Averbakh, 'Rasskazy veterana', p. 6, from the K. K. Smirnova family archive); 'Now, people stepped over them without feeling anything. The sight had become familiar. The snowdrifts were almost the height of a

person and people had not the strength to walk round the bodies' (Baikov, *Pamiat' blokadnogo podrostka*, p. 69).

46 Lazarev, 'Leningrad v blokade', p. 203.

47 Ibid.

48 See V. F. Chekrizov: 'One of a building's activists reports to the housing manager that a man has died in their apartment. Manager: "He's got a wife. Get her to sort him out and get him removed." "She's at death's door too." "Then we'll wait, and when she dies we'll move them both at the same time"' (V. F. Chekrizov, 'Dnevnik blokadnogo vremeni', *Trudy Gosudarstvennogo muzeia istorii Sankt-Peterburga*, *vyp.* 8, *SPb.*, 2004, p. 56); a letter from S. V. Soldatenkov to the *Istoricheskaia komissiia Soveta veteranov LGU* [Historical Commission of the Committee of Veterans of Leningrad State University]: 'I went into the mortuary and saw a woman lying face down, with her face in a shallow puddle. I went back to the reception desk for help and told them, "There's a live woman in there among the bodies." The official replied: "They took her out dead, she came to in the fresh air and now she's moved. What are we supposed to do? She's going to die anyway."' (*'My znaem, chto znachit voina . . .'*, p. 283).

49 E. P. Postnikova, 'Zapiski blokady', *OR RNB, fond* 1273, *listy* 2 verso – 3.

50 'On a sheet of plywood on a two-wheeled cart were three bodies sewn into rags, probably adolescents, judging by their size. A passer-by glanced at them and said, 'Oh, three dolls, dressed up this time"' (Konopleva, 'V blokirovannom Leningrade. Dnevnik', *delo* 3).

51 In a diary entry of 9 September 1941, N. A. Ribkovskii mentions queues a kilometre long outside canteens and snack bars (quoted in N. Kozlova, *Sovetskie liudi. Stseny iz istorii*, M., 2005, p. 258). This may have resulted from a panic after the bombing of the Badaev warehouses. See also A. A. Griaznov's entry of 24 September 1941: 'You have to queue for 3–5 hours before you can lunch in a canteen open to the public' (A. A. Griaznov, 'Dnevnik', *Chelovek v blokade*, p. 20).

52 Konopleva, 'V blokirovannom Leningrade. Dnevnik', 19 October 1941, *OR RNB*, *delo* 3, *list* 15; see also: 'I was phoning from the canteen. It was very crowded and there was uproar and fighting' (P. M. Samarin, 'Dnevnik', 12 January 1942, *RDF GMMOBL*, *opis'* 1–1, *delo* 338, *list* 841; see also E. I. Dmitrieva's memoirs: 'There was an urn of boiling water in the canteen, and there was a queue and even fighting over that' (quoted in V. D. Chursin, 'Soobshchaet 21–i o svoei gotovnosti', *Publichnaia biblioteka v gody voiny*, p. 124); 'In the lunch break, before we were allowed into the canteen, everybody gathered and there was squabbling which could lead to a fight' (B. Mikhailov, *Na dne voiny i blokady*, SPb., 2001, p. 40).

53 Ginzburg, *Zapisnye knizhki*, p. 740.

54 The March 1942 report to the City's Communist Party Committee of a team investigating how Leningrad canteens and cafes were functioning commented on an 'inconsiderate and formalistic attitude towards diners, who are treated in an uncouth manner' (*900 geroicheskikh dnei*, p. 267).

55 G. A. Kulagin, *Dnevnik i pamiat'. O perezhitom v gody blokady*, Lg., 1978, p. 153; see also the entry in I. D. Zelenskaia's diary for 20 September 1942: 'The least thing causes rudeness and disputes between those next to each other, and also with the waitresses. Every table is trying to attract the waitress's attention ahead of its neighbour' (I. D. Zelenskaia, 'Dnevnik', *list* 100 verso).

56 Likhachev, *Vospominaniia*, p. 473. Testimony about this may be overly emotional and overstated, but it cannot be ignored. See A. Lepkovich, 'People became so much ruder during this time. They changed out of all recognition' (A. Lepkovich, 'Dnevnik', 20 May 1942, *TsGAIPD SPb*, *fond* 4000, *opis'* 11, *delo* 59, *list* 18 verso); Anna Zelenova wrote to friends on 22 February 1942: 'We think constantly about food, squabble and despise each other because the circumstances we are in have exposed all our worst features' (A. I. Zelenova, *Stat'i. Vospominaniia. Pis'ma*, SPb., 2006, p. 115); see the entry in Mikhail Tikhomirov's diary for 21 January 1942: 'A crowd of people with buckets and other containers are squabbling and shouting. They are kneeling to draw water but jostling each other and spilling it' (*Dnevnik Mishi Tikhomirova*, SPb., 2010, p. 29).

57 See V. Bazanova's diary for 22 November 1941: 'I walk past the market and see queues. If you ask why they are queueing, the salesperson will reply irritably, "They don't know themselves. I've told them there's nothing here"' (V. Bazanova, 'Vchera bylo deviat' trevog . . .', *Neva*, No. 1, 1999, p. 129); F. A. Griaznov noted on 27 November 1941, 'Some people stubbornly stand at a shop door, ignoring the manager's warning that there have been no deliveries' (Griaznov, 'Dnevnik', p. 124).

58 A. O. Zmitrichenko (transcript of reminiscences), *900 blokadnykh dnei*, p. 93.

59 L. A. Khodorkov, 'Materialy blokadnykh zapisei. 17 ianvaria 1942 g.', *RDF GMMOBL*, *opis'* 1–r, *delo* 140, *list* 15.

60 See D. N. Lazarev's reminiscences of meals at the *Dom uchenykh* (Scholars Club) in October–November 1941: 'The person sitting on my left tells me he imbibed eight bowls of soup in a single day' (Lazarev, *Leningrad v blokade*, p. 196).

61 Zelenskaia, 'Dnevnik', 18 November 1941, *list* 33 verso.

62 Transcript of a communication by P. P. Trofimov, *NIA SPbII RAN*, *fond* 332, *opis'* 1, *delo* 126, *list* 20; Griaznov, 'Dnevnik', 6 December 1941, p. 138.

63 67 Griaznov, 'Dnevnik', 6 December 1941, p. 138.

64 M. I. Chaiko, 'Dnevnik', *Trudy Gosudarstvennogo muzeia istorii Sankt-Peterburga*, *vyp.* 5, p. 123.

65 'My legs have swollen and can't carry me. I fall over at the least impact' (M. M. Krakov, 'Dnevnik', 26 February 1942, *TsGAIPD SPb.*, *fond* 4000, *opis'* 11, *delo* 53, *list* 14).

66 I. Byl'ev, 'Iz dnevnika', *Khudozhniki goroda-fronta. Vospominaniia i dnevniki leningradskikh khuodzhnikov*, Lg., 1973, p. 333.

67 Bochaver, 'Eto – bylo', *listy* 51–2.

68 Ibid.

69 Vs. Ivanov, *Dnevniki*, M., 2001, pp. 203–4; see also the account of a conversation with a Red Army soldier on leave in the city: 'He says he would never have believed that people could be reduced to such a state and live' (entry for 21 February 1942 in *Dnevnik Mishi Tikhomirova*, p. 44).

70 Borovikova, 'Dnevnik', 15 January 1942, *list* 101; N. P. Zavetnovskaia to T. V. Zavetnovskaia, 22 December 1941, *OR RNB*, *fond* 1273, *list* 23 verso; M. V. Mashkova to S. M. Mashbits, 5 November 1941, *Publichnaia biblioteka v gody voiny*, p. 115; N. N. Erokhina (Klishevich), 'Dnevnik', 15 June 1942, *RDF GMMOBL*, *opis'* 1, *delo* 490, *list* 35.

71 See the entry for 17 January 1972 in Petr Kapitsa's diary: 'They look down or turn away ashamed their thin faces with their prominent noses, to keep us

from seeing their premature wrinkles, bruises and blotches below their eyes. If any of them chance to look up, it is with embarrassment' (P. I. Kapitsa, *V more pogasli ogni*, Lenizdat, 1979, p. 261).

72 As noted in the report of the Leningrad City Planning Commission for the period from 1 July 1941 to 1 January 1942, the number of footwear repair centres fell from 398 to 86, the bathhouses ceased to operate, as did most communal services centres and almost all the laundries ('Iz otcheta Lengorplana "Leningrad v period voiny i blokady"', *900 geroicheskikh dnei*, p. 297).

73 T. Nezhintseva, 'Rasskazhu o svoem muzhe', in Shestinskii, *Golosa iz blokady*, p. 348.

74 During the winter of 1941–2, 6,369 mains water supply points froze up (43 per cent of the total) (V. M. Koval'chuk, *900 dnei blokady. Leningrad. 1941–1944, SPb.*, 2005, p. 76).

75 Zelenskaia, 'Dnevnik', 10 December 1941, *list* 41 verso.

76 See E. Kapustina's memoirs of the student hostel in the Physics Institute of Leningrad State University: 'People were lying there, covered with a blanket and bits of material. I suggested we might wash but they refused, saying that afterwards they will be even colder' (Kapustina, *Iz blokadnykh dnei studentki*, p. 220).

77 B. P. Fedorov, secretary of the October district committee of the Komsomol [Young Communist League], recalled finding an emaciated man in an apartment on Glinka Street: 'When we looked more closely, we found his heels had been gnawed away by rats. He was alive, but lacked the strength to fight them off' (B. P. Fedorov (transcript of reminiscences), *Oborona Leningrada, 1941–1944. Vospominaniia i dnevniki uchastnikov, Lg.*, 1968. P. 467). Survivors of the siege remembered the rats with particular horror: 'A fat rat leapt off the face of my aunt who had died two weeks previously and bounded towards me' (Il'ia S. Glazunov, *Rossiia raspiataia*, vol. I, part 2, *M.*, 2006, p. 102); 'They devoured the engine oil, they devoured the dead lying at the factory awaiting their turn' (Ol'ga Grechina, 'Spasaius' spasaia', *Neva*, No. 1, 1994, p. 262); L. M. Arshintseva, the training officer of the Petrograd Office of Communications, reported that postmen were 'stumbling in the stairwells over deceased who were being gnawed by rats' (transcript of a communication by L. M. Arshintseva to *NIA* SPbII RAN, *fond* 332, *opis'* 1, *delo* 4, *list* 2 and verso); 'The limbs of many of the corpses are being gnawed. This primitive mortuary, together with the rats, will become an active source of infection' (letter of 6 February 1942 from M. F. Zybin, administrator of the dredger *Volkhov*, to the deputy chairman of the Leningrad Province executive committee, N. N. Shekhovtsov, *Vodokanal Leningrada. 1941–1945. Vodosnabzhenie i kanalizatsiia Leningrada v gody Velikoi Otechestvennoi voiny, SPb.*, 1995, p. 234).

78 Even in autumn 1942, 25–30 per cent of the workers at the Egorov factory were found to be infested with lice (V. M. Kapitonova, 'Dnevnik', 22 September 1942, *NIA SPbII RAN, fond* 332, *opis'* 1, *delo* 55, *list* 6).

79 V. Kuliabko, 'Blokadnyi dnevnik', entry for 17 September 1941, *Neva*, No. 1, 2004.

80 'I cannot be parted from my felt boots and winter coat', N. Bazhenov wrote in his diary on 15 May 1942. (N. V. Bazhenov, 'O tom, kak oni umirali . . . (Iz zapisnoi knizhki)', *OPI NGM*, *opis'* 2, *delo* 440, *list* 14). An acquaintance told G. Goppe in 1945, 'I still can't get the chill out of myself.' Asked which was

more terrible, the hunger or the cold, he replied, 'The cold, because you can't get used to it' (G. Goppe, 'Marshruty odnogo puteshestviia', *Deti goroda-geroia, Lg.*, 1974, p. 77).

81 See A. S. Savanina's story of someone who worked at the State Bank: 'She was always exceptionally dirty, smoky, and wearing a garment the like of which I can't think anyone was wearing before the war. She had pulled grimy, greasy rags out of somewhere and dressed herself in it all' (A. S. Savanina, 'Leningradskaia gorodskaia kontora Gosbanka v gody voiny', *Dozhivem li my do tishiny. Zapiski iz blokadnogo Leningrada, SPb.*, 2009, p. 226); the transcript of a communication by M. I. Skvortsov states, 'People came to us at the Party Committee leaning on sticks. They were terribly emaciated, dirty, and wrapped in rags' (*NIA SPbII RAN, fond* 332, *opis'* 1, *delo* 110, *list* 10); N. P. Kopaneva, ed., *Leningrad 1941–1942. Iz dnevnikov G.A. Kniazeva*, 7 February 1942, *SPb.*, 2005, p. 53.

82 E. Vechtomova, *Vopreki vsemu. Iz leningradskikh blokadnykh zapisei*, Literaturnoe nasledstvo, vol. 78, part 2, *M.*, 1966, p. 246.

83 Zelenskaia, 'Dnevnik', 15 March 1942, *list* 69.

84 Vs. V. Ivanov, *Dnevniki, M.*, 2001, p. 204.

85 Mashkova, 'Iz blokadnykh zapisei', 10 March 1942, p. 26.

86 Lepkovich, 'Dnevnik', 15 December 1941, *list* 8 verso.

87 G. M. Kok, 'Dnevnik. 22–25 dekabria 1941 g.', *TsGAIPD SPb., fond* 4000, *opis'* 11, *delo* 48, *list* 22 verso; 'Vospominaniia N. I. Zakaznovoi', quoted from Chursin, 'Soobshchaet 21–i o svoei gotovnosti', p. 130.

88 Chursin, 'Soobshchaet 21–i o svoei gotovnosti', p. 130.

89 See A. S. Nikol'skii's diary. 'Famine dictates manners. For example, one elderly, grey-haired scholar goes to lunch and licks the plate several times. Another, younger, less well-dressed fellow wearing a hat with earflaps and mittens which, for some curious reason he did not take off, took the bowl of soup offered by a waitress from the tray. It slipped in his hand, or rather his mitten, and some of it spilled on to a pile of used plates. Quite unperturbed, and paying no attention to the waitress's reproaches, he put the plate on the table, poured the spilled soup from the other plates into it and started drinking' (A. S. Nikol'skii, 'Dnevnik', 2 January 1942, *OR RNB, fond* 1037, *delo* 901, *list* 28).

90 Konopleva, 'V blokirovannom Leningrade. Dnevnik'.

91 Ibid.

92 Report of a team investigating the work of the Main Directorate of Leningrad Canteens and Cafes to the City Party Committee, March 1942, *900 geroiches-kikh dnei*, p. 267.

93 I. I. Zhilinskii, 'Blokadnyi dnevnik', *Voprosy istorii*, Nos. 5–6, 1996, p. 7.

94 *TsGAIPD SPb., fond* 25, *opis'* 2, *delo* 4464, *list* 69.

95 Ibid., *list* 72.

96 I. Metter, *Dopros, SPb.*, 1998, p. 51.

97 F. Makhov, '"Blok-ada" Rity Malkovoi', *Neva*, No. 9, 2005, p. 227.

98 A. P. Bondarenko, 'O blokade', P. K. Bondarenko family archive.

99 L. Razumovskii, 'Deti blokady', *Neva*, No. 1, 1999, pp. 30, 60.

100 'An energetic young woman with two little girls (one the cashier, the other in charge of marketing). "Come and buy! Oh, so tasty, just get it into your stomach!" were doing a brisk trade, scooping jars of something out of an enormous bucket' (Kok, 'Dnevnik. 22–25 dekabria 1941 g.', *list* 1).

101 Ol'ga Berggol'ts, *Vstrecha*, *SPb.*, 2003, p. 170.
102 V. F. Chekrizov, 'Dnevnik blokadnogo vremeni', 24 January 1942, p. 46.
103 P. I. Senichev, 'Leningradskii sudostroitel'nyi zavod im. A. A. Zhdanova v 1941–1943 gg., *"Ia ne sdamsia do poslednego . . ."*, *Zapiski iz blokadnogo Leningrada*, *SPb.*, 2010, p. 163.
104 Ibid.
105 A. S. Umanskaia, 'Dnevnik', 19 May 1941, *OR RNB, fond* 1273, *delo* 72, *list* 31.
106 The story of this siege survivor, who gave a school talk in 1979, was recorded by Ol'ga Grechina (O. Grechina, 'Spasaius' spasaia', p. 240). The note continues startlingly: 'She ate not only peat, but even raw fish heads, which her friend, who was a cleaner, brought her from the kitchen.'
107 We find one such description in Zhilinskii's diary: 'On Dibunovskaia Street, beside a rubbish tip, lies a woman with a child at her feet' (Zhilinskii, 'Blokadnyi dnevnik', 10 March 1941, p. 12); see also A. T. Kedrov: 'In one household a dead body was thrown from the top floor into the courtyard, which the residents then covered in rubbish' (Kedrov, 'Dnevnik', 16 February 1942, NIA SPbII RAN, *fond* 332, *opis'* 1, *delo* 59, *list* 119).
108 'I remember there was a puddle of soup in the street yesterday. A girl had spilt it, and several people got down on their knees to lick it up' (E. Levina, 'Dnevnik', in *Chelovek v blokade*, p. 164).
109 F. Makhov, '"Blok-ada" Rity Malkovoi', p. 226. Compare an entry in A. F. Evdokimov's diary: 'Coming out of the canteen, I stumbled in the corridor over an old man sitting there. He was slumped helplessly against the wall and, pulling dirty horse bones out of a rubbish container, was gnawing at them, like an envious wolf, with his broken teeth' (A. F. Evdokimov, 'Dnevnik', 5 December 1941, *RDF GMMOBL*, *opis'* 1–r, *delo* 30, *list* 75).
110 F. Makhov, '"Blok-ada" Rity Malkovoi', p. 226.
111 Ibid., pp. 226, 227.
112 G. Iurmin, 'Sankt-Leningrad', *Neva*, No. 1, 2004, p. 254; see also I. D. Zelenskaia, 'Every evening queues form in the canteen for leftovers' (Zelenskaia, 'Dnevnik', 3 December 1941, *list* 37 verso).
113 Zelenskaia, 'Dnevnik', 23 July 1941, *list* 92 verso.
114 Ibid., 12 December 1941, *list* 42 verso.
115 N. V. Frolov, '1–3 fevralia 1942 goda', *Kraevedcheskie zapiski. Issledovaniia i materialy*, *SPb.*, 2000, pp. 321–2. Frolov calls his wife 'Kitty'.
116 A. Fadeev, *Leningrad v dni blokady (Iz dnevnika)*, *M.*, 1944, p. 118.
117 N. N. Erokhina (Klishevich), 'Dnevnik', 15 June 1942, *RDF GMMOBL*, *opis'* 1, *delo* 490, *listy* 35–6.
118 Berggol'ts, *Vstrecha*, p. 162.
119 See Z. A. Ignatovich's entry about the head bookkeeper of the laboratory where she worked: 'All of us on the staff were struck by his exceptional good manners and tact, which did not even seem quite appropriate to his position. He very quickly lost weight and gave up the struggle: he stopped taking care with his appearance, no longer combed his hair, did not wash, and walked around looking quite lost. He took his place in the canteen before anyone else and waited impatiently to be served [with a nutrient powder – S. Ya.]. He would gobble up his own portion dry, and stare feverishly at the jar with the powder as other people were served. Then he would beg in a whining voice, "Let me lick the spoon, please"' (Z. A. Ignatovich, 'Ocherki o blokade Leningrada', *OR RNB, fond* 1273, *delo* 26, *list* 33).

120 'Otryvok iz doklada SD ob obstanovke vesnoi 1942 goda', *Zvezda*, No. 9, 2005, p. 182.

121 Inber, *Pochti tri goda*, 3 February 1942, p. 191.

122 'The mother kept saying in a heartbreaking tone, "Liulia, Liulia, what have you done to me! You have put me in my coffin alive." Liulia, desperately clutching a muff to her chest and staring fixedly ahead, whispered, "What a night this is going to be".'

123 See I. I. Zhilinskii's diary entry for 16 January 1942: 'We were cheated in the shop for a second time over the bread ration. The first time I was given 102 grams too little, and this time Olia was cheated out of 133 grams (Zhilinskii, 'Blokadnyi dnevnik', *Voprosy istorii*, Nos. 5–6, 1996, p. 27).

124 See A. I. Vinokurov's diary for 17 March 1942: 'Not infrequently a woman will have been queueing for an hour and hands the sales assistant her card, only to be told she has already received the food it entitles her to. Usually in such cases she starts crying or there is much swearing, accompanied by mutual insults. The saleswoman tries to persuade her the coupons have been used by the customer or her relative in a canteen' ('Blokadnyi dnevnik A. I. Vinokurova', p. 254).

125 V. B. Vraskaya, 'Vospominaniia o byte grazhdanskom v voennoe vremia', *OR RNB, fond* 1273, *list* 17. See also M. N. Feting on how her child was treated at his kindergarten: 'When my son fell ill, he was placed in an isolation unit where they were supposed to be put on an enhanced diet. When I visited him a few days later, I found he was so weak he couldn't stand. I asked him what he had been eating and he said he and the other children there had been told by the doctor they were not allowed to have any food. I gathered their rations had been eaten by the nurse!' ('Vospominaniia Mariny Nikolaevny Feting o voine i blokade Leningrada', *Ispytanie: Vospominanie nastoiatelia i prikhozhan . . .*, p. 125).

126 *Leningrad v osade. Sbornik dokumentov o geroicheskoi oborone Leningrada v gody Velikoi Otechestvennoi voiny. 1941–1944*, SPb., 1995, p. 253.

127 Ibid.

128 See L. K. Zabolotskaia: 'Zina and Marusia (when Marusia was working as a cook in a children's home) bartered a lot of good things for bread. For example, a wristwatch for 1 kg of bread' (L. K. Zabolotskaia, 'Dnevnik', *Chelovek v blokade*, p. 131).

129 L. Ratner, 'Vy zhivy v pamiati moei'. Vospominaniia blokadnogo mal'chika', *Neva*, No. 9, 2002, p. 149.

130 A. N. Mironova, 'Dnevnik', 3 March 1942, *TsGAIPD SPb., fond* 4000, *opis'* 11, *delo* 61, *list* 12.

131 As was emphasized in an information bulletin from the staff training department of the Leningrad City Party Committee on 26 March 1942, violations were noted specifically in the canteen of the Clara Zetkin factory ('The diners were cheated and there were instances of pilfering') and Canteen No.12 in Kirov district ('frequent instances of underweight portions in the soup and main courses') (*TsGAIPD SPb., fond* 25, *opis'* 2, *delo* 4464, *list* 68).

132 Minutes of a session of the Bureau of the Leningrad City Party Committee, 10 April 1942, *TsGAIPD SPb., fond* 25, *opis'* 2, *delo* 4464, *list* 11.

133 137 E. Gollerbakh, 'Iz dnevnika 1941 goda', in Shestinskii, *Golosa iz blokady*, p. 185.

134 138 L. Razumovskii, 'Deti blokady', p. 15.

135 139 Informatsiia Primorskogo RK VLKSM Leningradskomu GK VLKSM, 15 January 1942, *TsGAIPD SPb, fond* K-118, *opis'* 1, *delo* 78, *list* 5.
136 *900 geroicheskikh dnei*, p. 267. 'Many instances of underweight portions and undue moisture content of second courses' were noted in a resolution of the Leningrad City Party Committee of 10 April 1942 (*Protokol zasedaniia Biuro Leningradskogo gorkoma VKP(b)*, 10 April 1942, *TsGAIPD SPb., fond* 25, *opis'* 2, *delo* 4464, *list* 35).
　　See also M. M. Krakov on the serving of food in an 'enhanced diet' canteen: 'Satisfying, nutritious, delicious! But 15–20% gets stolen' (M. M. Krakov, 'Dnevnik', 5 May 1942, *TsGAIPD SPb., fond* 4000, *opis'* 11, *delo* 53, *list* 21); communication from chairman of the Vyborg district executive committee A. Ia Tikhonov about his visit to a sickbay: 'You go in and ask, "How are they feeding you?" You get the reply, "Not bad, only they don't give you enough. They're pilfering." Then they start telling you that the portions are underweight. They cheat you out of so-and-so many grams. If they're serving butter, you ask to have it on a piece of bread because if they put it on the porridge they'll cheat you' (transcript in *NIA SPbII RAN, fond* 332, *opis'* 1, *delo* 123, *list* 28 verso).
137 *TsGAIPD SPb., fond* 4000, *opis'* 11, *delo* 59, *list* 13 verso.
138 Quoted from *Budni podviga. Blokadnaia zhizn' leningradtsev v dnevnikakh, risunkakh, dokumentakh, SPb.*, 2006, p. 54.
139 *Dnevnik Mishi Tikhomirova*, 23 March 1942, p. 57.
140 T. Goryshina, 'Radi zhizni', *Neva*, No. 1, 1999, p. 192.
141 Grechina, 'Spasius' spasaia', p. 234.
142 One Leningrader describes how she protected firewood brought out from the basement. 'I ran into the courtyard, afraid there might be covetous eyes looking at our wood. Dragging the logs one by one would mean I couldn't keep an eye on the rest while I was doing it. The only solution was to keep the whole pile together by rolling them' (Maksimova, *Vospominaniia o Leningradskoi blokade*, p. 43).
143 Transcript of a communication by V. V. Korotkov, *NIA SPbII RAN, fond* 332, *opis'* 1, *delo* 69, *list* 20.
144 Transcript of a communication by V. P. Bylinskii, *NIA SPbII RAN, fond* 332, *opis'* 1, *delo* 22, *list* 5.
145 See Valentina Levina: 'Our aunt lost the place in our apartment where she lived and had to move in temporarily with the caretaker, who she found had taken our belongings' (V. G. Levina, *Ia pomniu . . . Zametki leningradki, SPb.*, 2007, p. 91).
146 V. M. Glinka, 'Blokada', *Zvezda*, No. 1, 2005, p. 183. On the topic of caretakers stealing possessions from empty apartments, see Likhachev, *Vospominaniia*, p. 456.
147 See Z. S. Livshits's comment upon learning that her neighbours were burgling apartments: 'All this is happening under the nose of housing managers who have their snouts firmly in the trough' (Livshits, 'Dnevnik', *Budni podviga*, p. 54).
148 E. S. Kots, 'Epizody, vstrechi, chelovecheskie sud'by', *Publichnaia biblioteka v gody voiny*, p. 191.
149 See N. P. Gorshkov's diary entries for 5 January 1942: 'under cover of darkness, thieves snatched bread from people coming out of the bakery and disappeared'; and 12 January 1942: 'There are more and more robberies. They

snatch bread and food ration cards, and seize paper bags from people coming out of bakeries and shops' ('Blokadnyi dnevnik N. P. Gorshkova', pp. 55, 62). Thieves also took advantage of 'darkness' in restaurants, according to D. S. Likhachev: 'The oil lamp was suddenly put out and thieves grabbed ration coupons and cards off the table' (D. S. Likhachev, *Vospominaniia*, p. 470); see also B. B. Kross, *Vospominaniia o Vove. Istoriia moei zhizni, SPb.*, 2008, p. 50; 'Vospominaniia o blokade', *Ispytanie*, p. 33; A.P. Zagorskaia, 'Dnevnik', 23 March 1942, *NIA* SPbII RAN, *fond* 332, *opis'* 1, *delo* 47, *list* 33.

150 M. S. Konopleva testifies, 'Thuggish behaviour has reached a stage where armed guards are being sent to bakeries' (Konopleva, 'V blokirovannom Leningrade. Dnevnik', 16 January 1942, *delo* 2, *list* 4). Such cases seem to have been rare: they are not mentioned by other siege victims. The guards in the bakery where Konopleva received bread were stood down the next day after themselves stealing a loaf of bread.

151 'People were talking today about the many cases of stealing of food and bread cards from women and, in particular, young girls sent by their mothers to the bakery or bread shop' ('Blokadnyi dnevnik N. P. Gorshkova', 4 February 1942, p. 72); 'Today, on Znamenskaya Street, a young woman snatched bread from a boy about ten years old, who had just bought it in the bakery. She was arrested. She explained she needed it to feed her hungry children' ('Blokadnyi dnevnik A. I. Vinokurova', 8 February 1942, p. 247). K. A. Karataeva recalled she would go to the bread shop with her sister because 'boys might snatch the bread' (K. A. Karataeva (transcript of reminiscences), *900 blokadnykh dnei*, p. 110); see also V. M. Lisovskaia (transcript of reminiscences), *900 blokadnykh dnei*, p. 156.

152 Zelenskaia, 'Dnevnik', 20 January 1942, *list* 56.

153 'In recent days there have been instances where individual citizens have assembled in groups to steal during deliveries on sledges and carts from bakeries to bread shops' (memorandum from the chief of the city police department to [chairman of the Leningrad City executive committee] P. S. Popkov, 30 January 1942, *Leningrad v osade*, p. 420; 'Yesterday evening on Razyezzhaya Street under cover of darkness several crates of bread loaves were stolen from a cart in motion by raiding adolescents, men and women' ('Blokadnyi dnevnik N. P. Gorshkova', 15 January 1942, p. 60). See also Levina, 'Dnevnik', 27 January 1942, p. 150.

154 Report from the head of the Main Directorate of Leningrad Canteens and Cafes to P. S. Popkov, 15 January 1942 (*Leningrad v osade*, p. 419).

155 Ibid. See the reminiscences of engineer V. I. Iakushev about events in late January 1942: 'Shortly before the end of the working day there was a bread delivery. There was not enough to go round. Those who got none rioted in the bakery' (V. I. Iakushev, 'Iz vospominanii o zhizni v blokadnom Leningrade', *Kraevedcheskie zapiski, vyp. 7, SPb.*, 2000, p. 295.

156 See a situation report from the Staff Training Department of the Leningrad City Party Committee to Andrey Zhdanov, 4 January 1942: 'Orphaned adolescents 14–15 years old are in a particularly difficult position. The children's homes do not take them in. The children mill around shops and bakeries and snatch bread and food from customers' (*Leningrad v osade*, p. 414).

157 Razumovskii, *Deti blokady*, p. 40.

158 Vraskaya, 'Vospominaniia o byte grazhdanskom v voennoe vremia', *list* 26.

159 A. I. Vinokurov told the tale of a boy of 15 who had helped himself to some-

one's bread and been detained by passers: 'He contrived to eat the lot while they were taking him to a policeman' ('Blokadnyi dnevnik A. I. Vinokurova', pp. 243–4).

160 Boris Kapranov, 'Dnevnik', 15 December 1941, *Budni podviga*, p. 42.

161 Likhachev, *Vospominaniia*, p. 471. Cf. V. Peterson's notes: 'One time I saw a boy being beaten in a street near our house. He had snatched a woman's bread ration as she was coming out of the bakery and fallen in the snow. Weary, debilitated people were kicking him, while he lay face down in the snow munching and munching' (V. Peterson, '"Skorei by bylo teplo". Vospominaniia o pervoi blokadnoi zime', *Neva*, No. 1, 2001, p. 172).

162 Here are a few: 'The bakery. A woman has received 200 grams of bread and leaves the counter. An emaciated man aged about 35 tears the bread out of her hands. He turns aside, hunches his shoulders and eats it greedily. People hit him. He says nothing and carries on chewing' (Khodorkov, 'Materialy blokadnykh zapisei', 12 January 1942, *list* 13); 'One time when bread was being issued a man grabbed it right off the scales and started eating it. The women hit him, but he shielded himself with his hands and carried on eating' (V. M. Lisovskaia (transcript of reminiscences), *900 blokadnykh dnei*, pp. 156–7; 'The sales assistant was issuing half a loaf of bread with a makeweight when suddenly, from behind our backs, a hand stretched out and grabbed our bread! We wailed, and the whole queue turned on the boy. They were punching him but he paid no attention and carried on chewing' (Mariia A. Gusarova, 'My ne padali dukhom', *Otkuda beretsia muzhestvo*, p. 96); 'I myself saw in a shop, a woman had just collected her bread from the sales assistant when a decent-looking young man grabbed the makeweight and started chewing it. The woman hit him, but he just bent over and carried on silently chewing' (Zhilinskii, 'Blokadnyi dnevnik', 16 January 1942, *Voprosy istorii*, Nos. 5–6, 1996, p. 26). See also the transcript of a communication by M. I. Skvortsov, *NIA SPbII RAN, fond* 332, *opis'* 1, *delo* 110, *list* 12; Livshits, 'Dnevnik', p. 174; interview with L. P. Vlasova, *Nestor*, No. 6, 2003, p. 81.

163 Z. A. Ignatovich, 'Ocherki o blokade Leningrada', *OR RNB, fond* 1273, *delo* 26, *list* 29.

164 'The girl paid no attention at all to the punches or the crowd which had gathered' (ibid., *listy* 29–30).

165 Ibid., *list* 30. Compare the story of a Leningrader about a boy she went to school with: 'He didn't even run away. He got down on his heels up against a wall and ate and ate. The whole queue went for him. The sales assistant told me, he hunched himself up, pulled in his head and shoulders, and kept the loaf wedged between his knees. People were punching him but he didn't notice the blows, just carried on eating. He managed to eat nearly the whole loaf' (Vol't Suslov, *50 rasskazov o blokade*, SPb., 1994, p. 86).

166 Suslov, *50 rasskazov o blokade*, p. 86.

167 See A. G. Usanova's account of how a workman seized her mother's bread. 'My mother was hammering on his back saying, "Give me back my bread," but he said, "I've eaten it"' (interview with A. G. Usanova, *Nestor*, No. 6, 2003, p. 251).

168 Zelenskaia, 'Dnevnik', 15 December 1941, *list* 43.

169 Interview with L. P. Vlasova, *Nestor*, No. 6, 2003, p. 81.

170 Z. V. Krasiukova, 'Iz dnevnika pamiati', *Leningradskaia nauka v gody Velikoi Otechestvennoi voiny*, SPb., 1995, pp. 102–3.

171 Interview with M. V. Vasil'eva, *Nestor*, No. 6, 2003, p. 62.
172 M. P. Pelevin, 'Povest' blokadnykh dnei', *OR RNB, fond* 1273, *delo* 36, *listy* 30–1.
173 Interview with Ignatova, *Chelovek v blokade*, p. 243.
174 V. A. Zavetnovskii to T. V. Zavetnovskaia, 5 February 1942, *OR RNB, fond* 1273, *list* 3 verso. Compare A. V. Smorodinova's reminiscences: 'If someone lost consciousness, they were given no care (as a rule, it would have been useless), and people helped themselves to their bread' (A.V. Smorodinova (transcript of reminiscences), *900 blokadnykh dnei*, p. 221).
175 Kulagin, *Dnevnik i pamiat'*, 23 June 1942, p. 161.
176 Ibid.
177 'In the morning, a corpse with bare feet has not been removed at No. 9 Proletkult Street (V. S. Liublinskii, 'Bytovye istorii utochneniia kartin blokady', 14 February 1942, in *V pamiat' ushedshikh i vo slavu zhivushchikh. Pis'ma chitatelei s fronta. Dnevniki i vospominaniia sotrudnikov Publichnoi biblioteki, SPb.*, 1995, p. 160); 'On the corner of Serpukhovskaya Street there is the body of a young woman with bare feet' (V. N. Nikol'skaia, 'V ocherediakh', *OR RNB, fond* 1037, *delo* 907, *list* 10); 'By the fence outside our block there is an old woman lying dead, with bare feet' (ibid. p. 12); see also Mikhailov, *Na dne voiny i blokady*, p. 54.
178 A. I. Vinokurov makes no bones about this. See *Blokadnyi dnevnik A. I. Vinokurova*, 28 February 1942, p. 250; see also the entry in Misha Tikhomirov's diary for 8 January 1942: 'Corpses just lying in the street are not uncommon. They don't usually have hats or anything on their feet' (*Dnevnik Mishi Tikhomirova*, p. 22).
179 See the entry in Khodorkov's diary for 28 May 1942: 'The body of a woman. Someone has already had the shoes off it' (*RDF GMMOBL, opis'* 1–r, *delo* 140, *list* 24).
180 Transcript of a communication by M. G. Aleksandrov, *NIA SPbII RAN, fond* 332, *opis'* 1, *delo* 2, *list* 38.
181 Grechina, 'Spasaius' spasaia', p. 250.
182 The mortuary at the Zhdanov factory, where the bodies of dead workers were stored, was guarded because 'live people were getting in and taking boots and clothes off the dead, and anything else they could' (P. I. Senichev, 'Leningradskii sudostroitel'nyi zavod im. A.A. Zhdanova v 1941–1943 gg.', p. 163).
183 L. I. Vorob'eva, 'Lunnye nochi voiny', *Otkuda beretsia muzhestvo*, p. 77.
184 'On the way out we saw people who had died lying right there in the street. They were clothed. On the way back, they had lost their fur coats and felt boots' (M. N. Kotliarova (transcript of reminiscences), *900 blokadnykh dnei*, p. 127).
185 Levina, 'Dnevnik', 23 February 1942, p. 158.
186 A. N. Mironova, 'Dnevnik', 23 March 1941, *TsGAIPD SPb., fond* 4000, *opis'* 11, *delo* 69, *list* 14.
187 Transcript of a communication by A.V. Smolovik, *NIA SPbII RAN, fond* 332, *opis'* 1, *delo* 113, *list* 14.
188 See the communication from G. Ia. Sokolov, deputy director of the Molotov factory: 'We received information that eleven mechanics from our factory have become street children: they do not spend the night at the hostel and go round canteens, steal ration cards from the sick, search the streets for deceased

persons, go through their pockets taking money and cards and removing their boots. They were dirty, infested with insects, ragged and swollen. When we caught them, they were very hungry and begged us for bread' (*NIA SPbII RAN, fond* 332, *opis'* 1, *delo* 117, *list* 4 verso).

189 Zhilinskii, 'Blokadnyi dnevnik', 30 January 1942, *Voprosy istorii*, No. 8, 1996, p. 3.
190 Ibid.
191 Glinka, 'Blokada', p. 178.
192 Ibid., pp. 178–9; compare A.A. Asknazii's notes: 'We came across bad people who were capable of taking a ration card, a piece of bread or a warm hat away from a person who was very weak' (A. A. Asknazii, 'O detiakh v blokirovannom Leningrade', *OR RNB, fond* 1273, *list* 13).
193 Zelenskaia, 'Dnevnik', 1 March 1942, *list* 65 verso.

2 Moral commandments

1 I. Metter, *Budni, Lg,*, 1987, pp. 356–7.
2 Ibid., p. 357.
3 Letter from V. Mal'tsev to M. D. Mal'tsev, 15 December 1941, *900 blokadnykh dnei*, p. 267.
4 K. Polzikova-Rubets, *Oni uchilis' v Leningrade*, 26 January 1942, *Lg.*, 1954, p. 82.
5 See Vladimir Mal'tsev's letter to his mother and sister: 'I feel very uncomfortable, sitting here without a job and wasting father's money. If the schools don't reopen I'll get a job' (V. Mal'tsev to Z. R. Mal'tseva and I. Mal'tseva, 22 October 1941, *900 dnei blokady*, p. 264). In her memoirs, I. A. Cherniavskaia mentions a family consisting of a 15-year-old boy, his mother and grandmother, all of whom were starving. The boy decided to go to the Elektrik factory: 'At least I'll be some use, and they'll give us 250 grams of bread' (I. A. Cherniavskaia, 'Istochnik sily', *Bez antrakta. Aktery goroda Lenina v gody blokady*, *Lg.*, 1970, p. 107).
6 A. S. Umanskaia, 'Dnevnik', 10 April 1942, *OR RNB, fond* 1273, *delo* 72, *list* 34 verso.
7 Daev, 'Printsipial'nye leningradtsy', *list* 91.
8 F. A. Griaznov, 'Dnevnik', 28 November 1941, p. 126; see also I. V. Turkov, chairman of the department of culture and propaganda of the Molotov factory about Grin'ko, the secretary of a workshop Party cell: 'I could see the man was weak and unlikely to make it back home. I said to him, "Go and get a meal in the restaurant. I'll give you the coupons." No matter how I tried, I just could not persuade him to take my coupons' (transcript of a communication by I. V. Turkov, *NIA* SPbII RAN, *fond* 332, *opis'* 1, *delo* 128, *list* 7 verso – 8).
9 Borovikova, 'Dnevnik', 10 January 1942, *list* 99 verso.
10 Mukhina, 'Dnevnik', 7 March 1942, *list* 91 verso.
11 A. Lepkovich, 'Dnevnik', 16 December 1941, *TsGAIPD SPb., fond* 4000, *opis'* 11, *delo* 59, *list* 9 verso.
12 Kulagin, *Dnevnik i pamiat'*, p. 218.
13 Ibid.
14 Kross, *Vospominaniia o Vove*, pp. 46–7.

15 F. A. Griaznov, 'Dnevnik', 28 December 1941, p. 170.

16 I. Metter, *Izbrannoe*, *Lg.*, 1999, p. 112.

17 Ibid.

18 Chekrizov, 'Dnevnik blokadnogo vremeni', 14 October 1941, p. 28.

19 Ibid., 29 January 1942, p. 48.

20 *Dnevnik Mishi Tikhomirova*, 30 December 1941, p. 18.

21 'Kseniia pours half into our cup and offers it to me. How hard it is to say no, but I do, nevertheless, force the word out, but stand there waiting to see if she will offer it a second time.' Compare V. M. Lisovskaia's memoirs: 'One day when we went there, Uncle Seva had decked the New Year's tree with sweets and mandarin oranges. He asked us, "Well, girls, are you hungry?" I said, "Yes!" but my sister dug me in the ribs and said, "Shush! You should be ashamed to ask for something to eat." We were very bashful' (V. M. Lisovskaia (transcript of reminiscences), *900 blokadnykh dnei*, p. 157).

22 Food ration cards were valid for 10 days.

23 Mukhina 'Dnevnik', *list* 73 verso.

24 Ibid.

25 E. A. Skriabina, *Stranitsy zhizni*, 15 September 1941, *M.*, 1994, p. 121.

26 A. P. Ostroumova-Lebedeva to L. Ia. Kurkovskaia, 13 January 1942, *Trudy Gosudarstvennogo muzeia istorii Sankt-Peterburga*, *vyp.* 5, p. 144.

27 Kuliabko, 'Blokadnyi dnevnik', 5 October 1942, p. 236.

28 'Vospominaniia o blokade Inny Timofeevny Balashovoi (Malikovoi)', *Ispytanie*, p. 67.

29 Ibid.

30 Ibid.

31 Interview with G. N. Ignatova, *Chelovek v blokade*, p. 250.

32 V. Glotser, *Marina Durnovo. Moi muzh Daniil Kharms*, *M.*, 2001, p. 125. [Daniil Kharms was arrested on 23 August 1941. He died in the psychiatric wing of Leningrad's Kresty prison hospital on 2 February 1942. – Tr.]

33 T. K. Val'ter and O. R. Peto, 'Odni sutki. Dekabr' 1941 g.', *OR RNB, fond* 1273, *delo* 51/1, *list* 20.

34 T. Kudriavtseva, *Fotografiia, kotoroi ne bylo*, *SPb.*, 2006, p. 16.

35 Pavlov, *Leningrad v blokade*, p. 174.

36 A. Adamovich and D. Granin, *Blokadnaia kniga*, *Lg.*, 1984, p. 123.

37 N. A. Lomagin, *Neizvestnaia blokada*, vol. II, *SPb.*, 2002. The NKVD (People's Commissariat of Interior Affairs) was the contemporary incarnation of the Soviet secret police.

38 N. P. Zavetovskaia to T. V. Zavetnovskaia, 9 February 1942, *OR RNB, fond* 1273, *list* 35.

39 Ibid.

40 B. P. Gorodetskii to his wife and daughters, 20 February 1942, quoted from S. Gorodetskii, *Pis'ma vremeni*, *Lg.*, 2005, p. 124.

41 Ibid.

42 Maksimova, *Vospominaniia o leningradskoi blokade*, p. 39.

43 Levina, *Dnevnik*, 17 January 1942, p. 148.

44 Ibid.

45 Transcript of a story, quoted from Shestinskii, *Golosa iz blokady*, p. 20.

46 Transcript of a communication by A. P. Ivanov, *NIA SPbII RAN, fond* 332, *opis'* 1, *delo* 53, *list* 8.

47 *Iz dnevnikov G. A. Kniazeva*, 7 January 1942, p. 39.

48 Ibid., 1 February 1942, p. 48.
49 Kulagin, *Dnevnik i pamiat'*, 22 March 1942, p. 147.
50 Zelenskaia, 'Dnevnik', 6 January and 2 April 1942, *listy* 50, 72 verso. See also 'Iz dnevnika Maii Bubnovoi', *Leningradtsy v dni blokady*, Lg., 1947, 20 December 1941, p. 224.
51 Zelenskaia, 'Dnevnik', 10 December 1941, *list* 41 verso.
52 See M. V. Mashkova on the subject of her neighbour Fisa, whose ration cards were stolen: 'She came to me several times, her legs collapsing, and begging for a piece of bread. I was not pleased, but gave her half my ration. I was irritated by the greedy way Fisa tried to cling on to her clothes and her life' (Mashkova, *Iz blokadnykh zapisei*, 21 April 1942, p. 476).
53 Olga Berggol'ts even mentioned this in a broadcast on Radio Leningrad: 'We not infrequently hear complaints along the lines of, "Oh, people nowadays are so rude and greedy and irritable"' (Olga Berggol'ts, *Govorit Leningrad*, in *Sobranie sochinenii*, vol. II, Lg., 1989, p. 206).
54 N. P. Zavetnovskaia to T. V. Zavetnovskaia, 5 February 1942, *OR RNB, fond* 1273, *list* 32 verso.
55 Ibid., 27 December 1941, *list* 24 verso.
56 G. Kabanova to M. Kharitonova, 2 April 1942, *RDF GMMOBL, opis'* 1-k, *delo* 5.
57 V. Kuliabko, 'Blokadnyy dnevnik', *Neva*, No. 3, 2004, p. 264.
58 Ibid. The 'Road of Life' was the route across the ice of Lake Ladoga which provided virtually the only access to Leningrad during the siege. There is information on the taking of bribes from evacuees on the Road of Life in a number of other documents. See a communication by L. S. Levin, the director of the evacuation centre at Borisova Griva: 'There were instances of extortion and looting by drivers and some of the evacuation centre staff, where evacuees gave large sums of money for a prompt place in the transports and to get across to the other side' (transcript of a communication by L. S. Levin, *NIA SPbII RAN, fond* 332, *opis'* 1, *delo* 77, *list* 22); there is also a communication from a member of staff at the same evacuation centre about the behaviour of one of the drivers: 'He took 1,000 rubles in cash from each person.' He also mentions that 'they would take vodka and spirits' (transcript of a communication by Ivanov, *NIA SPbII RAN, fond* 332, *opis'* 1, *delo* 77, *list* 44).
59 Zelenskaia, 'Dnevnik', 24 September 1941, *list* 19 verso.
60 Bazanova, 'Vchera bylo deviat' trevog . . .', 12 June 1942, p. 133.
61 Mukhina, 'Dnevnik', 21 November 1941, *list* 53 verso.
62 Ibid., 13 March 1942, *list* 92 verso.
63 Ibid., *list* 93.
64 Ibid.
65 Ibid., 3 January 1942, *list* 72 verso.
66 L. R. Kogan, 'Dnevnik', 21 February 1942, *OR RNB, fond* 1035, *delo* 1, *list* 15.
67 V. Kulyabko, 'Blokadnyi dnevnik', 10 September 1941, *Neva*, No. 1, 2004. p. 214.
68 Ibid.
69 Fadeev, *Leningrad v dni blokady*, p. 136.
70 A. O. Zmitrichenko (transcript of reminiscences), *900 blokadnykh dnei*, p. 93.
71 'In Leningrad, as before, part of the populace gorges itself while another part is starving' (Bazanova, 'Vchera bylo deviat' trevog . . .', p. 133); 'They say the

authorities lived better' (V. M. Lisovskaia (transcript of reminiscences), *900 blokadnykh dnei*, p. 157); 'Forbidden rumours circulated in those days, during the siege, about how they were living it up in Smolny' (Metter, *Dopros*, p. 50). A briefing from the staff training department and the department of agitation and propaganda of the Leningrad City Party committee sent to A. A. Zhdanov notes, for example, that in Shop No. 3 of Kirov district one of the customers commented, 'It's all very well for Popkov to make speeches, he's had plenty to eat but only feeds us with promises' (*Leningrad v osade*, p. 472).

72 'Parcels from the People's Commissar have been presented to forty-one individuals, causing offence to three times as many' (Kulagin, *Dnevnik i pamiat'*, 14 July 1942, p. 255). 'The saga of the "gift to the Academy of Sciences" has ended. Now ripples of sullen discontent of those who received short measure or nothing at all will spread in all directions' (*Iz dnevnikov G. A. Kniazeva*, 24 May 1942, p. 62). Animosity towards those who received incentives, which many considered unmerited, was reflected in the 'anti-Soviet' remark of someone working at a bakery (who was, incidentally, a Party member) and which found its way into an NKVD report: 'The Germans put all their money into preparations for the war, but we fritter ours away on 100,000–ruble bonuses' ('Soobshchenie UNKVD LO NKVD SSSR 21 aprelia 1942 g.', *Mezhdunarodnoe polozhenie glazami leningradtsev. 1941–1945*, SPb., 1996, p. 41).

73 *Iz dnevnikov G. A. Kniazeva*, pp. 25–6.
74 Likhachev, *Vospominaniia*, p. 461.
75 'Blokadnyi dnevnik N. P. Gorshkova', p. 88.
76 Ibid.
77 Konopleva, 'V blokirovannom Leningrade. Dnevnik', 1 July 1942, *delo* 2, *list* 91.
78 Ibid.
79 *Iz dnevnikov G. A. Kniazeva*, 23 January 1942, p. 46.
80 Likhachev, *Vospominaniia*, p. 461.
81 Zelenskaia, 'Dnevnik', 9 October 1942, *list* 102.
82 Ibid. See also the entry for 5 September 1942. 'If we stop working, we will see the traditional picture: the bosses will fix themselves up in the greatest possible comfort, and the rest will have to run around and make whatever arrangements for themselves they can' (ibid., *listy* 98 – 98 verso).
83 'The catering staff bring dinner and breakfast, and of course it is ration coupon-free' (Chekrizov, 'Dnevnik blokadnogo vremeni', 25 March 1942, p. 65).
84 Zhilinskii, *Blokadnyi dnevnik*, 2 January 1942, p. 21.
85 V. Kuliabko, 'Blokadnyi dnevnik', 2 February 1942, *Neva*, No. 3, 2004, p. 263.
86 Quoted from N. Ia. Komarov and G. A. Kumanev, *Blokada Leningrada. 900 geroicheskikh dnei. 1941–1944*, M., 2004, p. 142.
87 Transcript of a communication by A. L. Plotkin, *NIA* SPbII RAN, *fond* 332, *opis'* 1, *delo* 102, *list* 34.
88 V. Kuliabko, 'Blokadnyi dnevnik', *Neva*, No. 3, 2004, p. 263.
89 N. P. Zavetnovskaia to T. V. Zavetnovskaia, 9 February 1942, *OR RNB, fond* 1273, *list* 35 verso.
90 A. I. Kochetova to her mother, 24 December 1941, *RDF GMMOBL, opis'* 1–k, *delo* 5.

91 Ibid., 9 January 1942.
92 Ibid.
93 Berggol'ts, *Vstrecha*, p. 241.
94 Ibid.
95 Mashkova, *Iz blokadnykh zapisei*, 18 February 1942, p. 17.
96 Ibid.
97 Liublinskii, *Bytovye istorii utochneniia kartin blokady*, p. 157.
98 N. E. Gavrilina recalled her mother: 'She looked terrible, although she was only thirty-five: so terrible that elderly people offered her their seat in the tram' (N. E. Gavrilina, 'Vospominaniia o blokade', NIA SPbII RAN, *fond* 332, *opis'* 1, *delo* 150, *list* 12). See also a letter from N. P. Zavetnovskaia to T. V. Zavetnovskaia of 5 February 1942 where she describes one of her acquaintances: 'She was a young woman, but in two weeks turned into an old lady. Her mouth became all twisted' (*OR RNB, fond* 1273, *list* 33).
99 'Vospominaniia Travkinoi Zoi Sergeevny o blokadnom Leningrade', *NIA SPbII RAN, fond* 332, *opis'* 1, *delo* 149, *list* 5.
100 Metter, *Izbrannoe*, p. 109.
101 Berggol'ts, *Vstrecha*, p. 240.
102 Kulagin, *Dnevnik i pamiat'*, pp. 185–6 (dated April 1942).
103 Ibid.
104 See a letter from V. S. Liublinskii, who was deputy chief of staff of the Kuibyshev District Air Defence Unit: 'I found myself next at table to our commissar. He was embarrassed by the disproportion of our meals. Mine was 200 grams of pearl barley porridge with 10 grams of butter: his was 300–350 grams of the same porridge with 30–40 grams of butter, plus three good pieces of fried meat, plus coupon-free white bread. He put a piece of meat on my plate' (V. S. Liublinskii to A. D. Liublinskaia, 7 July 1942, *V pamiat' usheds-hikh i vo slavu zhivushchikh*, p. 238).
105 A. O. Zmitrichenko (transcript of reminiscences), *900 blokadnykh dnei*, p. 92.
106 Likhachev, *Vospominaniia*, p. 487; see also Maksimova, *Vospominaniia o leningradskoi blokade*, p. 39.
107 M. Pelevin, 'Povest' blokadnykh dnei', *OR RNB, fond* 1273, *delo* 36, *list* 26.
108 Likhachev, *Vospominaniia*, p. 471.
109 O. P. Solov'eva, 'Vospominaniia o perezhitoi blokade iunoi zashchitnitsy goroda Leningrada. (1941–1945 gody)', *OR RNB, fond* 1273, *delo* 25, *list* 8; see also an entry in Georgii Kulagin's diary about their factory canteen: 'You start looking sideways at the plates of neighbours who have not yet finished eating their meal, and always think they have been given a larger portion than you' (Kulagin, *Dnevnik i pamiat'*, 23 March 1942, p. 150).
110 V. G. Grigor'ev, *Leningrad. Blokada. 1941–1942*, SPb., 2003, p. 46.
111 Moldavskii, *Stranitsy o zime 1941–42 godov*, p. 355.
112 Byl'ev, *Iz dnevnika*, p. 333.
113 Interview with L. P. Vlasova, p. 70.
114 S. D. Kotov, *Destskie doma blokadnogo Leningrada*, SPb., 2002, p. 36.
115 She said later that she encountered 'the sympathy of strangers when I was exchanging things from home for a piece of bread' (G. M. Stepanova (Kabanova), 'Avtobiografiia', *RDF GMMOBL*, Akt 49–55).
116 Mashkova, *Iz blokadnykh zapisei*, p. 20.
117 Khodorkov, 'Materialy blokadnykh zapisei', 13 January 1942, *list* 13.
118 E. Solov'eva, 'Sud'ba byla - vyzhit'', *Neva*, No. 9, 2006, p. 232.

119 Interview with G. N. Ignatova, p. 256.
120 E. S. Tiis (transcript of reminiscences), *900 blokadnykh dnei*, p. 241.
121 Arkhiv Tsentra ustnoy istorii Evropeiskogo Universiteta v Sankt-Peterburge [Archive of the Oral History Centre of the European University in St Petersburg].
122 *Budni podviga*, p. 60.
123 Ibid., p. 134.
124 Ibid., p. 140.
125 Ibid.
126 Ibid., pp. 124–5.
127 The 'feeding' of highly placed officials evidently occurred not only in this nursery but also in other children's institutions. L. M. Lotman, who worked in a children's home, related that, after a drawing competition there, the judges, who were leading lights in the Union of Artists, were invited to a 'sumptuous evening meal and tea.' Two of the best educated of the kindergarten teachers (one of whom was Lotman) were detailed to engage them in conversation, but warned that their task was to 'talk about art, and most certainly not to participate in the tea drinking and repast'. The director of the children's home evidently had a very clear idea of whom it was appropriate to feed at the children's expense and whom not to bother with. See L. M. Lotman, *Vospominaniia*, *SPb.*, 2007, p. 92.
128 'Many live in sickbays. They come to work later, leave earlier, and are excused physical labour' (E. G. Levina, 'Pis'ma k drugu', *Leningradtsy v dni blokady*, *Lg.*, 1947, p. 206). 'Many swell and die of starvation. Those who have weakened are often given a holiday without pay, I suppose so they can have a good rest' (Borovikova, 'Dnevnik', *list* 90).
129 Sharypina, *Za zhizn' i pobedu. Iz zapisok partorganizatora*, *Deviat'sot dnei*, p. 143.
130 Zelenskaia, 'Dnevnik', 24 September 1942, *list* 19 verso.
131 Konopleva, 'V blokirovannom Leningrade. Dnevnik', 22 May 1942, *delo* 2, *listy* 74–5.
132 Memoirs of N. V. Shirkova, E. V. Shun'gina family archive, note dated January 1942.
133 V. Kuliabko, 'Blokadnyi dnevnik', *Neva*, No. 1, 2004, p. 219.
134 Berggol'ts, *Vstrecha*, p. 362.
135 N. P. Zavetnovskaia to T. V. Zavetnovskaia, 5 February 1942, *OR RNB, fond* 1273, *list* 30.
136 Ibid.
137 A. S. Nikol'skii, 'Dnevnik', 2 January 1942, *OR RNB, fond* 1037, *delo* 901, *list* 27.
138 *Blokadnyi dnevnik A. I. Vinokurova*, 28 February 1942, p. 251.
139 Grigor'ev, *Leningrad. Blokada*, p. 43.
140 Zhilinskii, 'Blokadnyi dnevnik', *Voprosy istorii*, Nos. 5–6, 1996, p. 9.
141 Interview with L. P. Vlasova, p. 81.
142 Interview with V. A. Alekseeva, *Nestor*, No. 6, 2003, pp. 49–50.
143 Ibid., p. 39.
144 G. Glukhova, *I byl sluchai . . .*, p. 221.
145 Interview with M. V. Vasil'eva, p. 63.
146 Khodorkov, 'Materialy blokadnykh zapisei', 2 January 1942, *list* 9.
147 Razumovskii, *Deti blokady*, p. 51.

148 Ibid.
149 A.V. Sirotova, 'Gody voiny', *OR RNB, fond* 1273, *list* 60.
150 T. K. Val'ter and O. R. Peto, 'Zapiski vyezdov skoroi pomoshchi', *OR RNB, fond* 1273, *opis'* 5211, *list* 15 verso.
151 A. Lepkovich, 'Dnevnik', *TsGAIPD SPb., fond* 4000, *opis'* 11, *delo* 59, *list* 5.
152 See M. S. Konopleva's diary, which lists hospitals which have been destroyed: 'There soon won't be a single hospital the Germans haven't bombed' (Konopleva, 'V blokirovannom Leningrade. Dnevnik', *list* 93).
153 Polzikova-Rubets, *Oni uchilis' v Leningrade*, 18 December 1941, p. 67.
154 N. P. Zavetnovskaia to T. V. Zavetnovskaia, 5 February 1942, *OR RNB, fond* 1273, *list* 31.
155 'Blokadnyi dnevnik N. P. Gorshkova', 8 March 1942, p. 85.
156 A. Lepkovich, 'Dnevnik', *TsGAIPD SPb., fond* 4000, *opis'* 11, *delo* 59, *list* 5 verso.
157 Borovikova, 'Dnevnik', 14 September 1941, *list* 39 verso.
158 Peterson, 'Dnevnik', 20 October 1941, *delo* 86, *list* 3.
159 Polzikova-Rubets, *Oni uchilis' v Leningrad*, 1 January 1942, p. 73.
160 *Pamiat' o blokade*, p. 44.
161 Daev, 'Printsipial'nye leningradtsy'.
162 F. A. Griaznov, *Dnevnik*, 14 November 1941, p. 103.
163 Ibid.
164 Chursin, 'Soobshchaet 21–i o svoei gotovnosti', p. 151.
165 Inber, *Pochti tri goda*, 4 January 1942, p. 174.
166 A. V. Sirotova, 'Gody voiny', *OR RNB, fond* 1273, *list* 60.
167 R. Belevskaia, *Cherez pokoleniia. Pamiat'. Pis'ma o voine i blokade*, vyp. 2, Lg., 1987, p. 220.
168 Transcript of a communication by M. N. Abrosimova., *TsGAIPD SPb., fond* 4000, *opis'* 10, *delo* 307, *listy* 27–8.
169 'Vospominaniia', quoted from S. Kotov, *Detskie doma blokadnogo Leningrada*, p. 164.
170 G. I. Kozlova, 'Moi studencheskie gody (Stranitsy vospominanii byvshei studentki priema 1940)', *'My znaem, chto znachit voina . . .'*, p. 202.
171 V. P. Kondrat'ev, 'Vesomyi vklad', *V osazhdennom Leningrade. Vospominaniia uchastnika geroicheskoi oborony o bor'be s golodom i sozdanii v usloviiakh blokady prodovol'stvennykh resursov*, Lg., 1974, p. 40.
172 Ibid., p. 41.
173 T. Sil'man and V. Admoni, *My vspominaem*, p. 294.
174 Transcript of a communication by M. N. Abrosimova, *TsGAIPD SPb., fond* 4000, *opis'* 10, *delo* 307, *list* 37; transcript of a communication by A. P. Ivanov, *NIA SPbII RAN, fond* 332, *opis'* 1, *delo* 53, *list* 7 verso; transcript of a communication by Z. V. Vinogradova, *NIA SPbII RAN, fond* 332, *opis'* 1, *delo* 24, *list* 7; transcript of a communication by M. N. Skvortsov, *NIA SPbII RAN, fond* 332, *opis'* 1, *delo* 110, *list* 8 verso; transcript of a collective of housewives and housekeepers at the Malaia Okhta enterprise; *NIA SPbII RAN, fond* 332, *opis'* 1, *delo* 146, *list* 13; 'Dnevnik pionerskoi druzhiny 105–i shkoly', *Deti goroda-geroia*, p. 136; 'Vospominaniia Travkinoi Zoi Sergeevny o blokadnom Leningrade', *NIA SPbII RAN, fond* 332, *opis'* 1, *delo* 149, *list* 6; Vitenburg, *Pavel Vitenburg*, p. 282.
175 Transcript of a communication by M. N. Abrosimova, *TsGAIPD SPb., fond* 4000, *opis'* 10, *delo* 307, *list* 19.

176 Transcript of a communication by A. P. Alekseeva, *NIA SPbII RAN, fond* 332, *opis'* 1, *delo* 3, *list* 11.
177 A. R. Dzeniskevich, V. M. Koval'chuk, G. L. Sobolev, A. N. Tsamutali and V. A. Shishkin, *Nepokorennyi Leningrad. Kratkii ocherk istorii goroda v period Velikoi Otechestvennoi voiny*, Lg., 1985, p. 118.
178 A. V. Burov, *Blokada den' za dnem*, Lg., 1979, p. 267.
179 In the Krasnogvardeiskii district, in the course of one and a half years, 46,000 items of warm clothing and 85,000 gifts were collected for the front (I. P. Barbashina, A. I. Kuznetsov, V. P. Morozov, A. D. Kharitonov and B. I. Iakovlev, *Bitva za Leningrad. 1941–1944*, M., 1984, p. 198); 15,000 items of crockery were collected for hospitals by medical workers of the Russian Red Cross (L. I. Levitskaia, transcript of a communication and a report on the work of the Red Cross Society in the period 22 June 1941 –31 December 1942, *TsGAIPD SPb.*, *fond* 4000, *opis'* 10, *delo* 276, *list* 16).
180 See the communication by Secretary of the Dzerzhinsky district Party committee, Z. Vinogradova: 'The population not only brought items but our women sewed and knitted warm clothes. Housewives sewed underwear. An old lady decided to knit mittens (she had three sons at the front). Her building was bombed. She lived on Vsevolozhskaia Street and brought fifteen pairs of mittens and socks all that way in the winter, on foot because the public transport was not functioning. She was sixty-five. Can you imagine her walking from Vsevolozhskaia? How many kilometres that is?!' (transcript of a communication by Z. V. Vinogradova, *NIA SPbII RAN, fond* 332, *opis'* 1, *delo* 24, *list* 6).
181 As N. V. Mansvetova, a member of the council coordinating the collection of items, noted in her memoirs: 'People brought everything they had. They donated good, high-quality items: boots, mittens, warm underwear, hats, socks, quilted winter jackets, and skeins of wool' (Mansvetova, *Vospominaniia o moei rabote v gody voiny*, p. 551). Worshippers and servers at the Cathedral of the Transfiguration gathered about 100 towels, bandages and items of warm clothing. They made 25 stoves for military hospitals (M. V. Shkarovskii, *Tserkov' zovet k zashchite Rodiny*, SPb., 2005, p. 56; Borovikova, 'Dnevnik', 12 October 1941, *list* 65 verso).
182 Zelenskaia, 'Dnevnik', 7 December 1941, *list* 39.
183 In September 1941, 900 people visited the front-line units as workers' delegates ('Spravka otdela agitatsii i propagandy gorkoma VKP(b) sekretariu Gorkoma VKP(b) A. I. Makhanovu', *900 geroicheskikh dnei*, p. 109). In the Time of Death, the number was probably fewer.
184 Borovikova, 'Dnevnik', 1 November 1941, *list* 69.
185 A. P. Zagorskaia, 'Dnevnik', 28 January 1942, *NIA SPbII RAN, fond* 332, *opis'* 1, *delo* 47, *list* 21.
186 See entries in Borovikova's diary: 'I took a look at myself in the mirror – just wrinkled skin and bones. I could only hope I would be sent again to the front to take gifts to the soldiers at New Year' (entry for 14 December 1941); 'I'm as thin as a rake. I so want to gorge myself, I can't believe it. The only consolation is that it looks as if I am going to the front. That may revive me a bit' (entry for 23 February 1942, Borovikova, 'Dnevnik', *listy* 89, 93). We find similar entries in the diaries of the actors F. A. and A. A. Griaznov, who gave concerts in military units they were paired with. They invariably mention that

they hope to be fed there. See F. A. Griaznov, 'Dnevnik', *Dozhivem li my do tishiny? SPb.*, 2009, p. 118; A. A. Griaznov, 'Dnevnik', *Chelovek v blokade, SPb.*, 2008, pp. 75, 80.

187 Transcript of a communication by P. P. Trofimov, *NIA SPbII RAN, fond* 332, *opis'* 1, *delo* 126, *list* 16.

188 On this correspondence, see the transcript of a communication by G. A. Maliarov, *NIA SPbII RAN, fond* 332, *opis'* 1, *delo* 83, *list* 20; transcript of a communication by Z. V. Vinogradova, *NIA SPbII RAN, fond* 332, *opis'* 1, *delo* 24, *list* 9.

189 Interview with M. V. Vasil'eva, pp. 63, 64.

190 N. L. Val'ter, 'Rabotat', borot'sia i pobedit'', *Bez antrakta*, p. 205.

191 Borovikova, 'Dnevnik', 18 November 1941, *list* 76 verso.

192 Zelenskaia, 'Dnevnik', 9 October 1942, *listy* 102 verso – 103.

193 V. S. Liublinskii to A. D. Liublinskaia, 6 May 1942, *Publichnaia biblioteka v gody voiny*, p. 230.

194 See the interview with A. G. Usanova. 'You're walking along the street and you see a white headscarf, wool, painted lips. It's a profiteer, of course it is. She's stolen the lot' (*Nestor*, No. 6, 2003, p. 251).

195 Samarin, 'Dnevnik', 8 January 1942, *list* 79.

196 Bezobrazova (transcript of reminiscences), *900 blokadnykh dnei*.

197 Berggol'ts, *Vstrecha*, pp. 239–40.

198 Livshits, *Dnevnik*, 12 April 1942, pp. 56, 57.

199 Mashkova, *Iz blokadnykh zapisei*, 23 March 1942, p. 33.

200 In a letter sent on 9 April 1942 to the chairman of the Committee on the Arts of the Council of People's Commissars, B. I. Zagurskii, head of the Arts Directorate of the Leningrad City Executive Committee, enthuses about theatre-goers who are willing to pay 400 grams of bread for a ticket (A.V. Burov, *Blokada den' za dnem*, p. 164). A telling commentary on this is a tale told by V. A. Opakhova, published in the *Blokadnaia kniga* of A. Adamovich and D. Granin. At just this time, in the spring of 1942, she and her daughter, on the verge of starvation, tried to go for walks in the city in the hope it would take their minds of the feelings of hunger.

201 Mashkova, *Iz blokadnykh zapisei*, 23 March 1942, p. 33.

202 Liublinskii, *Bytovye istorii utochneniia kartin blokady*, p. 166.

203 *Blokadnyi dnevnik A. I. Vinokurova*, p. 253.

204 L. R. Kogan, 'Dnevnik', 10 February 1942, *OR RNB, fond* 1035, *delo* 1, *list* 7.

205 Iu. Bodunov to his family, 16 December 1941, *RDF GMMOBL, opis'* 1–k, *delo* 5.

206 D. S. Likhachev, *Vospominaniia*, p. 482.

207 Secret report from the head of the Leningrad province NKVD directorate, 5 September 1942, *Leningrad v osade*, pp. 436–7.

208 Kniazev, *Iz dnevnikov G. A. Kniazeva*, 5–6 March 1942, p. 58.

209 Ibid.

210 A. F. Evdokimov, 'Dnevnik', 7 September 1942, *RDF GMMOBL, delo* 30, *list* 107. It is significant that even children were talking about it. M. A. Tkacheva (born 1930) said she very much liked a boy who 'was different. Compared to the rest of us, he was really blooming.' The schoolchildren were asked one time to talk about their parents: 'Vova got up and said, "My mum works in a canteen." None of us would talk to him for several days after that' (interview with M. A. Tkacheva, *Nestor*, No. 6, 2003, p. 235).

211 G. I. Kazanina to T. A. Konopleva, 19 October 1942, *OR RNB, fond* 1273, *delo* 4, *list* 2 verso.

212 R. Bidlak, 'Rabochie leningradskikh zavodov v pervyi god voiny', *Leningradskaia epopeia. Organizatsiia oborony i naseleniia goroda, SPb.*, 1995, p. 183.

213 A. R. Dzeniskevich, *Nakanune i dni ispytanii. Leningradskie rabochie v 1938–1945 gg.*, *Lg.*, 1990, p. 88; transcript of a communication by P. P. Trofimov, *NIA SPbII RAN, fond* 332, *opis'* 1, *delo* 126, *list* 20.

214 Transcript of a communication by G. Ia. Sokolov, *NIA SPbII RAN, fond* 332, *opis'* 1, *delo* 117, *list* 4.

215 Transcript of a communication by L. N. Arshintseva, *NIA SPbII RAN, fond* 332, *opis'* 1, *delo* 4, *list* 2 verso; transcript of a communication by S. V. Usov, *NIA SPbII RAN, fond* 332, *opis'* 1, *delo* 131, *list* 37 verso; letter from the director of the Frunze factory to the Krasnogvardeiskii District Executive Committee, 12 February 1942, *Nestor*, No. 8, 2005, p. 26.

216 Transcript of a communication by M. I. Skvortsov, *NIA SPbII RAN, fond* 332, *opis'* 1, *delo* 110, *list* 10.

217 Transcript of a communication by A. E. Efimov, *NIA SPbII RAN, fond* 332, *opis'* 1, *delo* 46, *list* 17.

218 Transcript of a communication by A. G. Egorova, *NIA SPbII RAN, fond* 332, *opis'* 1, *delo* 42, *list* 6.

219 Kapranov, *Dnevnik*, p. 42.

220 Ibid.

221 Quoted from *Leningrad v osade*, p. 260. Compare with V. F. Chekrizov's diary: 'If those in charge of the canteen were not so busy pilfering, there is more than enough food being delivered for everyone' (Chekrizov, 'Dnevnik blokadnogo vremeni', p. 75).

222 *Leningrad v osade*, p. 260.

223 Secret briefing from the head of the Leningrad province NKVD Directorate to A. A. Zhdanov, 5 September 1942, ibid., p. 437.

224 In the secret briefing to A. A. Zhdanov of 5 September 1942, a sentence from a private letter is quoted: 'When you see the brazenness of the glutted canteen staff, you feel very depressed' (*Leningrad v osade*, p. 437).

225 Razumovskii, *Deti blokady*, p. 41.

226 Zabolotskaia, 'Dnevnik', *Chelovek v blokade*, p. 131.

227 Gotkhart, 'Leningrad. Blokada', p. 38.

228 Ibid.

229 There were grounds for this. See the memoirs of F. D. Litvin: 'My mother, in the same bakery where she got food in return for her ration coupons, swapped a watch for bread with the sales assistant' (F. D. Litvin, 'V tiazhelye vremena net polutonov', *Ispytanie*, p. 117); in E. G. Levina's diary we read, 'I know the manageress at the bakery used stolen bread to buy four gold watches, two sewing machines and three gramophones' (E. G. Levina, *Dnevnik*, 16 January 1942, p. 147).

230 A. T. Kedrov, 'Dnevnik', 29 January 1942, *NIA SPbII RAN, fond* 332, *opis'* 1, *delo* 59, *list* 101.

231 'Iz dnevnika Gal'ko Leonida Pavlovicha', 18 January 1942, *Oborona Leningrada. 1941–1944. Vospominaniia i dnevniki uchastnikov, Lg.*, 1968, p. 517. Hatred of the profiteer, a person not only greedy, heartless and immoral, but also entirely capable of becoming an enemy of his own country,

is to be found in almost all the writings about the siege. See A. Lepkovich's diary: 'Who is having an easy time in Leningrad at present? Only swindlers and cheats who do not care about their people or their Motherland' (A. Lepkovich, 'Dnevnik', 23 February 1942, *TsGAIPD SPb.*, *fond* 4000, *opis'* 11, *delo* 59, *list* 10 verso); also the diary of N. P. Osipova: 'Forced today to exchange a dress and skirt with a canteen waitress for bread. That's how it is: some people die, and others are doing very nicely out of it' (N. P. Osipova, 'Dnevnik', 10 December 1941, *NIA SPbII RAN*, *fond* 332, *opis'* 1, *delo* 93, *list* 17; also the diary of A. T. Kedrov: 'Their pockets are stuffed with money, of course, more than they can count, and they have more to eat than any of us' (A. T. Kedrov, 'Dnevnik', 29 January 1942, *NIA SPbII RAN*, *fond* 332, *opis'* 1, *delo* 59, *list* 101).

232 Information summary from the staff training department and the department of propaganda and agitation of the Leningrad City Party committee to A. A. Zhdanov, 14 January 1942, *Leningrad v osade*, p. 471.
233 N. P. Zavetnovskaia to T. V. Zavetnovskaia, 15 January 1942, *OR RNB*, *fond* 1273, *list* 29.
234 Ibid., 5 February 1942, *OR RNB*, *fond* 1273, *list* 32 verso.
235 El'iasheva, *My ukhodim . . . My ostaemsia . . .*, p. 206.
236 A. I. Kochetova to her mother, 24 December 1941, *RDF GMMOBL*, *opis'* 1–k, *delo* 5.
237 Berggol'ts, *Vstrecha*, p. 176.
238 Entry for 24 January 1942 in the diary of [Harry Aesop], quoted from A. Krestinskii, 'Dnevnik Kharri Ezopa', *Deti goroda-geroia*, p. 297.
239 Zhilinskii, 'Blokadnyi dnevnik', 25 January 1942, *Voprosy istorii*, No. 7, 1996, p. 10.
240 L. Konnova, 'Ia zhila v Leningrade v dekabre sorok pervogo goda . . .', *Kraevedcheskie zapiski*, *vyp.* 7, *SPb.*, 2000, p. 306.
241 Maksimova, *Vospominaniia o leningradskoi blokade*, p. 44.
242 Bazanova, 'Vchera bylo deviat' trevog . . .', 3 April 1942, p. 130.
243 Quoted from A. Adamovich and D. Granin, *Blokadnaia kniga*, p. 128.
244 Samarin, 'Dnevnik', *list* 89.
245 Inber, *Pochti tri goda*, p. 18.
246 Gusarova, *My ne padali dukhom*, p. 96.
247 444 A .F. Evdokimov, 'Dnevnik', 5 December 1941, *RDF GMMOBL*, *opis'* 1–r, *delo* 30, *list* 75.
248 *Pamiat' o blokade*, p. 110.
249 Ibid., pp. 112–13.
250 Ibid., p. 113.
251 Ibid.
252 L. Druskin, *Spasennaia kniga. SPb.*, 2001, p. 133.
253 Gel'fer, 'Dnevnik', 20 March 1942, *listy* 17 – 17 verso.
254 V. Kuliabko, 'Blokadnyi dnevnik', 7 October 1941, *Neva*, No. 2, 2004, p. 237.
255 *V pamiat' ushedshikh i vo slavu zhivushchikh*, p. 181.
256 Borovikova, 'Dnevnik', 7 February 1942, *list* 110.
257 Gotkhart, 'Leningrad. Blokada', p. 36; I. S. Glazunov, *Rossiia raspiataia*, vol. I, book 2, p. 97; Lazarev, *Leningrad v blokade*, p. 199.
258 N. N.Erofeeva (Klishevich), 'Dnevnik', *RDF GMMOBL*, *opis'* 1–l, *delo* 490, *list* 27.

259 O. R. Peto, 'Dnevnik rozyska propavshikh v blokadu', *OR RNB, fond* 1273, *delo* 52/2, *list* 116.
260 Ibid.

3 The shifting boundaries of ethics

1 See the entry in I. D. Zelenskaia's diary for 6 February 1942: 'I took an order to the clinic for home visits for 20 persons, but the doctor refused to come out. She was swollen herself' ('Dnevnik', *list* 61 verso); see also the entry for 8 November 1941 in the diary of V. Peterson: 'A. P. is angry that there is nothing to eat, but how is that the fault of me and mother? Where are we supposed to find food?' (Peterson, 'Dnevnik', *list* 4).
2 Borovikova, 'Dnevnik', *list* 84.
3 A. Lepkovich, 'Dnevnik', 17 December 1941, *TsGAIPD SPb., fond* 4000, *opis'* 11, *delo* 59, *list* 10. Compare the diary of P. M. Samarin: 'Stashnevich sent a letter asking me to buy him grains and bread because he is dying of starvation. I am in the same situation myself. I can't get round to see him' (Samarin, 'Dnevnik', 12 January 1942, *list* 84).
4 A. Lepkovich, 'Dnevnik', 17 December 1941, *TsGAIPD SPb., fond* 4000, *opis'* 11, *delo* 59, *list* 10.
5 Zelenskaia, 'Dnevnik', 3 December 1941, *list* 37 verso.
6 Ibid.
7 A. A. Griaznov, 'Dnevnik', p. 63.
8 Ibid., 14 December 1941, p. 65.
9 Ibid., 15 December 1941.
10 Ibid.
11 B. P. Gorodetskii to his wife and daughters, 21 October 1941. Quoted from Gorodetskii, *Pis'ma vremeni*, p. 104.
12 Gel'fer, 'Dnevnik', 16 March 1942, *listy* 15 verso – 16.
13 Memoirs of N. V. Shirkova, E. V. Shun'gina family archive.
14 Ibid.
15 'Iz dnevnika Gal'ko Leonida Pavlovicha', 12 January 1942, p. 517.
16 A. A. Asknazii, 'O detiakh v blokirovannom Leningrade', *OR RNB, fond* 1273, *list* 14.
17 Zelenskaia, 'Dnevnik', 9 April 1942, *list* 73 verso.
18 Ibid., *delo* 72, *list* 53 verso.
19 Ibid., *listy* 53 – 53 verso.
20 Ibid., *list* 61.
21 Mel'nikovskaia, 'Dnevnik', *'My znaem, chto znachit voina . . .'*, p. 595.
22 *TsGAIPD SPb., fond* 4000, *opis'* 11, *delo* 53, *list* 36.
23 Ibid., *list* 37.
24 Konopleva, 'V blokirovannom Leningrade. Dnevnik', 5 October 1941, *list* 127.
25 Ibid.
26 Transcript of a communication by L. M. Arshintseva, *NIA SPbII RAN, fond* 332, *opis'* 1, *delo* 4, *list* 3.
27 E. A. Skobeleva, *Rodina moego detstva. 1940–1945 gg.*, SPb., 2004, p. 12.
28 A. F. Sokolov (transcript of reminiscences), *Oborona Leningrada*, p. 550.
29 Ibid.

30 M. P. Ivashkevich, 'Zamechatel'nye pomoshchniki', *V osazhdennom Leningrade. Vospominaniia uchastnikov oborony Leningrada, voinov i truzhenikov Oktiabr'skogo raiona, SPb.*, 1993, pp. 114, 115.
31 Levina, *Pis'ma k drugu*, 28 February 1942, p. 206.
32 Sokolov (transcript of reminiscenses], *Oborona Leningrada*, p. 565.
33 A. Ia. Blatin, *Vechnyi ogon' Leningrada, M.*, 1976.
34 Levina, *Dnevnik*, 4 April 1942, p. 158.
35 E. P. Lentsman (Ivanova), 'Vospominaniia o voine', *OR RNB, fond* 1273, *list* 4 verso. Compare with a communication from the deputy head of the Leningrad commercial port on work to clean the streets in March 1942: 'A woman came up to me, an accountant, and said, "I can't work: I'll die." "Well," I said, "everybody else is weak and they are managing to work. I am weak too but here I am wielding this pickaxe. Everyone has to work." I didn't let her leave, and she died at work that same evening' (*Dozhivem li my do tishiny*, p. 202).
36 Lentsman, 'Vospominaniia o voine', *list* 5 verso.
37 *Pamiat' o blokade*, p. 57.
38 Zelenskaia, 'Dnevnik', 19 March 1942, *list* 70; compare with E. M. Iukel'son's tale of the evacuation of a special skills school from Leningrad: 'The poor little kids were crying and asked the headmaster to include them among the evacuees. Some of the parents who were there asked him to do that too. Shirokov [the headmaster – S. Ya.] could see they were going to die. There was no way he could save them' (Sokolov, *Evakuatsiia iz Leningrada*, p. 99).
39 Shestinskii, *Golosa iz blokady*, p. 23.
40 G. M. Kok, 'Dnevnik. XII.1941–I.1942', *TsGAIPD SPb., fond* 4000, *opis'* 11, *delo* 48, *list* 2.
41 Metter, *Dopros*, p. 53.
42 Ibid.
43 See N. A. Bulatova's notes. 'When the evacuation began, Mother was completely against leaving Leningrad. It was downright dangerous to set out on a long journey with three children. In October 1942, however, they simply refused to issue us ration cards and we were ordered to leave' (Bulatova, 'Geroizm nashei mamy', *Otkuda beretsia muzhestvo*, p. 74). See also A. M. Smirnovskaia: 'Soon an order was issued that anyone who had two children would not be issued ration cards for food and must leave' (A. M. Smirnovskaia, 'Moi vospominaniia. 1941–42 g.', *OR RNB, fond* 1273, *delo* 24, *list* 3).
44 Solov'eva, 'Sud'ba byla - vyzhit'', p. 219.
45 S. I. Maletskii (transcript of reminiscences), *900 blokadnykh dnei*, p. 165.
46 Grechina, 'Spasaius' spasaia', p. 234.
47 See G. I. Glukhova, *I byl sluchai . . .*, p. 221; T. Kulikova, 'Syn', *Pamiat'. Pis'ma o voine i blokade, Lg.*, 1985, p. 340; L. A. Volkova (transcript of reminiscences), *900 blokadnykh dnei*, p. 78; Pavlova, 'Iz blokadnogo dnevnika', *Pamiat', vyp.* 2, p. 179; *Pamiat' o blokade*, pp. 37–8; E. A. Kondakova (transcript of reminiscences), *900 blokadnykh dnei*, p. 123.
48 O. N. Mel'nikovskaia, *Dnevnik*, 1 December 1941, pp. 592–3.
49 Transcript of a communication by V. P. Bylinskii, *NIA SPbII RAN, fond* 332, *opis'* 1, *delo* 22, *listy* 5 – 5 verso.
50 From the transcript of a communication by Mariia Pavlovna Fedorova, secretary of the Party organization of Bread factory No. 14, Dzerzhinskii

district, 27 December 1941, *Zhenshchina i voina. O roli zhenshchiny v oborone Leningrada. 1941–1944. Sbornik statei, SPb.*, 2006, p. 288.

51 Kulikova, 'Syn', p. 340.
52 L. Reikhert, 'Mat' i nas dvoe', *Pamiat'*, *vyp.* 2, p. 417.
53 S. Magaeva, *Leningradskaia blokada: psikhosomaticheskie aspekty, M.*, 2001, p. 52.
54 Polzikova-Rubets, *Oni uchilis' v Leningrade*, 26 November 1941, p. 55.
55 Ibid.
56 Levina, *Pis'ma k drugu*, p. 206.
57 *RDF GMMOBL, opis'* 1–l, *delo* 338, *list* 105.
58 E. P. Pavlova, 'Iz blokadnogo dnevnika', *Pamiat'*, *vyp.* 2, p. 193.
59 Konopleva, 'V blokirovannom Leningrade. Dnevnik', 14 April 1942, *delo* 2, *list* 57.
60 Quoted from A. Adamovich and D. Granin, *Blokadnaia kniga*, p. 29.
61 *V te dni. Leningradskii al'bom, Lg.*, 1946, p. 16.
62 M. P. Prokhorova (transcript of reminiscences), *Oborona Leningrada*, p. 449.
63 Z. A. Ignatovich, 'Ocherki o blokade Leningrada', *OR RNB, fond* 1273, *delo* 26, *list* 33.
64 Zelenskaia, 'Dnevnik', 7 December 1942, *list* 110.
65 Transcript of a communication by A. S. Ganzha, *NIA SPbII RAN, fond* 332, *opis'* 1, *delo* 28, *listy* 13 verso – 14.
66 Transcript of a communication by A. Ia. Tikhonov, *NIA SPbII RAN, fond* 332, *opis'* 1, *delo* 123, *list* 21.
67 This was reported by the director of the Svetoch factory, A. P. Alekseeva, talking about Zhdanov's speech to the secretaries of Party district committees (transcript of a communication by A. P. Alekseeva, *NIA SPbII RAN, fond* 332, *opis'* 1, *delo* 3, *list* 4.
68 Speech by E. F. Egorenkova, quoted from G. L. Sobolev, *Uchenye Leningrada v gody Velikoi otechestvennoi voiny, M.- Lg.*, 1966, p. 98.
69 Transcript of a communication by P. Kh. Murashko, *NIA SPbII RAN, fond* 332, *opis'* 1, *delo* 148, *list* 7.
70 Zelenskaia, 'Dnevnik', 25 April 1942, *list* 78.
71 Fadeev, *Leningrad v dni blokady. (Iz dnevnika)*, p. 114.
72 Ibid.
73 *Iz dnevnikov G. A. Kniazeva*, pp. 56 (9 February 1942), 58 (5–6 March 1942); 47 (26 January 1942); 43 (17 January 1942); and 56–7 (27–28 February 1942).

4 The influence of moral standards on people's behaviour

1 Metter, *Izbrannoe*, p. 117.
2 A. Kochetova to her mother, 31 December 1941, *RDF GMMOBL, opis'* 1–k, *delo* 5. Compare with the diary of F. A. Griaznov: 'In the morning we took a trip to Aunt Irus in the hope, I am ashamed to say, of a bite of food. We waited impatiently for her to treat us, as always, to an agreeable, delicious and varied breakfast' (F. A. Griaznov, 'Dnevnik', 20 December 1941, p. 156).
3 A. Kochetova to her mother, 31 December 1941, *RDF GMMOBL, opis'* 1–k, *delo* 5.
4 Ibid.

5 T. A. Kononova, 'Osazhdennyi gorod Leningrad', *OR RNB, fond* 1273, *opis'* 1, *delo* 1, *listy* 6 – 6 verso.

6 See the diary of P. M. Samarin: 'Lidukha [his wife – S. Ya.] brought two meals from the canteen, added three or four potatoes which we boiled and then fried, which were just delicious. Today we are being bourgeois! Our neighbours say now they have been reduced to just 125 grams of bread' (Samarin, 'Dnevnik', 15 December 1941, *list* 54). An entry in F. A. Griaznov's diary on the subject of visitors to the canteen reads: 'A woman asks the waiter to give her a second bowl of soup, which she drinks without bread. She stares avidly at those who are munching their small allocation of bread, and says loudly, "There, you see? I'm drinking it without bread, so I can give it to my son. He doesn't have enough, he's at college"' (Griaznov, 'Dnevnik', 14 November 1941, p. 103).

7 V. A. Prokhorova, 'Voina ne shchadila nikogo', *Otkuda beretsia muzhestvo*, p. 115.

8 T. A. Kononova, 'Osazhdennyi gorod Leningrad', *OR RNB, fond* 1273, *delo* 1, *list* 6 verso.

9 N. L. Mikhaleva, 'Dnevnik', quoted from T. A. Postrelova, 'Vypiski iz dnevnika N. L. Mikhaleva', *Zhenshchiny i voina. O roli zhenshchin v oborone Leningrada. 1941–1944 gg., SPb.*, 2006, pp. 301, 305.

10 Ibid., pp. 301, 302, 305.

11 A. N. Kube to V. D. Golovchiner, January 1942, *Neva*, No. 1, 1999, p. 199.

12 A. N. Kube to V. D. Golovchiner, late February 1942, *Neva*, No. 1, 1999, p. 200.

13 Ibid.

14 K. M. Ananian to M. M. Ananian, 7 March 1942, *OR RNB, fond* 1273, *list* 11 verso.

15 Ibid., *list* 1 verso.

16 Ibid., *listy* 2 – 2 verso.

17 A. V. Nemilov to I. I. Abramov, 11 January 1942, *'My znaem, chto znachit voina . . .'*, pp. 561–2.

18 A. Konnov, 'Stikhi 1942 goda', *Pamiat'*, p. 142.

19 Ibid.

20 A. N. Kubasov (transcript of reminiscences), *Oborona Leningrada*, p. 507.

21 Volkova, *Pervyi bytovoi otriad*, p. 181.

22 V. Kuliabko, 'Blokadnyi dnevnik', *Neva*, No. 3, 2004, p. 264.

23 Quoted from Khudiakova, *Za zhizn' leningradtsev*, p. 88.

24 Ibid.

25 Zelenskaia, 'Dnevnik', 25 November 1941, *listy* 36 – 36 verso.

26 See the reminiscences of one Leningrader: '[My mother] went to the Party district committee. The inspector was sitting there. Anyway, she went in and told her her daughter had lost her card. "I don't know how we're going to live. I have no one else now, no family, no one I know. We have no one to support us." She was really upset. "Yes, I just don't know what to do." My mother was crying. Anyway, the lady came over and she says quietly, "Don't worry, we'll re-issue your cards"' (*Pamiat' o blokade*, p. 120); see also R. Malkova's memoirs: 'They wouldn't give me my cards. I would go to the housing management and either the manager wouldn't be there or he wouldn't give me the cards. So I start crying and he gives me them for the next month' (F. Makhov, '"Blok-ada" Rity Malkovoi', p. 225).

27 A. S. Nikol'skii, 'Dnevnik', 2 January 1942, *OR RNB, fond* 1037, *delo* 901, *list* 27.

28 *Vystoiali i pobedili*, p. 15.

29 Transcript of a communication by I. V. Turkov, *NIA SPbII RAN, fond* 332, *opis'* 1, *delo* 128, *list* 8.

30 M. Liubova, 'Ob"ekt No. 136 (Zapiski direktora shkoly)', *Deti goroda-geroia*, p. 60.

31 See the information summary of 4 January 1942 from the staff training department of the Leningrad City Party committee to A. A. Zhdanov: 'Three children of four, six and eight years of age wandered around the city for five days after the death of their mother. Their father is in the army. Three other young children, Vera, Nina and Anfisa Razin, were in hardship after the death of their parents. For a long time they roamed the city in search of food, entirely without money' (*Leningrad v osade*, p. 414).

32 Transcript of a communication by G. S. Egorov, *NIA SPbII RAN, fond* 332, *opis'* 1, *delo* 41, *list* 5 verso.

33 Transcript of a communication by P. P. Trofimov, *NIA SPbII RAN, fond* 332, *opis'* 1, *delo* 126, *list* 20 verso.

34 Quoted from N. A. Lomagin, *Leningrad v blockade, M.*, 2005, p. 507.

35 Z. A. Miliutina, 'My zhili v blokadu . . . 1941–1944 gg.', *OR RNB, fond* 1273, *list* 10.

36 Mikhailov, *Na dne voiny i blokady*, p. 61.

37 Peto, 'Deti Leningrada', *OR RNB, fond* 1273, *list* 11.

38 Ibid., *list* 13.

39 Ibid., *listy* 13 – 13 verso. Compare the diary of I. I. Zhilinskii: 'A woman told me as we were going along that a mother had died in their family hostel. There were three children. Her relative arrived, gathered up all her possessions and, without seeing to her burial, took away her ration cards. The children are doomed to starve. A sick woman was taken from the hostel and a girl of about eight, hungry and lying in bed, loudly asked as they were leaving: "Lady, take me too. I'm still alive"' (Zhilinskii, 'Blokadnyi dnevnik', 10 March 1942, *Voprosy istorii*, No. 8, 1996, p. 12).

40 Volkova, *Pervyi bytovoi otriad*, pp. 182–3.

41 Ibid., p. 179.

42 See, for example, the entry in N. G. Gorbunova's diary for 16 November 1941: 'Today a little girl was brought to the children's home. Her mother had abandoned her at the district soviet. She is five. She told us very confidently that her name was Valia, and asked, "When are you going to take me to the children's home? I've had nothing to eat all day. Take me there soon"' (N. G. Gorbunova, *NIA SPbII RAN, fond* 332, *opis'* 1, *delo* 30, *list* 15 verso).

43 See M. N. Feting's reminiscences: 'Many of the mothers who brought children to the kindergarten looked like old women' (*Ispytanie*, p. 126).

44 A. T. Kedrov, 'Dnevnik', 11 February 1942, *NIA SPbII RAN, fond* 332, *opis'* 1, *delo* 59, *list* 106.

45 V. Kabanov to N. Kharitonova, March 1942, *RDF GMMOBL, opis'* 1-k, *delo* 5.

46 G. Kabanova to N. Kharitonova, 10 April 1942, *RDF GMMOBL, opis'* 1-k, *delo* 5.

47 Ibid.

48 Mukhina, 'Dnevnik', 5 March 1942, *list* 87.

49 Ibid., 15 February 1942, *list* 83 verso.
50 Ibid., 5 March 1942, *list* 87 verso.
51 Ibid.
52 Quoted from 'Otchet o deiatel'nosti Spaso-Preobrazhenskogo sobora za gody voiny, Iiun' 1943', *Leningrad v osade*, p. 550.
53 Ibid.
54 Ibid., p. 551.
55 Grechina, 'Spasaius' spasaia', p. 243.
56 Samarin, 'Dnevnik', 7 January 1942, *list* 78.
57 Mikhaleva, *Dnevnik*, 30 December 1941, p. 302.
58 N. P. Osipova, 'Dnevnik', 29 December 1941, *NIA* SPbII RAN, *fond* 332, *opis'* 1, *delo* 93, *list* 19.
59 M. P. Pelevin, 'Povest' blokadnykh dnei', *OR RNB, fond* 1273, *delo* 36, *list* 26.
60 V. N. Nikol'skaia, 'Nikolai Fedorovich', *OR RNB, fond* 1037, *delo* 907, *listy* 3–4.
61 Ibid., *list* 4.
62 Ibid.
63 Razumovskii, *Deti blokady*, p. 25.
64 Ibid., p. 56.
65 Likhachev, *Vospominaniia*, p. 454.
66 Samarin, 'Dnevnik', 9 January 1942, *list* 81.
67 *Blokadnyi dnevnik A. I. Vinokurova*, p. 248.
68 In this connection, see a memoir note by M. Durnovo, wife of Daniil Kharms: 'Two boys were coming towards me, one supporting the other. The second was dragging his feet and the other was almost hauling him. The latter was pleading, "Help! Help! Help! Help!" One of the boys began to fall and I watched in horror as he died. The other, too, began to collapse' (Glotser, *Marina Durnovo. Moi muzh Daniil Kharms*, p. 121).
69 Ronchevskaia, 'Vospominaniia o blokade Leningrada', *list* 4.
70 Ibid.
71 Borovikova, 'Dnevnik', 15 December 1941, *list* 89 verso.
72 E. I. Mironova, 'Voennyi dnevnik', 25 December 1941, *RDF GMMOBL, opis'* 1–l, *delo* 338, *list* 14.
73 Likhachev, *Vospominaniia*, p. 454.
74 B. P. Gorodetskii to his wife and daughters, 2 June 1942. Quoted from Gorodetskii, *Pis'ma vremeni*, pp. 136, 138.
75 A. A. Griaznov, 'Dnevnik', 19 December 1941, p. 68
76 Ibid., pp. 68–9.
77 'Sonia [his former housekeeper – S. Ya.] came by to get warm. We boiled some water for her, and tomorrow we will give her some firewood. In gratitude, she brought us a cup of wheat from the mill, a lump of dough and a large flatbread' (*Dnevnik Mishi Tikhomirova*, 17 January 1942, pp. 25–6); 'Plakkhin's aunt came to see him with some children and he gave them all coffee to drink . . . Plakkhin's aunt looked in and gave me a little sugar, even though I tried hard to decline it. What have I done for her that she wants to give me something like that? I gave the children some bread and some steamed cabbage stalk' (A. A. Griaznov, 'Dnevnik', pp. 33, 34 (entries for 13 and 14 October 1941)).
78 Interview with V. G. Grigor'ev, *Nestor*, No. 6, 2003, p. 102.
79 Grigor'ev, *Leningrad. Blokada*, p. 44.

80 Interview with V. G. Grigor'ev, p. 102.
81 Fadeev, *Leningrad v dni blokady (Iz dnevnika)*, p. 120.
82 Mikhaleva, *Dnevnik*, pp. 302–3 (entries for 31 December 1941 and 15 January 1942).
83 Ibid., p. 103.
84 Transcript of a communication by Z. V. Vinogradova, *NIA SPbII RAN, fond* 332, *opis'* 1, *delo* 24, *list* 12.
85 B. L. Bernshtein, 'Leningradskii torgovyi port v 1941–1942 gg.', *Dozhivem li my do tishiny*, p. 203.
86 Ibid.
87 Zelenskaia, 'Dnevnik', 31 January 1942, *list* 59 verso.
88 Ibid.
89 Letters from A. I. Kochetova to her mother, 24 and 31 December 1941, 9 January 1942, *RDF GMMOBL, opis'* 1–k, *delo* 5.
90 N. P. Zavetnovskaia to T. V. Zavetnovskaia, 12 May 1942, *OR RNB, fond* 1273, *listy* 53 verso – 54.
91 O. R. Peto, 'Deti Leningrada. 1941–1943', *OR RNB, fond* 1273, *list* 11 verso.
92 Makhov, '"Blok-ada" Rity Malkovoi', p. 229.
93 M. R. Faianson, 'Buket iz berezovykh vetok', *Bez antrakta*, p. 94.
94 S. Tsukerman, 'Druzhinnitsa', *Leningradtsy v dni blokady*, p. 34; A. P. Ostroumova-Lebedeva, *Avtobiograficheskie zapiski*, 4 May 1942, p. 287; A. R. Dzeniskevich et al., *Nepokorennyi Leningrad*, p. 118.
95 Letters were sometimes collective and sent on behalf of all the members of a family. (One was signed by a 12-year-old girl.) See a letter from the Sokolov family to the chairman of the Lenin District Red Cross Society, A. D. Iakunin (transcript of a communication by A. D. Iakunin, *NIA SPbII RAN, fond* 332, *opis'* 1, *delo* 144, *list* 36); *Leningradtsy v dni blokady*, p. 34. For the most, however, they were written individually. They have a stylistic unity and use the same figures of speech.
96 It is not inconceivable that some Leningraders saw thank-you letters as improving their chances of continuing to receive help. Velenova, one victim of the siege to whom a domestic squad member, V. Molotkova, brought meals every day, wrote, 'I am very glad that you sent me Valia. My health is poor, but I hope to get better soon and that you will look after me' (quoted from N. Khudiakova, *Za zhizn' leningradtsev*, p. 54).
97 *Deviat'sot dnei*, p. 203.
98 Khudiakova, *Za zhizn' leningradtsev*, p. 56.
99 Ibid., p. 94.
100 Volkova, *Pervyi bytovoi otriad*, p. 183.
101 Letter from E. Radeev, 18 January 1942. Quoted from *Leningrad v osade*, p. 551.
102 Ibid.
103 V. Kuliabko, 'Blokadnyi dnevnik', 31 January 1942, *Neva*, No. 3, 2004, p. 262.
104 Samarin, 'Dnevnik', 9 December 1941, *list* 49.
105 Ostroumova-Lebedeva, *Avtobiograficheskie zapiski*, 13 February 1942, p. 276.
106 Mashkova, *Iz blokadnykh zapisei*, 23 April 1942, p. 50.
107 Mukhina, 'Dnevnik', 21 November 1941, *list* 52.

108 Solov'eva, 'Sud'ba byla - vyzhit'', p. 218; *Pamiat'*, p. 347.
109 See G. A. Gel'fer's diary entries: 'I am forever indebted to Tania. I will try, if I
    live, never to forget this and will instil in Gitka [his wife – S. Ya.] the love and
    respect I feel for her. Tania saved herself and me from certain death' (22 April
    1942, *list* 19 verso); 'I am still being supported by my foreman. I have never
    before met such a straightforward and kind person. I am at a loss to know
    how to show my gratitude' (ibid., 9 May 1942, *listy* 21 – 21 verso).
110 Kuliabko, 'Blokadnyi dnevnik', 5–12 March 1942, pp. 265, 266, 267.
111 Mukhina, 'Dnevnik', 6 March 1942, *list* 90.
112 Ibid., *list* 91.
113 N. Shubarkina, 'Sestra i podruga', *Pamiat'*, p. 338.
114 K. Chikhacheva, 'Khlebnye kartochki', *Pamiat'*, p. 151.
115 Solov'eva, 'Sud'ba byla - vyzhit'', p. 218.
116 A. Samulenkova, 'Velikaia chelovechnost', *Pamiat'*, vyp. 2, p. 208.
117 E. Krivobodrova, 'Velikie uroki', *Pamiat'*, vyp. 2, p. 347.
118 R. Iakovleva, 'Dalekoe – blizkoe', *Pamiat'*, vyp. 2, p. 271.
119 Bochaver, 'Eto – bylo', *list* 34.
120 Kuz'menko, 'Kotelok perlovoi kashi', *Pamiat'*, p. 152.
121 E. K. Bokareva (transcript of reminiscences), *900 blokadnykh dnei*, p. 54.
122 R. Ozhogova, 'Dolg serdtsa', *Pamiat'*, vyp. 2, p. 244.
123 Glinka, *Blokada*, p. 183.

5 The family: compassion, consolation, love

1 'Iz dnevnika Maii Bubnovoi', 12 January 1942, p. 227.
2 V. N. Nikol'skaia, 'U tetki', *OR RNB, fond* 1037, *delo* 907, *listy* 6–7.
3 Ostroumova-Lebedeva, *Avtobiograficheskie zapiski*, p. 301.
4 N. P. Zavetnovskaia to T. V. Zavetnovskaia, 22 December 1941, *OR RNB,
    fond* 1273, *list* 23 verso.
5 Pavlov, *Leningrad v blokade*, p. 180.
6 Adamovich and Granin, *Blokadnaia kniga*, p. 25.
7 L. A. Volkova (transcription of reminiscences), *900 blokadnykh dnei*,
    p. 79
8 V. B. Vraskaia, 'Vospominaniia o byte grazhdanskom v voennoe vremia', *OR
    RNB, fond* 1273, *list* 16.
9 Kapitsa, *V more pogasli ogni*, p. 255.
10 Ostroumova-Lebedeva, *Avtobiograficheskie zapiski*, pp. 266, 286–7.
11 Mashkova, *Iz blokadnykh zapisei*, pp. 18, 19, 21, 51.
12 Ibid., p. 21.
13 S. A. Pavlova to S. A. Kondrat'ev, January 1942, *Trudy Gosudarstvennogo
    muzeia istorii Sankt-Peterburga*, vyp. 5, p. 180.
14 L. R. Kogan, 'Dnevnik', 1 and 22 February 1942, *OR RNB, fond* 1035, *delo* 1,
    listy 1, 15 verso.
15 Ibid., *listy* 26 verso, 34.
16 Ibid.
17 Memoirs of N. V. Shirkova, E. V. Shun'gina family archive.
18 The story of a member of a Komsomol household squad which was inspect-
    ing defunct apartments. Quoted from Kotov, *Detskie doma blokadnogo
    Leningrada*, p. 17; see also V.M. Lisovskaia's reminiscence of her mother, who

refused to be evacuated: 'She was afraid she would die and there would be no one to look after her children' (*900 blokadnykh dnei*, p. 158).

19 See the transcript of a communication by P. Kh. Murashko, *NIA SPbII RAN*, *fond* 332, *opis'* 1, *delo* 148, *listy* 6 – 6 verso.

20 Skobeleva, *Rodina moego detstva*, p. 14.

21 Ibid.

22 A. F. Evdokimov, 'Dnevnik', 16 December 1941, *RDF GMMOBL*, *opis'* 1–f, *delo* 30, *list* 77.

23 Ibid., *list* 86.

24 A. V. Sirotova, 'Gody voiny', *OR RNB*, *fond* 1273, *list* 59.

25 N. P. Zavetnovskaia to T. V. Zavetnovskaia, 5 February 1942, *OR RNB*, *fond* 1273, *list* 72 verso.

26 Ibid.

27 Quoted from Makhov, '"Blok-ada" Rity Malkovoi', p. 225.

28 Ibid.

29 I. V. Nazimov, 'Dnevnik', 18 February 1942, quoted from *Budni podviga*.

30 Ibid.

31 Shestinskii, *Golosa iz blokady*, p. 22.

32 V. A. Zavetnovskii to T. V. Zavetnovskaia, 5 January 1942, *OR RNB*, *fond* 1273, *list* 27 verso.

33 N. P. Zavetnovskaia to T. V. Zavetnovskaia, 5 February 1942, *OR RNB*, *fond* 1273, *list* 4 verso.

34 V. S. Liublinskii to A. D. Liublinskaia, 23 February 1942, *V pamiat' usheds-hikh i vo slavu zhivushchikh*, p. 273.

35 Note added by A. I. Kochetova on 2 January 1942 to a letter sent to her mother on 31 December 1941, *RDF GMMOBL*, *opis'* 1–k, *delo* 5.

36 Ibid.

37 F. L. Shuffer-Popova to V. Popov, 4 June 1942. Quoted from E. Lur'e, *Dal'nii arkhiv. 1922–1959. Semeinaia khronika v dokumentakh, dnevnikakh, pis'makh*, *SPb.*, 2007, p. 62.

38 Chekrizov, 'Dnevnik blokadnogo vremeni', pp. 33, 39 (entries for 24 November and 31 December 1941).

39 V. N. Dvoretskaia to V. A. Dvoretskaia, 20 October 1941, archive of V. G. Vovina-Lebedeva.

40 Ibid., 1 December 1941.

41 Ibid.

42 S. A. Dobrovol'skii (transcript of reminiscences), *900 blokadnykh dnei*, p. 100. See also V. B. Vraskaia's story about her daughter: 'Every day on the way to kindergarten she could see dead, frozen bodies in the street, but we always tried to avoid them and distract her attention' (V. B. Vraskaia, 'Vospominaniia o byte grazhdanskom v voennoe vremia', *OR RNB*, *fond* 1273, *list* 26).

43 E. S. Tiis (transcript of reminiscences), *900 blokadnykh dnei*, p. 240.

44 Ratner, *Vy zhivy v pamiati moei*, p. 142.

45 *Pamiat' o blokade*, p. 38.

46 Ibid., p. 40.

47 Solov'eva, 'Sud'ba byla - vyzhit'', p. 219.

48 A. N. Kubasov (transcript of reminiscences), *Oborona Leningrada*.

49 V. M. Ivleva, 'Dnevnik', 10 November 1941, *RDF GMMOBL*, *opis'* 1–l, *delo* 431.

50 B. Prusov, 'Pishu stikhi', *Pamiat'*, *vyp.* 2, p. 209 (quoting an entry in his diary for 15 December 1941).
51 I. S. Glazunov to O. K. Glazunova, 4 May 1942. Quoted from Novikov, *Dnevnik*, p. 107.
52 A. I. Kochetova to her mother, 24 December 1941, *RDF GMMOBL*, *opis'* 2–k, *delo* 5.
53 See A. F. Evdokimov's diary: 'Strength draining away. My temperature 35.4°. Legs swollen. Face beginning to swell. Found in a pan (old) some half-rotten beetroot and potato peelings. After washing it well and boiling it I drank with gusto two bowls of slops instead of cabbage soup. No letter from Grania [his wife – S. Ya.] for over two weeks. Is something wrong? Perhaps she is just as hungry as we are' (A. F. Evdokimov, 30 November 1941, *RDF GMMOBL*, *opis'* 1, *delo* 30, *listy* 73–4).
54 See letter from M. I. Turkina, sent from Leningrad to her family on 26 February 1942: 'Mother is giving blood for a fourth month already in order to get a worker's ration card and support her children' (quoted from I. P. Leiberov, *Neposlednie gody. Sbornik statei, ocherkov, dokumentov, SPb.*, 2005, p. 41).
55 Z. I. Moikovskaia, 'Otkuda beretsia muzhestvo', *Otkuda beretsia muzhestvo*, p. 46.
56 A. V. Nalegatskaia (transcript of reminiscences), *900 blokadnykh dnei*, p. 188.
57 Solov'eva, 'Sud'ba byla - vyzhit'', p. 220.
58 A. B. Ptitsyn (transcript of reminiscences), *900 blokadnykh dnei*, p. 207.
59 M. A. Galaktionova, 'Korennye peterburzhtsy', *Otkuda beretsia muzhestvo*, p. 69.
60 L. S. Levitan, 'Pis'mo drugu. 23 November 1941', *'My znaem, chto znachit voina...'*, pp. 530–1.
61 A. L. Ianovich, 'Dnevnik', 24 November 1941, *NIA SPbII RAN*, *fond* 332, *opis'* 1, *delo* 145, *list* 27.
62 Burov, *Blokada den' za dnem*, p. 91.
63 Berggol'ts, 14 November 1941, *Vstrecha*, p. 214.
64 Ibid., 14 January 1942, p. 315.
65 A. F. Evdokimov, 'Dnevnik', 5 December 1941, *RDF GMMOBL*, *opis'* 1–r, *delo* 30, *list* 75.
66 Ibid., 3 February 1942, *list* 82.
67 Ibid., underlined by A. F. Evdokimov.
68 V. M. Ivleva, 'Dnevnik', 2 December 1941, *RDF GMMOBL*, *opis'* 1–l, *delo* 431.
69 Ibid., 16 October 1941.
70 Transcript of a communication by V. P. Kobylinskii, *NIA SPbII RAN*, *fond* 332, *opis'* 1, *delo* 22, *list* 10.
71 Lentsman, 'Vospominaniia o voine', *list* 5 verso.
72 Letter from N. Makarova to her sister about the death of their mother, O. N. Makarova, 27 March 1942, *RDF GMMOBL*, *opis'* 1–l, *delo* 1418.
73 Gel'fer, 'Dnevnik', 12 May 1942, *list* 40.
74 Mukhina, 'Dnevnik', 8 February 1942, *list* 82.
75 Ibid., 11 February 1942, *list* 82 verso.
76 Ibid.
77 Ibid., 13 February 1942, *list* 83.
78 Ibid., 17 February 1942, *list* 84 verso.

79 Ibid., 5 March 1942, *list* 87 verso.
80 Ibid., *listy* 88 verso, 87 verso.
81 Ibid., *listy* 87 verso – 88 verso.
82 A. Fadeev, 'Iz zapisnykh knizhek. (1924–1950)', *Sobranie sochinenii*, vol. VI, *M.*, 1971.
83 Fadeev, *Leningrad v dni blokady (Iz dnevnika)*, p. 110.
84 Ibid., p. 142.
85 See communications from heads of children's homes to N. G. Gorbunova: 'What did the children talk about? Exclusively about food: how much bread they had been given, what kind of lunch, dinner, afternoon snack, breakfast, who ate how much, etc. They had no interest in their homes, their families, and none at all about what was happening in the war' (N. G. Gorbunova, 'Dnevnik', *NIA SPbII RAN, fond* 332, *opis'* 1, *delo* 30, *list* 6 verso); and to M. K. Ivanova: 'We admitted children who had spent several days next to their mother's body. These children talked about nothing other than asking for food. When they recovered a little, still the only thing they would talk about was food' (transcript of a communication by M. K. Ivanova, *TsGAIPD SPb., fond* 4000, *opis'* 11, *delo* 350, *list* 4 verso).
86 Fadeev, *Leningrad v dni blokady (Iz dnevnika)*, pp. 144–5.
87 See the reminiscence of R. S. Lebedeva: 'Children sitting close to the stove pounced on newcomers and searched their pockets. My sister and I had bread, small pieces. They took it off us, fought over them, then picked the crumbs up off the floor' (quoted from N. B. Rogova, 'Chistye rodniki pamiati ili malye velichiny, sviazuiushchie zhizn'', *Zhenshchiny i voina*, p. 87).
88 Ibid., p. 146.

6 The family: ethics

1 See, for example, Shestinskii, *Golosa iz blokady*, p. 48.
2 Likhachev, *Vospominaniia*, pp. 471–2.
3 Razumovskii, *Deti blokady*, p. 88; Peterson, *'Skorei by bylo teplo'*, p. 172.
4 Likhachev, *Vospominaniia*, p. 479.
5 V. M. Lisovskaia (transcript of reminiscences), *900 blokadnykh dnei*, p. 156.
6 One young Leningrader (in 1942, she was 10 years old) recalled her elder brother asking her to buy the bread: 'He sent me because, he said, "Verushka, I'll only eat it. I'll never be able to bring it all back home. You go"' (*Pamiat' o blokade*, p. 129). See also Dmitry Likhachev's memoirs: 'Many asked sales assistants to give them makeweights so they could eat them on the way back home' (Likhachev *Vospominaniia*, p. 496).
7 Mukhina, 'Dnevnik'.
8 O. R. Peto and T. K. Val'ter, 'Dnevnik vyezdov skoroi pomoshchi. 14 December 1941', *OR RNB, fond* 1273, *delo* 52/1, *list* 13.
9 G. A. Guzynin, 'Kogda govorili pushki', *Bez antrakta*, p. 14; Peto and Val'ter, 'Dnevnik vyezdov skoroi pomoshchi. 2 December 1941', *list* 12.
10 Ostroumova-Lebedeva, *Avtobiograficheskie zapiski*, 25 September 1941, p. 259.
11 Mashkova, *Iz blokadnykh zapisei*, 20 February 1942, p. 18.
12 Ibid., 1 March 1942, p. 22.
13 Ibid., 7 March 1942, p. 25.

14 Zelenskaia, 'Dnevnik', 31 January 1942, *list* 59 verso; see also L. Ratner's memories of how he and his mother tried to move in with relatives because an unexploded bomb had fallen near their home: 'They were not very pleased to see us. They only had one small room and there were already three of them in it. We did, nevertheless, spend one night with them, and in the morning my mother said, "Let's go home." We did' (Ratner, *Vy zhivy v pamiati moei*, p. 142).

15 Ibid., p. 145.

16 A. B. Davidson, 'Pervaia blokadnaia zima', *Otechestvennaia istoriia i istoricheskaia mysl' v Rossii. XIX–XX vekov, SPb.*, 2006, p. 543.

17 Zelenskaia, 'Dnevnik', 15 November 1941, *list* 32 verso; G. D. Golodnova, 'Moia okraina', *Otkuda beretsia muzhestvo*, p. 114.

18 Mikhailov, *Na dne voiny i blokady*, p. 78.

19 Reminiscences of A. Neishtadt. Quoted from Mikirtichan, *Rol' Leningradskogo pediatricheskogo instituta v spasenii zhizni detei v gody voiny i blokady*, p. 185.

20 Razumovskii, *Deti blokady*, p. 60.

21 Magaeva, *Leningradskaia blokada*, p. 51.

22 L. M. Aleksandrova (transcript of reminiscences), *900 blokadnykh dnei*, p. 14.

23 Makhov, '"Blok-ada" Rity Malkovoi', p. 224.

24 See the speech by Chairman of the Leningrad City executive committee P. S. Popkov at a meeting of the Leningrad City Party committee on 9 January 1942: 'In the Kirov district we have this kind of fact. A mother had died and been buried. An old woman has been left, after the death of her daughter, with two children. The old lady is ill and cannot get out of bed. We found she was lying there, keeping the two children warm with her body' (*Leningrad v osade*, p. 282).

25 Ratner, *Vy zhivy v pamiati moei*, p. 144.

26 Ibid., p. 147.

27 Ibid., p. 148.

28 Daev, 'Printsipial'nye leningradtsy', *list* 102.

29 Ibid.

30 S. P. Blizniuk (transcript of reminiscences), *900 blokadnykh dnei*, p. 47; K. L. Mikhailova (transcript of reminiscences), *900 blokadnykh dnei*, p. 185; V. V. Alekseev (transcript of reminiscences), *900 blokadnykh dnei*, p. 31.

31 Makogonenko, *Pis'ma s dorogi*, pp. 126–7.

32 Berggol'ts, *Vstrecha*, p. 50.

33 Likhachev, *Vospominaniia*, pp. 492, 494.

34 See M. S. Smirnova's memoirs: 'One member of staff was being evacuated, but her mother was in bed sick and being left behind. She moaned, "Water, water . . ." Leaving for the "mainland", the daughter said, "Take care of my mother." She agreed with the caretaker that she would keep an eye on the old lady' (Chursin, 'Soobshchaet 21–i o svoei gotovnosti', *Publichnaia biblioteka v gody voiny*, p. 141).

35 There were also cases like the following: in a report from Librarian Mogilianskii about the death of the folklore specialist, N. P. Andreev, written on 5 November 1942, we read: 'It transpired that at the time of his death N. P. Andreev had been abandoned by all his relatives and died alone. He was buried by the housing management many days after his death' (*Publichnaia biblioteka v gody voiny*, p. 293).

36 Likhachev, *Vospominaniia*, pp. 494, 492.

37 See a letter from E. A. Shchurkina to T. A. Konopleva: 'A few days ago I received two letters from Kira. She is now living in Yaroslavl. Her mother has been left behind in Leningrad, almost at death's door. How the poor girl is suffering. She begs us not to judge her too harshly' (*OR RNB, fond* 1273, *delo* 2, *listy* 2 – 2 verso).

38 Zelenskaia, 'Dnevnik', 25 February 1942, *listy* 63 – 63 verso.

39 K. A. Karataev (transcript of reminiscences), *900 blokadnykh dnei*, p. 111; L. Shcherbak, 'Mama – glavnyi khirurg', *Pamiat'*, *vyp.* 2, p. 389; Magaeva, *Leningradskaia blokada*, p. 31; *Pamiat' o blokade*, p. 111; Aleksandrova, 'Ispytanie', *Leningradtsy v dni blokady*, p. 191.

40 Quoted from D. Granin, *Tainyi znak Peterburga, SPb.*, 2002, p. 64.

41 See V. Bazanova's diary: 'I saw my school friend, Natka. Her father died and now her mother has died. Without telling Natka, she bartered something at the market for a piece of butter, ate the lot, and died shortly afterwards' (entry of 3 April 1942); 'From Nina, I heard the fate of two sisters. Her mother had a difficult death from starvation: she kept screaming that she wanted to live. The older sister is still alive, because she helped herself to her family's last crumbs and stole wherever she could' (Bazanova, 'Vchera bylo deviat' trevog . . .', pp. 131, 139). See also the memories of E. A. Kondakova: 'One time they gave everyone a tin of condensed milk against their ration cards. We put our little sister out on to the street, and sat and gorged ourselves. Rimka [her sister – S. Ya.] wanted to go home but we did not let her' (Kondakova (transcript of reminiscences), *900 blokadnykh dnei*, p. 124). M. S. Konopleva gives another example of the erosion of family ethics in her diary. Children's ration cards were to be re-registered at school in connection with their being given an additional 100 grams of bread: 'Parents had to entrust the cards to the children for re-registration, but many cards were never brought back home. Some children swapped or sold them, relying on the extra 100 grams they would be getting at school, and also, of course, on their mothers not leaving them without bread at home and giving them some of their ration' (Konopleva, 'V blokirovannom Leningrade. Dnevnik', *delo* 2, *list* 80).

42 A. O. Zmitrichenko (transcript of reminiscences), *900 blokadnykh dnei*, p. 92.

43 *Pamiat' o blokade*, p. 115. Compare with the story of a girl admitted to a children's home: 'Someone picked my pocket of our ration cards. Mum somehow got hold of something but gave almost all of it to me. I did not want to, but took and ate it and she starved. I saw her first getting thinner and thinner, and then she began to swell up' (quoted from L. Raskin, 'Deti velikogo goroda (Leningradskie deti v dni Otechestvennoi voiny)', *Zvezda*, Nos. 5–6, 1944, p. 70).

44 *Pamiat' o blokade*, p. 111.

45 Peterson, *'Skorei by bylo teplo'*, p. 173.

46 V. Peterson, 'Iz blokady – na Bol'shuiu zemliu', *Neva*, No. 9, 2002, p. 153; see also Solov'eva, 'Sud'ba byla - vyzhit'', p. 220.

47 See the reminiscences of N. E. Gavrilina: 'Mum was admitted to the Kuibyshev district hospital. I went to see her every day, not only because I wanted to see her but also because she shared the soup they gave her with me' (N. E. Gavrilina, 'Vospominaniia o blokade', *NIA SPbII RAN, fond* 332, *opis'* 1, *delo* 150, *list* 12).

48 Solov'eva, 'Sud'ba byla - vyzhit'', p. 219.

49 Nalegatskaia (transcript of reminiscences), p. 192.

50 N. P. Zavetnovskaia to T. V. Zavetnovskaia, 29 December 1941, *OR RNB*, *fond* 1273, *list* 25 verso.

51 Sil'man and Admoni, *My vspominaem*, p. 248.

52 L. Koshkin, 'Na postu', *Pamiat'*, *vyp.* 2, p. 384; see also Likhachev, *Vospominaniia*, pp. 470–1.

53 Kapitsa, *V more pogasli ogni*, 14 and 17 January 1942, pp. 257, 258.

54 Reminiscences of A. O. Sokolova in Bochaver, 'Eto – bylo', *list* 32; E. Pavlova, 'Iz blokadnogo dnevnika', 12 February 1942, *Pamiat'*, *vyp.* 2, p. 191.

55 *Pamiat' o blokade*, p. 85.

56 Memoirs of N. V. Shirkova, E. V. Shun'gina family archive.

57 'Mother has also become very weak. I try to make sure she does not deprive herself: she keeps wanting to refuse food in favour of Vladimir [her son – S. Ya.]' (A.V. Smirnova, 'Po sledam svoei zhizni', *OR RNB, fond* 1273, *list* 29).

58 I. Sinel'nikova's reminiscences, Razumovskii, *Deti blokady*, p. 54.

59 *Pamiat' o blokade*, p. 115.

60 It turned out that the girl's mother had died and her little sister at home was crying and asking for something to eat' (Z. V. Miliutina, 'My zhili v blokadu . . . 1941–1944 gg.', *OR RNB, fond* 1273, *list* 10).

61 *Zhizn' i smert' v blokirovannom Leningrade. Voenno-meditsinskii aspekt, SPb.*, 2001, p. 163.

62 Interview with V. A. Alekseeva, p. 41.

63 Ibid. See also an entry in V. Peterson's diary: 'Mother is lying there ill and probably hungry. I brought her 25 grams of bread and 25 grams of jelly. She is very happy' (V. Peterson, 'Dnevnik', 6 January 1942, *TsGAIPD SPb., fond* 4000, *opis'* 11, *delo* 86, *listy* 8 – 8 verso).

64 V. B. Vraskaia, 'Vospominaniia o byte grazhdanskom v voennoe vremia', *OR RNB, fond* 1273, *list* 16.

65 See the entry in E. Mukhina's diary of 18 December 1941, 'Today at school we were given not jelly but *prostokvasha* yogurt made from soya milk, a quarter of a litre. It tasted very good. I brought it home and shared it with mother and Aka. They liked it very much too' (*list* 65 verso); see the entry for 12 January 1942 in M. M. Bubnov's diary: 'I went to school, got two servings of soup, and Mum diluted it with water' ('Iz dnevnika Maii Bubnovoi', p. 227).

66 See the entry for 6 January 1942 in E. Mukhina's diary about the New Year's party at the theatre, where the children were given a meal: 'I rushed home because my mummy was waiting there hungry. We had agreed that for dinner that day we would have whatever I brought home from the theatre (*list* 75).

67 Solov'eva, 'Sud'ba byla - vyzhit'', p. 221.

68 See the entry for 26 April 1942 in B. Bazanova's diary: 'I took one porridge with eggs home and Mum and I ate it together. Of course, it isn't enough for Mum, but I bring what I can' (Bazanova, 'Vchera bylo deviat' trevog . . .', p. 132); entry for 30 December 1941 in E. Mukhina's diary: 'So, today, Mum brought three bowls of yeast soup and two cups of cocoa. Today, though, I brought very little, only the solids from my soup and one meat patty' (*list* 69).

69 M. A. Gulina, L. A. Tsvetkova and I. A. Efimova, 'Soznatel'nye i bessoznatel'nye komponenty psikhologicheskikh posledstvii travmy voennogo vremeni u leningradskikh detei, perezhivshikh blokadu i evakuatsiiu', *Zhenshchiny i voina*, p. 225. See also the reminiscences of A. V. Nalegatskaia: 'In the basement of the hostel where we lived there was a children's centre. We sometimes received thin soup with grains, mostly wheat, floating in it.

Sometimes Alla [her 4-year-old daughter – S. Ya.], when she received the soup and was ravenously drinking it, would say, "I'll leave some for you, Mummy", but unintentionally drank it all. It really was not very much' (A. V. Nalegatskaia (transcript of reminiscences), *900 blokadnykh dnei*, p. 188).

70 V. Vladimirov, 'Dnevnik', *RDF GMMOBL, opis'* 1–1, *delo* 385, *list* 28.

71 Ibid., *list* 34.

72 Mukhina, 'Dnevnik', 6 January 1942, *list* 74 verso.

73 'Vospominaniia o blokade Niny Timofeevny Balashovoi (Malikovoi)', *Ispytanie*, p. 57.

74 E. P. Bokareva transcript of reminiscences), *900 blokadnykh dnei*, p. 53.

75 V. Vladimirov, 'Dnevnik', 14 February 1942, *RDF GMMOBL, opis'* 1–1, *delo* 385, *list* 16.

76 V. V. Churilova, 'Detskie vospominaniia o voine i blokade', *OR RNB, fond* 1273, *listy* 9–10. Here are some other examples: I. Sinel'nikova, who was in a children's reception centre, would help her sister: 'We found a rope and I would lower down to her everything we were given in the morning' ('Vospominaniia I. Sinel'nikova', L. Razumovskii, *Deti blokady*, p. 55). V. B. Vraskaia would ask to be allowed to go back home from her sickbay, complaining that she found it difficult to get to sleep: 'I did not just visit my family, but brought them treasures I had saved up: pieces of butter, some sugar, cheese and glucose' (V. B. Vraskaia, 'Vospominaniia o byte grazhdanskom v voennoe vremia', *OR RNB, fond* 1273, *list* 24).

77 Polzikova-Rubets, *Oni uchilis' v Leningrade*, p. 55.

78 Levina, *Dnevnik*, 9 May 1942, p. 170.

79 Zhilinskii, 'Blokadnyi dnevnik', *Voprosy istorii*, Nos. 5–6, 1996, p. 26.

80 *Dozhivem li my do tishiny*, p. 202.

81 Solov'eva, 'Sud'ba byla - vyzhit'', p. 219.

82 Zelenskaia, 'Dnevnik', 15 March 1942, *list* 69.

83 171 V. M. Ryzhkova (transcript of reminiscences), *900 blokadnykh dnei*, p. 218.

84 Ibid.

85 Mashkova, *Iz blokadnykh zapisei*, 28 May 1942, p. 53.

86 Khodorkov, 'Materialy blokadnykh zapisei', 8 April 1942, *list* 22.

87 Ibid.

88 A. N. Mironova, 'Dnevnik', 3 March 1942, *TsGAIPD SPb., fond* 4000, *opis'* 11, *delo* 69, *list* 12 verso.

89 Transcript of a communication by L. S. Levina, *NIA SPbII RAN, fond* 33, *opis'* 1, *delo* 77, *listy* 6, 7, 9, 10.

90 Transcript of a communication by A. D. Iakunina, *NIA SPbII RAN, fond* 33, *opis'* 1, *delo* 144, *list* 32.

91 I. V. Nazimov, 'Dnevnik', 25 January 1942, p. 133. See the reminiscences of D. Moldavskii: 'I knew that at funerals you were supposed to be sad and wipe away a tear, but there was none of that. All I felt was hungry' (Moldavskii, *Stranitsy o zime 1941–42 godov*, p. 362).

92 El'iasheva, *My ukhodim . . . My ostaemsia . . .*, p. 209.

93 *TsGAIPD SPb., fond* 4000, *opis'* 11, *delo* 86, *listy* 6 verso, 7.

94 Ibid., *delo* 59, *listy* 17, 19.

95 *RDF GMMOBL, opis'* 1–1, *delo* 338, *listy* 43, 57, 59, 62, 73, 75–7.

96 Konopleva, 'V blokirovannom Leningrade. Dnevnik', *delo* 2, *list* 64.

97 *Neva*, No. 9, 2002, p. 147.

98 Skobeleva, *Rodina moego detstva*, p. 13.
99 Interview with A. M. Stepanova, p. 188.
100 Ibid., p. 184.
101 Kulagin, *Dnevnik i pamiat'*, p. 162.
102 'It is surprising that deaths now are not mourned. On the contrary, people always add in a particular tone of voice, "Now at least they don't stop the ration cards of dead people until the end of the month"' (Zhilinskii, 'Dnevnik', 2 January 1942, *Voprosy istorii*, Nos. 5–6, 1996, p. 21). Z. A. Ignatovich wrote about a boy in a queue who told her about his mother's death: 'That means I've got about another ten days of my Ma's ration left' (Z. A. Ignatovich, 'Ocherki o blokadnom Leningrade', *OR RNB, fond* 1273, *delo* 26, *list* 6).
103 Zhilinskii, 'Blokadnyi dnevnik', *Voprosy istorii*, No. 8, 1996, p. 10.
104 Quoted from V. Kalendarova, 'Rasskazhite mne o svoei zhizni', *Pamiat' o blokade*, p. 222. Compare with A. Lepkovich's diary entry of 24 December 1941: 'I met the 7-year-old daughter of Musia [his friend – S. Ya.], who said in great excitement, "Uncle Arkadii, my Mummy has died." I asked why she was so pleased, and she said, "Of course I am. I get to keep her ration cards"' (*TsGAIPD SPb., fond* 4000, *opis'* 11, *delo* 59, *list* 11 verso).
105 Interview with a Leningrader caught in the siege. Quoted from Kalendarova, 'Rasskazhite mne o svoei zhizni', p. 116.
106 See the reminiscences of V. Nikol'skaia: 'There is a hallway beside the bread shop. A commotion at the door. A body, sewn into a sheet, is being brought out on a sledge. Young people are pulling it, with two old ladies behind. They are making the sign of the cross. "Christ be with you! Christ be with you!"' (Nikol'skaia, 'V ocherediakh', *OR RNB, fond* 1037, *delo* 907, *list* 9). See also Smirnova (Iskander), *Dni ispytanii*, p. 196; Muranova, *Tsentral'nyi gosudarstvennyi arkhiv rabotal vsiu blokadu*, p. 169; Inber, *Pochti tri goda*, 2 January 1942, p. 70.
107 Konopleva, 'V blokirovannom Leningrade. Dnevnik', 6 January 1942, *delo* 2, *list* 17.
108 Ostroumova-Lebedeva, *Avtobiograficheskie zapiski*, 16 November 1941, p. 266.
109 N. A. On'kova, 'Vospominaniia o tiazheloi leningradskoi blokade', *OR RNB, fond* 1273, *delo* 20, *listy* 9–10; V. M. Lisovskaia (transcript of reminiscences), *900 blokadnykh dnei*, p. 156; reminiscences of I. Sinel'nikova, in Razumovskii, *Deti blokady*, p. 54.
110 See A. Lebedev's diary entry for 18 January 1943: 'In the winter of 1941–2 I was giving out planks for coffins for museum staff who had died, but soon we ran out. I said crossly, "Tell me, how much does a dead person need a coffin? The living need firewood more"' (A. Lebedev, 'Iz dnevnika', *Khudozhniki goroda-fronta*, p. 356).
111 Mashkova, *Iz blokadnykh zapisei*, 1 March 1942, p. 22; compare with the entry for 14 February 1942 in A. F. Evdokimov's diary: 'Today I was walking past a cemetery and saw a terrible picture. A pit had been created by exploding dynamite and more than a hundred mutilated human corpses had been flung into it (not placed, but flung). Near the pit was a pile of naked dead people, some without legs, some headless, and most stripped of flesh. It was a scene I will remember for the rest of my life' (*RDF GMMOBL, opis'* 1–r, *delo* 30, *list* 84).

112 Interview with A. M. Stepanova, p. 187.
113 Ivanov, *Dnevniki*, p. 208. Compare with the reminiscences of A. V. Andreev: 'We were going along a path to the far side of the Neva. There was the frozen body of a woman with a child. When we came back, she was still there. The next day, the child had disappeared and so had the woman's legs. If it was rats, the bones would have been left. When we went by the next day, there was only the woman's head. They had even made off with the trunk' (interview with A. V. Andreev, p. 262).
114 See the reminiscences of B. L. Bernshtein: 'Here, in the yard, someone was "hunting" the body of a big man for a very long time. He was evidently being hidden. At first he was in the hallway, then he was moved to the entrance of the Local Air Defence Unit, then to the cloakroom' (Bernshtein, *Leningradskii torgovyi port v 1941–1942 gg.*, p. 207). On the butchering of flesh from corpses, see also A. P. Zagorskaya, 'Dnevnik', 30 January 1942, *NIA SPbII RAN, fond* 332, *opis'* 1, *delo* 47, *list* 22; transcript of a communication by E. I. Miliutina, *NIA SPbII RAN, fond* 332, *opis'* 1, *delo* 86, *list* 20; transcript of a communication by M. I. Skvortsov, *NIA SPbII RAN, fond* 332, *opis'* 1, *list* 10 verso; Kross, *Vospominaniia o Vove*, p. 44; interview with E. I. Obraztsova, p. 240; T. K. Velikotnaia, 'Dnevnik nashei pechal'noi zhizni v 1942 g.', *Chelovek v blokade*, p. 95; Vitenburg, *Pavel Vitenburg*, p. 281.
115 A. P. Grigor'eva, 'Vospominaniia', P. K. Bondarenko family archive.
116 Inber, *Pochti tri goda*, p. 70.
117 Ibid., p. 70.
118 *Leningrad v osade*, p. 324.
119 Already on 31 December 1941, V. Pasetskii noted in his diary that what you most commonly saw being pulled along in the street were 'corpses swaddled in white sheets, and coffins were very rarely to be seen' (V. Pasetskii, 'A vse-taki stranichku Shillera ia uspel otkhvatit'', *Neva*, No. 5, 2003, p. 104).
120 N. V. Baranov, *Siluety blokady. Zapiski glavnogo arkhitektora goroda*, Lg., 1982, pp. 56–7; see also the reminiscences of N. V. Shirkova about her father's funeral in January 1942: 'The corpses that were brought were stacked like logs on top of each other. If [the coffin] was of poor quality, it was immediately broken up to fuel a fire round which the workers could warm themselves' (memoirs of N. V. Shirkova, E. V. Shun'gina family archive); reminiscences of R. M. Kopilenko about the working of the local air defence unit at the cemetery: 'Our soldiers (and this was the practice of everybody working there) removed the body from the coffin, broke the coffin up, and used it to fuel fires to warm themselves a little' (transcript of a communication by R. M. Kopilenko, *NIA SPbII RAN, fond* 332, *opis'* 1, *delo* 67, *list* 23). The women from the Svetoch factory who were loading bodies at the People's Club on Gorky Prospekt, if anyone brought a dead person in a coffin, 'tied ropes round the boards from the coffins and dragged them to the factory'. There was a shortage of firewood there too, and it was only a short drive (transcript of a communication by A. P. Alekseeva, *NIA SPbII RAN, fond* 332, *opis'* 1, *delo* 3, *listy* 7 verso – 8.
121 See a letter sent by one survivor of the siege to V. Kh. Vainshtein in January 1990. She went to work at the cemetery because the rations there were more generous (*OPI NGM, fond* R-20, *opis'* 2, *list* 2 verso).
122 V. B. Vraskaia, 'Vospominaniia o byte grazhdanskom v voennoe vremia', *OR RNB, fond* 1273, *list* 23.

123 Memoirs of N. V. Shirkova, E. V. Shun'gina family archive.
124 See the very similar notes of V. Bazanova ('You can only get coffins made or people buried in exchange for bread and oilcake') and M. S. Konopleva ('The gravediggers will do their job only if paid in bread') (Bazanova, 'Vchera bylo deviat' trevog . . .', p. 129; Konopleva, 'V blokirovannom Leningrade. Dnevnik', *delo* 2, *list* 4 verso).
125 This may have occurred in the course of only a few weeks. T. Nezhintseva had her father-in-law buried in a coffin and a separate grave on 3 January 1942, but her mother-in-law on 26 January 1942 in a mass grave and 'swaddled', without a coffin (T. Nezhintseva, *Rasskazhu o svoem muzhe*, p. 348).
126 M. N. Kotliarova (transcript of reminiscences), *900 blokadnykh dnei*, p. 128; A. D. Duchkov (transcript of reminiscences), *900 blokadnykh dnei*, p. 89; Z. Dicharov, 'Alekha s Maloi Okhty', in Shestinskii, *Golosa iz blokady*, p. 409.
127 N. Makarova to her sister, 27 March 1942, *RDF GMMOBL, opis'* 1–1, *delo* 418.
128 Ibid.
129 O. Berggol'ts to her sister, early 1942. Quoted from E. Binevich, 'Rozhdeny v Leningrade', *Neva*, No. 5, 2003, p. 188.
130 Ibid.
131 Z. A. Ignatovich, 'Ocherki o blokade Leningrada', *OR RNB, fond* 1273, *delo* 26, *list* 9.
132 Transcript of a collective of housewives and housekeepers at the Malaia Okhta enterprise: *NIA SPbII RAN, fond* 332, *opis'* 1, *delo* 146, *listy* 14–15.
133 N. M. Suvorov, *Sireny zovut na posty. Stranitsy blokadnogo dnevnika*, Lg., 1980, p. 45.
134 N. Makarova to her sister, 27 March 1942, *RDF GMMOBL, opis'* 1–1, *delo* 418.
135 T. G. Ivanova, 'Vospominaniia', *Chelovek v blokade*, p. 218.
136 I. K. Stadnik, 'V osazhdennom Leningrade', *40 let velikoi pobedy. Sbornik vospominanii sotrudnikov klinicheskoi polikliniki-uchastnikov Velikoi Otechestvennoi voiny i trudovogo fronta, OR RNB, fond* 1273, *list* 51; compare with an entry in the diary of V. N. Nikol'skaia: 'Dead bodies in the streets, parks, boulevards and rubbish dumps' (V. N. Nikol'skaia, 'Dnevnik v Leningrade vo vremia blokady s 1941 po 7 fevralia 1942', *OR RNB, fond* 1037, *delo* 907, *list* 19).
137 V. Gapova, 'Odna zima', in F. Abramov, *O voine i pobede*, SPb., 2005, p. 165.
138 Skobeleva, *Rodina moego detstva*, p. 14; E. Pavlova, 'Iz blokadnogo dnevnika', 14 December 1941, *Pamiat'*, *vyp.* 2, p. 287; Ostroumova-Lebedeva, *Avtobiograficheskie zapiski*, 1 January 1942, p. 271.
139 See the reminiscences of L. Shcherbak about events in February 1942: 'We walked along Liteiny Prospekt. Many little sledges with dead bodies which people had not had the strength to take all the way to the cemetery and had abandoned' (*Pamiat'*, *vyp.* 2, p. 389); letter from S. A. Reiser to V. S. Baevskii, 26 December 1981: 'One day, going to the Public Library, where I worked, from No. 11 Nevsky Prospekt, where I lived, I counted *seven* corpses in the street: people who had fallen on their way somewhere or been thrown out of buildings so they did not have to be buried' (quoted from A. Baevskii, *Roman odnoi zhizni*, SPb., 2007, p. 412).
140 E. Mironova, 'Blokada i front', *RDF GMMOBL, opis'* 1–1, *delo* 449; see also the diary entry of N. P. Gorshkov: 'There are many instances where those

accompanying a coffin dump it somewhere in the street without taking it all the way to the cemetery, and then make themselves scarce' ('Blokadnyi dnevnik N. P. Gorshkova', 6 January 1942, p. 56); also the memoirs of V. G. Grigor'ev: 'Those who died were carried to the stair landing or the courtyard and just left there. Those who were strong enough would carry the corpse to the park and put it in a slit trench we had dug in the summer for the population to take shelter' (Grigor'ev, *Leningrad. Blokada*, p. 40).

141 See the diary entries of G. A. Kniazev and M. S. Konopleva: 'The family were unable to get the bodies buried within six to ten days, and in the end decided to dump the corpse in a deserted street and leave it for the police to collect' (*Iz dnevnikov G. A. Kniazeva*, 1 January 1942). 'Often relatives dump corpses for the police to deal with, to avoid all the trouble of burying them' (Konopleva, 'V blokirovannom Leningrade. Dnevnik', 3 February 1942, *OR RNB, fond 368, delo 2, list 35*).

142 Shul'kin, 'Vospominaniia balovnia sud'by', p. 152.

143 Mashkova, *Iz blokadnykh zapisei*, 22 March 1942, p. 32.

144 N. Kartofel'nikov, 'Prostaia sud'ba', *Pamiat'*, p. 180.

145 Konopleva, 'V blokirovannom Leningrade. Dnevnik', 20 September 1941, *list* 94.

146 See the reminiscences of A. B. Davidson: 'From mid-November visits to relatives and friends, unless they lived next door or nearby, all but ceased' (A. B. Davidson, 'Pervaia blokadnaia zima. Vospominaniia', *Otechestvennaia istoriia i istoricheskaia mysl' v Rossii XIX–XX vekov, SPb.*, 2006, p. 543).

147 Z. Dicharov, 'O tekh, kto ne geroi ...', in Shestinskii, *Golosa iz blokady*, p. 153.

148 Polzikova-Rubets, *Oni uchilis' v Leningrade*, p. 65.

149 Lentsman, 'Vospominaniia o voine', *list* 4 verso.

150 E. Ia. Dan'ko to V. P. Bianki, 6 December 1941, in Bianki, *Likholet'e*, p. 99.

151 A. Kube, to V. D. Golovchiner, in *S Vasil'evskogo ostrova na ulitsu Marata*, p. 194.

152 Kuliabko, 'Blokadnyi dnevnik', 10 September 1942, *Neva*, No. 1, 2004, p. 213.

153 N. P. Zavetnovskaia to T. V. Zavetnovskaia, 5 April 1942, *OR RNB, fond* 1273, *list* 55 verso.

154 Ibid. See also Gotkhart, 'Leningrad. Blokada', p. 40; Zhilinskii, 'Blokadnyi dnevnik', *Voprosy istorii*, Nos. 5–6, 1996, p. 16.

155 Shvarts, *Zhivu bespokoino*, pp. 623, 658; Sil'man and Admoni, *My vspominaem*, p. 250; Berggol'ts, *Govorit Leningrad*, p. 235.

156 Kuliabko, 'Blokadnyi dnevnik', 14 September 1941, *Neva*, No. 1, 2004, p. 217.

157 See the reminiscences of R. Malkova: 'I made friends with a girl at school and began to visit her. Sometimes she gave me cabbage soup and bran' (Makhov, '"Blok-ada" Rity Malkovoi', p. 225); also the reminiscences of I. Balashova (Malikova): 'I saw my little friend, Nina. She handed me a small package. Inside was a piece of white bread bun generously spread with condensed milk' (*Ispytanie*, p. 54).

158 Ostroumova-Lebedeva, *Avtobiograficheskie zapiski*, 1 January 1942, p. 221.

159 Ibid., p. 262; Novikov, *Dnevnik*, 3 May 1942, p. 216.

160 L. A. Tikhonova (transcript of reminiscences), *900 blokadnykh dnei*, p. 249.

161 Borovikova, 'Dnevnik', 15 January 1942, *list* 101.

162 Fadeev, *Leningrad v dni blokady (Iz dnevnika)*, p. 133.

163 'Iz dnevnika Gal'ko Leonida Pavlovicha', 18 January 1942.
164 Nezhintseva, *Rasskazhu o svoem muzhe*, p. 344.
165 Smirnova (Iskander), *Dni ispytanii*, p. 196.
166 T. D. Rigina, *Karel'skoe studencheskoe bratstvo*, p. 37. Sen Sen tablets were usually used to disguise the fact that someone had been drinking.
167 Moikovskaia, *Otkuda beretsia muzhestvo*, p. 48.
168 Memoirs of N. V. Shirkova, family archive of E. V. Shun'gina.
169 A. V. Smirnova (Iskander), *Dni ispytanii*, p. 197.
170 V. S. Liublinskii to A. D. Liublinskaia, 25 February 1942, *Publichnaia biblioteka v gody voiny*, p. 225.
171 Liublinskii, *Bytovye istorii utochneniia kartin blokady*, p. 158.
172 A. I. Zapadalov, 'Nesostoiavshiisia iunga', *Neva*, No. 1, 2004, p. 229.
173 Solov'eva, 'Sud'ba byla - vyzhit'', p. 278.
174 S. A. Reiser, *Vospominaniia. Pis'ma. Stat'i, SPb.*, 2006, p. 33.
175 E. Vechtomova, 'Malen'kaia doch' bol'shogo vremeni', *Golosa iz blokady*, p. 337; *Zhenshchiny i voina*, p. 302; Byl'ev, *Iz dnevnika*, p. 333; A. N. Kube to V. D. Golovchiner, *S Vasil'evskogo ostrova na ulitsu Marata*, p. 200.
176 'Mum's friend had a cat called Mukha, so she went and asked if she could have Mukha to feed us, her hungry children' (L. A. Volkova (transcript of reminiscences), *900 blokadnykh dnei*, p. 78); someone who was a 'long-standing acquaintance' of T. Maksimova's family asked for their cats, referring to the fact that he had three sons' (Maksimova, *Vospominaniia o leningradskoi blokade*, p. 39).
177 See T. Maksimova's memoirs: 'Mum offered our guest some hot water from the samovar and brought out the only food we had for that day, two "siege" sweets, a mixture of husks and saccharine, each of which weighed 5–7 grams' (Maksimova, *Vospominaniia o leningradskoi blokade*, p. 39).
178 Khodorkov, 'Materialy blokadnykh zapisei', *listy* 10–13.
179 A tale told by Z. Likhacheva, quoted from Likhachev, *Vospominaniia*, p. 465.
180 Polzikova-Rubets, *Oni uchilis' v Leningrade*, 27 January 1942, p. 83; Reikhert, *Mat' i nas dvoe*, p. 414.
181 Reikhert, *Mat' i nas dvoe*, p. 414.
182 *Pamiat' o blokade*, p. 43. See also the transcript of a communication by Iu. P. Marugina, *NIA SPbII RAN, fond* 332, *opis'* 1, *delo* 149, *list* 21.
183 V. G. Daev, *Pinkevich, Zoshchenko i drugie. SPb.*, 2000, p. 47; Kotov, *Detskie doma blokadnogo Leningrada*, pp. 171, 193. There is a description in O. R. Peto's diary of the history of V. Kuznetsov's family. His wife asked her neighbour, whom she was living with because it was warmer there, to take the children after her death to the October District Council. The lady duly came and put in each of the boys' coat pockets 'a note with their names'. The family's fate was tragic, nevertheless: one of the children died right there in the council building, while the other was evacuated, but his father was never able to find him again (O. R. Peto, *Dnevnik rozyska propavshikh v blokadu, OR RNB, fond* 1273, *delo* 51/2, *listy* 81–2). See also a note of the tale of the child Andronov, who was admitted to a children's home after his mother's death: 'I was taken in by our neighbour, who washed me in the tub and dressed me in clean clothes' (quoted from Raskin, *Deti velikogo goroda*, p. 70).
184 L. A. Tikhonova (transcript of reminiscences), *900 blokadnykh dnei*, p. 249.
185 Volkova, *Pervyi bytovoi otriad*, p. 181.
186 Tale told by T. Loginova, quoted from Razumovskii, *Deti blokady*, p. 58.

187 Magaeva, *Leningradskaia blokada*, p. 39.
188 Razumovskii, *Deti blokady*, p. 56.
189 Il'in, *Ot blokady do pobedy*, p. 181.
190 Maksimova, *Vospominaniia o leningradskoi blokade*, p. 43.
191 Quoted from Raskin, *Deti velikogo goroda*, p. 69.
192 Nikol'skaia, 'U tetki', *OR RNB, fond* 1037, *delo* 907, *list* 6.
193 Samarin, 'Dnevnik', 2 April 1942, *list* 109.
194 Ratner, *Vy zhivy v pamiati moei*, p. 147.
195 Reikhert, *Mat' i dvoe nas*, p. 413.
196 E. A. Kondakov (transcript of reminiscences), *900 blokadnykh dnei*, p. 123.
197 L. I. Lavrent'eva and V. N. Soboleva (transcript of reminiscences), *900 blokadnykh dnei*, p. 152
198 Entry for 13 January 1942 in the diary of schoolboy A. Kargin, quoted from A.V. Burov, *Blokada den' za dnem*, p. 123; see also entry for 23 February 1942, 'In the morning we did a swap with a housewife in our building. We gave her 50 grams of dried potato and she gave us 50 grams of dried onion' (ibid., p. 147).
199 Maksimova, *Vospominaniia o leningradskoi blokade*, p. 46.
200 Ibid.
201 See the reminiscences of Z. Likhacheva. Quoted from Likhachev, *Vospominaniia*, p. 448.
202 See the reminiscences of E. A. Skobeleva: 'In order to move, they needed a truck, and you could only get one in exchange for firewood. So our neighbours one floor up told the head of the military hospital about our firewood, they got their removal, and we were left with no firewood' (Skobeleva, *Rodina moego detstva*, p. 12).
203 Interview with L. P. Vlasova, p. 69.
204 Quoted from Kotov, *Detskie doma blokadnogo Leningrada*, p. 186.
205 Mashkova, *Iz blokadnykh zapisei*, 5 March 1942, p. 24.
206 Glazunov, *Rossiia raspiataia*, vol. I. book 2, p. 103.
207 Likhachev, *Vospominaniia*, p. 466.
208 V. Kuliabko, 'Blokadnyi dnevnik', *Neva*, No. 1, 2004, p. 219.
209 R. V. Mashukova (Kruglova) (transcript of reminiscences), *900 blokadnykh dnei*, p. 174. See also interview with G. N. Ignatova, p. 254.
210 Quoted from *Pamiat' o blokade*, p. 112.
211 Ibid., p. 83.
212 Interview with A. A. Vostrova, *Nestor*, No. 6, 2003, p. 89.
213 Mashkova, *Iz blokadnykh zapisei*, 3 April 1942, p. 40.
214 Interview with T. I. Sakharova, *Nestor*, No. 6, 2003, p. 200.
215 K. F. Fedorova (transcript of reminiscences), *900 blokadnykh dnei*, p. 264.
216 E. Tikhomirova (Spasskaia), 'Kotel mannoi kashi', *Pamiat'*, *vyp.* 2, p. 241.
217 Mukhina, 'Dnevnik', 15 February 1942, *list* 83 verso.
218 E. Krivobodrova, 'Velikie uroki', *Pamiat'*, p. 346.
219 The reminiscences of K. P. Dubrovina, quoted from Adamovich and Granin, *Blokadnaia kniga*, p. 91.
220 Ibid., p. 92.
221 Mashkova, *Iz blokadnykh zapisei*, 17 February 1942, p. 15.
222 Solov'eva, 'Sud'ba byla - vyzhit'', p. 220.
223 Interview with a siege survivor, quoted from *Pamiat' o blokade*, p. 112.
224 Ibid.

225 Sharypina, *Za zhizn' i pobedu*, p. 144.
226 Kabytova, *Ob odnoi leningradskoi blokadnoi sem'e*, p. 255.
227 T. D. Kholmovskaia, 'Teatr – voennyi ob"ekt', *Bez antrakta*, p. 215.
228 M. A. Sadova, 'Biblioteka v osazhdennom gorode', *Publichnaia biblioteka v gody voiny*, p. 172.
229 Solov'eva, 'Sud'ba byla - vyzhit'', p. 220
230 The reminiscences of V. Tikhomirova, quoted from L. Razumovskii, *Deti blokady*, pp. 59–60.
231 A. F. Evdokimov, 'Dnevnik', *RDF GMMOBL*, *opis'* 1–r, *delo* 30, *list* 82.
232 *Iz dnevnikov G. A. Kniazeva*, 5 January 1942, p. 37.
233 'At work, Tsvetkova, a courier, brought aspic made from belts of some sort and offered me a little. I ate it, naturally' (Samarin, 'Dnevnik', 9 January 1942, *delo* 332, *list* 81).
234 Z. A. Miliutina, 'My zhili v blokadu . . . 1941–1942 gg.', *OR RNB, fond* 1273, *list* 9.
235 'What a nightmare starvation is! Today I begged a piece of bread in the security section, and enough tobacco to roll 2–3 cigarettes' (Samarin, 'Dnevnik', 18 January 1942, *list* 90).
236 A. Samulenkova, 'Velikaia chelovechnost'', *Pamiat'*, *vyp.* 2, p. 208; see also the reminiscences of L. Shul'kin about evacuation of the workers of the Kirov factory: 'Four days before departure, two sisters from the workshop appealed to me for help. They had lost their bread ration cards and needed to get through the next four days. I gave them my card for those days. I survived on oilcake, of which I had a small supply' (Shul'kin, 'Vospominaniia balovnia sud'by', p. 153).
237 Likhachev, *Vospominaniia*, p. 477.
238 Berggol'ts, *Vstrecha*, p. 157.
239 Krivobodrova, 'Velikie uroki', *Pamiat'*, pp. 346–7.
240 'Vospominaniia S. S. Kazakevich', *Publichnaia biblioteka v gody voiny*, p. 133.
241 'Vospominaniia M. M. Cherniakova', *Publichnaia biblioteka v gody voiny*, p. 146.
242 Nalegatskaia (transcript of reminiscences), *900 blokadnykh dnei*, p. 189.
243 V. Kuliabko, 'Blokadnyi dnevnik', *Neva*, No. 2, 2004, p. 241.
244 Konopleva, 'V blokirovannom Leningrade. Dnevnik', 9 January 1942, *delo* 2, *list* 19.
245 The reminiscences of G. A. Ozerova, quoted from Adamovich and. Granin, *Blokadnaia kniga*, p. 102.
246 T. Dorofeeva, 'Takaia byla rabota', *Pamiat'*, *vyp.* 2, p. 201.
247 Khodorkov, 'Materialy blokadnykh zapisei', *list* 7.
248 *Iz dnevnikov G. A. Kniazeva*, 23 January 1942, pp. 46–7.
249 Nikiforov, 'Iz dnevnika zamestitelia direktora po MPVO i okhrane zavoda im. Marti (Admiralteiskaia sudoverf)', *Vystoiali i pobedili*, p. 15.
250 Smirnova (Iskander), *Dni ispytanii*.
251 Ibid.
252 N. A. Rakhmalev (transcript of reminiscences), *TsGAIPD SPb.*, *fond* 4000, *opis'* 10, *delo* 298, *list* 17. Compare with a communication from A. S. Trifonov, administrator of the Party Central committee at Hydro-electric Power Station No. 1: 'At the initiative of the Party bureau it was decided to give all supplementary rations to the most skilled workers. The power station was able in the main to retain its old production staff, although as a

consequence we had some losses among the auxiliary work force' (transcript of a communication by A. S. Trifonov, *NIA SPbII RAN, fond* 332, *opis'* 1, *delo* 125, *listy* 7–8); see also a communication by a member of the Sudomekh shipbuilding factory committee: 'We began to support people by admission to the sickbay and through enhanced diets. The main workers bucked up, but auxiliary workers continued to suffer malnutrition and be weak' (transcript of a communication by K. A. Eremeev, *NIA SPbII RAN, fond* 332, *opis'* 1, *delo* 44, *list* 13). When E. G. Levina argued that she should not be admitted to the sickbay because 'other people are more ill', she was told, 'This is a commercial decision to support those we most need' (Levina, *Dnevnik*, 20 March 1942, p. 163).

253 Transcript of a communication by A. I. Chistiakov, *NIA SPbII RAN, fond* 332, *opis'* 1, *delo* 138, *list* 5 verso.

254 V. Kuliabko, 'Blokadnyi dnevnik', *Neva*, No. 2, 2004, pp. 242, 243.

255 On his birthday, B. B. Piotrovskii received a present from I. A. Orbeli, director of the Hermitage, of 'a piece of wood glue' (B. B. Piotrovskii, *Stranitsy moei zhizni, SPb.*, 1995, p. 199).

256 Z. A. Ignatovich, 'Ocherki o blokade Leningrada', *OR RNB, fond* 1273, *delo* 26, *list* 33.

257 Entry for 2 August 1942 in S. M. Glazovitskaia's diary, quoted from Bochaver, 'Eto – bylo', *list* 91.

258 M. S. Krasnov (transcript of reminiscences), *TsGAIPD SPb., fond* 4000, *opis'* 10, *delo* 298, *list* 26.

259 P. I. Senichev, *Leningradskii sudostroitel'nyi zavod im. A. A. Zhdanova v 1941–1943 gg.*, p. 163.

260 Transcript of a communication by A. A. Kuskova, *NIA SPbII RAN, fond* 332, *opis'* 1, *delo* 76, *list* 9.

261 Transcript of a communication by M. Ia Tiapkina, *NIA SPbII RAN, fond* 332, *opis'* 1, *delo* 129, *list* 129.

262 Transcript of a communication by I. V. Turkova, *NIA SPbII RAN, fond* 332, *opis'* 1, *delo* 8, *list* 7.

263 Transcript of a communication by G. S. Egorova, *NIA SPbII RAN, fond* 332, *opis'* 1, *delo* 41, *list* 3 verso; transcript of a communication by A. P. Alekseeva, *NIA SPbII RAN, fond* 332, *opis'* 1, *delo* 3, *list* 6 verso.

264 Dzeniskevich, *Nakanune i v dni ispytanii*, p. 103.

265 Transcript of a communication by G. M. Itel'son, *NIA SPbII RAN, fond* 332, *opis'* 1, *delo* 54, *list* 7.

266 V. Kuliabko, 'Blokadnyi dnevnik', *Neva*, No. 2, 2004, p. 243.

267 A. Askinazii, 'O detiakh v blokirovannom Leningrade', *OR RNB, fond* 1273, *list* 9.

268 Z. A. Ignatovich, 'Ocherki o blokade Leningrada', *OR RNB, fond* 1273, *delo* 26, *list* 34.

269 Polzikova-Rubets, *Oni uchilis' v Leningrade*, pp. 70–1, 78.

270 358 M. N. Abrosimova (transcript of reminiscences), *TsGAIPD SPb., fond* 4000, *opis'* 10, *delo* 307, *list* 18.

271 359 A. V. Smirnova (Iskander), *Dni ispytanii*, p. 196.

272 Quoted from Chursin, 'Soobshchaet 21–i o svoei gotovnosti', *Publichnaia biblioteka v gody voiny*, p. 139.

2

7 Party and government

1 *900 geroicheskikh dnei*, p. 40.
2 *Iz dnevnikov G. A. Kniazeva*, p. 46.
3 See M. S. Konopleva's diary: 'It is difficult to get ration cards reinstated, and possible only for those for food. Instead of Category 1 the applicant is downgraded to Category 3: "Dependants"' (Konopleva, 'V blokirovannom Leningrade. Dnevnik', 1 July 1942, *delo* 2, *listy* 90–1).
4 'Blokadnyi dnevnik N. P. Gorshkova', 4 February 1942, p. 73.
5 Ginzburg, *Zapisnye knizhki*, pp. 725–6.
6 'Intellectuals wanted to change. Those not subject to mobilization wanted to do something useful immediately: work in a military hospital, offer their services as translators, write a newspaper article and even refuse to accept a fee. These good intentions and wishes were fed into a mechanism entirely incapable of coping with such a psychological response. With its usual crudeness and mistrust of the goodwill of those it was responsible for, it rejected people for one sector and forced them to work in others' (ibid, p. 732).
7 V. A. Ivanov, 'Osobennosti realizatsii chrezvychainykh mer po podderzhaniiu v blokirovannom Leningrade rezhima voennogo vremeni', *Gosudarstvo. Pravo. Voina. K 60–letiiu Velikoi pobedy*, SPb., 2005, p. 475.
8 Ibid., p. 110.
9 Ibid.
10 El'iasheva, '"Papa" Voznesenskii', p. 147.
11 Chursin, 'Soobshchaet 21-i o svoei gotovnosti', *Publichnaia biblioteka v gody voiny*, p. 150.
12 Ibid.
13 'Vospominaniia S. S. Kazakevich', quoted from *Publichnaia biblioteka v gody voiny*, p. 133.
14 See the reminiscences of M. S. Smirnova: 'At first we were given 800 grams of bread, then 500, then 400. I went to see Egorenkova. "I have worked here so many years! Give me a worker's ration card." "Impossible." "Then transfer me to work as a caretaker." "Forget it!" She was a rude woman, harsh' (quoted from *Publichnaia biblioteka v gody voiny*, p. 138).
15 Note of a conversation with E. F. Egorenkova, quoted from *Publichnaia biblioteka v gody voiny*, p. 127.
16 Metter, *Dopros*, p. 50.
17 K. L. Mikhailova (transcript of reminiscences), *900 blokadnykh dnei*, p. 184.
18 Mashkova, *Iz blokadnykh zapisei*, 1 March 1942, p. 22.
19 Fadeev, *Leningrad v dni blokady. (Iz dnevnika)*, p. 119.
20 N. P. Zavetnovskaia to T. V. Zavetnovskaia, 5 February 1942, *OR RNB, fond* 1273, *listy* 30 – 30 verso. See A. T. Kedrov: 'I met trucks fully loaded with corpses. Some of the women passing by muttered, "Ours are being taken in their hundreds to the cemetery and we say nothing about it, but in Finland twelve children died of hunger and we're shouting about it from the rooftops"' (A. T. Kedrov, 'Dnevnik', 12 January 1942, *NIA SPbII RAN, fond* 332, *opis'* 1, *delo* 59, *list* 91.
21 Quoted from Lomagin, *Neizvestnaia blokada*, book 1, p. 224.
22 Fadeev, *Leningrad v dni blokady (Iz dnevnika)*, p. 134.
23 Quoted from Lomagin, *Neizvestnaia blokada*, book 1, p. 224.

24 Ibid., pp. 224–5.
25 Glinka, *Blokada*, p. 191.
26 Pavlov, *Leningrad v blokade*, p. 175.
27 A. Gordin, 'Iz blokadnykh zametok', quoted from Lomagin, *Leningrad v blokade*, p. 473.
28 Pavlov, *Leningrad v blokade*, p. 175.
29 E. S. Lagutkin (transcript of reminiscences), *Oborona Leningrada*, p. 399.
30 El'iasheva, '"Papa" Voznesenskii', p. 147.
31 I. A. Averkiev (transcript of reminiscences), *Oborona Leningrada*, p. 491.
32 'Iz otcheta Otdela narodnogo obrazovaniia Lengorispolkoma o rabote s 22 /6–41 po 1/1–42', *900 geroicheskikh dnei*, p. 362.
33 Ibid.
34 Transcript of a communication by R. M. Kopilenko, *NIA SPbII RAN, fond* 332, *opis'* 1, *delo* 67, *list* 8.
35 Transcript of a communication by A. Ia. Tikhonov, *NIA SPbII RAN, fond* 332, *opis'* 1, *delo* 123, *list* 17 verso.
36 'Protokol zasedaniia Biuro Leningradskogo gorkoma VKP (b) 10 April 1942', *TsGAIPD SPb., fond* 25, *opis'* 2, *delo* 4464, *list* 10.
37 Ustvol'skaia, *Vospominaniia leningradki*, p. 99.
38 Transcript of a communication by R. I. Bushel', *NIA SPbII RAN, fond* 332, *opis'* 1, *delo* 21, *list* 11.
39 Bidlak, *Rabochie leningradskikh zavodov v pervyi god voiny*, p. 179.
40 Transcript of a communication by A. M. Grigor'ev, *NIA SPbII RAN, fond* 332, *opis'* 1, *delo* 32, *list* 10.
41 Entry for 5 March 1942 in N. A. Ribkovskii's diary, quoted from Kozlova, *Sovetskie liudi*, p. 268.
42 402 Ibid., pp. 268–9.
43 403 Transcript of a communication by A. P. Alekseeva, *NIA SPbII RAN, fond* 332, *opis'* 1, *delo* 3, *list* 6 verso.
44 Bernshtein, *Leningradskii torgovyi port v 1941–1942 gg.*, p. 205.
45 Levina, *Pis'ma k drugu*, 28 February 1942, p. 201.
46 Shul'kin, 'Vospominaniia balovnia sud'by', p. 153.
47 Nalegatskaia (transcript of reminiscences), *900 blokadnykh dnei*, p. 190.
48 Kotov, *Detskie doma blokadnogo Leningrada*, p. 176.
49 'I got a job with the district soviet, 200 rubles a month, as a clerk. There is a reasonable canteen, which is why I went for the job' (V. N. Dvoretskaia to V. A. Dvoretskaia, 1 December 1941, Archive of V. G. Vovina-Lebedeva); 'I had a meal in the canteen of the district Party committee. There were about 25 people on the books for full communal feeding. In the morning we got a cup of tea, not hot, no sugar, and accompanying a spoonful and a half of porridge. For lunch we usually had cabbage leaf and core soup, followed by patties made from substandard (cured) offal or casein fritters. In the evening, a glass of tea and half a spoonful of porridge. Bread in accordance with the ration standard' (A. S. Savanin, 'Leningradskaia gorodskaia kontora Gosbanka v gody voiny', *Dozhivem li my do tishiny*, p. 226); 'The food in the canteen [of the Komsomol City Committee – S. Ya.] was like anywhere else, and issued against your ration cards. Nevertheless, you did sometimes get additional dishes of vegetables and other non-meat products. This canteen, although it did not satisfy your hunger, did at least keep us from starving. In the spring a canteen was opened for Party activists and we began to get

better fed' ('Vospominaniia E. A. Sokolovoi o rabote Instituta istorii partii pri Leningradskom OK KPSS v gody Velikoi otechestvennoi voiny', *TsGAIPD SPb, fond* 4000, *opis'* 18, *delo* 486, *listy* 50 – 50 verso).

50 Koval'chuk, *900 dnei blokady*, pp. 91–2.
51 Ibid., p. 91.
52 Grechina, 'Spasaius' spasaia', p. 278.
53 Litvin, 'V tiazhelye vremena net polutonov . . .', *Ispytanie*, p. 118.
54 Metter, *Dopros*, p. 50.
55 V. Kochetov, *Ulitsy i transhei. Zapiski voennykh let, M.*, 1965, pp. 148, 176.
56 'Vospominaniia E. A. Sokolovoi', *TsGAIPD SPb., fond* 4000, *opis'* 18, *delo* 486, *list* 55.
57 B. P. Fedorov (transcript of reminiscences), *Oborona Leningrada*, pp. 465, 468.
58 M. I. Gorbachev (transcript of reminiscences), *Oborona Leningrada*, p. 459.
59 Transcript of a communication by A. A. Kuskov, *NIA* SPbII RAN, *fond* 332, *opis'* 1, *delo* 76, *listy* 1 – 1 verso.
60 *900 geroicheskikh dnei*, p. 241.
61 *Iz dnevnikov G. A. Kniazeva*, 6 January 1942, p. 34.
62 A. A. Dolinina, *Nevol'nik chesti, SPb.*, 2004, p. 323.
63 Letter from I. Iu. Krachkovskii to P. S. Popkov, 19 March 1942, quoted from Dolinina, *Nevol'nik chesti*, p. 324.

8 Strangers

1 Speech by chairman of the Leningrad City executive committee P. S. Popkov at a meeting of the Leningrad City Party committee, 9 January 1942, *Leningrad v osade*, p. 282.
2 Kotov, *Detskie doma blokadnogo Leningrada*, p. 33.
3 Transcript of a communication by M. N. Abrosimova, *TsGAIPD SPb., fond* 4000, *opis'* 10, *delo* 307, *listy* 23, 33, 40.
4 Ibid., *listy* 41–3.
5 M. P. Prokhorova (transcript of reminiscences), *Oborona Leningrada*, p. 451.
6 A. N. Mironova, 'Dnevnik', 20 January 1942, *TsGAIPD SPb., fond* 4000, *opis'* 11, *delo* 69, *list* 10 verso.
7 See transcript of reminiscences of A. N. Tikhonova in Kudriavtseva, *Fotografiia, kotoroi ne bylo*, p. 23.
8 Khudiakova, *Za zhizn' leningradtsev*, p. 55.
9 On the rescuing of children in the Dzerzhinskii children's reception and reallocation centre, see Kotov, *Detskie doma blokadnogo Leningrada*, p. 26.
10 Transcript of a communication by E. G. Bronnikova, *TsGAIPD SPb., fond* 4000, *opis'* 10, *delo* 350, *list* 19.
11 Ratner, *Vy zhivy v pamiati moei*, p. 148.
12 Transcript of reminiscences of I. Sinel'nikova in Razumovskii, *Deti blokady*, p. 55.
13 See *Blokadnyi dnevnik A. I. Vinokurova*, 4 January 1942, p. 240.
14 It was for the 'scandalous state of their reception centres' that the heads of the Kuibyshev and Vasileostrovsky children's reception and reallocation centres were dismissed from their posts in spring 1942 (ibid., p. 24).

15 Mashkova, *Iz blokadnykh zapisei*, 18 February 1942, p. 17.
16 Transcript of reminiscences of V. Tikhomirova, in Razumovskii, *Deti blokady*, p. 60.
17 N. G. Gorbunova, 'Dnevnik', *NIA SPbII RAN, fond* 332, *opis'* 1, *delo* 30, *list* 6; A. N. Mironova, 'Dnevnik', 28 January 1942, *TsGAIPD SPb., fond* 4000, *opis'* 11, *delo* 69, *list* 10 verso; transcript of a communication by A. Ia. Trifonov, *NIA SPbII RAN, fond* 332, *opis'* 1, *delo* 123, *list* 17 verso; transcript of a communication by A. D. Iakunina, *NIA SPbII RAN, fond* 332, *opis'* 1, *delo* 144, *listy* 33–4.
18 Note of a tale told by K. N. Galchenkova, in Razumovskii, *Deti blokady*, p. 50.
19 Razumovskii, *Deti blokady*, p. 50.
20 Ibid.
21 Note of a tale told by K. N. Galchenkova, quoted from Razumovskii, *Deti blokady*, p. 50.
22 Fedorov (transcript of reminiscences), *Oborona Leningrada*, p. 467.
23 Mashkova, *Iz blokadnykh zapisei*, 17 February 1942, p. 15. Compare with the recollection of S. Gotkhart: 'At first, people who still had some strength left did respond to this. If they saw someone had fallen but was still alive, they would lift them to their feet, and sometimes even help them to get back home. Then, however, there came a time when people became dulled and insensitive. They would just keep walking' (Gotkhart, 'Leningrad. Blokada', pp. 43–4). Compare with the memories of L. P. Vlasova: 'So, I'm walking along and I lift this one man up and he walks for a bit and falls down again. And on the way back he's frozen to death. Well, I couldn't pull him about, I was a young girl. This man, well dressed he was, and he fell and I helped him to sit down somewhere. I says to him, "You have a sit and then go to your work." You weren't allowed to be late for work. I go back, and he's frozen. That was the first one I saw, but then there was so many of them you came across. I didn't get involved' (interview with L. P. Vlasova, p. 68); 'To start with I always helped them back up if they were alive. There was one old man I pulled and pulled, but it didn't help' (El'iasheva, *My ukhodim . . . My ostaemsia . . .*, p. 288).
24 Shvarts, *Zhivu bespokoino*, p. 617.
25 See the letter from N. P. Zavetnovskaia to T. V. Zavetnovskaia, 4 February 1942: 'I was in Alexander Park and fell in the snow and just could not get back up. The passers-by were so used to people falling they didn't try to help, just left them to die' (*OR RNB, fond* 1273, *list* 33); compare the recollection of L. El'iasheva: 'By that time we had got used to the fact, if you can get used to it, that there were people lying there you just could not help' (El'iasheva, *My ukhodim . . . My ostaemsia . . .*, p. 208).
26 Khodorkov, 'Materialy blokadnykh zapisei', *list* 9.
27 Glinka, *Blokada*, p. 178.
28 *Publichnaia biblioteka v gody voiny, SPb.*, 2005.
29 Zhdanova-Stepunina, 'Iz dnevnika', *Pamiat'*, p. 136.
30 See the note of the story of an elderly intellectual lady who told Alexander Werth that in the streets and on the stairs you had to step over dead bodies. People had simply stopped noticing them (Vert (Werth), *Rossiia v voine 1941–1945 gg.*, p. 240); letter from M. I. Turkina to D. P. Turkin, 26 February 1942: 'Someone might collapse in front of us, and people would just step over them and go on their way. In the morning, on your way to work, you step

over quite a few bodies, frozen into the ice or just lying in the snow' (I. P. Leiberov, *Neposlednie gody. Sbornik statei, ocherkov, dokumentov*, *SPb.*, 2005, p. 41); reminiscences of Z. V. Ianushevich: 'Nobody helps up people who have slipped and fallen. Everyone passes by, stepping over them, paying no attention' (Ianushevich, *Sluchainye zapiski*, pp. 62–6).

31 Khodorkov, 'Materialy blokadnykh zapisei', 13 January 1942, *listy* 13, 14.
32 Gotkhart, 'Leningrad. Blokada', p. 44. Compare the interview with that of another Leningrader: '"So I'm walking along and I see someone has fallen, but I know if I try to help them back up I'll fall down too and I won't be able to get up either." That was very often how they explained it.' Another Leningrader passed on something her mother had told her: 'I was going to the factory. This man was alive, and he says, "Give me your hand or I'm going to freeze to death here." And she bends down to him and says, "Please forgive me. I can't give you my hand. I'm very weak, I can hardly walk myself. I need to get to the factory now, and then make it back home. I just don't have the strength. You'll pull me and I'll fall. Forgive me." She turned away and left him, without giving him her hand' (*Pamiat' o blokade*, p. 114).
33 See M. V. Mashkova's remark about someone who had fallen down and whom she tried to rescue: 'It was inevitable he would die', because 'the ambulance didn't take people who were dying' (Mashkova, *Iz blokadnykh zapisei*, 12 February 1942, p. 15); compare with the reminiscences of D. S. Likhachev: 'Several people who had been found in the street were lying in the reception area [of the clinic – S. Ya.]. I asked, "What is going to happen to them now?" I was told, "They will die." "But can't they be taken to hospital?" "We don't have the transport, and anyway they don't have the food there to give them. They really would need a great deal of food, because they are in an extreme state of malnutrition"' (Likhachev, *Vospominaniia*, p. 456).
34 Kochetov, *Ulitsy i transhei*, p. 190. Compare with the diary of M. S. Konopleva: 'I went today to the chemist's shop on Kirochnaia. Two men were in there dying, and a woman who was asking for help. The old chemist shrugged helplessly: they had no medicine to cure starvation' (Konopleva, 'V blokirovannom Leningrade. Dnevnik', 16 January *delo* 2, *list* 24).
35 E. Postnikova, 'Zapiski blokady', *OR RNB, fond* 1273, *listy* 9 – 9 verso.
36 V. Semenova, 'Legenda i byl'', *Pamiat'*, p. 131.
37 Glinka, *Blokada*, p. 178.
38 Related by A. P. Serebriannikov to the staff of the Public Library. Quoted from I. V. Aleksakhina, ed., *'Iz pisem frontovykh let*, *SPb.*, 1995, p. 25.
39 Kapitsa, *V more pogasli ogni*, 14 January 1942, p. 257.
40 Mikhailov, *Na dne voiny i blokady*, p. 51.
41 *Pamiat' o blokade*, p. 114.
42 Ibid., pp. 84–5.
43 El'iasheva, *My ukhodim . . . My ostaemsia . . .*, p. 208.
44 Note of a story told by V. E. Skorobogaten'ko, quoted from D. Granin, *Tainyi znak Peterburga*, *SPb.*, 2002, pp. 63–4.
45 Daev, 'Printsipial'nye leningradtsy', *list* 100. Compare with the reminiscences of B. Mikhailov: 'By the descent there is an icehole on the Neva. This is the second day an old man has been lying there with a mug in his frozen hand. Nobody helped him' (Mikhailov, *Na dne voiny i blokady*, p. 51).
46 See the reminiscences of M. A. Cherniavskaia about falling into a hole near the Passazh arcade. 'The other women gasped and moved away from the

hole. They wouldn't have been able to help me anyway.' She was rescued by a man who arrived on the scene. 'He silently pulled me out of the water, silently filled my bucket, and equally silently went on his way' (M. A. Cherniavskaia, 'Istochnik sily', *Bez antrakta*, p. 109); see also the reminiscences of L. Koshkin: 'We brought water from the River Fontanka, and helped enfeebled people to get back up the icy snowdrift to the embankment' (L. Koshkin, 'Na postu', *Pamiat'*, *vyp.* 2, p. 184).

47 See V. Inber's story: 'We were not walking, we were running under a continuous barrage of fire when suddenly, near the corner bakery, from the icy pavement we heard a tremulous plea: "My dears, my children, help me!" An old lady had fallen in the darkness. We helped her up and were about to rush on when we heard, "My children, my precious children! I have lost my food ration cards. How will I get by without them? Help me, my dears!" She was fumbling about in the dark. I was beside myself with fear and weariness and said, "Find them yourself! We can't help you any more." I. D. [her acquaintance] said nothing. He just bent down, looked for them and found them. Then we helped her back to the street. (Inber, *Pochti tri goda*, pp. 162–3).

48 Daev, Printsipial'nye leningradtsy', *list* 100.

49 Ibid., *list* 84.

50 Mikhailov, *Na dne voiny i blokady*, p. 55.

51 See N. P. Gorshkov's diary entry for 24 January 1942: 'People coming in the other direction would draw attention to signs of incipient frostbite, and their fellow Leningraders would start vigorously rubbing parts of their face' ('Blokadnyi dnevnik N. P. Gorshkova', p. 64); also the memories of D. Moldavskii:, 'How many times, when I was dragging myself to the university and stopped, someone I didn't know would come up to me and say, in a weak voice, "Don't stop. Keep moving!"' (Moldavskii, *Stranitsy o zime 1941–42 godov*, p. 355).

52 Kapustina, *Iz blokadnykh dnei studentki*, p. 219; G. I. Nikiforov, 'Iz dnevnika zamestitelia direktora po MPVO i okhrane zavoda im. Marti (Admiralteiskaia sudoverf')', *Vystoiali i pobedili*, p. 15.

53 See the diary of N. L. Mikhaleva for 31 January 1942: 'I saw a young woman whose legs gave way beneath her and she collapsed helplessly in the snow. They just could not get her back to her feet and another woman was holding her baby' (Mikhaleva, *Dnevnik*, p. 304); one young Leningrader remembers, after their mother died, setting off with her brother to the children's reception centre: 'On Ligovsky Prospekt my brother fell down and could not get up again. A man who was passing carried him in his arms to the reception centre' (quoted from Kotov, *Detskie doma blokadnogo Leningrada*, p. 199; see also Mikhailov, *Na dne voiny i blokady*, p. 74).

54 Mikhailov, *Na dne voiny i blokady*, p. 55.

55 L. R. Kogan, 'Dnevnik', 13 March 1942, *OR RNB, fond* 1035, *delo* 1, *list* 41 verso.

56 'Nobody in Leningrad had ever heard the word "dystrophic", but now you hear it everywhere, at work, in the queues, on the tram' (*Blokadnyi dnevnik A. I. Vinokurova*, p. 282).

57 V. S. Liublinskii to A. D. Liublinskaia, 29 July 1942, *V pamiat' ushedshikh i vo slavu zhivushchikh*, p. 180; see V. Bazanova's diary: 'Leningraders! . . . Half of them use "dystrophic" as a term of abuse. By the way, when they see a victim of starvation they say, "Look out! Here comes a right dystrophic

bag of bones"' (Bazanova, 'Vchera bylo deviat' trevog . . .', p. 143); also
V. G. Daev's memoirs, 'I shuddered in my hospital bed when I heard the
nurse call out cheerfully, "Hey, dystrophics, get out your spoons, dinner's on
its way." How can she not be ashamed to shout that word out loud?' (Daev,
'Printsipial'nye leningradtsy', *list* 88).
58 Ivanov, *Dnevniki*, 24 November 1942, p. 203.
59 *Blokadnyi dnevnik A. I. Vinokurova*, p. 282.
60 See V. Suslov's tale of a quarrel with his friend. '"You utter dystrophic!"
he swears at me. "Dystrophic yourself!" I retort, offended.' See also
V. Golovanova's reminiscences about children in the siege: '"Dystrophic" and
"starveling" were their most damning insults' (V. Golovanova, '"Distrofik"',
in Anat. Petrov, 'Tetrad' v kleenchatoi oblozhke', *Neva*, No. 1, 1999, p. 399);
see also the reminiscences of N. Tikhonov: 'A boy, thin, with swelling in his
sunken cheeks, was throwing sods of turf at a girl. The girl stood up to her full
height and shouted ringingly, "Oh, you pathetic dystrophic!" The word "dystrophic", that pitiful, cheerless, winter word, had become a term of abuse even
among children.' (Tikhonov, *Leningrad prinimaet boi*, p. 25). It is noteworthy
that Tikhonov's sketches were published in 1943, when officialdom was still
trying to downplay the truth about the siege.
61 Daev, 'Printsipial'nye leningradtsy', *list* 88.
62 Khivilitskaia, *Simptomatologiia*, p. 164.
63 Transcript of reminiscences of N. Ivanova, quoted from Razumovskii, *Deti
blokady*, p. 59.
64 M. Pelevin, 'Povest' blokadnykh dnei', *OR RNB, fond* 1273, *delo* 36, *list* 57.
65 Khivilitskaia, *Simptomatologiia*, p. 164.
66 Bianki, *Likholet'e*, p. 172. He also clearly remembered the 'fixed smile which
never left their faces'. He too regarded it as a symptom of degeneration:
'Smiling, they report their news: "My mother has died." "My daughter got
buried under the rubble in a bomb shelter." They keep smiling' (ibid.).
67 Kulagin, *Dnevnik i pamiat'*, 3 June 1942, p. 218.
68 Mashkova, *Iz blokadnykh zapisei*, 16 April 1942, p. 45.
69 Ibid. Compare with E. G. Levina: 'Dystrophy nowadays evokes no pity but
a slight feeling of contempt. They have become mere ballast. We recognize
them from their silhouette, their voice, the uncleanliness people find so repellent' (Levina, *Dnevnik*, 3 June 1942, p. 172). See also the descriptions of a
dystrophic she knew: 'He was walking down Nevsky Prospekt in a fur-lined
pyjama jacket, felt boots with galoshes, unshaven and dirty on a warm summer's day' (ibid.). O. Grechina also commented that dystrophics, afraid of
the cold, 'often went out wearing a quilt over their head and body' (Grechina,
'Spasaius' spasaia', p. 249).
70 Zelenskaia, 'Dnevnik', 10 December 1941, *list* 40 verso.
71 G. Kholopov, 'Nevydumannye rasskazy o voine', *Deviat'sot dnei*, p. 234.
72 V. Bazanova, who considered herself a dystrophic, could not even bring
herself to enrol at a drama studio because she was afraid of being bullied.
(Bazanova, 'Vchera bylo deviat' trevog . . .', p. 146). She had good reason.
When she was studying in 1942 at a vocational school she noticed she was
often given short measure in the canteen: 'I was a dystrophic, so I was invariably given only water' (ibid., p. 143).
73 Likhachev, *Vospominaniia*, pp. 475–6.
74 See the reminiscences of A. Terent'ev-Katanskii: 'There it is, the sickbay for

dystrophics. Again the stronger boys are beating them up' (A. Terent'ev-Katanskii, 'Nerazorvavshiisia snariad', *Neva*, No. 1, 2001, p. 217); see also Razumovskii, *Deti blokady*, p. 43.

75 *Blokadnyi dnevnik A. I. Vinokurova*, p. 251.

76 Information from the Primorsky district committee of the Komsomol to the Leningrad City committee of the Komsomol, *TsGAIPD SPb.*, *fond* K-118, *opis'* 1, *delo* 78, *list* 4.

77 Zelenskaia, 'Dnevnik', 4 January 1942, *list* 49.

78 See G. A. Kniazev's diary entry for 16 January 1942: 'I asked our former driver at the academy whether he knew whose body that was being taken away yesterday in such a strange state. "Oh, that was a cleaner from the main building." "Why was she so messed up, with even her hair trailing behind in the snow?" "Oh, she had no family"' (*Iz dnevnikov G. A. Kniazeva*, p. 41).

79 K. Ia Anisimova, 'Shkoly v dni blokady', *Vystoiali i pobedili*, p. 48.

80 Kapranov, *Dnevnik*, 20 December 1941, p. 45. A Leningrad Province NKVD secret report to A. A. Kuznetsov of 28 November 1941 noted, 'Living conditions for the population awaiting evacuation are extremely unsatisfactory. Most hostels are unheated and lack bedding. The hostels are dirty, have no water, the sick are not accommodated separately. The hostel for evacuees at 10 Saltykov-Shchedrin Street is cold. For 362 evacuees there are only 42 (sets) of bedlinen, the others sleep on the floor. The hostel at No. 4 Lazaretnyi Lane is poorly heated because, owing to lack of transport, no coal has been delivered. For 474 people there are just 100 beds' (*Leningrad v osade*, SPb., 1995, p. 274).

81 Konopleva, 'V blokirovannom Leningrade. Dnevnik', 9 June 1942, *delo* 2, *list* 82.

82 Kok, 'Dnevnik', *TsGAIPD SPb.*, *fond* 4000, *opis'* 11, *delo* 48, *listy* 20 verso, 21 verso.

83 See the reminiscences of V. G. Daev about the basement where the vocational schoolchildren warmed themselves up, and cooked a dog in a cauldron. They had to go two city quarters away from their hostel because there were evidently no dogs left any nearer (Daev, 'Printsipial'nye leningradtsy', *list* 82). Even more striking is his comment, 'In November, we students were jealous of the vocationals. They were said to be getting three meals a day in their boarding schools. Their food evidently wasn't up to much' (ibid.).

84 Information from the Primorsky district committee of the Komsomol to the Leningrad City committee of the Komsomol, 15 January 1942, *TsGAIPD SPb.*, *fond* 118, *opis'* 1, *delo* 78, *list* 5.

85 Grigor'ev, *Leningrad. Blokada*, pp. 37–8.

86 Daev, 'Printsipial'nye leningradtsy', *list* 82.

87 'We had had many vocational schools, but all that was left of them were a lot of hungry boys. As soon as the sales assistant put food down on the counter, they would grab it and put it in their mouth' (interview with A. G. Usanova, p. 251). 'The vocational school boys crowded round me at the exit and managed to pull one ration away' (memories of S. Kazakevich, quoted from Chursin, 'Soobshchaet 21-i o svoei gotovnosti', *Publichnaia biblioteka v gody voiny*, p. 133).

88 *Blokadnyi dnevnik A. I. Vinokurova*, 27 January 1942, p. 244.

89 Quoted from Lomagin, *Neizvestnaia blokada*, book 2, p. 276.

90 *Leningrad v osade*, p. 288.

91 Daev, 'Printsipial'nye leningradtsy', *list* 82.
92 Transcript of a communication by Ivanova, *NIA SPbII RAN, fond* 332, *opis'* 1, *delo* 79, *list* 38.
93 Transcript of a communication by V. P. Bylinskii, *NIA SPbII RAN, fond* 332, *opis'* 1, *delo* 22, *list* 7 verso.
94 Nazimov, 'Dnevnik', 25 January 1942, *Budni podviga*, p. 132.
95 Grigor'ev, *Leningrad. Blokada*, p. 45.
96 M. E. Petrovicheva (Sudakova), M. B. Sapegina, I. A. Egorova (Koroleva) and E. P. Platunova (Shteinberg), 'Mnogomu uchilis' na khodu', in P. F. Gladkikh, *Zdravookhranenie i voennaia meditsina v bitve za Leningrad glazami istorika i ochevidtsa*, SPb., 2006, p. 93.
97 A. A. Asknazii, 'O detiakh v blokirovannom Leningrade', *OR RNB, fond* 1273, *list* 10; on the mortality rate of vocational school pupils see also an interview with V. G. Grigor'ev, p. 104; 'Informatsiia Primorskogo RK VLKSM', 15 January 1942, *TsGAIPD SPb., fond* K-118, *opis'* 1, *delo* 78, *list* 5.
98 See I. D. Zelenskaia: 'The queues stand outside the shops as if glued there, even when the doors are locked' (Zelenskaia, 'Dnevnik', 27 November 1941, *list* 37); also the entry for 2 November 1941 in A. P. Ostroumova-Lebedeva's diary: 'Everywhere there were huge queues standing outside empty shops, with no idea whether any food was going to be delivered' (Ostroumova-Lebedeva, *Avtobiograficheskie zapiski*, p. 264); also the memoirs of L. Razumovskii: 'The manager comes out and says there has been no delivery of grains, there is no meat or pasta either. An outburst of indignation, but nobody leaves. Everybody is demanding something, shouting. To carry on queueing is awful, but they are also afraid of leaving. What if? We carry on queueing, in silence, for an hour, maybe two. Many people give up and go away' (Razumovskii, *Deti blokady*, p. 28).
99 Mashkova, *Iz blokadnykh zapisei*, 1 March 1942, p. 22.
100 *Blokadnyi dnevnik A. I. Vinokurova*, p. 244.
101 Daev, 'Printsipial'nye leningradtsy', *fond* 1274, *list* 89.
102 Inber, *Pochti tri goda*, 25 December 1941, p. 167.
103 Razumovskii, *Deti blokady*, p. 27.
104 Mukhina, 'Dnevnik', 25 December 1941, *list* 67.
105 Tale told by Z. V. Ostrovskaia, quoted from Adamovich and Granin, *Blokadnaia kniga*, pp. 94–5.
106 Mashkova, *Iz blokadnykh zapisei*, p. 16. see also the diary entry for 25 December 1941 of M. M. Krakov: 'Joy on everyone's face! The people are so happy and congratulate each other' (M. M. Krakov, 'Dnevnik', *TsGAIPD SPb., fond* 4000, *opis'* 11, *delo* 53, *list* 4); F. A. Griaznov: 'The shop manager comes out and congratulates everybody on the supplementary ration. People kiss each other, irrespective of gender' (F. A. Griaznov, 'Dnevnik', p. 167); N. M. Suvorov, 'In the bakeries everyone was cheering and so pleased' (Suvorov, *Sireny zovut na posty*, p. 39).
107 A. Lepkovich, 'Dnevnik', 24 December 1941, *TsGAIPD SPb., fond* 4000, *opis'* 11, *delo* 59, *list* 11 verso.
108 Levina, *Pis'ma k drugu*, p. 203.
109 Mikhailov, *Na dne voiny i blokady*, p. 61; interview with A. N. Tsamutali, p. 263.
110 Lentsman, 'Vospominaniia o voine', *listy* 3 verso – 4.

111 'Iz dnevnika Maii Bubnovoi', 28 January 1942, p. 230.
112 N. N. Erokhina, 'Dnevnik', 24 November 1941, *RDF GMMOBL, opis'* 1–1, *delo* 490, *list* 31.
113 Mikhaleva, *Dnevnik*, 24 January 1942, p. 300.
114 Daev, 'Printsipial'nye leningradtsy', *list* 80.
115 See the reminiscences of E. P. Lentsman: 'When a lot of people had gathered, some energetic soul issued consecutive numbers as if to legitimize the queue, and bearing these numbers many went back home for a drink of hot water. Meanwhile, another energetic soul comes along and hands out their numbers. We come back after a while and people won't let us into the queue because we have the "wrong" numbers. Big argument' (Lentsman, 'Vospominaniia o voine', *OR RNB, fond 1273, list* 3 verso).
116 Gotkhart, 'Leningrad. Blokada', p. 46; Ratner, *Vy zhivy v pamiati moei*, p. 140.
117 Konopleva, 'V blokirovannom Leningrade. Dnevnik', *list* 71.
118 Ibid., *list* 156.
119 'Blokadnyi dnevnik N. P. Gorshkova', p. 74.
120 Zelenskaia, 'Dnevnik', 27 November 1941, *list* 37.
121 N. P. Zavetnovskaia to T. V. Zavetnovskaia, 5 February 1942, *OR RNB, fond* 1273, *list* 33.
122 S. Ya. Meerson, 'Iz dnevnika blokadnoi shkol'nitsy', *OR RNB, fond* 1273, *list* 4. See also E. Skriabina's diary: 'Huge queues. The stronger push out the weaker.' (E. Skriabina, *Stranitsy zhizni*, 12 October 1941, *Lg.*, 1994, p. 125); also: 'About 400 people are queueing, but from the other direction there are seventy people or more at the entrance pushing aside those in the queue. Shrieking cursing, wailing' (F. A. Griaznov, 'Dnevnik', 30 November 1941, p.129); 'Swearing, rudeness, people pushing unceremoniously into the queue. Brazen bullying. Naturally the weaker and more polite people often come off worse' (Zhilinskii, 'Blokadnyi dnevnik', 4 January 1942, *Voprosy istorii*, Nos. 5–6, 1996, p. 24); 'An almighty crush, churning about in a chaotic queue of starving people. The cashier's desk and counter got smashed' (Levina, 'Dnevnik', 6 February 1942, p. 154).
123 Razumovskii, *Deti blokady*, p. 28.
124 V. M. Lisovskaia (transcript of reminiscences), *900 blokadnykh dnei*, p. 157.
125 G. A. Kniazev, *Dni velikikh ispytanii. 1941–1945. Dnevniki*, 22 December 1941, *SPb.*, 2009, p. 359.
126 Z. A. Ignatovich, 'Ocherki o blokade Leningrada, *OR RNB, fond* 1273, *delo* 26, *list* 6.
127 See the reminiscences of V. I. Gredasova: 'We see a long queue, bread being sold against ration cards. We join it. We see someone collapse, a woman. No one pays any attention because they can hardly stand up themselves. A boy shouts, "Mum! Mum!", but the woman has died' (Gredasov (transcript of reminiscences), *900 blokadnykh dnei*, p. 83.
128 Mikhaleva, *Dnevnik*, p. 304.
129 A. Ia. Tomashevskaia, 'Ia uslyshala vzdokh tolpy . . .', *Pamiat'*, *vyp.* 2, pp. 198, 199.

9 Concepts of civilization

1 L. Ratner wrote harshly, and perhaps defiantly, about this. Those who survived the Time of Death typically reacted very strongly against the hushing up of details about it, even by the focus on stories and personalities which became part of the legend: 'Now when you hear or read about the siege of Leningrad you might suppose the most important things which happened were the fact that the Theatre of Musical Comedy never closed, that Shostakovich wrote his Seventh Symphony and Olga Berggol'ts her poetry. Actually, none of the people around me knew anything about those things. All we knew was starvation, cold and misery' (Ratner *Vy zhivy v pamiati moei*, p. 149).
2 See Gel'fer's diary entry for 30 January 1942: 'Everybody is talking only about food and deaths. Nothing inspires people to greater things' (Gel'fer, 'Dnevnik', *list* 8).
3 B. Zlotnikova, 'Dnevnik', *TsGAIPD SPb.*, *fond* 4000, *opis'* 11, *delo* 40, *listy* 2 – 2 verso.
4 Ibid., *listy* 8, 8 verso (entry for 7 November 1941).
5 Ibid., *list* 14.
6 Ibid., *list* 18.
7 Ibid. (entry for 6 January 1942).
8 Ibid., *list* 19 (entry for 25 July 1942).
9 Ibid., *list* 20.
10 Quoted from report of the Nazi *Sicherheitsdienst*, p. 81.
11 See entry in N. A. Ribkovskii's diary for 15 March 1942: 'Today there is an operetta. Not a ticket to be had at the box office. A vast crowd of enthusiasts at the theatre. The whole lot crushing each other, like starving people seeking bread, ready to pounce on any ticket without asking the price' (quoted from Kozlova, *Sovetskie liudi*, p. 263).
12 Note of a tale told by I. Z. Drozhzhina, quoted from Aleksandrova, *Ispytanie*, p. 191.
13 Shvarts, *Zhivu bespokoino*, p. 668.
14 *Iz dnevnikov G. A. Kniazeva*, 16 January 1942, pp. 41–2.
15 Kok, 'Dnevnik', 18 December 1941, *TsGAIPD SPb.*, *fond* 4000, *opis'* 11, *delo* 48, *list* 14 verso.
16 O. Iordan, 'Velichie dukha', *Deviat'sot dnei*, p. 113.
17 Levina, *Pis'ma k drugu*, p. 207.
18 Zlotnikova, 'Dnevnik', 8 December 1941, *list* 3 verso.
19 M. D. Tushinskii to T. M. Vecheslova, 13 April 1942, *OR RNB*, *fond* 1273, *listy* 7–8.
20 Mukhina, 'Dnevnik', 22 November 1941, *list* 56 verso.
21 Ibid., 18 March 1942, *list* 94.
22 Ribkovskii, *Dnevnik*, 23 February 1942, p. 216.
23 Mukhina, 'Dnevnik', 20 April 1942, *list* 108.
24 Smirnova, *Dni ispytanii*, p. 192.
25 Ibid., pp. 192–3.
26 Ibid., p. 193.
27 B. V. Asaf'ev, 'Moia tvorcheskaia rabota v Leningrade v perve gody Velikoi Otechestvennoi voiny', *Sovetskaia muzyka*, No. 10, 1946, p. 92.
28 Ibid.

29 Letter from G. E. Lebedev, quoted from P. K. Baltun, *Russkii muzei – evakuatsiia, blokada, vosstanovlenie, M.,* 1981, p. 55; A. G. Beliakov and V. A. Rozhdestvenskii clearly also had an eye on the censor in the letters they wrote to their families.
30 Bochaver, 'Eto – bylo', *list* 74.
31 M. M. Krakov, 'Dnevnik', *TsGAIPD SPb.*, *fond* 4000, *opis'* 11, *delo* 53, *list* 9.
32 Vert (Werth), *Rossiia v voine 1941–1945 gg.*, p. 241.
33 Bianki, *Likholet'e*, p. 166.
34 Gel'fer, 'Dnevnik', 30 January 1942, *list* 8.
35 S. Ya. Meerson, 'Iz dnevnika blokadnoi shkol'nitsy', *OR RNB, fond* 1273, *list* 6.
36 Razumovskii, *Deti blokady*, p. 40.
37 Lentsman, 'Vospominaniia o voine', *list* 6.
38 Bianki, *Likholet'e*, p. 180.
39 G. Kabanova to N. Kharitonova, 10 April 1942, *RDF GMMOBL, opis'* 1-k, *delo* 5.
40 Ivanov, *Dnevniki*, p. 208.
41 E. N. Sorokina, 'Stranitsy blokadnykh let', *Bez antrakta*, pp. 160–61.
42 M. K. Petrova, 'V osazhdennom i svobodnom Leningrade. Iz vospominanii', *OR RNB, fond* 576, *delo* 5, *list* 2.
43 'Blokadnyi dnevnik N. P. Gorshkova', 24 January 1942, p. 66.
44 M. P. Prokhorova (transcript of reminiscences), *Oborona Leningrada*, p. 446.
45 Ibid.
46 Metter, *Izbrannoe*, p. 108.
47 Ronchevskaia, 'Vospominaniia o blokade Leningrada', *list* 4.
48 Polzikova-Rubets, *Oni uchilis' v Leningrade*, p. 58.
49 A. Poliakov, 'Tri epizoda', *Pamiat'. Pis'ma o voine i blokade, Lg.*, 1985, p. 140. These 'novellas' were fantasies only, of course, by the standards of the siege. See a letter sent by T. D. Rigina from Leningrad in December 1941: 'We dream constantly about porridge, soup, and in general anything edible, especially butter, meat and sweet things' (quoted from Rigina, *Karel'skoe studencheskoe bratstvo*, p. 37).
50 Polzikova-Rubets, *Oni uchilis' v Leningrade*, p. 58.
51 Bazanova, 'Vchera bylo deviat' trevog . . .', 22 October 1941, p. 128.
52 Ostroumova-Lebedeva, *Avtobiograficheskie zapiski*, p. 262.
53 Borovikova, 'Dnevnik', 10 October 1941, *list* 58 verso.
54 Mukhina, 'Dnevnik', 27 February 1942, *list* 86.
55 Ostroumova-Lebedeva, *Avtobiograficheskie zapiski*, 1 January 1942, p. 271.
56 Zelenskaia, 'Dnevnik', 5 December 1941, *list* 38.
57 Entry for 23 February 1942 in A. Kargin's diary, quoted from Burov, *Blokada den' za dnem*, p. 147.
58 M. M. Krakov, 'Dnevnik', 23 January 1942, *TsGAIPD SPb., fond* 4000, *opis'* 11, *delo* 53, *list* 8.
59 Razumovskii, *Deti blokady*, p. 20.
60 G. Solsberi, *900 dnei. Blokada Leningrada, M.*, 2000, p. 310.
61 A. Kochetova to her mother, 24 December 1941, *RDF GMMOBL, opis'* 1-k, *delo* 5.
62 Gel'fer, 'Dnevnik', 30 January 1942, *list* 8 verso.
63 V. S. Liublinskii, *Bytovye istorii utochneniia kartin blokady*, p. 175.

64 Ribkovskii, *Dnevnik*, 15 August 1942, p. 261.
65 A. L. Asknazii, 'O detiakh v blokirovannom Leningrade', *OR RNB, fond* 1273, *list* 8.
66 Mukhina, 'Dnevnik', 16 November 1941, *list* 51.
67 Shestinskii, *Golosa iz blokady*, p. 52.
68 Grigor'ev, *Leningrad. Blokada*, p. 42.
69 Mukhina, 'Dnevnik', 3 January 1942, *list* 72 verso.
70 V. G. Votintseva, '1941–1942 god', *OR RNB, fond* 1273, *list* 2.
71 See diary entry of T. K. Velikotnaia: 'Father was continually thinking about porridge made from any grain. He told me every night that before we went to work we should make it a habit to eat porridge' (Velikotnaia, *Dnevnik nashei pechal'noi zhizni v 1942 g.*, p. 86).
72 See the reminiscences of M. A. Bochaver: 'Sometimes, when we talked about what it would be like after the war, we would imagine the kind of feast we would have to mark the victory, and what a party we would organize at home' (Bochaver, 'Eto – bylo', *list* 53).
73 Mukhina, 'Dnevnik', 22 November 1941, *list* 57.
74 Levina, *Dnevnik*, 9 August 1942, p. 180.
75 E. A. Shubin, 'Blokadnye dnevniki pisatelei', *Literaturnyi Leningrad v dni blokady*, M., 1973, p. 269.
76 *Iz dnevnikov G.A. Kniazeva*, 10 September 1941, p. 23; A. P. Nikulin, 'Dnevnik', 14 January 1942, *TsGAIPD SPb., fond* 4000, *opis'* 11, *delo* 48, *list* 26.
77 T. A. Kononova, 'Osazhdennyi gorod Leningrad', *OR RNB, fond* 1273, *delo* 1, *list* 6.
78 Mansvetova, *Vospominaniia o moei rabote v gody voiny*, p. 357; Mukhina, 'Dnevnik', 3 April 1942, *list* 94.
79 Levina, *Pis'ma k drugu*, p. 204.
80 E. Uchitel', 'Dve vstrechi', *Deviat'sot dnei*, p. 155.
81 A. S. Umanskaia, 'Dnevnik', *OR RNB, fond* 1273, *delo* 72, *list* 39.
82 A. Lepkovich, 'Dnevnik', 12 December 1941, *TsGAIPD SPb., fond* 4000, *opis'* 11, *delo* 59, *listy* 5 verso – 6.
83 Quoted from Burov, *Blokada den' za dnem*, p. 84.
84 M. D. Tushinskii to T. M. Vecheslova, 12–15 October 1941, *OR RNB, fond* 1273, *list* 4 verso.
85 Ibid.
86 [M. Iu. Konisskaia to I. V. Shcheglova, 15 December 1941], *Istoriia Peterburga*, No. 6, 2006, p. 77. Compare with the entry in V. Kuliabko's diary for 24 December 1941: 'Yes, starvation has powerfully affected everything, but I need at all costs to get through all this in order to see my dear ones again, and to see the liberation of my Motherland' (V. Kuliabko, 'Blokadnyi dnevnik', *Neva*, No. 2, 2004, p. 242).
87 A. P. Nikulin, 'Dnevnik', 10 January 1942, *TsGAIPD SPb., fond* 4000, *opis'* 11, *delo* 82, *list* 1.
88 Ibid., *list* 2.
89 Ibid., 13 January 1942, *listy* 22–3.
90 Ibid., *list* 50.
91 Ibid., 14 January 1942, *list* 30.
92 See the reminiscences of V. G. Daev: 'The image of a Leningrader collapsing from starvation has often been used in fiction. Unfortunately, they are

regularly forced to make theatrical gestures, flinging their arms wide, utter-
ing lofty phrases. Everything was much more straightforward. An enfeebled
person before collapsing tries to clutch at some support. He might collapse
in the middle of the road, but only if he had first slipped or stumbled' (Daev,
'Printsipial'nye leningradtsy', *list* 100).

93 Nikulin, 'Dnevnik', 14 January 1942, *TsGAIPD SPb.*, *fond* 4000, *opis'* 11, *delo*
82, *list* 32.
94 Bochaver, 'Eto – bylo'.
95 'Fragmenty blokadnykh pisem A. G. Beliakova', *Neva*, No. 9, 2002, p. 222.
96 Iu. Bodunov to his family, 16 December 1941, *RDF GMMOBL*, *opis'* 1–k,
delo 5.
97 'I promised to write to you about the young man I met in the park during the
army exercises. He has a little sister too, but much younger than you. He is
nine years old and she is seven. They get on well together, although his sister
is very wasteful. He goes to get the bread and to the canteen too. All that,
the young man has to do himself' (V. Mal'tsev to I. Mal'tseva, 1 May 1942,
Deviat'sot dnei, p. 271).
98 A. S. Nikol'skii, 'Dnevnik', *OR RNB*, *fond* 1037, *delo* 901, *list* 25.
99 V. S. Liublinskii to A. D. Liublinskaia, 23 January 1942, *Publichnaia biblioteka v gody voiny*, p. 222.
100 Polzikova-Rubets, *Oni uchilis' v Leningrade*, 7 January 1942, p. 73; Mashkova,
Iz blokadnykh zapisei, 25 February 1942, p. 20.
101 'A few days ago I read my diary and felt ashamed that everything in it was so
dull and empty' (E. Pavlova, 'Iz blokadnogo dnevnika', 14 September 1941,
Pamiat', vyp 2, p. 182); 'I've just reread my whole diary. How petty I've become.
I think and write only about food, when there are masses of other things to write
about apart from that' (Mukhina, 'Dnevnik', 22 November 1941, *list* 56).
102 *Leningrad v osade*, p. 228.
103 Ibid., p. 283.
104 M. S. Krasnov (transcript of reminiscences), *TsGAIPD SPb.*, *fond* 4006, *opis'*
10, *delo* 298, *listy* 25–6.
105 Ibid., *list* 25.
106 Solov'eva, 'Sud'ba byla - vyzhit'', p. 219.
107 Burov, *Blokada den' za dnem*, p. 149.
108 Ibid., p. 93.
109 Ibid., p. 72.
110 Koval'chuk, *900 dnei blokady*, p. 92; transcript of a communication by A. T.
Pimenov, *TsGAIPD SPb.*, *fond* 4000, *opis'* 10, *delo* 307, *list* 8.
111 Mansvetova, *Vospominaniia o moei rabote v gody voiny*, p. 558.
112 M. I. Gorbachev (transcript of reminiscences), *Oborona Leningrada*, p. 459.
113 'Iz dnevnika Gal'ko Leonida Pavlovicha', 4 January 1942, p. 515.
114 Ibid., 12 January 1942, p. 516.
115 I. S. Namochilin, 'Dnevnik', 19 January 1942, *TsGAIPD SPb.*, *fond* 4000,
opis' 11, *delo* 79, *list* 22 verso.
116 Ibid., 21 January 1942, *list* 23.
117 'Iz dnevnika Gal'ko Leonida Pavlovicha', 7 December 1942, p. 531.
118 Likhachev, *Vospominaniia*, p. 473; see also M. S. Konopleva's diary entry for
26 January 1942, *OR RNB*, *fond* 368, *delo* 2, *list* 30.
119 L. R. Kogan, 'Dnevnik', 3 February 1942, *OR RNB*, *fond* 1035, *delo* 1,
list 2.

120 See the report of the Nazi *Sicherheitsdienst* about the situation in Leningrad in spring 1942: 'Disgraceful propaganda on cardboard posters assiduously depicts terribly mutilated women' (*Zvezda*, No. 9, 2005, p. 81).
121 Kochetov, *Ulitsy i transhei*, p. 160.
122 Samarin, 'Dnevnik', 16 December 1941, *list* 55; see also Bazanova, 'Vchera bylo deviat' trevog . . .', 8 December 1941, p. 129.
123 Mukhina, 'Dnevnik', 8 September 1941, *list* 38 verso.
124 From the transcript of a meeting of the board of the Leningrad Province Union of Soviet Writers, 26 November 1941, *Leningrad v osade*, pp. 504–5.
125 Borovikova, 'Dnevnik', 4 January 1942, *list* 97.
126 Peterson, *'Skoree bylo by teplo'*, p. 171.
127 Ibid., p. 208.
128 Berggol'ts, *Govorit Leningrad*, p. 208.
129 Ibid., p. 240.

10 Self-control

1 Tarasenkov, *Iz voennykh zapisei*, p. 26.
2 Sel'tser, 'Dnevnik', 18 October 1941. Quoted from Glezerov, *Ot nenavisti k primireniiu*, p. 48.
3 M. D. Tushinskii to T. M. Viacheslova, 12–15 October 1941, *OR RNB, fond* 1273, *list* 4.
4 Record of a story from E. K. Beletskaia, quoted from V. Togo, *Poteriavshii rodinu plachet vechno*, M., 2001, pp. 103–4.
5 Record of an account by I. S. Drozhzhina, quoted from Aleksandrova, *Ispytanie*, p. 189.
6 Zlotnikova, 'Dnevnik', 15 November 1941 *list* 23.
7 Zelenskaia, 'Dnevnik', 7 December 1941, *list* 39.
8 Ibid., 29 October 1941, *list* 25 verso.
9 Ibid., 7 December 1941, *list* 39.
10 Ibid., 22 November 1941, *list* 35.
11 Polzikova-Rubets, 27 December 1941, *Oni uchilis' v Leningrade*.
12 Mukhina, 'Dnevnik', 23 November 1941, *list* 58.
13 Ibid.
14 V. Mal'tsev to M. D. Mal'tsev, 21 December 1941, *Deviat'sot dnei*, p. 273.
15 Ibid.
16 Druskin, *Dnevniki*, 25 November 1941, p. 123.
17 Ibid., pp. 122–3.
18 Ibid.
19 Ginzburg, *Zapisnye knizhki*, pp. 184–5. Compare with the reminiscences of V. Sosnora: 'They lie about the siege. Ask how I suffer and I will reply, mythically' (V. Sosnora, *Proza, SPb.*, 2001, p. 545).
20 Ginzburg, *Zapisnye knizhki*, p. 184.
21 Ibid., pp. 184–5.
22 See entries in G. A. Kniazev's diary for 29 September and 6–8 October 1941 (*Iz dnevnikov G.A. Kniazeva*, pp. 27, 29).
23 Inber, *Pochti tri goda*, p. 173.
24 Khodorkov, 'Materialy blokadnykh zapisei', *list* 8.
25 M. M. Krakov, 'Dnevnik', *TsGAIPD SPb.*, *fond* 4000, *opis'* 11, *delo* 53, *list*

6. Later, on 3 May 1942, E. Levina reports in her diary that 1 May presents from other towns and villages were inscribed, 'To the Heroes of Leningrad' (Levina, *Pis'ma k drugu*, p. 209).

26 See the entry in A. Beliakov's diary for 10 September 1942 (A. Beliakov, 'Blokadnye zapisi', *Neva*, No. 1, 2005, p. 245).

27 Vs. Vishnevskii to A. Ia. Tairov, 10 October 1942, *Neva*, No. 1, 2005, p. 220. Compare with the entry in A. Beliakov's diary for 10 September 1942: 'Truly, they are heroes' (Beliakov, 'Blokadnye zapisi', p. 245).

28 Ginzburg, *Zapisnye knizhki*, p. 185.

29 I. Metter's comments are particularly caustic: 'Flies out of Leningrad, and that turns out to be an act of heroism. "All it would take would be to encounter one Messerschmitt"' (Metter, *Izbrannoe*, p. 110).

30 See the notes of actor V. R. Gardin, where this feeling is expressed with such unfeigned, biting sarcasm that one suspects it is fuelled not only by patriotic emotion but by personal antipathy. 'The evacuation of Lenfil'm at a time when my native city has become the arena of events which will go down in the history of the world would be totally baffling for me if I did not know, as they say, not just to the bottom of my heels but to a depth three metres beneath them, nearly every member of my cinematographic milieu. At meetings, in the studio, the whole lot of them, with the appropriate emotion in their voice and expressive gestures, said things they not only did not believe but which they well knew were the opposite of what was going to happen' (V. R. Gardin, 'Vospominaniia o dniakh blokady', *OR RNB*, *fond* 1273, *opis'* 1, *delo* 163, *listy* 23–32 verso). Notably, he later struck out this text, probably to avoid offending many people.

31 Zlotnikova, 'Dnevnik', 25 July 1942, *listy* 5 verso – 6.

32 Kapitsa, *V more pogasli ogni*, 8 February 1942, p. 272.

33 Levina, *Pis'ma k drugu*, 31 January 1942, p. 203.

34 Daev, *Pinkevich, Zoshchenko i drugie*, p. 37.

35 K. M. Ananian to M. M. Ananian, 8 January 1943, *OR RNB, fond* 1273, *list* 9 verso; see also Kochetov, *Ulitsy i transhei*, p. 325.

36 Metter, *Izbrannoe*, p. 106.

37 Polzikova-Rubets, *Oni uchilis' v Leningrade*, 16 September 1941, p. 34; Shvarts, *Zhivu bespokoino*, p. 661; Kulagin, *Dnevnik i pamiat'*, 16 July 1942, p. 259.

38 Druskin, *Spasennaia kniga*, p. 133.

39 Shvarts, *Zhivu bespokoino*, p. 560.

40 Compare with the explanations of a woman who accepted evacuation, the manager of a boarding school in Molotov province, in a letter to K. Polzikova-Rubets: 'I am ashamed that I left Leningrad. You know, I left not because I was afraid but because I felt I was needed more among the children than in the situation in Leningrad' (Polzikova-Rubets, *Oni uchilis' v Leningrade*, 16 September 1941, p. 34).

41 Shvarts, *Zhivu bespokoino*, p. 661.

42 Kulagin, *Dnevnik i pamiat'*, 16 July 1942, p. 254.

43 V. Kaverin, *Epilog, M.*, 1997, p. 258.

44 A. S. Berman, 'Dnevnik'. Quoted from *Budni podviga*, 9 December 1941, p. 110.

45 Ibid., 7 August 1942, p. 179.

46 Ibid., 10 December 1941, p. 111.

47 Quoted from Adamovich and Granin, *Blokadnaia kniga*, p. 52.
48 O. R. Peto, *Deti Leningrada*, *OR RNB, fond* 1273, *listy* 10, 10 verso.
49 Inber, *Pochti tri goda*, p. 176.
50 Sharypina, *Za zhizn' i pobedu*, p. 144.
51 Ibid.
52 *Pamiat' o blokade*, p. 111.
53 Borovikova, 'Dnevnik', 15 December 1941, *list* 90.
54 A. M. Grigor'ev (transcript of reminiscences), *Oborona Leningrada*, p. 413.
55 Entry in the diary of N. A. Ribkovskii, quoted from Kozlova, *Sovetskie liudi*, p. 266.
56 'Protokol sobraniia chlenov VLKSM zavoda No. 5 NKSP', *TsGAIPD SPb., fond* K-118, *opis'* 1, *delo* 79, *list* 94.
57 'Protokol sobraniia chlenov VLKSM zavoda "Krasnaia Bavariia" 14 maia 1942', *TsGAIPD SPb.*, *fond* K-118, *opis'* 1, *delo* 79, *listy* 12 – 12 verso. Compare the excuse of a Komsomol member who was threatened with expulsion for failing to pay her membership dues for three months: 'I did not pay because someone had pickpocketed my ration cards and I am in great need now. I was ill. I will receive money tomorrow and will pay the dues in full' ('Protokol sobraniia chlenov VLKSM zavoda "Leninskaia iskra", 12 avgusta 1942 g.', *TsGAIPD SPb., fond* K-118, *opis'* 1, *delo* 79, *listy* 33–4).
58 B. M. Eikhenbaum, *Raboty o L've Tolstom*, *SPb.*, 2009.
59 I. Paperno, *Sovetskii opyt, avtobiograficheskoe pis'mo i istoricheskoe soznanie: Ginzburg, Gertsen, Gegel'*, NLO, vol. LXVIII, *M.*, 2004, p. 104.
60 On the structuring of descriptions in accordance with the typology of genres, styles, characters and their actions, see the analysis by L. Ginzburg of the memoirs of Saint Simon: L. Ginzburg, *O psikhologicheskoi proze*, *Lg.*, 1977, pp. 143–4, 160–3.
61 L. N. Tolstoi, *Polnoe sobranie sochinenii*, vol. XXX, *M.*, 1951, pp. 18–19.
62 V. S. Liublinskii to A. D. Liublinskaia, 23 February 1942, *V pamiat' ushedshikh i vo slavu zhivushchikh*, p. 174.
63 Mashkova, *Iz blokadnykh zapisei*, 18 February 1942, p. 17.
64 Mukhina, 'Dnevnik', 25 May 1942, *list* 134 verso.
65 Gel'fer, 'Dnevnik', 19 January 1942, *list* 4.
66 Ibid.
67 Ibid., *listy* 7 – 7 verso.
68 V. Mal'tsev to Z. R. Mal'tseva and I. Mal'tseva, 22 October 1941, *Deviat'sot dnei*, p. 273. 'In the past you had to do things because of other people, but now it doesn't matter whether I keep the place clean or not, because I am the only person likely to be using it' (ibid.).
69 Ibid.
70 Mashkova, *Iz blokadnykh zapisei*, 5 March 1942, p. 18.
71 Ibid., 21 April 1942, p. 20.
72 Ibid., 23 April 1942.
73 Ibid., p. 49.
74 Ibid.
75 Druskin, *Dnevniki*, p. 133.
76 Ibid., p. 134.
77 Ibid., p. 135.
78 Ibid., p. 133.
79 Ibid., p. 135.

80 The reference is to the philosophical treatise Druskin was working on at this time.
81 Druskin, *Dnevniki*, p. 134.
82 Ibid., p. 147. A typing error has been corrected to read '1941', which corresponds with a chronology of Druskin's life and works, appended to the text of the diaries.
83 Ibid.

Leningraders in the Time of Death: human and superhuman

1 Glinka, *Blokada*, p. 191.

Index

from neighbours 195–6
recorded in diaries and letters
283–4
to colleagues 202
to friends 185, 186–9
hoarding 14, 42, 79
issued to hungry children 136
looking for 60–1
monitoring the distribution of 288
for Party officials 219–21
porridge 9, 10, 51
privileges 217–18
quarrelling within families over
173–4
self-justification arguments around
84–6
sharing 54, 291, 324
with colleagues 199–200
in families 164–72
introspection on 311, 316
with neighbours 192–3
stealing within families 170–2,
173
in tales of the siege 268
talking about 5, 18, 212, 269–72,
273, 274–6, 323
theft of 23
and dystrophics 244
from canteens 20–1
vocational schoolboys 246
thinking about 258, 263
see also bread; ration cards; soup
food rations
butter 45, 251
and honesty 32–5
increase in 16, 249
privileged 33, 45–6
reduction in 3, 4, 248
see also bread; ration cards
food substitutes/surrogates 4, 15–16,
189
conversations in queues about
248–9
fraud involving 19
given to neighbours 193
industrial manufacturing ingredients
203–4
sharing with colleagues 199
in tales of the siege 268
talking about 271

footwear
stolen from dead bodies 26, 27
frail people, stealing from 23
fraud 19–20, 22, 29
involving ration cards 19, 20, 22, 70,
79, 249
friends 183–90
death of 184–5
expressing sympathy with 184
help extended to 185–6
moving in with 156–7, 185
visiting 185
to ask for help 104–5, 189–90
Frolov, N. V. 18
funerals 8, 175, 176–83
coffins 176–8, 182, 183, 268
gravediggers 178
graves 178–80
symptoms of moral depravity 180–3
future times, tales of 274–7
Fyodorov, B. P. 220
Fyodorov, M. P. 94
Fyodorova, Klavdia 196

Galaktionova, M. A. 145
Galko, Leonid 73, 84, 187, 289
Galuzin, A. 115
Ganzha, A. S. 98
Gapova, Valentina 181
Garshin, Vladimir 4
Gelfer, G. A. 78, 83, 148, 267, 272,
310
introspection in diary entries 313–14
gifts
as acts of charity 62
expressing gratitude for 118–19
food 35, 47, 54, 82
by senior comrades 219
compassion in families 138–9
eating undeliverable food 82–3
exchanges between neighbours
192–3
expressing gratitude for 119, 120,
124–5, 127–8
recorded in diaries and letters
283–4
to colleagues 202
to friends 185, 186–9
sharing with friends 188–9
for soldiers 65–6